THE MEANINGS OF DRESS

THE
MEANINGS
OF DRESS

Mary Lynn Damhorst   Iowa State University

Kimberly A. Miller   University of Kentucky

Susan O. Michelman   University of Massachusetts—Amherst

Fairchild Publications
New York

Executive Editor: Olga Kontzias
Assistant Editor: Lori Applebaum
Production Editor: Iris Bass
Copy Editor: Susan Casal
Art Director: Mary Siener
Production Manager: Priscilla Taguer

Interior Design: Jeanne Calabrese
Cover Design: Lisa Klausing

Library of Congress Catalog Card Number: 99:72451

ISBN: 1-56367-165-4

GST R 133004424

Printed in the United States of America

CONTENTS

PREFACE

All three of us were in the same quandary. What should we assign as reading material for our classes on the social, psychological, and cultural aspects of dress? Our classes cater to an increasingly diverse body of students—young, older, international, male and female, minority and mainstream. And each of us teaches with a substantial number of freshmen in our classes—students new to the college experience. How can we engage students in the subject matter and in the wide array of resources that can facilitate learning?

We've each tried a number of approaches: text that covered some but not all of what was included in our courses; text that was too advanced; individual readings on reserve in the library or available through a copy center; and handouts that summarized elemental concepts. All of us found that resources offering minority perspectives and global diversity were limited in availability or fairly absent from texts.

This book does not answer all teaching needs for introductory classes on the social, psychological, and cultural aspects of dress. But we've created a resource that we think is a valuable supplement to existing and future textbooks. *The Meanings of Dress* provides readings that are compelling and that expand our notions of what dress does for the individual and society. It introduces basic concepts likely to be covered in classes related to dress and psychology, sociology, cultural studies, and consumer behavior.

This book is about dress, that is, all the things human beings do to the surfaces and appearance of their bodies. Dress is an essential part of human experience. Perhaps because of its closeness to the body, dress has a richness of meanings that express the individual as well as groups, organizations, and the larger society in which that person lives. Understanding its function helps us relate to other cultures, facilitates our interactions with others, and moves us to reflect upon and understand ourselves. We can also gain insight into how and why consumers buy clothing and other products related to dress.

Emphasis on Diversity

Diversity is an important fulcrum for the book. We have tried to incorporate perspectives offered by a variety of disciplines, cultures, and issues. We look to voices of multiple authors to help us understand dress.

These authors vary in gender, ethnicity, cultural backgrounds, age, and work roles. We hear from academics, journalists, business professionals, novelists, and students. They demonstrate how dress is a central factor in most areas of everyday life, such as work, school, sports, rituals and celebrations, intimate relationships, fantasy and play, and aging and development throughout a person's lifespan. The authors talk about dress and the body as a means of communication, but one that also contributes to problems of stereotyping, discrimination, and exclusion from power in society. They describe the richness of meanings associated with the body and dress that varies as a result of age, gender, sexual orientation, ethnicity, culture, immigration, position in society, and era. Dress is also examined as a reflection of larger social processes such as fashion systems, political conflict, hegemony, technological changes, organizational evolutions, generational experiences as well as cultural change in general.

The Meanings of Dress takes an interdisciplinary approach. Articles are selected from psychology, sociology, anthropology, material culture, history, communications, semiotics, aesthetics, consumer behavior, marketing, business management, consumer economics, popular culture, gender studies, feminist scholarship, minority studies, and more. Dress is a multifaceted phenomenon. One viewpoint is just not enough.

Plan of the Book

Writings and visuals from popular magazines, newspapers, scholarly journals, books, advertisements, and cartoons contribute the illustrative material of the book. Some of the articles are carefully selected reprints, while others are new and written specifically for this book. Our aim was to build a collection of scholarly, but easy-to-read works.

Chapter 1 introduces the essential concepts used throughout the book, including those of culture, self, identity, social role, meaning, and fashion. Chapter 1 establishes the centrality of diversity, pluralism, relativism, and holism to understanding dress.

Chapters 2 through 13 introduce a variety of concepts and issues and include pedagogy and readings. Key terms and concepts are emphasized in bold in the chapter introductions. Each article is highlighted in its chapter introduction to explain the relevance of the article to chapter issues and themes. Suggested readings at the end of each introduction encourage the reader to further explore topics. The learning activity also at the end of each introduction, helps students experience the ideas and concepts in the chapter. Discussion questions following each reading encourage critical thinking about the articles. In general, chapters are arranged in a micro to macro organization, starting with discussion of some basic components of human life in relation to dress and moving to larger societal systems. Throughout all chapters, however, we consider the perspectives of individual, group, and larger society and culture.

The integral relationship of the body to dress, self, and society is introduced in Chapter 2. Chapters 3 and 4 unpack the process of communication and the creation of meanings of dress through human interaction.

Chapters 5 through 10 focus on various social roles and how dress helps us express, perform, and experience those roles. Gender and sexual identity, are examined in relation to the self within various cultural contexts in Chapter 5. Chapter 6 examines how individuality and conformity are essential to dressing the self for various identities. Chapter 7 focuses on the function of dress in the work environment. Chapters 8 and 9 chart dress as a reflection of age roles throughout the lifespan, from infancy to elder years. Race, ethnicity, and social class are roles examined in Chapter 10. The chapter addresses the importance of body and dress to issues of minority status, hegemonic power, and exclusion and inclusion from power bases.

Moving to still larger systems in society, Chapter 11 examines the fashion process as part of the dynamics of cultural change. Religion is the focus of Chapter 12. Religious ideology is a major influence on larger cultural organization and values, and dress is a reflection of religion. Finally, Chapter 13 takes a macro look at dress as a part of cultural change.

The Meanings of Dress ends with Chapter 14, a look at major societal trends in the near future that may affect dress. Future shifts of age and ethnic representation, technology as it affects modes of access to procuring goods, and environmental issues are examined for impact on dress and how we think and feel about the body. Consideration of multiple scenarios closes the book with a useful exercise on the complexity of dress in society.

ACKNOWLEDGMENTS

This book of readings and activities is the result of the collective efforts of many individuals. We thank all our helpers for their generous time, effort, and support.

We would like to thank the Department of Textiles and Clothing at Iowa State University for allowing graduate assistants to help with various aspects of the book. In particular, we thank Harriet McLeod, Cai Guise-Richardson, Jennifer Ogle, and Mary Alice Casto for their energetic and often innovative efforts at locating articles and visuals. Eunah Yoh, Carol Hall, and especially Sherry Shofield-Tomschin were instrumental in getting the endless array of permissions completed and organized.

We thank the writers who willingly let us include their work. They have told engrossing and valuable stories. We especially thank the contributors of original manuscripts for their enthusiasm for the book and their willingness to lend to our editorial requirements.

We thank Jo Moreno, University of Rhode Island, for helping us "test drive" the book.

Our editor, Olga Kontzias, deserves endless praise for her patience at our plodding progress. She served as an astute guide to the intricacies of publishing a text, performed miracles at getting the visuals compiled, and was an extraordinary cheerleader. Her energy for this project was essential. Many others at Fairchild Publications assisted in the preparation of this book. Mary Siener, the art director at Fairchild Books, was bound by e-mail for many months.

Mary Lynn Damhorst would like to thank her colleagues Jane Farrell-Beck, Nancy Miller, and Ann Marie Fiore for funneling interesting articles and cartoons her way. She also thanks her parents Florence and Clarence Damhorst for their support of her multiyear efforts. Her Mom clipped articles faithfully over the years and her Dad even pitched in as a fact checker. She also thanks her students in her Appearance in Society class during the spring of 1998. Their completion of evaluations of the readings tested was most helpful in shaping the book. Of course, her coeditors were the most essential part of the team. It would not have been possible to assemble such a diverse and rich array of material without working together. Their great efforts at writing, editorial feedback as they developed the chapters, and camaraderie during the long process made this book one of the most valuable experiences of her life.

Kimberly A. Miller would like to thank Jill Buckland, reference librarian at W.T. Young Library, University of Kentucky, for her prompt and able assistance. She would also like to thank The College of Human Environmental Sciences at the University of Kentucky for granting her a sabbatical leave, which allowed time for the completion of the book. The support of Charles Lee Spillman, for his patience and willingness to review drafts of the manuscript is deeply appreciated.

Many people helped Susan O. Michelman directly and indirectly in the production of this text. First, she would like to thank her coeditors, who were wonderful to work with in both good and difficult times. Second, she would like to acknowledge the many students she has taught in Dress and Culture at the University of Massachusetts since 1995 who shared their interest and enthusiasm in this topic. They motivated her to provide them with a textbook that would draw them into critically thinking about the diversity of human appearance. Their ideas have greatly enriched her thinking. She must also thank the Center for Teaching at the University of Massachusetts, which awarded her a Lilly Foundation Teaching Fellowship in 1995 to work on developing this course. Some of the creative ideas about teaching that she shared with colleagues from other disciplines that year are woven into this textbook. Her acknowledgments would not be complete without thanking her family. Her husband John who patiently listened to her ideas and critiqued her writing for years, almost consistently gives her great and realistic feedback. Her son Adam and daughter Adria always kept her abreast of contemporary culture. Her father-in-law, Irving Michelman, patiently proofread many pages for her. For those of you who have inspired her thinking on the topic of the meanings of dress, she thanks you all.

Readers selected by the publisher were also very helpful. They include M. Lynn Alkire, Central Missouri State University; Linda Arthur, University of Hawaii; Diane Frey, Bowling Green State University; Melody Lehew, Kansas State University; Charlene Lind, Brigham Young University; Elizabeth Lowe, Queens College; Nancy Oliver, Northern Arizona University; and Sarah Schmidt, UNC-Greensboro.

1999
           Mary Lynn Damhorst
             Kimberly A. Miller
            Susan O. Michelman

CHAPTER 1
Introduction

Mary Lynn Damhorst

AFTER YOU HAVE READ THIS CHAPTER, YOU WILL COMPREHEND:

- How dress is a multifaceted behavior.

- How dress is a part of culture and society, reflecting how people think and organize themselves.

- Fashion is collective behavior.

- How meanings of dress are relative to cultural, historical, social, and individual context.

- The relationship between dress and the self.

- The value in diversity in dress across cultures.

    . . . appearance is a primary mark of identification, a signal of what they consider themselves to be.

Banner, American Beauty (1983, p. 3)

This book is a compilation of readings about **appearance**, including all aspects of the human body that have the potential to be observed by other human beings. We focus particularly on **dress**, which we define as any intentional modification of appearance (see Kaiser, 1990; Roach-Higgins & Eicher, 1992). Dress is what people do to their bodies to maintain, manage, and alter appearance; therefore, dress is behavior.

Dress includes more than clothing—those three-dimensional objects that enclose and envelop the body in some way (Roach-Higgins & Eicher, 1992). Dress includes a wide array of other supplements and attachments to the body, such as makeup, nose rings, masks, shoes, headdresses, wigs, and hair plugs. Dressing may include application of chemicals, heat, and light to change color, texture, and odor, as in perfumes, deodorants, tanning, facial peels, hair straightening or curling, tattoos, scarification, and branding. Removing noticeable portions of the body can also be an act of dress, such as cutting hair, shaving a beard, removing a facial mole, removing fat through liposuction, or getting a nose job. Dieting and exercise are also, in part, a type of dress—if those activities are undertaken to change weight, muscle definition, or body shape in any way. Extremes of purging or self-starvation can also be dressing activities when adopted as strategies toward losing weight. The dressed (or even undressed) body is very much a project under continual construction (Brumberg, 1997).

Roach-Higgins and Eicher (1992) contend that dress is intentional, but in accidental circumstances, this requirement of intention becomes complex. For example, getting splashed and covered with mud by a passing truck is not an act of dress, but how one deals with mud all over one's clothing is an act of dress, even though there might not be complete freedom of choice in how the mud problem is solved.

Dress and appearance are worthy of study because they are laden with meanings. Appearance and dress often provide the most immediate and apparent visual cues about age, gender, ethnicity, social status, and social roles. The shape of the body, as we shall examine in Chapter 2, has significant meanings. In addition, dress protects the body from the environment—physical, psychological, and social. It expresses relationships, steers individuals to approach or avoid others, shapes actions toward others, reflects how people feel about themselves, and expresses personal values and values of the society in which an individual lives. Dress is more than the mere objects and materials people put on their bodies. Dress can be a sign or symbol that refers to and stands for **meanings** not inherent in the material or object.[1] In sum, the physical body when dressed reflects the "social body" or surrounding societal system (Turner, 1991). Chapter 4 examines the complex array of meanings that can be expressed through dress.

Dress is a chronicle of any time in history. As fashions or norms of dressing change over time, trends in technology, the economy, religion, the arts, notions of morality, social organization, and patterns of everyday living are reflected in dress. Chapter 13 looks at societal changes reflected in dress. We can learn much about people in any society through the way they dress and the meanings assigned to their dress. For example, Ellen Melinkoff in *What We Wore* (1984) compared the late 1960s and early 1970s to the previous 10 years:

> The hippie look was many things: sloppy, creative, unstudied, studied, uniform, eccentric, and most of all, casual. That casualness is its legacy. Of course, true hippie garb went to the extreme of casualness, unkempt. But it drew our attention to just how uptight, plastic, cookie-cutter-correct we had been in our dress.
>
> Whether in Jackie Kennedy A-line outfits or Mary Quant minis, we dressed in packs. The only avenue open to us to impress other people was through correctness. The hippies spit on that idea. They felt clothes should be a form of expression and people should be comfortable as well. (p. 170)

PREVAILING CONCEPTS

Several themes and concepts are introduced in this first chapter so that we can draw on them in the following chapters and readings. The concepts include culture and society, fashion, relativism, self, diversity, and pluralism.

A Cultural Perspective

Culture is an elusive and complex concept. Throughout the lifetime of an individual, culture surrounds and shapes the individual in ways that are barely recognizable to the individual.

Linton (1936) pointed out that culture is a complex whole that includes any capabilities and habits held by members of a society. Culture is a system that is learned and reflected in behavior patterns characteristic of the members of a society (Hoebel, 1958). The behavior patterns under focus in this book are the many forms of dress. In taking a cultural perspective to understand dress, a **holistic** approach must be adopted in which all aspects of a culture are considered as shaping the meanings of dress and the choices people make when choosing forms of dress.

WHAT PEOPLE THINK. Spradley (1972) neatly summarized culture as ". . . what people know, feel, think, make, and do" (p. 6). What people know and think are the mentifacts of a culture, which include ideas, ideals, values, knowledge, and ways of knowing. Knowing how to dress is a part of any cultural knowledge base. How, indeed, do so many people know they should wear jeans on their legs and not on their heads? This seemingly obvious rule is very much a part of many cultures today, as jeans are a garment worn by people all around the globe. We will examine the complexity of unwritten rules for dress in Chapter 3.

In any one appearance, a person may express personal and cultural values simultaneously. For example, a culture that creates changing fashions may be expressing a general belief that change and newness are positive (Sproles & Burns, 1994). In contrast, a culture that values tradition and doing things the old way will likely produce clothing that changes very little over time, as among old order Amish groups in the United States who wear clothing similar in style to what Amish wore in the 1800s.

People also learn meanings of different styles or types of dressing—another component of cultural knowledge. Note the many dress features that are used in the United Technologies ad to create the image of a car thief in the United States (see Figure 1.1). For viewers of the ad who are familiar with large U.S. urban areas, the combination of dress items in that ad image may elicit a **stereotype**, or a network of meanings assigned on the basis of appearance. In the ad text—the advertiser gives further information that the man is a thief and not someone whom many people want hanging around their neighborhood. Appearance stereotypes are mentifacts shared by members of a cultural group.

Stereotypes are based on limited information, such as appearance, and result in a network of inferences about characteristics of the person. Even though the stereotype rarely fits any individual completely, believers of the stereotype generalize its characteristics to all members of the group. The stereotyper tends to be blinded to other characteristics that make the individual unique. Some individuals hold to a stereotype so rigidly that they become **prejudiced** against a group and discriminate against the group regardless of information that the stereotype is unfair or untrue. When a stereotype is widely held in a culture, prejudicial treatment of the group on a broad scale is likely to occur in that society.

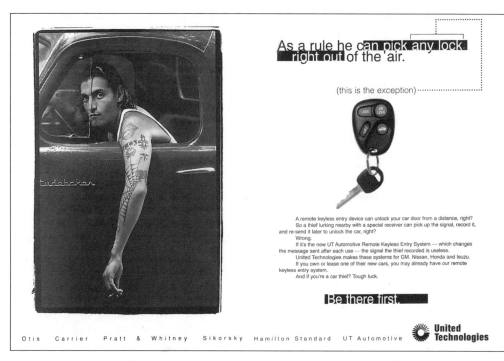

FIGURE 1.1 *Advertisers use appearance cues to present images that evoke stereotypes. In the context of this ad, the man appears to be someone you might not trust with your car.*

What makes stereotyping particularly dangerous is that many people are unaware that they apply a stereotype consistently to a group. Human beings have a natural tendency to attempt to classify others into familiar types to simplify the task of making sense of the surrounding social world. Only by recognizing that we all, at some time, use stereotypes can we become more diligent at avoiding erroneous stereotyping and labelling.

WHAT PEOPLE DO. What people do are the **sociofacts** of a culture. Sociofacts are social behaviors or how people organize themselves in relation to one another. In fact, the term **society** is often used to refer to a group of people living and working together in a systematic way. George Herbert Mead (1934) contended that society requires coordinated interaction of individuals. Dress can help in coordinating interaction. For example, uniforms can help people know whom to ask for help if an auto accident has occurred and whom to ask for water in a restaurant. Dress gives clues as to the age of individuals, their gender, and their attractiveness—all helpful in deciding, for example, who to ask to dance at a campus bar (even though dress cues can be deceiving). In some cultures dress helps identify who should be accorded special respect and courtesies and who should be ignored or barred from entry to "polite" public areas.

Societies often have a group that dominates and leads minorities and less powerful groups in society. This situation of dominance is referred to as **hegemony**. The powerful group tends to set standards for behavior and ways of thinking (Gramsci, 1971). We will examine how hegemony in the United States has an influence on standards of attractiveness (Chapter 2), business appearance norms (Chapter 7), gender dress (Chapter 5), and social status of ethnic groups (Chapter 10).

Social organization is reflected in and facilitated by dress in many facets of society. In fact, fashions cannot exist without coordinated interaction of individuals acting as a collective in wearing similar looks, lengths, and silhouettes. **Fashion** is a way of behaving that is temporarily adopted by a discernable portion of members of a social group as socially appropriate for the time and situation (Sproles & Burns, 1994). Without some similarity and coordination in behavior among individuals, a society would have only unique, idiosyncratic expressions rather than fashion. We will look at the individual and group behaviors that shape fashion systems in Chapter 11.

WHAT PEOPLE MAKE. What people make are sometimes called the **artifacts** of culture. Dress includes manufactured and handmade objects and materials. These objects also are products of the processes and technologies a culture develops to make things. Both sociofacts and mentifacts become encoded in artifacts, such as dress, made by people in a culture. Chapter 12 looks at how the sociofacts and mentifacts of religion are reflected in dress.

The Relativity of Meanings

Throughout the readings in this book, the authors do not merely describe dress and physical features of individuals or cultural groups, but continually strive to understand the meanings dress and the body have for those individuals and societies. Dress and the body have meanings that are relative to culture and historical times. For example, Mamie Van Doren (see Figure 1.2a) was a popular pinup girl in the United States during the 1940s. Her thighs, ample according to present U.S. standards, might preclude someone like Mamie from attaining national popularity as a sex symbol today. She was considered quite shapely and attractive 50 years ago. Compare the photo of Mamie with the photo of 1990s U.S. supermodel Kate Moss (see Figure 1.2b). Similarly, a woman in Jamaica is more apt to be considered attractive if she is pleasingly "plump," a larger body ideal than is currently fashionable in mainstream United States. (Sobo, 1994).

Meanings are not usually handed down by some inhuman force of cultural or political correctness, however. Meanings are created by individuals living day by day within cultures and interacting daily with the objects and materials of dress. As Herbert Blumer (1969) proposed, the meanings of things (e.g., objects, ideas, behaviors) are directly attributable to the social interaction one has with others. Meanings emerge as people hear others talk about the way people look, see each other interact with others dressed in certain ways, and act together toward those people on the basis of appearance. Meanings of dress and appearance are created, maintained, and modified as individuals collectively deal with dress and the people wearing that form of dress.

It is people, then, who assign meanings to dress and who develop shared consensus about what dress means. To create shared meanings about any type of dress in most cultures in the world today requires a convoluted process of meaning transfer and transformation. Various media, such as fashion magazines, films, and television shows contribute greatly to the transfer and transformation of meanings of dress around the world. Meanings may constantly change as people of diverse ages, shapes, roles, and backgrounds decide to wear the same style. The types of occasions to which they wear the style and the activities for which the style is worn influence meanings assigned to the style.

FIGURE 1.2A *Mamie van Doren was a popular pinup and actress during the 1940s, admired most for her "vital statistics."*

FIGURE 1.2B *Supermodel Kate Moss has remarkably different body dimensions in comparison to Mamie van Doren. Kate represents the epitome of the thin body ideal of the 1990s.*

Time and number of adopters are important factors in development of dress meanings. For example, Lind and Roach-Higgins (1985) found that dress worn to express radical and liberal political ideas on U.S. college campuses in the 1970s became less clear in meaning as more and more students adopted the styles originally worn by and associated only with radical students. The meanings changed from "radical" and "political liberal" to "general campus fashion." The same type of dissolution of meanings has occurred more recently with the adoption of rap dress and grunge-look dress throughout suburbs and small towns in the United States. Adolescent wearers of these styles are not a part of the groups who innovated the looks

Change in fashion over time adds to the relativity of meanings of dress as fashion ideas **diffuse** or spread throughout a society (Sproles & Burns, 1994). New ideas for fashion may first be introduced by designers or innovative individuals. Fashion magazines, advertising, retail displays, and celebrities may promote the style as "fashionable," "the latest thing," and "attractive." If a significant number of consumers decide to adopt the style, it actually becomes a fashion, though only certain segments of consumers may wear the style. The style may take on added meaning of representing the groups or lifestyles of people who adopt the new look. For instance, a style might be associated with women in business executive roles in New York City. Then several years later, when the style is no longer featured as new and fewer people wear it, its meaning may change to "passé," "boring," "dowdy," or "out of it." (For example, see Figure 1.3.)

The Individual Self

When do individuals get to be themselves in the midst of all this collective action and shared meanings? Symbolic interactionist Mead (1934) proposed that the **self** is defined through interaction with other people. Dress is part of our interactions with others who act toward us, in part, on the basis of the meanings of our dress. Dress is part of defining self identity to others; we choose items that reflect our interests, personality, roles, membership in groups, age, gender, socioeconomic status, and more. Of course, some situations or roles limit the amount of choice in self-expression; an extreme example of conformity is found in dress of prison inmates who wear uniforms that mask personal identity and emphasize only the prisoner role (Goffman, 1961).

Learning about the self is a lifelong process (examined in Chapters 8 and 9). Cooley (1902) suggested that we use other people as mirrors to tell us who we are in a "looking glass self" process. Continuous presentation of **programs** of dress (programs could include other types of behavior, of course) and reflection upon others' **reviews** or reactions to dress allows an individual to gain a sense of how others see the self and assign meaning to the self (Stone, 1962). We use others in this process of **self-indication** to learn who we are (Blumer, 1969). Meanings of dress are part of what is learned through the self-indication process.

An integral part of the self are the roles we take on. **Roles** are positions that people occupy in a group or society (Biddle & Thomas, 1966). These positions are defined by social relationships; people take on roles in relation to other persons. Performance of a role is guided by social expectations for the role player's behavior (including dress), knowledge, and attitudes. Adult individuals tend to have multiple roles that define parts of the self. At any one time, a man may be 42 years old (age role), male (gender role), Puerto Rican (ethnic role), a chef and a boss to junior chefs (employment roles), a father, a husband, a brother, a son (family roles), a best friend of another man (social role), and a coach for a girls' soccer team (community leadership role). He may express some of these roles through dress, but not all of these roles in any one appearance. These roles are parts of the puzzle that make up the man's **identity**.

FIGURE 1.3 *Personnel interviewers rated this suit as attractive and highly appropriate for business interviews in 1985. Today, the outfit looks a bit frumpy and out-of-date.*

Other aspects of identity include unique personal traits and interests that are not necessarily role related. The Puerto Rican man might run five miles alone every morning and think of himself as defined in part by running. He, in a sense, has many identities that make up his total self. We would need to examine his total wardrobe to begin to grasp the multiple identities of this man, but some of his identity might never be expressed through dress.

Can anyone truly be an individual if we rely on others to tell us who we are and how to behave in roles? To be a human being, interaction with other human beings is essential. It is the complex combination of unique experiences and reviews from a wide array of others that makes every individual a unique self. Given some amount of personal freedom, we have the human capacity to choose from reviews we receive to define the self. We can decide whose compliments or insults about our hair to consider valid when getting a haircut. Or we may choose to get the regulation haircut for army recruits because we want to become part of that occupational group (see Figure 1.4). To some extent, however, cultures limit the choices we have. Some haircuts might never be considered or known as a possibility in some cultures. Chapter 6 examines the concepts of individuality and conformity.

A World of Diversity

While people in cultures throughout the world are diverse in the way they dress and the meanings they assign to dress, a network of connections—business, political, media, electronic, migratory, family, and friendships—has emerged among nations to make the

FIGURE 1.4 *New U.S. Army recruits on their daily run sport regulation haircuts. Recruits must learn to think, act, follow orders, and dress like soldiers so that they can function as a fighting unit.*

present day world a shrinking "global village." Many of us no longer live in isolation from other cultures outside our borders. In addition, within any society multiple cultures may be living together or in close proximity. The United States is a prime example of a society that incorporates people from many cultures within its boundaries. The United States is a multicultural society.

Appreciating cultural difference in dress is a complex process, especially when confronted with an appearance that is culturally quite different from one's own. The scarification patterns on the face of the Kamo woman in Figure 1.5 might be difficult for some of you to look at if you are not used to seeing this type of body modification. But in her own community in Northern Nigeria, she is probably considered attractive and appropriate.

Keep in mind, however, that dress in the United States may look ugly or ridiculous to people in other cultures. High heels, lipstick, and tanning practices seem strange or even dangerous from other cultural viewpoints. Dress that is commonly accepted in one's own country may be considered inappropriate or immodest in another culture. For example, exposure of women's bare upper arms is seen as immodest in many Moslem cultures, even during hot weather. To prevent insults when traveling in those cultures, women from Europe and the United States may cover up more than they would at home during hot weather.

We have attempted to include articles in most chapters that give viewpoints from cultures outside the United States or from minority groups within the United States. One reason for including diverse perpectives is to encourage a move away from **ethno-centrism**—the judging of people from other cultures and backgrounds by one's own cultural standards and beliefs. To function adequately in the global and multicultural workplace and neighborhoods of today requires development of the ability to accept and respect differences and to strive for relativity in understanding. The perspective of **pluralism**—the acceptance of differences in others while not necessarily wanting to adopt those differences for the self—is increasing in the United States (Light, 1988). It is a perspective that will be increasingly expected on the part of mature individuals in the United States and will be a requirement for getting and keeping many jobs now that a great variety of business and government organizations have become global in their customer/client base and span of operations.

The added benefit of pluralism is the depth of understanding of the self that comes from developing skill in analyzing one's own personal reactions to diversity. In addition, moving away from a smaller ethnocentric way of thinking to seeing and appreciating a wide array of possibilities for dress adds richness to life. It is fun and rewarding to expand our ideas about what is attractive, aesthetically pleasing, and interesting. Awareness of variety in the world facilitates creativity in dressing and expressing the self.

FIGURE 1.5 *A Kamo woman in Northern Nigeria has scarification designs on her face.*

Summary

In this chapter, we have considered how dress is meaningful human behavior that includes a wide array of modifications to the body. Dress may reflect many aspects of cultures, including the ways that people think, organize themselves, behave toward others, and know how to make things. Individual choice in dress is strongly shaped by culture, fashion (if present in the culture), and the social roles the individual performs. However, a unique self may be expressed through dress due to the complex mix of role identities and individual preferences held by any individual. In the shrinking global society of today, acceptance of diversity of appearances due to individual and cultural differences is becoming a highly important social skill.

Notes

1. We do not delve into the technical difference between "*sign*" and "*symbol*" in this text and use the terms interchangeably. Various scholars use the two terms differently, and there is wide disagreement as to how the terms apply to dress. See John Lyons, 1977, *Semantics, Vol. 1*, Cambridge University Press, for discussion of varying definitions in the field of semiotics.

References

Banner, L. W. (1983). *American beauty*. New York: Alfred A. Knopf.

Biddle, B. J., & Thomas, E. J. (1966). *Role theory; concepts and research*. New York: Wiley.

Blumer, H. (1969). *Symbolic interactionism: Perspective and method*. Englewood Cliffs, NJ: Prentice-Hall.

Brumberg, J. J. (1997). *The body project*. New York: Random House.

Cooley, C. H. (1902). *Human nature and the social order*. New York: Charles Scribner's Sons.

Goffman, E. (1961). *Asylums: Essays on the social situation of mental patients and other inmates*. Garden City, NY: Doubleday.

Gramsci, A. (1971). *Selections from the prison notebooks of Antonio Gramsci*, trans. by Q. Hoare and G.N. Smith. London: Lawrence and Wishart.

Hoebel, E. A. (1958). *Man in the primitive world: An introduction to anthropology* (2nd ed.). New York: McGraw-Hill.

Kaiser, S. B. (1997). *The social psychology of clothing: Symbolic appearances in context*. (2nd ed. rev.). New York: Fairchild.

Light, P. C. (1988). *Baby boomers*. New York: Norton.

Lind, C., & Roach-Higgins, M. E. (1985). Fashion, collective adoption, and the social-political symbolism of dress. In M. R. Solomon (Ed.), *The psychology of fashion* (pp. 183–192). Lexington: Heath/Lexington Books.

Linton, (1936). *The study of man: An introduction*. New York: D. Appleton-Century.

Mead, G. H. (1934). *Mind, self, and society*, ed. by Charles W. Morris. Chicago: The University of Chicago Press.

Melinkoff, E. (1984). *What we wore: An offbeat social history of women's clothing, 1950 to 1980.* New York: Quill.

Roach-Higgins, M. E., & Eicher, J. B. (1992). Dress and identity. *Clothing and Textiles Research Journal,* 10 (4), 1–8.

Sobo, E. J. (1994). The sweetness of fat: Health, procreation, and sociability in rural Jamaica. In N. Sault (Ed.), *Many mirrors: Body image and social relations.* New Jersey: Rutgers University Press.

Spradley, J. P. (1972). *Culture and cognition: Rules, maps, and plans.* San Francisco: Chandler Publishing.

Sproles, G. B., & Burns, L. D. (1994). *Changing appearances.* New York: Fairchild.

Stone, G. P. (1962). Appearance and the self. In *Human behavior and the social processes: An interactionist approach* (pp. 86–118), ed. by A. M. Rose. New York: Houghton Mifflin.

Turner, B. S. (1991). Recent developments in the theory of the body. In *The body: Social process and cultural theory* (pp. 1–35), ed. by M. Featherstone, M. Hepworth, & B. S. Turner. London: Sage Publications.

The Body in Cultural Context

Kimberly A. Miller

AFTER YOU HAVE READ THIS CHAPTER, YOU WILL COMPREHEND:

- Frameworks for viewing the body and dress.

- The process of critical thinking about the body.

- How to identify and critically analyze U.S. cultural ideals for men and women.

- Cultural stereotypes and their potentially negative consequences.

- A feminist critique of cultural ideals for women.

- Cultural alternatives to the U.S. ideal of thinness.

The purpose of this chapter is to engage the reader in a critical thinking process about the body. The body has many possibilities for adornment; it can be considered a canvas for self-expression. Most of the readings in this chapter focus on body weight, which reflects a Euro-American—and increasingly global—obsession. But other body issues are also presented such as muscle shape and size, men's height, and mehndi (henna hand tattoos) (see "Designs for the Hands" in Chapter 3). Body piercing and tattooing are forms of body adornment that have become increasingly popular in recent years, especially among young people. Body piercing includes those piercings that are visible in public settings (e.g., lip, nose, and eyebrow rings) and those that are not typically visible in public settings (e.g., genital, nipple and navel rings). Similarly, tattooing can be publicly viewed or hidden. Hair loss for men—and women—can lead to the use of wigs or toupees; hair dyes that give the illusion of more hair; or hair transplants. Altering the body through surgical procedures has become increasingly common (with both men and women) and include facial peels, liposuction, and face-lifts. Regular visits to the dermatologist can alter the body by removal of skin tags, moles, and warts in an effort to achieve a smooth and even skin tone. Most hair salons will remove facial hair by waxing lips, chins, and eyebrows. Clearly, there are numerous ways to dress the body. This chapter will draw on the reader's sensitivity to explore the many ways that we adorn and alter our bodies.

FRAMEWORKS FOR VIEWING THE BODY

Because the body is so rarely observed without clothing, dress and the body are closely connected; hence the need to address the body in a discussion about dress. Several scholars have devised ways to view the clothed body, and their work provides a basis for not only viewing the body but also for performing research studies on dress. Roach-Higgins and Eicher (1992) created a classification system for types of dress and their properties. Body modifications and supplements can be classified according to their respective properties. For example, skin can be transformed by tattooing (modification), which alters its color (property) and surface design (property). Body piercing not only modifies the body's skin but allows for a ring to be attached to the body (supplement).

Susan Kaiser (1997) proposed a contextual perspective when viewing the body and dress. Awareness of the social, cultural, and historical influences at any given time is essential to understanding dress and its meaning, according to Kaiser. The contextual perspective draws from perspectives in sociology, psychology, and anthropology and allows the researcher to understand meanings below the surface. Mary Lynn Damhorst (1989) created a model that considers the context of a person's dress and appearance. Underlying the contextual model are two premises: (1) in real life, we seldom see clothes divorced from social context, and (2) it has been demonstrated that interpretations of clothing vary along contextual lines (Damhorst, 1985).

Still other scholars view and study dress with an emphasis on visual perception. Marilyn DeLong (1998) presented a method for analyzing appearance that includes a sensitivity to visual aesthetic dimensions of perception. Robert Hillestad (1980) used a structural approach to explore interactions between the body and clothing. Whether approaching the study of the body from a social, psychological, cultural, historical, or aesthetic perspective (or a combination of perspectives), one overarching concept remains clear: The body and all its attachments communicate volumes of information about an individual, a society, a culture, or a time in history.

CRITICAL THINKING ABOUT THE BODY

To begin the process of critically thinking about the body, it is instructive to examine one's own cultural ideals. A **cultural ideal** is the type of person a culture identifies as highly desirable or attractive. Princess Diana and Tom Cruise are two examples of ideals from British and U. S. cultures; you can probably think of many others. When we examine a cultural ideal, we begin by asking questions.

- Where did these ideals come from? (This informs us of our ethnic heritage.)
- When did these ideals develop? (This provides a historical context.)
- Who do these ideals benefit? (Gives us an idea of the cultural rewards for ascribing to an ideal.)
- Who do they hurt? (Tells us the negative consequences for not ascribing to an ideal.)

After the reader has examined his or her cultural ideals, it is especially informative to compare ideals from several cultures. This chapter is intended to generate critical questions about cultural ideals.

The readings in this chapter will certainly stimulate your thinking about the body. You may agree with some of the ideas presented in the readings and disagree with others. That's fine; there are no absolute right or wrong answers. Rather than deciding what is right or wrong, there is value in examining these issues so you can decide how you feel about them personally.

ANALYZING U.S. IDEALS

Before embarking on an examination of the dress and appearance of persons from many cultures, it is helpful to create a list of characteristics of the cultural ideal for U.S. women and men. Each semester I enlist the help of students in my courses at the University of Kentucky to create this list. What are the ideal characteristics for women? What are the ideal characteristics for men? The "thin-but-toned" ideal is often a topic of discussion as students point out that just being thin is not enough. "Tall, dark, and handsome," "no pain, no gain," and "one can never be too rich or too thin," are often mentioned as the list develops.

This exercise is often fun and invigorating, and most students are eager to chime in; momentum builds. Other students sit quietly and watch with skepticism as the list of characteristics fill the chalkboard. After the list is complete, we step back and take a hard look. How many people can actually attain these ideals? Ten percent of the U.S. population? Five percent? Less than five percent? How realistic are these ideals to the average man and woman in the United States? What are the payoffs for approximating the ideal? What are the risks for not being anywhere near the ideal or intentionally challenging the ideal? The readings in this chapter should help you arrive at some answers to these questions.

For some students, this is an eye-opening and informative exercise. Perhaps they were subconsciously aware of U.S. ideals, but to see them written on the chalkboard is especially revealing. Other students may have decided long before my class that these ideals are nonsense or unfairly discriminatory and have decided not to be held hostage to the cultural standards being discussed. Obviously, each individual chooses the extent to which they will be affected by these ideals. No doubt, the exercise prompts each person in the room to reflect on her or his decision about how to deal with these issues personally.

As students and I collaborate on the list, there is often a few nervous giggles in the room and perhaps one brave soul who challenges the class exercise. Their giggles indicate the students' uneasiness with the ludicrous list unfolding on the chalkboard. My response to a challenge of the exercise is that we can identify cultural standards without necessarily agreeing with or perpetuating them. As a matter of fact, this exercise often has the opposite effect. Some students feel empowered by the class discussion to pick and choose which characteristics to embrace and which ones to ignore. Ultimately, students are well versed in popular culture (thanks to the media age in which they have grown up) and are familiar with the ideals whether they ascribe to them or not. Not surprisingly, the same list of characteristics occurs semester after semester indicating the enduring nature of cultural ideals in the United States.

Ideals and Power

The "root of power" for women and men is also part of our class discussion. Typically, women are viewed as powerful if they are attractive and fit the cultural ideal. Men are deemed powerful if they have high earning ability or potential. Clearly, one is based more on the physical body while the other is based on skills/abilities. And since we know that physical bodies are likely to decline with age, and skills and earning power are likely to increase with age, we begin to notice some interesting gender differences. Susan Kaiser (1997) regarded these gender differences as an artificial dichotomy between agonic and hedonic power or "doing versus being".

Agonic power refers to power that is active and direct, in other words "doing." while **hedonic power** is indirect and passive and relates to "being." The cultural ideal for men is more toward the agonic end of the continuum. The ideal for women is more toward the hedonic end of the continuum. Women achieve their power in society through being attractive and spending time and energy on their appearance. Men achieve their power in society through "doing" and spending time and energy achieving skills. Kaiser refers to this dichotomy as artificial because we all know women who are highly skilled and men who are preoccupied with their appearance (see "You're So Vain" in Chapter 9).

Ideals and Gender

Given the previous information about cultural ideals and social power, it seems logical that men and women would pursue activities that are rewarding. But when did these expectations of men and women begin? Gendered dress expectations for the 20th century were possibly affected most by late-19th century ways of thinking. Because of the industrial revolution and growing capitalism in the United States, men's dress and demeanor of the late-19th century took on a somber appearance. The three-piece business suit came into use at this time and set the stage for men's business wear during the 20th century. Fred Davis (1988) compares the strong desire for economic success to men's restricted dress code.

During the 19th century, women's dress continued to follow the same elaborate dress code it had followed for centuries. In large part, this was because men and women were assigned different daily tasks. Because men would be interacting with others in the business world (i.e., public sphere) his dress had to be taken seriously. Because women would be at home raising children and managing households (i.e., private sphere) her dress could follow the whims of fashion. How has dress changed for men and women in the 20th century compared to the late-19th century?

There are definite minimum dress expectations for both men and women. For example, women are not supposed to have facial hair and men are not supposed to have large breasts. But there is a big difference between minimum expectations and ideal expectations. **Stigma** is assigned to those who do not (or cannot) meet minimum dress expectations. Physical disabilities, obesity, hair loss, and postmastectomy are all conditions that can cause a person to be socially stigmatized. Most people are judged physically attractive if they *exceed* minimum expectations and demonstrate some effort toward approximation of the cultural ideal. Since no one is perfect and certain ideal characteristics are simply not genetically transmitted to all (i.e., long legs), generally society is accepting of the ordinary person.

Is it easier for men to achieve the ideal than it is for women? Certainly men and women are socialized differently about topics of dress and appearance. This socialization leads to less tolerance in society for men who adopt traditional feminine dress (i.e., manicured nails) as compared to women who adopt traditional masculine dress (i.e., trousers). Men, however, are not exempt from the pressure of living up to an ideal. Three readings in particular are especially informative about ideals and the male body. "The 1997 Body Image Survey Results," "Tattooing: Another Adolescent Risk Behavior Warranting Health Education," and "Mission Impossible" address both the obsession we have with body weight and the difficulty of reaching and maintaining the thin-but-toned ideal. Male responses were outnumbered by female responses to "The 1997 Body Image Survey Results," but the number of men who are dissatisfied with their bodies is growing. We learn from the survey results that men and women are both concerned about body weight but each is concerned with different issues. For instance, men exercise primarily to add bulk and gain weight, women exercise primarily to lose weight. Men also report (more often than women) that exercise makes them feel better and relieves stress. There is one issue on which men and women agree; the stomach is the body part they both find most troublesome. Even though appearance is the area where women gain most power in society, men are increasingly susceptible to appearance ideals (see "Turning Boys Into Girls" in Chapter 13) and are resorting to more traditional female behaviors—such as cosmetic surgery—to deal with the pressure.

Tattooing may once have been regarded a masculine behavior because of its association with men in the military, but the increased media coverage about tattoos may be one reason why more girls than boys today are getting tattoos. Of the 213 tattooed adolescents who responded to a recent survey, 55 percent were girls and 45 percent were boys. According to "Tattooing," more girls (55 percent in 1997) are receiving tattoos compared to a previous study (35 percent in 1994). Girls may consider tattoos a fashion accessory, however, the permanent nature of tattoos negates the changing nature of fashion. Boys may consider tattoos less of a fashion item and more a means to show toughness. Adolescents are growing and changing individuals, as pointed out by the article's authors, therefore a tattoo selected at age 14 is likely (among 30 percent of respondents in the 1997 study) to lead to disappointment, embarrassment, and low self-esteem. This is an unfortunate occurrence when adolescents are struggling with body image issues.

"Mission Impossible" reports on the body concerns of adolescent boys. Skipping showers after gym class is one way to avoid feelings of inadequacy when a young man compares himself to male models in Calvin Klein ads. We know that more men suffer from eating disorders today than ten years ago. Indications are that men are expected to live up to cultural standards of attractiveness more so today than in the past. Consequently, 11 percent of high school boys are using steroids. However, even with ever-increasing pressure on boys to meet the ideal, boys are twice as likely to be satisfied with their appearance than girls. In summary, both women *and* men are becoming less satisfied with their bodies.

Ideals and the Individual

How much impact does a cultural ideal have on an individual? Ideals are pervasive through the media. Airbrushed photographs of fashion models and the use of body doubles in popular movies are two ways that unrealistic ideals are perpetuated. It is often youth who are most vulnerable to these seductive and unattainable ideals. Researchers typically blame the ideal of thinness for incidents of anorexia and bulimia among adolescents. Another finding from "The 1997 Body Image Survey Results" exemplifies the impact of the thinness ideal. Fifteen percent of women and 11 percent of men who responded to the survey said they would trade more than five years of their lives to be at their ideal body weight. These are astounding findings! People are actually willing to trade years of their lives for an "ideal." Ultimately, comparing one's own body to unreachable ideals leads to feelings of inadequacy.

In some way, all of the readings in this chapter address a person's body image. **Body image** is the mental picture one has of her or his body at any given time (Fisher, 1968). You may know someone who has a great body. Then, after you get to know her or him, you discover that the individual is very critical of his or her own body. This is an indication that a perfect body does not guarantee a positive body image. "The 1997 Body Image Survey Results" notes that the growing chasm between our actual bodies and our preferred ones is troubling. Why are we so dissatisfied?

Several researchers have looked for a connection between body perception and self-esteem. **Self-esteem** involves individual feelings of self-worth (Rosenberg, 1985). Not surprisingly, when we feel better about our bodies, we feel better about ourselves. "Mission Impossible" reports that adolescents will go to dangerous lengths to look like their favorite movie stars. Because most models starve themselves to maintain their weight and their photographs are airbrushed to make them appear even thinner, it is nearly impossible for a normal teenager to look like her favorite idol. Comparing one's self to a cultural ideal is a self-defeating exercise for anyone, but especially for adolescents who may not have developed a stable sense of self-worth. "The 1997 Body Image Survey Results" also points out the myth that many diet programs reinforce: Weight loss equals improved self-esteem. Whereas that may be true in some cases, a more reliable route to improved self-esteem would be to develop self-acceptance regardless of how one measures up to the cultural ideal.

Tattoos may increase positive feelings about body image temporarily, but tattoos can have long-term negative body image consequences for adolescents. In "Tattooing," researchers report that many adolescents surveyed (83 percent) reported initial pleasure with their tattoo, and 81 percent reported continuing pleasure. Despite the short-term pleasures with tattoos, 30 percent of adolescents surveyed were later dissatisfied with their tattoos and report low self-esteem when showing others their tattoos. The long-term commitment inherent in tattoos may outweigh the short-term benefits when tattooed as an adolescent. The health risks are also important to adolescents. The risk of HIV/AIDS was cited by 18 percent of respondents in the 1997 study as one reason for not obtaining a tattoo. It would appear that the risks of a tattoo far outweigh the benefits; however, media influence and social acceptance can be powerful motivators.

Body cathexis is the degree of satisfaction with the body (Secord & Jourard, 1953). Body dissatisfaction is incredibly high among the 1990s U.S. population according to "The 1997 Body Image Survey Results" and "Mission Impossible." Dissatisfaction with the body leads to excessive exercise and dieting, self-induced vomiting, and plastic surgery. Siebert's "The Cuts That Go Deeper" in Chapter 3 discusses just how far is too far when it comes to reshaping bodies through plastic surgery. The extent of self-hatred is alarming, especially when it is estimated that 50 percent of all nine-year-old girls have dieted. Certainly all this obsessiveness surrounding the body begs the question: Why don't we like what we have? The suggested reading by Gaitskill, "The Fat Girl in Everyone," discusses how horrified we are of being fat. "The 1997 Body Image Survey Results" article ends with an interesting discussion about what this obsession with the body really means. Are we so complacent as a culture that we have nothing better to do than worry about a few extra pounds?

To critically analyze U.S. cultural ideals for men and women is a process of examining our present-day society. Who benefits from all this hype surrounding thinness? Who loses? Where will all this focus on the body lead us as a nation? As a global player on economic and social issues? These are instructive questions that do not have easy or immediate answers.

CULTURAL STEREOTYPES

A person's body carries with it a set of characteristics that are categorized by others. When meeting someone for the first time and prior to that person speaking, we assume their age, sex, body weight/size, ethnic background, level of attractiveness, and how much effort they put into their appearance. First impressions are often lasting ones; even though a first impression may be inaccurate, we are often reluctant to let go of our initial assessments. Because humans do not have the time to mentally process each individual they encounter daily, we develop shortcuts to manage this visual information overload. Unfortunately, these shortcuts can often lead to stereotypes that often result in discrimination against the stereotyped group. For example, "Tattooing" reports that adults view tattoos as deviant behavior, and that perception may lead some adults to stereotype tattooed adolescent as deviants. But adolescents view tattoos more positively than adults. Adolescents consider tattoos as objects of self-identify and body art. Cultural stereotypes can be long-standing among older persons, while cultural changes among younger persons occur quickly and often regardless (or in spite) of past connotations.

"Fat Chance in a Slim World" relates a personal story of discrimination related to body size. The expression "Don't judge a book by its cover" is familiar to most people. However, the reality is that appearance *does* count. "Fat Chance in a Slim World" illustrates the negative consequences of cultural stereotypes, one of which is stigmatization. To **stigmatize** a group is to brand them as unworthy of respect. Take for example the statement: All overweight people are lazy and have no self-control. This stigmatization often leads to prejudiced behavior in which all large-size persons we encounter are treated the same despite their individual differences.

Short males suffer negative social consequences similar to those of overweight women. In "Heightism: Short Guys Finish Last" we learn that the western height ideal for men is six feet two inches tall. The author of this article gives a somewhat tongue-in-cheek summary of the consequences of being a short male. A few of those consequences include: being accused of having a Napoleon complex even though one is normally assertive; lower salaries; fewer mating opportunities; and lower professional status. A lower salary is a serious consequence given that it will ultimately affect a person's quality of life. In the United States, tall men and thin women are rewarded with better-paying jobs, more dating opportunities, and higher social status. It is no wonder that Americans will go to extreme lengths to attain an ideal body weight and level of attractiveness. "Heightism: Short Guys Finish Last" ends with a powerful plea to treat all individuals as just that—individuals.

When we consider the global marketplace, cultural stereotyping can be especially fatal to success in business. Many businesses today serve customers from a wide array of cultural, ethnic, and racial backgrounds, resulting in a wide variation of physical characteristics. The fast pace of doing business presents additional challenges to resist stereotyping as a means of saving time. One must carefully balance the need to get things done quickly with the understanding that an individual's background cannot be assumed or stereotyped.

FEMINIST CRITIQUES OF THE CULTURAL IDEAL

"On The Muscle" provides an interesting critique of traditional feminine ideals. Although not about body weight specifically, this article focuses on the muscular female body and its ability to shake up traditional definitions of male/female difference. Written from a feminist perspective, "On The Muscle" covers several key societal issues related to the female body. Female bodybuilders challenge the traditional view of the passive and helpless female. This once prevalent view of women is believed by feminists to originate from a **patriarchical society**; that is, a society that traces descendants through the father and makes men the center of hegemonic power. Female bodybuilders pose a threat to patriarchy because their well-developed, visible muscles are perceived as strong and, traditionally, muscles were under the sole proprietorship of males. In patriarchical societies, the female is supposed to be less powerful than, and even subordinate to, males. The author of "On The Muscle" compares fear of female body builders to that of homophobia; i.e., the fear of homosexuals. The author makes the argument that both female bodybuilders and homosexuals challenge the traditional patriarchy by daring to thrive without connections to the heterosexual male power base. In other words, female bodybuilders and homosexuals are not dependent on a heterosexual male for money, power, or sexual pleasure.

On perhaps a more practical level for most women, "The 1997 Body Image Survey Results" indicates that feminist beliefs may offer women some protection from the thin ideal. Of those respondents who described themselves as feminists, only 32 percent were strongly dissatisfied with their overall appearance compared to 49 percent of women who described themselves more traditionally. This finding was also related to actual behaviors in preventing weight gain. Twice as many traditional women (40 percent) vomit to control their weight compared to those claiming to be feminists (24 percent). Furthermore, it is entirely possible for more than one female ideal to be present at any given moment. See "The Athletic Esthetic," in Chapter 5 for a discussion of three concurrent feminine ideals.

CULTURAL STANDARDS OF BEAUTY

Perhaps another way to protect oneself from unrealistic ideals and gain some perspective is to look at several other cultures' definitions of beauty. One connecting factor among all cultures is that we are all human beings. And as humans we simply are not satisfied with what nature has given us. It seems to be human nature to "improve" upon the characteristics we were born with. Because all cultures define an ideal for its members, most individuals will spend time and energy trying to attain that ideal. As social beings, we also want acceptance from others. One way to demonstrate that need for acceptance is the effort put into some approximation of one's cultural ideal.

One of the purposes for identifying U.S. ideals through the class exercise described earlier is to acknowledge cultural biases and cultural ethnocentrism before viewing other cultures and their practices. **Ethnocentrism** is the belief that one's own culture has the "right" way to do things. But when we make comparisons cross-culturally, can one honestly say that there is a difference between wearing high-heeled shoes and the bound lily foot? Is scarification any different than having a face lift or a nose job? Euro-American ideals often seem harsh when compared to other cultures.

"Is Thin In? Kalabari Culture and the Meaning of Fatness," offers the reader a cross-cultural comparison of body ideals for females. The Kalabari body weight ideal for women has been traditionally much heavier than the American ideal. The Kalabari ideal, however, is currently being affected by a global ideal that draws heavily from western culture. The globalization of female beauty is creating ambivalence among young Kalabarian women regarding their traditional definition of female beauty.

We can find many non-Western cultures that traditionally define a large-size body for women as ideal; however, we will use three examples to exemplify the encroaching globalization of female beauty. The Kalabari is one example. Another example can be found in a Polynesian culture. "The Miss Heilala Beauty Pageant" gives the reader a specific example of how the globalization of Euro-American ideals of female beauty is affecting the Miss Heilala Beauty Pageant and the Tongan definition of female beauty. Ideals of female beauty from the United States, Australia, and New Zealand make it increasingly difficult for pageant officials to continue to emphasize traditional characteristics such as eyes and facial expression over a thin body ideal. Large body size has traditionally been a mark of Tongan beauty. Teilhet-Fisk notes in her article that there is a Tongan expression that literally means "to look fat is to look well." American concepts of beauty seem particularly superficial when compared to those of Tongan women.

A third example of a culture that rejects the thin body ideal is Jamaica (Sobo, 1994). In Jamaican culture, thinness symbolizes a person's detachment from others. A thin person in Jamaica is viewed as someone who has low status and is not loved or cared for by others—just the opposite of Euro-American beliefs. One unfortunate consequence of the globalization of female beauty is that one day (if not already) all women may look alike and we will lose the diversity of the past.

Summary

In this chapter, we hope to make the process of "reading the body" a more conscious one. Rather than disregarding the categories in your head and the ten-second (or less) process of putting a person in one category or another, we hope that you will become more aware of how much information you may currently take for granted. This information is important because you may be acting on it in ways in which you are unaware. If you ignore or disregard people because of their appearance, this behavior may not be serving you well. The consciousness of reading the body becomes especially important in a global economy as students graduate from college and begin careers with individuals from various ethnic backgrounds. One can no longer assume that they will spend their career working with people who look "just like me."

Suggested Readings

Gaitskill, M. (1991, December). The fat girl in everyone. *Allure*. (pp. 42, 44, 46.)

Halprin, S. (1995). *"Look at my ugly face!"* New York: Penguin.

Wolf, N. (1991). *The beauty myth: How images of beauty are used against women*. New York: Doubleday.

Selected Images of Pregnancy through Time

Objective: To examine cultural standards of pregnancy over time.

Pregnancy is an interesting stage of a woman's body that is associated with social and emotional expectations. For example, in the Arnolfini Wedding Portrait from 1434 (see Figure 2.1) the bride appears to be pregnant when in reality she is not. Her appearance is fulfilling a social expectation. In Europe at that time, great emphasis was placed on replenishing the society because of losses resulting from wars and plagues.

Most Americans reacted similarly after World War II by replenishing society, resulting in the Baby Boom generation. Postwar fashions for women are often noted for emphasizing a woman's reproductive capacities (Storm, 1987). A common example of this is Dior's New Look in 1947.

Moving ahead to the early 1970s, we see women exposing their pregnant bellies unapologetically (see Figure 2.2). One might assume that these women are hippies or women who adopted the philosophy of "let it all hang out" quite literally. No bashful pretenses here!

In the 1980s, Princess Diana (see Figure 2.3) took a very conservative approach to her dress for impending motherhood. Note the details of Princess Diana's dress: ruffles around the neck and wrists; white hose; and black patent leather shoes with bows. It appears as if Princess Diana is dressed as the child she is about to have! Certainly the social expectations of Diana would have greatly affected her choice of dress while pregnant with the future King of England. This is quite a shift from the previous 1970s illustration!

Also during the 1980s, there was a need for more professional dress than what Princess Diana was wearing (Miller, 1985). Many women in the 1980s were working to establish a career before having a family. You can imagine how difficult it might be for a lawyer or medical doctor to instill confidence in her abilities while wearing ruffles and bows to the office (see Belleau, Miller & Church, 1988). Several companies during the 1980s developed a line of maternity clothing especially for the professional woman (see Figure 2.4).

Now let's turn our attention to the 1990s. Demi Moore was pictured on the cover of *Vanity Fair*, pregnant and nude in 1992 (see Figure 2.5). Quite a bold step for Demi and *Vanity Fair* that resulted in an interesting reaction to this issue. Some cities in the United States required that the magazine arrive wrapped

FIGURE 2.1 *In Jan van Eyck's Arnolfini Wedding Portrait (1434), the bride is conforming to the 15th-century body ideal for European women.*

FIGURE 2.2 *Exposing their abdomens, these women from the early 1970s are visually challenging societal expectations of pregnant women.*

FIGURE 2.3 *Princess Diana conservatively dressed in maternity attire.*

in brown paper (much like pornographic magazines) while other cities banned the sale of the magazine issue completely. These reactions raise some interesting questions. Why was the cover of *Vanity Fair* so disturbing that it had to be covered or completely banned? Are Americans so uncomfortable with the sight of a pregnant woman (a natural state of the body) that this picture had to be covered up?

It would appear as though Demi Moore was making a brave and somewhat risky career move by posing nude for the magazine cover. It would *not* seem likely that she was interested in initiating a national debate on the societal expectations of pregnant women. During the Victorian era in America, women were expected to stay at home and out of view when they were "in the family way." Demi very visibly challenged that old notion. How would you describe Demi Moore's body? Do you consider her body beautiful or repulsive? If you were the parent of small children, would you have left this issue of *Vanity Fair* on the coffee table in the living room for your children to see? Why or why not?

FIGURE 2.4 *Career maternity apparel worn by profes-sional women in the 1980s.*

FIGURE 2.5 *Demi Moore challenges American sensi-tivities by appearing pregnant and nude on the cover of Vanity Fair in 1992.*

Writing Activity

Write a paragraph or two about your thoughts on why the Demi Moore photograph was covered in brown paper or banned. Also include any ideas that came to mind while you looked at the images of pregnant women (real or imagined). How have ideas about preg-nancy changed over time? How have those changes been reflected in dress? In the 1990s, concern for body weight affects women's decisions regarding childbirth. More women are deciding not to have children because of the potential weight gain and dif-ficulty in losing pregnancy weight. What implications does the decision not to have chil-dren have for our society? Also, consider the social class and status of the women illus-trated. How might Princess Diana's status affect her dress as compared to the women from the early 1970s?

Group Activity

After writing down your thoughts, divide into small groups and share your ideas with your fellow classmates.

References

Belleau, B. D., Miller, K. A., & Church, G. E. (1988). Maternity career apparel and perceived job effectiveness. *Clothing and Textiles Research Journal*, 6 (2), 30–36.

Damhorst, M. L. (1985). Meanings of clothing cues in social context. *Clothing and Textiles Research Journal*, 3, 39–48.

Damhorst, M. L. (1989, July). *A contextual model of clothing sign systems*. Paper presented at the Colloquium on the Body and Clothing as Communication, Institute of Marketing Meaning, Indianapolis, IN.

Davis, F. (1988). Clothing, fashion and the dialectic of identity. In D. R. Maines & C. J. Couch (Eds.), *Communication and Social Structure*. Springfield, IL: Charles C. Thomas.

DeLong, M. R. (1998). *The way we look: dress and aesthetics* (2nd ed.), New York: Fairchild

Fisher, S. (1968). Body image. In D. Sills (ed.), *International encyclopedia of the social sciences*, Vol. 2. New York: Macmillian.

Hillestad, R. (1980). The underlying structure of appearance. *Dress*, 5, 117–125.

Kaiser, S. B. (1997). *The social psychology of clothing* (2nd ed. rev.). New York: Fairchild.

Miller, K. A. (1985). *Clothing preferences for maternity career apparel and its relationship to perceived job effectiveness*. Unpublished master's thesis. Louisiana State University, Baton Rouge.

Roach-Higgins, M. E. & Eicher, J. B. (1992). Dress and Identity. *Clothing and Textiles Research Journal*, 10, 1–8.

Rosenberg, M. (1985). Self-concept and psychological well-being. In R. L. Leahy (Ed.), *The development of the self*. Orlando, FL: Academic Press.

Secord, P. F., & Jourard, S. M. (1953). The appraisal of body cathexis: Body-cathexis and the self. *Journal of Consulting Psychology*, 17, 343–347.

Sobo, E. J. (1994). The sweetness of fat: Health, procreation, and sociability in rural Jamaica. In N. Sault, ed., *Many Mirrors: Body image and social relations*. Rutgers University Press.

Storm, P. (1987). *Functions of dress*. Englewood Cliffs, NJ: Prentice-Hall.

1 The 1997 Body Image Survey Results

D. M. Garner

For the past three decades, women and, increasingly, men have been preoccupied with how they look. But the intense scrutiny hasn't necessarily helped us see ourselves any more clearly. While as individuals we are growing heavier, our body preferences are growing thinner. And thinness is depicted everywhere as crucial to personal happiness. Despite the concerns of feminists and other observers, body image issues seem to be only growing in importance.

When most people think of body image, they think about aspects of physical appearance, attractiveness, and beauty. But body image is so much more. It's our mental representation of ourselves; it's what allows us to contemplate ourselves. Body image isn't simply influenced by feelings, and it actively influences much of our behavior, self-esteem, and psychopathology. Our body perceptions, feelings, and beliefs govern our life plan—who we meet, who we marry, the nature of our interactions, our day-to-day comfort level. Indeed, our body is our personal billboard, providing others with first—and sometimes only—impressions.

With that in mind, Psychology Today decided it was time for another detailed reading of the state of body image. The landmark PT national surveys of 1972 and 1985 are among the most widely cited on the subject. We wanted to try and understand the growing gulf between actual and preferred shapes—and to develop the very revealing picture that can be seen only by tracking changes over time. We asked David Garner, Ph.D., to bring his vast expertise to our project. Garner, the director of the Toledo Center for Eating Disorders, is also an adjunct professor of psychology at Bowling Green State University and of women's studies at the University of Toledo. He has been researching and treating eating disorders for 20 years, heading one of the earliest studies linking them to changes in cultural expectations for thinness. From measurements of *Playboy* centerfold mod-

els and Miss America contestants, he documented that these "model women" had become significantly thinner from 1959 to 1979 and that advertising for weight-loss diets had grown correspondingly. A follow-up study showed the trend continuing through the late 1980s.

Garner, along with Cincinnati psychotherapist Ann Kearney Cooke, Ph.D., and editor at large Hara Estroff Marano, crafted five pages worth of questions and in our March/April 1996 issue we asked you how you see, feel, and are influenced by your bodies. The response was phenomenal: about 4,500 people returned questionnaires from every state, not to mention Europe, Israel, Puerto Rico, Pakistan, Saudi Arabia, South Africa, New Zealand, Peru, Australia, Japan, and China. Ten months after the questionnaire hit the newsstands, responses are still coming in. Many of you supplemented your surveys with pages pouring out heart and soul. And though you could reply with complete anonymity, a whopping two-thirds chose to include names, addresses, and phone numbers. Some of you even included pictures!

Our statistical analyses were conducted on the first 4,000 responses—3,452 women and 548 men (86 percent women, 14 percent men)—a much wider gender split than in our readership as a whole, which is 70 percent women and 30 percent men. (See "Who Responded to the Survey," below.) The predominantly female response clearly says something about the stake women have in this topic. Participants were primarily Caucasian, college-educated, in their early to mid thirties, middle-income, and heterosexual. Women who responded range in age from 13 to 90 and weigh between 77 and 365 pounds (89 women weigh 100 pounds or less; 82 women weigh more than 250 pounds). Men

	Women	Men
Total number	3,452	548
Average age	32	35
Actual weight	140	180
Desired weight	125	175
Height	5'5"	5'11"
Caucasian	87%	82%
College grad +	62%	54%
Income: $50,000 +	39%	38%
Heterosexual	93%	79%
Bisexual	4%	8%
Health problems	36%	30%

HOW YOU DESCRIBE YOURSELVES
What you have to say about yourselves:

	%Women	%Men
Relationship-oriented	74	63
Career-oriented	62	56
Happy person	69	66
Spiritually oriented	66	53
Feminist	55	20
Traditional in values	44	43
Athletic	33	45
Pro-choice	73	64
Politically conservative	21	28
Strong belief in astrology	16	14

range in age from 14 to 82 and weigh between 115 and 350 pounds. You describe yourselves as relationship-oriented, pro-choice, intellectual, politically liberal, and spiritual. At the top of your worry list are financial matters and romantic relationships. A significant segment described health problems that vary from relatively minor ailments to cancer and AIDS.

APPEARING TO BE DISSATISFIED

The 1997 Psychology Today Body Image Survey shows there's more discontent with the shape of our bodies than ever before. Okay there are some things we like about our appearance: height, hair, face, feet, and the size of our sex organs generate the most approval. In the span between face and feet, our primary sex organs are a small oasis of favor amidst a wasteland of waist land. Apparently there's little pressure to change the things that we can't see or change. Of course, these areas tend not to be repositories for the accumulation of fat—that object of abhorrence. In contrast, the negative focus remains on our visible attributes, the ones that display fat—the ones that can presumably be controlled or corrected with enough self-discipline.

Fifty-six percent of women say they are dissatisfied with their overall appearance. Their self-disparagement is specifically directed toward their abdomens (71 percent), body weight (66 percent), hips (60 percent), and muscle tone (58 percent). Men show escalating dissatisfaction with their abdomens (63 percent), weight (52 percent), muscle tone (45 percent), overall appearance (43 percent), and chest (38 percent).

Weight dissatisfaction means one thing to men and something entirely different to women. The overwhelming majority of women—89 percent—want to lose weight. How much? The average woman's weight is 140 pounds; the preferred weight is 125 pounds. Only 3 percent of the women who say they are dissatisfied with their bodies want to gain weight; 8 percent want to stay the same. By contrast, 22 percent of the men who say they are dissatisfied with their bodies want to *gain* weight. (See "Men and Body Image," page 34.)

The survey also shows a correlation between body dissatisfaction and body weight—those who are more dissatisfied tend to be heavier. In fact, the average weight of the most dissatisfied women is about 180 pounds; the least dissatisfied weigh in at 128 pounds. Both groups have an average ideal weight that's lower than their actual weight; however, in the former group

WHAT SHAPED YOUR BODY IMAGE WHEN YOU WERE YOUNG?

Some of the facts that figure into body image:

	%Women	%Men
Physical		
My personal feelings about weight	58	35
Interpersonal		
Being teased by others	44	35
My mother's attitude about my body	31	13
My father's attitude about my body	23	11
Positive sexual experiences	26	28
Sexual abuse	18	7
Cultural		
Movie or TV celebrities	23	13
Fashion magazine models	22	6
Sports figures	7	16

it's fifty pounds away from reality, compared with three pounds for the least dissatisfied.

How important is it for people to be the weight they want? We put the question in stark terms and asked, "How many years of your life would you trade to achieve your weight goals?" The findings are astounding: Fifteen percent of women and 11 percent of men say they would sacrifice more than five years of their lives; 24 percent of women and 17 percent of men say they would give up more than three years. These answers make us regret not testing the extremes and offering 10- and 20-year options. Still, we can confidently conclude that a significant minority of you believe life is worth living only if you are thin.

A rather drastic measure of weight control is cigarette smoking. Statistics reveal that smoking is on the rise among young women. Robert Klesges, Ph.D., and colleagues at the University of Memphis have repeatedly shown that smoking is used by many women for weight control. While we didn't specifically ask whether you smoke, we did ask whether you smoke to control your weight. About 50 percent of women and 30 percent of men say they puff away to control the pounds.

EXTREME WEIGHT CONTROL

To control my weight during the past year, once a week or more:

	%Women	%Men	Eating Disorder*	No Eating Disorder
Induced vomiting	6	1	23	1.5
Abused laxatives	6	3	17	3
Took diuretics	5	4	10	4
Used diet pills	12	6	20	9

Women identifying themselves as having a diagnosed or undiagnosed eating disorder.

Body dissatisfaction has very different implications for people depending upon how heavy they are. Among those well above normal weight, body dissatisfaction is a painful expression of despair, but understandable given the cultural stigma of being fat. However, an equivalent amount of self-loathing on the part of thin people suggests a different kind of problem—distortion on top of dissatisfaction. Thin women distort reality by seeing themselves as fat. Today this type of distortion is rampant and has become the norm. It explains why so many women are susceptible to eating disorders, where the pursuit of thinness is driven by faulty perceptions rather than reality. One hundred and fifty-nine women in our sample are extremely underweight—and 40 percent of them still want to lose weight. Many have eating disorders, to be described later.

AGE AND BODY IMAGE

A number of national studies have shown that body weight is increasing among American adults. Moreover, epidemiologic studies find that body weight increases with age. For both men and women it tends to increase during the first five decades of life, then decline on the way to our inevitable destiny. Although the pattern of gradual weight gain during adulthood recently sparked a public health frenzy, leading to such programs as C. Everett Koops Shape Up America, an analysis of 13 major studies of weight change by Reuben Andres, M.D., of the Gerontology Research Center in Baltimore, Maryland, found that people who put on some pounds during adulthood survive longer than those who maintain or even lose weight.

Our findings confirm that body weight usually increases with age. On average, both men and women tend to put on five to ten pounds per decade, a trend that stops between the ages of 50 and 59. Weight declines slightly after age 60.

Since satisfaction with our appearance is so closely tied to how much we weigh, particularly for women, it's logical to assume that our self-disparagement would gradually increase over a lifetime. But that's not what we found. The youngest women, ages 13 to 19, are both the thinnest and the most satisfied with their appearance, however

54 percent of them are still dissatisfied. The number barely increases to 57 percent among women ages 20 to 29. And it remains at around this level, even though women gained five to ten pounds each succeeding decade.

We can't say for sure how these young women will feel as they get older; a survey, of course, taps different women at each age, not the same women over time. Nevertheless, the magnitude of self-hatred among young women is astonishing. Despite being at a weight that most women envy, they are still plagued by feelings of inadequacy. The good news is that even though women gain weight with age, they don't become more dissatisfied as they get older. In fact, there's some evidence that as they age they gain insight and appreciation of their bodies' abilities.

Induction into our culture's weight concerns is happening for women at younger ages. Girls today not only have more weight concerns when they're young, they also lack buffers to protect their psyches. Kids don't know themselves well and have not yet developed many competencies to draw on. It's easier for them to look outside themselves to discover who they are—and find themselves lacking. While we may not be able to draw conclusions about them based on the experiences of older women, we can only hope that over time they develop the insight of this 55-year-old woman from Pennsylvania: "From age 15 to 25, I was very concerned about my body image and went on many diets. As I matured, I realized that personality and morals are more important than how you look and stopped beating myself up and accepted my body. Now I don't worry about my weight but I do eat healthfully and exercise moderately."

In contrast to women, only 41 percent of young men ages 13 to 19 say they are dissatisfied with their appearance. The figures stay about the same for men ages 20 to 29 (38 percent), then spike to 48 percent among 30- to 39-year-olds. They decline again for the 40 to 49 age group (43 percent) and increase for men ages 50 to 59 (48 percent). Again, in contrast to women, a significant proportion of dissatisfied men want to *add* body mass, not lose it. But the critical point is that men as a group are more satisfied with their appearance, although the number who are

THE WEIGHT OF INFLUENCE: FACTORS FOSTERING POSITIVE BODY IMAGE
What's instrumental in making you feel good about your body?

	%Women	%Men
Physical		
Exercising regularly	64	62
Losing weight	62	39
Feeling thin	53	24
Accepting my body the way it is	50	36
Wearing flattering clothes	46	21
Interpersonal		
Compliments on my appearance	48	44
Love from another person	43	44
Positive sexual experiences	40	41
Good relationships	33	34
Emotional		
Confidence in my abilities	39	38
Feeling effective as a person	39	36
Meditating	11	9

THE WEIGHT OF INFLUENCE: FACTORS FOSTERING NEGATIVE BODY IMAGE
What's instrumental in making you feel bad about your body?

	%Women	%Men
Physical		
Gaining weight	66	37
Not exercising regularly	44	36
Looking at my stomach in the mirror	44	33
Looking at my face in the mirror	16	15
A certain time in my menstrual cycle	29	—
Interpersonal		
My partner's opinion of my appearance	40	29
Being around someone critical	32	19
Someone rejecting me	26	24
Relationships not going well	24	21
Negative sexual experiences	20	16
Emotional		
Not feeling confident	22	18
Being in a bad mood	15	9

tormented about their weight and shape appears to be growing.

THE LOCUS OF FOCUS

Because we were interested in discovering what was most instrumental in creating positive and negative feelings about your bodies, we asked how your body image is influenced by certain aspects of physical appearance: gaining weight, feeling thin, looking at your face in the mirror, looking at your stomach in the mirror. Exercise was also included, because we use it to change our body weight and shape.

We assumed focusing on features like the face and the stomach—the latter the bearer of fat and of children—would produce highly-charged feelings, both good and bad. However, we were specifically interested in trying to understand the relative impact of different physical features on body feelings—the locus of focus. We also wanted to measure how physical aspects of appearance stack up against interpersonal factors, such as being rejected, receiving compliments, being teased, and sexual experiences, as well as emotional components, like feeling effective as a person and overall happiness.

When it comes to what causes negative feelings, gaining weight is at the top of the list for everyone: two-thirds of women and about a third of men say its a very important cause of their disapproval of their bodies. And the stomach, not the face, is the prevailing locus of disapproval for both men and women. Looking at your stomach in the mirror is an extreme downer for 44 percent of women and 33 percent of men—compared to the face, which was a downer for 16 percent of women and 15 percent of men.

Women are hit with a very specific source of body antipathy: more than 75 percent say that "a certain time in the menstrual cycle" is an important cause of negative feelings about their bodies. And a fear of fatness may be perverting women's attitudes toward pregnancy and childbearing. About a third of women say that, for them, pregnancy itself is an important source of negative body feelings.

If these feelings are strong enough, its only reasonable to assume that they may affect some women's decisions to have kids. As one 25-year-old Maryland woman offers: "I love children and would love to have one more—but only if I didn't have to gain the weight." A 43-year-old woman from Georgia proselytizes against pregnancy: "I tell every young girl that if they like the way their body looks, don't get pregnant. It messes up a woman's body."

While interpersonal factors are the cause of negative feelings about the body for fewer people, they are highly influential for a significant minority. Forty percent of women and 29 percent of men say their partner's opinion about their appearance is very important to their body image. About a quarter of all respondents say the same goes for someone rejecting them. Thus there's a major connection between the way we feel about our body and the way we perceive others feel about it. One 54-year-old New York woman says: "Since my partner sees me as beautiful, I feel beautiful." This interpersonal connection seems to take root early, as a 17-year-old woman from New York explains: "My partner's feelings about me and my looks mean everything to me. If my mate had an unfavorable opinion, that would be devastating."

What impact does our mood have on our feelings about our body? The survey, as well as other research, suggests a potentially deadly two-way self-perpetuating process. When we feel bad about anything, our body satisfaction plummets, and when we hate our body, our mood takes a dive. A 39-year-old Connecticut woman captures the vicious cycle: "When I'm in a bad mood about anything, I get more critical of my body. When I am more critical of my body, I lose confidence in my abilities." A 35-year-old woman from Pennsylvania illustrates the process: "When I am in a bad mood about something else, my focus often goes right to my body weight and I either feel fat or I obsess about food."

The connection between mood and body is critical; it suggests that body dissatisfaction is not a static entity but rather is governed, at least in part, by our general emotional state. When we feel bad about something else, our bodies get dragged down in the negative tide.

Among the many aspects of body image we looked at was the role of certain life orientations.

DO FASHION MODELS INFLUENCE HOW YOU FEEL ABOUT YOUR APPEARANCE?

What's the media's impact on how we see ourselves?

	%Women	Extremely Satisfied Women	Extremely Dissatisfied Women	%Men
I always or very often:				
Compare myself to models in magazines	27	17	43	12
Carefully study the shapes of models	28	18	47	19
Very thin or muscular models make me:				
Feel insecure about my weight	29	12	67	15
Want to lose weight	30	13	67	18
Feel angry or resentful	22	9	45	8

For example, we compared women who call themselves feminists with those who view themselves more traditionally. There are no differences between the groups in average body weight. But 32 percent of feminists, compared with 49 percent of traditional women, are strongly dissatisfied with their overall appearance. When asked more specifically about their weight, 24 percent of feminists and 40 percent of traditional women are extremely dissatisfied. The differences translate directly into behavior—twice as many traditionally oriented women vomit to control their weight as women claiming to be feminists. It appears that feminist beliefs confer some behavioral protection.

When we asked what leads to positive feelings about your bodies, the results generally mirrored the findings about negative feelings, but there are some interesting differences. Weight-related factors tended to top the list of sources of positive feelings paralleling the results for negative feelings. Exercise generated the greatest source of positive feelings. But moderate exercise, we found, goes a long way. People who exercise a lot do not seem to feel any better than those who exercise moderately.

And while both men and women identify a few circumstances that could crash their feelings about their bodies, you point out more factors that bolster it. About twice as many people judge sexual experiences as a source of good feelings rather than bad. For both sexes, interpersonal and emotional factors more often serve to reinforce, not punish. This is encouraging news; it implies that there are many avenues for us to improve our feelings about our bodies.

When we asked what shaped your body image during childhood and adolescence, most women and a significant minority of men reiterate the cultural theme that thinness is the key to happiness. But interpersonal factors also weigh heavily on most of us during development, and women rank them more important than men.

For many, teasing during childhood or adolescence had a crushing affect on body image. So much so that the extent of the damage can't be captured by a questionnaire. The narratives paint a graphic picture of the pain. As one 59-year-old Illinois man recounts: "Being teased when I was a child made me feel bad about my body for years and years." A 37-year-old woman from Ohio admits: "No matter how thin I become, I always feel like the fat kid everyone made fun of." An 18-year-old Iowa woman says: "The memories absolutely haunt me and make me feel like something is wrong with me."

By far, however, the dominant factor that regulates our feelings about our appearance is our body weight—actual body weight as well as attitudes about it. The weight of this influence is staggering compared to other factors. Body weight alone accounts for 60 percent of our overall satisfaction with our appearance; all other physical features combined add only 10 percent more to our level of satisfaction. This suggests a simple solution—just change your weight and happy times will follow. Unfortunately it's not that simple.

EXERCISE: THE NEW HOLY GRAIL?

Virtually everyone surveyed says they exercised during the past year—97 percent of both sexes. And exercise gets high marks when it comes to breeding positive body feelings (by a narrow margin for women, a substantial majority for men). Seventy-six percent of women and 86 percent of men report exercising at least two hours a week; 20 percent of women and 27 percent of men exercise five or more times a week for at least 30 minutes. There's a modest relationship between the amount of time spent exercising and satisfaction with appearance, and this is stronger for men than women.

On the surface, it appears that exercise is an uncomplicated remedy for achieving harmony with our bodies. But a closer look at our findings tempers this conclusion. More than 60 percent of women and 40 percent of men indicate that at least half of their workout time is spent exercising to control their weight. And for a significant proportion of both sexes—18 percent of women, 12 percent of men—all exercise is aimed at weight control.

But all that exercise is not leading to body satisfaction, since 88 percent of these women and 79 percent of these men say they are dissatisfied with their appearance. By contrast, among those who exercise for weight control less than 25 percent of the time, only a third are dissatisfied with their appearance. For many women, exercise is simply one more weapon in the weight-control war, a practice that mutes its ability to boost body satisfaction.

However, heavier women say the more they exercise, the bigger the boost to body satisfaction. Among women who weigh more than average, 30 percent of those who exercise more than five times a week are satisfied, compared to 20 percent who exercise less than once a week.

Whether or not exercise is effective as a method of weight control, it does tend to make

THE BIG BAD BODY
The dissatisfaction we feel toward our bodies has not only risen since 1972, the rate at which it's rising is accelerating:

| | 1972 Survey% | | 1985 Survey% | | 1997 Survey% | |
	Women	Men	Women	Men	Women	Men
Overall appearance	25	15	38	34	56	43
Weight	48	35	55	41	66	52
Height	13	13	17	20	16	16
Muscle tone	30	25	45	32	57	45
Breasts/chest	26	18	32	28	34	38
Abdomen	50	36	57	50	71	63
Hips or upper thighs	49	12	50	21	61	29

us feel better about our appearance. It also improves both health and mood.

SEX AND BODY IMAGE

Sexual experiences affect our body image and our body image affects our sexual liaisons. You describe this reciprocal relationship poignantly. Body image affects sexual experiences: "The less attractive I feel, the less I desire sex," says a 31-year-old woman from Louisiana. "If at all possible I avoid sex; however, if it should happen, I am unwilling to let go. I have the feeling I may be vulgar to my partner."

Sexual experiences affect body image: "A bad sexual experience makes me feel embarrassed about my body," admits a 19-year-old Texas woman. Sexual abuse amplifies this self-abasement: "Having been sexually assaulted brought a lot of body hatred, and a desire to not have a body," a 24-year-old woman from Illinois says.

As has been the case for so many other variables in the 1997 Survey, weight gets in the middle of the picture. One 20-year-old Missouri woman states: "I try to lose weight for boyfriends. When I am fat, I know that no one wants to be with me. I feel like unless I have a good body, no decent guy wants me!"

The connection between sexual experiences and body image is affirmed in our overall findings. More than a third of all men (40 percent) and women (36 percent) say that unpleasant sexual experiences are moderately to very important in causing negative feelings of their body. But an even greater percentage—70 percent of men and 67 percent of women—feel that good sexual experiences contribute to satisfactory feelings about their bodies. Few believe they are irrelevant (6 percent of men and 7 percent of women).

Twenty-three percent of women consider sexual abuse moderately to very important in having shaped their body image in childhood or adolescence. That's twice the number of men—10 percent—who think so, perhaps reflecting the difference in rates of abuse between men and women. But the vast majority of men (85 percent) and women (74 percent) declare that it's almost or completely irrelevant, no doubt indicating their lack of personal experience.

The personal accounts of some respondents leave no doubt as to the devastating effects of sexual abuse. An 18-year-old woman says: "As a young child, I was sexually abused by my father. I grew up feeling as though there was something inherently dirty and evil about my body." Abuse is clearly a dominant factor in body image for members of both sexes, but it's not ubiquitous, unlike such factors as teasing by others (73 percent of women and 57 percent of men) and personal feelings about weight (79 percent of women and 56 percent of men).

Intriguingly, those who are dissatisfied with their bodies are much more inclined to view negative sexual experiences as important than those who are body-satisfied. Only 15 percent of women who are extremely satisfied with their bodies say that negative sexual experiences are very important in determining their body image (42 percent say that negative sexual experiences are completely irrelevant). In contrast, 41 percent of body-dissatisfied women regard negative sexual experiences as very important (only 16 percent say they are completely irrelevant). The same is true for men.

Sexual and physical abuse are important contributors to body dissatisfaction—but again primarily it's women who have been sexually abused who think so. Sexual abuse is judged very important by 30 percent of women who are extremely body-dissatisfied, versus 13 percent of the extremely body-satisfied group. Women who feel good about their bodies and have not been victims of abuse just don't grasp the damage abuse can do to feelings about the body.

EXTREME WEIGHT CONTROL

Eating disorders occur when a person's intense preoccupation with their "fatness" leads them to extreme measures to control their weight. Considerable research indicates that anorexia and bulimia are outgrowths of a negative body image and, further, that today's epidemic increase in eating disorders is related to the intense pressure put on women to conform to ultraslender role models of feminine beauty.

MEN AND BODY IMAGE

In general, men say they are more satisfied with their bodies than women. And weight plays a less important role in shaping their feelings about their bodies. A little over 12 percent of the men who responded to our survey say they're gay. In general, gay men are more concerned about their weight and have more eating concerns.

	%All Men	%Gay Men	%Women
I am extremely or somewhat satisfied with my body	57	44	44
Gaining weight is very important in making me feel bad about my body	37	46	66
Feeling thin goes a long way toward making me feel good about my body	24	34	53
Do you ever diet?	58	70	84
Have you ever been diagnosed with an eating disorder?	3	9	14
Do you think you have an eating disorder but haven't been treated?	5	17	14
Do You Use:			
Diet pills	5	12	10
Laxatives	2	6	4
Diuretics	3	8	4
Vomiting	1	3	4

A remarkable 84 percent of women and 58 percent of men report having dieted to lose weight. A sizable proportion of respondents say they have resorted to extreme and dangerous weight-control methods in the last year: 445 women (13 percent) and 22 men (4 percent) say they induce vomiting; more than a third of each of these groups vomit once a week or more. Fourteen percent of women (480) and 3 percent of men (16) say they have actually been diagnosed with eating disorders. Among the very underweight women in our survey, 31 percent (49) indicate they have been diagnosed with an eating disorder. And 11.5 percent of women and 2 percent of men say they have an eating disorder but have never received treatment, although the type of eating disorder was not specified.

Vomiting was more common among those who say they have been diagnosed (23 percent), less common among those who identify themselves as having untreated eating disorders (11 percent). Perhaps most surprising is that 1.5 percent of women (38) vomit for weight control and don't feel they have an eating disorder!

Laxative abuse for weight control is common among those diagnosed with eating disorders (17 percent) and those self-identified (9 percent). It is also reported by 3 percent of women (72) who don't feel they have eating disorders.

Vomiting and laxative abuse seem to be increasingly accepted as "normal" methods of weight control. And eating disorders themselves have become the object of envy, gaining celebrity status with each new high-profile victim. There's even evidence that eating disorders acquire a positive patina with media exposure—even if it's negative—and that actually helps spread them by social contagion. This was driven home by a patient I recently saw. When told she really didn't meet the diagnostic criteria for an eating disorder, she burst into tears. "I tried so hard to get an eating disorder, to be like [a high profile gymnast]," she lamented, "but I guess I can't even get this right."

Not surprisingly, one of the keys to helping people overcome eating disorders is fostering the development of a positive body image. Unfortunately, this means swimming against the cultural stream, as it's extremely hard to avoid ubiquitous thin-is-beautiful messages. Studies of prime-time television indicate that programs are dominated by people with thin body types and thinness is consistently associated with favorable personality traits. But one of the most interesting aspects of the psychology of appearance is that not everyone succumbs to the same pressures.

MEDIATING SELF-PERCEPTION

The media play an important role as a cultural gatekeeper, framing standards of beauty for all of us by the models they choose. Many observers, including eating-disorder specialists, have encouraged producers and editors to widen the range of beauty standards by including models more representative of real women. But often they respond by saying that more diversity will weaken sales; recently *Vogue* magazine acknowledged the outrage toward gaunt fashion models—but denied there's any evidence linking images of models to eating disorders.

The 1997 Body Image Survey gathered direct information on this issue and more generally on the media's impact on self-perception. The results are nothing short of fascinating. Forty-three percent of women report that "very thin or muscular models" make them feel insecure about their weight. This is true for only 28 percent of men. Just under half of women (48 percent) indicate very thin models make them want to lose weight to look like them; 34 percent

of men agree. Though drawn to and driven by the image of fashion models, 34 percent of women declare they are angry and resentful at these presumed paragons of beauty, as are 15 percent of men.

The impact of the media, however, is somewhat selective, affecting most strongly those who are dissatisfied with their shape, and who are generally heavier and farther away from the cultural ideal. Women who are extremely satisfied with their weight compare themselves to and study the shapes of models less than half as often as women who are body-dissatisfied.

Even more striking, 67 percent of the women who are dissatisfied with their bodies say that very thin or muscular models make them feel insecure about their weight very often or always (versus 12 percent of body-satisfied women). Sixty-seven percent also say models make them want to lose weight (versus 13 percent of body-satisfied women), and 45 percent say models make them angry or resentful (versus 9 percent of body-satisfied women).

Similarly, those who say they have been diagnosed with an eating disorder report being highly influenced by fashion models. Forty-three percent compare themselves to models in magazines; 45 percent scrutinize the shapes of models. Forty-nine percent say very thin models make them feel insecure about themselves, and 48 percent say they "make me want to lose weight to be like them."

Clearly, body satisfaction, a rather rare commodity, confers relative immunity to media influence. But the existence of a large number of women who are drawn to media imagery but resent the unreality of those images is cause for concern. It suggests they are experiencing an uncomfortable level of entrapment. We wonder how long it will take for their resentment to be unleashed full force on the fashion industry and/or the media—and in what form.

Women and, to a lesser degree, men are not only affected by images in the media, they also want to see themselves represented differently. They're clamoring for change and willing to put their money on their predilections. The overwhelming majority of all respondents—93 percent of women, 89 percent of men—want models in magazines to represent the natural range of body shapes; 82 percent of women assert they are willing to buy magazines containing heavier models, as do 53 percent of men, even though most still believe that clothes look better on thin models.

One 30-year-old woman captures the feeling: "The media portray an image of the perfect woman that is unattainable for somewhere between 98 to 99 percent of the female population. How are we supposed to live up to that standard that is shoved in our faces constantly—I hate it."

THE SHAPE OF THINGS TO COME

More than ever before, women are dissatisfied with their weight and are fighting it with relentless dieting and exercise. Thinness has become the preeminent yardstick for success or failure, a constant against which every woman can be measured, a gauge that has slowly permeated the male mentality. Yet the actual body weight of women in the U.S. has increased over the last 30 years, and consumer pressure for weight-loss products is surging.

Research shows that dieting to lose weight and fear of fatness are now common in girls as young as nine years old—and escalate dramatically during adolescence, particularly among those at the heavier end of the spectrum. The risk of developing an eating disorder is eight times higher in dieting 15-year-old girls than in nondieting 15-year-old girls.

The 1997 Body Image Survey results and cumulative clinical experience suggest there is merit to becoming comfortable with yourself even if you don't conform to current cultural body-size ideals. Some people are naturally fatter, just as others are naturally thinner. Despite a $50 billion-a-year diet industry, conventional treatments for obesity are an abysmal failure. Traditional dietary and behavioral treatments may have an effect in the short term, but they do not produce lasting and clinically significant amounts of weight loss. They are no match for the genetic and biological factors that regulate body weight. They certainly reinforce the myth that weight loss is the preferred route to improve self-esteem. Perhaps the wisest course is to get plenty of exercise—and accept yourself the way you are rather than try to mold yourself into a narrowly defined and arbitrary ideal, no matter how widely pictured it is.

Preoccupation with body image is undoubtedly not good for our mental health, but it also seems to be a metaphor for something larger in the culture—if we could only figure out what. Over a decade ago, the late social critic Christopher Lasch argued that our culture of mass consumption encourages narcissism, a new kind of self-consciousness or vanity through which people have learned to judge themselves not merely *against* others but *through* others' eyes. The "image" projected by possessions, physical attractiveness, clothes, and "personality" replace experience, skills, and character as gauges of personal identity, health, and happiness. We are thrown into a chronic state of unease, perfect prey for an array of commercial "solutions."

Psychiatrists and psychologists have also weighed in on the meaning of body image issues. At the 1996 meeting of the American Psychological Association, Yale psychiatrist Alan Feingold, M.D., received an award for detailing differences in body-image pressures on men and women. Dr. Feingold contends that pressure on women to look good is not only growing but reflects intensified competition for dwindling resources; after all, looks confer a kind of status to women. Others point to role conflicts for women; power issues; a mother-daughter generational rift; and the possibility that in a world of rapidly shifting realities, we seize on the body as an island of certainty—numbers on a scale represent quantifiable accomplishment. Perhaps it's all of these; the body is a big screen on which we now project all of our anxieties.

BOX 1

A Very Revealing Picture:
Psychology Today's 1997 Body Image Survey Findings

• Body image is more complex than previous research suggests. It's influenced by many factors, including interpersonal factors, individual factors such as mood, and physical factors like body weight. Cultural pressures also play their part. Which factors are most important vary from person to person.

• Body dissatisfaction is soaring among both women and men—increasing at a faster rate than ever before. This is the great paradox of body preoccupation—instead of insight, it seems to breed only discontent. But a revolution in the way women see themselves—may be brewing.

• How important is it for people to be the weight they want? Fifteen percent of women and 11 percent of men say they would sacrifice more than five years of their lives to be the weight they want. Twenty-four percent of women and 17 percent of men say they would give up more than three years.

• Among young women ages 13 to 19, a whopping 62 percent say they are dissatisfied with their weight. And it gets a bit worse with age: Sixty-seven percent of women over age 30 also say they are unhappy with how much they weigh.

• While body hatred tends to stay at about the same level as women age, today's young women may be more vulnerable to self-disparagement as they get older. They are being initiated into feelings of body dissatisfaction at a tender age, and this early programming may be difficult to undo.

• Body dissatisfaction afflicts those women who describe themselves as feminists (32 percent) as well as those who say they are more traditional (49 percent). Nevertheless, feminist beliefs seem to confer some behavioral protection: Feminists say they are less willing to use drastic measures like vomiting to control their weight.

• Physical factors, such as gaining weight, are the most common cause of negative feelings about the body. Nevertheless, relationships also have an impact. If your mate doesn't think you look great, you're likely to feel devastated.

• Pregnancy is increasingly being seen not as a normal body function but as an encumbrance to body image. And some women say they are choosing not to have children for this reason.

• More than 75 percent of women surveyed say that menstruation, another normal body function, causes them to have negative feelings about their bodies.

• Bad moods wreak havoc on women's feelings about their bodies. Women get caught in a vicious spiral: emotional distress causes body loathing; disgust with their body causes emotional distress.

• Teasing during childhood or adolescence has an indelible effect on women's feelings about their bodies. Women say that the negative fallout can last for decades—no matter what shape they're currently in.

• What's a quick way to feel good about your body? Good sex. The survey found that in general, good sexual experiences breed high levels of body satisfaction.

• Sexual abuse is an important contributor to body dissatisfaction—but only women who have been sexually abused think so. Other women don't grasp the damage abuse can do to feelings about the body. The experience of sexual abuse seems to create a divide that mirrors the general cultural debate over the validity of allegations of sexual abuse.

• What's the most reliable way to develop positive feelings about your body—to say nothing of your health? Respondents say it's exercising—just for the pleasure of it.

• Curiously, most people say that when it comes to weight control, exercising does not boost body satisfaction. Only women who are very heavy disagree.

• It's no longer possible to deny the fact that images of models in the media have a terrible effect on the way women see themselves. Women who have eating disorders are most influenced by fashion models.

• A model backlash has already begun. Although images of fashion models are intended to inspire identification and emulation, more than three out of ten women say they make them feel angry and resentful. They make more than four out of ten women feel insecure. Women say they are dying to see models that are more representative of the natural range of body types.

BOX 2

One of the major goals of the 1997 Body Image Survey was to learn about how people have remade their image. Though we anticipated receiving a few brief suggestions, we were inundated with your personal accounts of change. We have summarized your suggestions but kept your words. Try and discover what factors play a role in your struggle with your body. And be deliberate about creating a lifestyle that increases your chances for ending the war with your body.

1. Develop criteria for self-esteem that go beyond appearance. One way to make appearance less important is to develop other benchmarks for self-evaluation. A 51-year-old woman from California summarizes the approach: "By achieving in other areas, balancing successes and failures, searching where positives are possible." A 53-year-old Washington man says, "focusing on succeeding at work, participating in sports, and friendships have helped me overcome my negative body feelings."

2. Cultivate the ability to appreciate your body, especially how it functions. One middle-aged woman writes: "I have often wanted to write an article called 'I Have a Beautiful Body.' No, I don't look like Jane Fonda. I look like a normal 46-year-old woman who has had three children. But my body is beautiful because of all it does for me. I have two eyes that can see, a large nose for smelling, a large mouth for eating and smiling, two hands that can hold and hug, two breasts that have

nursed three sons, an abdomen that was home to three babies, two legs that can walk everywhere I want to go, and two feet to take me there."

"I have extremely red hair and as a child I hated it because it was so different," says a 20-year-old woman from California. "I have come to realize that my hair is a beautiful and exotic part of me. Now I cherish it."

3. Engage in behavior that makes you feel good about yourself. "When I have negative thoughts and feelings about my physical appearance, I try to behave in ways that will turn them around, like exercise and buying a piece of clothing that enhances my appearance," says a 30-year-old Missouri woman.

"Although Rubenesque at age 54, I currently model nude for a local university art school, meditate daily to focus inward, and enjoy dancing, swimming, archery, art, and my writing projects," says a Georgia woman.

4. Reduce your exposure to noxious images. "I stopped buying fashion magazines completely when I was about 24," says a 30-year-old woman from Michigan. "Comparing myself to the models had a very strong and negative impact."

"One of the things that helped me become more accepting of my body was the realization that it was okay to be female," says a 67-year-old woman from Ohio. "It sounds hokey, but watching old movies starring Sophia Loren and Ava Gardner helped. These women had shoulders, and breasts, and

hips, and are some of the sexiest women I have ever seen."

5. Exercise for strength, fitness, and health, not just weight control. "When I was able to stop focusing on how my body looked and began experiencing what it could help me accomplish—climbing, swimming, cycling, surviving in the wilderness—it made me feel extremely satisfied," says a 28-year-old woman from Louisiana.

"About a year ago I started walking every day for about an hour," says a 22-year-old woman from New York. "Because I was walking I felt so good. I also lost 10 pounds, but that didn't matter. My attitude changed because I cared about my health."

6. Seek out others who respect and care about your body; teach them how to talk about and touch your body. "The most recent experience that has helped has been a lover," says a 67-year-old Ohio woman. "He makes me glad to be in this body with this shape and these dimensions."

7. Get out of abusive relationships. "If my partner didn't like my appearance, he would no longer be my partner," says a 31-year-old woman from Alabama. "I eliminate the negative."

8. Identify and change habitual negative thoughts about your body. "I constructed a tape of positive self-talk with personal goals and feelings I want to achieve," says a 25-year-old Washington woman. "When I have a bad attitude about my body, I pop in my tape. It really helps improve my self-image."

"When I look in the mirror at my body I always try to say nice things rather than cringe," continues the wise-beyond-her-years 25-year-old.

9. Decode more complicated thoughts about the body. Are negative thoughts and feelings about your body distracting you from other issues that are really bothering you? A 60-year-old woman writes: "A factor that has helped me come to terms with my body was recognizing that much of my relationship prob-lems had more to do with shyness and lack of social skills than physical appearance. Once I worked on my people skills, I found that I worried less about my appearance."

10. If you can't get over your bad body image, consider seeking professional help. "I was bulimic for 12 years," says a 36-year-old woman from Oregon. My recovery was based on individual counseling, support from friends, and a hell of a lot of hard work on my part."

11. Control what you can, forget about what you can't. "As far as negativity about my physical appearance," says a 33-year-old woman from Michigan, "I've had one simple rule: work on improving what you can realistically change, and don't spend time worrying about the rest."

DISCUSSION QUESTIONS

The 1997 Body Image Survey Results

1. What finding surprised you the most? Why?

2. When you consider that individuals at the end of the 20th century have more conveniences and better health care than any generation previous to them, why the obsession with thinness?

3. Do you agree with the concluding statement of the article that "the body is a big screen on which we now project all of our anxieties"? Why or why not?

4. Can you identify any cultural or societal issues that may have had an impact on the "growing gulf between actual and preferred [body] shapes"?

2 Mission Impossible

Karen S. Schneider

Plato said that we behold beauty in the eye of the mind…and that's still the problem. In his 25-year career, for example, director Joel Schumacher has worked with, among others, Demi Moore, Julia Roberts and Sandra Bullock. But, he says, "I have never worked with a beautiful young woman who thought she was A) beautiful or B) thin enough."

In Hollywood, such insecurity is not without reason. At last March's Academy Awards ceremony, actress Alicia Silverstone, 19, the fresh-faced sensation of *The Crush* and *Clueless*, did the unthinkable: She appeared in public despite the fact that, like many of her teenage peers around the country, she had just added on 5 or 10 pounds. Was she congratulated for the self-confidence and assurance it took to be herself? Hardly. The tabloids, noting Silverstone's role in the next *Batman* sequel, blared out lines like "Batman and Fatgirl" and "Look Out Batman! Here Comes Buttgirl!" and *Entertainment Weekly* sniped that Alicia was "more *Babe* than babe." Silverstone won't comment on the commotion; Schumacher, who is directing her in the upcoming *Batman and Robin*, says he was startled by the meanness of the stories: "The news coverage was outrageous, disgusting, judgmental and cruel. What did this child do? Have a couple of pizzas?"

In a word, yes. In the moral order of today's media-driven universe—in which you could bounce a quarter off the well-toned abs of any cast member on *Melrose Place* or *Friends*, fashion magazines are filled with airbrushed photos of emaciated models with breast implants, and the perfectly attractive Janeane Garofalo can pass for an ugly duckling next to Beautiful Girl Uma Thurman in the current hit movie *The Truth About Cats & Dogs*—the definition of what constitutes beauty or even an acceptable body seems to become more inaccessible every year.

The result? Increasingly bombarded by countless "perfect" body images projected by TV, movies and magazines, many Americans are feeling worse and worse about the workaday bodies they actually inhabit. The people being hurt most are the ones who are most vulnerable: adolescents.

"There is a tremendous stigma in our society about being fat," says Thomas Cash, professor of psychology at Old Dominion University in Norfolk, Va., and author of *What Do You See When You Look in the Mirror?* "Kids aspire to be thin, but just any kind of thin isn't sufficient—now it has to be thin *and* toned. If people compare themselves with these unrealistic standards, they can only conclude they are born losers."

"We're evolving toward an unnatural view of beauty," says Los Angeles social psychologist Debbie Then, "thin women with huge breasts and stick legs like those of a 12-year-old. What real women's bodies look like is labeled wrong and unattractive." Says Mary Pipher, author of *Reviving Ophelia*, the current bestseller about the psychological and physical health of teenage girls: "Research shows that virtually all women are ashamed of their bodies. It used to be adult women, teenage girls, who were ashamed, but now you see the shame down to very young girls—10, 11 years old. Society's standard of beauty is an image that is literally just short of starvation for most women."

In 1972, reports Cash, 23 percent of U.S. women said they were dissatisfied with their overall appearance; today, that figure has more than doubled, to 48 percent. An exclusive *People* poll conducted in May confirms that women are three times as likely as men to have negative thoughts about their bodies (see Box 1, page 42)—and the younger they are, the unhappier they are. Since 1979, Miss America contestants have become so skinny that the majority now are at least 15 percent below the recommended body weight for their height. (Medically, the same percentage is considered a possible symptom of anorexia nervosa.) In the past 30 years, the voluptuous size-12 image of Marilyn Monroe has given way to the size-2 likes of *Lois & Clark* star Teri Hatcher.

But perhaps the most distressing evidence comes from teenage girls themselves. "There's not a second in my life that I don't think about some aspect of how I look," says Sarah Goldberg, 18, a college-bound high school senior from Chicago. The desire for thinness was fueled by "almost anybody I saw in movies," concurs Anne Marie Gibbons, 18, who attends an all-girl boarding school in Troy, N.Y., and who until recently suffered from anorexia. "I always wanted to look like the person on the magazine cover, whether it was Niki Taylor, Kate Moss or Sharon Stone."

"I have a friend who's thin and gorgeous, and she's always commenting on how much she hates her body," says Adrienne Seele, 15, of Chevy Chase, Md. "And I think, 'Wow, if she thinks that about her body, what does she think of mine?'"

According to a study recently commissioned by Girls Incorporated, a Manhattan-based organization dedicated to promoting self-confidence in women, of 2,000 teen and preteen boys and girls polled about their viewing habits, 15 percent of girls (and 8 percent of boys) diet or exercise to look like one of the many images they soak up on TV. "My friends and I love *Melrose Place* and *90210*," says 17-year-old Ali Jatlow of Potomac, Md., who will enroll in Cornell University come fall. "We plan our schedules around them. But it's so depressing. I read that Tori Spelling weighs 105 lbs. [and is 5'5"], and I'm, like, 'How can she be that tall and weigh so little?'"

Not all young women, of course, compare themselves to the stars. "Just because I see someone on TV doesn't mean I have to feel bad about myself," says Roshanda Betts, a 19-year-old sophomore at Texas A&M. As an African-American, Betts is not alone in her thinking. A 1995 University of Arizona survey of black high school students found that 70 percent of teenage African-American girls are satisfied with their bodies. But according to a 1993 survey conducted by *Essence* magazine, 54 percent of black women are at high risk for developing an eating disorder. "It's become a generational and class issue," says Audrey Chapman, a Howard University psychology professor. "Many middle-class blacks who are assimilated into the white culture—and teenagers too—want to be thin, thinner, thinnest." The exposure of more and more nude bodies on cable TV and in movies has raised the stakes for everyone. "There is enormous pressure for teenage girls to be thin," says Shirley Damrosch, a clinical psychologist at the University of Maryland who has done numerous studies on body image and attractiveness. "And early sexual activity doesn't help. If you are naked and having sex, someone saying you have a little surplus can be devastating to young women."

Ad agencies, the fashion industry and magazines clearly play their part. As Diane George of Milwaukee, Wis., asked *People* in a letter last month: "Is it really necessary to include the height and weight of your 50 Most Beautiful People in the World?...Beauty comes in all shapes and sizes."

Another sign that the problem is getting worse is that it's also getting worse for men and boys. "We see more eating disorders in men than we did 10 years ago," says Dr. Arnold Andersen, a professor of psychiatry at the University of Iowa who specializes in eating disorders and body image among men. (The National Association of Anorexia Nervosa and Associated Disorders estimates that 1 million males suffer from anorexia or bulimia.) High school boys, an article in *The New York Times* noted recently, are skipping showers after gym class. Dr. David Bernhardt, a specialist in pediatrics and sports medicine at the University of Wisconsin-Madison, speculated that the boys, bombarded by images of highly buffed male bodies, were feeling comparatively inadequate and thus more reluctant to let their own bodies be seen. Studies show, he added, that up to 11 percent of high school boys used anabolic steroids. "The No. 1 reason cited by the boys," Bernhardt told the *Times*, "is body image." Zack Fine, a 17-year-old senior at Francis W. Parker School in Chicago, is into soccer, baseball, theater—and, just now, trying to take a few pounds off his 180 lb., 6' frame. "The men in Calvin Klein ads are Adonises," he says. Though hardly realistic, he adds, "I'd like to look like that."

But even with the added pressure, boys are far more comfortable with themselves than are

Poll: The Skinny on Fat and Self-Perception

What's important in determining attractiveness? A new body-image poll, conducted for People by Marketing & Research Resources, Inc., of Frederick, Md., finds that what matters is weight—specifically, your own. Only 5 percent of women consider weight the principal characteristic in rating the attractiveness of others. Instead, they said "overall appearance" mattered most in assessing others. But when women are asked to rate their own attractiveness, weight looms as the dominant factor among 17 percent. (Men were twice as likely to name "physical fitness and conditioning" as weight in determining attractiveness, while women placed "facial features" slightly ahead of conditioning.) The poll, a random sample of 1,017 Americans between the ages of 13 and 59, conducted May 16 through May 19, also found that:

• Teenagers are more likely to have negative feelings about their appearance than adults: 45 percent say they experience unhappiness or dissatisfaction with their appearance one or more times a week, compared to 39 percent of those in the 35–59 age group. The younger you are, it seems, the more often you are dissatisfied about your appearance.

• Similarly, women are significantly less happy with their bodies than men: One-half of all women report frequent dissatisfaction with their appearance, versus fewer than one-third—31 percent—of men.

• Southerners expressed the highest level of dissatisfaction, with 45 percent answering that they were dissatisfied with their bodies once a week or more. Residents of the Northeast report the lowest level of dissatisfaction (34 percent). Midwesterners (41 percent) and Westerners (43 percent) fill out the national profile.

---

girls. The *People* poll found that boys expressed dissatisfaction with their appearance at almost precisely half the rate of girls. "Boys are more objective," says Andersen. "They don't buy into the culture of dieting until they're 15 percent above their normal or ideal weight." And the feedback they receive is different. "From the minute genders are assigned, people react differently to boys and girls," says Pipher. "They say, 'Look at those thighs. He'll be a great football player,' to a boy. To a girl they say, 'Look at those eyelashes. She'll really be a head-turner.'" As Cash points out, while acne and voice changes can get a guy down, when a boy hits puberty he gets muscles; girls get hips. "He thinks, 'I'm getting strong,'" says Cash. "She thinks, 'I'm becoming fat.'" Faced with pressures from every direction, 75 percent of America's teenage girls, by one estimate, resort to diets. "I like thinness," says Wendy Levey, a 17-year-old junior at Manhattan's Dalton School who is a member of the track team and the human rights committee—and weighs 97 lbs. at 5' even. "I'm not happy if I think I look fat in what I'm wearing. Kate Moss looks so cool in a bathing suit. I don't know if I'm conditioned [to think this way] or if it's just me," she adds, "but I don't think anything could make me abandon my desire to be thin."

Not surprisingly, there has also been an increase in demand for quick fixes. According to the American Society of Plastic and Reconstructive Surgeons, the number of girls 18 and younger getting liposuction rose from 472 to 511 from 1992 to 1994 (the most recent data available). "The other day a teen came with a picture of the stars on *Beverly Hills, 90210*," says Chicago plastic surgeon Dr. Anthony Terrasse. "I counseled her on the role of exercise and diet as a first step before considering surgery."

Still, the most alarming response of all to body image anxieties is self-imposed starvation.

Nationally, the reported incidence of both anorexia and bulimia has doubled since 1970, according to the American Psychiatric Association. And, say experts, the patients are getting younger and younger. "I have an 11-year-old patient who won't eat because she's terrified of developing hips," says Deborah A. Newmark, a Washington psychotherapist. "She read on a cereal box that if she runs up and down the stairs 15 times she'll burn 300 calories."

Experts are not alone in their concern. In L.A., actress Jennifer Crystal, 23, daughter of Billy Crystal, worries when she returns to visit her alma mater, Brentwood School, and sees "the girls keep getting thinner and thinner." At Northwestern University in Evanston, Ill., where she graduated with a degree in performance studies in 1994, bulimia was so common among students, she says, that "the pipes in one sorority house kept getting clogged because so many people were throwing up in the sinks." Director Schumacher says the teenage daughters of his friends are also afflicted; one recently told him she belongs to a bulimia clique in her New Jersey high school. "I don't know what's going to happen to this generation of females," he says. "This obsession with being skinny is insane."

It only gets worse when the desire is to be skinny *and* buff. Many teens are unaware of the intense work that goes into the physiques they are trying to emulate. Linda Hamilton rigorously pumped iron to get the biceps she made famous in 1991's *Terminator 2*. Angela Bassett combined a weight-training program with a low-fat diet to sculpt her body for 1993's *What's Love Got to Do with It?* Even so, some of the most beautiful stars choose or are required to use body doubles for nude or seminude scenes—as, for example, Julia Roberts in *Pretty Woman*. (Shelley Michelle, who stood in for Roberts and runs the casting agency Body Doubles and Parts, told *InStyle* that at least 85 percent of body doubles have breast implants.) "I was shocked when I found out it wasn't her body," says Brandi Dickman, a fitness enthusiast who worked out twice a day to shed 20 pounds before entering college. "Everyone thinks she's so pretty, yet in Hollywood they didn't feel even *her* body was good enough."

The fact is, stars often battle the beast of body image as fiercely as their fans do. Janeane Garofalo is pretty, but at 5'1", by Hollywood standards she's not tall enough. Silverstone may be tall enough but—at the Oscars at least—she wasn't thin enough. Princess Diana—who

BOX 2
The Facts About Figures

1%–4% Percentage of high school and college girls who have either anorexia or bulimia

0.5%–1% Percentage of girls who had bulimia or anorexia in 1976

33-23-33 Average measurements of a contemporary fashion model

36-18-33 Projected measurements of a Barbie doll, in inches if she were a full-sized human being

5'4"–142 The average height and weight of an American woman

5'9"–110 Average height and weight of a model

33% Percentage of American women who wear a size 16 or larger

80% Percentage of women who diet

25% Percentage of men who diet

50% Percentage of American women on a diet at any one time

50% Percentage of 9-year-old girls who have ever dieted

$10 billion Revenues of the diet industry in 1970

$33 billion Revenues of the diet industry today

10% Percentage of teenagers with eating disorders who are boys fought bulimia for years—is thin enough but, as a supposed ripple of cellulite that recently made headlines suggests, she is still not considered sufficiently toned.

After Gabrielle Carteris of *90210* decided to become an actress 20 years ago, she recalls, an agent dismissed her with the blunt "You're not attractive enough for the world of acting." Comedian Jackie Guerra, who appeared in the WB sitcom *First Time Out,* had a hard time selling her full-size figure to Hollywood. But she is still amazed when she recalls the producer who told her, "Jackie, I'd rather have you smoke two packs a day than eat more than 1,000 calories a day."

Casting directors say they would like to broker talent but inevitably are forced to factor in looks. "I've always thought of myself as 'essence casting,' to get the actor who evokes intrinsic beauty, love and joy," says Elina DeSantos, who cast *Dead Poets Society* and such daytime soaps as *Days of Our Lives.* "But I know she better not be fat, no matter what her essence, because a director just won't hire her."

"People are poised like vultures to attack imperfection," says Lindsay Chag, who cast the sitcom *Anything But Love.* "I see a lot of actresses who are incredibly talented and very sexy, but if they are not thin enough, I can't bring them further."

Some casting directors, meanwhile, wonder why screenwriters don't create roles physically diverse enough. *Thelma & Louise* and *Something to Talk About* screenwriter Callie Khouri is clear on the subject: "I never say a character is thin or fat because she will be cast as a thin person anyway. When you are dealing with the major actresses, all of them together might make up a size 14."

While some power brokers in the fashion and entertainment industry accept some responsibility for the overwhelmingly thin and unrealistic human products offered up for public consumption, the *most* accountable party, it seems, is the other guy. Model agencies point their fingers at fashion magazines ("It's the editors who book the girls," says Stuart Cameron of New York

City's Women modeling agency). Movie people blame television ("Take all the daytime soaps and you'll see actresses who have that body type—very slender with big fake breasts," says Schumacher). Television executives dodge the bullet too. "There *are* no overweight actresses that come in to read for me," says Darren Star, creator of *Melrose Place* and *Beverly Hills, 90210.* "The ones that read for me are very attractive people. Besides, people have always looked at movies and television to create their myths. To confuse the fantasy with reality is a mistake."

Whoever is to blame, Mary Pipher, for one, is concerned. "It makes me angry," she says, "the needless suffering by women who are putting energy into losing weight when they could be focusing on making themselves better people, making the world a better place. We need a revolution in our values. We need to define attractiveness with much broader parameters."

Nancy Friday, author of the recently published *The Power of Beauty,* agrees. "The quest for superficial beauty really intensifies with no secure sense of self to fall back on," she says. "People are desperate to be around people who are comfortable in their skin. They are hard to find, but after that flash in the pan of gold chains, tattoos and pierced skin, what you really want to be around is people who are themselves, so you can relax and be yourself."

Screenwriters Stephanie Garman and Holly White had just that sort of redefinition in mind a couple of years ago when they wrote a script called *Fat Chance.* The concept: An aging screen star, whose battle with obesity had made tabloid headlines for two decades, appears on a talk show and announces that she has had it with dieting and has learned to love herself the way she is. Inspired, millions of women across the country follow suit. "No one bought it," says White. Too bad; a lot of women out there would have loved the proposed ending: On a beach one afternoon, a couple of chubby women in swimsuits watch as a super-slim sunbather in a bikini walks by. "Isn't it a shame," says one to the other. "She has such a pretty face."

BOX 3
Teen Weight Wars:
Voices from the Trenches

"Sometimes a magazine article about bulimia will be followed by a skinny model in the latest fashions. They could be naturally thin, or they could be starving to death."
—Danielle Pier, 13
  Brookline, Mass

"In the transition to high school I kind of got lost. I wanted to be a part of things, and I felt like everybody around me was thin, so I thought if I got thin like they were, everything would be perfect. I linked having the perfect body to being liked by other people."
—Jessica Green, 15
  Richmond, Va.

"I've overheard guys say Pamela Anderson is the most beautiful woman on earth. The camera always zooms in on her breasts. It makes me mad. Young girls who are having an identity crisis say, 'I'm ugly because I don't look like her.' We can't all look like her."
—Roshanda Betts, 19, Dallas

"I was babysitting for this little girl—she couldn't have been more than 8—and she asked me how many calories a bottle of Clearly Canadian had. She's 8 years old! What does she need to be thinking about that for?"
—16-year-old, Richmond, Va.

"I always thought I was fat. In high school everybody was thin and perfect. There was a lot of pressure to be beautiful. I wanted to look as slender and sleek as Kate Moss. I thought people like Cindy Crawford were overweight."
—Debra Burock 18
  Coopersburg, Pa.

"I have a friend who thinks the Calvin Klein ads with the anorexic, pouty-eyed, open-mouthed models are the epitome of gorgeous women. I just see them as sick. It's like saying you have to be sick to be attractive."

—Adrienne Seele, 15
  Chevy Chase, Md.

"It's hard to get girls if you're overweight. People look at you differently.... Sometimes I take diet pills. They're prescription. I haven't learned how to deal with it better. If I need to lose 10 pounds and need to do it fast, I'll take the diet pills."
—Jamie Laden, 17
  Englewood, N.J.

"I have so much I want to do with my life, I can't let something like 10 or 15 pounds get in my way. I'm so much more than my body size, and I don't have any time for those who would judge me just on what I look like."
—Genevieve Gonzales, 17
  San Diego

DISCUSSION QUESTIONS

Mission Impossible

1. Is it impossible to escape the media's image of thinness for males and females? Or, are there elements that allow an individual to successfully combat the unrealistic ideals portrayed by the media? If so, what are those elements?

2. Do you think the waif model ideal of the 1990s is becoming less prevalent? Can you identify other decades in history when an ultra-thin ideal was also prevalent? Given this information from the past, can you forecast when there will be another waif wave?

3. It is interesting to note that African American women are somewhat more protected than Caucasian women from the thin ideal. Why do you think this happens?

4. In at least two places in this article, statements are made that indicate people who buy into the thin ideal are confusing fantasy with reality. How do you feel about this issue?

3 Tattooing: Another Adolescent Risk Behavior Warranting Health Education

Myrna L. Armstrong
Kathleen Pace Murphy

Adolescence is filled with psychosocial pressures, biological turmoil, and struggles for independence. Adolescents are challenged to describe who they are and what they want to become. Often, they are preoccupied with themselves, their appearance, and the opinions of others; they obtain many ideas from peers, role models, and the media. Today, tattooing is on the rise with at least 7 million adults already tattooed (Armstrong, Stuppy, Gabriel, & Anderson, 1996). Prevalence and popularity of tattooing have also been demonstrated among adolescents (Armstrong & Gabriel, 1994; Armstrong & McConnell, 1994b).

BACKGROUND
Tattooing and Health Risks

The most common health risks of tattooing are infections and allergic reactions (Anderson, 1992; Long & Rickman, 1994). Transmission of blood-borne diseases also are possible because small to moderate amounts of bleeding occur during tattooing. A large incidence of hepatitis B (13 cases) resulted in New York City banning tattoo artists in 1961; no similar large scale cases have since been reported. Additionally, "transmission of HIV by tattooing is possible," but no documented cases of human immunodeficiency virus (HIV) or acquired immune deficiency syndrome (AIDS) have been located (Long & Rickman, 1994, p 616).

Risks with Adolescent Tattooing

For almost 30 years, physicians in England have voiced concerns about amateur tattooing and the associated problems of embarrassment, shame, and social disgrace (Balakrishnan & Papini, 1991; Mercer & Davies, 1991; Thomson & McDonald, 1983). All of these physicians recommend health education about tattooing.

In the United States, there are a few descriptive medical articles about adolescent tattooing. Fried (1983) suggested adolescent tattooing expressed "aggression, sexuality, and rebellion" (p. 239), whereas Litt (1994) suggested gang association in amateur tattooing. Farrow, Schwartz, and Vanderleeuw, (1991) identified "an impulsive personality style, deviant behavior, and drug abuse" (p. 187) as common characteristics. Health education was recommended; however, no specific programs were cited.

In the nursing literature, only one study in the United States has been conducted on adolescent tattooing. Armstrong and McConnell (1994b) queried 642 adolescents in six Texas high schools. Among the nontattooed adolescents ($n = 537$), over a third (33%, $n = 177$) were interested in tattooing. The percentage of tattooed adolescents ($n = 105$) was 8.6%. Many reported academic grades of As and Bs (69%, $n = 72$). The number of those with studio or amateur tattoos was almost equal. The average age for the first tattoo was 14 years of age with the earliest tattooing reported at 10 years of age. Over half (57%, $n = 60$) had one tattoo, whereas 40% ($n = 42$) had two or more tattoos.

Three areas of risk were investigated by Armstrong and McConnell (1994b), namely the psychosocial risks of purchase (vulnerability with the procedure), possession (problems encountered while having the tattoo), as well as health risks (potential diseases, allergies, or infections after tattooing). Purchase and possession risks

Armstrong, M. L., & Murphy, K. P. (1997, November) Tattooing: Another risk behavior warranting health education. *Applied Nursing Research(10)*4, pp. 181–189. Copyright © 1997 by W. B. Saunders.

were documented in this study "as evidenced by whimsical decision making, the young age at tattooing, the short time-frame for decisions, the visual messages in their tattoo designs, the exposed body locations, and the lack of support by parents, siblings, and the public" (Armstrong & McConnell, 1994b, p 123). No health risks were documented, but the potential of blood-borne diseases existed as many (70%, $n = 73$) report some bleeding during their tattooing procedure.

A second study was undertaken to examine various regions in the United States and build on the previous level of knowledge. The purposes of this exploratory study were two-fold, (a) to examine adolescent interest in tattooing, and (b) to identify the characteristics and associated purchase, possession, and health risks of tattooed adolescents.

METHODS

Little is known about the tattooed adolescent, so a descriptive design similar to the Armstrong and McConnell (1994b) study was used in this quantitative study. A 72-item self-reporting, anonymous, scannable bubble form survey tool was used. The survey tool was divided into two parts. The first section was designed for all respondents and included five demographic and general questions about tattooing. The second part was specifically designed for adolescents with tattoos; it contained questions regarding choices about tattooing, health risks, the purchase experience, their feelings about their tattoos, the responses from others, and the purpose of the tattoo. The reading level of the survey was at the 7th grade level.

Procedure

School nurses were recruited through a variety of school health networks and asked to facilitate distribution of the survey. Eight sites received surveys. Survey distribution instructions included information to maintain the respondent's anonymity and confidentiality. The school nurse, the classroom teacher, and the accessibility of students in the 7th grade through the 12th grade all entered into the decisions of how classrooms were chosen for survey distribution.

From the 3,650 surveys that were distributed, 2,212 (61%) were returned.

RESULTS

Usable data were collected from 2,101 adolescents (53% [$n = 1,113$] girls and 47% [$n = 988$] boys) from 8 junior or senior high schools across the United States. Ethnic representation included White (77%, $n = 1,618$), Hispanic American (8%, $n = 168$), Asian American (7%, $n = 147$), African American (5%, $n = 105$), and others (3%, $n = 63$).

All subjects were asked their interest in tattooing and reasons for refraining from tattooing. A majority of the subjects (55%, $n = 1,156$) were interested in tattoos. Reasons for not obtaining a tattoo included permanent markings (23%, $n = 483$); AIDS/HIV or other diseases (18%, $n = 378$); parental disapproval (16%, $n = 336$); and pain (12%, $n = 252$). Cost was not a deterrent (3%, $n = 64$). Over one-fifth of the respondents (22%, $n = 462$) stated there was no reason keeping them from getting a tattoo.

After these questions, subjects without tattoos ($N = 1888$, 90%) were thanked for their participation and exited from the survey while the remaining tattooed subjects ($N = 213$, 10%) completed the rest of the questions.

Tattooed Adolescents

The 213 tattooed adolescents (55% [$n = 117$] of girls and 45% [$n = 96$] of boys) provided information about their decisions and experiences before, during, and after the tattooing. Ethnic representation of the tattooed subjects were 61% Whites ($n = 129$), 21% Hispanic Americans ($n = 45$), and 10% others ($n = 21$); Asian Americans remained the same (8%, $n = 18$). Over half of the subjects (61%, $n = 129$) had one tattoo whereas 39% ($n = 84$) had two or more tattoos. Some of the subjects (10%, $n = 21$) documented as many as six.

PURCHASE EXPERIENCE. The mean age of their first tattoo was 14 years ($SD = 2.5$) with most (87%, $n = 185$) obtaining their tattoos from 12 to 17 years of age. Over half of the tattooed adolescents (52%, $n = 111$) had obtained their first tattoo during grades 7 to 9, whereas another third (35%, $n = 75$) obtained their first tattoo during the 10th or 11th grade.

Self-reported letter grades revealed tattooed adolescents with As and Bs (56%, $n = 119$) at the time of tattooing; these grades remained for the majority of the sample (59%, $n= 126$). Several remarks (11%, $n = 23$) were received on the comment sheets expressing their thoughts about the association of grades and tattoos, for example, "grades have nothing to do with tattoos." Over one third reported major changes and stress in their lives (39%, $n = 83$) at the time of tattooing.

Numerous reasons were reported for obtaining the tattoo such as "just wanted one" (44%, $n = 94$), wanted to be independent/express oneself (23%, $n = 49$), and "for the heck of it" (16%, $n = 34$). Less than one third of the parents (28%, $n = 60$) were aware of the tattooing intention and 17% ($n = 36$) signed consent forms; now, 62% ($n = 132$) of the parents know about the tattoo.

The majority of tattooed adolescents (57%, $n = 121$) labeled themselves "risk takers" at the time of tattooing and this remains a consistent belief (58%, $n = 124$). Often, friends or a group of people (70%, $n = 149$) were with them before tattooing. During their tattooing, other friends (37%, $n = 79$) were also tattooed. Alcohol, drugs, or both, were used by some tattooed adolescents (28%, $n = 60$) before the tattooing. Only 7% ($n = 15$) believed their friends applied pressure to obtain the tattoo.

POSSESSION EXPERIENCES. Questions were asked about their personal response to the tattoo as well as reactions from friends and family. Many report initial pleasure with their tattoo (83%, $n = 177$) and continuing pleasure (81%, $n = 173$). Body sites were equally distributed between concealed (51%, $n = 108$) and exposed areas (49%, $n = 105$). When asked to describe how their tattoos were helpful, 50% ($n = 107$) replied "it made me feel special and unique." The tattoo was not helpful to other respondents (30%, $n = 64$); they cited disappointment, embarrassment, and low self-esteem. Many chose not to answer these questions (56%, $n = 119$). Family support for the tattoo was low in comparison to positive responses from their friends.

HEALTH EXPERIENCES. Repeated needle injections of a foreign substance could predispose subjects to health risks. Red and yellow pigments were selected by 47% ($n = 100$) of the tattooed adolescents, but only a small group of them (14%, $n = 30$) reported short-term irritations. No blood-borne diseases were reported but 68% ($n = 145$) cite small to large amounts of bleeding during the procedure, so the potential exists.

PURPOSE OF THE TATTOO. Twelve statements were presented as possible purposes of the tattoo; no additional write-in comments were received. The most agreed-upon statement related to personal identity, "be myself, I don't need to impress people anymore" (81%, $n = 173$). Most of the respondents disagreed or rejected the other statements (Table 1).

STUDIO VERSUS AMATEUR TATTOOING. Of the total group of tattooed adolescents, 42% ($n = 119$) obtained studio tattoos whereas 54% ($n = 94$) reported amateur tattoos. Those with amateur markings started younger, were in lower grade levels when they started (grades 7 to 9, 68%), had more tattoos, and reported lower academic grades (Bs and Cs, 70%). Straight pins or sewing needles, pens, pencils, or other homemade devices (45%, $n = 42$) were used for the tattooing; many were done in the home (66%, $n = 62$). Few gang-related tattoos were reported (5%, $n = 5$), yet several ($n = 13$) describe tattooed dots on their hands and face (the configuration of the dot can explain a certain gang).

ENFORCEMENT OF TATTOOING REGULATIONS. State tattooing regulations (Tope, 1995) were compared with the respondent's location. Massachusetts, which prohibits all tattooing, in this study had a 6% rate of tattooing, with 17% of those adolescents obtaining parental consent. Illinois and North Carolina prohibit tattooing of minors. Study data indicate rates of 10% and 6% respectively, with low rates (15% and 30%) of parental consent. California permits tattooing of minors with parental consent. Respondents from this state had the highest tattooing rate (14%), with 5% obtaining parental consent.

TABLE 1

Reported Purpose for Tattooing in Adolescents (n = 213)

Item	Strongly Agreed/ Agreed (%)	Strongly Disagreed/ Disagreed (%)	N
Be myself, I don't need to impress anyone anymore.	81		173
Improve my social position.		92	196
Do what another person expected.		89	190
Do what friends suggested.		88	187
Do what someone in my group strongly urged me to do.		88	187
Make new personal associations and friendships.		87	185
Help me be more acceptable to my friends.		86	183
Do what people who love me say is important.		85	181
Help me separate from my other life experiences.		85	181
Help me obtain more status and prestige.		84	179
Help me feel better about myself.		79	168
Help people judge me for who I really am.		64	134

DISCUSSION AND IMPLICATIONS

This research expands on earlier work by Armstrong and McConnell (1994b) and queried adolescents (N = 2101) regarding their interest in tattooing and major reasons to refrain from tattooing. Two findings were of interest regarding both groups of nontattooed adolescents. First, they agreed on the same reasons for refraining from tattoos, namely permanent markings and the concern of AIDS and other diseases. Secondly, tattooing interest in this study was 55% compared to 33% in the Armstrong and McConnell study (1994b), conducted 2 years previously. This tattoo interest could be attributed to regional differences as well as increased role models and coverage about tattoos in the media.

Data from the tattooed adolescents were similar to the Armstrong and McConnell study (1994b). The similarities include the academic grades, the single and multiple tattooing, the bleeding during the procedure, the exposed body locations, the major changes and stress, and the responses from families and friends. Both groups were in strong agreement about the purpose of their tattoo, "be myself, I don't need to impress anyone anymore." Profiles of those with amateur and studio tattoos were also the same.

Several experiences occurred with greater frequency in this study than in the Armstrong and McConnell study (1994b). There was an increased number of girls (55% from 35%), more impulsiveness in the decision for tattooing (52% from 41%), an increase of risk takers (57% from 45%), and an earlier age ratio (ages 12 to 17 from 14 to 18 years of age) when the tattoos were obtained.

Findings indicate that adolescents who want a tattoo will obtain one, regardless of money, regulations, or risks.

Proactive development of credible health education for all three educational levels of schools (elementary grades, junior high, and senior high) becomes important, the mean age (14) in tattooing and the young age of one respondent who started tattooing at 8 years of age. Yet, developing education for adolescents is challenging, especially when many adolescents believe they have a "right to have a tattoo" (Armstrong & McConnell, 1994a, p. 28). Careful incorporation of the two major areas that cause the nontattooed respondents the most concern with tattooing would be important to address within health education. Thus, informed decision-making could be promoted in health education by incorporating information about the possibility of blood-borne diseases, permanent markings, and themselves as growing and changing people. Hopefully this will produce dissuasion, or at least minimize risks, by encouraging specific questions if they insist on tattooing (Armstrong & McConnell, 1994a).

As noted in the subjective data provided by the respondents, the view points of the adolescents and adults about tattooing differed, in both studies. Adolescents view the tattoos as objects of self-identity and body art whereas adults perceive the markings as deviant behavior. From the adolescent's perspective, they were very positive about their tattoos with the majority describing how the tattoo(s) were helpful in "feeling special and unique." Yet, parental response for the tattoos was consistently low, around the 10% range. Some respondents describe disappointment, embarrassment, and low-self-esteem experiences when others viewed their tattoo(s). This is unfortunate at a time when adolescents are concerned about themselves, their image, and their appearance.

For tattooed adolescents, psychosocial and health risks are compounding adolescence, a time already filled with psychosocial pressures. Tattooing in adolescents is increasing and needs to be added to the "growing lists of previously ignored, important public educational issues" (Armstrong et al., 1996, p. 415).

References

Anderson, R. R. (1992). Tattooing should be regulated. *New England Journal of Medicine, 326,* 207.

Armstrong, M. L., & McConnell, C. (1994a). Promoting informed decision-making about tattooing for adolescents. *Journal of School Nursing, 10* (2). 27–30.

Armstrong, M. L., & McConnell, C. (1994b). Tattooing in adolescents, more common than you think: The phenomenon & risks. *Journal of School Nursing, 10*(1). 22–29.

Armstrong, M. L., & Gabriel, D. C. (1994). Adolescents and tattoos: Marks of identity or deviancy? *Dermatology Nursing 6,* 119–124.

Armstrong. M. L., Stuppy. D. J., Gabriel, D. C., & Anderson, .R. (1996). Motivation for tattoo removal *Archives of Dermatology, 132,* 412–416.

Balakrishman, C., & Papini, R. (1991). Removal of unwanted tattoos. *British Journal of Plastic Surgery, 44,* 471.

Farrow, J. A., Schwartz, R. H., & Vanderleeuw, J. (1991). Tattooing behavior in adolescence. *American Journal of Diseases in Children, 145,* 184–187.

Fried, R. I. (1983). The psychodynamics of tattooing: A review. *Cleveland Clinic Quarterly, 50,* 239–242.

Litt, I. F. (1994). Self-graffiti?, Self-image?, Self-destruction?: Tattoos and adolescents. *Journal of Adolescent Health Care, 15,* 198.

Long, G. E., & Rickman, L. S. (1994). Infectious complications of tattoos. *Clinical Infectious Diseases, 18,* 610–619.

Mercer, N. S. G., & Davies, D. M. (1991). Tattoos: Marked for life [Letter]. *British Medical Journal, 303,* 380.

Thomson. W., & McDonald, J. C. H. (1983). Self-Tattooing by schoolchildren. *Lancet, 2,* 1243–1244.

Tope, W. D. (1995). State and territorial regulation of tattooing in the United States. *Journal of the American Academy of Dermatology, 32,* 791–799.

Tattooing

1. Why is tattooing so attractive to adolescents despite the cost, health risks and permanent nature of a tattoo?

2. How have perceptions of tattoos changed over time? For example, adults consider tattoos as deviant behavior and adolescents consider tattoos as an expression of self-identity.

3. If you were to conduct the next research study on adolescent tattooing, what information would you be interested in learning? Consider information that was not covered by Armstrong and Murphy. What information was missing from their study? How would you approach adolescents for the study? Would you go to the mall or to schools? Would you interview adolescents or hand out a written questionnaire?

4. Consider the five frameworks introduced in Chapter 2 for viewing the body. Which framework or frameworks would work best for designing a study about tattoos? Why?

4 Fat Chance in a Slim World: We Believe It's the Size of a Book's Cover That Counts

Jack Levin

A black woman in Philadelphia wrote recently complaining about the way she was treated by other people. Among other things, she rarely dated, had few friends, and was forced to settle for a job for which she was overqualified. Moreover, passengers on buses and trains often stared at her with pity or scorn, while workers at the office rarely included her in their water-cooler conversations.

The letter writer attributed these difficulties not to her gender or race, but to the fact that she was vastly overweight by conventional standards. Her letter brought to mind the unfortunate victims of such illnesses as cancer, heart disease, and Alzheimer's, who have the unavoidable symptoms of illnesses over which they have little, if any, control. But they are typically treated with compassion and sympathy.

Curiously enough, fat people frequently receive contempt rather than compassion, unless their obesity can be attributed to some physical ailment (such as a "glandular condition"). Otherwise, they are seen as having caused their own problem by some combination of excessive impulsivity and lack of moral fiber. Not unlike prostitutes, ex-cons, and skid row bums, they may be regarded as lacking in the self-control and willpower necessary to lead a healthy, normal life. In addition, this discrimination has been directed more often at women than at men over the years.

The term *fat person* is therefore more than a description of somebody's weight, body type, or illness; more often than not, it is also used to stigmatize an entire group of human beings by making their belt size an excuse for prejudice. The lady from Philadelphia may have been correct: Research suggests that people who are overweight by our standards are often viewed as undesirable dates and mates. They frequently have trouble getting married, going to college, obtaining credit from banks, or being promoted. In short, they are excluded, exploited, and oppressed.

Discrimination against fat people is, of course, only one expression of a much more general tendency in our culture: the tendency to judge others by their looks rather than their intelligence, talent, or character. Study after study suggests we believe that "what is beautiful is good!" That is, attractive individuals are more likely to be preferred as dates, to be popular with their friends, to be cuddled and kissed as newborns, to achieve high grades in school, to be disciplined less severely by their parents, to be recommended for jobs after personal interviews, and to have their written work judged favorably.

By conventional American wisdom, fat is as ugly as thin is beautiful. We are so infatuated with being slim and trim that it is indeed hard to imagine anything else. Yet the desirability of particular body types and body weight varies from culture to culture. Beginning with the ancient world, fat has not always been universally despised. Instead, fat people were often respected, if not admired, throughout history. Even Cleopatra was fat by our standards, although by the standards of her own time and culture, she was a raving beauty. Renoir's French impressionist masterpieces similarly portray a version of the female body that today is considered massive, huge, and fat rather than beautiful. And in cultures where food was in short supply, obesity has often been used to demonstrate personal success. Under such circumstances, rich people could afford to eat enough to be fat and therefore to survive. Skinny was therefore a sign of neither good health nor beauty, but a symptom of poverty and illness.

Until the roaring twenties, the large and voluptuous version of feminine beauty continued to dominate in our culture. But the flappers changed all that by bobbing their hair, binding their breasts, and, by some accounts, trying to resemble "adolescent boys." While many women of the 1920s moved toward feminine power, others retreated from it by shrinking their bodies through fad diets. The result was that, during this era, the suffragette movement succeeded and women got the vote, but many men felt threatened. All of a sudden they preferred women who were small, petite, and thin— women who looked powerless.

Given the importance of physical attractiveness in defining the value and achievement of females, it should come as no surprise that American women have come under extreme pressure to be unrealistically slim and trim. This may have made many women dissatisfied with their bodies and mistakenly convinced them that mastery was possible only by controlling their weight. Women constitute 90% of those afflicted with the eating disorder anorexia nervosa and are the majority of those who join organizations such as Weight Watchers and Diet Workshop. Women are also more likely than men to suffer from compulsive overeating and obesity.

Since the women's movement of the 1960s, we seem to have become even more preoccupied with being slim and trim. *Playboy* centerfolds and contestants in the Miss America pageant have become increasingly thin. Leading women's magazines publish more and more articles about diets and dieting. Physicians offer drastic medical "cures" such as stomach stapling for obesity and liposuction surgery for "problem areas" like "saddlebag" thighs, "protuberant" abdomens, buttocks, "love handles," fatty knees, and redundant chins. And the best-seller list inevitably contains a disproportionate number of books promising miraculous methods of weight reduction.

In the face of all this, signs of an incipient cultural rebellion against crash dieting and irrational thinness have emerged. Popular books like Millman's *Such a Pretty Face*, Orbach's *Fat Is a Feminist Issue*, and Chernin's *The Obsession: Reflections on the Tyranny of Slenderness* have taken their place in bookstores alongside the diet manuals. But, rather than urging obedience to the conventional standards of beauty, these new books expose the dangers to physical and mental health of rapid and repeated weight loss. Rather than focusing on individual change, they place the blame for our excessive concern with being skinny on sexism and the socialization of women to absurd cultural standards.

The merchants of fashion have also sensed a cultural change in the offing. Growing numbers of dress shops now specialize in "designer fashions for size 14 and over" and "flattering designs in better plus size fashions." Moreover, based on a good deal of evidence from around the world, physicians have revised their weight standards so that what was formerly considered 10 or 15 pounds overweight is now regarded as optimal.

As a final element in this dynamic, organizations such as the National Association to Aid Fat Americans (NAAFA) have helped fat people—even those who are considered obese—to gain a more favorable self-image. Rather than automatically advising its members to diet, NAAFA calls attention to the fact that fat people are often the victims of prejudice and discrimination. It recognizes the dangers in rapid and repeated weight loss and focuses instead on improving the ways fat people are treated on the job, as customers, and in social situations. Taking its cue from black organizations, which reject words originating in the white community such as *Negro* and *colored*, NAAFA prefers to use the word *fat* rather than *overweight* or *obese*. In this way, it refuses to conceal the issue in euphemisms and emphasizes that "fat can be beautiful!"

Unfortunately, however, our culture continues to give fat people a double message. On the one hand, we advise them to be themselves and to accept their body image regardless of social pressures to conform to some arbitrary standard of beauty. On the other hand, we urge them to go on diets so that they will no longer be fat. While the rhetoric may confuse, it is also revealing. All things considered, our aversion is deeply embedded in our culture and is likely to remain with us for some time to come.

DISCUSSION QUESTIONS

Fat Chance in a Slim World

1. Why is there a cultural bias toward fat men? Why are fat men a non-issue while fat women are met with strong attitudes of disdain?

2. Why are cancer and heart disease victims afforded compassion while those who are overweight are met with contempt?

3. You have just arrived at your freshman dorm and met your assigned roommate who is 100 pounds overweight. Do you ask to be reassigned to another roommate? Why or why not?

5   Heightism: Short Guys Finish Last

When George Bush was America's president and Daniel Ortega was Nicaragua's, Mr. Ortega threatened to cancel a local peace deal that the Americans had painstakingly brokered. Hearing the news, an enraged Mr. Bush grasped for an insult worthy of the offence. "That little man," he snarled repeatedly, dripping contempt. "That *little* man."

Actually Mr. Ortega is 5 foot 10 inches (1.78 metres) tall, which makes him a fraction of an inch taller than the average American—and not that much shorter than Mr. Bush, who is 6'2". Yet when Mr. Bush was searching for an atomic but not obscene insult, it was stature that he immediately seized upon. In that respect, he was not being presidential: merely, rather, primate. For the primate *Homo Sapiens* tends to sort its males by height.

Every boy knows, practically from birth that being "shrimpy" is nearly as bad as being a chicken, and closely related at that. Call a man "little", and he is understood to be demeaned. When Mr. Bush called Mr. Ortega "that little man", his primate-male cerebellum knew what it was doing. It was engaging in what may be the most enduring form of discrimination in the world.

The bias against short men hurts them. It is unfair. It is irrational. So why is it not taken seriously? A serious question: especially if you happen to be short.

FIRST THE BAD NEWS

On the advice of our lawyers, we pause here for a mental-health notice. Tall men are invited to forge on, as are women (for whom it is weight, not stature, that is life's bane—but that is another story). Short men, however, proceed at their own peril. What follows will depress them.

Height discrimination begins from the moment male human beings become vertical. Give 100 mothers photographs of two 19-month-old boys who resemble each other closely,

except that one is made to look taller than the other. Then ask the mothers which boy is more competent and able. The mothers consistently pick the "taller" one. As boys grow, the importance of height is drummed into them incessantly. "My, how tall you are!" the relatives squeal with approval. Or, with scorn, "Don't you want to grow up big and strong?"

Height hierarchies are established early, and persist for a long time. Tall boys are deferred to and seen as mature, short ones ridiculed and seen as childlike. Tall men are seen as natural "leaders"; short ones are called "pushy". " If a short man is normally assertive, then he's seen as having Napoleonic tendencies," says David Weeks, a clinical psychologist at Royal Edinburgh Hospital. "If he is introverted and mildly submissive, then he's seen as a wimp."

Dr. Weeks is 5'2", so he may have an axe to grind. But he can prove his point. Turn, for example, to the work of two American psychologists, Leslie Martel and Henry Biller, whose book "Stature and Stigma," (D.C. Heath, 1987) is especially useful.

Mr. Martel and Mr. Biller asked several hundred university students to rate the qualities of men of varying heights, on 17 different criteria. Both men and women, whether short or tall, thought that short men—heights between 5'2" and 5'5"—were less mature, less positive, less secure, less masculine; less successful, less capable, less confident, less outgoing; more inhibited, more timid, more passive; and so on. Other studies confirm that short men are judged, and even judge themselves, negatively. Several surveys have found that short men feel less comfortable in social settings and are less happy with their bodies. Dustin Hoffman, that 5'6" actor,

---

is said to have spent years in therapy over his small stature.

The western ideal for men appears to be about 6'2" (and is slowly rising, as average heights increase). Above that height, the advantages of extra inches peter out, though very tall men do not, apart from hitting their heads, suffer significant disadvantages. And medium-sized men do fine (though they typically will say they would like to be taller, just as women always want to be thinner). The men who suffer are those who are noticeably short: say, 5'5" and below. In a man's world, they do not impress. Indeed, the connection between height and status is embedded in the very language. Respected men have "stature" and are "looked up to": quite literally, as it turns out.

One of the most elegant height experiments was reported in 1968 by an Australian psychologist, Paul Wilson. He introduced the same unfamiliar man to five groups of students, varying only the status attributed to the stranger. In one class, the newcomer was said to be a student, in another a lecturer, right up to being a professor from Cambridge University. Once the visitor had left the room, each group was asked to estimate the man's height along with that of the instructor. Not only was the "professor" thought to be more than two inches taller than the "student"; the height estimates rose in proportion to his perceived status.

It is little wonder, then, that when people meet a famous man they so often say, "I expected him to be taller." If you still doubt that height matters, look around. At the palace of William III at Hampton Court, London, you will see door knockers above eye level: the better to make callers on the king (who was, in fact, decidedly short) feel, literally, lowly. Or sit across from your boss in his office, and see who has the higher chair.

NOW THE WORSE NEWS

Perhaps heightism is just a western cultural prejudice? Sadly not. In Chinese surveys, young women always rate stature high among qualifications for a future mate. Indeed, the prejudice appears to be universal.

In the 1960s and 1970s, Thomas Gregor, an anthropologist at America's Vanderbilt University, lived among the Mehinaku, a tropical forest people of central Brazil who were amazed by such new-fangled gadgets as spectacles. Among the Mehinaku, attractive men should be tall: they are respectfully called *wekepei*. Woe unto the *peritsi*, as very short men are derisively called (it rhymes with *itsi*, the word for penis). Where a tall man is *kaukapapai*, worthy of respect, the short one is merely laughable. His lack of stature is a moral as well as physical failing, for it is presumed to result from sexual looseness during adolescence.

"No one wants a *peritsi* for a son-in-law." Mr. Gregor writes. By many measures—wealth, chieftainship, frequency of participation in rituals—tall men dominate in tribal life. They hog the reproductive opportunities, too. Mr. Gregor looked at the number of girlfriends of Mehinaku men of varying heights. He found a pattern: the taller the man, the more girlfriends he had. As he explained, "the three tallest men had as many affairs as the seven shortest men, even though their average estimated ages were identical."

He went on to note that the Trobriand Islanders of the Pacific, the Timbira of Brazil, and the Navajo of America were among the many other traditional cultures that also prize male height. "In no case have I found a preference for short men," he said. Among anthropologists, it is a truism that in traditional societies the "big man" actually is big, not just socially but physically.

It is not hard to guess why human beings tend instinctively to defer to height. Humans evolved in an environment where size and strength—and good health, to which they are closely related—mattered, especially for men. Indeed, they still matter, albeit less than they did. Other things being equal, large males are more to be feared and longer-living; an impulse to defer to them, or to prefer them as mates, thus makes good evolutionary sense. Perhaps the impulse is softened in a modern industrial society. But how much? Consider six aspects of a supposedly advanced culture.

- **Politics**. In all but three American presidential elections this century, the taller man has won. By itself this might be a coincidence.

And of course some short politicians thrive (examples include France's François Mitterrand and Britain's Harold Wilson). But the pattern is still clear, and is also found in:

- **Business**. A survey in 1980 found that more than half the chief executives of America's Fortune 500 companies stood six feet tall or more. As a class, these *wekepei* were a good 2½ inches taller than average; only 3% were *peritsi*, 5'7" or less. Other surveys suggest that about 90% of chief executives are of above-average height. Similarly for:

- **Professional status**. Looking at several professions, one study found that people in high-ranking jobs were about two inches taller than those down below, a pattern that held even when comparing men of like educational and socioeconomic status. Senior civil servants in Britain, for instance, tend to be taller than junior ones. Shorter people also have worse:

- **Jobs**. Give job recruiters two invented resumés that have been matched except for the candidates' height, as one study did in 1969. Fully 72% of the time, the taller man is "hired". And when they are hired, they tend also to earn rather more:

- **Money**. In 1994 James Sargent and David Blanchflower, of America's Dartmouth College, analysed a sample of about 6,000 male Britons whose progress was monitored from birth to early adulthood. Short teenaged boys made less money when they became young adults (aged 23) than their taller peers—even after other attributes, such as scores on ability tests or parents' social status, were factored out. For every four inches of height in adolescence, earnings went up more than 2% in early adulthood. Another survey, of graduates of the University of Pittsburgh, found that those who were 6'2" or taller received starting salaries 12% higher than those under six feet.

Not only do tall people grow richer, rich people grow taller. They enjoy well-nourished childhoods and better health. The stature-success nexus further bolsters the social preference for height. And that preference is expressed in a coin that is even more precious than money, namely:

- **Sex**. Mating opportunities are, at least in evolutionary terms, the ultimate prize of status. And here is the final humiliation for short men. When 100 women were asked to evaluate photographs of men whom they believed to be either tall, average or short, all of them found the tall and medium specimens "significantly more attractive" than the short ones. In another study, only two of 79 women said they would go on a date with a man shorter than themselves (the rest, on average, wanted to date a man at least 1.7 inches taller). "The universally acknowledged cardinal rule of dating and mate selection is that the male will be significantly taller than his female partner, write Mr. Martel and Mr. Biller. "This rule is almost inviolable." For short men, the sexual pickings are therefore likely to be slim.

SO WHY DON'T YOU CARE?

Is there, then, no good news for short men? No: there is none. And if, having read this far, you do not believe that height discrimination is serious, you are no doubt a tall person in the late stages of denial. Or, perhaps, you cringe at the thought of yet another victim group lining up to demand redress. Surely the notion of SHRIMPS (Severely Height-Restricted Individuals of the Male Persuasion) as an oppressed social group is silly, and the idea of special protections or compensatory benefits for short men preposterous? Actually, no—unless all such group benefits are equally dubious.

In general, the kinds of discrimination worth worrying about should have two characteristics. First, bias must be pervasive and systematic. Random discrimination is mere diversity of preference, and comes out in the wash. But if a large majority of employers prefers whites, for instance, then non-whites' options in life are sharply limited. And second, bias must be irrational: unrelated to the task at hand. If university mathematics faculties discriminate against the stupid, that may not seem fair (not everyone can master set theory); but it is sensible.

In politically correct terms, people who share an unusual characteristic that triggers pervasive and irrational aversion have a strong claim to be viewed as a vulnerable minority group. Is the discrimination against SHRIMPS, then, pervasive? Plainly so. Is it irrational? Except in a few rare cases in which height might affect job performance, obviously. Is it hurtful? Just ask any of the parents who clamour to put their little boys on growth hormones. Will it disappear of its own accord, as people become more enlightened? Be serious. Try to imagine that a century hence, when genetic engineering allows designer children, parents will queue up for shorter boys.

In some respects, indeed, SHRIMPS have it worse than members of ethnic minorities. Jews, Asians and other ethnics often favour each other for jobs, marriages and the rest. If they are disadvantaged within the majority culture, they may at least be advantaged in their own. But short men are disfavoured by more or less everybody, including other short men. If they want to flee, they need to find another planet.

Yet no country seems to have any antidiscrimination protections for SHRIMPS. America now has laws that ban discrimination against 70% or more of its population, including women, the elderly, blacks, Hispanics, Asians, Pacific islanders, Aleuts, Indians, and the handicapped — extending to people with back problems or glasses. Britain bans discrimination against women and nearly every ethnic or cultural group, Rastafarians excepted. But SHRIMPS? The whole issue, if it ever arises at all, is simply laughed off.

What accounts for this peculiarity? America's Equal Employment Opportunity Commission, which oversees the antidiscrimination laws, now boasts a man who has given the subject some thought. He is Paul Steven Miller, who is 4'5" tall. To be exact, he is an achondroplastic dwarf. Medically speaking, a dwarf has a recognisable genetic condition marked by short limbs, average-sized trunk, moderately enlarged head, and so on. This is regarded as a disability in America, and is legally protected against discrimination.

Mr. Miller favours protections for such little people. But he opposes extending protections to the "normally" short — men like America's labour secretary, Robert Reich, who is 4'10" and hears no end of it. (Bill Clinton, looking at a model of the White House made from Lego, commented: "Secretary Reich could almost live in there.") Why protect Mr. Miller but not Mr. Reich? Because, Mr. Miller says, one cannot protect everybody. "It would be totally unwieldy to let everybody in." Quite true. But convenient, too, to draw the line so as to include him but exclude a raft of other claimants. Convenience is not a principled reason for leaving short men to suffer their fates.

Indeed, it is hard to find any principled reason. Most of the obvious excuses for excluding SHRIMPS from the list of disadvantaged groups do little but show how arbitrary is the concept of any "group". For example, one might argue that there is no obvious line that demarcates a man short enough to be a SHRIMP. True enough; but in a world where blood mixes freely, there is equally no clear way to distinguish, for instance, a "Hispanic" from an "Anglo", or an American Indian from a "white" man.

Perhaps a "minority group", then, must be an ethnic or hereditary grouping? Plainly not. If women, homosexuals and people in wheelchairs may be minority groups, then surely short men can qualify. American Hispanics have nothing in common except the "Hispanic" label itself (they are mostly identified solely by their names). At least SHRIMPS are all detectably short.

In the West, the past quarter-century has been an era of awakening group consciousness. Blacks and women, Asians and indigenous peoples, homosexuals and the disabled — one by one, all have come to embrace group-based identities and protections. The obese are now reaching for group status; and, in truth, they too have a case. So why not short men? Logically, there seems no way out.

WEE MEN OF THE WORLD, UNITE!

Accordingly, *The Economist* demands that the European Convention on Human Rights grant SHRIMPS the protections that other disadvantaged minorities have already won. The United Nations should hold global conferences on the status of SHRIMPS. American federal contractors should be checked for height, to see that

SHRIMPS get their fair share. Employers should bend over backwards to recruit and promote SHRIMPS, and should be fined for allowing workers to disparage them. Elite universities should make sure that they include sufficient numbers of SHRIMPS among their students and faculties. Not least, newspapers that snidely refer to short men as "SHRIMPS" should be subjected to long lawsuits, and the authors concerned should be sent for sensitivity training (even if they are only 5'7", and write anonymously).

Then again, perhaps not. Knowing that short young men earn less money than other young men is, certainly, interesting. Knowing that only 9% of American Hispanics, as against 24% of non-Hispanics, hold a university degree is also interesting. But what do such facts imply? One does well to remember that they are mere statistical compilations, averages that blur together individuals who have virtually nothing in common. A "Hispanic", for instance, is a mere Spanish-sounding name masquerading as a human being. A SHRIMP, similarly, is no more than a mark on a tape measure.

To convert adjectives into pronouns—as in "a SHRIMP", or "a black" or "an Asian" or "a homosexual"—is to seize upon a single element of a person's make-up and cast into the background everything else. This kind of thinking may be useful as a tool of social analysis; as a basis for public policy, however, it is treacherous. For centuries, short men have shrugged their shoulders and carried on. They, at least, still see themselves, and are seen by others, as variegated individuals, not as a monotonal social group. That may be the best approach to all such human characteristics.

DISCUSSION QUESTIONS

Heightism: Short Guys Finish Last

1. Just as women are pressured to live up to thin ideals, so do men have a set of ideals to measure up to. How would you compare the plight of overweight women to that of short men? For example, overweight women can diet and exercise to lose weight but short men cannot diet or exercise to become taller.

2. How do you feel about the relationship of financial and quality-of-life issues to men's height? Do you agree with the author's suggestion that heightism should be regarded as the equivalent of sexism, ageism, and racism? Why or why not?

6   On the Muscle
Laurie Schulze

WORKING (IT) OUT: FEMINIZING MUSCLE

"Here She Is, Miss, Well, What?" asks the title of an article on female bodybuilders in *Sports Illustrated*. The implication is clear: the female bodybuilder is very difficult to position within any existing cultural map of the feminine (see Figure 2.6). But the problem cuts through gender into sex, as the opening lines of the same article reveal. "We always knew women could never build muscles, at least not, uh, real women."[1] The female bodybuilder threatens not only current socially constructed definitions of

FIGURE 2.6 *A female bodybuilder flexes her muscles and challenges the traditional view of women as passive and weak.*

femininity and masculinity, but the system of sexual difference itself. In a recent review of the documentary on women's bodybuilding, *Pumping Iron II: The Women* (1985), a male film critic calls the muscular female body a "kind of self-imposed freak of nature."[2] A *Newsweek Magazine* article quotes the "typical response" to Bev Francis, a world champion power lifter turned bodybuilder: "That *can't* be a woman."[3]

This body is dangerous. The deliberately muscular woman disturbs dominant notions of sex, gender, and sexuality, and any discursive field that includes her risks opening up a site of contest and conflict, anxiety and ambiguity. Some popular materials suggest that female bodybuilding is "redefining the whole idea of femininity." Some pose the question in terms of "how far" a female bodybuilder can go and still remain a "woman."[4] The most pervasive tendency, however, seems to be a recuperative strategy, an attempt to pull her back from a position outside dominant limits into a more acceptable space.

What Stuart Hall and other critics have called the "framing" function of popular forms can be traced in the ways in which popular magazines, particularly those magazines addressed to a female readership, work on the image of the female bodybuilder.[5] Rather than claiming that she redefines the idea of femininity, the notion of femininity is deployed to redefine her in hegemonic terms.

If the figure of the female bodybuilder is controversial, disturbing, and transgresses established notions of what a woman is "supposed to look like," she is also capable of being positioned in a more normative regime. The fitness phenomenon of the 1980s saturates advertising and popular materials with representations of sleek, athletic female bodies. National newsmagazines like *Time* splash the leotard-covered "new ideal of beauty" across their covers.[6] "Working out," being "in shape" (and possessing the capital and leisure necessary to do so) are the new markers of feminine sexuality, desirability, and status. "Jock chic" is glamorous, high fashion, enviable.[7] With a little work, the female bodybuilder—even though she oversteps the limits of that normative map of female physicality—can be contextualized in familiar discursive and representational space. Those elements that can be assimilated to one of the accepted maps of femininity are included, and those elements that cannot be absorbed are marginalized or excluded. This redefinition takes the form of attaching certain markers of femininity to the figure of the female bodybuilder, markers that anchor her to established and accepted values. Muscle is rephrased as "flex appeal," her heterosexuality and heterosexual desirability are secured, and female bodybuilding is freighted with an ideology of control aligned with notions of competition in the workplace.

What is generally referred to as the "fitness phenomenon" indicates a shift in the definition of the "ideal body" of the 1980s (for both women and men) towards the more muscular body. Chronicling the fashions in body types over the last thirty years, Alexandra Penney details the changes in the "ideal body." In the 1950s, the popular ideal for men was the "well-muscled" look, while the ideal type for women was "big bosomed and round hipped" and "well fed." In the 1960s, what Penney terms the "whippet look," the female type summed up by the model Twiggy, became fashionable for both men and women. With the 1970s, the well-maintained "healthy" body—the result of jogging and swimming—became normative for both men and women, but the "slim-line" look still controlled the overall shape this ideal body assumed. In the 1980s, however, the ideal body carries more muscle mass and is more defined, the male displaying the visible muscles of the weight-trained athlete, and now even women are using weights to "strengthen their muscles and to develop rounder contours."[8] The new female ideal of beauty, featured in a *Time* cover story, is now "taut, toned and coming on strong."[9]

The contemporary trend in fitness and current notions of health demand that women engage in the "kind of exercise that produces greater muscle definition," according to one popular magazine, which points out that "while it was very difficult to sell the defined look to women in the '70's, today a full 50 percent of the nation's 4.2 million Nautilus users are female."[10] The terms in which this is expressed articulate the commodification of the body in consumer culture. A complex net of social, economic, and ideological determinants activates the ideal body, and it is clear that fitness-related industries stand to profit if a particular female body type becomes a marketable commodity.

The normative ideal of beauty today, then, is invoked in language like "slim," "strong," "sinuous," "athletic," and "healthy." And it is against this notion of what the ideal woman's body is supposed to be that popular discourse often positions the female bodybuilder. In magazines, the professional female bodybuilder is placed either at the limits of the ideal or just beyond its boundaries. The kind of difference constructed for her in this dominant discourse of feminine beauty is posed in terms of "excess." If the female bodybuilder has transgressed the ideal, there is an attempt to ease her back into the space secured by the ideal, emphasizing certain features, suppressing others, and papering over contradictions. By examining the inscription of what Hall would refer to as the "preferred reading" of the female bodybuilder in these texts, I hope to reveal some of the specific strategies by which this domestication of a potential challenge to dominant definitions of a feminine body is accomplished.[11]

The form of address used in many articles in popular women's magazines sets a reassuring tone. Articles on bodybuilding frequently frame the issue in terms of a question for which they supply the answer. "Women's Bodybuilding: What's In It For You?" one article asks.[12] The "you" is obviously not a female bodybuilder, not one of "them," but the implication is that the regimen of the

female bodybuilder could have positive effects for the "normal" woman. Typically, the articles detail those benefits in ways that connect the female bodybuilder to the feminine norm.

One strategy is to allege that weight-training for women will enhance their heterosexual desirability, and here we again find confirmation of Adrienne Rich's insight about the "compulsory" nature of heterosexuality in the way this sexuality is attached to sport.[13] Patriarchy and homophobia combine in complex ways to link female bodybuilders with lesbianism, and denying this linkage is critical to the project of framing female bodybuilding within dominant systems of meaning. The female bodybuilder must be anchored to heterosexuality: if she is not, she may slip through the cracks in the hegemonic system into an oppositional sexuality that would be irrecuperable. Female bodybuilders quoted in these magazines almost always mention "boyfriends" and their delight in the increased (sexual) attention they receive from men attracted to their physicality.[14] An interview with athlete Patrice Donnely (who played the role of Tory, a pentathlete involved in a lesbian relationship in *Personal Best* [1982]) quotes her as saying "Men have always loved my body. My boyfriend loves to show it off. He'll say to friends, 'Hey, watch Patrice flex!'"[15]

This set of meanings constructed around the female bodybuilder guarantees that weight-training makes women "more sensual." As one writer puts it, "a woman who is more aware of her physicality will...be more aware of her sexuality... sex is, after all, a form of exercise for two."[16] But of course the implication is that the exercise partner can only be male. The ultimate heterosexual, then, is an athlete, since it is now popular wisdom that weight-training increases sexual endurance.[17] That women's newly acquired sexual stamina is cut to the measurements of male desire is clearly stated.[18] For it is common sense in this discourse that *her* body work must enhance *his* sexual pleasure.[19]

Another strategy that domesticates women's bodybuilding and makes weight-training more easy to market to women is the discourse of reassurance that allays the main fear that "normal" women have about weight-training: that they will develop "excessive" muscles. A *Vogue* article elaborately protests that the "natural" differences between males and females prevent any "masculine" muscle bulk resulting from weight-training for the "average woman." The fleshed-out argument goes like this:

> ...for most women, the question of excessive musculature is moot, partly because they have such low levels of the basically male hormone testosterone, but mostly because only a scant minority have the genetic make-up that will allow them to develop a so-called masculine physique. Besides having to work harder for their muscles—as much as six hours a day in the gym...women bodybuilders must diet more strictly than men to reduce their naturally higher levels of body fat, then take diuretics to get rid of the water in their skin to achieve the veiny "rippled" effect that the judges are after. Given these facts of life, the best the average woman can hope for is a sleek, sinewy look.

The article concludes, quoting a female bodybuilder: "There is no way to change biology."[20] Biology—this system of meaning allegedly beyond work, beyond sociality, beyond ideology—is invoked to defuse the threat female bodybuilding poses to sexual difference and gender differentiation. Those few women who do develop "masculine" muscles are biological exceptions and fanatics. If you are biologically average and use weight-training in moderation, there is no danger of acquiring the kind of physicality that will challenge the status quo. On the contrary, you will achieve the "sleek, sinewy look" that conforms to the ideal body.

And the argument goes further to reassure women that the difference between flexed and unflexed muscle is the difference between normality and excess. *Glamour* explains to its readers that competitive bodybuilders deliberately "pump up" their muscles before a contest, and that the muscle size one sees in photographs of women bodybuilders is the result. This difference is illustrated with two side-by-side photographs of a female bodybuilder labeled "Ellen with muscles flexed for competition" and "Ellen with muscles relaxed." The female bodybuilder—when not "being a bodybuilder"—looks "just like everyone else."[19] The female bodybuilder is then invisible,

except on the contest stage. This carefully brackets the threat of excessive muscularity off from the "normal" social world and confines it to the bodybuilding subculture. It also assures women who are thinking about working out with weights that they need not fear a loss of privilege or social power; despite any differences that may result from lifting weights, they will still be able to "pass." *These* muscles are a difference that won't make a difference.[20]

Channeling bodybuilding into the mainstream usually involves linking it to self-improvement, self-confidence, and self-control, and from there to the new woman who must acquire more assertiveness if she is to compete with men in the labor force. Pointing out that half of all American women are now employed full time, a recent article goes on to say that competing with men requires restructuring the female body to "fit the new *fashion* [emphasis mine: notice how social and economic equality between men and women is discursively translated into a 'fashion'] of equality."[21] According to *Glamour*, "delicate wrists [and] voluptuous curves are no longer *au courant*. These old markers of the feminine have now become 'liabilities,' and must be replaced with the self-confident look of health and a firm body."[22] The new body is positioned as a "dress for success" fashion statement, an essential part of the image necessary to climb the corporate ladder.

Finally, the new developed body is mainstreamed as a support for the merger of work, leisure, and consumption. Mike Featherstone, in "The Body in Consumer Culture," connects "body maintenance" with "marketability of the self." With industrialization and the development of mass production and consumption, "workers who had become used to the rhetoric of thrift, hard work and sobriety, had to be 'educated' to appreciate a new discourse centered around the hedonistic lifestyle entailing new needs and desires." This new discourse took up the ideology of continual self-improvement and self-maintenance, and one of the avenues for developing new markets was the stimulation of consumer desires connected with the body and the self, combined in contemporary currency in the notion of "lifestyle."

Advertising in the early 20th century organized a new critical attitude towards the body and imagined a "world in which individuals are made to become emotionally vulnerable, constantly monitoring themselves for bodily imperfections which could no longer be regarded as natural." This body may be a carrier of "youth, beauty, energy, fitness, movement, freedom, romance, exotica, luxury, enjoyment, fun," but these benefits are not simply given. The desired and desirable qualities of the body in consumer culture are "plastic." In other words, their achievement requires work on the part of the individual. Thus it is that a certain state of anxiety is created. If an individual is not attractive, it is his or her (perhaps especially her) own fault. An improperly serviced body is the responsibility of the owner. Since the way one looks is a "reflex of the self," bodily imperfections are read as a symptom of "laziness, low self-esteem, and even moral failure." Body maintenance is a conduit to pleasure, social acceptance, and self-worth.[23]

Popular discourse harnesses female bodybuilding to this regime of hedonism and self-maintenance. It positions the bodybuilder's body as a site of heterosexual pleasure, romance, youth, fun, and beauty. Under the aegis of body maintenance, the female bodybuilder can be pulled into the hegemonic system, circulated with the ideas of hard work, self-discipline, competition, and success. Weighted down with markers of the patriarchal feminine and hailed as capitalist subject, the female bodybuilder can be transformed into a less problematic phenomenon. But only less problematic. Whether relegated to the margins of the cultural system as a freak, or recuperated as the site of "flex appeal," the female bodybuilder continues to cause considerable ideological strain.

Notes

1. David Levin, "Here She Is, Miss, Well, What?," *Sports Illustrated*, 17 March 1980, 66.

2. Richard Corliss, "Real People in a Reel Peephole," *Time*, 6 May 1985, 86.

3. Charles Leerhsen and Pamela Abramson, "The New Flex Appeal," *Newsweek*, 6 May 1985, 82.

4. Charles Gaines and George Butler, "Iron Sisters," *Psychology Today* (November 1983): 67.

5. See Stuart Hall, "Culture, the Media and the 'Ideological Effect,'" *Mass Communication and Society*, ed. James Curran, Michael Gurevitch, and Janet Woollacott (Beverly Hills: Sage Publications, 1979), 315–48; Stuart Hall, "Encoding/Decoding," *Culture, Media, Language*, ed. Stuart Hall, Dorothy Hobson, Andrew Lowe, and Paul Willis (London: Hutchinson, 1980), 128–39.

6. Richard Corliss, "The New Ideal of Beauty," *Time*, 30 August 1982, cover.

7. Alexandra Penney, "Showing Some New Muscle," *New York Times Magazine*, 15 June 1980, 58.

8. Penney, "Showing Some New Muscle."

9. Corliss, "The New Ideal of Beauty," 72.

10. Leerhsen and Abramson, "The New Flex Appeal," 83.

11. Hall, "Encoding/Decoding."

12. Linda Gordon, "Women's Bodybuilding: What's In It For You?," *Glamour* (October 1981): 116.

13. Adrienne Rich, "Compulsory Heterosexuality and Lesbian Existence," *Signs* 5, no. 4 (Summer 1980): 631–60.

14. Jim Calio, "Shades of Charles Atlas," *People*, 26 May 1980, 87.

15. Corliss, "The New Ideal of Beauty," 76.

16. Corliss, "The New Ideal of Beauty."

17. Calio, "Shades," 87. Bodybuilder Lisa Lyon states that "your sexual endurance is better" as a result of weight-training.

18. "Strength… The Good Reason Women are Weight Training," *Vogue* (September 1983): 316; Leerhsen and Abramson, 83.

19. Gordon, "Women's Bodybuilding," 116.

20. Calio, "Shades," 87.

21. Corliss, "The New Ideal of Beauty," 72–77.

22. Janice Kaplan, "The New Ideal Female Body: Standards of Feminine Appeal are Definitely Changing," *Glamour* (July 1981): 58.

23. Mike Featherstone, "The Body in Consumer Culture," *Theory, Culture and Society* 1 (Autumn 1982): 18–26.

On the Muscle

1. Why are female bodybuilders considered odd or different by mainstream culture?

2. Do you agree with Schulze's analysis of female bodybuilders from a feminist perspective? Why or why not?

3. Is the presence of female bodybuilders in society a positive or negative step for men and women in general? Why?

4. What does the author mean by stating "The female bodybuilder threatens...the system of sexual difference? Explain.

7 Is Thin In? Kalabari Culture and the Meaning of Fatness

Susan O. Michelman
University of Massachusetts-Amherst

It will be of no surprise to those reading this article that most women in America today aspire to an aesthetic of thinness and are constantly seduced into thinking that "you can neither be too rich nor too thin." Although this is historically quoted from the Duchess of Windsor, the statement bears contemporary truth because many women equate thinness with happiness and financial success (Bordo, 1993).

How dominant an ideal is this aesthetic of thinness? Every culture ascribes to a body ideal for both men and women. A body ideal is a size, age, and a combination of physical attributes that society deems to be the most desirable for each gender. For example, the current popular ideal for American women emphasizes a youthful, slim, athletic, and well-toned physique. Although most apparel designers both promote and design for this image, in reality, only a small percentage of the population fit these stringent criteria. Recent studies have found that the average American woman is 5 feet 4 inches tall, weighs 142 pounds, and wears a size 14.

Not every culture on the globe ascribes to an ideal of slimness. As the apparel industry is both motivated by and addresses an increasingly diverse multicultural market, both designers and merchandisers will need to be sensitive to cultural body ideals. Asia's rapidly expanding market of fashion consumers is an example of this trend. Currently, some Indonesian designers are attaining success by designing for Asian women's tastes and body size, frequently smaller in proportion to an American or European woman's body frame.

In each historic era, the American women's body ideal has changed based upon society's motivations and resulting characteristic forms of dress. At the turn of the 20th century, women's corsets enhanced an S-shaped ideal with an ample bustline, tiny waist, rounded hips, and long hair. Couturier designers, such as Charles Worth, extolled these ideals in lavish, hand-constructed designs for wealthy women. Only 20 years later, along with the advent of mass production of apparel and social changes such as women attaining the vote, the "flapper era" extolled a youthful, slim, almost boyish physique for women, with short, bobbed hair. This ideal for women was literally the antithesis of designs at the turn of the century.

My objective in writing this article is to demonstrate that there is no one universal body ideal for women. I will discuss the tradition of *iria* among the Kalabari people of Nigeria. In 1990, I

Original for this text.

did fieldwork and research among the Kalabari (Michelman, 1992). In contrast to American culture, I discovered that fatness or plumpness is considered a sign of beauty for Kalabari women. Understanding the body ideals of another culture, the Kalabari, will help you gain a greater understanding of the diversity and cultural meaning of body ideals, particularly for women (Michelman & Eicher, 1995; Michelman, 1995).

THE KALABARI AND THE TRADITION OF IRIA

The Kalabari are an ethnic group who reside in the Niger River delta of southern Nigeria in West Africa (Figure 2.7a). The Kalabari form a distinct cultural and linguistic subgroup that is a comparatively small population of approximately one million within the total Nigerian population of 120 million. The eastern Niger River delta, where the Kalabari live, is a saltwater swamp. Exploitable resources from this environment are limited, and people have relied primarily on occupations of fishing, salt-making, and trading, along with exchanging produce from inland areas. Although most Kalabari are Christians, precolonial beliefs and practices still pervade their daily and ritual life.

Kalabari dress has been examined by several authors from different points of view. Erekosima and Eicher have discussed the concept of cultural authentication expressed through Kalabari dress (Erekosima, 1979; Erekosima & Eicher, 1981). Through trade, foreign goods and European cloth were introduced into the Niger River delta area as early as the 16th century (Alagoa, 1972, p. 291). The Kalabari incorporated these western items into their indigenous system of dress and aesthetics, modifying them to make them part of their own ethnic identity.

The Kalabari celebrate the female appearance known as *iria*, a cultural celebration of womanhood characterized by dress and body modifications. *Iria* marks the period of transition in the female life cycle from late childhood through childbirth. According to Akobo's (1985) accounts of the oral tradition of *iria*, in early puberty, young women underwent the ceremony of *ikuta de* (i.e., decoration with beads)

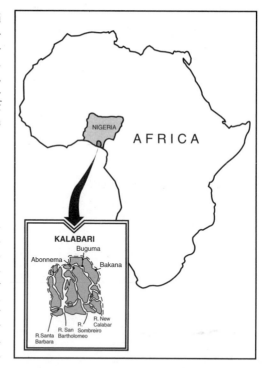

FIGURE 2.7A *The Kalabari reside in the Niger River delta of southern Nigeria in West Africa.*

which was a cultural acknowledgement of their femininity. As adolescents, these young women performed the *pakiri iwain* ceremony where they became "social debutantes." With subsequent ceremonies and physical maturity, they revealed less of their bodies to the public. *Konju fina* was the ceremony that indicated their readiness for marriage. *Bite sara* was peformed when they became betrothed, with the final stage *iriabo* indicating their childbearing status. (See Figure 2.7b.)

After the adolescent "coming out," Kalabari men were historically able to openly admire the young woman's appearance and approach the parents concerning marriage. As the female body matured and rounded out, clothing became less important as it obstructed the visibility of the body's development. Well-developed breasts and, more important, protruding buttocks indicated the ability to wear wrappers properly. Wrappers are large, rectangular pieces of

FIGURE 2.7B *Examples of how two Kalabari women incorporated western items into their indigenous system of dress and aesthetics, modifying them to make them part of their own ethnic identity.*

FIGURE 2.7C *Historic portrait reveals the desirable state of roundness in Kalabari women.*

cloth that are literally wrapped around the body at the waist and extend to the ankles. Wrappers are worn by both men and women.

Historically, after the birth of their first child, a woman stayed in a fattening room for about two months, necessitating a substantial financial commitment from the woman's and husband's family (Daly, 1984). While in the fattening room, the woman was attended by other female family members, who nurtured the *iriabo*'s child while the woman was instructed in dance. Dancing was performed publicly at the end of the confinement.

Today, because of contemporary demands of education and employment, women are less willing to devote time to complete the full process of becoming an *iriabo*. *Iria* is now performed by women at cultural events and particularly at family funerals.

Nonetheless, cultural ideals of female beauty are still associated with public acknowledgement and approval of female fecundity. The ideal adult Kalabari female figure is "substantial and thick or plumpy" (Daly, 1984). The expression "to be up to a woman" is to be rounded, particularly in the breasts and buttocks. The practice of seclusion or fattening after pregnancy further enhances the image of the plump Kalabari woman. Historical photographs reveal women in the desirable state of roundness. (See Figure 2.7c.)

The midsection of the female Kalabari body is emphasized by clothing more than any other area. This body aesthetic, admired by both Kalabari men and women, indicates an intense interest in recognizing and revering the reproductive capacity of the female. There is no apparent comparable interest in a plump body for Kalabari males.

BODY IDEALS IN CROSS-CULTURAL CONTEXT

Even among the Kalabari of Nigeria who have an essential cultural belief in the beauty of a plump female body, contemporary influences conveyed through international media are having their effect by creating ambivalence about plumpness, particularly among younger women. The globalization of body ideals is a contemporary issue and makes it impossible for them to exist in cultural isolation.

The Kalabari women and their desired body aesthetic are a striking contrast to the images of thin women prevalent in American media. By understanding that there are cultural alternatives to this ultra-thin image, readers may begin to think more critically about alternative ideals of beauty. Dress, in all cultures, has a unique and critical role because of its proximal relationship to the body. The body and how we dress are a medium of culture, a powerful symbolic form, a surface on which the rules, hierarchies, and ideologies of a culture are inscribed. Mary Douglas (1982), suggested that the human physical body in any culture symbolically represents important aspects of the social "body." How the physical body serves as a medium of expression varies with ethnicity, and religious and political beliefs. This could include ideals related to modesty, size, and importance of various body parts — some that are covered and some not. Body ideal varies from culture to culture and can change over time.

References

Akobo, D. I. (1985). *Oral traditions of Buguma: Iria ceremony a case study*. Department of Library Studies: University of Ibadan.

Alagoa, E. J. (1972). *A history of the Niger delta*. Ibadan, Nigeria.

Bordo, S. (1993). *Unbearable weight: Feminism, western culture, and the body*. Berkeley: University of California Press.

Daly, M. C. (1984). *Kalabari female appearance and the tradition of iria*. Unpublished doctoral dissertation. University of Minnesota, St. Paul.

Douglas, M. (1982). *Natural symbols*. New York: Pantheon Books.

Erekosima, T. V. (1979). *The tartans of Buguma women: Cultural authentication*. Paper presented at African Studies Assoc.: Los Angeles, CA.

Erekosima, T. V., & Eicher, J. B. (1981). Kalabari cut-thread and pulled-thread cloth. *African Arts, 14* (2), pp. 48–51, 87.

Michelman, S. (1992). *Dress in Kalabari women's societies*. Unpublished doctoral dissertation. University of Minnesota, St. Paul.

Michelman, S. O. (1995). Social change and the symbolism of dress in Kalabari women's societies. *Family and Consumer Science Research Journal, 23* (4), pp. 368–392.

Michelman, S. O. & Eicher, J. B. (1995). Dress and gender in Kalabari women's societies. *Clothing and Textiles Research Journal. 13* (2), 121–129.

DISCUSSION QUESTIONS

Is Thin In? Reflections on the Kalabari

1. Can you identify any ethnic influences on your current body weight/size? If so, what are the ethnic influences? If you cannot identify any ethnic influences on your current body weight, why not?

2. Why do you think the midsection of the plump traditional female Kalabarian figure (emphasized by clothing) is the body part many American women try to de-emphasize? Reflect on the different ideologies that

would lead to such opposite approaches to viewing the body.

3. Speculate as to why Kalabari men do not also have a plump body ideal.

4. Would you characterize the following statements as ethnocentric? Why or why not? "What they do in Africa has nothing to do with me. I don't care what people think about me being too skinny. They are not me."

8   The Miss Heilala Beauty Pageant: Where Beauty Is More than Skin Deep

Jehanne Teilhet-Fisk

Introduction

When I went to the Kingdom of Tonga in Western Polynesia in June of 1981, it was to study *ngatu*, tapa cloth. But the excitement surrounding the Heilala Festival preempted the women's attention, and mine as well.[1] Tonga is a constitutional monarchy, an independent kingdom protected by England that struggles against growing pluralism to maintain a stratified society where the chiefly and/or noble (*'eiki*) ranks are socially differentiated from commoners (*tu'a*).[2] As Campbell and others have noted, this struggle is manifested in tensions "arising between the new economy and the old social order, just as they have arisen between the new economy and the old political order" (Campbell 1992, 227). These tensions in turn are articulated in the debate over "beauty" that emerges in the Miss Heilala Beauty Pageant.

I started my study of the Miss Heilala Beauty Pageant with the premise that I was studying ethno-aesthetic systems. I soon realized, however, that the Miss Heilala Beauty Pageant is vested with multiple political and cultural meanings that are put into play around different perceptions of beauty. In the Miss Heilala Beauty Pageant, I discovered, beauty is more than skin deep.

THE MISS HEILALA BEAUTY PAGEANT

"Beauty" and Tongan Identity

The beauty pageant is a focal point of the Heilala Festival that is held annually from late June through early July in Nuku' alofa, the capital of Tonga. The Heilala Festival week is a recent invention filled with cultural events, craft competition, church pageantry, spectator sports, parades, nightclub revelry, and ancient dances. The Festival, a cultural tribute to the king Taufa'ahau

Tupou IV, was also designed to promote tourism and instill pride in "the Tongan way." The Festival is timed to coincide with His Majesty's birthday on July 4th, which is proclaimed a public holiday. Thus the Festival, its beauty pageant, and the king's birthday (an occasion entrenched in cultural protocol) are complementary events. While his Majesty is the symbolic keystone of the Heilala Festival—which, according to local sources, was named in 1979 after "the flower of our royal family"—younger members of the royal family also legitimize and sanction the beauty pageant.

An outgrowth of a beauty pageant organized as a charity fund raiser in the 1950s by a member of the royal family, today's Miss Heilala pageant is the official forum for selecting a woman to represent Tonga against other Polynesians at the Miss South Pacific Pageant, before going on to the Miss World or Miss Universe competitions. In addition to representing a Tongan identity in international competitions, the Miss Heilala Pageant is a popular way of maintaining links with the many Tongans living abroad. Roughly 60,000 Tongans live abroad, compared to the 100,000 who live in Tonga (Campbell 1992, 223).[3] Thus, the Miss Heilala Beauty Pageant represents an important means of sustaining a "Tongan" community, one that agrees on certain values that can be put into public practice when all its diasporic segments return once a year. At the same time, however, the organizational structure of international beauty pageants imposes on the Miss Heilala Beauty Pageant practices and ideas that run counter to Tongan identity. For example, the inclusion of an internationally-mandated bathing suit competition compromises traditional avoidance *tapus* (taboos) that prohibit men from gazing upon any portion of their sister's body that would normally be clothed.

These tensions between local and global standards of behavior are most evident in the conflict between Tongan identity as it is defined and enacted in Tonga, and as it is defined and enacted by the expatriates or "Tongan Nationals" who return to Tonga for this pageant.[4] The local and expatriate Tongan perspectives ultimately run counter to each other. This contradiction functions at the levels of language, the economy, the political order, and national ideology, and leads directly into the most personal, private, and powerful features of identity: kinship, family, body, sexuality, and relations between the sexes. These contradictions, tensions, and conflicts become most clear in simple questions about what constitutes "beauty."

The local Tongan community has its own perception of beauty, *faka' ofo'ofa*, that goes far beyond the surface of physical attributes and is deeply entrenched in social and moral values that uphold and emphasize the family, kinship, church, and a nationalist ideology based on constitutional monarchy. Tongan expatriates, especially those born abroad, have a different and narrower definition of beauty, one not embedded in Tongan cultural values. The expatriates' ideas about beauty can also differ depending on whether they come from the United States, Australia, or New Zealand. These expatriate ideals are affected by global notions of beauty that are less culture-specific, but are based generally upon Euro-American preferences. The Miss Heilala Beauty Pageant is a key site where these different aesthetics articulate and conflict.

THE 1993 MISS HEILALA FESTIVAL

All agree that the 1993 Heilala Festival was exceptional—it had more of everything including an all-time record of nineteen pageant contestants, more than half of them from overseas. Everyone wanted to make the 1993 event a spe-

cial celebration for the King's seventy-fifth birthday, the Silver Jubilee of their Majesty's coronation, and the installation of two nobles. It lasted fifteen days and nights, and Tongans of all ages came from other islands and from overseas to participate as audience, congregation, performers, or contestants in a panoply of events.

In a Tonga caught in a transition era "in which the indigenous and the foreign are unequally and unevenly blended" (Campbell 1992, 228), the Heilala Festival instills a sense of allegiance, community, and social interdependence, by bringing the indigenous and the foreign together. The band concerts, children's talent shows, spectator sports, float parade, gay beauty pageant, and the nightly events of the Miss Heilala Beauty Pageant tend to incorporate and express changing attitudes toward modernization, the new economy, formal education, and authority. Other occasions are culturally indigenous and promulgate the old social and political order with gala affairs that pay tribute to the *'eiki* class. These events include elaborate dances performed by entire villages, contrapuntal singing groups contending for honors, lavish invitational (birthday and jubilee) feasts, regal installations of nobles, and handicraft competitions designed to maintain the quality and integrity of ancient media.

The interaction of these events distributed all over *Nuku' alofa*, produces new relationships and dialogues that can either pit older values against contemporary ones or bind them together. This process is especially visible in the beauty pageant—a modern vehicle that is not Tongan, but that nonetheless helps to define, communicate, and package Tongan culture, identity, and pride.[5]

A *Tongan Perspective on Beauty Pageant Practices*

The 1993 Miss Heilala Beauty Pageant had five separate judging events for all contestants. Four of these events—Miss Talent Quest, Miss Tau'olunga, Miss South Pacific, and Miss Heilala Ball—were open to the public, who purchased separate tickets for each. The fifth event, the Tongan–English interview, took place in private at a special luncheon attended by contestants and judges. Although the five events are evenly weighted in final marks, the prizes differ, with the largest prize of 2,000 *pa'anga* (exchanged at a little less than the United States dollar) and a round-trip ticket to the United States of America and London going to the winner of the coveted Miss Heilala title. Contestants must be part Tongan (as one informant put it, "one-quarter, one-half—any part"), single, and between the ages of eighteen and twenty-four.

In spite of the impressive awards and the broad entry criteria, local women are hesitant to enter the Miss Heilala competition. Indeed, all of the Tongan contestants I interviewed in 1993 reported being "talked into" entering by their mother, aunt, or girlfriend. One of the reasons they gave for their hesitancy was that it is "un-Tongan" to put oneself on public view. This rationale is grounded in normative gender practice in which women tend to avoid public exposure, "preferring instead spectator or humble positions" (Marcus 1978a, 242).

It is difficult to generalize about Tongan women because their individual ranks and social roles differ in their positions as sisters, aunts, wives, and/or queens. Whereas houses, land, titles, and secular powers are passed down through men, honor, mystical knowledge, abstract power, and political veto rights are passed down through women. Sisters therefore have powers and rights that they lack as wives. Even a commoner woman has more influence as a sister than as a wife. The influence wielded by Tongan sisters is bolstered by brother-sister avoidance practices.

In Tonga, sisters command respect and avoidance from their brothers, a practice embedded in a descent system where the father's side outranks the mother's, but where sisters outrank brothers, thus giving the father's sister and her children the highest rank. The father's sister has ritual or mystical powers and material rights over her brother's children (Goldman 1970; Rogers 1977; Marcus 1978a, 1978b; Bott 1981; Biersack 1982; James 1983, 1988). The father's eldest sister has the highest rank and is called *mehekitanga*. She is usually the *fabu* or the woman "who is ceremonially or ritually superior in a par-

ticular social context" (Rogers 1977, 167). Although the practice is now less common, brothers tend to defer to the superior status of their female siblings by according them *faka'a-pa'apa*, respect and honor. Out of respect for their sisters, brothers are under pressure to avoid situations that might compromise their sister's and classificatory sister's honor.

The Miss Heilala Beauty Pageant as a Reflection of Social Hierarchy

The Miss Heilala Beauty Pageant is structured to reflect the Tongan social order. The zenith of the social hierarchy is represented by the H.R.H. Crown Prince Tupouto'a, who is the official patron of the festival and installs Miss Heilala. His sister, H.R.H. Princess Salote Mafile'o Pilolevu Tuita, promotes the Miss Tonga/San Francisco Beauty Pageant in the United States and brings the winner(s) back to compete in the Miss Heilala Pageant. Without the royal family's approval, there would be no Miss Heilala contest for, as Kaeppler has observed, "innovation in Tonga takes place downward from the top of stratified society" (1993, 95). All official Festival events are honored by the appearance of the royal and noble families and various "VIPs." Their presence gives honor to the contestants and valorizes their role as representatives of the Kingdom at local, national, and international events. The royal family's presence also assures the allegiance of the local participants and community at large and helps prevent the use of the Festival as a platform for oppositional or anti-royal views.

The more educated middle-class Tongans and nobles often act as judges. Tongan judges must bridge the social order, while balancing their place within the Tongan social order and professional community. Therefore, their social obligations and relationships influence their judgments and sway their votes. Should a patron or judge of higher social rank indicate that a particular contestant (maybe his sister's daughter or girlfriend) must place first in a certain event, then the other judges and/or those tallying the votes will obey out of respect. Independent auditors, computer systems, and Euro-American judges are slowly being introduced to bring an element of "objectivity" and change into "the Tongan way," but the final tallies for the winner of the different titles are never made public, so modernization usually loses to Tongan protocol.[6]

The winner of the pageant is never crowned "Queen" or "Princess," as in American pageants, nor would a noble's daughter enter such a contest.[7] Many of the contestants are from the *tu'a* class (commoners and/or rising middle class). These commoners are, in some sense, more elevated in the local hierarchy than expatriate contestants, Tongan, or part-Tongan nationals. These non-local Tongan frequently enter the pageant without understanding or even thinking about their social class or place in the local social structure. From their perspective, they might also be considered as being outside the social structure altogether.

Indeed, these Tongan expatriates conventionally come to the Miss Heilala competition with Euro-American egalitarian and individualistic ideology, believing that they will be judged on the basis of beauty and talent. In 1993, several of the non-local Tongan contestants I interviewed were convinced that they would win the title or at least place as first runner-up, particularly because Miss Tonga/New Zealand had won the Miss Heilala title in 1992. But this did not happen.

"BEAUTY" AT THE LOCAL AND GLOBAL JUNCTURE

Although it includes several practices that conflict with local Tongan norms and social arrangements, the Miss Heilala Pageant does not pose a direct threat to the old political order. It does, however, rearrange social relations, and thus furnishes an entry into modern reforms that question social hierarchy and hereditary privilege. It is also a place where many kinds of unresolved tensions come to a head at the local and global juncture.

One kind of tension between local and global standards in the pageant is created by the inequality in financial assistance given by the sponsors. In its early years, the pageant was sponsored by the *'eiki* class and the heads of extended families, but that has given way to sponsorship by corporations like Benson & Hedges and Royal Beer, who want the contestants to promote their products.[8] In 1993 some of the locals complained that the Tongan expatriates got the "richest" sponsors, and that without better sponsorship the locals could not keep up with the new styles.[9] This inequality also pitted the Tongan expatriates against each other (i.e., Miss Tonga/San Francisco and the other women from California, Miss New Zealand Tonga Tourist Association, Miss Australia Tongan Tourist Association) and against the local contestants from the main island (Tongatapu), as well as against the other island candidates (Ha'apai and Vavau), and this in turn kindled regional factionalism.

Factionalism at the local, global, and regional level was also apparent when the California-Tongan contestants were constantly singled out and taunted by the audience for the way they dressed and the way they spoke Tongan. The Californians were not prepared for the old ways; as one contestant from California explained in a personal interview, "I brought my shorts and pants and then, well, I was told, 'We don't want you wearing shorts, not even around the hotel.' I was amazed because even though I am part Tongan, I was not born here, and I wasn't raised knowing their culture, knowing how strictly conservative they are" (Tongan-American, June 30, 1994). Californians were also charged, more than any other expatriate group, with being "snobs" and propagating American attitudes and change. While local Tongans will frequently allude to tourists (and Euro-American videos, television shows, and movies) as undesirably "other," they tend to tolerate casual dress and "progressive ways" without adopting them. There is a grave problem, however, when non-local Tongan contestants "return" with the same dress styles and values as tourists. Local adolescents and children become confused: since these expatriates are Tongan, not *papālangi* (European), they don't understand why their parents are opposed to their adopting American fashions.

Diasporic Tongans are thus caught in a double-bind. The only venue in the entire festival that is readily open to their participation is the pageant. Yet when an expatriate wins the Miss Heilala title (which has happened on several occasions lately; in 1990, 1992, and 1994), local Tongans are less than pleased. As they put it to me, they do not want Tonga represented locally or abroad by an expatriate who they perceive as being more *papālangi* than Tongan. It sends a confused signal to the local Tongan youth about Tongan identity.

Factionalism and Cultural Unity

Global standards and the inclusion of expatriates in the Miss Heilala Beauty Contest has generated local discontent and factionalism, but has also promoted cultural unity and the essentialization of a Tongan identity overseas. When Princess Pilolevu moved to San Francisco, California with her husband to open the Tongan Consulate, she became more aware of these complex issues of identity and Tonganness; one result was the first official "Miss Tonga/San Francisco Pageant" in 1993.[10]

I interviewed some former Miss Heilala contestants who were attending the Miss Tonga/San Francisco Pageant in 1994. They all affirmed that the 1993 Miss Heilala pageant had a profound affect on their sense of identity and cultural pride in being Tongan. Within the pageantry, amid the subtle plays of status rivalry and conspicuous consumption, there lies an affirmation and even celebration of ethnic identity and national pride in being Tongan—indigenous or expatriate—in a global world. When the Tongans from abroad return for the Heilala Festival they may not share the values of the local Tongan community, but they do share in the value of being Tongan. As an older expatriate from New Zealand explained to me, "When you are Tongan you always know who you are. You are never to be anything less than the very best. The constitution of Tonga is Tonga, King, God and my heritage, so that's always implanted in a Tongan's heart." After a pause this expatriate added, "though in this generation, here and overseas, it kind of got lost somewhere."

Miss Tau'olunga: The Retention of Tongan Culture

To keep the "Tongan way" from getting lost, the Heilala Festival and Beauty Pageant uses categories that reaffirm and strengthen Tongan ethnic identity, cultural pride, and language. The judges "assess the contestant's knowledge of both the Tongan and English languages, of Tongan culture and their general knowledge" (*Heilala '93* 1993, 9). The beauty pageant also has the unique Tongan category of Miss *Tau'olunga*, which has the most sub-categories and awards the most prizes.

The official Festival booklet *Heilala '93* explains that "while all events rank equally for marks toward the award of the title, the one aspect of this pageant which is unique to Tonga, and which distinguishes this pageant from other beauty contests, is the Miss *Tau'olunga* evening." The *Tau'olunga* is the classic solo dance of Tonga culture, traditionally performed by the daughters of the royal family and nobility.[11] Every aspect of the presentation—the costume, the set-piece movements, the grace and art of their execution, the charm and beauty of the dancer—are strictly marked. The *Tau'olunga* is more than a dance; "it is an expression of the essence of Tongan culture, combining beauty, skill, respect and modesty…" (*Heilala '93* 1993, 8).

The Miss *Tau'olunga* evening is the cultural highlight of the Miss Heilala Pageant and always has been. The likelihood that this event would ever be performed in an international setting is very doubtful as its definition of beauty is expressly Tongan. This is the event where the local women excel, with grace and dignity. A Tongan friend explained, "We believe everyone has a double that only comes out when you dance. Your double is pure, ethereal, really perfect, it goes into the core of Tongan culture which is trying to bring out the best in people, and the *Tau'olunga* epitomizes this cultural affect. It is always a family's pride, a village's pride, so if Miss Ha'apai wins then the whole of the Ha'apai island wins."

The *Tau'olunga* is the only event that is judged solely by Tongans in the Tongan language and with Tongan aesthetics. Judges look for beauty, chiefly motions, facial expression, and body-foot coordination, while allowing room for creativity, intent, and the ability to invoke feeling (Heilala Festival Week Program, 1985, 17). Miss Tonga/New Zealand thought that the expatriates had difficulty performing the *Tau'olunga* "properly, the real Tongan way, as it is the most difficult dance in all the South Pacific." A former judge confirmed that "overseas girls have trouble winning this section: they don't grow up knowing how to dance it."

Local Tongans believe that expatriate contestants in the *Tau'olunga* event are given too much leeway, and often ridicule their awkward performances. Her Royal Highness explained: "There aren't enough teachers of Tongan dance for them to be able to understand the movements and like it. Hula and Tahitian is very popular, you can look in the telephone book and find a hula teacher in Foster City [California] who was born in Hawaii. So they dance the hula to show their pride in being Polynesian." Many of these women will perform a Polynesian dance for the contest as a way of saving face for not being able to execute the *Tau'olunga* as well as the local contestants.

In former years, the *Tau'olunga* was always accompanied by a small, often spontaneous group of men and/or women who would share the stage, their exaggerated movements and jovial antics drawing attention to the dancers' beauty, grace, and skill. This is called *tulafale* and is one of the ways that Tongans express their pleasure with the beauty of a dancer's movements. When the Tongan Tourist Association assumed greater control over the Miss Heilala Beauty Pageant in 1980, this part of the *Tau'olunga* was eventually cut from the program because, I was told, it was "distracting" and "lacked a sense of professionalism." Another way of expressing pleasure is by shouting words of praise, *māile*, or making a *fakapale*, placing paper money or presents upon the dancer. *Fakapale* is the customary way to raise money for charitable funds, and it has been retained as part of the *Tau'olunga* event.

In 1993, the committee added a new element to the *Tau'olunga* competition, giving extra points for original dance compositions and original dance costumes. The goal, according to the director of the Tongan National Center, is "to preserve and maintain Tongan traditions." These costumes are made from vibrant colors of freshly picked leaves. The intricate patterns and the means and methods of making the ancient forms are cherished family secrets.[12]

Miss South Pacific: The Antithesis of Miss Tau'olunga, or Whose Notion of Natural Beauty?

The high value placed on the Miss *Tau'olunga* event is reflected in the prizes awarded—the winner receives 500 *pa'anga*, and a trip to Honolulu—in contrast with the winner of the less valued Miss Talent Quest who only receives 250 and no trip. While local Tongans perceive Miss *Tau'olunga* as the personification of Tongan beauty and skill, Miss Talent Quest is seen as being caught in a transition, and Miss South Pacific is denounced as being anomalous and anti-Tongan. Indeed, Miss South Pacific is the event that causes the biggest rift between local Tongans, expatriate Tongans and the foreign audience at large. The conflict centers on the way "natural beauty" is interpreted and displayed in the "beach wear" section of the event, where contestants are judged in "Polynesian costume and beach wear" on "poise, natural beauty, modesty and figure" ("Briefing Papers for Miss Heilala Contestants" 1993).[13] The conundrum is whether the judges and contestants should make decisions based on Euro-American norms of body aesthetics that are the standard in international competitions, or repudiate these norms in deference to Tongan notions of beauty.

In Tonga, the body and the moral behavior associated with the body are not separate from ideals governing kin relations, relations between the sexes, brother-sister avoidance, and the social order at large. As among Polynesians, Tongans have always symbolically mapped potency and hierarchical significance onto the parts of the somatic body. Polynesians were famous for using the body as a medium of artistic expression. Their purpose was to mark a person's position in the social group in formal or public situations rather than personal embellishment. Therefore the notion of judging the body as a reflection of the individual, rather than a sign of one's rank, social status, and origins, is not the Tongan way. The somatic body mirrors ideals of Tongan society, which are reflected by the elite class and in the performance of the most elite dance (the *Tau'olunga*) and these ideals are ranked, just as is the society.

Throughout Polynesia the head is considered the most *tapu* (taboo) part of the body (along with the genitals and upper thighs). The head is the seat of thought and rationality, and the top of the head is the repository of *mana* and *tapu*.[14] Because hair is on the top of the head, it too held sanctity. With the advent of Christianity, hair now means less than it once did. Tongan women still cut their hair at the death of their father as a form of respect and submission to his role as chief of the family. In public, at church, or on formal occasions, women's hair is kept neat and tidy, worn in a bun or other restricted fashion. Hair should only be worn loose while performing a ceremonial dance or in the privacy of one's home. Long loose hair has associations with a liminal state or with sexuality. Unkempt hair is associated with a death in the family, expressing a distraught feeling. Tongan hair types range from frizzy to straight, short to long, and black to brown. The international beauty pageant places a different emphasis on hair; *papālangi* judges have a stereotype of Polynesians with straight, long, silky black hair worn freely over their shoulders. Tongan hair does not always comply with this stereotype, and so some contestants have taken to using straightening agents.

According to local standards of beauty, the face should be well defined, with well-set dark eyes framed by expressive eyebrows, a full mouth, and a high forehead. Few use makeup, since it is thought that a beautiful face does not need lipstick, rouge, or eye shadow. Eyes and expressive eyebrows are of great communicative importance in Tonga. The beauty of the face is radiated by its expressiveness—a canon of the *Tau'olunga*. Large body size was also a mark of beauty and rank in Tonga. There is an expression in Tongan which literally means "to look fat is to look well." In Tonga, fattened body and light skin were signs of high social rank. The present King Taufa'ahau Tupou IV allegedly weighed close to 400 pounds in his prime.

The Tongan body was therefore subject to cultural regimens and regulations, and was judged according to indigenous standards. Fatness symbolizes community well being, and Miss Heilala should be pleasingly plump according to this canon, where the human body represents the social body. Small hands and fingers were also a sign of high status, of membership in elite classes that did no manual labor. Soft, supple hands are also an important aesthetic element in Tongan dances.

In Tongan public life, womens' genital region and thighs are never exposed. Movement of the upper legs and hips are restricted, even in dance, and it is still considered vulgar to show movement in or expose the upper legs in Tonga. A Miss Heilala chaperon told me that "Tongan women should never show their thighs or wear bathing suits, and when they finally uncover their legs in the privacy of their own home [especially on the wedding night] they should be fair, smooth, soft, and unmarked, never 'dressed' with panty hose." Women should also sit with their legs to the side.

Tongans of high rank are distinguished, especially the women, by lighter skin protected from the sun and kept smooth and soft with specially scented Tongan oils. Though the contestants come from the more common class, they too admire lighter skin and refrain from basking in the sun, keeping their skin soft with oil. Oil has a specific meaning in Tonga, where its sheen on a bride signifies virginity. When the bride shines and glistens, she is being presented for all to bear witness to her virginity. The dancer of the *Tau'olunga* must also glisten with oil, as a symbol of her alleged state of virginity. All of the contestants must be single, and in Tonga great pride is expressed in a woman who remains a virgin until she is married. When a young woman reaches twenty-one years of age her parents often give her a big party to thank her for remaining a virgin.

Ethno-aesthetic values such as shininess (*ngingila*) pervade all of the traditional Tongan arts, but the only time in the Festival pageant when the contestants can draw upon these values is in the *Tau'olunga* event. The audience waits with a kind of Durkheimian "effervescence" for the entry of the contestants who appear dripping in oil that shimmers off the reflected light as it glides down their color-rich costumes and their arms. She is a majestic image of grandeur, *sino molu*, a soft, supple body.

But this aesthetic is no longer unchallenged. A local Tongan closely associated with the pageant sums up the ways local and international aesthetics collide in the pageant:

> Papālangi elements have crept into the basis of judging. What is regarded in America and Europe as a fat person would be regarded here as a kind of beauty in size, we like traditional size and stature. Slimness was never a part of our principles by which we judge beauty. We admire *sino molu*…and when we judge beauty we first look at the face and rank its ability to attract people. Hair is not as important as it is to Europeans, it ranks after the face and size.

The Tongan notion of natural beauty reflects and valorizes the ideals embodied in the essence of royalty and, at the same time, these ethno-aesthetic ideals conflict with the winning values of the international scene.

The Swimwear Event: Where Local and International Perspectives Collide

When the swim wear event was made a part of the Miss Heilala Beauty Pageant, the pageant committee tried to accommodate Tonga's notion of natural beauty, modesty, and the unique social conventions by listing the event as a sub-section of the "South Pacific Evening." Contestants are given the option of wearing traditional Tongan swimwear—a wraparound skirt or a sarong—in lieu of the "official international" one piece bathing suit with a sarong. Nevertheless, the event is still perceived locally as a cultural travesty, as immoral, and as an embarrassment. No cash prize is given. As one local Tongan explained, "Local Tongan girls would not wear bathing suits, they think this is un-Tongan." As

an after-thought this Tongan added, "Nice well rounded limbs and large size do not show up too elegantly when Tongans wear bathing suits."

In 1993 some California contestants unintentionally flaunted social convention by appearing in the standard swimwear "costume" of international competitions: a one-piece bathing suit, hosiery, high heels, and a sarong or jacket. This caused eyebrows to raise. They did not walk barefoot but paraded down the platform in heels, then they turned and took off their upper garment. These actions were disruptive, and they caused a number of brothers and male cousins to immediately leave the stadium following the avoidance taboo. One of the men told me that it was very embarrassing for him and that if he had stayed he would have been forced to prevent other men from looking at his cousin and this would have caused a fight. Another man also reported being upset by the expatriate parade of bathing suits. "Women should be clothed, it is offensive to Tongans to see unclothed women. A few of the contestants are my cousins. To see a 'sister' dressed in that nature is bad to witness."

Miss Tonga/San Francisco defended the actions of the California contestants by arguing that "the girls coming from overseas anticipated wearing a swimsuit, not beachwear. The bathing suit section is a big part of the whole international competition and we thought it was important here." The expatriate Tongans from California did not understand the controversy they had caused. What is interesting is that the pageant committee had been unwilling to come to terms with the conflict.

Conclusion

The Miss Heilala Beauty Pageant brings together the different ways that local Tongans and expatriates perceive beauty; sometimes the systems of aesthetics collide. The ethno-aesthetic system embedded in older social, cultural, and moral values remains dominant, and the pageant system, borrowed from abroad, is used by Tongans to assert the dominance of the local over the foreign. The standards of international beauty pageants that Miss Heilala's expatriate contestants bring with them to the pageant bring out and objectify local Tongan ideas about the body, gaze, and proper behavior between siblings. When expatriate contestants arrive from their distant diasporic homes to compete, they are forced to confront the most personal, private, and powerful features of their "Tongan" identity: kinship, the family, and the body. They are forced to question the basis of their identity, and to acknowledge the superiority of the local Tongan way.

Meanwhile, blame for the changing values seen in the Miss Heilala contest is placed on its *papālangi* elements, including its "foreign" standards of beauty and the swimsuit event that are required in the international competitions. While few tourists can actually secure seats at the Miss Heilala Pageant, and those who do are put off by the noise and crowds, Tongans rationalize this foreign contest as a concession to tourists. Nevertheless, there is accommodation and change within the pageant itself that promises some long term changes in local values. These changes can take many forms, but it is apparent that the Miss Heilala pageant may always be dealing with two kinds of cultural aesthetics, which are linked with two different attitudes toward a cultural identification bifurcated by national boundaries.

What remains clear is the fact that beauty is more than skin deep, and Tongans will continue to be at odds with the standards of natural beauty set by the international pageant. Yet the pageant works because the expatriates can participate in a way approximately equal to the locals. The Tongan details allow the locals to accept the form, at the same time vesting the whole with real relevance to their culture.

Notes

I would like to express my appreciation to H.R.H. Princess Salote Mafile'o Pilolevu Tuita for her support of this project, and to extend my gratitude to the following people who made it possible: Joyce Anna Afeaki, Sesilia Cornett, Tupou'ahome'e Faulupa, Samantha Fisk, Melesungu Fonongaloa, Papiloa Foliaki, Joana Sālote Forbes, Futa Helu, Rosetta Johansson, Tafolosa Kaitapu, Michelle Nui, 'Ana Michelle 'Otuafi, Rosie Havea, Maopa Helmuli Pulu, Ruperta Fulivai, Sikahema Rodriguez, Dorothy Salamasina, Irene Schaumkel, Sandra Schoonderwoerd, Afuha'amango Taomoepeau, Mele Hola Telefoni and Katri Vaa'ivak. To the many Tongans who have helped answer my questions, I can only express my gratitude for their generosity in allowing me to publish what they know better than I. These acknowledgments do not in any way bind the persons mentioned to my interpretation, for it is only that—an interpretation. And finally, this essay could not have been written without the patience and help of all the editors: Colleen Ballerino Cohen, Richard Wilk, and Beverly Stoeltje.

1. The initial Heilala Festivals were informal, so much so that my daughter was allowed to participate as a flower girl in 1988. In 1993 I judged the Tui Kahoa Kakala and Tui Sisi Kakala contest (traditional garlands worn around the neck or waist on ceremonial and festive occasions), and I was also given permission by H.R.H. Princess Salote Mafile'o Pilolevu Tuita to videotape aspects of the pageant. During this period I lived in the room next to the Tongan-New Zealand contestant and her chaperones, whom I accompanied everywhere they went. In 1994 I was one of the judges for the evening gown competition at the Miss Tonga/San Francisco pageant. Everyone involved knew that I was studying the pageant, and all gave me permission to use their names. I have chosen, however, to give them anonymity.

2. Tongan principles of social status and societal rank are based on primogeniture, genealogy, purity of descent line, and complex marital exchanges. Commoners (*tu'a*), though emancipated from forced labor in 1862, are still socially differentiated from the chiefly and/or noble ranks (*'eiki*). This is a stratified society where all ranks and groups are differentiated from each other by systems of exchange (Kaeppler 1971; Rogers 1977; Biersack 1982; Teilhet-Fisk 1991; Campbell 1992).

3. Tongan emigration has increased dramatically since 1975. As Campbell (1992, 223)

points out, "Some impression of the impact of emigration can be seen in the fact that the 1986 census gave the population of Tonga as 94,535, only 4.6 percent higher than the 1976 census estimate. The crude rate of natural increase without emigration would have been perhaps five times that figure."

4. Tongans in general classify the expatriates as "Tongan Nationals" regardless of their actual citizenship because of their continuing strong commitment to the ideology of the Tongan family (Cowling 1990, 192–96, 202).

5. Although billed as a tourist event, the pageant attracts more expatriates than tourists. In 1993, foreign tourists comprised only 20 percent of the visitors coming to Tonga, whereas "Tongan Nationals" make up at least 80 percent..." (Fonua 1993, 9). Unlike most events that attract tourists, the Heilala Festival is not "staged" for an uninformed audience of tourists. Tourists are certainly welcomed and many events are explained in English, but unless they have a patient Tongan friend or tour leader who gently leads them through the gatherings and finds them a place where they can sit and/or see, tourists do not enjoy the festival. Even fewer attempt to come to the one event designed with tourists in mind, the beauty pageant.

6. When I served as a Euro-American judge in a craft competition and a beauty pageant, the point criteria were not made clear, and in one situation the total points added up to one hundred and twenty rather than the one hundred stated. The system imposes a Euro-American system of evaluation that is "un-Tongan" and is, thus, basically ignored. Tallied points do not follow the aesthetic principle of *heliaki*. *Heliaki* is "characterized by never going straight to the point but alluding to it indirectly" (Kaeppler 1993; 6). It is difficult to apply the point system to an interpretation and allusion particularly in the case of a beauty pageant that embodies so many cultural elements.

7. A Tongan with a long association with the Miss Heilala Beauty Pageant reported that there must have been chiefly women in the early stages when they were raising money for a worthy project "but it is not the kind of thing chiefly girls should take part in. There is a good reason behind this: they would be ashamed if they didn't win over a girl of lower social status. The judges would be at fault."

8. This in turn generates conflict with Christian censure of smoking and drinking.

9. Some felt that the expatriates should bring their own sponsors from abroad. Most of the American Tongans agreed that they had the better sponsors, but they were quick to point out that they paid their own way over and brought their own competitive apparel. It was suggested that the problem rested in the hands of the local sponsors who did not want to compete with rival companies based in the United States that might use the sponsorship as a way of getting into a new Tongan market.

10. She encouraged and helped sponsor a number of Tongan-Americans entered in the 1993 Miss Heilala Beauty Pageant. "In the two years I have been here, I have really learned to appreciate the difficulties the Tongan people in California are experiencing. I sympathize with them. At the same time, they have a whole generation of Tongan kids growing up here, some are even identifying with blacks rather than Polynesians. They don't know what Polynesian is, their parents don't have time to tell them what Polynesian is or what even Tongan is. They have lost their identity. Tongans here learn Tongan as a second language, they learn everything Tongan as a second culture, as a foreigner."

11. The *Tau'olunga* is considered Tongan, even though Tongans freely acknowledge its origin is Samoan. "*Tau'olunga* is an amalgam of many elements. Its music is adapted from Western music traditions. Its name and manner are borrowed from Samoa. Its movements and role are Tongan" (Kaeppler 1993, 29). Tongans have embraced the *Tau'olunga* as being a chiefly dance which pays honor to the old political order.

12. This concern for preserving "traditional" materials was expressed in the 1994 pageant when Her Royal Highness used bark cloth (real and imitation) as a medium for modern fashions. She introduced a new event, the cultural Tapa night. The idea for this event stems from the work of Finau, a contemporary fashion designer who first used tapa cloth to honor the King and Queen when they came to the Polynesian Cultural Center Celebrations (Hawaii) in 1993. In 1994 the princess invited him to display his tapa cloths at the Miss Tonga/San Francisco Pageant. Some of the people were upset, because the winning dress was made from Fijian tapa, *masi*. Finau felt that the outfits should only be made from indigenous tapa cloth (or cloth printed with Tongan tapa designs) because "it elevates the value of our culture" (personal communication).

13. Kololiana 'Otuangu's article in her new publication, *Tongan Women* (1994), addresses these broader issues and suggests that "a committee should sit down and work out new rules and…decide whether the contestants should represent only a South Pacific country or whether they should open it up for participants from migrant communities in places like Australia and the United States of America. Decisions need to be made on judging criteria. Should the pageant for example pursue a *Palangi* criteria of beauty with full make up or a traditional island kind of beauty?" ('Otuangu 1994, 20).

14. Tongans share with other Polynesians a concept of *mana* and *tapu*. Mana has been interpreted as a kind of supernatural power, divine force, authority, and generative potency (Shore 1989, 139–43). To speak of mana is always to imply tapu or taboo. "As an active quality, tapu suggests a contained potency of something, place or person. In its passive usage, it means forbidden or dangerous for someone who is *noa*" (Shore 1989, 144). This notion of being tapu is still present in Tonga today. The heads of the royal family should always sit higher than commoners. Therefore the head of the contestant must be held high and with dignity if she is to embody the essence of Tonga.

DISCUSSION QUESTIONS

The Miss Heilala Beauty Pageant: Where Beauty is More than Skin Deep

1. Did it surprise you to learn that Euro-American concepts of beauty may be encroaching on beauty pageants held on other continents around the world? Do you consider this globalization of beauty a positive or negative development? Why or why not?

2. Had you ever imagined a beauty pageant in which the female contestants were not expected to have slim figures? Or a pageant in which facial expression and eyes were more important than body size? Had you ever imagined a culture that believed "to look fat is to look well"? Why or why not?

3. What do the Kalabari women and the Tongan women have in common? What would be the outcome or benefits if American women ascribed to heavier body ideals?

CHAPTER 3

Dress as Nonverbal Communication

Mary Lynn Damhorst

AFTER YOU HAVE READ THIS CHAPTER, YOU WILL COMPREHEND:

- The substantial complexity underlying communication through dress.

- The basic components of the structure of dress communication systems.

- Why people put together appearance according to "rules" or guidelines for dress shaped by cultural, historical, and group factors as well as personal tastes and preferences.

- The characteristics of the present era in time that influence the way consumers "produce" appearances.

We express much through dress, including our personal identities, our relationships with others, and the types of situations in which we are involved. A phenomenal amount of information is transmitted in one appearance, and human beings have an amazing capacity to make sense of a substantial amount of detail in a very short time. In this chapter we will consider both the complexity of communicating through appearance and those factors that influence messages sent through dress. In Chapter 4 we will look more closely at the types of meanings conveyed and the process of creating meanings about the self and society through dress.

WHAT IS NONVERBAL COMMUNICATION?

Dress is one of several modes of nonverbal communication, that is, communication that does not necessarily involve verbal expression through speaking or writing.[1] Other types of nonverbal communication include facial expressions, physical movement and actions (kinetics), the physical distances people maintain from one another (proxemics), touch (haptics), the sound of the voice while delivering verbal communications (paralinguistics), and hand gestures. All of these types of nonverbal communications involve behaviors that are informative and meaningful to people.

Dress serves as a backdrop while other forms of communication—verbal and nonverbal—occur. Unlike many other modes of communication, dress often tends to be stable or unchanging for many hours of the day. Dress, then, is usually **nondiscursive** behavior rather than behavior that dynamically changes or unfolds moment by moment as do words in a conversation or movements in a dance (McCracken, 1988).

Two different definitions of communication are useful in understanding dress. One definition, mapped out by Burgoon and Ruffner (1974), contains a number of premises about sending and receiving messages:

1. *Communication is an interactive process among two or more people.* Television and other media communications send messages to a vast audience. The message sender may never interact directly with most viewers, but an interaction nonetheless occurs. For example, when thousands of young women attempted to copy Jennifer Aniston's (of *Friends*, an NBC sitcom) hairstyle in the mid-1990s, it became clear that she had an impact on her audience. Her hairstyle conveyed meanings that many wanted to adopt as part of personal identity. (See Figure 3.1.)

2. *Communication involves the sending of messages to at least one receiver who, for a complete act of communication, sends a feedback message to the original sender.* Feedback messages sent via dress are not always obvious and overt. Occasionally, one may receive a direct compliment or insult about dress. Or a long stare or whistle may be the feedback. In many instances, lack of comments serves as feedback that nothing was terribly wrong with one's appearance. Getting a job or a date may indicate that one's dress was appropriate. Of course, addressing someone as "Ma'am" when the person addressed is male might indicate a misinterpretation of dress or an insult or joke that questions the gender appropriateness of dress.

3. *Communication is a process that is ongoing and dynamic in which commonly shared meanings are negotiated and created to*

FIGURE 3.1 *Jennifer Aniston of* Friends *helped make the shag hairstyle popular during the 1990s.*

reach common understanding. According to the three-part definition of communication, sender and receiver must come to a minimal level of agreement about the meanings of dress for a complete communication interaction to occur. This may happen to some extent in purposeful efforts at impression management, such as dressing for a job interview, wedding dress, or a uniform for a job role. But for most dress, wearer and observer never converse specifically about dress and often do not completely agree on what each other's dress means (Tseèlon, 1992). Dress is so **polysemic** (i.e., sends a great amount of messages all at one time) that it is difficult to find agreement on all the meanings packed into one appearance.

A second, broader definition of communication emphasizes that dress is "**the production and exchange of meanings**" (Fiske, 1990, p. 2). A wearer puts clothing, hairdo, accessories, and grooming together to produce an appearance and may assign meanings to that assembled appearance. Each observer of that appearance may agree on some meanings but may also have a unique interpretation of the appearance. Disagreement does not mean that communication stops or fails. It is the sum of how wearer and observers interact (or do not interact) on the basis of appearance that produces meanings for the wearer and the observers.

Throughout much of the world during the late 20th century, dress meanings tend to be vague and hard to verbalize. A picture, such as an appearance, tells a thousand words, but those thousand words are difficult to pin down. In addition, changing fashion trends continually modify meanings of dress, adding further to lack of clarity of meanings. Umberto Eco (1962) refers to this vagueness of meanings as **undercoding**; meanings of dress in U.S. society today are coded only generally and imprecisely, leaving much to the imagination of the perceiver. The Rhonda Perlmutter III cartoon by Roz Chast (Figure 3.2) derives its humor from the fact that dress today can rarely be read so literally and specifically.

In contrast to "modern" attire worn throughout the world today, dress in traditional cultures tends to change slowly over time and may incorporate long-used symbols that are steeped with meanings. The kimono described in "Flow of Kimono" by Liza Dalby are traditional Japanese garments that are clear in meaning to those who know the code of kimono. Similarly, some uniforms in mainstream U.S. society, such as police and military uniforms, rely on long familiar symbolic components to express the role of the uniform wearer.

The Structure of Dress Communication Systems

CHANNELS OF TRANSMISSION. Dress as a communication system is extremely complex. In any one appearance, messages may be sent simultaneously through a variety of channels. Berlo (1960) defined **channels** of communication as the five physiological senses. We often study how dress is used to communicate via the visual channel. However, we might also send messages via the hearing channel (e.g., the clanging of bangle bracelets, the tapping of heels on an uncarpeted floor, the rustle of taffeta) or via the sense of smell (e.g., perfumes, deodorants to mask body odor, new leather). The sense of touch is inherent in perceiving clothing, as textiles have a tactile component. We can often look at a fabric and guess that it is soft (e.g., corduroy, velvet) or slick (e.g., vinyl). These sensory transmissions may have meanings for observers. For example, many business dress advisors suggest that clanging jewelry and obvious perfumes convey an image that is less than professional in the office environment (Fashion Workshop, 1989; Fiore & Kim, 1997; Rosch, 1988).

FIGURE 3.2 *Roz Chast cartoon in a 1988* New Yorker *magazine proposes an absurd level of specifity in meanings of dress.*

Notice that we have not discussed the sense of taste. Perhaps because of the low level of development of that sense in humans, it is not commonly used as a message channel in dress. Other than berry-flavored lipsticks, only a few amusing and/or erotic novelty dress products are flavored. We won't describe those here.

GRAMMAR. An array of things may be combined on the body to compile a dressed appearance. When hairdo, facial grooming or makeup, clothing, scents, jewelry, shoes, and accessories are all combined, a tremendous amount of organization has taken place. The **rules** we use to put all of these components together on the body are loosely held guidelines for what is appropriate, fashionable, and attractive. The rules are a sort of **grammar** of dress. We learn the grammar of dress through the media and through groups and families to which we belong.

Any dress grammar rules can be broken; however, some rules are held seriously in some societies. For instance, in most communities in the United States today, it is against the law for women to go topless and for men to display genitals in public. These laws stem from moral taboos related to a sense of modesty and sexual behaviors. Among the Old Order Amish in the United States, purposeful violation of rules about skirt length or exposure of buttons on certain garments could be cause for excommunication from the group. Violating the grammar of Amish dress (see Figure 3.3) is a sign of questioning and abandoning the rules that are rooted in religious identity of the group (Schweider & Schweider, 1975).

For most of what we wear, however, rules are not seriously enforced but are shaped by personal tastes, fashion trends, and group habits and conventions. For example, many people in the United States tend not to wear red and pink garments together in one ensemble. However, a print or multicolored garment may combine those two colors in ways that appear attractive. In addition, fashion trends may be changing the "no-red-with-pink" rule, as well as other rules.

ELEMENTS OF DRESS SIGNS. Some of the elementary components of clothing that may convey messages are listed in Figure 3.4 within the inner oval of the diagram. These are "perceptual elements" that are the integral units of fabric and apparel that can be perceived by human beings. Many of these elements are the basic elements of design (Davis, 1996; Fiore & Kimle, 1997). Some of the elements have multiple subcomponents that influence meaning; for example, color has hue (the color family), value

FIGURE 3.3 *Amish women watching swimmers. The Old Order Amish have strict rules for dress style, shirt length, and head coverings.*

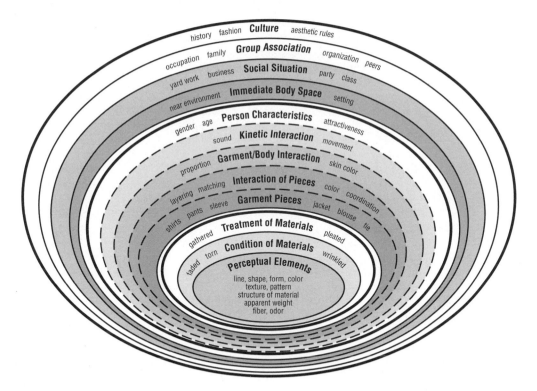

FIGURE 3.4 *Model of clothing in context.*

(lightness versus darkness), and intensity (brightness versus dullness). Fiber names can be meaningful (i.e., silk is a luxury fiber) as are fabrics such as denim (Berger, 1984). These elementary units are relevant for clothing, but other aspects of dress such as hair, tattoos, and shoes have different sets of elementary perceptual units. The "Young Japan Is Dyeing" article examines recent meanings of hair color in Japan, where dyeing hair brown indicates that a person is "youthful" and "nonconforming." Natural, undyed black hair color is perceived as more conforming.

During the 20th century in North America, rounded design lines and flowing and delicate, translucent fabrics (such as voile) may be worn by women but are not traditionally seen in men's dress. Men tend to wear angular lines and sturdy, smooth, "hard" woven fabrics (McCracken, 1985). These differences in lines and fabrics reflect differences in traditional concepts of what is male (e.g., active, sturdy, strong) and female (e.g., soft, fragile). Today, women borrow masculine fabrics and design lines freely, as they take on roles and behaviors traditionally reserved for men. The increasing incorporation of menswear symbols into womenswear is helping (along with other societal changes) to obscure the traditional gender meanings of design lines and fabrics.

CONTEXT OF USE. In any appearance, a great number of perceptual elements are combined according to or in violation of some rules of grammar. It is how elements are combined and placed on the body, who wears them, and in what situation they are worn that shapes meanings of perceptual elements. Combinations of elements and surrounding situations make up **context** (cf. Bateson, 1979). Figure 3.4 maps components of context that may shape meanings of clothing.

The remaining inner ovals of Figure 3.4 pertain to clothing materials and how they influence meanings. Condition of fabrics such as stains or tears could degrade the impression given by a job applicant. The meaning of fading and tears can vary with the whims of fashion, however. Distressed and stonewashed jeans as well as prewashed and sandwashed silks and linens have been popular recently for casual clothing. Treatments of materials such as gathers may add fullness and softness to clothing, whereas pressed pleats may appear precise and sharp.

The next several layers of the clothing context model (Figure 3.4) relate clothing to the body of the wearer. Garment pieces become familiar objects in a culture and are usually associated with coverage of one area of the body. Certain arrangements of elements (i.e., lines, shapes, fabrics, patterns) within a garment piece may then add meanings. For instance, denim jeans are a highly familiar garment symbol worldwide.

Garment pieces are combined in an ensemble with accessories and worn on the body. In some cultures, infinite arrangements and meanings are possible. In "Women's Job Interview Dress: How the Personnel Interviewers See It," Damhorst and Fiore examine the complex rules that interviewers used to assess appropriateness of women's suits for management-level job interviews. A surprising diversity of styles were acceptable for job interviews, given certain limitations.

When placed on the body, the wearer's shape fills out the garment, and skin and hair coloring interact with garment elements. "Designs for the Hands" describes how various lines drawn on the hand for traditional Indian mehndi interact with the shape of the hand.

Body size also influences meanings of clothing. Clayton, Lennon, and Larkin (1987) found that garments worn by larger-size female models tended to be evaluated as less fashionable. This could pose a problem in marketing to larger-size women via catalogs and magazine ads. Do larger-size women themselves see plus-size models as less fashionable than slim models? Certainly, more research is warranted. To approach the size issue cautiously, many mail-order firms feature plus-size models that are actually only a size 12 or 14, larger than average fashion models (size 4 to 6) but not in the size ranges offered in women's larger sizes (16W and up). (See "Plus-Size Modeling" in Chapter 10.)

Body movement may add meanings to clothing. In "Flow of Kimono," Liza Dalby explains how movement and posture is essential for achieving a graceful presentation of kimono. Displaying the same movements while wearing modern dress makes an individual look pigeon-toed and awkward.

Numerous characteristics of the wearer can influence interpretation of clothing meanings. For example, an ice-cream stain on the shirt of a toddler may be perceived as cute or amusing, but might not be so cute on a 42-year-old. Similarly, during the 20th century in the United States, cross-dressing (wearing dress of the opposite gender) is often more acceptable when women are doing the borrowing.

The outer layers of the model in Figure 3.4 relate to the situation surrounding the wearer. Let's leap to the outer rim and examine the all-encompassing context of culture (Firth, 1957). Elements and grammar of clothing take on meaning in cultural context. Consider the color red, for example. Red is an appropriate color for traditional Chinese bridal dresses, but what would the meaning of red convey in an American bride's dress? Similarly, red is the traditional color for funerals in Ghana, Africa, but is not usually an appropriate color to wear to funerals in the United States.

Moving to the "group association" level of the model, groups and organizations vary with each culture and over time. In North America, the medical doctor's white coat is associated with laboratory science, cleanliness, purity, godlike control over life, and impartial treatment of all—concepts relevant to 20th-century medicine (Blumhagen, 1979). At the end of the century as doctors take on a more egalitarian role with patients and emphasize preventive medicine, many doctors are abandoning the white coat for street wear more similar to patients' attire. Similarity and casualness are expected to reduce barriers to effective communication, essential to fully assessing the patient's health status. However, some patients feel more comforted by the white coat, a familiar symbol of medical authority and expertise.

Families are social groups, but each family may have its own subculture within the larger culture, shaped by socioeconomic factors, parental style and values, and family lifestyle. One family may have strict rules that its female children cannot wear make-up until they are 17. Other families may allow girls some use of make-up even at age six.

Dress helps us define social situations. Some social critics fear that the invasion of casual dress into business organizations will degrade the seriousness and professionalism of business interactions, while some workers enjoy the relaxed tone set on "casual days." Similarly, a party to which everyone wears tuxedos and formal gowns might have a different atmosphere or definition than a party to which everyone wears T-shirts and jeans.

Finally, immediate surroundings of space and people can influence interpretations of dress. Damhorst (1984–1985) asked employees of private business firms in Texas to describe what they thought was happening in different pictures of men and women interacting in various office settings. Dress of the pictured people clearly shaped stories told about the pictures and influenced meanings of adjacent persons' dress (see Figure 3.5).

a   b

FIGURE 3.5 *The two stimulus pictures (Damhorst, 1984–1985), with formality of clothing worn by the man and woman reversed, elicited different stories. The respondents in the study described the informally dressed woman in (a) as causing problems for the man who was "obviously" high in status and competence. In contrast, the woman in (b) was seen as managerial and having to reprimand or fire the incompetent worker who was crouching behind his desk.*

To sum up the model of clothing in context, it is not individual colors or garment pieces that dominate an appearance to create meanings. How all elements are combined on the body within cultural context is crucial for meanings. As Roach-Higgins and Eicher (1992) emphasized, dress is an assemblage. How the wearer uses clothing and other components of dress in context makes dress meaningful.

THE PRESENT-DAY CULTURAL "MOMENT"

The present situation in U.S. culture very much shapes how consumers assemble appearances and send messages through dress. The characteristics of U.S. culture, as well as many cultures around the world, at the end of the 20th century are sometimes referred to as **postmodern** (Gitlin, 1989). We will not try to pinpoint when postmodernism started, will not assume that now is totally different in every way from prior eras, or trace the philosophical or political bases of postmodern theory; the term simply is useful in summarizing some present-day trends in consumer life. Morgado (1996) thoroughly analyzes postmodern influences on dress. We will focus our look at four characteristics of consumer culture—eclecticism, nostalgia, questioning of rules, and simulation—that are reflected in how we purchase and present our appearances today.

Postmodern appearances are **eclectic** in that consumers often mix-and-match a diverse array of styles and influences in any one appearance or throughout a wardrobe. For example, African-inspired fabrics (e.g., kente cloth) are sewn into American styles; a Peruvian-knitted alpaca sweater may be worn with jeans. Consumers and designers borrow fabrics, hairstyles, jewelry, and diverse symbols across cultures, making the market for clothing very globally inspired. Postmodern consumers are prone to mix diverse brands and designers in one appearance and buy parts and pieces of an ensemble at an array of price levels. Buying separates and mixing them with diverse accessories is quite common. Consumers mix-and-match not just to save money but to have more freedom in putting unique looks together. Susan Kaiser in "Identity, Postmodernity, and the Global Apparel Marketplace" describes how consumers actively put looks together to "produce identity."

Perhaps because the postmodern era is occurring while we move into a new millenium, people might become **nostalgic** for times past as we know we are leaving them behind. Fashion trends tend to highlight a past decade every few years. Currently, flared pant legs are inspired by 1970s bell-bottoms. Tie-dyeing, popular in the 1960s, reemerged in the late 1980s and early 1990s. "Vintage Jeans Hot in Japan" describes a recent Japanese nostalgia for very classic and authentic Levi blue jeans, dated as far back as the 1950s and earlier. (This is global borrowing for the Japanese too, as jeans were a U.S. product back in those decades.)

Questioning of traditions and rules seems to be a given during the current times (Featherstone, 1991). We see this in dress in fashionable combinations of masculine and feminine symbols, casual combined with formal, and interesting mixes of fabrics that challenge old rules about not mixing patterns in one look (see Figure 3.6). Young people also tear jeans and consider them more fashionable than new tidy ones. During a time when many traditional aspects of culture such as gender roles, sexuality, bases of economic power distribution, and ethnic hegemony are questioned, it is no wonder that questioning of traditional rules for dress should occur.

Finally, Baudrillard (1983) suggested that during the postmodern era, **simulations** are becoming as valuable as what is real and rare. Since the late 1980s, animal prints and fake furs have been featured even in top designer lines, perhaps to save endangered species while affording enjoyment of natural forms. We also live in an era when cosmetic surgery is on the rise. It seems to be increasingly acceptable to modify the natural body and acquire a "simulated" perfect figure or face. This trend probably is increasing because of technological innovations that allow us to simulate materials (and bodies) effectively. Siebert in "The Cuts That Go Deeper" wonders how far this quest for the perfect body will go.

Kaiser in "Identity, Postmodernity, and the Global Apparel Marketplace" discusses the overall trends in postmodern consumer culture—choice, creativity, and resulting complexity and confusion. With so many consumers mixing and matching, breaking old rules in novel ways, and borrowing across cultures and times it becomes increasingly difficult to read appearances clearly (and it takes greater time to make decisions while getting dressed in the morning). Communicating through dress is increasingly complex.

Summary

In summary, the vast complexity of communicating through dress has become heightened during the postmodern era. Old rules of dress are questioned, symbols are borrowed and used out of historical and cultural context, and what is real can be simulated and faked. Communicating through dress may less often involve clearly shared meanings. The perceiver may have to work hard at making sense of an appearance produced during postmodern times. Nevertheless, dress is still significant human behavior that takes on a rich array of meanings within the surrounding context of individual wearer, social interactions, family, organizations, and culture.

FIGURE 3.6 *This 1995 Todd Oldham design shows a non-traditional contrast of patterns in the pairing of zigzag tube top with spotted skirt.*

Notes

1. Verbal communications may be transmitted via dress, as when a brand logo (e.g., Calvin Klein Jeans, Tommy Jeans from Hilfiger) is emblazoned on a garment or a saying is printed on a message T-shirt.

Suggested Readings

Barnard, M. (1996). *Fashion as communication*. London: Routledge.

Gitlin, T. (1989). Postmodernism defined, at last! *Utne Reader*, July/August, pp. 52–61.

McCracken, G. (1988). *Culture and consumption*. Bloomington: Indiana University Press.

Morgado, M. A. (1996). Coming to terms with *postmodern*: Theories and concepts of contemporary culture and their implications for apparel scholars. *Clothing and Textiles Research Journal*, *14* (1), 41–53.

How Postmodern Are You?

Objective: To examine your own and other's dress to see whether characteristics of postmodernism are evident.

Procedure

Read Susan Kaiser's article "Identity, Postmodernity, and the Global Apparel Marketplace" in this chapter. Then break up into small groups of three to five people and examine what each of you are wearing for postmodern components. Consider clothing, accessories, and more permanent forms of dress such as tattoos and piercings. Think about the following:

1. Trace when and where you bought each of the items you are wearing. Did you obtain them from a wide variety of sources and places?

2. Are you wearing only one brand of clothing?

3. How did you decide to accessorize and coordinate pieces?

4. Do you always wear the pieces you have on today in exactly the same combinations, or do you mix-and-match any of the items you are wearing with other items in your wardrobe?

5. Do any of the items you are wearing have special meanings for you?

6. What identities are you expressing in your present appearance?

7. List what you find that reflects each component of postmodern times and explain briefly. Some items might fit under more than one component. Consider whether you are wearing an ensemble that is, in any way:

   Eclectic

   Nostalgic

   Violating traditional rules

   Simulation

Compare across groups in class to find out what people are wearing that fits with postmodern characteristics.

References

Barnard, M. (1996). *Fashion as communication.* London: Routledge.

Bateson, G. (1979). *Mind and nature.* New York: E. P. Dutton.

Baudrillard, J. (1983). *Simulations.* P. Foss, P. Patton, & P. Beitchman, Trans. New York: Semiotext(e), Inc.

Berger, A. A. (1984). *Signs in contemporary culture.* New York: Longman.

Berlo, D. K. (1960). *The process of communication.* New York: Holt, Rinehart and Winston.

Blumhagen, D. W. (1979). The doctor's white coat: The image of the physician in modern America. *Annals of Internal Medicine, 91,* 111–116.

Burgoon, M., & Ruffner, M. (1974). *Human communication*. New York: Holt, Rinehart and Winston.

Clayton, R., Lennon, S. J., & Larkin, J. (1987). Perceived fashionability of a garment as inferred from the age and body type of the wearer. *Home Economics Research Journal, 15,* 237–246.

Damhorst, M. L. (1984–1985). Meanings of clothing cues in social context. *Clothing and Textiles Research Journal,* 3(2), 39–48.

Davis, M. L. (1980). *Visual design in dress*. Englewood Cliffs, NJ: Prentice-Hall.

Eco, U. (1976). *A theory of semiotics*. Bloomington: Indiana University Press.

"Fashion workshop: Real life cues to clothes for your job." (1989, October). *Glamour,* pp. 203–206.

Featherstone, M. 1991. *Consumer culture and postmodernism*. London: Sage.

Fiore, A. M., & Kimle, P. A. (1997). *Understanding aesthetics: For merchandising and design professionals*. New York: Fairchild.

Fiore, A. M., & Kim, S. (1997) Olfactory cues of appearance affecting professional image of women. *Journal of Career Development, (4)* 247–264.

Firth, J. R. (1957). *Papers in linguistics, 1934–1951*. London: Oxford University Press.

Fiske, J. (1990). *Introduction to communication studies*. London: Routledge.

Gitlin, T. (1989). Postmodernism defined, at last! *Utne Reader,* July/August, pp. 52–61.

McCracken, G. (1985). The trickle-down theory rehabilitated. In M. R. Solomon (Ed.), *The psychology of fashion,* pp. 39–54. Lexington, MA: Lexington Books.

McCracken, G. (1988). *Culture and consumption*. Bloomington: Indiana University Press.

Morgado, M. A. (1996). Coming to terms with *postmodern*: Theories and concepts of contemporary culture and their implications for apparel scholars. *Clothing and Textiles Research Journal, 14* (1), 41–53.

Roach-Higgins, M. E., & Eicher, J. B. (1992). Dress and identity. *Clothing and Textiles Research Journal, 10* (4), 1–8.

Roscho, L. (1988, October). The professional image report. *Working Woman,* pp. 109–113, 148.

Schwieder, E., & Schwieder, D. (1975). *A peculiar people: Iowa's Old Order Amish*. Ames: Iowa State University Press.

Tseëlon, E. (1992). Self presentation through appearance: A manipulative vs. a dramaturgical approach. *Symbolic Interaction, 15* (4), 501–513.

9 Young Japan Is Dyeing (It's Anything but Natural)

Nicholas D. Kristof

If a few space aliens landed in Japan and conducted some scientific research, they might conclude that elderly Japanese have gray hair, middle-aged Japanese have black hair and young Japanese have brown hair.

This is because to be young in Japan these days, at least young at heart, is to dye one's hair brown—or, as it is called in Japanese, chapatsu, or tea hair. Of course, there are youthful black heads left in Japan, but those people might as well wear white socks and crew cuts and signs saying, " Kick me."

"Those guys with black hair—even if they say a joke, it's not funny," said Yukie Yamamoto, an 18-year-old college student, shaking her head with disgust. "Brown-haired guys make better boyfriends, because they're more fun to hang around with."

The rush to dyed hair is sociologically interesting because bleaching one's hair was traditionally regarded as the mark of a social dropout or delinquent, a litmus test of non-ambition. Even now, most schools ban brown hair, and big companies and Government ministries are very reluctant to hire someone with dyed hair for any responsible position.

Thus, at least for some Japanese, tea hair is a bit like long hair was for some men in the West: an assertion of individuality, a signal that one will not just be another obedient cog in the machinery, an act of rebellion. But in Japan, the rebellion lasts only until it is time to join the machinery.

"I have a job interview tomorrow, so I've got to dye my hair black again tonight," said Yuki Makiguchi, an 18-year-old college freshman sporting tea hair. "It's part-time work as a math tutor, and if I had this hair, I'd never get the job. They wouldn't hire me like this—no way!"

The boom in tea hair has set off a bit of a debate, mostly because many older people think the trend is unwise, unhealthy and un-Japanese.

"Behind the fashion, there is I think a deep-rooted inferiority complex toward Westerners, which may make people think that black hair is uncool," a reader wrote in a letter to the editor of the Asahi Shimbun, a major national newspaper. "I hope that they value their identity as Japanese and Asians."

Other critics fight back not just with words. A police chief and his deputy on the northern island of Hokkaido were dismissed this year after a ruckus in a bar that began when the chief spotted a young man with brown hair.

"Why do kids these days dye their hair?" the chief asked, before pouring a mug of beer over the young man's head.

Some sports figures have sported brown hair, but the general manager of the Yakult Swallows, the champion baseball team in Japan last year, announced this spring that he would ban tea hair on all players. He said he found it distracting.

The cat-and-mouse game over hair color is played with greatest sophistication in the nation's high schools and junior high schools. Most schools have rules banning tea hair, but a huge proportion of students claim to be part of the small minority of Japanese who have naturally brown hair.

"Once a month we have to get our hair checked by the teacher at school," said Remi Sato, a 16-year-old high school girl. "If it's brown, then we have to bring in a childhood photo to show that it's always been brown."

The policy does not seem very effective, for Miss Sato's hair is undeniably colored brown. She shrugged and explained that the teachers had given her "guidance," but it seemed to have been left at that.

"'The act of dying hair is banned," Miss Sato said. "So dying it black again would be illegal, too." Still, the teachers occasionally take action. The winner in an 800-meter race at a junior high school track meet last year climbed the stand to get his gold medal, and officials noticed that he had brown hair. They denied him the medal even though the boy asserted that the color came from "overuse of a hair dryer."

Young people say that brown hair promotes an image of casualness and informality, while black hair conveys seriousness. Both men and women said that as a result, there is a tendency to look for brown-haired dates but black-haired spouses.

"If I were just playing around, I'd prefer a girl with tea hair," said Tomotaka Hamohara, a 19-year-old college student. "But for a girlfriend, I'd like a black-haired girl."

An industry group conducted a survey last fall suggesting that 44 percent of working women in their 20's have dyed their hair, along with 38 percent of high school students.

Occasionally young people dye their hair shades of orange, purple or green, but those are a tiny minority regarded by the rest of society as fascinating zoo animals—the orange-crested guitarist, the glow-green mohawk with earrings—and they stand about as much chance of entering mainstream careers as pandas or gazelles do.

Brown, on the other hand, is the "in" fashion, and it seems that the only models getting any work these days are those with tea hair. With, a women's magazine for Japanese in their 20's, has a special section in the May issue about "New Hair Styles for Spring." Of the 31 models shown, every one has hair at least a little bit brown.

If the idea of brown hair is to assert oneself, it may seem counterproductive to be individualistic in precisely the same way as everyone else. But in Japan, perhaps even more than in the West, young people sometimes rush in new directions at the same time.

"Back in the States, the point of fashion is to look different," said Miho Teruya, a 16-year-old girl who lived in Boston for several years. "But here, you follow fashions to look the same."

Miss Teruya said her brown hair is natural and runs in the family, adding that her grandmother was summoned for interrogation by the police during World War II about her brown hair. But Miss Teruya said brown hair is now becoming so widespread that she is thinking of a change.

"Four years ago, I was happy that I was the only one with brown hair," she said. "But now that everybody has it, I'm thinking about dying my hair black."

DISCUSSION QUESTIONS

Young Japan Is Dyeing

1. What meanings did brown hair have in Japanese culture in 1996? And why?

2. Why would brown hair be unlikely to have the same meanings in mainstream U.S. culture?

10 Women's Job Interview Dress: How the Personnel Interviewers See It

Mary Lynn Damhorst
Ann Marie Fiore
Iowa State University

Women have moved into management and professional roles in unprecedented numbers since the 1970s. For example, in 1980 women held 21.8 percent of management, marketing, advertising, and public relations roles in business. By 1990, however, women held 30.6 percent of those roles (Bureau of the Census, 1992). As individuals and groups take on new roles, they are apt to adopt appropriate symbols to help them learn and carry off their new roles (Solomon, 1983). But what *is* appropriate dress for women in their new business roles? As women dress themselves for employment in the traditionally man-tailored world of business, should they wear severely tailored pantsuits and ties similar to those worn by men, or should women opt for another look?

In this study we looked at women's interview dress for management-level jobs in the Midwest and examined employment interviewer evaluations of appropriateness of job applicant dress. Data was collected in 1991, more than a decade after women began their influx into business employment. The degree of similarity to and variation from men's business dress norms can tell us much about women's changing business roles. As Warren (1949) proposed, role behaviors such as dress go through a phase of change and experimentation while roles go through a period of change.

The overall goal of the study was to identify aesthetic components of women's apparel that are appropriate in the business employment interview situation for managerial applicants in the midwest United States. Responses from male and female employment interviewers were compared to examine whether men and women have different standards for business dress. The findings have practical consequences for women who are entering new roles in the business world.

METHOD

The respondents included 37 female and 24 male human resource managers and employment interviewers at 61 businesses randomly selected from the Des Moines, Iowa, Chamber of Commerce business directory. We excluded businesses directly involved in selling clothing to avoid interviewers who might be more interested in fashion than the average interviewer. Age of the interviewers ranged from 26 to 62 years. The firms they represented varied in size from 14 to 4,200 employees.

Our data collector showed each interviewer 100 color photographs of women's skirted suits and a few dresses selected from current mail-order catalogs, which included a wide variety of style characteristics. Posture of models could not be controlled, but each photo included a full length, front view of a standing model. Hair and facial features as well as background were cut away to eliminate contribution of those cues. Pictures were mounted on separate sheets of neutral gray paper and encased in clear film folders.

The interviewers sorted the pictures into piles they thought differed in level of appropriateness for a middle-management employment interview with their firm. After sorting, the interviewers described their reasons for ranking the outfits. Statistical cluster analysis identified groups of outfits with highest appropriateness, mid-level appropriateness, and low appropriateness. We then devised a complex visual analysis system to measure aesthetic characteristics of the suits and dresses in each group.

Original for this text.

RESULTS

In general, male and female interviewers ranked the suits similarly. Interviewers judged 22 of the 100 outfits as high in appropriateness for management-level employment interviews. These 22 suits and dresses all had some components of classic tailoring, reminiscent of men's business suits, usually including a tailored sleeve that was eased at the natural shoulder line or slightly extended and padded from the shoulder line; skirts were straight or flared slightly through pleats or fullness; garment silhouettes were fitted, but never extremely tight. The jackets might contain a traditionally tailored lapel and collar, but also were collarless or had collars of varied styles.

Interviewers seemed to have a flexible set of rules for judging appropriateness of job interview dress. There were only two absolute rules for appropriate interview dress.

Absolute Rules

Skirts above the knee were consistently ranked as low in appropriateness, regardless of other garment characteristics. In 1991, short shirts were fashionable, but apparently not yet appropriate for the formal job interview. (Today, a skirt an inch or two above the knee may be appropriate now that we are more used to seeing them.) Kanter (1977) suggested that management personnel are expected to look modest. Our job interviewers in the early 1990s also felt that sexy appearances could be distracting or send an unprofessional message in the office.

The most appropriate designs were also fairly symmetrically balanced. Asymmetry is interesting but may focus too much attention on the applicant's clothes rather than what she is saying. The perceiver may have to expend substantial cognitive energy trying to comprehend the complexity of an asymmetric outfit (Berlyne, 1974).

Bendable Rules

Other characteristics of outfits in the most appropriate cluster were common in the top ranked suits. These "rules" were flexible, however, and could be violated as long as the remainder of the ensemble contained appropriate features. For example:

- Necklines did not reveal much bare skin; jewelry or a scarf could fill in an open neckline area
- Sleeves were usually full length, set-in, and tailored
- Jacket lengths extended from just below the waistline to mid-hip area
- Jackets were worn closed
- Skirts were not tight or full
- Low-contrast plaids and prints could be worn in the upper body area or throughout the suit, but rarely in the skirt alone
- Prints were angular and highly ordered patterns (i.e., plaids)
- Fabrics were smooth and simple dense structures, not complex laces or knits
- No screaming bright colors or very bright yellows
- Hosiery varied in color but was sheer rather than opaque
- Accessories and jewelry were limited in number and not conspicuous in size or scale
- Neckline and upper body were the focal emphasis of designs
- Waistlines were fitted or indicated by belts or structural features
- Garments did not envelop the body with great volume of material, but were also not skin tight
- Forms were "crisp" and structured rather than drapey and droopy, or gathered and puffy
- Styles were not highly casual nor formal for evening or wedding occasions.

Overall, the appropriate outfits were not visually complex (see Figure 3.7a, b, and c). However, each appropriate outfit included some unique design feature that distinguished the garments from severe masculine-style tailoring. Dissimilar to men, women may need to include some small deviations from traditional tailoring to show that they have an aesthetic sense and that they are in tune with the times. Silhouettes were up-to-date but not slavish to the latest fashion

a b c

FIGURE 3.7 *Three of the suits ranked as highly appropriate by the personnel interviewers contain many components of traditional business suit tailoring. Note variety in skirt styles, jacket length and styling, jewelry, and blouse patterns. Suit colors were (a) grey tweed, (b) green, and (c) gold.*

trends. Although a wide variety of jacket collar styles and garment colors and fabrics were acceptable, a guiding principle—that interview dress should not be distracting or demanding of too much attention—was paramount. Up to two deviations from the bendable rules were possible; more than two deviations led to ranking of the outfit as either middle or low in appropriateness. Even one violation of the absolute rules or extreme deviation of bendable rules could relegate the outfit to low appropriateness (see Figure 3.8a, b, and c).

Interviewer Gender Differences

Male and female interviewers differed in a few ways. Women and men agreed on ten of the suits as highly appropriate. Women felt that nine more of the outfits were appropriate for inter-

views, including two dresses without jackets. Women also ranked far more of the suits as low in appropriateness than did the men.

The most appropriate suits as judged by men included less variety in color than did the women's most appropriate cluster. Men basically went for gray, beige, navy, tan, and black—that is, neutrals. However, they did approve a green suit and golden tan suit. Men liked black so much that a visually busy black-and-white print suit was included in their highly appropriate group. Female interviewers included more variety, such as pinks, magenta, and lighter colors. Women may consider a wider array of colors as appropriate because they are not socialized to the restricted color codes that men learn from a young age (Scherbaum & Shepherd, 1987).

Women also considered a few tailored dresses as highly appropriate apparel for job

a   b   c

FIGURE 3.8 *Three of the suits ranked as highly inappropriate contained two or more violations of rules. These suits are: (a) too casual with khaki fabric and too sexy in the low neckline, short skirt, and asymmetric sarong style skirt; (b) too casual with the waist-length bomber jacket and asymmetric opening; (c) too short and fussy in neckline detail.*

interviews, whereas men's top-ranked cluster included only suits. Men may be so accustomed to seeing the jacket layer symbol that they require an outer layer as a sign of business competence (Scherbaum & Shepherd, 1987).

To a slight degree, female interviewers had a higher tolerance for narrower skirt silhouettes that emphasized body shape. One wonders if the male interviewers were more moralistic than female interviewers, more worried about consequences of dress for sexual harassment, or more attuned to sexual meanings of women's dress.

Similarly, a raised or high, rounded neckline on a plain surface was appropriate to female interviewers, but men needed some breakup of space at the neckline to move the eye up toward the face (see Figure 3.9). Perhaps men are used to seeing this breakup of visual space on men cre-

ated by a contrasting tie, shirt, and jacket. Or perhaps (for an alternative and jaded interpretation), men are so accustomed to objectifying women's bodies and perusing them visually that they need every crutch possible to keep their attention on the woman's face and what is being said.

Overall, women accepted more aesthetic variety in top-ranked outfits and relegated more suits to lowest ranks. This could possibly be the result of women's greater confidence in evaluating women's dress. Men might not be as confident in judging when suits are completely inappropriate. Women are socialized to develop more sophistication in analyzing aesthetics of appearances. Gender norms incline women to emphasize aesthetics and attend to the aesthetics of the body. Women may make more complex judgments of women's dress than do men.

FIGURE 3.9 *Suit ranked as highly appropriate by the women but slightly less appropriate by the men has a high rounded neckline that does not visually break up neckline space to emphasize the face.*

Conclusions

A skirted version of the traditional men's business suit seems to serve as a basic reference framework to which women's business dress is compared and interpreted. However, the notable variety in colors and design details among appropriate suits and dresses indicated that both male and female interviewers used rules for interpretation of dress flexibly and complexly. A relative degree of variation from the standard classic business suit seemed to determine appropriateness. Only skirt length and degree of asymmetry were rules from which deviations were not allowed. The general similarity in male and female personnel interviewer rankings of suits indicates societal, or at least business community, consensus on meaning of aesthetic symbols in women's business dress.

The findings give evidence of women's changing "fit" into business roles. Greater variety in color and design detail was acceptable in the 1991 interview dress than was acceptable in men's business dress. Women are allowed to exercise an elaborated code of colors, fabrics, and design details as long as they borrow some of the restrictions of the men's business suit code. Variety in women's business dress has been found by other researchers (Kimle & Damhorst, 1997; Solomon & Douglas, 1987).

Various interpretations of the consequences of variety in women's business dress are available. We will consider only a few here. Naomi Wolf (1991) contended that greater acceptance of aesthetic play in women's business dress was actually a "plot," encouraged by the male power structure and society in general, to keep women "below the glass ceiling" in the hierarchical structure. Women are encouraged to look somewhat feminine and even considered threatening if they look too masculine. Their more feminine, gender-emphasizing appearances keep them from looking truly businesslike and professional and will limit their progress in reaching top levels in the business community (Wolf, 1991). Are women then doomed to lower levels in business?

An alternative interpretation considers variety in women's business dress as a positive trend. As a significant proportion of women are moving into management and professional positions in industry and government, women may gain more power and confidence to develop role dress that reflects female gender traditions. Women are participating in the creation of social and cultural institutions and norms (Kaiser, 1991). They are partially adopting symbolic forms that have helped men to operate in the capitalist patriarchy of the business arena but are adjusting those symbols to integrate aesthetic variety into their work role clothing. Women have become an active and contributing part of the business community. That male and female interviewers evaluated some variety positively indicates that women are succeeding at shaping the meaning of professionalism in dress.

References

Berlyne, D. E. (1974). The new experimental aesthetics. In D. E. Berlyne (Ed.), *Studies in the new experimental aesthetics* (pp. 1–24). New York: Wiley.

Bureau of the Census. (1992). *Statistical abstract of the United States* (112th ed.). Washington, D.C.: United States Department of Commerce, Economics and Statistics Administration.

Kaiser, S. B. (1991). Gender relations, clothing, and appearance: Discovering a common ground with feminist thought. In S. B. Kaiser, & M. L. Damhorst (Eds.), *Critical linkages in textiles and clothing subject matter: Theory, method and practice* (Special Publication 4, pp. 220–222). Monument, CO: International Textile and Apparel Association.

Kanter, R. M. (1977). *Men and women of the corporation*. New York: Basic Books.

Kimle, P. A., & Damhorst, M. L. (1997). A grounded theory model of the ideal business image for women. *Symbolic Interaction, 20,* 45–68.

Scherbaum, C., & Shepherd, D. (1987). Dressing for success: Effects of color and layering on perceptions of women in business. *Sex Roles, 16*(7/8), 391–399.

Solomon, M. R. (1983). The role of products as social stimuli: A symbolic interactionism perspective. *Journal of Consumer Research, 10,* 319–329.

Solomon, M. R., & Douglas, S. P. (1987). Diversity in product symbolism: The case of female executive clothing. *Psychology of Marketing, 4* (3), 189–212.

Warren, R. L. (1949). Social disorganization and the interrelationship of cultural roles. *American Sociological Review, 14,* 83–87.

Wolf, N. (1991). *The beauty myth*. New York: William Morrow.

DISCUSSION QUESTIONS

Women's Job Interview Dress

1. How is the "interaction of pieces" level of the clothing in context model (Figure 3.4) reflected in the decisions the employment interviewers made about appropriateness of women's dress for job interviews?

2. What differences in gender socialization influenced differences in how male and female interviewers evaluated the outfits?

3. Given the flexible rules guiding appropriateness of women's dress for job interviews and the differences in perceivers, could women have some difficulty knowing what to wear to a management-level job interview? How would you recommend they deal with the difficulty?

4. For other types of jobs, would the same rules apply for appropriate interview dress for women?

Mehndi is the word in Hindi used to describe henna, henna painting, and the resulting designs. Henna is a plant best known to us as a natural product used to color and condition the hair. Henna painting is an ancient cosmetic and healing art whereby the dried leaves of the henna plant are crushed into a powder, then made into a paste that is applied to the body to safely dye the skin. This is done in elaborate patterns and designs, traditionally on the hands and feet. The result is a kind of temporary tattoo, often reddish in color, which will last anywhere from several days to several weeks. The process is absolutely painless and in no way harmful to the skin. In fact, henna is said to condition the skin as it beautifies the body.

Mehndi is practiced in many parts of the world. From the deserts of North Africa to the villages of northern India, magnificent designs blossom and vanish upon the hands and feet of women as they have for thousands of years. Most commonly associated with romantic love and the ritual of marriage, henna designs are an integral part of bridal adornment in Hindu, Moslem, and Sephardic traditions.

Mehndi is an art form that traditionally has been practiced exclusively by women. In North Africa, Asia, the Middle East, or any Indian or Moslem community, you will find women who decorate themselves with henna. It is taught and practiced largely in the oral tradition, with recipes and patterns passed from one generation to the next. Henna designs may be used in the East to celebrate a special occasion, much the way one in the West might bake a cake or a favorite holiday food. It's that natural and that integral. But while mehndi retains an aura of festivity and well-being, it remains a sacred practice intended not just to beautify the body but to invite grace and good fortune into one's home, one's marriage, and one's family. It is a kind of talisman, a blessing upon the skin.

Henna painting in its purest form is largely improvisational and intuitive. Ancient symbols and motifs are subject to the whim and imagination of the artist, and great emphasis is put on the singularity and originality of each interpretation.

This art has always involved a marriage of the personal and the traditional, spreading slowly from one culture to another over thousands of years and taking on new meaning with each incarnation. Now we become a part of this evolution by discovering for ourselves what mehndi means today.

RITUAL ORIGINS

Despite the variety of cultures that practice the art of henna painting, its primary use in each one remains the same, and that is to decorate the hands and feet of the bride (and sometimes the groom) for the wedding ceremony.

One theory regarding the origin of henna painting as a ritual practice links it to the defloration of the bride and the appearane of hymeneal blood. This connection becomes less abstract when one considers the color of the henna and the duration of its stain in relation to the menstrual cycle. Another link can be found in the poetry and folklore of India, where mehndi is often referred to as love juice.

Mehndi marks a *samskara*, or rite of passage, in a woman's life. In classical India tradition, there is no formal ceremony at the time of puberty to celebrate the young girl's coming of age. This time usually coincides with the celebration of marriage. Mehndi is therefore associated with the sexual initiation into womanhood, as well as the union of husband and wife.

The essence of this ritual is transformation. The girl who becomes a bride stands at the threshold of another existence. The joining together of the man and woman in wedlock "encapsulates the creative activity which spawned the universe," as Richard Kurin points out in

Roome, L. (1998) *What Is Mehndi?* In *Designs for the Hands: The timeless art of henna painting.* New York: St. Martins.

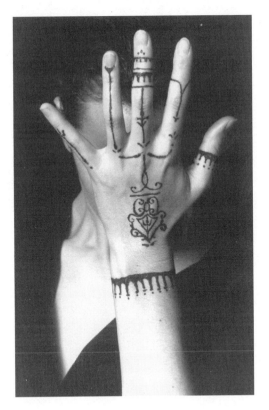

FIGURE 3.10 *Hand and wrist with mehndi design.*

Aditi, The Living Arts of India. When a girl is initiated into womanhood through marriage, the realm of the sexual unfolds before her, as does the medium of henna painting. Like lovemaking, this becomes part of her vocabulary of expression. It will be shared at every celebration or festivity. She will explore it for the rest of her life, unless she is widowed, in which case she will usually abandon the art.

THE ART OF MEHNDI

In order to understand the art of mehndi, it is important to understand the role of bodily adornment in the places where this art form is practiced. For at least five thousand years, the people of India have devoted inexhaustible creativity and energy to the invention of ornamentation and designs that celebrate the human

form through the medium of adornment. This is a spiritual endeavor, and in the words of author Oppi Untract, "By adorning the visible, material body, they also seek to satisfy a universal longing for the embellishment of its intangible counterpart: the human spirit."

In India, there is a special term *(shringar)* that is used to describe the beauty of a woman's creativity. The concept of shringar is a particularly lovely one. A woman displays her shringar in the act of creative expression. She may do it with a gesture or in a great work of art. She may reveal it in the way that she adorns herself or another. Shringar is the power of beauty beneath the surface, and mehndi is one of the many ways that such beauty is made manifest.

The *Solah Sringar* mentions mehndi as one of the sixteen adornments of a woman, though mehndi is also included in the *Kama Sutra* as one of the sixty-four arts for women.

Adornment in India is usually motivated by religious beliefs and has none of the stigma of vanity and materialism that it has in the West. It is associated with transformation and transcendence. Ceremonial painting is considered sacred work, and beautification a form of worship.

THE INVISIBLE AND THE UNSPOKEN

Mehndi is a language. It is not just a beautiful art form. It asks the woman to have a dialogue with the universal, and it provides the words by which to have that dialogue.

In Morocco, animism—the belief that all objects and living beings possess a soul—figures greatly in the practice of any and every craft and art form. Beyond this notion of soul is the idea that certain objects and animals contain mystical power and positive energy. These magical properties are referred to as *baraka*.

The concept of baraka is key in attempting to understand the role of henna painting in Moroccan society. Belief in the existence of baraka makes every moment and mundane task an opportunity for spiritual meditation. Simple acts of day-to-day life—cooking, weaving, or cleaning—become a form of worship, prayer, or what some might consider magic.

All things contain baraka, but in varying degrees. The henna plant was said to be the prophet Mohammed's favorite flower and as a result is believed to have much baraka. It is therefore respected as part of Islamic tradition and is used by the Moslem people for blessings, protection, and purification.

Similarly, the Hindus believe that Lakshmi, the goddess of prosperity, dwells in henna designs. A Hindu woman will paint her hands with henna to feel Lakshmi's presence and earn her favor, but this can happen only if she is worthy. If the woman is not worthy or shows no respect for the customs that she has learned, it is taken as an affront to the goddess, and is thought to have serious consequences.

HENNA AS ORACLE

The tradition of henna painting is supported as much by superstition as by celebration. In the words of André Malraux, "All art is a revolt against man's fate," and for centuries women have tried to predict and influence their futures through the medium of mehndi. The very word *mehndi* originally meant religious guide.

One of the most common superstitions about mehndi has to do with the color of the henna on a bride's hands. If the color is deep and red, it is said that the love between the husband and wife will be strong and long-lasting. Henna is often the first gift from the bridegroom to the bride, and it is therefore thought that the color speaks of the love he will feel for her.

There are many ways in which men and women use henna as an oracle. Sometimes a dot of henna will be put on the forehead to determine the fortune of the man or woman: if it stains, it is thought to signal good luck.

HENNA FOR PROTECTION

Although henna's use as a divining vehicle is not to be minimized, its more popular function is the attempt to influence the events of the future.

Women in every country practicing henna painting offer their designs to the spirits, gods, or goddesses in an effort to appease them and win their favor.

In Morocco there is a very clear understanding that symbols of protection are "the only action a human can take in the face of *mektoub* (destiny), the determining force behind every individual's life." Often henna is used to guard against misfortune. It is used for its magical powers and in some ways is practiced in the spirit of witchcraft. Different patterns and depths of color of the henna are thought to please the various spirits *(djoun or djun)*. A woman will often have a henna party in order to placate a spirit or to make a particular request. For instance, if her child is sick, she might promise to have a henna party to honor a particular spirit who she believes could answer her needs and heal her child. Whatever the nature of her request, if she fails to follow through with her promise, it is believed that great misfortune could befall her.

Such practices may be dismissed as purely superstitious by the nonbeliever, though perhaps it would be wise to consider their deeper significance. After all, despite the great advances of technology and all the comfort and protection it affords us, man still remains defenseless before the whim of fate. Ultimately, we know nothing more than our prehistoric ancestors about why we are alive on this planet, and though we effectively distract ourselves from the inevitability of death, our lives lead us forward into the unknown.

Contemplating mehndi's traditions may help deepen an awareness of our relationship to life's fundamental mysteries. The traditional use of henna is similar to prayer, and, whether it reveals a regret, a request, a fear, or a superstition, it admits to the presence of forces beyond our comprehension—forces infinitely greater than ourselves.

DESIGNS FOR THE HANDS

The art of mehndi is a tribute to the hands. In this unusual medium where leaf is to skin as paint is to canvas, a magical relationship occurs between the hands and the healing dye left upon them. Henna stains the palms a deeper and more lasting color than any other part of the body. Just as the beautiful designs of mehndi distinguish and accentuate the uncommon nature of the hands, so should we.

A WELL-TRAVELED BRIDGE

It is easy to take our hands for granted. They serve constantly. We rely on our hands for countless everyday tasks. They are the facilitators—those with which we give and receive. But whether making money or music, farming the land or healing the sick, our hands remain our most-traveled bridge to each other. It is the hands that we join in greeting or farewell, in worship or in wedlock.

Mehndi celebrates the hands as a miracle of creation and a vehicle of love. It focuses our attention on the sacred nature of the hands' activities. Here instrument in turn becomes canvas. From the hand to the hand, the henna flows a deep red into patterns of personal meaning, defined by and redefining tradition.

Mehndi is a unique form of painting because it not only honors but requires contact. Human touch—itself a medium of expression—adds another dynamic dimension to this work. The unlikely result of one person's desire to paint and another's desire to be painted is that they will probably end up holding hands for quite some time. This is an uncommon way of getting to know someone and an important opportunity for both people involved.

HEALING HANDS

As well as a celebration, mehndi provides a much needed vacation for the hands. Henna painting requires that the recipient be free of all responsibilities for the duration of the application, which can last as long as a full day and evening. Taking the time out to do this is in itself a healing thing, and when done in the proper spirit, it can be a rare and welcome break from the hectic routine of day-to-day life.

There are many healing elements in this practice aside from the medicinal properties already mentioned. Many women suffer the ill effects of having their hands in water for a good part of the day. For centuries, henna has been called upon to soften and rejuvenate the skin in the same way that it conditions and revitalizes the hair.

The process of having mehndi done involves important elements of massage and meditation. It requires stillness and concentration, as well as sustained physical contact with another person. The paste is cool and soothing to the skin; fingers must remain extended, hand open, and palm upturned. Of the many healing elements of mehndi, not the least is the warmth and comfort of having one's hand held.

SENSITIVITY AND SENSUALITY

More sensitive than any other part of the body, aside from the mouth and tip of the nose, the human hand contains up to thirteen hundred nerve endings per square inch. The hand generates heat, an essential ingredient in the henna painting process. This, as well as the thickness of skin, makes the inside of the hand the primary canvas for this form of painting. The Hindu bride will have the backs of her hands painted as intricately as the palms, with the idea that each hand then becomes two, and she will have four hands with which to give pleasure to her husband.

Henna painting celebrates and accentuates the erotic and sensual beauty of the hands. For Westerners it provides a way to feel touched by the exotic. There is something magical and exciting about having one's hands decorated with henna while knowing that for centuries it has been associated with romantic ritual.

THE FINGERS

The fingertips are a good place to begin discussing the sensual nature of designs for the hands. Fingertips may be dipped in henna. This is a traditional method of finger work in India, and though it may seem extreme to us, it is deeply associated with eroticism and feminine beauty. It is also a popular technique in Middle

Eastern henna, as evidenced in the *Juti* and *Rawayid* styles of the United Arab Emirates.

Henna will stain the fingernails a deep and lasting color that will remain several months and grow out with the nail. Several thousand years ago in Egypt, it was considered ill-mannered to venture out without one's nails hennaed. Nowadays, with the popularity of elaborate nail painting, an organic product that dyes the nails instead of covering them is an interesting option. In India, women decorate their nails with mehndi designs after having a child, as these designs are thought to bring protection, good luck, and a speedy recovery to the new mother.

The fingers are a very dynamic part of the mehndi experience. Some of my favorite mehndi designs involve only the fingers. For the mehndi artist, working with the fingers poses a challenge because they are narrow surfaces with vanishing horizons. They take the color quite well, though designs on the back of the fingers may fade a little faster than those on the inside. Traditionally, finger patterns are done in a number of ways. They may simply decorate the top or inside of the hand or wrap like rings or ribbons around each finger. Patterns may be done to match bracelets or rings or to imitate traditional Indian jewelry. For instance, a ring of henna on every finger may be joined by a thin thread of color to a central medallion on the top of the hand, which is then joined to the wrist. This produces an effect best described by imagining tiny chains attaching one's rings to the top of one's bracelet. Of course there are many simpler options. A small design painted at the base of the thumb or running up the side of the palm to the pinkie can be very lovely.

My favorite finger designs are from the Moroccan tradition. Sparse and striking in their simplicity, they often cover only a single finger or area of the fingers. There are many exciting variations of this form. Some designs extend from a single finger over the top of the hand to the wrist.

THE BACK OF THE HAND

The back of the hand is an elegant surface for mehndi designs. One of the most versatile designs for the hand is that of vines, which weave and wrap their way unpredictably from fingertip to wrist. Fluid, graceful, and simple to do, the creeping vine drawn on the back of the hand is known in India as *B hai ki bal*. Connected with happiness and well-being, vines are a great way to incorporate scars, age spots, or any irregularities of the complexion into the design.

The back of the hand is a temperamental surface. If the skin is tanned and dry, it can be difficult for the color to take. People who use their hands a lot often think they will have a longer lasting pattern if they do the back of the hand instead of the palm. This is not true. With few exceptions, mehndi will last the longest on the palm. For those concerned with longevity, it is important to stress that designs on the back of the hand may fade (with average washings) in anywhere from a week to ten days.

The top of the hand provides an entirely different painting experience than the palm. Specific designs seem better suited to a convex surface than to a concave. Perhaps this has to do with the function of the parts. The palm evokes images of opening and offering (the sun, a flower, or a mandala), whereas the back of the hand acts more as a shield—closing, clenching, defending. Many of the motifs I choose for the top of the hand draw their inspiration from ironwork or symbols of protection, such as those used in Morocco to deflect the evil eye.

THE PALM

For the henna artist, the human hand is an incredible canvas full of mystery and character, and the palm is its center. It's already-existing patterns and lines provide a perfect springboard for the imagination—an irresistible invitation to innovation and improvisation. The color of the skin on the inside of the hand is often much lighter than that on the back of the hand. This, as well as the temperature and thickness of the skin, yields dazzling results when mehndi is used on the palm. If proper care is taken and the mud is left on overnight, the pattern will turn a deep red color with crisp, clearly defined edges. When the hand is unusually warm, the color may even turn black.

Circular or spiral designs are compelling shapes to use in the center of the palm and are my patterns of choice. Concentric circles, evenly spaced as in a target, provide the perfect foundation for an intricate mandala. Embellishing this central form is a traditional technique in mehndi and an exciting improvisational format for the artist. The more elaborate work is usually done within the circle, leaving negative space around the outside of the motif.

TRADITIONAL DESIGNS FOR THE HANDS

Frequently people ask for the traditional hand designs. These take a variety of forms. Traditional could mean the *Nagsh* patterns of the United Arab Emirates, the sublime geometric patterns of Marrakesh, or the elaborate filigreed work of Pakistan.

In India, traditional mehndi is dense and intricate like a lace glove. One traditional format for this work is the use of a square or rectangular border that covers the entire palm. This is referred to as Old Mehndi. I have see many beautiful examples of this technique, which creates its own frame for a magnificent and intricate field of design.

It is a popular custom in India to choose a symbol or design for the palm that may then be incorporated into or enhanced by the mehndi patterns. Paisleys, vines, peacock feathers, or spirals fill the palm from fingertip to wrist, often surrounding a central motif, like a peacock or *sakaspara* (a type of sweet shaped like a diamond).

According to Indian palmistry, the right hand symbolizes the man, and the left, the woman. Mirror images in henna paintings are intended to show the union of the masculine and feminine principles.

Among my favorite mirror patterns is the figure of a bird, wings spread across the palms and backs of both hands. Actually, there are four birds, one on each hand, whose bodies form on the pinkie side, each with a wing wrapping round the palm and back of the hand and two more which form when the hands come together. The bird is considered a spiritual messenger traveling between the heavens and the earth.

One couple asked to have one bird painted on each of their hands. One of them was leaving on an airplane trip the next day, and they wanted a picture taken of their hands together, forming one bird. Their hope was to reunite before the henna pattern faded.

FRONT AND BACK

Full hand work frequently extends beyond the palm or back of the hand onto the wrist. I have already mentioned that the skin on the top of the hand may not take the color as deeply as the palm. The skin of the wrist and the arm poses a different challenge. Not only will the dye not take as deeply, but the color may be different from the rest of the hand. (Color and intensity may also vary from the inside of the wrist to the top.) Hair on the skin, which usually begins at the wrist, prevents the thin lines of henna paste from lying directly against the skin; chances are that the color will not take. In cases like this, bold, simple designs are a better choice.

Despite the inconsistencies of skin types, hair, or temperature, the wrist and the arm present exciting possibilities for accentuating and elaborating upon hand and finger designs. Full hand work traditionally trails off the palm in an intricate, tapered edge. For the Hindu or Moslem bride, it is often a point of great pride to extend the mehndi up as much of the arm as the wedding dress will show. The length and intricacy of the mehndi are admired as would be an expensive necklace or garment. It is an indication of wealth, taste, and stature.

Variations on these elaborate traditional forms can be elegant and exciting. One example is a lacelike cuff that extends from the wrist like a sleeve, with the fingers remaining bare. Or perhaps a pattern all around the outline of the hand, following the same line as a pencil tracing but running all the way down the sides of the arms? The possibilities are infinite.

In keeping with the true nature of mehndi, no two patterns are ever exactly alike, just as no two hands ever could be. This art form visually enhances an area so seasoned with sensory experience, so full of the life force and energy, that in the best of cases it will feel as though the dye is bringing a power, already present, to light.

Designs for the Hands

1. Both the process of applying henna and mehndi designs have meanings. List the many meanings associated with this traditional practice. Do any of the meanings reflect the larger society in which mehndi is practiced?

2. How does the hand interact with henna designs to lend meaning to mehndi?

12 Kimono Schools

Liza Dalby

Geisha may be the only definable group of women in Japan today who, as a matter of course, wear kimono every day. New members of the profession obtain help in getting dressed from their ex-geisha mothers and their colleague sisters. They soon learn the proper way to move by example and practice. A middle-class woman who takes up kimono as a hobby does not have this surrounding environment to learn from, so instead she may actually take lessons from one of the recently established kimono schools. These institutions capitalize on the fact that many women with the means and desire to cultivate a kimono image do not quite have the required knowledge or confidence. They give classes that range from basic kimono wearing to advanced techniques of tying the *obi* in facsimiles of daffodils or folded cranes.

The kimono schools try to convince the public that they alone hold the secret to kimono success, by having appropriated one particular mode of wearing the garment and elevating it to an ideal. The text of one school calls for an elderly lady to wear her kimono "with dignity"; a middle aged woman, or "missus," to wear it "composedly"; and a young girl to wear hers "neatly and sprucely." All this originates from bourgeois notions of how the upper crust once dressed—and, in particular, from the somewhat stiff samurai class tradition, where propriety was

the sole aim of women's dress and demeanor. That the kimono has been and can be very sexy and alluring seems to be systematically ignored by the schools.

A certain amount of judicious padding will help most women achieve a better kimono line, to be sure, but the numerous figure-fillers advocated by the kimono schools mold a woman's figure into an absolute cylinder. A towel around the waist, a V-shaped bust pad that adds substance to the upper chest, a bust suppressor to flatten the breasts, and a back pad to fill in the curve of the lower spine are items recommended as kimono foundation garments. Various sorts of clips and elastic velcro bands are sold to keep the collars in place and the front overlap neat. Such gadgetry is a substitute for the ease that comes with familiarity in wearing kimono. Geisha somehow manage to stay put together without all these aids.

When I first began to wear kimono, I used towels and handkerchiefs here and there as padding devices, as well as alligator clips to keep my underkimono in place. As I became more accustomed to wearing kimono every day, and as

FIGURE 3.11 *Contrast in eras: Geisha in traditional kimono passes pedestrian wearing modern dress on the street.*

my entire way of moving became more attuned to its constraints, I found I could do without all the clips and padding and still maintain a neat appearance. A novice kimono wearer will usually tie the obi too tight, cutting off breath and appetite, yet will still somehow come apart after several hours. A geisha, or other experienced woman, can tie the obi so that it is well secured but not constricting. One of my plump geisha friends, for instance, said she always wore kimono when she was invited out to dinner so she could eat more.

LEARNING A FOREIGN CLOTHING

We are revealed by clothes more than we are clothed by them. Only a sincere attempt to wear foreign dress makes us realize the extent to which we are not just naked without familiar clothing: we are stripped of part of ourselves. A garment as demanding as the kimono, for example, requires a whole new personality, and, like learning a foreign language, it takes a while before we are no longer self-conscious.

"You look like a rabbit, hopping along like that," the sarcastic auntie at the Mitsuba would jibe during my early days of attending parties as one of the geisha. I would then forget the errand I had been sent on while I concentrated on my manner of walking. Eventually the proper movements became natural, but in absorbing them I discovered that I had developed another self in kimono. By no accident are the relatively small gestures of Japanese body language gauged to the kimono, but I was surprised to find that after a while, I actually felt awkward speaking English when dressed as a geisha. American English body language simply does not feel right in kimono.

Much presence of mind is required to switch back and forth easily between Western and Japanese dress. Few geisha can do it. On the whole, they tend to look awkward in dresses and skirts. The stunning and sophisticated older geisha I met at a banquet one evening seemed dowdy on the street the next day in her two-piece navy blue knit. When they wear Western clothes, geisha scrape their feet along as they are used to doing in their zōri. Their manner of walking with turned-in feet, which makes a kimono rustle delicately, looks simply pigeon-toed in shoes and a dress. They seem to be wearing invisible kimono, gesturing as if long sleeves were quietly constraining their arms.

Almost every geisha I know has a weakness for kimono and a passion for collecting them. This is above and beyond the necessity of acquiring the basic number for each season that is considered a geisha's working wardrobe. Kimono are the single greatest expense in a geisha's budget. When a young woman begins her geisha career she will have had to purchase at least ten of them, along with obi, to see her through the changes of season in proper attire. About ten thousand dollars is needed to purchase a minimum wardrobe. A young geisha is thus likely to start her career in debt for the loan to buy kimono.

An old proverb says that Osaka people are *kuidōraku*—prodigal in their expenditures on the delights of eating—whereas Kyoto people would eat plain rice in order to lavish their money on clothes *(kidōraku)*. The Kyoto geisha exemplify their city's stereotype perfectly. I know from my own experience, too, that it is difficult to be satisfied with a bare minimum number of kimono. Once wearing kimono becomes a habit, the desire to have a chestful of kimono and obi becomes an addiction. In Kyoto, where the affectionate local dialect term for kimono is *obebe*, women talk about the enviable state of being *obebe mochi,* having lots of kimono. Every geisha wants to be obebe mochi, and she will spend thousands of dollars a year to add to her kimono collection.

Geisha will appear before guests only in silk kimono and, further, only in certain kinds of silk kimono. Although kimono today can be thought of first of all as native dress, as counterposed to Western dress, within the realm of Japanese clothing a number of important distinctions define which kimono can be worn on what sort of occasion.

DISCUSSION QUESTIONS

Kimono Schools

1. How is movement a part of the grammar of wearing kimono and modern street attire?

2. What parts of the clothing in context model (Figure 3.4) are referred to in factors affecting kimono meanings?

13 Identity, Postmodernity, and the Global Apparel Marketplace

Susan B. Kaiser
University of California at Davis

Today, a visit to another country—or even to another city or state in our own country—often yields surprises when observing *what is available* for purchase, *what* people are actually wearing, and—in some cases, most significantly—*how* people are wearing what they are wearing. For example, one might see the same basic products everywhere, but worn in a variety of ways. Jeans, baseball caps, T-shirts, or other fairly basic items may be worn in many different ways: tight or baggy; shaped in a variety of ways; tucked or loose; and the like. So, it is not only what we buy, but also how we wear what we buy that expresses our identities: that is, who we are and how we see ourselves at any point in time. We can shape these ideas in relation to ourselves as individuals, as well as the groups and communities to which we belong, and even the nations or societies in which we live.

The idea that appearance styles, or "looks," are *negotiated* as people influence each other on what to wear and how to wear it is fundamental in understanding social processes of fashion (Kaiser, Nagasawa & Hutton, 1991; Kaiser, 1997). Places and communities have identities, too. The latter, in fact, is no longer restricted to

Original for this text.

geographic location. Global technologies, the worldwide production and distribution of apparel, and the circulation of images of style across national and cultural boundaries all contribute to what might be characterized as a larger, complicated negotiation of global style, or international dress (Eicher, 1992). It is possible to be influenced not only by immediate, local, culture(s), but also by globally circulating images and commodities. Constructing and reconstructing appearance and, in part, identity, becomes a process of figuring out how we "fit" in and "depart" from a vast array of possible looks. The contemporary social and economic conditions that shape the global apparel marketplace and our multiple possibilities for shaping identity within it are often referred to as "postmodernity" (Lyon, 1994). The commodities and images that were once only available through travel or other cross-cultural contact are now globally and quickly produced, distributed, and consumed. In the process, more and more global locations are touched by "global style" in some way, as apparel manufacturers search around the world for (a) new sources of labor that are less expensive, more timely in response, and higher in quality, and (b) new consuming markets. A nation's level of economic development influences whether it will be regarded as a source of labor or a consuming market, or both. Yet the picture is even more complicated than that: Pockets of poverty exist within relatively wealthy nations, and pockets of wealth exist within relatively impoverished nations. The issue of who can afford to buy which goods in the global marketplace becomes one that is ethical, as well as economic.

What is for sale in the postmodern, global marketplace? Objects, images, and the marketers' constructions of reality. On a daily basis, consumers around the world are bombarded with new ideas and possibilities, whether they can afford to buy them or not. If one can afford to participate, it is possible to be part of larger (even global) communities ranging from the business world to leisure interest groups (e.g., rap or reggae or country western music; skateboarding or biking or golfing) and more fundamental identity-based communities (e.g., gay and lesbian; African diasporas; youth) to the

more local hometown community where someone lives. Magazines, catalogs, and television and internet shopping help to bring a world of possibilities for consuming and shaping identity to the fingertips of global consumers.

How do we make sense of who we are and who we are not in the context of postmodernity: a time characterized by media and commodity saturation, in a marketplace that may seem more global than personal? And how does fashion influence individual and collective searches for identity? The term *fashion* implies change; it also implies processes of imitation and differentiation. To some extent, we want to express our inclination and ability to belong to certain groups and communities. Yet somehow we balance this desire with assertions of individual uniqueness. Almost 100 years ago, sociologist Georg Simmel, who has been described by some as one of the earliest postmodern thinkers, noticed this interplay between imitation and differentiation in fashion change (Simmel, 1904). Even more generally, he indicated that in times of intense societal change or transition, we (collectively) become more concerned about representing who we are by how we consume: by what we buy and how we use and display it in our expressions of identity to others (Lyon, 1994).

Identity politics are involved in processes of imitation and differentiation. The word "fashion" is related to the Latin word *factio*, which implies faction or political distinctions (Barnard, 1996). Issues of gender, race and ethnicity, sexuality, nationality, social class, age, and leisure-time preferences all enter into the creation of the groups in which we see and do not see ourselves. These issues have always been factors in how we consume fashion. Since the late 1960s and early 1970s, however, we have become more aware of these issues due to social movements and related academic areas of study (i.e., feminist, ethnic, and cultural studies). The media have also played a huge role in shaping a larger cultural awareness of identity politics. In 1997, when Ellen "came out" as a lesbian on her television situation comedy, a whole media discourse (on talk shows, in magazines, and on the internet) emerged to learn more and express views about diverse sexualities.

In addition to promoting awareness of differences through a complex expression and discovery of identity politics, postmodern culture seems to thrive on the juxtaposition of component parts from different social, cultural, and historical contexts. Traditional categories and boundaries collapse, or at least budge, as they are stretched by a bending, blending, and blurring of ideas and images (e.g., gender blending, retro looks, subcultural fusions). It is not so much that this idea of mixing and blending is completely new. The history of clothing and appearance styles has probably always relied on blending to some extent. But now there are technological and economic conditions that bring all of these possibilities into our televisions and computers. And there is a lot of profit to be made. Consider the following:

- Gender and sexual blending is evident in media that highlights drag or cross-dressing. A "lesbian chic" look (short hair, black pantsuits, masculine black shoes) becomes widely popularized in films, television, and in the workplace.

- The growth of casual businesswear creates a need to mix and match separates, potentially blurring a number of boundaries: formality, status, gender, age, and the like.

- Junior high girls wear dresses to dances and parties that would once be reserved for women who are adults: very long dresses (with slits) or very short, sexy black evening dresses worn with high-heeled, strappy black sandals.

Appearance styles ("looks") tend to be eclectic, visually stimulating, and confusing when consciously contemplated. How can we explain this complexity of style in the contemporary marketplace, and what is the impact on our perceptions of identity? On a cultural level, through talk shows or other interactions with media, as well as through "global style" per se, we seem to be collectively working through ideas or conducting "cultural conversations" about *what* appearances say about individual, community, national, and global identities. We are also interested in *how* and *why* we rely on style to work through ideas. These self-examining tendencies are often characterized as indicating a kind of *postmodern reflexivity*. This reflexivity refers, for example, to the media analysis of media coverage (e.g., "Are we paying too much attention to political scandals, showing the same images over and over until they become imprinted in viewers' minds?"), to the self-conscious and critical examination of fashion and beauty issues by fashion and beauty magazines whose pages depict thin models, at least some of whom have undergone breast augmentation surgery (e.g., "Is plastic surgery really necessary?"), and to public discussions of dress codes in the context of concerns regarding gang symbolism (e.g., "Will school uniforms really eliminate violence?").

Are we losing ourselves in a sea of surface-level judgments? In some ways, images are almost amazingly important for politicians and celebrities, as well as for the public in general. Consider the number of times and the variety of ways in which Madonna has "remade" herself. A whole page on the World Wide Web—"Hillary's Hair"—is devoted to Hillary Clinton's changing hairstyles. And, consider the popularity of "makeovers" on daily talk shows. Witness the increase in elective cosmetic surgery, the explosion of the fitness market, incidences of eating disorders, and the importance of designer or status labels in more and more contexts (including the football field).

Or, are we reaching new heights of understanding about ourselves and developing new, integrated ways of relating to one another? In a recent (1998) visit of the Pope to Cuba, communist leader Fidel Castro greeted him in a business suit: a symbol of western, masculine capitalism. The international media reported on the political significance of this stylistic choice and its global, economic consequences. Did this signal the fall or decline of communism in Cuba? Or is it possible that new models of government could emerge, combining some of the most humane, equitable, and freedom-inspired qualities of communism and democracy with capitalism? Although the media did not comment on it, Castro's trademark beard remained intact. Consistent with his speeches, he seemed to be conveying the idea that his country was moving in new directions and creating new syntheses or collages of political ideas, rather than portraying a mere capitulation to western, capitalist democracy.

In the everyday context, style affords an outlet for experimenting with a whole host of changing boundaries and collages of ideas and identities. Most likely, those who experiment the most with style have the most to gain from new aesthetic and status boundaries—namely, women, ethnic minorities, and working-class youth. Those whose physical appearances coincide with traditional notions of power (i.e., northern European white male heritage) seem to have the most to lose from changing aesthetic and status boundaries (for example, any move away from the century-old and remarkably stable, male business suit).[1] Yet there are signs that these boundaries are indeed changing, as evident in the "casualization" of businesswear (that is, the move away from suits toward a mixing and matching of separates, for at least some days of the week). And those who seemingly have the most to lose are participating in the shift to "casual Fridays" or even "casual weeks." Women and ethnic minorities have probably had some visual influence on this trend, because their relative tendency to be "more into style" has added variety and complexity into the visual culture of the workplace. On the other hand, some women and ethnic minorities in mid-management positions worry that the casual businesswear trend may serve to "keep them in their places," with the glass ceiling intact (Janus, 1998).

So style, in many ways, seems to be a "mixed bag." Signs of progressive change, whether anticipated or reflected through style, coincide with the suggestion—so embedded in modern, western thought—that playing with appearances is shallow or superficial. About 100 years ago, Oscar Wilde (gay author and leader in the "aesthetics movement" who espoused "art for art's sake") said, "It is only shallow people who do not judge by appearances." In other words, the true mystery of our realities may reside in the visible, tangible, and taken-for-granted realm of appearances. We may be able to express something about ourselves and our cultures through the medium of personal appearance that we are unable to get across through other means.

In the postmodern cultural context it seems as though a lot of the pieces of the puzzle that compose our realities are "up for grabs" or dislodged from their usual locations and juxtaposed with one another in a way that does not seem to fit. Shared yearnings lead us to search for new ways of understanding our identities and communities (hooks, 1990). Simultaneously, advanced-stage or global capitalism compels us to want and "need" more than ever. The promise of improving ourselves (for a price) is alluring and intoxicating, as evident in slogans such as "Shop 'til you drop," "When the going gets tough, the tough go shopping," and "Truth, knowledge, new clothes." Are we in the process of shaping new realities or merely serving as pawns in the marketplace? Let's consider this question by exploring three topics close to the heart of postmodernity: choice, confusion, and creativity.

CHOICE

Eclecticism is the degree zero of contemporary general culture: one listens to reggae, watches a western, eats McDonald's food for lunch and local cuisine for dinner, wears Paris perfume in Tokyo and "retro" clothes in Hong Kong. (Lyotard, 1988)

Choice is often regarded as the mainstay of freedom. In the global context, the desire for and availability of consumer goods is equated with progress. To a great extent, freedom and democracy are associated with an unlimited range of options in the consumer marketplace. And in the capitalist apparel marketplace, the range of choice is tremendous because goods are produced and distributed worldwide. (Often, textiles and apparel are the first items produced in nations taking the first steps toward becoming more industrialized.) The assortment of styles, colors, and textures is enormous, if not overwhelming. In the apparel marketplace, at least in the industrialized nations, the world is at our fingertips. Yet another trend seems to contradict this idea of increased variety in the marketplace.

In some ways, there is a globalization of style, with some looks (often those associated with western capitalism, modernity, and democracy) having the most global potency. At the same time, the choice *within* a given store or community seems to have increased, drawing from (and often appropriating) all kinds of cultural and subcultural traditions and innovations.[2] This tendency toward both increased variety within geographic locations and a homogenizing effect across locations represents a global paradox. Still, catalogs stuffing the mailboxes of middle-class consumers defy any problems with geographic access. The concept of choice itself becomes more complicated and harder to interpret.

Perhaps it is easiest to comprehend choice by examining its limits. The limits to choice are primarily economic. Not everyone can afford the latest, most popular brand of shorts for their children. Not everyone can afford to travel and to be inspired by diverse cultural expressions of style. Not everyone can afford to diversify their wardrobes to engage in a daily, pleasurable, and postmodern play with style. And often those who actually make our clothes (i.e., apparel workers around the world, including those who live in immigrant communities in postmodern cities such as Los Angeles), are least likely to be able to afford to purchase the clothes for which their labor is responsible.

Yet in many modernized societies, even within very basic categories of commodities, including those at lower price points (e.g., disposable diapers, coffee, pantyhose), there can be a confusing array of choices. Buying even seemingly generic or standard items (e.g., Nike shoes, Levi jeans) requires complicated thought processes as one contemplates the range of features from which to select, the statement he or she will be making, and the contexts in which the item is likely to be worn:

- A woman in her thirties goes to a discount outlet shopping mall to buy a pair of athletic shoes and is confronted with a large store filled with thousands of boxes. What she thought would be a generic item actually presents a vast array of options. She must make numerous choices. Which brand should she choose? Should she go with high tops or the standard models? What color does she want? Will she be using the shoes for aerobics, step class, walking, running, playing tennis or basketball, or some combination thereof? Does she really need the $200 shoes with the air pumps? Can she wear the shoes for multiple functions even though they are intended for specific functions? Should she select leather, vinyl, or canvas? How do the shoes compare in terms of how they fit and feel? And what can she wear with them?

- The same woman stops at a convenience store on her way home to buy pantyhose for the next day. She wants a quick and easy decision, after the multiple choices she has confronted in her purchase of athletic shoes. She walks over to a display of pantyhose in egg-shaped containers. What size is she: A, B, or Queen? She briefly checks the height and weight table to confirm her size and then begins to address the other choices she must make: color, sheer versus reinforced toe, control top versus sheer-to-the-waist versus regular top, and so forth. As she makes her choice, she must: (a) consider what garments she will wear with the pantyhose, (b) analyze her figure and examine how she feels about it, and (c) debate whether the sheer styles will be less durable.

- A nine-year-old boy goes to the department store with his father to buy some jeans for school. The two of them are confronted with rows and rows of jeans, folded neatly in shelves built into the wall. Once they find what they think is his size, they unfold the jeans to examine the stylistic variations. Does he want basic indigo blue or some fashionable color? Faded (and if so, *how* faded)? Preshrunk or shrink-to-fit? Zipper or button fly? Standard five-pocket, or extra pockets on the legs, and if so, how low can they be without suggesting gang membership? Flared, straight leg, or "pipe" style? Then, when beginning to try on some of the options to arrive at the best "fit," questions surface regarding how long, how baggy, and how low the jeans should be worn. And what are the current features and ways of wearing jeans that are associated with gang involvement? Does the school have a dress code—implicit or explicit?

Thus, even in the realm of standard or basic items, the range of choice is evident in today's marketplace. Choice can also be subtle, but still require a great deal of thought and attention. In some ways, choices that are not obvious or readily visible when entering a store may be even more complicated. On the surface, one is making a "basic" purchase. So why does so much thought need to go into the decision-making? Why are there so many issues to be weighed?

Perhaps we need new ways of thinking about choice in a global economy. For example, how do we *perceive* choice, and how do these perceptions compare with what apparel producers and marketers are trying to achieve? Whose cultural traditions and innovations become a part of the package of choice, and who receives credit for these traditions and innovations? Who profits? What are the effects of the complexities of choice? One possibility is that too much choice may create a feeling of overload that contributes to a preference for simplicity. Hence, the now "classic" popularity of black and (more recently) dark brown or gray, after every conceivable color combination has been seen on the body and head; the return of basic jeans after the heyday of designer jeans in the 1970s; the return to unisex disposable diapers by one manufacturer, after a decade of gender-coded diapers (for example, blue or male-patterned and "functionally altered" diapers for males). Yet even these "simpler" styles reflect a diversity of choices; the choices are merely more subtle.

Hence, choice can lead to confusion, ambiguity, and a desire for relief. At the same time, diversity in the marketplace can contribute to a celebration of style. The postmodern marketplace allows for a creative search for and expression of identity. In some ways, it is easier to figure out who we are *not* than it is to affirm a positive identity. In the retail setting, one can survey the options visually, scanning and eliminating the more obvious expressions of "not me," or identity *not* (Freitas et al., 1997). Then comes the even more complex process of gauging, mixing and matching, and the fine-tuning of possible, positive identity expressions ("me" or, more accurately, multiple "me's"). Even if one is not

inclined to revel in the play of appearances, a certain amount of energy, in addition to money, is required to put together an appearance. Hence, choice contributes to confusion on the one hand and creativity on the other.

CONFUSION

Culture is in a process of recycling: everything is juxtaposable to everything else because nothing matters. (Gitlin, 1989)

Schizophrenic…an experience of isolated, disconnected, discontinuous material signifiers which fail to link up into a coherent sequence. (Jameson, 1983)

Postmodern eclecticism can foster ambiguity. U.S. culture, for example, is not sending straightforward messages about what is fashionable. We are bombarded with a diverse array of everyday looks of the people around us (intensified in an urban context); commodities in stores; images advertised and promoted in fashion magazines; appearance styles we see in films and television sitcoms; mail catalogs; and music videos.

There is likely to be a confusion about issues of time (e.g., are we looking forward or backward?), place (e.g., is there a local look anymore?), and existence (e.g., why are we so caught up in image?). Image and style seem to be in a constant state of flux:

- Apparel manufacturers traditionally produced only a few lines of garments per year, and retailers could reorder successful styles. Today, some produce as many as twelve lines per year and do not accept reorders.

- One can observe a vast range of styles in media such as music videos. Moreover, characters in the videos frequently change their looks numerous times in the space of a few minutes, suggesting that identity is changeable in the flick of a second. A somewhat similar pattern is found in Hindi films produced in Bombay, India.

- Youth subcultures seem to multiply overnight, and they stylistically blend into one another. The visual images that identify them precede verbal labels (e.g., punk or post-punk, new age, gothic, motorhead, boardhead, skater, or surfer).

Part of our confusion about culture and fashion probably stems from ambivalence, which has always been with us but is probably intensified in the postmodern context. In fact, we seem to be ambivalent about capitalism itself: We both love and hate what capitalism represents and promotes (Wilson, 1985). We also seem to be ambivalent about our identities, and fashion can give aesthetic form to unconscious tensions linked to gender, age, and status (Davis, 1992). And we are probably ambivalent about our own absorption in issues of style, appearance, and image; they seem both trivial and practical, superficial and complex, personal and global. At any rate, the stage is set for experimentation. Fashion seems to provide a way of articulating individual and cultural ambivalences that are not easily expressed otherwise (Kaiser, Nagasawa & Hutton, 1991; Kaiser, Nagasawa & Hutton, 1995). In any case, ambivalence and confusion provide creative fuel for aesthetic exploration.

CREATIVITY

According to the French sociologist Jean Baudrillard (1975), it is not so much a matter of *being* the self as it is *producing* the self. To consume is to produce again. Part of what we produce as consumers are our appearance styles. In addition to its relation to the word *factio*, the term "fashion" also derives from the Latin *facere*, which means "to make or to do." Using fashion as a verb or a process in this way, we can consider how fashioning appearance style is one way—a visual and creative way—of producing identity. In African American culture, the term "style" is often used similarly as a verb or process, in a way that implies that styling is a way of producing not only identity, but also a sense of community with others (Hall, 1993). That is, it becomes a process of creating a cultural bond with others.

We could argue about whether or not we are more likely to experiment with our appearance styles, and hence, our identities, in the postmodern context. Is our current level of "producing

identity" at a record high, historically speaking? Clothing historian Rachel Pannabecker (1997) suggests that although there do seem to be some unique aspects of contemporary appearance styles, they need to be examined in the context of larger, historical trends.

What we do know is that today, more than one look can simultaneously be regarded as fashionable. As clothing scholar Jean Hamilton (1990) comments, it becomes an issue of *looks* for spring, rather than a single look for spring. So there are many ways that we can create our appearance styles and still be considered fashionable. This seems to represent a shift toward a greater plurality of popular styles, perhaps to parallel an increasing awareness of what it means to live in a multicultural society. Yet we also live in a global society, as noted earlier, and our clothes are being produced in a larger array of places around the world, as apparel and retail companies search for or "source" new locations with lower labor costs for sewing clothes. And, perhaps in part as a result, there is a stronger emphasis on mixing and matching separates, because the pieces that are produced and worn together are produced, and often purchased, in different locations. These pieces come together, somehow, in our wardrobes and our appearances.

So on a daily basis, we engage in the process of managing our appearances, almost unconsciously using our creative abilities. I recently asked a close friend, Carol, and my son, Nathan, to describe where and when they obtained the different pieces comprising their ensembles. Carol, who is 30 years old and from Louisiana, is now living in California and is dressed for a Sunday afternoon play we are attending together. Nathan, who is 20 years old and a student, has come home for Sunday dinner. Both are dressed casually and comfortably, and the total looks they have created are understated and well coordinated. Yet a discussion about each article comprising the look reveals a more complex state of affairs:

- Carol, who is 30 years old, is wearing black straight jeans (relaxed fit) pants bought at GAP and made in the United States. She has on a black leather belt (made in Italy) with antiqued brush silver (scroll design) hardware; her sister bought it for her as a birthday gift while they were shopping together at The Limited a few years ago. Her long-sleeved brown knit top buttons up the front and has a V-neck. It was made in Taiwan, but she bought it at Lerner New York in Baton Rouge, Louisiana. She is wearing a black "pleather" vest over it, made of 100% polyurethane. It was made in China, and she bought it at a discount store in Baton Rouge, for seven dollars (where all separates are seven dollars), a few years ago, when she was on a tighter budget. She has only worn it once before, but really likes the way it fits. And this is the first time she feels as though she has *really* worn it. She is wearing dark brown boots with heels; she bought them at Mervyn's in Woodland, California, and they were made in China. She's also wearing knee-high black socks purchased at Sears in Sacramento, California; she actually had meant to buy trouser socks. She is also wearing a scarf of 100% polyester that was made in Italy. It is square, with a black border and different shades of beige in an abstract design. She "borrowed" it from her sister. She's also wearing a silver ring with a swirl design; she bought it in San Francisco from an Asian street vendor for five dollars. She is also wearing a sterling silver ring with a V-shaped design; she got it at Rich's department store in Atlanta, in one of her favorite neighborhoods (and stores). She is also wearing silver antiqued drop earrings from The Limited; they were a Christmas gift from her sister. There is another, identical pair that is currently circulating between her and her sisters. Her watch, which she wears every day, is a silver chained style; it was made in Japan, and she bought it at a time that she was consciously moving toward wearing silver. She bought the watch in Marietta, north of Atlanta, at Sears in the Galleria shopping center. She is also carrying a black, leather Etienne Aigner purse; it has a drawstring style with gold hardware and a detachable shoulder strap with a fixed shorter strap that can be worn over the wrist, "lady style." It has a matching wallet. She bought it at an outlet mall in Gonzales, Louisiana. She is also wearing a new fragrance (Clinique Wrappings), made in the United States. Overall, she realizes that her outfit is the result of six years of acquisition of goods, although she has never worn all of these pieces together before. She put the overall look together (especially her boots) to go with her recent, short-cropped haircut. She calls the whole outfit a typical "sister style" outfit. The term has a double meaning. She associates the look and some of the component parts with her sisters; they would all "fit" together with a look like this. In a larger sense, the outfit also represents "sistuh style"; it is a "constructed" and "achieved" look that she associated with the process and outcome of African American female styling.

- Nathan, who is 20 years old, begins by describing his gray and black baseball cap with "Oakley" embroidered into it. The cap was made in Bangladesh. He purchased the cap for five dollars from a street vendor in Mexico during spring break about a year ago. After purchasing the cap, he began to compare it with other caps with the same brand name, and he's noticed that the "a" on his cap is shaped differently. He is wearing a T-shirt that says "Glacier Point: Coolest Apartments in Davis." The T-shirt was given to him by his apartment complex about six months ago to celebrate its grand opening. The T-shirt was made in Jamaica. Over the T-shirt, he's wearing a gray, long-sleeved pullover top with a collar and cuffs and a small white stripe as a trim. He bought it at GAP in Sacramento, California, a few months ago, but it was made in the northern Mariana Islands. He's also wearing GAP jeans, worn loose but not too baggy, and just long enough to "scrunch" over his shoes. The jeans were made in the United States. He's also wearing black Nike high tops, with a "swoosh" trademark symbol. He bought them in Texas on a family trip to visit relatives almost a year ago. They were made in Indonesia. He doesn't remember where he got his white socks; he pulls them straight up, but not quite all the way. His Guess watch was a Christmas present from his parents. He realizes that he has only worn this complete outfit a couple of times, but it is a fairly typical "student" outfit for him.

Whether or not we are conscious of it, a lot of effort and eclecticism goes into our created selves. On a routine basis, we assemble elements from different times and places in our lives. The objects themselves are produced in an even wider range of locations throughout the world. The net result of our coordinating efforts may be subtle, or it may reveal a mood celebrating the possibilities of color, texture, and form. In any case, we are participating in a process of producing identity when we construct our looks. Perusing the labels indicating the country of origin also reminds us of the labor "behind the scenes," although this labor, in many ways, remains invisible in a global economy.

Some appearances may seem more postmodern than others, but the point is not one of classifying appearances or styles as traditional, modern, or postmodern. Instead, what seems to capture the idea of postmodern best lies in minding, managing, and perceiving appearance styles and component parts from a perspective that is perhaps more tolerant of diversity and ambiguity, more exploratory, and more "constructed" of elements from various places around the world. We are fashion consumers in a larger, global marketplace that is profit-motivated, often exploitative of developing societies, and endangering to a sense of place. The upshot of the contradictions that seem to be part and parcel of postmodernity is as follows: There is a promise of a new way of seeing the world as at once pluralistic and democratic, expressive and creative. But there are also cultural and personal costs associated with this new insight—namely, the possible threat of further exploitation on a global scale, a blurring of cultural traditions into a vast uniform global context, and a confusion between who we are and how we look. These may be the ultimate choices to which fashion in the postmodern context refers.

Perhaps we will be able to arrive at some form of synthesis through new imagery, new social arrangements, and new ways of viewing ourselves. Hopefully, such a solution will be kinder and gentler to women, ethnic minorities, and people of developing nations. We are at a critical juncture in our global society, and fashion plays a part in shaping and defining this juncture. Consciously or unconsciously, we are both commodity consumers and identity producers as we manage our appearances and continue to create ourselves and our communities. With increased awareness of identity politics, global inequities, and industry and media influences, perhaps we can create new, more complex understandings, as well.

Notes

1. The "sack suit" emerges from a longer process of a masculine move away from anything feminine, frivolous, or fussy (see Paoletti, 1985).

2. There is an ongoing debate in the textiles and apparel field on whether the range of choice increases or decreases in the context of global capitalism (see Kaiser, Nagasawa, & Hutton, 1995; Kean, 1997; Kaiser, Nagasawa & Hutton, 1997; Kaiser, 1997).

References

Barnard, M. (1996). *Fashion as communication*. New York/London: Routledge.

Baudrillard, J. (1975). *The mirror of production* (M. Poster, trans.). St. Louis, MO: Telos Press.

Davis, F. (1992). *Fashion, culture, and identity*. Chicago, IL: University of Chicago Press.

Eicher, J. B. (1995). Cosmopolitan and international dress. In M. E. Roach-Higgins, J. B. Eicher, & K. K. P. Johnson, (Eds.). *Dress and identity* (1995) New York: Fairchild Publications.

Freitas, A. J., Kaiser, S. B., Chandler, J., Hall, C., Kim, J-W., & Hammidi, T. (1997). Appearance management as border construction: Least favorite clothing, group distancing, and identity . . . not! *Sociological Inquiry* 67 (3) 323–335.

Gitlin, T. (1989). "Postmodernism defined, at last!" *Utne Reader* July/August (4), pp. 52–61.

Hall, C. (1993). *Toward a gender-relational understanding of appearance style in African-American culture*. Master's thesis, University of California at Davis.

Hamilton, J. (1990). "The silkworms of the East must be pillaged": The cultural foundations of mass fashion. *Clothing and Textiles Research Journal* 8(4):40–48.

hooks, b. (1990). *Yearning: Race, gender, and cultural politics*. Boston, MA: South End Press.

Jameson, F. (1983). Postmodernism and consumer society. In H. Foster (Ed.), in *The anti-aesthetic: Essays on postmodern culture* (pp. 111–125). Port Townsend, WA: Bay Press.

Janus, T. (1998). *Negotiations @ work: Analysis of the casual businesswear trend*. Master's thesis, University of California at Davis.

Kaiser, S. B. (1997). *The social psychology of clothing: Symbolic appearances in context* (2nd edition revised). New York: Fairchild Publications.

Kaiser, S. B., Nagasawa, R. H., & Hutton, S. S. (1991). Fashion, postmodernity and personal appearance: A symbolic interactionist formulation. *Symbolic Interaction* 14(2), 165–185.

Kaiser, S. B., Nagasawa, R. H., & Hutton, S. S. (1995). Construction of an SI theory of fashion: Part 1. Ambivalence and change. *Clothing and Textiles Research Journal* 13(3), 172–183.

Kaiser, S. B., Nagasawa, R. H., & Hutton, S. S. (1997). Truth, knowledge, new clothes: Responses to Hamilton, Kean, and Pannabecker. *Clothing and Textiles Research Journal* 15(3), 184–191.

Kean, R. (1997). The role of the fashion system in fashion change: A response to the Kaiser, Nagasawa and Hutton model. *Clothing and Textiles Research Journal* 15(3), 172–177.

Lyon, D. (1994). *Postmodernity*. Minneapolis, MN: University of Minnesota Press.

Lyotard, J. F. (1988). *The postmodern condition: A report on knowledge* (G. Bennington, & B. Messumi, trans.). Minneapolis, MN: University of Minnesota Press.

Pannabecker, R. (1997). Fashioning theory: A critical discussion of the symbolic interactionist theory of fashion. *Clothing and Textiles Research Journal* 15(3), 178–183.

Paoletti, J. B. (1985). Ridicule and role models as factors in American men's fashion change, 1880–1910. *Costume* 19, 121–134.

Simmel, G. (1904). Fashion. *International Quarterly*. Reprinted in *American Journal of Sociology* 62 (May 1957): 541–558.

Wilson, E. (1985). *Adorned in dreams: Fashion and modernity*. London: Virago Press.

DISCUSSION QUESTIONS

Identity, Postmodernity, and the Global Appparel Marketplace

1. How is fashion currently a part of identity politics?

2. How is fashion in the United States global?

3. How does postmodern emphasis on choice and creativity cause confusion? Is confusion an essential part of postmodern dress? What does it accomplish?

14   Vintage Jeans Hot in Japan

Tokyo, Japan (AP)—Like so many shoppers, Yo Murata was happy when he found that perfect pair of blue jeans: Comfortable yet classic, broken-in, but sturdy. And the price was right—Only $2,500.

"I wanted to buy ones like I used to wear as a teenager," the 44-year-old fast-food franchise owner explained. "Because they bring back memories of my good old days."

A vintage-jeans craze in Tokyo has given rise to about 100 boutiques catering to connoisseurs of faded denim and old-style copper rivets. And the demand has pushed prices up to levels normally associated with haute couture.

Murata's purchase was two years ago, and he regards it as a great buy. These days, a pair of the same vintage jeans—Levi's, circa 1950—fetch around $5,000.

SEVERAL WEEKS PAY

Conspicuous consumption was common during Japan's free-spending 1980s, but several years of recession created a strong demand for discounted goods. Vintage jeans though, seem to be an exception to the backlash against big spending. Luxury designer wear may have lost its lustre, but somehow it's OK to drop a splashy amount of money on down-home denim.

The $2,500 that Murata paid is the average monthly entry-level salary at major Japanese companies.

Murata said if he could find another pair he'd snap it up in a minute.

"I would pay that much if I can find a pair that fits me, because they are so attractive and high quality," he said. "The 1950s models have nicer color and they are sturdier."

Until several years ago, Levi's from the early 1950s were priced at $40–60, only slightly more expensive than the ordinary models, said Hideyuki Kawamura, manager of the Tokyo boutique Delaware.

"The price has skyrocketed since recent years....Many people began fighting for a limited number of pairs in stock," Kawamura said.

HOW TO BE HIP

As is common with Japanese fads, demand is fed by trendy magazines that provide readers with detailed instructions on how to be hip. Usually, this involves a purchase.

"Jeans are the champion of vintage goods....They often cost as much as a car," said the August issue of Goods Press magazine. But it said they were worth it "because they're so precious."

Price varies according to jeans' age and conditions. For vintage fans, the dream jeans are Levi Strauss from as early as 1930s, which go for thousands of dollars.

Customers search for the leather back patch and the logo on the red tab. They turn the jeans inside out to see if the famous hidden copper rivets for the back pockets are there. The stitches and seams must be all cotton and yellowish.

The demand shows no sign of slowing, purveyors say.

"When it comes to used and surplus stock jeans, the boom is still continuing," said Hideo Wakni, manager at the Tokyo-based used clothes outlet Voice. "We have at least one customer a day who buys $1,000 pair just like that."

The boom has sent floods of Japanese buyers to the United States, inflating the price of used jeans around Los Angeles. Now reasonably priced high-quality vintage models are hard to find, said Yoshifumi Yamamoto, an owner of the Delaware boutique.

Vintage Jeans Hot in Japan

1. How did the 1994 Japanese fad for recycled jeans reflect postmodernism?

2. The vintage jeans market is also lucrative in the United States. Are North Americans buying vintage jeans for the same reasons as do Japanese consumers?

15 The Cuts That Go Deeper

Charles Siebert

"Now, what is it you'd like done?" Tracy Martin asked as I took a seat beside her and stared into a wall-size mirror. Martin, a tall, slender blonde in her early 30's, is a computer-imaging technician and health educator at the Institute for Aesthetic and Reconstructive Surgery in Nashville, the country's first all-purpose plastic surgery center and one of the most advanced facilities of its kind in the world. Founded seven years ago at Nashville's Baptist Hospital, the institute features a staff of 22 plastic surgeons, its own state-of-the-art surgical unit and private recovery suites, a wide variety of pre- and post-operative cosmetic salon services, a fitness center, a skin-assessment center and a separate resource center with a library, a video room and a year-round program of free seminars to educate both patients and doctors about the latest developments in plastic surgery. Each year at the institute, thousands of people visit the computer-imaging center; there, the designs they have on themselves are modified by, and electronically melded with, the designs now made possible by modern plastic surgery.

As Martin fixed my image on her computer—it has a big TV-size screen with a camera mounted on top—I sat reviewing the institute's extensive makeover menu. Starting from the top, it includes:

Hair replacement surgery. Through a variety of techniques, among them "scalp reduction, tissue expansion, strip grafts, scalp flaps or clusters of punch grafts (plugs, miniplugs and microplugs)."

Brow lift. To minimize creases in the forehead and hooding over the eyes.

Blepharoplasty. To cut away excess skin and fat around the eyes, eliminating drooping upper eyelids and puffy bags below.

Otoplasty. To reshape ears.

Rhinoplasty. To reduce, increase or reshape the nose.

Collagen and fat injections. To enhance the lips or plump up sunken facial skin.

Liposuction. To remove fat deposits.

Chemical peel. To eliminate wrinkled, blemished, unevenly pigmented or sun-damaged skin.

Dermabrasion. To remove scarring from acne using a high-speed rotary wheel or laser surgery.

Rhytidectomy (face lift). To tighten sagging skin and the underlying facial muscles over which the skin is then redraped.

Facial implants. To change the basic shape and balance of the face (building up a receding chin, adding prominence to cheekbones, etc.).

Brachioplasty. To lift and tighten upper-arm skin.

Augmentation mammoplasty (breast enlargement).

Mastopexy (breast lift).

Gynecomastia (male breast reduction).

Abdominoplasty (tummy tuck).

"Well…" I began, having no idea where to begin, feeling a bit embarrassed (even in my journalistic play-acting mode) at the prospect of conducting before a stranger that private, contentious exchange we all have with our reflections. I felt as if I were at the barbershop, except that it was me, not just my hair, that was about to be cut and styled, actually a kind of mega-cut: my various requests to be carried out on the once-removed image of myself on Martin's computer screen. "Well, what do you think I need?"

"Men always do that," Martin said, laughing. "They always make me tell them what I think they need. Women will just come right out and say, 'Look, I've got this huge stomach—fix it.'"

She then took up her imaging wand and, I suppose to spare me any further discomfort, began to go at what she kindly referred to as "the most common problem areas for men." She shaved away the slight sag that 40 years of living has left beneath my chin, then lightly brushed off the spray of wrinkles about my eyes. Next, she set to work on—I'll call it—the singularity of my nose.

"It's not that I have anything against yours," she explained, eagerly whittling it away to what even I, as I watched over her shoulder, recognized to be some ideal—by Western Civilization's standards, at least—of a perfectly proportioned nose.

She placed the wand back in its holder and pushed a button; within seconds I was holding a single before-and-after Polaroid, the old and the renovated me, framed side by side. I sat staring at it, caught somewhere between an immediate recognition of the obvious improvement and an incipient sense of disappointment in my own delight over it—of rebuke at my own vanity. This, of course, sounds like an internal argument that one might conduct over the prospect of actually having plastic surgery performed. But for an ever-growing number of people there is no such conflict.

Not long ago, cosmetic plastic surgery was more or less the exclusive province of the rich and the famous, changing one's profile being, to most people, a high-profile pursuit. But in recent years, with the steady advancement of cosmetic surgery techniques, and with the advancing age of youth-clutching baby boomers, there has been what might be called a growing democratization of the desire to redo oneself, a greater willingness to challenge that age-old notion of growing old gracefully. There were nearly 400,000 esthetic surgeries performed in the United States in 1994, the last year for which records are available. Of these, 65 percent were done on people with family incomes under $50,000 a year, even though health insurance does not cover cosmetic surgery. Meanwhile, according to a survey by the American Society of Plastic and Reconstructive Surgeons, the number of people who say they approve of esthetic surgery, either for themselves or others, has increased 50 percent in the last decade. And among those undergoing cosmetic repairs are more and more men and a surprising number of men and women under 30—pioneers in what might be called preventive physical renovation.

This growing acceptance of plastic surgery may reflect more than America's peculiar inability to let go of youth or the advances in surgical techniques (which, for instance, allow one to have an endoscopic brow lift for $2,100 and be back at work in a week). We are witnessing a fundamental change in our thinking about the body. As ridiculous as this may sound, we now spend far more time with our bodies. Not only are we living longer, but a good many of us are doing so in less physically demanding ways. In an automated, computer-driven world of office-tower days, there is more idle time than ever, time to reassess, to argue and to tinker, to both remark and—in the form of tattoos and various body jewelry that have become so popular among youth—mark upon our increasingly disengaged, physically disappointed selves. Selves that, with the proliferation of Instamatic cameras and video camcorders and computer-imaging machines, we now routinely contemplate from afar.

It is as though we are collectively experiencing with our bodies that same dull shock that we have all felt upon hearing our voices on a tape recorder for the first time. We have achieved, in a sense, a complete objectification of the body, the body as a separate and increasingly obsolete entity, a "meat cage," to borrow a phrase popular among the denizens of cyberculture. Moreover, with magazine and television ads daily driving home to us the disparity between ourselves and some one or other bodily ideal, we are going to health clubs in ever-increasing numbers just to work on our bodies, to physically re-engage them, shape them, make them as hard and sculptured as the very machines that have displaced them. And we are going, in ever-increasing numbers, to places like the Institute for Aesthetic and Reconstructive Surgery, not only to resculpture the parts of ourselves that exercise can't reach but, in some cases, to alter ourselves in ways that go beyond the relatively surface manipulations of "esthetic" surgery.

There are advanced procedures that entail, for example, breaking apart and reconfiguring, like so many new puzzle pieces, the skeletal orbits of the face and skull. These methods are, of course, most often used to repair severe birth defects or disfigurements resulting from accidents. But given the growing acceptance of cosmetic surgery and the increasing refinement of modern surgical techniques, the day may not be far off when people will be regularly availing themselves of the most drastic reconstructive surgeries for purely esthetic purposes. Just how far will people be willing to go in their pursuit of that ideal of beauty? And what of this pursuit, even in its less radical manifestations? Are we, in fact, whittling away at something deeper than creases and wrinkles and layers of fat?

Take another look at yourself, the vessel you've awakened with and spoken to for years, your ally or antagonist (depending on your self-image) but no longer your only option. Somewhere between an inviolable temple and a useless meat cage fall our present-day selves — not so much temples as temperable clay; less prisons than points of departure.

Posted on a white marker board, outside the automatic doors that lead to the institute's four operating rooms, was the surgery schedule for Tuesday, Jan. 23. There was to be a 7:30 A.M. endoscopic brow lift, lower-lid skin excision and blepharoplasty on a 43-year-old female; a 9:30 A.M. nasal revision on a 51-year-old male; a 10 A.M. ultrasonic liposuction of a 46-year-old female's abdomen, inner and outer thighs and knees; a midday bilateral cheek implant and lower-eye skin excision on a 38-year-old male; and at 1:30 P.M., an augmentation mammoplasty bilateral on a 20-year-old female.

Stopping first at the pre-op unit where patients are prepped for surgery, I stepped into a sterile one-piece "bunny suit" and then passed down the hallway through the automatic doors to O.R. No. 14, where Dr. G. Patrick Maxwell, the institute's founder and medical director, would be performing the early-morning brow lift and blepharoplasty. Various attendants and scrub nurses were moving about in the white light, readying equipment and implements. Maxwell was still back in one of the pre-op unit's mini-hospital rooms, drawing plans for the surgery on his patient's body. All plastic surgery patients are prepped this way, turned into human contour maps—concentric circles, hash marks and arrows drawn in black marker to guide surgeons past an existing face, belly or thigh toward a more desirable one.

Maxwell's patient arrived in O.R. No. 14 partly sedated, her forehead mapped with vertical lines running from the top of her outer eyelids up to her hairline and little arrows marked alongside indicating the general direction her brow would be going. Maxwell, a lean, handsome man in his late 40's, was dressed in hospital blues and a pair of black high-top Nikes. He had a surgeon's light strapped to his head like a miner's lamp. Stepping to the table, he took up a huge hypodermic filled with a clear liquid and began injecting it into the woman's forehead.

"This is epinephrine," he said for my benefit in his soft Southern drawl, the woman's forehead slowly expanding. "It promotes vasal constriction and helps reduce the bleeding."

He picked up his scalpel and, just above the woman's hairline, made three small vertical incisions through the soft tissue right down to the bone. As I stood by, I found myself recalling a conversation I'd had with Dr. Joseph M. Rosen, a plastic and reconstructive surgeon at the Dartmouth-Hitchcock Medical Center in Lebanon, N.H. "It used to be we just removed excess skin," he had told me. "But now esthetic surgery involves changing the shape and structure of the underlying bones and soft tissue. Some esthetic surgery involves changing the entire craniofacial structure."

Rosen is hardly your typical plastic surgeon. I first came upon his name in a recently published book, "Escape Velocity: Cyberculture at the End of the Century," by Mark Dery, a cultural critic of the on-line world. Rosen teaches a course at Dartmouth College's Thayer School of Engineering called "Artificial People: From Clay to Computers" and will tell you, without blinking, that making a winged human is entirely possible using arm-to-torso skin flaps. (These flaps wouldn't actually enable you to fly, but you could glide like a flying squirrel from perch to perch.) When I asked him about the prospect of more and more people opting to have their faces reconstructed for esthetic reasons, he said, somewhat impatiently: "Yes, that's already happening, but what's interesting is, how does a kangaroo jump as high as it does? What happens is that one of its muscles is modified just like a rubber band that gets loaded heavily and then fires. So what stops a basketball player from coming in and having me do the same thing technically to his legs?"

Rosen went on to say. "The thing about plastic surgery is that it's the only surgery that's also a philosophy. Dr. Ambroise Paré, the father of modern surgery, talked back in the 16th century about how the task is to fix the defects of nature. That defines the field, and on a given day, we are called upon to assist any number of chest, abdominal or eye surgeons when they have problems. But then on top of it all we actually operate on people who are normal. It's amazing that we're allowed to do that, the idea that we can get a permit to operate on someone who is totally normal is an unbelievable privilege. In a way it's the ultimate surgery."

Maxwell was by now deep inside the forehead of the middle-aged woman whose brow no longer pleased her. Having picked up his endoscope—essentially a thin tubular probe with a camera on the end—he was inserting it into one of the scalp incisions. The deep red inner terrain

of the woman's forehead appeared on the monitor above the operating table. Through another of the incisions Maxwell inserted a long, thin scalpel.

"Only a few years ago with this type of surgery, we'd have to make an incision from ear to ear," he explained, running his finger along the woman's scalp line, "and then peel the face down to work on the layers beneath. There'd be a bigger scar, a lot more trauma and swelling and a lot longer recovery time. This patient will be up and back to work in seven days." For the next half-hour or more, I watched as scope and scalpel moved in careful tandem, working their way toward the muscle above the woman's nose. "This is the corrugator muscle, the frown muscle," Maxwell said as he began cutting it away. "This procedure will minimize the chance for a scowling appearance."

With each snip, I imagined the ghosts of the myriad worries that furled this woman's forehead flying free: there, the times she troubled over school exams; there, the long waits for loved ones who were late; and there, the years of confusion and doubt. I thought of Tracy Martin in computer imaging telling me about her own brow lift a few days before. I had asked her, at one point, to furrow her brow. She tried. Her forehead didn't move. "I can't," she said. "And it doesn't bug me at all. I don't want to grimace."

Once Maxwell had withdrawn both endoscope and scalpel, the woman's forehead was irrigated with antibiotic solution, the skin bulging outward into a smooth cask. Maxwell pressed it back flush again the skull bone, bloodstained liquid gushing from the incisions above. He signaled me over, bid me to look down where the narrow beam of his headlamp shone into one of the incisions. "Do you see that thin layer there?" he asked, his scalpel tip pointing to a bright scrim of red tissue called the galea, a Latin word meaning "leather helmet." The blade flicked. There was a faint rip, then only white. "That's the skull," Maxwell said.

Next, he took up a small silver hammer and then held up between his thumb and forefinger the tiniest metal post. "Just like picture hangers you'd put in a wall," he said, tapping one into the woman's skull, then repeating the procedure on the opposite side of her forehead. Two long stitching strings were then threaded into the soft undertissue just above the woman's eyebrows. When Maxwell took hold of the loose ends, her forehead stretched upward slightly and smoothed out. Images of some favorite furrowed faces ran through my mind—Auden's, Lincoln's, Simone Signoret's, my father's—as Maxwell tied the strings to the posts, hanging on his middle-aged patient the picture of a new, unblemished brow.

Cosmetic surgery has long been considered a willful violation of not one but two basic Judeo-Christian precepts: that which forbids tampering with the body, desecrating its temple, and that which preaches against the kind of excessive vanity thought to motivate such a desecration. But in recent years, as the cost has grown less prohibitive and the trauma less severe, and as we have begun seeing more and more flesh—and judging it by standards set by magazines, movies and the like—cosmetic surgery has come to be seen as a kind of condoned cheating.

"There is that notion that we shouldn't disturb what's been given us," Rosen says. "But we're much better at it now. And after all, our society is very much caught up with appearances. In California now it seems sort of uncommon to find someone who hasn't had work done. In places like rural New England there is still a resistance because, I would argue, when you're in a small village and everyone knows who you are and you're very much a part of the community matrix, it really doesn't profit you much to change your appearance. But in a place like New York City, it's easier to make that step across into a new area."

Purely cosmetic plastic surgery is a modern phenomenon, its advent being, appropriately enough, coincidental with the rise in the mid- to late 19th century of the great urban industrial centers, where a person's countenance—freed from the confines of the provincial village—could become a fully anonymous, publicly paraded entity. The nose was the focal point of the earliest cosmetic procedures. According to Blair O. Rogers's "History of the Development of Aesthetic Surgery," which I came upon in the institute's library, a surgeon in Berlin named Johann F. Dieffenbach is credited with performing, in the mid 1800's, the first rhinoplasties. In 1881, an otoplasty to correct protruding ears was done at the Manhattan Eye, Ear and Throat Hospital; in 1895, the first breast augmentation was tried in Heidelberg, using a transplanted tumor from the patient's back. The first tummy tuck was undertaken four years later, and not long after the first eyelid surgeries and face lifts. Bit by bit, a scheme for the body's full reshaping was beginning to take shape.

Of course, the earliest techniques left a lot to be desired. During the first two decades of the 20th century, for example, cosmetic surgeons were injecting low-melting paraffin into patients' faces and then sculpturing their features as though working up figures for a wax museum. The immediate effects were often quite stunning, but people eventually began dropping dead from huge wax clots in their arteries. The first face lifts had their problems too. They entailed making various S- or quarter-moon-shaped excisions along the hairline or just behind the ears and then stitching together the opposite sides of the opening. There were no deadly side effects from these operations, but the great elasticity of skin rendered their effects fleeting. In her later years, a desperate Marlene Deitrich is said to have resorted to gathering up and securing her own recurring postlift sags by sticking hat pins into the scalp beneath her wig.

Nose jobs became more popular in the 50's and 60's, as white ethnic girls were taken to New York or Los Angeles by their mothers to obtain smaller Protestant prows. But few ventured beyond their noses, for even that operation meant blackened eyes and, later, the staring and whispering of pious neighbors. Even into the 1970's, radical cosmetic surgery meant the one sudden pullback of an aging notable's face: images of Phyllis Diller struggling to clamp her teeth down on that cigarette holder come to mind.

Now, however, you can have your breasts or your buttocks resculptured into a variety of shapes. Ultrasonic liposuction can emulsify end draw away liters of fat with a fraction of the bruising and blood loss that result from traditional liposuction. Along with the full facial reconfigurings available, there is a whole new array of supplemental surgeries, like pectoral and calf implants and the recently devised and increasingly popular phalloplasty, in which the penis can—with varying degrees of success—be lengthened and (with fat injections or skin grafts) thickened. Beyond this, some plastic surgery experts suggest that in the near future bodily changes will take place outside the operating room with fat-burning pills, anti-aging growth hormones that promote muscle and bone growth and the application of laboratory-grown skin cells that will, in effect, give people a new coat of actual skin.

In the information age, cosmetic surgery might best be construed as a kind of real-life morphing, traveling in place, a palliative—more lasting than a mere change of clothes or a new hairdo—for our growing inability in a seemingly speeded-up world to sit still in our own skins. People like Cindy Jackson, the founder of the Cosmetic Surgery Network, a consulting company for people contemplating surgical revision, have often been cited as an example of this new tendency toward extreme shape-shifting. In the past eight years, Jackson, 40, has undergone more than 20 cosmetic surgery procedures—face and brow lifts, two nose jobs, lip surgery, tummy tucks, liposuctions and breast implants—all by way of incrementally morphing herself in the general direction of her declared female paradigm, the Barbie doll. Transforming a human body to Barbie's specifications is beyond the capabilities of even today's cosmetic surgery wizards. "They've done dimensional studies," Rosen says. "In order to be Barbie you'd have to be about 6 feet, 7 inches and 120 pounds. You'd have to have a number of ribs removed. I think it would be physically impossible to be Barbie." Still, Jackson presses on in her mission literally to live up to what she calls the contemporary Western feminine ideal. In her most recent revision, surgeons sawed off a portion of her jawbone so that her chin, like Barbie's, would be even in profile with her upper lip. Jackson believes that there is nearly limitless potential for changing the body, that "your body doesn't have to be static through its entire life."

Another well-known modern shape-shifter is Orlan, a French performance artist and professor of fine arts at the École des Beaux Arts in Dijon. She has had nine plastic surgery operations since 1990, each one part of a work in progress called "The Ultimate Masterpiece: The Reincarnation of St. Orlan." Her idea is to embody the classical Western ideal of feminine beauty, arming her plastic surgeons with a computer-generated blueprint for her new face, a composite of features drawn from Renaissance masterpieces: Mona Lisa's forehead, the eyes of Gérôme's Psyche, the chin of Botticelli's Venus, the mouth of Boucher's Europa, the nose of a 16th century Diana. Each procedure has been "performed" before a small art-world audience; all are on videotape, and one, in 1993 at the Sandra Gering Gallery in New York, was broadcast by satellite to art galleries around the world.

Her operating "theater" is usually decorated with crucifixes, plastic flowers and fruits. Surgeons, attendants and the patient herself sport scrubs designed by Orlan or top fashion designers like Paco Rabanne. Opting for local rather than general anesthesia, Orlan remains conscious throughout and choreographs the entire proceeding, reading from various psychoanalytic and literary texts and interacting with her audience via telephone or fax. All excised pieces of Orlan—hair, skin, fat—are preserved in petri dishes and later sold as "reliquaries" of the flesh of St. Orlan. She sees herself as a kind of modern-day martyr, not only to her art but also to the cause of questioning "the standards of beauty imposed by our society by using the process of plastic surgery to a different end than the usual patient does."

Of course, the majority of plastic surgery patients are not looking for a full-scale identity change. They want to have their original selves refined or renewed—motivated by that age-old desire to undo the effects of aging. Not only has life expentancy increased, but, as a recent study by the National Institutes of Health revealed, our quality of life has as well, creating, in turn, a greater disjuncture between the way people feel and the way they look, a disjuncture that people are resorting to cosmetic surgery to mend.

But the motivation is often more than mere vanity. A growing number of middle-aged workers, men especially, now have to compete with those much younger than themselves for positions in a more service-oriented, image-driven work place. The very nature of work is changing, shifting from the mills and factories—places where brow lifts and tummy tucks tend not to be the hot topic of conversation—to the world of suits, sales and first impressions. Or, as Tracy Martin in computer imaging put it, "Men just have to put their best face forward more now than ever before."

And this idea that we are how we look is not limited to the work place. According to "From Head to Soul," one of the brochures I picked up in the institute's lobby, "We are judged approximately 93 percent on what we do not say." The author of this conclusion, Joyce Knudson, is a member of the Association of Image Consultants International, and offers a special training program in image enhancement. "It has been shown time after time," she goes on to explain, "that attractive people get more and keep more jobs, have more friends, and have better family relationships."

It is this apotheosizing of "image" in conjunction with the refinement of modern surgical techniques—the increasing ease and efficacy with which cosmetic surgery can, in essence, implement attractiveness—that is prompting what may be the most age-resistant and image-conscious generation of men and women in history to explore their own plasticity.

"So many of us baby boomers grew up with the illusion of eternal youth in a self-indulgent environment," said Christiane Haemmerlein, the institute's paramedical esthetician. "And now the techniques to help maintain that youthful appearance are all available."

Haemmerlein, an incredibly fresh-looking 40-year-old, had the fat around her eyes removed 10 years ago and plans to have more work done soon. The current trend in plastic surgery is for people to have a number of mini-lifts, -nips and -tucks starting say, in their late 20's, to take advantage of the elasticity and suppleness of younger skin.

"I feel if you can look at your parents, then you can start to see something in yourself that is going that way," Martin said. "I know my dad has heavy eyelids, and I thought, When I'm 30, my eyelids are going to be past the point of no return. So with surgery I was able nip that in the bud, and now I won't get to where I'm not happy with my eyes."

One afternoon at the institute I witnessed a breast augmentation. The patient, a 20-year-old who, although she possessed what Maxwell and everyone else in O.R No. 12 agreed were perfectly shaped breasts, wanted larger ones, much larger, in fact, than Maxwell was willing to make them.

"I'm not going to do anything weird," he said to me as his surgical assistants injected air into the test implants he had just inserted in the young woman's chest, her breasts slowly rising. "There are extremes that people want that are inappropriate, and so it's a matter of understanding where a patient is coming from, whether they're emotionally and psychologically stable and whether what they want is attainable. In this case, it came down to the patient and I understanding what her perception of larger breasts meant, not just the size of the cup, but the shape and the look of the cleavage, what she wants to see when she goes like this." Maxwell squeezed his upper arms inward on his own chest.

"O.K," he said. "Lift her up, please."

The operating table was tilted almost straight upright. In the brash light, with all but the patient's upper torso wrapped tightly in surgical blankets, her full, taut breasts unswayed now by gravity, it was as though we were viewing a marble bust from antiquity. I thought of something Rosen had said when I asked him how a surgeon decides on the shape of a given altered part. "I once asked that of a well-known plastic surgeon I work with," he answered, "and he told me he went to the Louvre and studied art, and that while he was aware of many different standards and measuring systems, he ultimately decided by what looked right and nice."

Maxwell also had a theory about esthetic standards. "Now, if she were a New York City fashion model, walking the runways in Armani or Calvin Klein, she probably would have been happy with the breasts she has," he said. "A lot has to do with regional preferences. In the South and West, big breasts are the thing, whereas in the East the enlargements are more modest, and in the Midwest there's nothing. My final dialogue with this patient was that I would make her as large as I can and yet still be within the parameters of normal that she and I discussed."

Maxwell eyed his patient another moment. He had a few cubic centimeters of air taken out of the left breast; then he returned to the table, removed the test implants and inserted the permanent saline-solution ones. He stepped back once more and then nodded his approval. That's good," he said. "They'll sit more naturally when the swelling goes down."'

Nothing in this new image-driven world is necessarily inalterable. In essence, we have arrived at a whole other way of thinking about our physical selves—the body not as a fixed-cast that we inherit from our parents and begrudgingly grow old in, but as pliant putty, a work in progress.

"My husband doesn't pay much attention to this plastic surgery stuff," Haemmerlein, the esthetician, said. "And I tell him, 'You better watch out or I'm going to look like your daughter one day.'"

Maxwell's 12:30 patient—a 41-year-old male whose birth date, I happened to note on his chart, is but a few days from my own—emerged from prep looking like some remote tribesman all done up in war paint: a modern-day man briefly bearing the ritual markings of a primitive one in order to obtain a whole new face. He was to have the very procedures performed on him that Martin had imaged on me: a lipoplasty of the area under his chin and a blepharoplasty of the upper and lower eyelids. He was also scheduled for a "bilateral buccal fat pad removal" (taking out the fat pads in his cheeks), although two hours into the surgery, Maxwell was still working on the chin area, where excessive bleeding and scar tissue from an old cosmetic surgery operation was rendering a fairly routine procedure something of a struggle.

As I stood by watching yet another mound of bloodied gauze being extracted from the patient's opened chin pouch, I thought that if he or any of the others whose surgeries I had attended in the past two days, could have watched as well—could have seen the detached forehead flaps, the excised eyelid skin, the torrents of blood, the liters of cream-colored lique-fied fat flowing out through ultrasonic liposuction tubes—then they might have opted not to go through with them. And then it occurred to me that it is precisely our obliviousness to such detail that cosmetic surgery pivots around: it's a total obsession with surface, with appearances. The plastic surgeons and operating room assistants have to pry behind our person (from the Latin "persona," meaning "mask worn by an actor") to snip, pull, buttress and rehang the underpinnings of our identities. The patients want only the restored and completed picture.

When Maxwell finished with his patient's chin, he set to work on the face, carefully cutting away sliver moons of skin from the upper and lower eyelids, removing pockets of fat from the sacks below the eyes. For the sake of symmetry, he had one of his assistants keep track of just how much tissue he was removing from each side by laying it out in a pattern that roughly mirrored the source from which it was taken: a nether-face of skin and fat building on a blue towel atop the patient's chest.

I stepped outside and made my way to the surgeon's lounge for a breather. One of the surgical unit's scrub nurses was leaning against a counter in her hospital blues, eating lunch. I asked her if it didn't wear her down after a while, watching so many of these surgeries. She just shrugged and said that the only thing that really bothered her was people who had liposuction when it was exercise they needed.

Given the number of institute employees I had already encountered who had opted for plastic surgery, I inquired if she, too, hadn't had some work done. She nodded in a way that suggested I was a bit dim to have even asked. "My breasts and my eyes," she said. I mentioned, so as not to feel too excluded, that I had, from time to time, considered doing something about my chin. "You could use a little work on your eyes, too," she said. "Those upper lids." I started looking about for a bit of glass in which to review myself when a young female surgeon I had seen chatting with Maxwell in the O.R. the day before walked by with her face all marked up for her own operation, scheduled for later that afternoon.

I felt as if I were trapped in some bad sci-fi film: "The Invasion of the Visage Snatchers."

My mind flashed back to a scene I had taken in the day before. Maxwell had invited me up to his office to talk, and then had showed me into an adjacent dark room, where he took out sheet upon sheet of slides—"before" and "after" shots of the many patients he had operated on. I glimpsed a cavalcade of bared breasts, bellies, buttocks and thighs; of anonymous refashioned faces—each set displaying remarkable changes and yet the whole of them, the composite photo, exposing something far more poignant about self-perception and the lengths some people will go in pursuit of that ideal of beauty.

The montage underscored at once the disparity between our actual and our longed-for selves, and the degree to which our notion of who we are is determined by the way we look. In each of the "after" photos the subjects bear slightly startled expressions, as though they have just crossed over into some unchartered terrain. Our identities are so inextricably tied up with the face we view in the mirror, and the way we think others view it, that changing it can be deeply traumatizing. We are each, in a sense, the compendium of a lifetime's worth of self-assessments—prolonged stares and passing glimpses at our selves. Even those who opt for cosmetic surgery often haven't fully considered the psychological impact of such alterations.

"A lot of work is done here modifying people's expectations," said Rose Ann Miller, the institute's administrative director. "People might think they want to look a certain way, but if it's very different, and they look in the mirror for the first time, it can be a shock. The mind still has to envelop that new image."

And yet despite these attempts to modify desires and expectations, people tend to approach their surgeries with a very clear notion of what they want and a fearless conviction about obtaining it. "Most people are very accurate about their facial shortcomings," said Dr. Joseph B. DeLozier, a craniofacial expert at the institute. "They are very direct about what they don't have and what they want. They often walk in with pictures of what they want, especially when it comes to the nose. They'll say, 'Give me that nose.'"

One 55-year-old face-lift recipient told me she couldn't wait to leave the institute and show off her new visage. "I'm very excited," she said, her bandages having just recently been removed, her face still slightly swollen and blotched red from the added laser surgery she had had to remove surface wrinkles. "I can't wait to heal, get on some makeup and get back out there. It's kind of like an adventure."

The newly refined art of plastic surgery has begun to present us with unprecedented options that may forever change the lifelong argument we conduct with our physical selves. What happens, the question becomes, if the face we are born with no longer has to be the one we settle for? If surgeons can entirely rearrange a person's visage, if homeliness, whatever that is exactly, is remediable, why then wouldn't an adolescent, for example, who is deeply unhappy with his or her appearance and suffering horribly for it, just avoid the slings and arrows altogether by having it changed?

DeLozier is doing more and more cosmetic surgeries on young people. "They make up a big part of my practice," he said. "Of course, we have to be a little careful, because the face is often still growing at that stage, and you can make somebody worse if you operate on parts of the face before it has completely developed."

I asked him if the extreme alterations now possible presented psychological problems for the recipients, literal identity crises.

"They do have a new identity," he said, "but with our ability to show people what they will look like ahead of time, it's most often not an issue. If people come in with fairly normal features telling you they can't stand their face, then I will spend a lot of time trying to make sure they're being realistic about what surgery is going to do for them. People will confuse their appearance with their personality and their place in life and expect a radical change in their appearance to make their life better. But if you operate on someone who is psychologically fine, then they usually have little trouble embracing their new appearance."

I began to imagine a world of entirely altered faces, one in which it will seem unnatural not to have been altered, unnatural to be natural; a population surgically amended toward some lowest common denominator of face in the same way that local regional accents are said by linguists to be blurring into that nondescript entity known as "nightly news anchor speak." If the amending of a person's perceived esthetic shortcomings is to become as routine as a tonsillectomy, then what effect will this have, in turn, upon that so-called character-building process by which we overcome our obsession with appearances and get on to more essential matters; the process by which those who have felt daily slighted because of their "unattractiveness" fight back in the form of achievements far more substantive and lasting than mere appearance? Might necessary and useful anger get diluted by an epidemic of attractiveness, diminishing, in turn, the level of creativity and achievement as well?

The fact is that for all the apparent radicalness of cosmetic surgery, it is, in the end, radically conformist—a form of slavish obeisance to an outwardly imposed standard of beauty. Will the new advances in plastic surgery help to foster some bleak Orwellian (or is that Orlanian?) nightmare in which we all become slaves to a culturally imposed, uniform standard of beauty, or will the overwhelming majority of us, despite the increasing availability of high-tech and relatively painless reshaping options, continue to prefer and proffer to the world our original faces for what they are—infinite variations on a theme called beauty?

As I left the surgical unit, one of the few unrevised workers that I spoke with at the institute said that she had been considering having some work done. "But then," she said, a nicely furrowed frown indicating a still-intact corrugator muscle, "I looked at my nose in the mirror and thought, That's my father there, and that's my mother right there in the upper eyes."

DISCUSSION QUESTIONS

The Cuts That Go Deeper

1. How have the meanings of cosmetic surgery changed over the past 30 years?

2. What is the "philosophy" of cosmetic surgery, and what are its ironies?

3. What fundamental changes in our thinking about the body are reflected in increasing acceptance of cosmetic surgery?

4. If cosmetic surgery continues to become more and more common, what kind of meanings could slight defects and flaws in appearance develop?

5. Do you agree with the author's cautions and concerns about cosmetic surgery?

CHAPTER 4

Dress in Human Interaction

Mary Lynn Damhorst

AFTER YOU HAVE READ THIS CHAPTER, YOU WILL COMPREHEND:

- The vast array of meanings that can be communicated through dress.

- The processes through which meanings of dress can develop.

- How the meanings of dress are culturally and socially constructed.

- Why the meanings of dress, even traditional dress, are dynamic and, in some ways, always changing.

- How meanings of dress reflect the self and society.

An endless variety of meanings may be communicated through dress. The roles we play, the culture we live in, our gender, age, and personal interests and preferences all may be indicated through dress and appearance. We express identity through dress and use dress to help us get jobs done, prop up self-confidence, and sometimes to have fun. Certain events and ceremonies are made important or festive with special attire.

Recall from Chapter 1 that meanings of symbols such as clothing are something other than the clothing object itself. Dress refers to or indicates qualities or meanings more abstract than the actual physical objects of dress. For example, dress makes visual proclamations such as "this person is male," "the wearer is competent at her job," "this person is fashionable," "this person is Nigerian," "I'm attending a black-tie affair," "I completed the 1996 10 K Fox Valley Run," or "I wanna be like the Spice Girls." Many dress messages are such that we might feel a bit silly having to verbally pronounce them upon first meetings with others.

McCracken (1988) contended that, because dress remains fixed or unchanged during most interactions, it tends to communicate stable characteristics of the wearer. Keep in mind, however, that many of us change our clothing and sometimes other aspects of grooming every day or several times a day. The "stable" characteristics we communicate may be stable only for a few hours. On one day, a student might throw on a sloppy sweatsuit to go to class because he's having a bad day and doesn't want to pay much attention to dress. Usually, however, that same student rarely wears sweats to class, preferring jeans and sweaters. Another student might dress in sweats every day; his attire might indicate personal attitudes about school, self, and dress. The meanings of his dress may be far more complex than not caring about his appearance, however. In the student's mind, and to the group he hangs out with, sloppy may be "cool." Surface-level interpretations do not always accurately tap the meanings of dress.

Table 4.1 lists three general types of dress messages with some examples of these three classifications of dress meanings. Dress refers to or indicates abstract characteristics of the wearer, relationships the wearer has with others, and the type of situation in which the wearer is involved. These three types of messages help to summarize the vast array of meanings that dress can convey.

Multiple Identities

As discussed in Chapter 1, the self includes many identities. In any one appearance, an individual expresses only a small portion of those identities. Business women in Des Moines, Iowa, expressed several aspects of identity in their business appearances every day (Kimle & Damhorst, 1997). They communicated stable roles such as female gender,

TABLE 4.1
Types of Dress Messages

Personal Characteristics
  Traits
  Values, attitudes, interests
  Lifestyle
  Mood

Relationships
  Cultural background
  Group membership
  Group roles—family, occupation, friendship, gender
  Status, prestige

Definition of Situation
  Intention to act
  Orientation—formal, casual, serious, playful

office manager, and age, as well as situational meanings such as casual days or formal presentations to important clients. The business women realized that they also carefully planned their appearances to express subtle aspects of their positions and capabilities in the business community. For example, they incorporated what were traditionally masculine suit-style components to express characteristics of efficiency, seriousness, and professionalism, but they tried not to look too masculine; they attempted to express a feminine aesthetic and attractiveness without looking too feminine or too sexy; they dressed to look up-to-date and savvy about fashion without being too fashion-forward; appearing conservative and businesslike was important, but indicating some small degree of individuality was necessary to avoid looking mindlessly conforming. The business women seemed to juggle an array of meanings in their appearances, but avoided taking any meanings to extremes. None of the women, however, reported that she ever tried to express in her work dress that she was a mother, that she loved hiking or tennis, or that she was trying to find a new mate. All of the women had other roles and characteristics, but none of them ever expressed all aspects of themselves in their work dress. Any adult appearance will have an array of meanings, but no appearance indicates everything about the self.

Rituals, Celebrations, and Deep Meanings

Ritual dress such as graduation gowns or prom tuxedos may mark important transitions and events in life. Figure 4.1 shows young women in cotillion ball dresses for a traditional celebration that introduces young women to their community and marks their passage into adulthood.

At times, more individualistic behaviors such as a haircut or getting a tattoo may signify a life transition such as a divorce or career change, as in "Memorial Decoration"

FIGURE 4.1 *Debutantes at New York cotillion ball all wear white.*

by Sanders. Some dress, such as sorority pins or wedding rings, may do more than serve as a badge of membership or status. For some, such items symbolize deep attachments and interpersonal connections.

Meanings of dress may be more than personal. In "Bird Feathers" sacred meanings invested in feathers incorporated into Native American dance dress connect the wearer to the essential spirit of tribe, totemic animal, and nature. Sacred religious dress (e.g., priest or pastor vestments) and some governmental dress (e.g., judicial robes, queen's regalia) may hold profound meanings that symbolize important values and principles of society (see Figure 4.2).

"Costume" Histories

In "Saving Grace" in Chapter 9, Jackie White reports that many consumers store and save clothes, shoes, and jewelry as mementos that have built up meanings over the years. Everyday dress accumulates meanings over time that remind the owner of his or her past and self-identity. Even the mundane experiences of purchase, use, and maintenance of

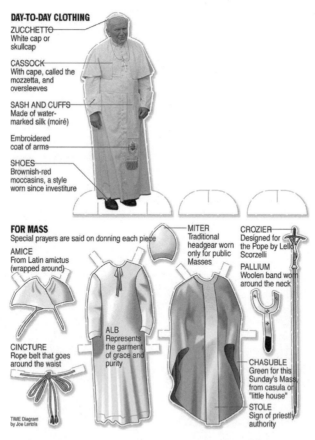

FIGURE 4.2 *Papal paper dolls? The Pope wears garments steeped in religious significance and hundreds of years of tradition.*

dress may add personal meanings to dress (McCracken, 1986). Objects of clothing and adornment may remind us of special experiences we had while wearing that item or of a time when we felt especially attractive or comfortable. Garments can become companions, of sorts, who have accompanied the wearer through many of life's journeys.

Some types of dress develop a history beyond personal experience and capture the history of the times in which they were worn. The denim blue jean, invented in the 1840s by Levi Strauss, has a history spanning more than 150 years. First developed for gold miners, lumberjacks, ranchers, and other workers developing the western frontier, the durable and functional blue jean soon was adopted by laborers throughout the United States. Independence, hard labor, and unpretentiousness are some of the original meanings of jeans that still are associated with the garment today (Morgado, 1981). Wilson in "Rebel, Rebel" (Chapter 13) traces the 20th-century history of blue jeans and new meanings that have been added over time.

LEARNING AND PRODUCING THE MEANINGS OF DRESS

The histories described above involve accumulation of meanings over time in dress. Some other meaning processes we will explore are meaning through association, symbolic interaction and discourse, individual perceiver constructions of interpretations, media and marketing productions of meanings, and role socialization.

Association

Dress may develop meanings as the result of long years of association with a group or type of people. In "Memorial Decoration" Clinton Sanders discusses how tattoos became historically associated with marginal and deviant groups in western societies, thereby imparting a hint of deviance in the act of tattooing even today when it has become fashionable. In contrast, among the Maori in New Zealand, and islanders of Motua in Papua, New Guinea, tattooing is a normative, common form of dress. (See Figure 4.5.)

In "Scent of a Market" Wilkie describes how certain scents become associated with pleasant or unpleasant events and experiences, shaping personal and cultural preferences for scents. We respond to some scents through a conditioned reflex as the scent becomes integrally connected to something or someone who is repellent or attractive.

Black leather motorcycle jackets are worn by a variety of individuals but are associated with biker gangs. To play on this association as deviant but chic, the J. Peterman Company featured a black motorcycle jacket on its Fall 1998 catalog (Owner's Manual No. 70). The jacket is subtitled, "A Masterpiece of Intimidation," alluding to the fearful reputation of bikers.

Some components of dress have deeply rooted meanings developed through a complex interplay of societal and personal associations. The following excerpt from *Arranged Marriage* by Claitra Banerjee Divakaruni (1995) describes how a young woman and her mother in contemporary India use traditional meanings of colors to express personal concerns and agendas:

> We had some arguments about this sari. I wanted a blue one for the journey, because blue is the color of possibility, the color of the sky through which I would be traveling. But mother said there must be red in it because red is the color of luck for married women. Finally, father found one to satisfy us both: midnight blue with a thin red border. (p. 20)

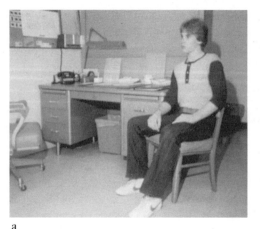

a   b

FIGURE 4.3 *Police and high school counselors described the boy differently when he wore (a) neat dress versus (b) messy dress.*

Producing Meanings

Not all meanings of dress have long histories of development. As mentioned in Chapter 3, meaning is a continual process of production and exchange. In the **symbolic interaction** process outlined by George Herbert Mead (1934), an individual tries out a behavior such as a new haircut, others react to that behavior, and the individual reflects on the reactions to the behavior. Based on these reactions and the individual's reflections upon and feelings about others' reactions, he will decide whether to continue wearing the new haircut or perhaps wear a hat to hide it. A continual process of presentation of appearance and reflection on reviews or feedback from others responding to appearance develops meanings of appearance over time. Gregory Stone (1962) referred to this process as **discourse**. Repeated patterns of appearance become integrated as components of self-identity. An individual may have to **negotiate** with others the meaning of appearance to move all parties to new understandings of the meaning of dress. For example, an adolescent girl may spend a great deal of time trying to convince her parents that piercing her navel is quite acceptable.

Groups may be involved in presenting programs of appearance to the surrounding public to develop a group identity. Catholic nuns' habits are dress symbols with a long history of meanings. Since the 1960s, when many orders discarded the habit for secular clothing, nuns have had to negotiate appropriate appearances for their role as women religious with their constituencies and with the church. Appearing in society as women rather than cloaked nuns has redefined the role and identity of these women. "From Habit to Fashion: Dress of Catholic Women Religious" in Chapter 12 explores these issues.

Organizations and institutions may make purposeful efforts to establish meanings of dress. For example, the Boy Scouts of America revised the uniform for Boy Scouts in the early 1980s. Their official introduction and handbook established the **denotative** or official meaning of their dress. However, an organization does not always control the **connotations** or implied meanings of dress. The khaki-colored uniforms for Boy Scouts may appear a bit militaristic to some observers.

Perceiver as Part of Production

The wearer or the organization establishing a dress symbol is not the only party involved in producing and exchanging meanings. The perceiver's unique characteristics—such as age, gender, attitudes and values, occupation, social class, and culture—influence interpretations of dress. Littrell and Berger (1985–1986), for example, found that occupational backgrounds influenced the interpretations of dress of an adolescent boy by police officers and high school counselors (see Figure 4.3). Counselors discussed the boy in relation to the types of school problems or concerns he might have. Police considered whether the boy was in trouble with the law. The observer takes an active role in making sense of appearances; the responses of the observer to dress may shape the meanings of dress for the wearer.

Media and Marketers as Producers of Meanings

The various forms of media constantly present images that shape meanings of appearances throughout the world. The movie *Raiders of the Lost Ark*, for example, firmly established the brown leather bomber jacket and hat worn by the star, Harrison Ford, as symbols of the independent, intrepid adventurer. Retailers, such as Banana Republic,

"...a YOUNG WOMAN dressed in a stunning white and purple outfit with an enormous hat."

—J. Cameron, "Titanic" screenplay scene direction

April 10, 1912. The Titanic prepares to depart.

Rose DeWitt Bukater steps onto the dock and into our lives. She had wanted to wear black; fortunately (in this case) her fiancé insisted otherwise.

Exact reproduction of Rose's boarding suit, which helped win an Academy Award for costume designer Deborah L. Scott. Fully-lined. Cream wool with contrasting Purple velvet trim, including covered buttons. The high-waisted, ankle-length skirt has two slits for ease of walking.

Rose's Boarding Dress (No. AAV10217). Price: $695. Imported. Women's sizes: 4 through 12. Comes with guarantee that you will look stunning, too, but have smoother sailing.

Rose's Boarding Blouse (No. AAV10218), exact reproduction in fine Cream cotton; fetching lace trim at rounded collar and down the front, covered placket, slim Black silk charmeuse tie. Price: $145. Imported. Women's sizes: 4 through 12.

"Hockley, she is splendid."

Rose's Boarding Hat. (No. AAV10219). Reproduction in Purple straw with oversized silk taffeta bow and trim; that big brim (21" across, a bit more manageable than the original) frames your face gorgeously. Price: $350. One adjustable size fits all.

FIGURE 4.4 *J. Peterman catalog offered replicates of Rose DeWitt Bukater's cruise departure suit in their Christmas 1998 Gift Book No. 4.*

hurried to provide glamour-seeking consumers with similar jackets and hats after the movie debuted in 1981. In its Christmas 1998 Gift Book No. 4, J. Peterman offered copies of costumes seen in the movies *Titanic* and *L. A. Confidential*. It remains to be seen whether these movies will have an influence on fashion over the following years. (See Figure 4.4.)

Media is integral to the fashion industry. Fashion magazines regularly present proposals of what might become the latest fashions. The industry is continually attempting to manage the meanings of dress through packaging, advertising, and store layouts, as is shown in the article "Scent of a Market." It is up to consumers, of course, to make the final purchase decisions that will turn new styles into fashions.

Ogle and Damhorst (in press) found another example of media involvement in shaping dress meanings. In popular press, magazines, newspapers, and other work dress advice articles targeted at women during the late 1980s and early 1990s, an ongoing dispute revolved around the issue of sexually suggestive clothing in the workplace. A number of authors adamantly denounced all revealing and provocative styles as unfit for the office. They felt that women's work clothes should not attract the sexual attention of male colleagues to avoid undermining of the woman's authority and reputation and to reduce chances of sexual harassment. In contrast, just as many other authors claimed the opposite, that suggestive and even seductive dress allows women to use their sexuality to their advantage in the business arena. Sexiness was considered a sign of assertiveness by these authors and conducive to emphasizing professional power. They felt that women's well-earned confidence in business roles should enable them to depart from conservative and masculine suit styles. The promoters of sexiness suggested a tough but feminine, sexy but authoritative look achieved through suggestive, but not showy garments. The authors taking opposite sides on this issue never argued openly in their articles. Nevertheless, dress-for-success articles seemed to serve as a grandstand for negotiation of new standards of appearance for women in business.

IMPACT OF MEANINGS

Meanings of dress often have implications for the wearer beyond personal expression. Because of its personal meanings, dress may act as a facilitator and help the wearer get things done, such as a job or a task. Dress may help an individual engage in fun or creative activities. Some individuals also become intensely involved in dress for aesthetic or fetishistic purposes. Of course, the meanings of dress may elicit stereotypes that move observers to treat the wearer in a way that has negative or positive consequences. Dress also serves as therapy, to help the individual bolster self-esteem, cope with problems, or escape from stress.

Dress as Facilitator

Think back to the last time you wore a costume. Did you act differently while wearing the costume? Miller et al. (1991, 1993) examined how costumes facilitate play and celebration. The wearer becomes disguised and anonymous in some costumes, lending more freedom to perform acts that are silly, uninhibited, and sometimes illegal. In other cases, the costume puts the wearer in a role that is not ordinary for the wearer. This can enable taking on the fantasy role or acting as someone other than one's self.

Olson describes the "war paint" that Drake University football player Mark Goldsberry wears for every game in "Bulldog with Character Makeup." Mark's painted face readies and focuses him for the game and inspires his teammates to play well. Dress sometimes energizes and motivates both wearer and observer.

Creativity and the Fun of Expression

Personal expression can be fun and creative. In "Hail to the T," Reed regales the history of the T-shirt as a portable billboard. T-shirts may sport humor, reminders of places or events, reports of accomplishments, art works, status brands, political ideas, or favorite rock groups. T-shirts scream out the wearer's interests, tastes, and involvements more explicitly than do most items of clothing.

We play with dress in a variety of ways. People sometimes wear costumes to enjoy a different identity or to associate with a person or role that one can never truly attain. For some, dress can serve as a fetish, eliciting sexual excitement or fantasies (Steele, 1996).

The aesthetic components of dress may be meaningful and provide enjoyment to the wearer or observer as well (Fiore & Paff, 1997). McLeod (1998), for example, found that African American business men often described a strong aesthetic involvement in their work dress. Some experienced pleasure in the feel of a high-quality suit fabric or a pant leg that draped perfectly. Many felt a certain joy in looking professional and attractive in a business suit. Purchasing attire and dressing for work (i.e., purchasing a tie, shirt, and suit that go together perfectly) was, in part, a creative experience.

Stereotypes

As we learned in Chapter 3, dress is an assemblage, and the clothing, hair, accessories, and grooming assembled on the body sends out a network of information. In some cases, a certain "look" or assemblage of dress may come to be associated with a certain type of wearer, and all who wear that look may risk classification as that type of person.

In some cases, just one component of appearance, such as skin color, can elicit a stereotype. Individuals from ethnic minority groups may use dress to overcome negative stereotypes assigned to their ethnicity. Chapter 7 includes several readings (by Russell, Schneider, and McLeod) in which African Americans describe how they use professional dress to facilitate impressions of competence and credibility in job roles. In contrast, Rodriguez in "Complexion" (see Chapter 10) describes how his dark skin color gave him many identity challenges as he grew up in California during the 1950s. Darker skin color at that time was associated with lower-status minorities.

Dress as Therapy or Escape

We have all heard of compulsive shoppers who go bankrupt because of an insatiable need to buy clothes. Other individuals use attention to appearance not only to bolster self-confidence but to compensate for lack of self-esteem (Holloman, 1989). John Littrell in "Employing Clothing for Therapeutic Change in Brief Counseling" describes how he encourages counseling patients to use clothing to help solve problems and make progress in the therapy process.

Many individuals use dress to help them escape in small ways from problems. Lynne Taetzsch in "Fighting Natural" (1994) described how she bleached her hair to help her cope with larger struggles and dissatisfactions during her life. She recalls one incident of "hair therapy" (p. 247):

At twenty-seven I arrived at Newark Airport with one suitcase and my nine-month-old baby in my arms. When my father and sister picked me up, they made such a fuss over the baby that no one put my suitcase in the car. It was gone, of course, when my father went back to get it. I had come home once again after a failed attempt at living in California—this time with my husband John who had never found a job in the four years we'd lived in L.A. So there I was with the clothes on my back, my baby, and a fist-ful of debts.

Everyone felt sorry for me, of course—a young woman alone in the world with her baby. One of my brothers handed me twenty dollars to ease the pain. I immediately went out and bought a box of Clairol silver blond. Perhaps if I could look in the mirror and see someone else, this life wouldn't really be happening to me.

Summary

In this chapter we have discussed how a vast array of meanings may be communicated through dress. In general, these meanings indicate characteristics of the wearer, relationships of the wearer with others, or situations in which the wearer is involved. Meanings of dress are produced and developed through diverse and complex processes, involving individuals, groups, media, and historical accumulations of meanings. In addition to all of these, meanings of dress often have implications for the wearer. Some meanings associated with certain aspects of dress or appearance may have negative consequences for the stereotyped wearer. The implications are not always negative, however. Dress can facilitate activity and creativity, and may bolster confidence in the self, or may serve as an escape from problems or stress.

Suggested Readings

Blumhagen, D. W. (1979). The doctor's white coat: The image of the physician in modern America. *Annals of Internal Medicine, 91,* 111–116.

Foster, P. (Ed.) (1994). *Minding the body: Women writers on body and soul.* New York: Bantam Doubleday Dell Publishing Group.

Melinkoff, E. (1984). *What we wore: An offbeat social history of women's clothing, 1950 to 1980.* New York: Quill.

Stone, G. P. 1962. Appearance and the self. In A. M. Rose (Ed.), *Human behavior and social processes: An interactionist approach,* pp. 86–118. New York: Houghton Mifflin.

LEARNING ACTIVITY

Trying on a New Identity[1]

Objective: To examine how dressing in a way that is out of the ordinary for yourself makes you feel and causes you to reflect upon your identity. Using systematic observation techniques, record other people's reactions to your dress, your reactions to reviews, and comparisons of self to others.

Procedure

Select one of the following dress incongruities in planning the dress you will wear for at least six hours during one day to produce one or more of the following meanings:

1. *Situational incongruity*: Dress that is inappropriate for the occasion or situation such as clothing that is much too formal for class or clothing inappropriate for the weather.

2. *Role incongruity*: Dress that is inappropriate for a role, such as wearing dress that is too mature, too youthful, or that is appropriate for a role you do not hold.

3. *Personality incongruity*: Dress inconsistent with your self-image or lifestyle and worn in the presence of friends who know you well. Examples could be major changes in the amount of makeup or jewelry you normally wear or changes in the tightness or sexiness of your clothing.

4. *Off-key or faux pas*: Dress appropriate to your situation, role, and personality but with one mistake such as a zipper unzipped, noticeable stains or holes, or unmatched socks.

Wear your dress incongruity for at least six hours in one day. Try to wear it on a day when you will be seen by and interact with a variety of people you know, as well as people you know very little or not at all.

It is most instructive and fun to pretend that nothing is different about yourself. Let others react to you before explaining to them that what you are doing is an experiment.

Recording Your Experience

Carry a notebook to record your reactions and the reactions of others as the experiment progresses. Record information on the following:

- Positive and negative responses.

- Responses from males and females.

- Verbal and nonverbal responses.

- Responses from acquaintances, friends, and strangers.

- Your feelings and thoughts about yourself before you venture out wearing the costume and as the experiment progresses.

- Comparisons of self with others' appearances.

---

1. Thanks to Mary Littrell, Darlene Fratzke, and the belated Ruth Marshall for help in developing this exercise over years of experimentation.

Also, describe the places you went, situations you were involved in, types of people with whom you interacted, types of people you were seen by but with whom you did not specifically interact, date and times of day for each entry in your recordings, and weather conditions you may have experienced.

Questions to Ponder

1. Were the reviews you received consistent with your program of dress? Consistent with your expectations? Consistent with any part of your self?

2. Was your self validated or challenged during the experiment? In what way? Plot how your feelings about your dress and yourself changed during the day.

3. What factors may have affected your accuracy in interpreting responses from others?

4. Did you learn anything about how people respond to others on the basis of appearance? What types of meanings did various others seem to assign to your dress?

5. Did you learn anything about yourself—your capabilities, the influence others have on how you feel, your reliance on appearance to project a preferred identity?

6. Will you ever dress this way again?

References

Divakaruni, C. B. (1995). *Arranged marriage*. New York: Doubleday.

Fiore, A. M., & Paff, J. (1997, July). *Facilitating the Integration of Textiles and Clothing Subject Matter by Students Part One: Dimensions of a Model and Taxonomy*. Paper presented to the Confluences: Fashioning Intercultural Perspectives Conference of the International Textile and Apparel Association and Université de la Mode, Lyon, France.

Holloman, L. O. (1989). Self-esteem and selected clothing attitudes of black adults: Implications for counseling. *Journal of Multicultural Counseling and Development, 17*, 50–61.

Kimle, P. A., & Damhorst, M. L. (1997). A grounded theory model of the ideal business image for women. *Symbolic Interaction, 20*, 45–68.

Littrell, M. A., & Berger, E. A. (1985–1986). Perceiver's occupation and client's grooming: Influence on person perception. *Clothing and Textiles Research Journal, 4*(2), 48–55.

McLeod, H. (1998). *African American male executive dress: Issues of aesthetics, conformity and ethnic identity*. Unpublished Master's thesis, Iowa State University, Ames.

McCracken, G. (1986). Culture and consumption: A theoretical account of the structure and movement of the cultural meaning of consumer goods. *Journal of consumer Research, 123*, 71–84.

McCracken, G. (1988). *Culture and consumption*. Bloomington: Indiana University Press.

Mead, G. H. (1934). *Mind, self, and society*. Chicago: The University of Chicago Press.

Miller, K. A., Jasper, C. R., & Hill, D. R. (1991). Costume and the perception of identity and role. *Perceptual and Motor Skills, 72,* 807–813.

Miller, K. A., Jasper, C. R., & Hill, D. R. (1993). Dressing in costume and the use of alcohol, marijuana, and other drugs by college students. *Adolescence, 28*(109), 189–198.

Morgado, M. (1981). *The blue jean thing.* (slide set and script). Honolulu: University of Hawaii.

Ogle, J. P., & Damhorst, M. L. (in press). Dress for success in the popular press. In K.P.P. Johnson and S. J. Lennon (Eds.), *Power and appearance.* Oxford, England: Berg.

Steele, V. (1996). *Fetish: Fashion, sex & power.* New York: Oxford University Press.

Stone, G. P. (1962). Appearance and the self. In A. M. Rose (Ed.), *Human behavior and social processes: An interactionist approach,* pp. 86–118. New York: Houghton Mifflin.

Taetzsch, L. (1994). Fighting natural. In P. Foster (Ed.), *Minding the body: Women writers on body and soul,* (pp. 233–247). New York: Bantam Doubleday Dell Publishing Group.

16 Memorial Decoration: Women, Tattooing, and the Meanings of Body Alteration

Clinton Sanders

"We have always been tattooers from mother to daughter," declared the old woman. "But there must have been one who started it," said the interpreter, "and where did she get her talent from?" "From a sheikh." "But from what sheikh?" The reply was long in coming, but at last she blurted out: "Let's say it was Satan."[1]

The human body is a compelling and eminently flexible instrument of communication. For thousands of years, cultures have required, condoned, or condemned physical alterations because of their coded meanings in the daily drama of social interaction. Some modes of body change are easily assumed and discarded. Clothing, makeup, hairstyle, and other transient forms typically are used to communicate the person's understanding of a specific situation or event, to mark a break from the ordinary round of events, to indicate change in status through the life-cycle, and to identify one as a participant in a particular subgroup.

Both Nuban men and women of the Sudan, for example, use elaborate body painting to enhance the beauty of their bodies and to signify their clan membership. From the time they are betrothed at the age of six until they are married, Nuban women oil and apply ocher to their bodies daily, using colors appropriate for their father's clan section. Following marriage and childbirth, the woman changes the color to suit her husband's clan. The painting communicates social connectedness and reproductive status as well as providing a means of expressing and enhancing the wearer's unique sense of her individual beauty.[2] For other reasons, the woman in our own culture uses makeup to accentuate and enhance her beauty as it is socially defined and to inform others about her interests and, to some extent, her ideological orientations. During the "first wave" of the women's movement, makeup became imbued with considerable meaning as it symbolized one's acceptance or rejection of commercial, male-imposed conceptions of female attractiveness. At the same

FIGURE 4.5 *Traditional moko chin tattoo on Maori woman. Huia Hono Nahuia is a prominent elder of Rotorua, New Zealand.*

time, the young woman's ability to exercise control over her "madeup" self was commonly a source of familial conflict, for it symbolized her movement away from parental/paternal supervision and connection to her age and gender peers.[3]

Sanders, Clinton, "Memorial Decoration: Women, Tattooing, and the Meanings of Body Alteration," *Michigan Quarterly Review* (Winter 1991) Copyright © 1997 by W. B. Saunders.

While modes of body alteration such as makeup, hairstyle, and clothing mark transient—and often conflictual—social identities and changes, they are easily modified should they lose their various attractions or communicative significance. Permanent body alterations, on the other hand, tend to carry more weighty symbolic baggage. In most cultural contexts, infibulation (piercing), cicatrization (scarification), body sculpting, tattooing, and other forms of permanent corporeal change represent commitment, lifelong status, and permanent identities. Commonly, this assumption of a new social identity—and, consequently, the repudiation of the old identity—is accompanied by ritual. As befitting rites of significant social connectedness, these communal acts of permanent body alteration entail considerable pain. For example, the legs and arms of Kayan women in Borneo are ornately tattooed with traditional animal designs. Being tattooed below the elbow is particularly important since undecorated arms are defined as indicating cowardice—that the woman was unable to endure the pain of the procedure.[4] Such marks act both to distinguish the marked person from other individuals and symbolically to incorporate her as a member of the group.

The following discussion focuses on a common mode of permanent marking—tattooing—as it is directed at and understood by women. Following a brief overview of women's tattooing in folk and tribal cultures, I will present an account of the purposes and social consequences of the tattoo for women in contemporary American society.

WOMEN AND TATTOOING IN FOLK AND TRIBAL CULTURES

Tattooing fulfills three general purposes as it is practiced and defined in non-western cultures. As mentioned above, it defines the wearers cumulative or permanent identity both within and outside of the tatooed person's social group. One of the oldest verifiable examples of tattooing was found on the mummified body of an Egyptian priestess dated about 2,000 B.C. Egyptian tattooing was practiced exclusively upon women, especially dancers, singers, and priestesses in the service of Bes, the deity associated with recreation. These tattoos afforded protection as well as publicly identifying them as devotees of Bes.[5]

In addition to its connection to religious practice, tattooing has been and is used to identify one's membership in groups whose members share activities and skills in common. In seventeenth and eighteenth century Japan, large-scale tattoos depicting samurai, dragons, gods, and other traditional figural themes enjoyed great popularity. This tattoo practice (irezumi after "ire," meaning "to insert" and "zumi" referring to the pigment) was fashionable particularly among middle-class merchants forbidden by "sumptuary laws" to wear the silks, brocades, and precious metals reserved for the nobility. The complex and intensely beautiful tattoo work, which allowed one to display wealth while formally abiding by the law, provided a moderately subtle means of nose-thumbing directed at the traditional elites. By the mid-nineteenth century (the late Edo period), full-body tattooing had filtered down the class structure and identified workers and members of certain guilds (firefighters, butchers, porters). Though irezumi was largely employed by men, geishas also adopted it as an occupational identifier and as a decorative enhancement of their commercial, sexual, and entertainment activities.[6] While most nineteenth-century Japanese tattooists were male, it was not uncommon for young women to become proficient in the practice as well.[7]

The most common identity function of the female tattoo is in communicating the woman's marital status and genealogical background. This purpose was most complexly realized among the Maoris of New Zealand. First encountered by Western explorers in the late eighteenth century, moko tattooing was practiced by both men and women. The black spirals, waves, flowing lines, and geometric designs of moko were inscribed principally on the face, neck, legs, and buttocks. Placement and design had distinct meaning, and the knowledgeable person could "read" the wearer's social rank, lineage, honorable acts, special skills, and relationships. Women's moko was not commonly as extensive as that worn by men. It was usually limited to designs on the lips and chin. However, because of their lineage some women carried more extensive designs. They were socially regarded as men and given the rights and privileges enjoyed by chiefs. Women were particularly honored for their mastery of valued skills, and poets, weavers, teachers, and dyers of cloth were highly respected and identified by their facial tattoos. Due largely to the influence of Christian missionaries, the practice of *moko* began to decline in the early twentieth century. However, women were more likely to continue to be tattooed than were Maori men. Currently, with the resurgence of interest in cultural backgrounds and customs among the Maori, young women in particular are once again acquiring this mark of their heritage.[8]

Because it accentuates and calls attention to the physical differences between men and women, tattooing, like other modes of body alteration, is related to the definitions of beauty and erotic appeal which comprise the complex system of meaning constituting culture. Tattooing beautifies and enhances sexual attractiveness. On the Papuan island of Motua, for example, women's tattoos are expressly seen as a means of provoking sexual interest. The application of tattoos is done in stages with the young girl receiving her first design on the stomach around age ten. Somewhat later, tattoos are added to her face although the central portion of the face is left unmarked unless the girl is from an important family. At puberty the young woman's back, arms, and upper chest are tattooed, followed later by application of designs on the rest of her chest and inner thighs. Like *moko*, the tattoo images are abstract and highly meaningful, denoting family accomplishments and honors. After the woman is married, a final V-shaped design is added to her chest signifying sexual fidelity to her husband.[9]

The third major function of the tattoo in tribal and folk cultures involves magical or protective utility. Although tattooing is proscribed in Islamic cultures as a desecration of the divine creation, the practice continues to be common among the women in nomadic groups of Yemen. Typically applied by women tattooists to the lower lip and chin, tattoos are seen as providing a magical protection from physical ailments—particularly eye problems, sterility, and venereal diseases—and as sustaining the good health of the wearer. The tattoo is especially beneficial in this regard if mother's milk is mixed with the pigment and if the tattoo procedure is accompanied by the recitation of a verse from the Koran.[10]

Similarly, Ainu women living on the northernmost island of Japan believe that facial tattoos provide good health, afford protection from the pains of menstruation, and guarantee a happy afterlife. The Ainu woman's tattoo was once regarded as so significant that untattooed women were excluded from participation in banquets and other group activities.[11]

This relationship between the tattoo mark and the afterlife is not uncommon in tattooing cultures. The spirits of Long Glat women of Borneo were seen as differentially honored based on the extensiveness of the tattooing they acquired in life. Those most heavily tattooed were allowed to gather pearls from the heavenly river, while those with only partial decorations were only permitted to watch.[12]

A BRIEF HISTORY OF TATTOOING IN THE WEST

The modern history of tattooing in Western culture begins with the voyages of Captain James Cook in the 1760s and his encounter with tribal tattooing in the South Pacific. Cook introduced the Tahitian word "ta-tu" (meaning "to strike" or "to mark"), and soon tattoo replaced "pricking" as the common English term for the practice. Many of Cook's officers and seamen were tattooed on his first voyage and, on a later expedition, Cook returned to England with a heavily tattooed Tahitian prince who became the first of a popular series of exotic tattooed "curiosities" to be exhibited in Europe. By the end of the nineteenth century, tattooing became something of a fad among the European aristocracy—both male and female— and members of the upper classes. Such dignitaries as Queen Olga of Sweden, Princess Weldemar of Denmark, Princess Anne of Bourbon-Parma, the Duchess of Marlborough, and Lady Randolph Churchill (Winston's mother) bore tattoos—most of them applied by Tom Riley, George Burchett, or Sutherland Macdonald, the best known tattooists of the time. The "tattoo rage" as it was dubbed by the press spread to the U.S. where in 1897 the *New York World* reported that 75 percent (!) of American society women were tattooed.[13] The tattoo fad among upper-class women in this country continued into the 1920s—prompted in part by the widespread publicity surrounding the discovery of the mummy of a tattooed Egyptian princess at Luxor.

In addition to small decorative tattoos, cosmetic tattooing also enjoyed considerable popularity from the turn of the century into the 1920s. Much of the work done on women by tattooists consisted of darkening eyebrows and lashes, applying permanent color to cheeks, and tattooing red lips. Tattooing had, however, a fairly short life as an accepted and fashionable practice. The press was quite active in condemning tattooing—especially as it was adopted by women and members of the elite. Tattooing was, as socialite Ward McAllister put it, suitable "for an illiterate seaman, but hardly for an aristocrat."

Relegated again to its "rightful place" as a custom of criminals, sailors, prostitutes, manual laborers, and other disreputable types, tattooing was reestablished as a symbol of social marginality. Like many other forms of physical deviance it found a home as a commercial curiosity in circuses, "freak" shows, and other exhibition settings in the early part of this century. The first "tattooed lady"—"La Belle Irene"—appeared in 1890. From that time through the Great Depression tattooed women dominated this corner of the amusement world. The appeal of tattooed women derived from the fact that they had to reveal considerable areas of their bodies in order for their designs to be appreciated by the public. Tattooed women also represented all that respectable women were conventionally expected to reject. Their body decorations clearly indicated to avid viewers that they were sexual, flamboyant, and "immoral." In order to deflect some of the stigma associated with their tattoos, a number of the women concocted stories in which they were captured by "savages" and forcibly tattooed or were compelled to acquire the marks after having been kidnapped by run-of-the-mill domestic criminals. Annie Howard, for example, who, along with her brother Frank, made up one of the most famous tattooed couples (they worked for Barnum and Bailey in the early 1900s), maintained that they had both been shipwrecked in the South Seas and forcibly tattooed. In actuality, much of Annie's work was done by her brother who eventually opened a tattoo shop in Boston when he retired from show businesses.[14]

WOMEN AND CONTEMPORARY TATTOOING

As my fieldwork took me more and more deeply into the social milieu of tattooing, I was consistently struck by the numerous differences between male tattoo recipients and the women who chose to alter/enhance their bodies in this way. In the studios I studied, forty to fifty percent of the clientele were women—a far higher proportion than I anticipated when I began the research.[15] The designs chosen and the area of the body upon which the person decides to carry the tattoo are issues which significantly distinguish men from women. While men typically have their tattoos inscribed on their arms, women tend to locate tattoos on the breast, back of the shoulder, hip/pubic area, or lower abdomen. These differences in placement are related to differing definitions of the function of the tattoo. Men commonly see the tattoo as a public symbol whereby they communicate aspects of their social identity to casual acquaintances and strangers in the course of everyday interaction. Women, on the other hand, are more concerned with the perceived unconventionality and possible stigmatization resulting from the tattoo mark. Rather than being a public declaration of self, for the woman the tattoo is a private decoration—a bodily enhancement meant for personal enjoyment and the private appreciation of those with whom she has intimate relationships.

Women also choose different designs than do men. Rather than selecting the cartoony, death-oriented, or aggressive images typically requested by men, women favor floral pieces, butterflies, gentle mythical beasts (the unicorn and Pegasus are quite popular), and colorful birds such as parrots or peacocks. Since exceptions to general rules are significant illustrations of those rules, I quote from a field conversation I had with a young woman who carried an unusual tattoo (a snake coiled around a large rose) on what is, for a woman, an unconventional body location (her bicep).

Sanders: How did you decide on that particular design?

Woman: I wanted something really different, and I'd never seen a tattoo like this on a woman before. I really like it, but sometimes I look at it and wish I didn't have it.

Sanders: That's interesting. When do you wish you didn't have it?

Woman: When I'm getting real dressed up in a sleeveless dress and I want to look…uh, prissy and feminine. People look at a tattoo and think you're real bad…a loose person. But I'm not.

The concern expressed by this woman about the negative symbolic baggage carried by tattoos in American society tells us why wearing a tattoo is both a liability and a pleasure. The tattoo is a "label" which potentially marks a person—especially a woman—as unconventional and, therefore, as possibly dangerous or at least unpredictable. However, our culture contains rather ambivalent messages about unconventionality, for "being different" is valued as well as condemned. Part of the power of the tattoo, then, derives from its ability to identify the bearer as uniquely individual and as unconcerned with the approval or disapproval of those who are unmarked and unknowledgeable. One woman expressed this point quite simply:

> I can't think of one compact reason [I got a tattoo]. They are pretty. But most of all they are a poke in the eye to people who don't have them—people who are straights or whatever.

The fact that women routinely choose "private skin" on which to have their tattoos placed raises a variety of issues that directly affect their service encounters with the tattooist and their experience in the studio. For one thing, the tattoo operation is more painful when directed at bony areas such as the hip or chest or sensitive spots like the breast or lower abdomen. Pain is the major focus of the questions asked by clients. The pain involved in getting a tattoo depends on body location, the tattooist's skill, and the customer's pain threshold and most people adjust to it fairly well after the initial jolt (tattooists refer to this adjustment as "settling to the needle"). A small proportion of clients—between two and five percent—pull away from the needle, become nauseated, or pass out. My observations verified a major item of general tattoo lore—these problematic responses almost always involve male customers. Women are far more able to cope with the discomfort of the tattoo experience. Tattooists account for this difference by saying that child-bearing makes women more accustomed to pain, women are used to having their bodies altered and worked on, or that women tattooees are more committed to the process than are men.[16]

The tattoo locations typically chosen by women require intimate exposure of the body. Most tattoo artists are male (though women are increasingly entering the practice), and the tattoo setting continues to be predominantly male-oriented. Many women clients are understandably uncomfortable about exposing their bodies in the company of gawking male strangers. Some studios now have curtained-off areas where women (or, in some cases, males receiving tattoos near their genitals) can enjoy a measure of privacy while being tattooed. Women themselves cope with the exposure issue in various ways. They wear clothes that will allow for the baring of the tattooed area while concealing the surrounding parts of the body, and they typically arrive at the tattoo setting in the company of female friends who provide support and a measure of protection.

Most tattooists are aware of the concerns of their women clients and adopt a businesslike, desexualized demeanor when working on women's bodies. One of my interviewees described her experience in acquiring a small tattoo on her breast.

> I remember changing my clothes right there in the room—just turned my back to the door. It's not that I wasn't aware that the artist was a male person, but it just wasn't threatening. I had my shirt off and he applied the outline. He was actually going to touch me. He was so close to me when he was bending over me…you just get a distance there. It's like when a doctor is examining your breasts or something, or a gynecological exam. His hands were warm and reassuring.…I didn't get the feeling that he was looking at me in any sexual way. I think he said later that he only sees two inches of flesh at once. He was also rather matter-of-fact. He said that I should be careful not to place the tattoo too near my nipple. To be explicit and talk about my body—my nipple—was rather matter-of-fact and reassuring.

In addition to defining the tattoo as a piece of "body jewelry" (a term commonly used by the women I interviewed), female tattooees consistently saw the tattoo as a symbolic object which demonstrated their connection to other people. The "vow" tattoo has a lengthy history in western tattooing[17] and both men and women commonly receive tattoos which represent their most valued relationships. While the permanence of the tattoo is symbolically important as an expression of a lasting association, human relationships are such that tattoos typically outlive most social connections. Many tattooists attempt to discourage clients from having other people's names permanently affixed to their bodies. The application of "coverup" tattoos over outdated vow tattoos is a major source of income in most studios. At times, given the intense focus on relationships with men which is still a consequence of the cultural understandings acquired by women, vow tattooing can be carried to rather sad extremes. Here is an account by a tattoo artist which is but one of a number of similar stories I encountered in the course of my research.

> [I have this customer whose] boyfriend is some hot soul musician....Every time she comes in she gets the same thing. She gets his name put on her thigh. I don't know, she's real nice looking but she has G—T about fifteen times on her thigh. I try to get her to let me put a heart or a butterfly or something on, but she just wants the name. Last time she was in she got something different. She got "property of" put before the name.

During the years I was immersed in the tattoo community, I noticed fewer women using tattoos in this way—to symbolically and permanently affix their relationships with men to their bodies. Prompted, I believe, by some of the significant changes in women's orientations as well as the broadening of the tattoo client base resulting in women from a wider range of sociocultural backgrounds acquiring tattoos, the women I encountered increasingly were using tattoos to celebrate themselves and commemorate significant transitions in their lives. One of the more thoughtful tattooists with whom I worked described this orientation as follows:

> I do see that many people get tattooed to find out again...to say, "Who was I before I got into

this lost position?" It's almost like a tattoo pulls you back to a certain kind of reality about who you are as an individual...it transfers you to that next step in your life....A woman will come in and say, "Well, I just went through a really ugly divorce. My husband had control of my body and now I have it again....I want a tattoo that says that I have the courage to get this, that I have the courage to take on the rest of my life. I'm going to do what I want to do and do what I have to do to survive as a person."

Another interviewee remarked:

> [My decision to get a tattoo] came at a time of transition. The tattoo is a marking of one point of my life to another. I was going through a divorce. I was doing something for me. I wanted this tattoo....I did this not for a husband, not for parents, not for a boss, not for anyone else but me....I was at a time in my life when I was primed to have a new experience. All of the things I had learned up to that point—you get married, you settle down, you have a family, you buy a house—do all the traditional things, copy your parents down the line—it wasn't working. My internal reason was to make a statement.

This heartening view of the symbolic import of the tattoo—as a representation of control over and pride in the physical self—was the dominant purpose expressed by women tattooees. They commemorated a renewed affirmation of who they were and marked the passing of one stage and movement into another, hopefully more satisfying, one. Yet, even if the future offered further disappointment and change—as it was sure to—the tattoo would remain to remind the bearer that she had exercised courage. As one woman poignantly described the meaning of her tattoo:

> In the future when I'm sitting around and bored with my life and I wonder if I was ever young once and did exciting things, I can look at the tattoo and remember.

Notes

This discussion is based on some seven years of ethnographic field work within the social world surrounding tattooing. Readers interested in exploring the larger phenomenon of tattoo production and collection—especially as tattooing has moved toward being defined as a legitimate artistic practice—should see Clinton R. Sanders, *Customizing the Body: The Art and Culture of Tattooing* (Philadelphia: Temple University Press, 1989)

1. Anthropological conversation with a Moroccan tattoo-woman quoted in Michel Thevoz, *The Painted Body* (New York: Rizzoli, 1984), p. 70.

2. James Faris, "Significance of Differences in the Male and Female Personal Art of the Southeast Nuba," Arnold Rubin, ed., *Marks of Civilization*, (Los Angeles: UCLA Museum of Cultural History, 1988), pp. 29–40.

3. As in contemporary western society, application of decorative body paint often occurs in situations of considerable sociability. For example, among the Kayapo of Brazil young women and wives gather three times a year to paint each other's bodies with complex, non-representational designs which have erotic significance and symbolically refer to the animal myths which are central to tribal cosmology. See Thevoz, p. 52.

4. R. W. B. Scutt and Christopher Gotch, *Art, Sex and Symbol* (New York: A. S. Barnes, 1974), p. 40.

5. See Robert Bianchi, "Tattoo in Ancient Egypt," Arnold Rubin, ed., *Marks of Civilization*, pp. 21–28.

6. See Donald Richie and Ian Buruma, *The Japanese Tattoo* (New York: Weatherhill, 1980) and Donald McCallum, "Historical and Cultural Dimensions of the Tattoo in Japan," Arnold Rubin, ed., *Marks of Civilization*, pp. 109–134.

7. Marcia Tucker, "Pssst! Wanna See My Tattoo…," *Ms.*, April 1976, p. 29.

8. See D. R. Simmons, *Ta Moko: The Art of Maori Tattoo* (Auckland: Reed Methuen, 1986) and Peter Gathercole, "Contexts of Maori *Moko*," Arnold Rubin, ed., *Marks of Civilization*, pp. 171–177.

9. Scutt and Gotch, p. 143. The eroticism of women's body alterations is especially emphasized among the Nuba of the Sudan. After the Nuban woman weans her first child a series of scars are cut into her back. These marks are defined as quite beautiful and are regarded as sexually arousing when felt by the woman's lovers during intercourse (Faris, pp. 34–35).

10. Victoria Ebin, *The Body Decorated* (New York: Thames and Hudson, 1979); Thevoz, p. 70.

11. Jerome Levy, Margaret Sewell, and Norman Goldstein, "A Short History of Tattooing," *Journal of Dermatologic Surgery and Oncology* 5 (11), November 1979, p. 852; Norman Goldstein and Margaret Sewell, "Tattoos in Different Cultures," *Journal of Dermatologic Surgery and Oncology* 5 (11), November 1979, p. 858. See also Richie and Buruma, pp. 13–14.

12. Jocelyn Paine, "Skin Deep: A Brief History of Tattooing," *Mankind* 6, May 1979, p. 42.

13. See Scutt and Gotch, pp. 165–178; George Burchett and Peter Leighton, *Memoirs of a Tattooist* (London: Oldbourne, 1958); W. D. Hambly, *The History of Tattooing and Its Significance* (Detroit: Gale Research, 1974 [1925]).

14. C. W. Eldridge, *Early Tattoo Attractions* (Berkeley, CA: Tattoo Archive, 1981); Robert Bogdan, *Freak Show* (Chicago: University of Chicago Press, 1988), pp. 241–250; Scutt and Gotch, pp. 151–160; Tucker, pp. 31–33.

15. In addition to the observations and conversations included in my fieldnotes, my information is drawn from six lengthy, semi-structured interviews with women tattooees and data drawn from a four-page questionnaire completed by clients in two studios and by tattoo enthusiasts attending the 1984 convention of the National Tattoo Association. Approximately one-third of the survey respondents were women. In general, the women tattooees were better educated than the men but reported significantly lower yearly incomes. For details, see Sanders, pp. 169–170.

16. Sanders, pp. 136–138; Tucker, p. 31.

17. Following the Battle of Hastings (1066), King Harald's mutilated body was identified by the name "Edith" tattooed over his heart.

Memorial Decoration: Women, Tattooing, and the Meanings of Body Alteration

1. What are or were meanings of tattoos among some groups of women in non-Western culture?

2. Who originally tattooed in Western culture, and how did those original tattoo wearers influence the meanings of tattoos even today?

3. How are relationships expressed or shaped by tattoos in U.S. culture?

4. How are tattoos gendered, that is, used differently by men and women?

5. Do you have any tattoos? If so, what meanings does the tattoo have for you? Has it affected your relationships with others?

6. Do tattoos on other people affect your impressions of them? If so, how? Do your impressions depend on the wearer and the tattoo design?

17   Bird Feathers

The origin of the feather is one of the many mysteries of nature. The feather itself is at least 140 million years old. Throughout these millions of years of change, the basic types of feathers have emerged essentially unchanged. Three types of feathers make up a bird's plumage. The down feathers, consisting of long, flexible, soft plumes, provide insulation. They are found on newly hatched birds and beneath the contour feathers of adult birds. Contour feathers cover the body, wings and tail of the adult bird and help establish the bird's body outline. At the base of the contour feathers are small growths of a third type called filoplumes, which are small, simple, hairlike feathers with a long shaft and a rudimentary brush of barbs.

A typical contour feather is attached to the skin by a hollow quill that has an opening in its base to permit entry of blood vessels, which furnish nourishment to the developing feather. When fully formed, the opening disappears and the feather becomes a dead structure. The quill extends as a shaft into the webbed or flattened portion of the feather, an intricate structure made up of hundreds of slender, parallel barbs.

Each barb in turn, has many tiny barbules projecting from it, which interlock to form an airtight supporting surface. The color of feathers is produced by pigments; by reflection of light; and by light refraction. When a feather becomes worn, it is lost through molting and replaced by new growth.

A single feather lying on the ground can cause one to stop, pick it up and really take notice of every aspect of the feather. Many Indian peoples believe the structure of a feather represents the journey one takes in life. The hollow portion, known as the quill, is considered the beginning of life. The shaft, the barb-bearing, solid part, is the path which leads to many experiences. The barbs that branch out from the shaft represent the choices and decisions made along the path, shaping one's perspectives and expanding the mind. It is believed that both sides of the feather hold feminine and masculine

"Bird Feathers," *The Wind River Rendezvouz*, Vol. 27, No. 3 (July, August, Sept. 1997). Copyright © 1997 St. Stephens Indian Mission Foundation, Inc.

FIGURE 4.6 *Man in feathered bustle and dance costume at powwow in Discovery Park, Seattle.*

An answer to the prayer is considered to be received by way of the feather's path.

A bird's life depends upon its feathers, but none is more important in flight than the strong, durable flight feathers of the wings and tail. Each bone and muscle beneath the wings and tail work together with the components of the feathers to make their aerial movements efficient and versatile. In the world of the Plains Indian, the feathers of an eagle were a representation of the spirit of the bird. The eagle wing (pinion) feathers implied strength and its tail feathers, primarily the center one, symbolized a sense of direction. Each of these feathers represented the life of the eagle along with its virtues.

In addition to the religious aspect, the feather is an identification to the wearer and is very symbolic. It might be a sign as to a position the wearer holds or it may signify membership in a particular tribe or society. The person may have an affinity for the bird. They may have seen that bird in a dream or on a vision quest while searching for direction in their life. (It is believed that seeing the bird lets the individual know it will listen and acknowledge their prayers.) The individual may have attained the feather through some sort of discipline or act of humanity. The bearer may have received it as a gift, passed on by a previous owner—the gift of a feather is highly valued by the recipient and considered a great honor. A feather is granted to a member of the armed forces who performed a heroic deed—much like a Plains warrior of the past being honored for his courage in battle. If a man earns enough feathers to attain a position of leadership, the feathers in his bonnet represent his virtues, they do not represent a war bonnet— a term used in many western Hollywood movies when referring to a chief's flamboyant feather headdress.

Women also earn eagle feathers through their achievements or passed on to them as a gift. An eagle plume is usually tied to a hair ornament such as a medicine wheel, then tied to the hair and worn on the left side of the woman's head. An eagle feather is generally fastened to the back of her head.

Every eagle feather is blessed in a traditional ceremony before it is granted so only good will

aspects. The female part of the feather (the dark or the inner half) reflects the gentle, nurturing, reflective side. The masculine part of the feather (the light or the outer half) reflects the solemn guardian and protector of the feminine side. A reality in the journey is constantly striving for balance of peace and harmony between good and evil.

Many different feathers are used on different occasions and are committed to many purposes. Prayers, chants and songs are used with feathers in traditional ceremonies, such as blessings, healings and cleansings, to call on the energy of different spirits as messengers. The feather is held aloft when a prayer request is made. The individual's use of a certain feather asks for the attention of the spirits of that particular bird, so their prayer will be comprehended.

be passed on to the owner. Use of feathers within Indian culture shows respect for the spirits of the sky. If the owner is respectful of the feather, it is believed that they will receive guidance throughout their life.

Feathers are seen in great abundance at Pow-Wows, adorning the traditional and fancy dancers' elaborate regalia, on ceremonial items and on other implements. Among the Indian peoples of this region, the male fancy dancer does not wear a bustle fashioned with eagle feathers. The traditional dancer's regalia include eagle feathers in their hair and a fan-shaped eagle feather bustle. Should an eagle feather drop to the ground from any dancer's regalia, the dancer does not pick it up. It requires a special prayer by a highly respected individual. The eagle feather is then picked up by this individual and returned to the owner.

An important factor is how a feather is used, not how beautiful it is or how the item was fashioned. The primary factor is the spiritual aspect. It is of the utmost importance what the owner feels when using the feather. The symbolism of birds and their feathers within Indian culture is being kept alive by parents teaching their children to carry on the traditions of their peoples.

DISCUSSION QUESTIONS

Bird Feathers

1. Traditional symbols develop meaning over time. What are the traditional meanings of feathers to Plains Indians?

2. How does the way a wearer behaves toward a feather affect its meaning?

18 Hail to the T, the Shirt That Speaks Volumes
J. D. Reed

We are standing outside the Hard Rock Cafe, the high-decibel, high-profile bistro on New York City's West 57th Street. The tail fins of a vintage Cadillac protrude from the wall above the entrance. To the right, a long line of people stand patiently on the sidewalk. But this crowd is not waiting to savor cheeseburgers or check out celebrities. Instead, they take turns ducking through a separate door that leads to the Cafe's clothing annex.

Most Saturdays a thousand or so people make it to the clothes counter, and many of them fork over at least $13 for a T-shirt. Altogether, Hard Rock Cafes in Dallas, Washington, D.C., London and other cities sell millions of T-shirts a year, bringing in almost as much cash as do the restaurant chain's food and drink.

The T-shirt, which first hit the national consciousness during World War II, has become the Big Mac of the international clothing industry. All over the world, billions of T's, garnished with a babble of words and images, are donned by men, women and children of every stratum of

Reed, J. D., "Hail to the T, the Shirt That Speaks Volumes," *Smithsonian* (April, 1992)

society. In the United States alone, more than one billion were sold in 1990.

T's have become such a familiar part of the visual landscape that little thought is given to the extraordinary stroll they have made down the fickle runways of fashion. Their significance goes beyond the level of mere couture—high or low. They are, in fact, an anthropologist's dream source for studying ongoing political, sexual, social and even verbal fashions. Unlike the graffiti at Pompeii, today's graffiti may wash away or get covered by layers of paint. Meanwhile, it is the T-shirt that will offer attentive future observers an extended, if quirky, index to the manners and mores of the late 20th century.

Consider the following scraps of cultural dialogue. T-shirt number one: JUST SAY NO. T-shirt number two: JUST SAY WHEN. To future anthropologists, some shirts will be easy to decipher. NUCLEAR POWER: ROTTEN TO THE CORE will lead them straight to 1979 and Three Mile Island. WE BELIEVE ANITA HILL and A WOMAN'S PLACE IS IN THE HOUSE (AND IN THE SENATE) will also provide an easy link to a specific period of history. Ditto for WE DON'T CARE. WE DON'T HAVE TO. WE'RE EXXON. But 500 years from now, what will scientists trying to reconstruct our world from the ruins of our culture do with: WHERE'S THE BEEF? or DIE, YUPPIE SCUM, not to mention T-shirt variations of elderly Mrs. Fletcher's TV-ad line I'VE FALLEN AND I CAN'T GET UP.

Essentially, the T-shirt began as underwear and graduated to outside work. Its origins are murky, though most likely nautical. One story goes back to a time when British sailors were ordered to sew short sleeves on their undershirts, to spare royal eyes the sight of hairy underarms. Another blames it all on undershirted long-shoremen unloading tea in 17th century Annapolis, Maryland. "Tea" became "T" and the rest is history. One thing is sure. In 1913 the U.S. Navy adopted the crew-necked, short-sleeved, white cotton undershirt, to be worn under a jumper, in part to cover sailors' chest hairs.

Ashore, T-shirt lineage is equally tantalizing. Before World War II, in the 1930s, the dread sleeveless singlet, with over-the-shoulder straps, a deep neck and totally exposed armpits, domi-

nated the underwear wardrobe of the American male But the T-shirt was a great leap forward, and by the late '30s Hanes and Sears, Roebuck started marketing cotton undershirts with short sleeves and a high neck for as little as 24 cents apiece. Sears introduced theirs in 1938. Giving credit to the seaman, they called it the "Gob"-style shirt and presciently proclaimed it both an outer garment and an undershirt—"It's practical, correct either way."

GABLE SHUCKED HIS DRESS SHIRT

They weren't called T-shirts then, and they didn't catch on, in part because in 1934 undershirts in general were dealt a serious blow by Clark Gable. The blunt instrument was the film *It Happened One Night*, in which Gable shucked his dress shirt to reveal that he wore nothing underneath. His costar, Claudette Colbert, seemed none too impressed, but American women liked the look, and their men were quick to follow Gable's lead. Undershirt sales plummeted. Waiting onstage, however, was World War II and an underwear revolution in the making. In 1941, as America was cranking up its war effort, the Navy called on its suppliers for millions of milky white, moderately high-necked, cotton-knit undergarments ever after to be known as skivvy shirts. The Marine Corps would get theirs in sage green. And after the war, the U.S. Army got on board, too, in olive drab.

For the millions of men and women who have served ever since in every theater of operations, but particularly in the tropics, T-shirts have been treasured gear. T's always look neat, and they wash easily. You can use them to polish belt buckles or shoes, or if necessary, press them into service as pillows or bandages. Most male escapees from the singlet have never worn anything so useful or comfortable. Thus it was that the T-shirt became *the* postwar undershirt—often, in warmer climates, the *only* shirt. It was an egalitarian item of costume, too, donned every day by men in every walk of life. Veterans (and their sons) simply felt naked without one.

For a while, the T-shirt suggested the kind of crewcut cleanliness and neatness indigenous to the new, postwar suburbs. Even Senator John F. Kennedy, millionaire navy hero and in many ways America's beau ideal, was photographed lounging about the garden of his Georgetown home in a T.

The most common place for the T-shirt, though, was on the back of the working man, for whom its comfort was essential. As a replacement for the armpit-revealing singlet as a man's only torso covering, the T-shirt came to serve as a proletarian symbol, a kind of sartorial pickup truck. Marlon Brando guaranteed the garment's place in the image of the American working class in the 1951 film, *A Streetcar Named Desire*. As Tennessee Williams' macho, mean-spirited, lowbrow lug Stanley Kowalski, Brando flexed and mumbled with animal sensuality, his rippling muscles shockingly visible beneath the form-fitting shirt.

JAMES DEAN FROZE THE LOOK

With Brando, too, in *The Wild One* (1954), the T-shirt debuted in its most enduring role, as battle flag of youthful rebellion. A young man who appeared in public in the 1950s wearing what middle-class moms and dads still thought of as underwear could set new standards for hormonal behavior. Between his duck-tail haircut and trademark pelvic thrust, Elvis Presley sported a T-shirt under a leather jacket and below a provocative sneer. In *Rebel Without a Cause* (1955), James Dean, T-shirted, jeaned and sporting a nylon windbreaker, froze the look—and the attitude.

Although the plain T has kept its macho appeal, the intervening years have had a gender-bending effect on the shirt's image. As early as 1959, in the film *Breathless*, Jean Seberg appeared in the masculine accouterments of short hair and a T-shirt with New York Herald Tribune emblazoned on the front. In it, Seberg seemed anything but masculine. In the following decade, as more and more women adopted the T, this formerly macho symbol evolved into a staple of a sexy new androgyny in fashion.

Young women stopped wearing blouses, knee-length skirts and pumps, and started wearing T-shirts with blue jeans or miniskirts. The T-shirt became the uniform of radical youth, male or female. In the mid-'60s, says Edith Mayo, a curator of political collections at the Smithsonian's National Museum of American History, it acquired a serious sort of radical chic, when the Student Nonviolent Coordinating Committee created an "SNCC uniform," a khaki T-shirt worn mostly with jeans and meant to symbolize the rural and working-class origins of many black citizens.

By the late '60s, T-shirts were being tie-dyed, painted and silk-screened with signs of peace and symbols of protest. It wasn't until the '70s, however, that decorated T-shirts exploded into an international forum for publicizing personal feelings, philosophies, political candidates and consumer goods.

For years, the only lettered shirts were those designed to identify college sports teams. The idea of wearing words—and of wearing underwear as outerwear, for that matter—first proved irresistible only to the country's children. They clamored for T's sporting the images of baseball heroes like Joe DiMaggio. In the mid-'50s, TV and film idols Fess Parker (as Davy Crockett) and Roy Rogers achieved their real immortality on kid-size shirts. T-shirts also began to be printed in small, local runs with the names of Little League teams, scout troops or summer camps.

The oldest painted T-shirt in the Smithsonian's collection is a child-size model that reads Dew-it With Dewey, a relic of New York Governor Thomas E. Dewey's ill-fated 1948 Presidential campaign against Harry Truman. Other Presidential slogans followed still on T's mostly cut to fit folks under voting ages. But as the baby boomers grew up, their T-shirts grew too.

It was not long before drag racers and surfers on the West Coast were taking designs they'd been airbrushing onto hot rods and surfboards and putting them on T's. Around the country, plain and tie-dyed T-shirts were becoming fixtures of young people's wardrobes. It was the Vietnam War, though, that dramatically thrust the shirt into the world of print and polemics. A nation of youth, teed off at their elders, got all T'd up to let everyone know about it.

Why tire your arms holding a picket sign when you could wear your complaint on your chest? For going to political rallies—or just heading out for a burger—T-shirts became the perfect two-in-one raiment. The country was developing a tendency to believe that opinion was more important than knowledge, a view that fitted these shirts to a T. Without your having to speak, everyone knew where you stood on the war, on the sexes, on the powers that be. T-shirts expressing views on every conceivable subject or making personal confessions were soon to follow. LIBERATE MARIJUANA, T shirts shouted. And IMPEACH NIXON. Or—proving that nothing stays simple—I'M A VIRGIN (THIS IS AN OLD SHIRT).

Just as people were getting accustomed to the talking T, a series of new technologies began making mass production of full-color images on cloth possible. "Suddenly this summer," a 1970 article in *Time* announced, "the undershirt is very much back in—but not as an undergarment. Violently colored and decorated with cartoon characters (Mickey Mouse), symbols of dissent (a marijuana plant) or simple slogans…the shirts are a bright new trend for the kids—and the Over-30s too." Four years later *Time* was still babbling on: "Thanks to novel techniques,…" its story ran, "major department stores…and hundreds of small T shops across the country let buyers pick from an almost limitless selection of designs and savings—or fashion their own." Manufacturers such as Fruit of the Loom dominated production of the shirts, but the decoration became (and remains) a cottage industry of extraordinary vitality and range.

"Clothes with pictures and/or writing…" wrote satirist Fran Lebowitz in her 1978 book, *Metropolitan Life*, "are an unpleasant indication of the general state of things.…If people don't want to listen to *you*, what makes you think they want to hear from your sweater?" This proved a minority opinion. Whether they thought people *wanted* to listen or not, Americans became more and more determined to let their figures do the talking. The year Lebowitz's book was published, roughly 500 million T-shirts were sold in the United States.

Indisputably, the 1970s were the golden age of the T-shirt. For the members of the Me Generation, T-shirts provided the perfect medium for asserting their individuality. And in a decade of "letting it all hang out," the T-shirt offered instant familiarity among strangers—an index for passers-by to what you thought, liked or wanted to be associated with.

SANDWICH BOARDS IN PORTABLE COTTON

Inevitably, the shirts have become collector's items, like postcards, pressed flowers or prom tickets. For the traveler the T replaced the suitcase sticker of the '30s and '40s, offering such messages as MY PARENTS WENT TO PARIS AND ALL I GOT WAS THIS LOUSY SHIRT (or, more lately, GEORGE BUSH WENT TO ROME AND ALL I GOT WAS THIS LOUSY RECESSION).

Folks could flaunt not only where they'd been but what races they'd run, concerts they'd seen, earthquakes and blizzards they'd survived. T-shirt merchandising schemes especially in cahoots with rock groups, popped up all over. T's were inspired by every fad, trial or even disaster that came along. Just as Desert Storm was being wrapped up in the Middle East, STORMIN' NORMAN FOR PRESIDENT T-shirts hit the streets.

Where in ages past, a small business might pay people to stalk the sidewalks wearing ankle-length sandwich boards announcing products or services, now—by selling logo-decorated T's for additional profit or simply giving them away—companies turned their customers into walking billboards. The T-shirt, whether promoting Budweiser or Bloomingdale's, became one of the great advertising mediums in the history of hype.

Paul Fussell, in his caustic social critique *Class: A Guide through the American Status System*, suggests that by wearing a brand name, an otherwise anonymous "prole" fuses himself with some successful commercial commodity—whether it be a pop star or a brand of pop—and becomes, "for the moment, somebody."

"And this need is not for the proles alone." Fussell graciously adds, citing T-shirts "stamped with the logo of *The New York Review of Books*,…or printed with portraits of Mozart and Haydn and Beethoven, which assure the world, 'I am civilized.'"

Novelist-critic Alison Lurie coined the term "legible clothing." But even she did not envisage the extensive legibility pioneered by T-shirt publisher R. Gilad Schamess, who last year started marketing short-short stories, each one brief enough to be printed a single shirt. Naturally he called them Tee Shorts.

T's reflect more than craziness, personal taste and mere consumerism. Political fervor no doubt mellowed in the '70s, but it certainly did not disappear. Women were asserting themselves, gays came out of the closet en masse, environmentalists were out to save the Earth — and their T-shirts conveyed their political agendas, along with provocative shots of humor.

With a little help from Gloria Steinem, a best-selling T asserted A WOMAN NEEDS A MAN LIKE A FISH NEEDS A BICYCLE. Today's career women prick our prejudices — and their own — with the sentiment OH MY GOD I FORGOT TO HAVE CHILDREN! Recently, African-Americans have been wearing images of Martin Luther King, Jr. and Malcolm X on tie-dyed backgrounds, and T's that tell passers-by IT'S A BLACK THING, YOU WOULDN'T UNDERSTAND.

Obviously the political left has offered flurries of T-shirt punches. Conservatives are not entirely T-shirt shy, either. When capital punishment was reinstated in Florida, for instance, supporters put out a shirt with the sentiment 1 DOWN, 131 TO GO.

The T's potential to provoke has not been ignored beyond our shores. In South Africa, black activists turned to the silk screen to record rage and, lately, a growing political power. At one point, in order to thwart protesters, Cape Town police banned T-shirts that bore the names or slogans of any one of 47 different anti-apartheid groups. Strongly criticized at home and abroad, the order was withdrawn by embarrassed officials.

Even in the United States, where T-shirt wearers are arguably protected by the First Amendment, many people think freedom of the T-shirt press has gone too far. Many American schools prohibit certain T-shirt messages, particularly those that celebrate sex or the use of cigarettes, alcohol or drugs. Outraged residents of resort areas such as Ocean City, Maryland, and

Rehoboth Beach, Delaware — where T-shirt merchants promise that they "print anything" — have waged war against the sale of obscene shirts. In that department, the T-shirt has tended toward soft porn. During the sexual revolution of the 1970s, wet-T-shirt contests were all the rage. And countless T's allowing wearers to drop a come-on line or a come-hither look in prose hit the market. Many showed an admirable stylistic brevity. AVAILABLE does well across a crowded room.

Some T-shirts are instructive. At Rutgers University's Cook College, student advisers used to wear T-shirts printed with a map of the campus, to help freshmen find their way. On their own T's, the freshmen wore a large X and the words YOU ARE HERE.

One of the T's great victories, won with a little help from the turtleneck, has been over the necktie. The male of the species will be forever grateful. For women, the T has provided an acceptable alternate to the hard-to-care-for blouse. In many offices, it is perfectly appropriate for both sexes to wear a simple, solid-colored, cotton T-shirt under a suit jacket.

In the 14th century, European nobility — bitterly resenting the rise of a moneyed merchant class — set up strict sumptuary laws forbidding upstarts from aping their betters by wearing ermine, brocade, jewels and other status symbols. In the case of such originally modest items of clothing as blue jeans and T-shirts, it is now the rich who are aping the working class, as Paris designer Coco Chanel once said they should.

Seventh Avenue designers offer unmistakably haute T's to a status-symbol-hungry clientele. Designers like Comme des Garçons do well with a flossy white T (at $50) that might be worn under a formal jacket to a dinner party. Others, like Calvin Klein, simply take the plain white T and put their label on it, selling a hefty amount of panache, albeit with a reasonable price tag ($9).

Popular-culture scholars now lament the fact that for years they didn't realize that the T-shirt would become one of the most garrulous and perhaps significant artifacts of 20th-century fashion. Still, not long ago, the Fashion Institute of Technology in New York was able to mount an exhibition presenting the events of 1991, from Desert Storm to the William Kennedy Smith trial, as recorded on T-shirts. Moreover, three divisions of the National Museum of American History—Costume, Community Life and Political History—have T-shirt collections.

The latest wrinkle is a creative collaboration between the T and something called Puff Paint. Squeezed from tubes in globs of many colors, it can turn a kid's T-shirt into a many-splendored fantasy in not-so-bas-relief. Heat-sensitive T-shirts that change color on the body are also a thing of the present.

Nobody knows when it will all end. But what seems perfectly clear is that as long as Americans feel the need to get stuff off their chests, the T-shirt is likely to stay on their backs.

DISCUSSION QUESTIONS

Hail to the T

1. How are message T-shirts part of cultural dialog?

2. Why is the T-shirt one of the most significant artifacts of 20th-century fashion?

19 Scent of a Market

Maxine Wilkie

The sensory delight of driving down a country road in the summer can quickly turn unpleasant when the scent of freshly mown grass becomes one of freshly killed skunk. The smell of a sizzling steak on the grill can make a man salivate while it makes his pregnant wife nauseous. An infant as young as two days old can identify his mother by her scent. People who lose their sense of smell often become depressed. Clearly, the sense of smell has a powerful effect on human thought and behavior.

A growing number of marketers are recognizing that the sense of smell can also be a powerful motivator for sales—and it's not just perfume that's winning by a nose. Businesses are sniffing out the connection between the sense of smell, memory, and mood. They are using this link to sell everything from body lotion to car wax. More remarkable is a line of products lumped under the new-age name of aromatherapy. They claim that certain fragrances released into the air have the potential to change the ambiance and mood of both work and home life.

The power of scent is no surprise to perfume manufacturers who have been promoting the sale of fragrance since the first alchemist figured out how to distill natural plant and animal essences into long-lasting scents. Last year, the $5 billion fine-fragrance industry offered 64 new fragrances. It's fueled by a multi-million-dollar advertising budget and counts on an ever-growing worldwide market to increase sales.

Wilkie, Maxine, "Scent of a Market," *American Demographics* (August 1995) Reprinted with permission. © 1995 American Demographics, Ithaca, New York.

Why is fragrance so important to the buying public? The key is a mixture of biological response, psychology, and memory. The limbic system is the most primitive part of our brain and the seat of immediate emotions. Certain odors elicit elemental emotional reactions because some fingers of the olfactory bulb dip directly into the limbic system. Smell, more than any other sense, is a straight line to feelings of happiness, hunger, disgust, and nostalgia—the same feelings marketers want to tap.

A PRIMITIVE SENSE

We shouldn't feel smug about our wonderful sense of smell. Humans are lightweights compared with other mammals, such as dogs, who rely more on smell than any other sense. Human beings lump individual odors into larger categories such as "turkey dinner." A dog, in comparison, can distinguish the onions from the sage in the stuffing and calculate how much butter is in the mashed potatoes. Smell might play a partial role in our attraction to, or repulsion from, another person, but a dog smelling another dog gets its life history in an instant.

Even with our less-than-perfect sense of smell, the chemistry involved in odors can still be a significant signal to the human animal. Just about every object emits odor molecules that float through the air. These molecules have particular shapes that perfectly match receptors randomly scattered throughout the mucus membranes of our nasal passages. Each receptor is connected to a nerve cell. When a molecule plugs into a receptor, it alters the shape of the nerve cell and sends a signal to the olfactory bulbs at the base of the brain. The olfactory bulbs act like a switching station; various smell impulses are combined, refined, interpreted, and sent along to the limbic system of the brain where the smell is recognized. There is no specific receptor for, say, pizza, but the olfactory bulbs are able to weave together the hundreds of odor molecules drifting off a pizza and come up with a coherent mental image of a steaming pie.

The mind has a strong memory for important smells that remind us of good or bad times, and these associations make up each individual's personal smell palate. Childhood scent memories can be especially strong. For many of us, the aroma of freshly baked chocolate-chip cookies is connected forever in the limbic system with contentment. Our mother's perfume is often lodged there, too. My sister maintains that she married her husband because he smelled exactly like the plastic Peter Pan doll of her childhood.

Culture also plays a major role in determining what is a pleasant smell and what is obnoxious. Certain spices smell normal in one culture, for example, while they make tourists gag. Life experiences can also alter the tenor of some smells; most people find floral scents pleasant, but to some, a bouquet only reminds them of funerals and death. The only universally pleasant smell is cola, which explains the global success of Coke and Pepsi.

Throughout much of recorded history and perhaps beyond, people have added fragrances to lotions and potions to mask unpleasant odors or create a certain ambiance. During eras when personal hygiene was less prevalent than today, women and men carried pomanders, balls of spices and flowers that overlaid their pungent body odor (and fought off infection, so they thought). Perfume as a mood setter and sexual attractant also has been around for a long time. Taking a cue from other animals, perfumers learned to extract the essential male animal sexual pheromone, musk, and use it as the basis for many perfumes. Although there is no scientific confirmation that animal musk excites people, or that humans have a sexually inviting musky odor of their own, about 20 kinds of synthetic musks are used today in perfume formulas.

Fragrances are complex entities that evolve on the skin because their various ingredients become volatile, that is, airborne, at different rates. Perfumers call these different levels "notes" and aim for certain top notes that dissipate quickly and lasting bottom notes that cling to the skin for hours. The ratio of oil to alcohol in a perfume also affects its lasting power. Perfumes are considered "aggressive" when the oil content is high compared with their alcohol content. A scent such as Giorgio Beverly Hills contains 34 percent oil, much higher than the average of 20 percent.

FRAGRANCE HAS A FUNCTION

Consumers commonly use two distinct types of fragrance, says Gabriella Zuckerman, a New York City-based consultant to the fragrance industry. One is functional and the other is not. "The functional fragrance signals some kind of benefit and is used more in treatment products," she says. "It subconsciously tells the consumer that this product will really do something. These fragrances reinforce the actual working of a product." She cites the addition of a mint smell to a product that cools as an example of a functional fragrance. Lemon and pine scents added to cleaning products are other cases in which fragrance plays a role in how the product is perceived to work.

Then there are playful fragrances—about 800 perfumes and colognes available at department stores, drugstores, and perfumeries in the U.S. Forty-two percent of men bought scent for themselves in 1994, as did 55 percent of women, according to Mediamark Research, Inc. of New York City. The gift market is also substantial: 26 percent of adults purchased perfume for men as gifts over the past year, and 29 percent purchased perfume gifts for women. Although a recent *Wall Street Journal* article claims that 75 percent of perfume business occurs during the holidays, when men most often buy perfume for women, women buying for each other dominate the market. Women also buy perfume and cologne for men more often than men buy such gifts for other men.

Three in four women used perfume or cologne in the six months before Mediamark Research surveyed them in spring 1994. Nine percent hadn't done so within the past seven days, but one in five spritzed themselves one to four times the week before the survey, while a little over one-third dabbed themselves five to seven times a week. Thirteen percent doused themselves with scent more than once a day. The largest contingent of such heavy users is found in the 25-to-34 age group, making up 23 percent of the heavy-use market. These young women are actually less likely than women aged 45 to 54 to heavily use perfume, but they outnumber their older counterparts.

Full-time working women are more likely than average to be heavy scent users, and they make up close to half of the overall women's market. Heavy use is above average among all major occupational groups except for women in professional specialties, such as nursing and teaching. Perfume use in general does not vary much by income, but women with household incomes of at least $30,000 are more likely than lower-income women to be heavy users. Single women are heavier users than married women, although married women out-number them. Likewise, Hispanic women tend to be heavier scent users than whites and blacks, but are out-numbered by both average-use groups.

Two-thirds of men used aftershave or cologne in the six months before they were surveyed, according to Mediamark. The heaviest users age-wise are those in the marriage or remarriage market, aged 18 to 24 and 45 to 54. As with women, single men are more likely than married men to heavily use cologne. In contrast with women, however, whose use rises with income, men with household incomes below $20,000 are more likely than average to use cologne more than once a day. Black men are much more likely than average to use aftershave or cologne heavily, while Hispanic men are somewhat more likely.

The $1.1 billion market for male fragrance is growing, not only because it has become more fashionable for men to wear scent, but because women use men's fragrances, too. It is estimated that 30 percent of men's fragrances are worn by women.

PERFUME IMAGES

Smell isn't everything when it comes to perfume. As an essentially inessential product that survives largely on image, the look is important, too. In a competitive market, packaging that stands out may get consumers' attention before they sample the product itself. In fact, clothing designers often develop a line of bottles first and then hire someone to produce a fragrance they feel matches the spirit of the design.

Among the plethora of sculpted bottles and crafted tubs recently launched, two lines stand out. Halston Borghese's Catalyst for men comes in chemistry flasks, test tubes, and beakers. Halston's aim is to remind men of their childhood chemistry sets, and, perhaps, to defeminize male fragrances. It hopes to attract men who buy fragrance for themselves rather than as gifts. Another striking package out last year was designed by Paris fashion bad boy Jean-Paul Gaultier. The bottle is a female torso, dressed in a copper or etched-glass bustier, but this elegant package comes doubled-wrapped in an industrial-looking tin can with the Gaultier name on it.

Multi-million-dollar advertising campaigns are now common in the perfume industry. Calvin Klein started the trend in the mid-1980s when it spent $17 million to introduce the highly successful Obsession with *film noir* TV spots and artsy magazine photographs. With sky-high development and advertising costs, the fragrance business has become a high-risk endeavor. "It's much harder to make a classic these days," says Dorothy C. Foster, president of DCF International, a New York City-based consulting firm for the fragrance and cosmetic industry. Using a star vehicle is not always a sure shot—Cher's personal fragrance bombed, while Elizabeth Taylor's White Diamonds is doing well. It's hard to say what will come of a recently introduced fragrance launched by world-renowned opera singer Luciano Pavarotti.

The fragrance industry is also prone to changing whims of fashion, says Annette Green, president of the Fragrance Foundation, a nonprofit educational arm of the fragrance industry. "Five years ago, the public was into very sexy, heavy, dramatic fragrances," says Green. "Today, there is a trend toward light, nonsexual, close-to-nature kinds of fragrances—food scents, citrus, vanilla—refreshing, sort of nonfragrance fragrances." Consultant Gabriella Zuckerman agrees: "The overall fragrance trend is toward fresh and transparent. People are also looking for a fun, uplifting, pleasant scent from their bath products, totally different from their classical fragrances."

In general, women at least are moving toward a "wardrobe of fragrances" rather than sticking to one classical scent. This shift toward a bathroom shelf cluttered with bottles is partially cost-driven. "Classical fragrances are quite expensive, so women use them sparingly, while they use bath products and other fun fragrance more extravagantly," says Zuckerman.

Calvin Klein is presumably on the forefront of expanding its fragrance business with the introduction of cK one, a scent aimed at both men and women. If nothing else, this makes gift-buying easier. Another way to increase sales is to expand beyond the domestic market. "A number of companies have been thinking globally," says DCF's Foster. "For example, Avon's Far and Away was designed to be sold all over the world and has done quite well."

Fine fragrance isn't the only arena undergoing changes. Adding lemon or pine to cleaning products doesn't necessarily do the trick anymore. "Lemon has a very cheap connotation," explains Zuckerman. "This is because so many of the rug sprays, room deodorizers, and bathroom deodorizers used an inexpensive version of lemon in the past." As a result, she feels that manufacturers need to develop more complex, interesting notes for functional products. "As society's taste gets more sophisticated in food, for example, people will be looking for more sophistication in fragrances in the functional market."

WORK HARDER, BUY MORE

One of the more remarkable trends in the fragrance industry is the notion that certain scents can motivate people to either work harder or buy more. Volunteers performed puzzle-solving tasks 17 percent faster when exposed to a floral scent, according to a study conducted by the Smell and Taste Treatment and Research Foundation of Chicago. The Good Housekeeping Institute found that proofreaders do much better when peppermint or lavender scents are piped into their atmosphere. A Japanese company discovered that lavender and jasmine soothed key-punch operators, while lemon increased production. Several companies now manufacture dispensers that emit scent into the atmosphere, covering thousands of square feet with fragrances designed to provide a particular motivating ambiance.

Some retailers have picked up on this research and believe that the right scent can compel shoppers to buy. Stores are now paying as much as $50,000 to fragrance experts to develop scents that match their store's clientele, or what they think their customers want to smell as they linger at the clothing racks.

Dr. Alan Hirsch, director of the Smell and Taste Treatment and Research Foundation, is one of the few people who has actually tried to test these claims. Although his work has been dismissed by some scientists, he has shown that people are more likely to buy Nike shoes and pay more for them when trying them on in floral-scented dressing rooms. The study states that this is the case even when the scent is too faint for people to notice. For stores that deal in the marketing of scent, pumping out their own product obviously has advantages. The natural body-lotion store, Natural Wonders, for example, sprays its own best-selling fragrance throughout its retail stores and maintains that sales are up because customers smell and buy.

These retailers represent just one arm of the new-age business of aromatherapy, which uses scents to calm, relax, relieve stress, or serve as a pick-me-up. As with perfume manufacture, essential oils are distilled from mounds of plant parts, flower, bark, and herbs. For example, it takes 4.5 million jasmine petals to produce 450 grams (about a pound) of jasmine oil. These oils are then released into the air by uncapping a bottle or heating the oil in a dish or on a light bulb. The point is to sniff up large amounts of pure odor molecules, which supposedly have therapeutic benefits because they change the body's chemistry.

Several cosmetic lines have expanded to include aromatherapy. Elizabeth Arden's spa line is based on the supposedly improving properties of scent. Estée Lauder's Origins line also offers mood-enhancing scents intended to improve the skin. The Aveda line has used the aromatherapy angle to sell its shampoos and skin products. The aromatherapy business expected to gross $230 million in 1995, according to the *Los Angeles Times*.

Annette Green feels the fragrance industry is moving away from strict "aromatherapy," which she calls a folk medicine based on massage techniques, and toward "aromachology," the science of the effect of scent on mood and behavior. Coincidentally or not, most effects discovered to date are related to food scents. Researchers at Yale University have shown that the smell of spiced apples can ward off a panic attack in some people and reduce stress levels, while lavender can promote alertness. By enclosing people in coffins and pumping in scents, Alan Hirsch has discovered that seashore and cucumber smells combat claustrophobia, while the scent of barbecue aggravates it. At the Sloan-Kettering Cancer Center in New York City, technicians are so convinced that scent has an effect on mood that they use sweet-smelling vanilla fragrance to relax people during some medical tests. And despite the fragrance industry's best aphrodisiac efforts, a study of perfumes revealed that the control scent, fresh cinnamon buns, was the only odor to induce sexual arousal in a sample of male medical students.

Because people change and cultures evolve, it's reasonable to expect further changes in the fragrance industry. It's more difficult to predict the direction of those changes. Today's lemon-scented Joy might become tomorrow's vanilla-scented Joy if the smell of vanilla becomes associated with cleanliness. Annette Green predicts a major trend toward scents with a proven link with behavior. "I identify these scents as smart scents—fragrances that offer more than a lovely fragrance."

Green thinks these scents will waft at us inside sensory enclosures, closets of smell, taste, and pleasure where we retreat for a few minutes at the end of a hard day. People who claim to suffer allergic reactions to particular scents would probably prefer that they be confined to such environments altogether. In fact, the School of Social Work at the University of Minnesota in Minneapolis has banned students and others from wearing scented personal products, including deodorants, in portions of one building on campus, primarily because an employee and student maintained that such fragrances make them ill.

Many in the medical community and general public remain unconvinced that multiple chemical sensitivity is a true malady, but even people who don't suffer ill effects may be irritated by men and women drenched in aftershave and perfume. Some people also object to the perfume swatches that now appear in major consumer magazines.

Even so, the fragrance industry continues to deluge consumers with new scents, images, and promises that their products will inspire, delight, and liberate us. For the vast majority, a little scent can go a long way toward setting the mood for love or food, work or serenity. Just as we crave variety in our diets, we appreciate variety in our perfume palate. The fragrance industry is counting on this to keep its cash registers ringing.

DISCUSSION QUESTIONS

Scent of a Market

1. What meanings do perfume marketers use to sell their brand of perfume?

2. What various approaches are taken by markers to produce those meanings of scents?

3. Do you wear scents? If so, what factors do you use in choosing a scent to wear?

20   Bulldog with Character Makeup

Jeff Olson

When Mark Goldsberry says he's wearing his game face, he's not kidding.

As always, it's applied with blue grease paint, sometimes three stripes on each side of his face, sometimes under the eyes, always inspired by a cross between Gene Simmons and the characters of "Braveheart." As always, it serves an inspirational purpose.

When Goldsberry puts on his game face Saturday for Drake's football game at San Diego, his motivation will be far more than theatrical. He'll recall last season, when he sustained a knee injury that doctors said would end his face-painting, football-playing career. He'll recall countless hours of rehabilitation, running and lifting weights. Then, as always, he'll go out and give 120 percent.

"It's symbolic," Goldsberry said of the war paint. "It means I'm ready for a battle, I'm ready to go after it. It's telling my team that I'm going to give it all I have on every play. I'm going to sell out and do everything I can."

The point isn't lost amid the violence. *Play every play like it's your last*, Goldsberry is telling his teammates, *because it just might be*. For a time after his knee popped last year during a victory against? Evansville, Goldsberry wasn't sure if he'd played his last game.

"There was serious doubt as to whether he'd ever be able to play again," Drake Coach Rob Ash said. "He worked extremely hard on his rehab. When it became apparent that he was

Olson, Jeff, "Bulldog with Character Makeup," *Des Moines Register*, Oct. 23, 1997. Copyright 1997, reprinted with permission by *The Des Moines Register*.

FIGURE 4.7 *Mark Goldsberry in face paint for the game.*

going to at least have a chance to play again, he ran and went through drills in a lot of pain. He drove himself to try to get ready to play again."

His teammates know what drove him to recover from the injury. It's the same strange force that continues to drive him.

"They know what goes through my head and what motivates me," Goldsberry said. "I motivate myself and get myself going. When I get myself going, then it spreads like wildfire. Everyone else gets going because I'm excited. They know Goldie's ready to go when he puts on his war paint."

The paint is just a reminder to his teammates of what Goldsberry put himself through just to play one more season of football. At the end of spring practice, when it was obvious that Goldsberry had recovered and would be an integral part of the Bulldogs' defense, he gave his teammates a speech they still quote.

"He told everybody, 'I will never, ever go less than 120 percent in any drill or any rep that I ever have the privilege of wearing a football uniform for,'" Ash said. "'I'll never know if that rep might be my last play. I'm going to make every one count. I'm going to make every one the best it can be. I'm never going to wear out, and I'm never going to let down.' It was awesome. It was inspirational for everybody. And he's carried through on that promise."

While the face-painting ritual is seen as a deadly serious part of Drake's motivational routine, Goldsberry plays a dual role as the team joker. He's been known to break into song, to quote lines from movies, and to draw laughter at the right opportunities.

"You might expect the team jester to be somewhat lackadaisical or inconsistent in his athletic performance," Ash said. "That's not what you get with Goldsberry. What you get with

Goldsberry is someone who knows exactly when to be loose and goofy and when to be totally focused and committed to what's going on."

He clowns because he loves the game, and because he said he feels as if his teammates take it too seriously. Football is important, he says, but not so important that it can't be fun.

"I like to joke around," he said. "Too many times, I feel people just go through practice like it's a job. The reason we play football—we don't get scholarships—is for the love of football. I just try to remind everyone with subtlety that this is a great sport. I've got four more weeks of this left. I'm never going to play football again."

Unless he lands a job with a really cool public relations firm after he graduates in May, Goldsberry will never smear blue paint on his face again. That's strictly for serious business.

"It's not for show-and-tell so everyone sees me painted up," Goldsberry said. "It's my way of saying, 'I'm ready to go.' I put it on right before we go out. Everybody knows. 'Goldie put on the paint. It's time to go out there and play a football game.' "

DISCUSSION QUESTIONS

Bulldog with Character Makeup

1. How was Mark Goldsberry's face paint a facilitator for Mark? For his team?

2. Do you ever dress in any way that motivates you to perform? Do you have dress that makes you feel lucky, powerful, or energetic? Why does the dress in question have this effect on you?

21   Employing Clothing for Therapeutic Change in Brief Counseling

John M. Littrell
Iowa State University

How recently have you worn a special article of clothing because you believed it would help you achieve a certain outcome? Perhaps it was your "lucky" T-shirt on the day of an exam. Or maybe it was a "special" pair of shoes that just made you feel good. We constantly use clothing to change the behavior of others—as well as ourselves. We cannot help but influence with the choices we make. Therefore, I found it surprising that professional counselors who are trained to help people solve problems have overlooked the power of clothing to assist in the change process. Little is written about how clothing may help clients wishing to make changes. Considering the many facets of clothing and human preoccupation with it, the lack of references to the therapeutic use of clothing is puzzling. The purpose of this article is to demonstrate how counselors can help clients

A portion of the article appeared in Littrell, J. M. (1998). Brief counseling in actions. Reprinted with permission of W. W. Norton and Company.

use clothing to move from one stage of change to another. Examples are provided from my use of clothing change in brief counseling with clients.

BRIEF COUNSELING AND THE STAGES OF CHANGE

Brief counseling is a relatively new development in helping clients make therapeutic change (de Shazer, 1994; Fisch, Weakland, & Segal, 1982; Furman & Ahola, 1992; Littrell, 1998; Littrell, Malia, & Vanderwood, 1995; O'Hanlon & Weiner-Davis, 1989; Talmon, 1993). As a brief counselor, I am committed to helping people alleviate their discomfort and reach their desired states as quickly as possible. Briefness is not endorsed for its own sake; rather, briefness is valued because it encourages clients to continue with their own lives without my assistance. Stated from a brief counseling perspective, my goal is to become quickly dispensable in my clients' lives.

In addition to brief counseling, I use a theoretical framework proposed by Prochaska, Norcross, and DiClemente (1994) to understand how clothing can be used as a vehicle for client change. Their proposed six-stage model describes how people change when dealing with problem behaviors. The six stages are: 1) **precontemplation** (denial of problem), 2) **contemplation** (acknowledgment of problem and serious thinking about solving it), 3) **preparation** (planning to take action on the problem within a month), 4) **action** (modification of behavior and environment), 5) **maintenance** (consolidation of gains and struggle to prevent relapse), and 6) **termination** (problem presents no temptation or threat). People may employ up to nine change processes (e.g., consciousness-raising, emotional arousal, environmental control, reward) at strategic times to make the transition from one stage to another, or to successfully complete a stage. My task as a counselor is to assist people in moving from one stage to another by employing appropriate therapeutic processes. For most clients, linear progression through the model is relatively rare; rather, recycling through various stages is common.

CASES INVOLVING THERAPEUTIC USES OF CLOTHING

This section is divided into four parts, each of which describes either movement from one stage of change to another, or movement within a stage.

Precontemplation/Contemplation

One of the most difficult tasks facing counselors is assisting people who do not think they have a problem. A change process most useful in moving people from precontemplation to contemplation is consciousness-raising. Case 1 illustrates how a nationally prominent therapist helped raise his client's consciousness by emphasizing clothing and appearance.

Contemplation/Preparation

People in the contemplation stage are intending to take action in the next six months, while those in the preparation stage are intending to take action in the next month. Emotional arousal (experiencing and expressing feeling about one's problems and solutions) and self-reevaluation (assessing feelings and thoughts about self with respect to a problem) are the two change processes that are most useful in helping people make the transition from contemplation to preparation.

Brief counselors believe their clients are doing their best at any given time to share their world views. Conveying trust in clients is facilitated by counselors adopting a stance of not knowing what is best for clients. When I work with clients I am aware in the short time we meet that I have very few clues as to how my clients live their lives. I have even fewer clues about what they want different in their lives. Confronted with my own lack of knowledge about who my clients are and what they want, I adopt a posture that says—trust the people you work with to be the experts in their lives.

In Case 2, the client is stuck in the contemplation stage. He has good intentions, but they are not yet being translated into serious preparation. The reliance of a client on his own life experiences is demonstrated in this case. The client's

CASE 1
Addressing the Issues

Historically, counseling/psychotherapy was considered a "talking cure." Counselors assumed that clients would only make behavioral changes to the extent that they talked about their problems and gained insight into them. Breaking from this framework, the clinical hypnotist Dr. Milton H. Erickson was a pioneer in helping clients to do something different—not just talk about it. He often assigned his patients tasks to carry out.

Erickson worked with a woman who was "somewhat overweight, very dirty and unkempt, and her clothes were loud and ill-fitting" (O'Hanlon & Hexum, 1990, p. 302–303). During therapy, Erickson provided explicit feedback about her appearance, including offering her a washcloth and instructing her to wash half her neck so she could see the contrast (Haley, 1973). In a subsequent session, Erickson gave her detailed instructions about how to dress for a dance. Erickson saw the woman for four sessions during which time she started grooming more attractively. Within a year the woman had married a college professor; five years later they had four children (Haley, 1973).

Erickson was clearly aware that some clients need to be jolted out of their states of denial. By providing explicit feedback on the woman's appearance, by providing her a self-demonstration (i.e., washing half her neck), and by giving detailed instructions about her attire, Erickson helped his client begin the move from precontemplation to contemplation, and on to action. He helped her use clothing and grooming to create a more socially acceptable appearance.

CASE 2
All the World Is a Stage

Calvin, who was a drama coach, and I worked together to help him reach his goal, which he stated as: "Getting the book that is within me written." He had received encouragement from others that his knowledge on the topic was abundant and that he really owed it to others to share it in print. To date he was using a "grind-it-out" pattern and the book had not written itself. Calvin was becoming an outstanding avoider of that which he professed to want.

Luckily, I suppressed my own ideas about what would work best in Calvin's world and stayed with the belief that he was the expert on his own life. Because Calvin was a drama coach, I asked him, "How could you take what you know about acting and apply it to your book writing?" Suddenly we were talking about how he taught his students to act. Calvin began to conceptualize his book writing as performing on the stage. I suggested he consider what costume he would wear while working on his book. Calvin said, "I'm going to wear an Indiana Jones outfit. I've already got the hat. My fingers will explore new territory as I seek adventure at the computer keyboard." As we drew additional parallels with the theater, Calvin became more animated. It looked as if he might leap from his chair and strike an Indiana Jones pose.

I spoke to Calvin on the phone in a follow-up just two weeks after our only session. Calvin told me he had begun writing while wearing his Indiana Jones hat. He expressed surprise that it was working so well. Calvin added, "This weekend I'm checking to see if Banana Republic has an Indiana Jones safari outfit." Calvin laughed and quipped, "I'm not depressed about the writing like I was because now I'm writing. It feels like I'm onstage in the spotlight. "

Paul had great plans for an exercise program. He wanted to walk for at least 30 minutes during his lunch hour. Despite his good intentions, Paul had actually gone walking only once or twice in the past month. At first Paul thought his problem was procrastination, because in examining his behavior he found that if the phone rang or someone came in with a question he invariably picked up the phone or talked with the person. He just couldn't turn down requests. At that point Paul began to conceptualize his problem as a lack of assertiveness.

I asked Paul to focus on exceptions by raising the question, "When in the past have you been able to go walking at noon regardless of anything else that was happening?"

Paul looked at me for a moment and then said, "In the past if I put on my walking shoes at noon then I would always go walking, regardless of whether the phone rang or someone wanted to talk." We coauthored Paul's statement into a small and powerful goal—"I will put on my walking shoes each and every noon at work." Paul's immediate reaction to his newly stated goal was one of relief and enthusiasm because he could achieve that goal. He gave up the "procrastinator" and "nonassertive person" labels and began to see his problem, as well as his solution, in a new light.

own understanding of his life allowed him to tailor a solution that fit perfectly for who he was. We met for only one session.

In this case, Calvin's level of emotional arousal was increased and he began the process of self-reevaluation. He was able to draw on his personal knowledge about his own life to better prepare. As the counselor, I reaffirmed that clients often possess considerable knowledge that can be tapped. My role was not to be a content expert but rather an expert at the process of finding solutions. While I facilitated my clients' search for solutions that worked, each client assumed responsibility for generating and implementing the new patterns that finally served as solutions. In this case I helped Calvin make a connection between what he did well and what he wanted to do. A specific costume to wear when he wrote was a key element in accessing a resourceful state for writing.

Preparation/Action

The move from the preparation stage to the action stage is facilitated by the change process of commitment (choosing and committing to act, or belief in ability to change). Two cases are offered to illustrate how this occurred in counseling sessions through the employment of clothing. Change from preparation to action occurred in Case 3 by introducing walking shoes. Change in Case 4 was facilitated using silk pajamas.

Finding exceptions can be challenging. Clients often have patterns from their prior experiences that may be useful in effectively dealing with the present. When Paul became aware of his exceptional behavior, his commitment to his goal was strengthened. The answer was as obvious as the walking shoes on his feet.

Case 4 illustrates how a client was able to use her own imagination to come up with a novel and humorous way to achieve her goal. The case also illustrates how the circumstances surrounding a case may be very serious, but this does not preclude the use of humor to assist a client. While the paperwork in this example is in the form of bills, the principles involved apply to the mound of paper that often appears on our desks. The quotes by Connie (the client) are from follow-up letters I received from her.

The silk pajamas from Victoria's Secret proved to be a pivotal point in our session. Connie had the skills and knowledge necessary to change, but she lacked the decisive commitment. The humor and excitement of the silk

CASE 4
I've Got a Secret

I met Connie in a workshop when she volunteered to be in a demonstration of brief counseling. During the workshop she stated her problem as follows:

"Since the death of my husband, I'm overwhelmed by the volume of stuff on my desk. This includes bills, invitations, insurance claims, correspondence, estimates for work to be done on the house, and notes concerning tasks which need to be handled. I believe I can do the work since I have two offices in which both desks are clean and all items are handled promptly. Still, this home situation seems so out of hand that I rarely can force myself to start on the project."

Connie's goal was rather straightforward. She wanted to be able to look at her desk and see a clean desk with possibly one or two items on top to be handled. More specifically, she wanted: 1) all of her bills paid on time, 2) cards and gifts sent out ahead of time, and 3) only a few envelopes on her desk, compared to the present mountain that rested there now.

Having arrived at a goal, I challenged Connie to come up with a plan to reach her goal by doing something different—but something different that was fun, interesting, or exciting. As we talked about what Connie could do to reach her goal she said the following:

I'm thinking, "How could this be fun?" I feel really good in the morning. I wonder about what would motivate me to change my behavior. I think I'll set my alarm for one-half hour earlier (5:30 A.M.) since I am most motivated at that time of day. I will work for one-half hour only—taking the project bit by bit instead of all at once—essentially changing the goal into a daily goal instead of the overwhelming one which I have now."

I shared with her that in my world 5:30 A.M. didn't exist, but that it sounded as though she was willing to do what she had come up with. Fun, interesting, or exciting ways to reach goals are not for all clients; however, Connie had a good sense of humor. Connie talked about getting up early to reach her goal, but I didn't hear much enthusiasm in her voice. It sounded like she was just going to go through the motions but without much enthusiasm. It was something that she said she would do, but I was skeptical. Because we had discussed doing something that was fun, interesting, or exciting, I challenged her to make what she would be doing more fun than what it sounded to me. She agreed that she could probably make the task more exciting.

During a break later that day, Connie said to me, "I'm going to order some silk pajamas from the *Victoria's Secret* catalog and I'm going to wear them only while doing desk work. I'll also enjoy a cup of coffee while on the task." As she told me this new plan I watched the nonverbal excitement and energy now being conveyed. Excitement and energy are what I'm looking for in terms of congruence between verbally stated willingness to do something and nonverbal body messages that are saying, "Yes, I am going to do this!" I asked Connie if she were willing to share her new, fun plan with the group. She readily agreed. During and following her sharing, Connie's mood and that of the group was best characterized as joy and high spirits manifested in laughter and merrymaking.

Our brief counseling session lasted approximately 30 minutes. A year later I sent Connie a follow-up evaluation form. In reply I received a letter from Connie and was delighted to read the following declaration:

"I am declaring your brief counseling on my desk problem a success because: 1) all of my bills are paid on time, 2) cards and gifts are out ahead of time, and 3) only a few envelopes are on my desk at this moment compared to the mountain which formerly rested there. I feel capable and powerful."

Connie proceeded to answer the following questions: What did you like best about the use of brief counseling? The least? What would you change if you had to do it over?

"What I liked best was the idea of it being brief. I counsel in two schools, which means I am the counselor for 800 children. I need lessons in brevity. Also, the thought of changing attitudes and looking at the possibility of being fun or silly about the problem opened up new thinking for me because the old certainly wasn't working."

Christine Simpson had written a sensitive and moving book about her daughter's coming to terms with her uncle's death by AIDS. Her book, *Jenny's Locket* (Simpson, 1996) had been published and now Christine was contacting all 50 state departments of education to have the book available for children. Christine had successfully completed 44 of 50 phone calls she wanted to make, but now she was stuck. She labeled herself a procrastinator. She asked herself why couldn't she complete the calls, because, after all, she had done most of them.

My initial response was to have her make the calls in a fun, interesting, and exciting way, because this particular technique seems to free people from viewing their problem as drudgery. Christine would have none of that. She just couldn't think of a way to make the remaining calls fun. In brief counseling, when something isn't working, the counselor needs to do something different.

I looked at Christine and said, "Christine, you have convinced me that there is no fun, interesting, or exciting way to make those phone calls. Maybe you're one of those persons who just has to grind it out. In fact, I suspect that for you to make those remaining phone calls is the equivalent of trudging through shit."

The change on Christine's face was amazing. She laughed and said, "You couldn't be more right!"

Sensing we were now on the right track, I added, "I have this picture in my mind of you standing near your desk making those last six calls wearing galoshes to protect your feet from all that shit you're standing in. Are you willing to get some galoshes and make those last six phone calls?"

Christine agreed to get a pair of galoshes from her husband and make the calls. Several days following our single session, I sent Christine a short, encouraging note with an attached picture of galoshes cut from a magazine. Several weeks later I received a letter from Christine. She wrote:

"I received your clipping of my galoshes and chuckled for the next day or so—and every time I look at them. At this point I have finally tacked the photo up at my desk. Well, I sat down to make those last six phone calls. I got all decked out to be the epitome of the absurd with my hubby's grassy, muddy boots on my feet and to my knees, emerald earrings, the whole nine yards. It was all I could do not to laugh when on the phone to Nevada, Ohio, Tennessee, New Hampshire, New York, and Kansas, but I did it.

Today I got a call back from my contact in Tennessee. You may think I am making this up, but I am not. She loved *Jenny's Locket* and is sending me the necessary paperwork so she can order 1600 books. One for each school in her entire state! In the past year I sold/gave away 1000 books. Today I matched that—and all because I got a kick in the rear at the right time."

I did not get a photograph of myself as you requested because no one else happened to be around. But that doesn't matter because I know in my heart and head what happened—and most importantly, someone believes in *Jenny's Locket* and will help me get it into the hands of children. Thank you so much for the "boot" in the rear! Galoshes are very special to me now."

---

pajamas opened up the way for Connie to make a commitment and to propel her from the preparation stage into the action stage.

Action

Successful action on a problem behavior is facilitated by four change processes: reward (rewarding self, or being rewarded by others, for making changes), countering (substituting alternatives for problem behaviors), environmental control (avoiding stimuli that elicit problem behaviors), and helping relationships (enlisting the help of someone who cares). In the final case, I employed galoshes to effect therapeutic change. The case involved only a single session with follow-up. Christine Simpson (the client's real name) had issued "A Call for Help."

Christine wore the galoshes and discovered that they actually transformed the phone calls from something she had to do into something she wanted to do. She appeared to use the helping relationship of counseling to engage in new actions. At the same time, the galoshes helped her control her environment by transforming the stimuli that elicited problem behavior (sitting at her desk in her office) into a room with manure on the floor for which galoshes were an appropriate and entertaining solution. Ironically, wearing galoshes to deal with the problem proved to be highly amusing to Christine and thus belied her earlier belief that the phone calls couldn't be fun, interesting, or exciting.

Conclusion

As counseling has evolved from exclusively a "talking cure" into more action-oriented approaches such as brief counseling, counselors have searched for new ways to effect therapeutic change. To date there have been only isolated reports in which brief counselors have used clothing to help clients reach their desired states. The integration of the cases presented in this paper with the stages-of-change model developed by Prochaska et al. (1994) offers a clear picture of how clothing may be employed across the stages of change.

On a personal note, the writing of this paper has afforded me the opportunity to place in a larger and much more systematic framework the therapeutic interventions I have employed over the years involving the use of clothing. I had not realized until I began thinking about this paper that I had used clothing to effect therapeutic change in a variety of counseling situations using multiple methods. Prochaska's model helped me realize that I was using clothing across the various stages of change and involving clothing in numerous change processes. My hope is that this paper will open the dialogue among counselors and scholars from the fields of textiles and clothing and psychology.

References

de Shazer, S. (1994). *Words were originally magic.* New York: W. W. Norton.

Fisch, R., Weakland, J. H., & Segal, L. (1982). *The tactics of change.* San Francisco: Jossey-Bass.

Furman, B., & Ahola, T. (1992). *Solution talk: Hosting therapeutic conversations.* New York: W. W. Norton.

Haley, J. (1973). *Uncommon therapy: The psychiatric techniques of Milton H. Erickson, M.D.* New York: Norton.

Littrell, J. M. (1998). *Brief counseling in action.* New York: W. W. Norton.

Littrell, J. M., Malia, J. A., & Vanderwood, M. (1995). Single-session brief counseling in a high school. *Journal of Counseling and Development, 73*(4), 451–458.

O'Hanlon, W. H., & Hexum, A. L. (1990). *An uncommon casebook: The complete clinical work of Milton H. Erickson, M.D.* New York: Norton.

O'Hanlon, W. H., & Weiner-Davis, M. (1989). *In search of solutions.* New York: Norton.

Prochaska, J. O., Norcross, J. C., & DiClemente, C. C. (1994). *Changing for good.* New York: William Morrow.

Simpson, C. (1996). *Jenny's Locket.* Nazareth, PA: Pearl Press.

Talmon, M. (1993). *Single session solutions: A guide to practical, effective, and affordable therapy.* Reading, MA: Addison-Wesley.

DISCUSSION QUESTIONS

Employing Clothing for Therapeutic Change in Brief Counseling

1. For which of the six stages of dealing with problem behaviors did Littrell present clothing examples?

2. Have you ever used clothing or other forms of dress to help you tackle a problem? What was the situation? Does it relate to any of the six stages of problem behavior therapy?

CHAPTER 5

Appearance for Gender and Sexuality

Susan O. Michelman

AFTER YOU HAVE READ THIS CHAPTER, YOU WILL COMPREHEND:

- Comparison of the cultural meaning of being a man or woman, and the link of gender norms to appearance.

- How gender is socially and culturally determined and is a significant component in the study of appearance.

- The diversity of human appearance that may be influenced by sexual orientation.

What do we notice in the first few seconds of encountering someone else? We usually notice skin color, age, body language, appearance (particularly if it is "different" and deviates from the norm) and most critically a person's sex—at least we think we see whether an individual is male or female. Actually, what we first notice is **gender appearance,** which we may correctly or incorrectly identify as a sign of their sex. What most people experience on a daily basis is related to fitting into socially accepted gender norms for dress.

Clothing does not have inherent meaning, it is culturally defined. Cultural norms and expectations surrounding the meaning of being a man or woman are closely linked to appearance. For example, in many Muslim societies, the practice of women's veiling quickly identifies gender as well as the cultural meaning of being a woman in that society. Women's lifestyles are secluded from the world outside the home, the domain of men. In Indonesia, the *sarong*, a rectangular piece of cloth wrapped and tied around the waist, is worn by both men and women. Similarly, the *wrapper*, in West Africa is worn by both sexes. In the culture of North America, the *sarong* and *wrapper*, which physically resemble our definition of a skirt, would rarely be seen on men except perhaps within the theatre, on film, or in the context of couture or *avant-garde* fashion. (See Figure 5.1.) Although currently somewhat limited to the young and brave, French designer Jean-Paul Gaultier recently designed skirts for men.

What then is meant when we use the terms gender and sex? Although many people use the terms interchangeably, the two terms do not have the same meaning. **Gender**, determined psychologically, socially, and culturally refers to "appropriate" behavior and appearance for males and females. Appropriate male and female behavior varies according to time and place. **Sex** refers to the biological aspects of maleness or femaleness. A person's sex is determined on the basis of **primary sex characteristics**, the anatomical traits essential to reproduction. One may assume that determining biological sex is a clear-cut process, but a significant number of babies are born **intersexed**. This is a broad term used by the medical profession to classify people with some mixture of male and female biological characteristics (Newman, 1995). For example, a **true hermaphrodite** is a person who is born with ovaries and testes. Why, then, is there no intersexed category? Parents of such children usually collaborate with a physician to assign their offspring to one of the two recognized sexes.

Secondary sex characteristics distinguish one sex from another. These are physical traits not essential to reproduction (e.g., breast development, quality of voice, distribution of facial and body hair, and skeletal form). Many of the articles in this text are concerned with such aspects of appearance. For example, the article "Athletic Aesthetic" by Brubach examines how some women currently envision their body ideal as one that is muscular and strong. This is in contrast to more typical 20th-century appearances of options for women.

Gender is a **social construction**. Frequently, differences between males and females are attributed to biology rather than the fact that they may be socially created. For example, the French painter Paul Gauguin noted this ambiguity about men and women

FIGURE 5.1 *A Kalabari man from Nigeria, West Africa, in traditional dress, which includes a wrapper, shirt, waist- and head-ties, and beads.*

which he recorded in a journal that he kept while painting in Tahiti in 1891. His observations were highly influenced by his recollections of the fashion norms of Europe during this period of the late 19th century, when women wore tightly laced corsets under their dresses. (See Figure 5.2a and b.)

> Among peoples that go naked, as among animals, the difference between the sexes is less accentuated than in our climates. Thanks to our cinctures and corsets we have succeeded in making an artificial being out of woman....We carefully keep her in a state of nervous weakness and muscular inferiority, and in guarding her from fatigue, we take away from her possibilities of development. Thus modeled on a bizarre ideal of slenderness...our women have nothing in common with us [men], and this, perhaps, may not be without grave moral and social disadvantages.
>
> On Tahiti, the breezes from forest and sea strengthen the lungs, they broaden the shoulders and hips. Neither men nor women are sheltered from the rays of the sun nor the pebbles of the sea-shore. Together they engage in the same tasks with the same activity....There is something virile in the women and something feminine in the men. (Gauguin [1919] 1985, pp. 19-20)

a   b

FIGURE 5.2. *The dress on the left in (a) follows the S-shaped silhouette that is more typical of the 19th-century. Gauguin's painting (b) illustrates his observations of Tahitian women.*

How then are we socialized into an appearance that is either masculine or feminine? This is determined by the culture in which a child is raised. **Socialization** is a learning process that begins immediately after birth and continues throughout life. It is a process that allows individuals to develop their human capacities, acquire a unique personality and identity, and internalize the norms, values, beliefs, and language needed to participate in society (Ferrante, 1995). Socialization involves the cultural context in childhood and adolescence in which individuals form their concepts of self. For example, when a child is born in any culture, the first question is almost always, "Is it a boy or a girl?" Although the answer to this question is based on a physical exam of genitalia, very quickly in a child's life, gender is established by others observing the way an infant is dressed by the parents. For example, in American hospitals newborn babies are given pink or blue blankets, identification bracelets, or even hair ribbons that give quick visual identification of their gender. Research has shown that children as young as two years of age classify people into gender categories based on their appearance (Weinraub et al., 1984). This is obviously long before they understand the meaning of the biological differences. The article "Day-Care Dress Up Not Amusing to Boy's Dad" points out that young children experiment with gender through dress up. This normal experimentation by the boy with feminine dress was interpreted by the father as "abnormal." In this chapter, we will be examining how gender and even sexuality does not exist as a binary opposition of male and female.

Gender socialization regarding appearance is closely linked to learned social roles. Children are highly influenced by gender-specific toys that serve to reinforce social stereotypes regarding femininity and masculinity. Some examples that have come under scrutiny for their influence on the development of children are Barbie for girls and G.I. Joe or Power Rangers for boys. Similarly, children's books and media images can reinforce stereotypical gender appearances. *Beauty and the Beast* and *The Little Mermaid* contain classic examples of beautiful young women whose lives are made perfect by a handsome prince. As children grow, they may begin to associate behaviors with gendered dress. The trend for very young children to wear designer clothing may contribute to their over-involvement and even preoccupation with appearance issues while they are very young and vulnerable.

THE SEXUAL IDENTITY KIT

Questions of gender are socially defined, but what about **sexual identity**? Do the anatomical differences in the reproductive systems of men and women provide a foundation for identifying the self as feminine or masculine? Present day debate on whether sexual identity is biological or constructed (as is gender) has been influenced by social movements dealing with sexual politics (Woodward, 1997). One important example is the **feminist** movement. In the broadest sense, a feminist is a woman or man who actively opposes gender dogma (i.e., learned patterns of behavior expected of males and females) and believes that self-image, aspirations, and life chances of both women and men should not be constrained by those scripts (Bem, 1993). For some people, the term feminist evokes negative images and stereotypes of mannish-looking women who hate men and who find vocations as wife and mother oppressive and unrewarding (Ferrante, 1995). In the article "A Visual Analysis of Feminist Dress," Kunkel analyzes the wide range of physical appearances of women who are self-designated feminists. Kunkel makes a strong point that there is no one physical stereotype.

What do you think of when you hear the word **sexism**? The male construction worker who whistles and shouts sexual comments at females passing by? The office worker who makes lewd comments about a coworker's appearance? Sexism refers to a system of beliefs and behaviors by which a group of people are oppressed, controlled, and exploited because of presumed gender differences (Anderson & Collins, 1992; Rothenberg, 1992). The Civil Rights Act, Title VII, defines **sexual harassment** as ". . . unwelcomed sexual advances, requests for sexual favors and other verbal or physical conduct of a sexual nature that are connected to decisions about employment or that create an intimidating, hostile, or offensive work environment." Feminist authors have sought to expand the definition of sexual harassment to include any coercive behavior imposed upon members of one gender by those of the other gender, which results in conditions of unequal power and is associated with gender differences (Wise & Stanley, 1987). Gender stereotypes figure strongly in the public's perceptions of both parties in harassment cases. Research consistently finds that the general public assumes that women who wear sexually provocative dress incite, and are in part responsible for, sexual harassment from coworkers (Johnson & Workman, 1992; Workman & Johnson, 1991). However, most evidence indicates that sexual harassment in the workplace is a power issue; an individual in a power position attempts to harass a subordinate regardless of how the individual dresses because the subordinate is an "easy," powerless target. Dress is an ambiguous form of communication, read incorrectly in many instances, and cannot be considered clear indication of intent of victims to "ask for" sex or sexual attention (Lennon, Lennon & Johnson, 1993).

Another type of harassment can be related to sexual preference. The article "Northampton Confronts a Crime, Cruelty," reports the violent and tragic consequences of **homophobia** or fear and harassment of individuals perceived to have a homosexual lifestyle. **Homosexuality** can be defined as same-sex sexual activity. Although this describes sexual experience, it does not necessarily include a long-term homosexual or gay lifestyle, because many heterosexual individuals have had homosexual experiences. Also, there are some individuals with **bisexual** desires and activities. A 15-year-old person such as the student described in the *Boston Globe* article may have conflict between sexual desires and activity and may be in a transition stage of sexual development without coming out to a more clearly defined homosexual, bisexual, or heterosexual resolution.

It is hoped that the materials presented in this book, as well as the reader's own thoughtful reflections will lead to an appreciation of diversity in culture as well as sexual orientation. The double tragedy of homophobic harassment and the victim's violent reaction should be most distressing for students of dress and culture because the article suggests that the harassment followed an intolerant, and perhaps incorrect, interpretation of dress and appearance.

Cross-Dressing

Popular culture is one venue for us to glimpse "queer practices," which play on masculine/feminine ambiguities with their deliberate exposure and celebration of the mismatch between gender and sexuality (Woodward, 1997). For example, as discussed in Hegland's article "Drag Queens, Transvestites, Transexuals: Stepping Across the Accepted Boundaries of Gender," **cross-dressers** are males who put on feminine dress or females who wear masculine dress for different purposes or effects. Culturally prescribed and proscribed gender norms, manifested by dress and appearance, can be challenged through social interaction. What happens when individuals step across the social boundaries of gender-appropriate dress and appearance by cross-dressing? How does the public respond when confronted with an incongruous or unfamiliar gender appearance? Recent popular movies such as *Tootsie*; *Mrs. Doubtfire*; *Priscilla, Queen of the Desert*; and *The Birdcage* have confirmed growing popular interest in gender-bending appearances of men cross-dressing as women. RuPaul, a male-to-female cross-dresser who has his own talk show on television, effects an appearance of a supermodel that is admired by some young women. *Victor/Victoria* was a popular play and movie that considered in a lighthearted way whether or not a woman can successfully "pass" as a man. This, of course, is Hollywood's interpretation of these gender issues. Does it work as well off-screen for those who cross dress? Hegland's article will give you a more realistic perspective.

Dress and Gender: A Historical Perspective

Examining dress historically gives us perspective on how the relationship between dress and gender has changed. During the 20th century up through the 1950s, men followed a **restricted code** for appearance, limited to angular design lines, neutral and subdued color palettes, bifurcated garments (i.e., pants) for the lower body, natural but not tight silhouettes, sturdy fabrics and shoes, and simple hair and face grooming (McCracken, 1985). This simple, restricted code helped them to focus on work and accomplishments rather than appearance. Their attire (except perhaps for the tie) did not tend to impede physical activity. In sum, men dressed for an agonic role in society. Spindler's article "Men in Uniformity" examines how men in our society typically dress to conceal aspects of their identity, which Spindler feels is not always true of women. She feels even the opportunity for men to let down their hair at work on "casual Fridays" has not released them from the burden of conformity, as they frequently adopt a "GAP-centric" uniform of T-shirts tucked into khakis or jeans.

Women, in contrast, had an **elaborated** code for appearance up through the 1950s. They could wear some of what men wore, and a lot more. Their unlimited options for fabrics, colors, design lines, and silhouettes gave them a useful bag of tricks for attending to their hedonic role, emphasizing pursuit of beauty and physical being. Their tight or flowing skirts, high heels, and nylons did not facilitate emphasis on physical activity, however. Women were encouraged to spend a lot of time on clothes, hair, weight control, and makeup to render themselves beautiful for men (who would marry and support women to have children). Women's engrossments in appearance, along with attending to men and children, could easily distract them from pursuing a full-time career.

Since the late 1960s, the pendulum has swung from men and women wearing distinctively different styles to an interest in so-called unisex and androgynous styles. **Androgyny** is defined as a mixing of masculine and feminine qualities in one person's appearance, while **unisex** refers to a style of clothing that could be worn by either men or women. For example, women have adopted some amount of androgyny in business dress. According to McCracken (1985), businesswomen in the United States avidly appropriated the business suit and its corresponding masculine body form in the early 1980s. He believes the motivation was a striving for women to be similar to their male counterparts in business settings, with shoulder pads, conservative fabrics, and a focus on the upper torso and head through contrasting shirt and tie. By the mid-1980s, however, women in business were increasingly moving away from a completely masculine look to a mix of feminine and masculine styling (Ogle & Damhorst, in press). Along with many business women softening their image, some U. S. men are showing less concern with a traditional masculine physical image, particularly in casual dress. Many men now wear soft pastel colors in shirts, in addition to jewelry, cologne, and skin products that were previously worn exclusively by women.

Goffman (1961) referred to the clothing and other necessary accoutrements of appearance as "identity kits." Today, these "kits" are being rapidly reevaluated according to social perceptions of gender, particularly as traditional social roles for men and women change. Men in the United States are now beginning to experiment with the torments of vanity, the prior domain of women. Men now account for around 25 percent of all cosmetic surgeries (see "You're So Vain" in Chapter 9). Clearly, men and women are not so different today in their obsession with appearance.

Summary

The articles in this chapter address multiple aspects of our gender appearance. Articles examine how we are socialized into gender, the relationship between sexuality and gender, the politics of appearance, and an examination of a historical practice in Chinese culture that constructed a feminine appearance. The articles allow you to critically reflect on your own thinking and ideas about appearance and its relationship to gender and sexuality.

Suggested Readings

Woodhouse, A. (1989). Sex, gender, and appearance. *Fantastic women: Sex, gender and transvestism* (pp. 1–16). New Brunswick, NJ: Rutgers University Press, pp. 1–16.

Barnes, R., & Eicher, J. (Eds.) (1992). *Dress and gender: Making and meaning.* Oxford, England: Berg Press.

Cahill, S. E. (1987). Directions for an interactionist study of gender development. In M. J. Deegan & M. Hill (Eds.), *Women and symbolic interaction.* Boston: Allen and Unwin, Inc.

Garber, M. (1992). *Vested interests: Cross-dressing and cultural anxiety.* New York: Routledge.

Goffman, E. (1976). *Gender advertisements.* New York: Harper Torchbooks.

Kessler, S.J., & McKenna, W. (1978). *Gender: An ethnomethodological approach.* Chicago: The University of Chicago Press.

Roach-Higgins, M., & Eicher, J. (1992, Summer). Dress and identity. *Clothing and Textiles Research Journal, 10,* (4), 1–8.

References

Anderson, M. L., & Collins, P. H. (1992). *Race, class, and gender: An anthology.* Belmont, CA: Wadsworth.

Bem, S. (1993). *The lenses of gender: Transforming the debate on sexual inequality.* New Haven: Yale University Press.

Davis, F. (1992). *Fashion, culture and identity.* Chicago: University of Chicago Press.

Ferrante, J. (1995). *Sociology: A global perspective.* NY: Wadsworth Publishing.

Gauguin, P. [1919] (1985). *Noa Noa: The Tahitian journal,* Trans. by O. F. Theis. New York: Dover.

Goffman, E. (1961). *Asylums.* Garden City, NY: Doubleday.

Johnson, K. K. P., & Workman, J., (1992). Clothing and attributions concerning sexual harassment. *Home Economics Research Journal, 21*(2), 160–172.

Lennon, T., Lennon, S. J., & Johnson, K. K. P. (1993). Is clothing probative of attitude and intent? Implications for rape and sexual harassment cases. *Journal of Law and Inequality, 11,* 301–325.

McCracken, G. (1985). The trickle-down theory rehabilitated. In M. R. Solomon (Ed.),*The psychology of fashion* (pp. 39–54). Lexington, MA: Lexington Books.

Newman, D. (1995). *Sociology: Exploring the architecture of everyday life.* Thousand Oaks, CA: Pine Forge Press.

Ogle, J. P., & Damhorst, M. L. (In press). Dress for success in the popular press. In K. K. P. Johnson & S. J. Lennon (Eds.), *Power and appearance.* New York: Berg.

Rothenberg, P. S. (1992). *Race, class, and gender in the United States.* New York: St. Martin's Press.

Weinraub, M., Clemens, L. P., Sockloff, A., Ethridge, T., Gracely, E. & Myers, B. (1984). The development of sex role stereotypes in the third year: Relationships to gender labeling, gender identity, sex-typed toy preference, and family characteristics. *Child Development 55,* 1493–1503.

Wise, S., & Stanley, L. (1987). *Georgie porgie: Sexual harassment in everyday life.* London: Pandora.

Woodward, K. (1997). *Identity and difference.* Thousand Oaks, CA: Sage Publications.

Workman, J. & Johnson, K. K. P. (1991). The role of cosmetics in attributions about sexual harassment. *Sex Roles, 24*(11/12), 759–769.

Appearance for Gender and Sexuality

Objective: To examine the intimate relationship between what we wear and our perceptions of gender.

This assignment will involve working with a partner to analyze which items of clothing are typically used only by males or females and which forms of dress are worn by both genders.

Procedure

Students should pair up. Ideally, females should pair with a male. This may not always be possible, however. Each student should obtain ten images from magazines, mail-order catalogs, or newspapers that depict items of clothing. To make the images slightly more ambiguous, cut off the head in the image. Try to pick some images that are more androgynous than others. Include some unisex clothing.

Show each image to your partner. Have your partner indicate if the item is typically worn by males or females. If the item is typically used by both males and females have your partner indicate "both."

Discuss and compare your responses with those of your partner. What are the items of clothing that are worn only by females? What items of clothing are worn only by males? What items are worn by both males and females?

Discussion

As a class, discuss why certain items of clothing are restricted to females. Why are some items worn predominantly by males? Analyze how dress has a role in reinforcing gender stereotypes. How have some of these "rules" of dress and gender changed within the past 10 to15 years? What social, economic, political, and ideological influences have affected gender and appearance issues? How might different cultures and their dress influence our typically "American" attitudes toward gender and appearance?

22   The Athletic Esthetic

Holly Brubach

A woman might train her body to excel in an astonishing variety of sports, to be precise and fast, to run with longer strides and to reach with her legs for the finish line, bettering her personal record by precious seconds, until eventually she wins three Olympic medals and commands such widespread admiration that she is called "the greatest athlete of all mankind for all time." But could she find a husband? That was the question with which the press confronted Mildred (Babe) Didrikson after her triumph in the track and field events at the Los Angeles Games in 1932.

A single woman, Didrikson was upheld as an example of the miserable fate that could befall young girls who grew too muscular. If the natural order decreed that women were "the weaker sex," then the woman who became strong disqualified herself from the attentions of the average man, who would no longer feel superior in her presence. In 1938, Didrikson set the matter to rest once and for all when she married George Zaharias, a 300-pound wrestler.

Hindsight enables us to see that Didrikson was the harbinger of a new ideal, and that most people at the time were simply not fitted to appreciate the beauty of a strong woman's body. Her glory, it seems, posed a threat to the existing order. Other women, for their part, were apparently content to aspire to the prevailing notions of the ideal female body. Those notions, reiterated and updated, persist in the images that surround us, and women persist in transforming their bodies accordingly, in an effort to endear themselves to the world.

But before setting out in pursuit of beauty, a woman must decide which—or rather, whose—idea of beauty she wants to pursue. Until recently, there were only two options. The first—the body, custom-built for clothes—is an image of women as they would like to see themselves. The second ideal—the body custom-built for sex—is a vision of women as men would like to see them. The end dictates the means, dividing women into separate camps. Some diet, in order to approximate the models in Vogue. Some get breast implants, in the hope of looking like the women featured in the Victoria's Secret catalogue.

It is only in the last few years, in ads for sneakers and sports clothes, in fitness magazines with circulations a fraction the size of Vogue's, that a third ideal has begun to emerge: the body custom-built for athletics. It is an ideal whose consequences are still unsettling and far-reaching. But at this point our fascination outweighs our trepidation. We made our way through "Terminator 2," riveted by the sight of Linda Hamilton's biceps. On Sunday nights, an audience of young girls tunes in to a television show whose host is their heroine, the pro volleyball star Gabrielle Reece. Condé Nast, the publishing empire whose titles include Vogue, Mademoiselle and Glamour, has announced its plans to introduce a new magazine about women and sports next spring. A woman—the basketball star Sheryl Swoopes—has, like Michael Jordan, had a sneaker named after her. Didrikson was simply born too soon. The ideal she represented was dismissed in her day, but it will not be put off any longer.

Back in the 1970's, at the onset of the so-called fitness craze, women's magazines that had been turning out perfunctory articles on calisthenics and spot-reducing, timed to coincide with the onset of bathing suit season, began directing their attention to the science of aerobics. Readers were exhorted to work up a sweat. Weight loss and muscle tone would follow. The argument for regular, vigorous exercise was not only esthetic but also medical, buttressed with quotations from doctors. Not that it needed buttressing—the women's movement and sexual liberation had predisposed women to the idea of taking responsibility for their bodies. Clothes and makeup were considered not for the trends they represented but as tools to be deployed at will, in the service of the magazines' larger subject: a woman's self-image. If the models pictured in these fitness articles weren't appreciably different from the models pictured in the fashion pages—if, in fact, at times they were the same models—the magazines could be forgiven: the women in aerobics classes at the time, even the die-hards, were mostly taut and lean, with muscles that weren't especially pronounced.

Since then, the glamour of fashion and the culture of fitness have pretty much parted company. As research has come out in favor of strength training, with weights or some other form of resistance as a supplement to cardiovascular workouts, bodies have changed, and women have acquired muscles that their mothers never had. Meanwhile, the narrow standard for the bodies that populate the pages of the fashion magazines remain unchanged. After a brief-and highly touted-moment a few years ago, when women who looked more ample and somewhat fleshier were being admitted to the ranks of the top models, the norm has reverted to the emaciated type that has predominated since Twiggy's heyday in the late 60's. In fact, the new generation of so-called supermodels—Kirsty Hume, Kate Moss, Shalom Harlow, Trish Goff, Amber Valletta—is stick-thin. Even Cindy Crawford and Claudia Schiffer, who star in their own exercise videos, look more toned than strong, their muscles lacking definition.

The fashion magazines have abdicated any responsibility for women's fitness. The exhortations are gone; the articles on the physiologic benefits of exercise are brief and infrequent, eclipsed if not replaced by first-person accounts of liposuction and other cosmetic surgery in keeping with the ideal body shown in the fashion pages. When, in 1979, Condé Nast inaugurated a magazine by the name of Self, to be devoted in large part to exercise and health, it cleaved the two ideals, freeing each to pursue its own course. From then on, Vogue could concentrate on the body best suited to the latest clothes, and women hungry for serious information about exercise were obliged to turn to special-interest magazines (of which Self is today only one of a dozen or so).

It's instructive to contemplate the differences between the various ideals for women and how the corresponding physiques are acquired. The fashion body is an achievement, arrived at by means of renunciation; it is the paradigm for an esthetic of purity, for a nunlike dedication to the cult of appearances and a capacity to forgo the sensual pleasure that food has to offer. In fashion photographs, the women who have attained this ideal strike aggressive poses, their limbs attenuated, angular and linear. Their faces, innocent and flawless, convey a certain smugness; their looks are outward evidence not of what they've done but of what they haven't done. They have risen above their bodies, subjugated them, pared them down to their essence of skin and bones. A tendency to appear frail and brittle lends these women an air of feminine helplessness: they must be handled with care. In a train station at rush hour, men would stop and offer to carry their suitcases.

Offers of another kind undoubtedly come the way of the odalisques in the Victoria's Secret catalogue, who are seen reclining, in various states of déshabille. Their attitude is languorous, passive and complacent, as if they were waiting for something to happen or for a man to come along. Their proportions are improbable, if not as preposterous as those of the women in Playboy and in pornographic magazines. Still, the Victoria's Secret types look like cartoon versions of real women, theirs bustlines selectively exaggerated to an extent that occurs rarely, if ever, in nature. (Because breast tissue is composed mostly of fat, a woman that bosomy would be fuller in the hips and thighs as well.) It seems safe to assume that this ideal, as embodied by these women, is the result not of what they've done but of what has been done to—or for—them: breast implants and, in some cases, liposuction. Even so, their legs and arms are never scrawny. Unlike fashion models, these women look as if they have an extra layer of upholstery gently cushioning the sharp corners of their joints.

These privileged glimpses of a life set in the boudoir are in stark contrast to the scenes in Women's Sports and Fitness, in which athletes streak across sunlit, wide-open landscapes. Caught in the act of biking, rowing, jogging, training for a triathlon, they look as if they refused to stop long enough to have their pictures taken. These women exude competence; they can carry their own suitcases. Their muscles, like the fashion models' slenderness, are hard-earned, but here the means is not abstinence but exertion. Though their bodies have been meticulously cultivated, their bodies aren't the point: the point is their ability to perform. What is most striking, given that it's the other two ideals that are calculated to please—to win the admiration of women or the affection of men—is the fact that these athletes seem content in a way that the other women don't.

And so, if women in our society are confused about what's required of them in order to qualify as beautiful, it's no wonder.

The progress of women in sports has been, admittedly, somewhat fitful, and the image of a muscular woman has been particularly slow to gain currency—perhaps to some degree because, deep down, our attitudes toward women's physical strength are conflicted. We applaud the notion of women at long last coming into their own. And yet, we wonder whether their achievement, by encroaching on what has traditionally been a man's prerogative, might in some way skew the balance between the sexes: women's gain is suspected of being men's loss.

Worse, women who have muscles are regarded by some people—men and women alike—as traitors to their sex, guilty of trying to become men. (Female body builders are widely regarded as the prime offenders. The trouble with this argument, and with this example, is that female body builders look not so much like men in general but like male body builders— their fellow subscribers to an esthetic that many, if not most, of the rest of us find grotesque.)

There is no underestimating the anxieties triggered by the prospect of women's physical strength. Will women, having laid claim to attributes we think of as manly, eventually usurp the positions that men have been occupying?

What if women injure themselves by trying to do what nature, in its almighty wisdom, never intended them to do? By inviting comparisons (if not competing directly) with men, who are biologically better equipped for most sports, are women setting themselves up for humiliation and defeat? Will muscles do away with the last trace of women's vulnerability—a quality that men have traditionally found attractive and touching?

And yet, muscles on women seem to serve a purpose. Anne Hollander believes that they are a way for women to take up space, as men do— to add physical substance, which, she says, "makes everyone take notice and listen to what you have to say and pay attention to your existence." A critic whose first book, *Seeing Through Clothes*, traced the parallels between artists' depiction of the nude body and fashionable dress, Hollander notes that, in other centuries, substance was something women achieved by means of the clothes they wore. "Queen Elizabeth I was a skinny little thing with a flat chest," she explains. "In order to make her presence felt she had to wear pounds of padded stuff that expanded her torso at the sides giving her the force she needed. It was absolutely not an option where she was concerned to have that narrow nymph's body, which was much admired in the love poetry of the time. That sort of woman had only indirect power."

At 6 foot 3 and 172 pounds, Gabrielle Reece commands respect and attention, too, but she's wearing a sports bra and briefs. The techniques available to Elizabeth I for colonizing the space around her would be impractical today, as would the avoirdupois of the imposing Victorian matron. We wear clothes that expose our bodies, and so the only acceptable way for us to add mass is to add muscle.

What is especially striking about the images of women we see in Nike ads or in the sports pages of the newspapers is that they come to us with so few precedents. From classical antiquity right up to our century, painters and sculptors have rendered women without muscles. (Michelangelo was one of the few exceptions.) Even Amazons, on the basis of their bodies alone, are indistinguishable from the goddesses of love; we recognize them by their short, one-sided tunics. The men in art, in a tradition descended from the Greeks, wear their muscles like a suit of armor just beneath the skin; no insult, physical or otherwise, could penetrate their strength. Their bodies are faceted, the surface subdivided into planes, like a Cubist painting. The women, however, tend to be enveloped in a blanket of fat. The transition from their ankles to their calves, from their calves to their knees, is made smoothly, uninterrupted by bones and tendons. Their thighs are lush. Their breasts are like peaches.

Judging from this cavalcade of inherited images, we might easily conclude that the guys in ads for Calvin Klein underwear look enough like the men we see in Poussin's paintings to be directly descended from them; it's the women today who look as if they're no relation to their predecessors. Along the road to independence, which has spanned the better part of our century, changes in the way women look and dress have ratified the changes in their lives. First, they cut their hair; then they seized on articles of clothing from men's wardrobes—trousers, shirts, hats, coats, even neckties and boxer shorts. Now women are appropriating the muscles in which men have outfitted themselves for so long. Hollander envisions a day in the not-too-distant future when men and women will look reasonably similar, meeting on some androgynous middle ground, with muscles on women much more commonplace. Then the woman's hairstyle will be different from the man's; her tattoos will be in different places; she'll pierce a different part of her body. Both may wear high heels; he still won't wear skirts. The process by which we alter our appearances in some ways and not in others is "irrational, the way it's supposed to be," Hollander says. "What looks right undergoes a change."

The course of fashion in the 20th century has been a long, slow striptease: first, the ankles came out from under long skirts; then the calves and the knees; the midriff; the thighs; the breasts. The vestiges of shame linger for a short time after the initial exposure, until eventually the sight of what had been hidden becomes familiar. Women's legs, when we first get a glimpse of them in photographs from the late teens and early 20's, in dresses that abruptly stop short at the knee, look awkward and hesitant at first, then energized, charged with a new awareness. With time, they grow confident and aggressive, accustomed to the attention of strangers.

As bodies, like other means of transportation—automobiles, trains and airplanes—have become increasingly streamlined, hips have been eliminated (in principle, if not in fact). Hips now strike us as excess baggage, slowing our pace, lowering our center of gravity, making us earthbound. Hollander notes that our three current notions of the ideal female body, as disparate as they may be, have this in common: none of them, not even the curvaceous one that incites men to sex, have hips. Hips are part of the equipment with which nature outfits women for motherhood, and motherhood these days is optional.

As the century has gone on, we have stripped women's bodies of anything extraneous—any padding, any surplus flesh, which in another era might have been considered decorative. In the process of lightening the load, bones have come into play. We now delight in watching the levers and pistons and hinges of the human machine in motion.

Will the tyranny of the body built for sports be any less punishing—or any healthier—than the tyranny of the body built for fashion? There is no reason to imagine that it will. Already, there is alarming evidence of eating disorders among female athletes, and the hormonal ramifications of rigorous training are yet to be defined. Like models, athletes have been genetically ordained. The 12-year-old who wants to grow up to look just like her heroine stands no more chance of turning out like Gabrielle Reece than she does of becoming the next Shalom Harlow, no matter how much time she puts in at the gym. As it turns out, the athletic ideal like the others, is beyond the grasp of all but a few. Even so, it seems reasonable to think that in the process of emulating her favorite sports star, a girl might gain a sense of pride in her body and its accomplishments. Which, in any case, is a far better hope than can be held out for those young girls who strive to resemble their role models by starving themselves.

It's one thing to allow that the muscular body constitutes a new ideal for women—that it is in fact beautiful. But the truth is that, despite the anxieties it provokes, it's also sexy. Muscles bestow on a woman a grace in motion that is absent from fashion photographs and other images in which the impact resides in a carefully orchestrated, static pose. Muscles also impart a sense of self-possession—a quality that is unfailingly attractive. This is not sex appeal conferred on a woman, as it's conferred on supermodels and sex goddesses. The athlete has come by her powers of attraction honestly. Other women's valiant attempts to make themselves beautiful—even when they succeed—are no match for the athlete's evident pleasure in her own articulate body.

It is a kind of fetishism—albeit a healthy one—that has taught us to appreciate women's bodies in detail. Our education has been gradual, requiring the better part of the last hundred years. Fashion designers, models and movie stars have been our tutors. We have learned to love a woman's pelvis, her hipbones jutting out through a bias-cut satin gown. We have come to admire the clavicle in its role as a coat hanger from which clothes are suspended. And, more recently, we have discovered elegance in the swell of a woman's quads, in the tapering form of her lats, in the way her delts square the line of her shoulders. Women, as they have gradually come into their own, have at last begun to feel at home in their bodies, which previously they were only renting. In athletes, we recognize women who own their bodies, inhabiting every inch of them, and the sight of their vitality is exhilarating. Our own potential has become apparent, thanks to their example. We want to be like them—alive all over.

DISCUSSION QUESTIONS

The Athletic Esthetic

1. How are muscles on women a reflection of changing social roles? How does this present-day popular image replace those of the past in defining femininity?

2. How does the "fashionable" body differ from the "muscular" one for women?

3. What does the future hold in relation to body ideals for women? What social, economic, historical, and political factors will influence this issue?

23　Day-care Dress Up Not Amusing to Boy's Dad

Lisa Respers

Woodlawn, Md.—When Henry Holmes picked up his 6-year-old son from the day-care center at the Social Security Administration's headquarters last week, he found the boy laughing and playing. And wearing a dress.

Holmes did not think it was funny.

"He was playing in this area they call 'housekeeping,' and he was wearing a shiny, white dress that resembled one a little girl would wear in a wedding," Holmes said.

Now that incident has sparked a dispute over teaching methods at the Social Secur-A-Kiddie Child Care Center's kindergarten program.

An irate Holmes has taken his son, Gerald, out of the program. The center, meanwhile, insists that such dressing up is not unusual or harmful. And the state, asked to investigate, says that dressing up is an appropriate part of a child-care curriculum.

After last week's incident, Holmes, a single parent, complained to officials at the center, which

occupies space in the Social Security's Operations Building but is not managed by the agency.

Linda Heisner, executive director of the Child Care Administration, said that "dress up" activities are considered an appropriate part of child-care curriculum.

Lindi Budd, executive director of the day-care center, said the facility provides clothing such as men's shirts and ties, dresses and high heels, and firefighters' and nurses' uniforms for children to use.

Holmes said he discussed the incident with his son and explained that other children might tease him.

To his dismay, he said, the boy responded, "I don't care."

Lisa Respers, Sun Staff. Article originally appeared in *The Baltimore Sun*.

DISCUSSION QUESTIONS

Day-Care Dress Up Not Amusing to Boy's Dad/ Respers

1. Why was the boy's interest in feminine dress a problem for the father and at the same time age-appropriate for the boy?

2. Give other examples of how young children explore social roles through appearance.

24   A Visual Analysis of Feminist Dress

Charlotte A. Kunkel
Luther College

This research began as I was simultaneously confronted with students' perceptions of feminist appearance and with an academic focus on dress signifying status. It came to me very clearly one day, when, after class, a student asked me if he "could meet one of those feminists." I inquired whether or not he thought I was a feminist. To my great surprise, he exclaimed, "You're not a feminist, you wear earrings!" I recognized in that moment that femininity and feminism are often perceived as opposing or competing social pressures in our culture.

The popular cultural image of femininity includes the characteristics of nurturance, passivity, and visual beauty. Conversely, feminists are frequently stereotyped as ugly, aggressive man-haters. Feminism, however, is a political position that denotes the theories and practices of social and economic equality of the sexes. Femininity is often interpreted as being at odds with a feminist philosophy of a woman's own control over and satisfaction with her body. Put more simply, there is a popular perception that cultural beauty ideals are not adhered to by feminists (e.g., they do not wear earrings or makeup).

I began asking myself how feminists' negotiate the body and self-presentation. Although much feminist writing theorizes the body, the dilemma of presenting and making sense of one's own appearance—in light of the cultural norms of femininity and a burgeoning feminist consciousness—is rarely examined in an empirical way. Rather, appearance studies are either theoretical or autobiographical in nature (e.g., Bordo, 1989; Brownmiller, 1984; Suleiman, 1986). In contrast, I ask: How do feminists dress? What meaning do they give to their appearances? Do they experience a dilemma of conflicting pressures to appear "politically correct" as a feminist and the dominant cultural norms to appear appropriately feminine? If so, how do they incorporate, mediate, resolve, or extinguish the dilemmas? Moreover, how do these "dilemmas" appear in and on the surface of the body?

In an effort to answer my question of how feminists present themselves, and make sense of their own dress, I completed the following study.

METHODS

Following Collier (1967) and Harper (1987), I employed a photo-elicitation methodology. Photo-elicitation involves photographing and then presenting the resulting photographs to the participants or informants to elicit responses. This process allows the researcher to access an understanding of the participants' interpretation of the event in question—of the photograph. This methodology is well-suited to feminist research because it allows for a collaborative and interactive research endeavor in which the role of participant is primary (Frankenberg, 1993; Reinharz, 1992; Westkott, 1990).

Participants were found through an advertisement requesting self-identified feminists who were willing to be photographed and interviewed about their appearance. I placed ads in three locations: a statewide liberal feminist organizations' newsletter; a local radical feminist publication; and a public university campus. Each volunteer then participated in a photo shoot in which they created their "self-portraits." I call them self-portraits because the volunteers not only decided upon the context, location, and time of the photo session, but they decided what dress to present as well. Further, I used a tripod and 35 mm camera with a self-timer to photograph participants. I invited the participants to look through the lens and adjust the camera as they liked. When the participant was satisfied, we set the self-timer. The participants then had ten seconds in which to "pose" or prepare for the camera to expose the film. Participants could take as many shots as they liked. I was not behind the camera in an effort to limit my bias as the photographer (Harper, 1994). I hoped the method

Original for this text.

would give the participants as much ownership over their photographs as possible.

We then arranged interview dates in which the participants and I would view their photographs. At each interview, I opened the discussion by inviting the participant to respond to each slide they had taken of themselves. I asked them to tell me what they saw, to talk about their appearance, to share what meaning they gave to the images, and whether or not they appeared to be feminist. Consequently, I inquired what feminism meant to them, how they came to that understanding, and what a feminist (and nonfeminist) looked like. I also asked them about the influence of popular cultural ideals of femininity and if components of feminism and femininity ever conflicted.

The 38 participants took a total of 202 photographs. Each participant took anywhere from two to 13 photographs, although the average number taken was five. Thirty-five self-identified feminists were interviewed. The participants ranged in age from 18 to 62, came from various religious and class backgrounds, and represented a number of racial and ethnic backgrounds, although participants were predominately white (83 percent). Respondents were primarily female, although several transgendered individuals (who identify, and I code, as women) and two men participated.

ANALYS IS

In this article, I will focus on the visual presentation and meaning of feminist self-presentation. The interpretation of symbols is the focus of study. My goal is to uncover the meanings given to feminist dress. Recognizing the often polysemic quality of symbols, the symbolist analyses used for the study involved three dimensions: 1) the "exegetical" or interpretive meaning from the informants—or simply, what they "say"; 2) the "operational" meaning that the researcher established from observation of the photographs—that is, what they "do"; and 3) the "positional" or contextual meaning of their dress (Turner, 1967).

RESULTS

For this sample of people, feminist presentation of self is diverse and eclectic, although not beyond normative cultural prescriptions of dress.

The photographic images do contain symbols of cultural or traditionally defined femininity. Practices of wearing flowers and frills, pearls, painted faces and nails, prepared or "big hair," heels, and hose all signify femininity. Femininity is also symbolized in body language—illustrated by head and body angles, big smiles, hand on the hip, taking up little physical space, and so on (Goffman, 1976; Henley, 1977).

Femininity is visually represented in the photographs. Imagine Connie[1], who illustrates the characteristic "feminine touch" by displaying dish detergent *lovingly* in her hands, while wearing a flowered print blouse and dark lipstick. Others suggest their femininity in their wearing of jewelry, long painted nails, and made-up faces. Similarly, Samantha and Jacqueline proclaim their femininity in their dresses, and Paula and Nancy through their permed and styled hair.

Feminine body language was also apparent in the images. Jill's body posture might be characterized as "body clowning" according to Goffman (1976), who argues that it represents subordinate status. Imagine a man in the same pose. Suddenly, it looks ridiculous. Others similarly tilt their heads at an angle, but take up little space. Taking up little physical space is symbolic of femininity and subordination as well, and is often illustrated in restrictive body postures. Some participants hid their arms and legs and literally scrunched their bodies together in the photographs.

Conversely, also present in the photographs are symbols of traditional power and strength-symbols which are often culturally coded "masculine"—and which are represented here in the wide and expansive body postures, in straightforward postures, "cocky" postures (Holly's thumb in her pocket), possessiveness (Kristen's arm raised above the fireplace), serious or non-smiling images, and sturdy or "no frills" postures. For example, Holly raises her fist in a show of power that highlights her studded leather wristband. Savannah presents a feminine image of power in a Venus figurine she has repositioned on her desk to be in the photograph. The voluptuous Venus figure is an ancient image of women's fertility and strength. This suggests that traditional femininity can also be powerful.

Moreover, many of the images contain these characteristics simultaneously—the photographs exhibit both traditionally subordinate femininities and images of power. For example, Holly chooses to have a photograph taken in front of a "Betty Boop" figurine contrasting its femininity with her resistance. Kristen displays a domineering posture while wearing a floral print dress. Rose wears a feminine pantsuit with slick hair and unpolished shoes standing on a chair in defiance of conformity.

What I find more remarkable, however, about feminist presentation of self is the interpretative meaning, or the participants' explanations they attach to their photographs and presentations of a feminist self. What an outsider or onlooker might interpret as feminine or powerful was interpreted by some of the participants in very different terms. In other words the feminist participants were redefining and creating feminist presentations of self out of the existing signs and symbols available to them. Participants talked about the meanings of their appearance and clothing in three common ways: 1) conformity, 2) rebellion, and 3) paradoxical testing of the boundaries of femininity and feminism.

Images of Conformity

Several participant's explanations or interpretations of their photographs contained overtones of appearing heterosexually attractive. For example, Dawn illustrates this when she explains:

> I know that I am feminist in some ways, but I know I'm not in others because I think, I guess, what you call "hard-core feminists" don't buy into any of the stereotypes of being female. That's also bad because then a lot of times they do turn out to be man-haters and sometimes they become lesbians or whatever. I think I'm about as feminist as I could be with what I believe. I do like men very much.

Dawn suggests that her feminism and her sexual orientation compete in her. Terry, Elaine, Jacqueline, and Paula also take pride in their feminine appearance and try to look "nice." Their explanation of "nice" is femininity. Diana illustrates this as she explains:

> I enjoy putting on makeup—I enjoy it and the heels and the whole bit. For work I try to look professional, but feminine, whether I'm in pants or a skirt or whatever I happen to be wearing. I think, to me, a stereotypical feminist tends to be more butch and androgynous.

Ironically, one participant thought she looked too nice or feminine. Faith saw her image in this way:

> Boy, I don't look like a politically active feminist kind. I feel like I look like a suburban housewife. Kind of dumpy body, sort of conservative haircut, sort of WASPy, sort of white-bread kind of face. I don't look like a streetwise person. With all of the flowers there, it just sort of adds to the innocence....Frumpy, dumpy, overfeminine.

Participants interpreted their images as nice—read feminine—and attractive, or ironically, as too nice, that is, too feminine. In contrast, there were negative connotations to not appearing feminine enough. When Connie saw the shot of herself, with her arms crossed in front of her body with stiff legs and no smile, she exclaimed, "Oh wow, there she is. There she is 'bitch-woman' 'femi-Nazi'." She interprets her nonsmiling image as negative, and interestingly, invokes the stereotypical feminist. Madeline describes her nonsmiling, chin-resting-on-her-raised-fist image as her "serious feminist" look, as did Marilyn. These postures are both in the classic masculine pose of Rodin's *The Thinker*. Participants saw their images through a lens of conformity—as conforming to traditional norms of femininity, or not. Only sometimes was this to their liking. Participants also saw their images as representing rebellion.

Images of Rebellion

Visual symbols of resistance were present in the photographs as interpreted by the participants. Some are more obvious than others. Mary, for example, chose a suffragette's costume for her photograph. She explains:

> I chose to have my picture taken this way because it showed a couple of different things to me. One is that feminists and suffragettes have been around a long time, and the fact that the Women's Chorus is very important to me...It has a banner with "Votes for Women"

across it. In those days, they didn't wear buttons, and I'm a very button-wearing person. Normally I have a minimum of one, usually three, and some of my pins. But I'm a very visually noisy person, so I like having this picture because it joins feminists across time, as well as being something I was involved in.

Mary clearly articulates her visual "noise," as well as its historical connection, to women's real and symbolic (visual) resistance. Others also interpret their photographs as visually resisting. For example, Regan notices that different shoes, her "...low black heels might look better with this" dress, but exclaims, "I was debating whether I should wear a different pair of shoes or not. Then I just said, 'forget it'." Similarly Toni sees her muscular legs as not conforming to feminine ideals.

Jacqueline, who appears very feminine in dress, interprets her appearance—specifically her pearls—as an image of strength. Although Paula has big hair and a made-up face, she describes herself, and her "...feminism is about strength and being bold" in her bright red and yellow print pants. Savannah illustrates well the power of body language. She describes herself as seen in Figure 5.3, as an image of strength:

> The position is okay. It looks pretty strong. It looks like a pretty good picture. I don't know about that chair. It's good for my back because it keeps my back straight up, but it's not meant to be a chair where you are really comfortable. I think it's a Victorian-era chair. You're meant to be a little lady sitting on it with your knees together and your toes pointed to the side and your hands on your lap...When I'm not in a situation where I think I've got to keep my legs together, I just go for comfort. But I think in taking the picture, I probably wanted to look square on to the camera. And because I was conscious that this was going to be a discussion of feminism, I think I wanted to present an image of strength. So, to be square on camera was the best way for me to do that—feet on the floor, none of this tippy toe stuff, none of this leg crossing. That might be ladylike, but to me it's not woman-like. I don't do it unless I'm really in a situation where I think I'm going to offend someone.

FIGURE 5.3 *Savannah seated in her women's room, a special room in her home.*

Squareness or a solid body posture means power to Savannah, in contrast to the feminine mannerisms of "tippy toe" and "leg crossing." The perceived dichotomy of femininity and strength is also articulated in this example. Several feminists combined the rebellion of Savannah and the conformity of others to present what in one participant's words were "images of paradox."

Images of Paradox

As the photographs alone convey, the feminist representations combine symbols of femininity and its rejection. Similarly, the participants' interpretations of their images also contained this paradox. Rose captured this, and the essence of her presentation, when I asked her if her body ever conflicted with her feminism. She responded:

Not for me but for others. For example, I think there is a paradox between having short hair, flat comfortable shoes and yet, dressing nicely and appearing nicely. This appearance presents a dilemma for those who want to box me in or put me in a box. I don't fit neatly into boxes—this is a part of my feminism—challenging the boxes.

In explaining her presentation of self, Rose depicts how intimately her appearance is a part of her feminism. Kristen also consciously presents a paradox. She explains:

I also like the contrast of what I was wearing and the kind of physical labor I had to put into the fireplace, contrasted with a dress that I wouldn't do any of that kind of work in. Even hunched over, I feel powerful. [What about it says powerful to you?] I'm looking straight at the camera, which feels presently powerful. Relaxed feels powerful to me. When I or anybody is tense, that feels like giving up or allowing whatever external tension or stress there is to disempower me. So if I'm feeling relaxed, that says powerful. And I look relaxed there.

Looking relaxed and straight at the camera symbolize strength for Kristen, as well as posing in front of her self-built fireplace. Interestingly, Kristen chooses to push the boundaries of strength by wearing a very feminine flowery dress for her pictures. Similarly, Marilyn dresses very femininely, and what might be considered conservatively, with a long skirt and a hat. Further, she poses provocatively with hands on hip and head, which also signals the sexual allure of femininity. Marilyn, however, interprets this photo as having mixed messages. She sees herself playing with symbols of femininity, and with nonconformity in her hats. Notice her photograph is in her "hat room." A room and habit (wearing hats) that she attributes to her uniqueness and nonconformity. Finally, Jamie (who claims not to have one look but many) offers that her whole life is embodied—her physical self included—by her feminism.

I recognized that everything about the way I was, the ways that were conflictual, had to do with not recognizing what my life view was—the way I raised my kid and everything—I'm a

feminist as much as anybody could possibly be one. One hundred percent.

Jamie sees the conflicts in her life, and in her appearance, as the essence of her feminism.

In review, the meanings of feminist self-presentation run the gamut of presentational styles and meanings. Participants both present and explain their appearances in terms of conforming to traditional feminine standards, rejecting those standards, and creating a combination of the two, presenting them simultaneously.

To complete a visual analysis, we must examine the positional or contextual meaning of feminist dress. I will discuss the symbolic dress of self-identified feminists in this study within the cultural context of the times. These three explanatory themes of participants' photographs, as conforming, rebellious, and paradoxical, echo the cultural ideals of femininity and the conformity it produces, even among feminists. Feminists do at times present and interpret their images as traditionally feminine. This is significant for a movement challenging the status quo. Femininity may signify acquiescence or subordination (Brownmiller, 1984; Henley, 1977; Collins and Lutz, 1993); however, rather than condemn femininely dressed feminists, feminist literatures suggests taking a "both/and" approach (Collins, 1990) and acknowledging the contradictions of living in a patriarchal culture (Westkott, 1990).

Feminists in this study also at times present images of cultural rebellion or a feminist resistance to the feminine norms. Images of power and strength as traditionally conceived or reconceived are symbolized. Further, they present an integration of feminist and feminine symbols as well as the redefinition of femininity from a feminist perspective. These observations correspond to feminist literature. Real-life feminists negotiate the cultural ideals of femininity and a feminist consciousness in context-specific and lifetime-specific ways such that the body is molded and given meaning through a feminist lens (Bordo, 1989; Fisher and Davis, 1993). Further, this lens is kaleidoscopic (Kourany, Sterba, and Tong, 1992, p. 28). Although some feminists saw traditional femininity as desirable, others rejected it and still others redefined and reclaimed it. Feminists are agents rather than passive in their self-presentation (Arthur 1993). Feminists have also redefined and reclaimed traditionally feminine symbols of power, as observed in the goddess image. Living in contradiction or simultaneously maintaining and challenging the patriarchy is symbolized in these participants' presentations and meaning-making of self.

Conclusions

Three themes emerged from participants' photographs and interviews. Feminists in this study conformed, rebelled, and integrated contradictory symbols of cultural femininity, feminist strength, and redefined femininity. Feminist self-presentation is complex and mediated by feminist philosophies that explain and make sense of multiple forms and meanings of dress. The multiplicity of feminisms also becomes apparent in this study and perhaps provides a lens of understanding. The diversity of presentations and meaning-making cannot be understood through one frame of reference. There is not just one feminist "box." As feminism is currently comprehended as a multiple-paradigmatic philosophy, it is not one unified whole, but is constantly being renegotiated. Certainly then, we should not expect one "look" or presentational style, at the same time recognizing that most participants emphasized that feminism is not a look at all, but a philosophy. Nevertheless, dress, images, bodies — presentations of self — are infused with culturally symbolic, and feminist, meaning.

Notes

1. All names of participants have been changed to ensure anonymity.

References

Arthur, L. B. (1993). Clothing, control, and women's agency: The mitigation of patriarchal power. In S. Fisher & K. Davis (Eds.). *Negotiating at the margins.* New Brunswick, NJ: Rutgers University Press. (pp. 66–84).

Ball, M. S., & Smith, G.W. H. (1992). *Analyzing visual data.* Qualitative Research Methods Vol. 24. Newbury Park, CA: Sage.

Bordo, S. (1989). The body and the reproduction of femininity: A feminist appropriation of Foucault, In A. Jaggar, & S. Bordo (Eds.), *Gender/body/knowledge: Feminist reconstructions of being and knowing* (pp. 13–33). New Brunswick, NJ: Rutgers University Press.

Brownmiller, S. (1984). *Femininity.* New York: Linden Press.

Collier, J., Jr. (1967). *Visual anthropology: Photography as a research method.* New York: Holt, Rinehart & Winston.

Collins, J. L., & Lutz, C. A. (1993). *Reading National Geographic.* Chicago, IL: University of Chicago Press.

Collins, P. H. (1990). *Black feminist thought.* New York: Routledge.

Fisher, S., & Davis, K. (Eds.) (1993) *Negotiating at the margins.* New Brunswick, NJ: Rutgers.

Frankenberg, R. (1993). *The social construction of whiteness: White women, race matters.* Minneapolis, MN: The University of Minnesota Press.

Goffman, E. (1976). *Gendered advertisements.* New York: Harper & Row.

Harper, D. (1994). On the authority of the image: Visual methods at the crossroads. In N. K. Denzin, & Y. S. Lincoln, (Eds.), *Handbook of qualitative research* (pp. 403–412) Thousand Oaks, CA: Sage.

Harper, D. (1987). *Working knowledge: Skill and community in a small shop.* Chicago, IL: University of Chicago Press.

Henley, N. M. (1977). *Body politics: Power, sex and nonverbal communication.* Englewood Cliffs, NJ: Prentice Hall.

Kourany, J. A., Sterba, J. P., & Tong, R. (Eds.) (1992). *Feminist philosophies.* Englewood Cliffs, NJ: Prentice Hall.

Reinharz, S. (1992). *Feminist methods in social research.* New York: Oxford University Press.

Suleiman, S. R. (Ed.) (1986). *The female body in western culture: Contemporary perspectives.* Cambridge, MA: Harvard.

Turner, V. (1967). *The forest of symbols.* Ithaca, NY: Cornell University Press.

Westkott, M. (1990). [1979]. Feminist criticism of the social sciences. In J. M. Nielsen, *Feminist research methods.* (pp. 58–68) Boulder, CO: Westview Press.

DISCUSSION QUESTIONS

1. According to Kunkel, why has the appearance of those women who call themselves feminist been stereotyped? What stereotype comes to your mind? How has this article addressed these issues?

2. Why is the term "feminisms" rather than "feminism" appropriate to this article on appearance?

25 Northampton Confronts a Crime, Cruelty

Jordana Hart

With his earring and black eyeliner, Matthew Santoni was a popular target for boys at Smith Vocational and Agricultural High School.

They would surround him, students recall, and spew "homo," "faggot," and "queer" at him, their words striking with rapier intensity.

Two weeks ago, Santoni, 15, apparently snapped. He allegedly stabbed to death a classmate, Jeffrey LaMothe, 16, amid the trendy boutiques and restaurants of downtown Northampton. LaMothe, according to many, was a ringleader of those who made Santoni's life miserable with their teasing.

While hundreds of teenagers came from schools all over the region to LaMothe's wake and funeral in Easthampton, described as the greatest convergence of young mourners ever at Sacred Heart Church, many other people focused on Santoni: Had teasing been the root of his rage?

LaMothe's murder cut to the core of this counter-culture college town. The affluent center of Massachusetts farm country, Northampton is also know for its open embrace of gay couples, many of whom have moved here from around the country to open businesses and start families.

"We think of Northampton as very progressive, so to hear that this kind of harassment is going on in our school system and that it might have led to such violence is very hard to accept," said Rebecca Lockwood, who runs youth programs, including one for gay and lesbian teens, at the Franklin Community Action Corporation in Greenfield, north of here.

"There is no excuse for that level of violence, no matter how persecuted you feel," Lockwood added. "But I think it gets really intense around sexual orientation, especially for young men. To be perceived as gay contradicts what young men are taught about being masculine."

Santoni never said he was gay, and he apparently was teased simply for his style of dress.

Now, amid increasing reports of school shootings and other acts of violence among young people across the country, specialists are paying more attention to youth culture and how harshly it treats those youngsters who are somehow different. Sexual orientation is but one subject of teasing: Looks, weight, family background, ethnicity, and race all register as fodder for teasers.

"The psychological damage of taunting, name-calling, exclusion, and other ways kids victimize kids is very extensive," said Ervin Taub, a professor of psychology at the University of Massachusetts at Amherst, who studies aggression among teenagers. "It is a significant issue, and one just beginning to be recognized."

Hart, Jordana, "Northampton Confronts a Crime, Cruelty." Boston Globe (June 8, 1998). Reprinted Courtesy of The Boston Globe.

Taub warned that parents and teachers must recognize when it is time to step in. "Adult passivity communicates things to kids. Perpetrators tend to interpret this" as tacit approval, he said.

On the sprawling campus of "the Voke," with its squat, red brick buildings set alongside wide-open fields, students said teasing is a familiar part of school life. Santoni, they said, looked like he was gay. And in the corrosive culture of high-school teasing, any distinguishing characteristics are fuel for taunts.

"It's all the time," said junior Becky Ely, 17, surprisingly stoic as she described a year of torment at the vocational school. "The boys call me slut, bitch. They call me a 10-timer, because they say I go with 10 guys at a time. I put up with it because I have no choice. The teachers say it's because the boys think I'm pretty."

Santoni's lawyer, Alan Black, said the boy, from nearby Florence, pleaded not guilty in Northampton District Court May 26 to a charge of murder. He is being held without bail at Plymouth County House of Correction and will be arraigned in Hampshire County Superior Court tomorrow.

Sources said Santoni had complained to administrators about the harassment, and that LaMothe was suspended from school. Ely said she, too, recently complained about the teasing to school officials, who have declined comment on either case.

The jabs at students like Ely and Santoni are hardly unique to this school of 516 students. Taunting and teasing have long been as basic to American high school culture as proms, geeks and jocks, specialists say. Just ask the overweight teenager in thick glasses. Or the girl who everyone says went all the way on a first date. Or the guy with an earring called "homo" or "faggot."

"Teasing happens a lot," said Joseph Laboute, a ninth-grader at Smith Vocational. "If you know them, you know how much they can take. But it is different if it's someone you don't know."

Smith Vocational itself is in a curious situation, existing as it does in what may well be one of the nation's most socially tolerant towns. Principal Veronica Carroll says the school has students who come from 29 towns—ranging from Northampton and Amherst to tiny farm towns like Goshen and Hatfield.

"I think of the school as a safe haven, but it is a lot of work to make it safe," said Carroll, who started teaching there in 1976. "There is less tolerance among kids in general."

Carroll declined to speak about the stabbing and what may have led to it. Since LaMothe's murder, she said, teachers have been meeting with students in small groups to talk about grieving and tolerance. "We have lost two students," she said. "There are rumors about taunting and about what kids were saying."

Carroll also said teachers have suggested starting a Gay/Straight Alliance, similar to those at 140 other Massachusetts high schools.

Lockwood, the youth-center counselor, said gay youngsters at meetings in Greenfield and across the state talk constantly about being harassed, and what it feels like to be ignored, or hear students toss around anti-gay invectives.

"I sat alone in French class because no one would sit next to me," said Emily DeLisle, a 10th-grader at Bromfield High School in Harvard, who came out to her parents and schoolfriends a year ago. "Kids told new students to stay away from me because there were rumors that I was gay. It never bothered me not to fit in with the popular kids, but I want friends and I want people to like me."

Meanwhile, Northampton residents continue to struggle with the realization that their city, known for its acceptance, is not immune to acts of taunting and violence.

Last week, hundreds of people gathered on the steps of Northampton City Hall for a rally against hate crimes, propelled by a May 23 attack by four young men on two others perceived to be a couple. Since that attack, which was reported to police, two others have come to light, said the Rev. Victoria Safford of the Unitarian Society, who has presided over same-sex marriages.

Teaching tolerance "is difficult, painful and dangerous, but it must be done," Safford said. "It is not that we have bad, homophobic children. We have frightened adults who have not done their own homework, and until they are willing to face that, we will continue raising violent, and homophobic children."

Northampton Confronts a Crime, Cruelty

1. Although not specifically stated in the article, what do you think was the nature of the young man's appearance that caused him to be labeled gay? How is this issue related to homophobia?

2. Why is it dangerous to stereotype someone's sexual preference based on their appearance?

26   Men in Uniformity

Amy M. Spindler

In the infinitely less complicated world of my childhood, there was a board game called Mystery Date. While I've forgotten most of the rules, what I do remember is a front door that lay in the center of the board like a hatch leading to a dungeon. As Mystery Date's television commercial explained, you opened the door and discovered your date. "Is he a dream?" the voice-over asked the girls playing the game as they ooohed. "Or a dud?" At which point the girls went: "Awwwwwww." The only thing separating the crudely cartooned Dream from the Dud, however, was his clothes. Dream wore a tux; Dud wore the kind of nerdwear that intimated a lifetime commitment to Ted Baxter. No matter who the girl was whose luck ran out, the response was always the same: She'd grab the little door and slam it in Dud's face.

These days, as a fashion critic watching men's wear shows, I sometimes play the Dream or Dud game as a reality check. Models are, as the profession demands, great looking, with corresponding physiques. Just as with the board game, it's the clothes that make the difference. If you slammed the door on any of these men, it would be because of what he's been made to wear on the runway. And clothes that can turn Dreams into Duds are too powerful for mere mortals.

But when I try to play the game in the street, I've discovered that the rules of Mystery Date no longer apply. Men have submerged themselves in such deep camouflage you can no longer tell the Dreams from the Duds just by opening the door and looking. Dreams and Duds, these days, dress pretty much the same.

Mark Twain once said, "Biographies are but the clothes and buttons of the man." If so, I think the converse should also be true: Clothes should be the biography of the man.

This leads to the fundamental difference between the way that women and men, in general, dress. Women dress to show how they see themselves. Men dress as they want others to see them. Women reveal, however coyly, a little bit about themselves. Men dress almost always to conceal everything about themselves.

Which is why there is something poignant about how men perceive that great tapestry of expression, the necktie. I was at a wedding recently where one guest was proudly showing off his tie, printed with bottles of Veuve Cliquot Champagne. Casual observers might assume it was just another unattractively patterned tie. But its wearer was satisfied he was revealing something intensely personal: the company where he works.

The industry is strewn with such ties, brandishing optical illusions, or pointillism of the Kama Sutra, marijuana leaves, college insignia. There is even a line made expressly for doctors, adorned with images of body organs. If I look closely enough, and can identify the organ, I may be inclined to strike up a conversation. "You must be a urologist!" I might say, discerning a sea of kidneys.

But then again, I could be wrong. They could be all too cleverly disguised Veuve Clicquot bottles.

The most pathetic example of the male's search for self-expression through neckties is the Jerry Garcia-designed Deadhead tie. What is a Grateful Dead fan doing with his throat being clutched by the symbol of corporate servitude?

The only thing worth noting about a Grateful Dead tie is that it's a baby boomer's take on the trend of a younger generation—connecting clothes and music. What has driven MTV, rap groups like Naughty By Nature and record executives like Tommy Boy's Monica Lynch and Def Jam's Russell Simmons into the fashion business is that, for young men particularly, the music they listen to and the clothes they wear have become inexorably linked. There are the silver jackets of ambient techno music fans, the baggy trousers of hip hoppers, the babyish pinks and blues of rave kids.

But try making any melodic match-ups in midtown Manhattan on the average work day. If there is any music that could be ascribed to men in their conformist suits, it's the sort being piped into the conveyances lifting them to their offices. Aside from the occasional summer seersucker that appears on city streets as frequently as a screened-in porch, the clothes most businessmen wear to work can only be described as drab. Few ventured to try the whimsical white linen suits that appeared on so many spring and summer runways. Despite men's fashion magazines' labored instructions (look at everything we can do with even a simple, boring pin-striped suit!), most men are more than willing to wear simple, boring pin-striped suits in the simple and boring way.

The solution for all this conformity might have been casual-dress Fridays, providing an opportunity for men to let their hair down at work. But Casual Fridays seem on the way to inventing a second sort of uniform: Gap-centric T-shirts tucked into khakis or jeans, worn with loafers.

Evidently, the idea of Casual Fridays was too modest a proposal. What if the marketing minds had invented Fantasy Fridays, where men would be directed to dress for the occupation they wish they had chosen? It's not as though men don't have unfulfilled dreams. I was at a recent Rolling Stones concert in Giants Stadium, watching Mick Jagger flail around on stage, when my friend, an executive at a cable network, confessed he would trade everything to be a rock star. Jagger was wearing a silk celery-colored pirate shirt, a purple vest with tails, and black pants that laced up the back. My friend was wearing khakis and a dress shirt.

He may never be a rock star, but with Fantasy Fridays, he could dress like one: he could don a skull ring, a top hat festooned with devil's horns, an Edwardian jacket and football pants. He could wear a kilt like Axl Rose, or mud and a diaper like the Red Hot Chili Peppers. And he'd still have his hands free to shuffle millions of dollars of other people's money around.

Obviously, wanting to be a rock star has more to do with the adulation of 100,000 fans at $55 a head than with the freedom to hop about dressed like a member of his satanic majesty's service. Nor do I ever remember Mystery Date players longing to open the door to find Mick Jagger's twin. (Keith Richards is another story.)

But somewhere between Mick and the Gap is Dream dressing for men in the 90's. What makes Jagger sexy on stage is not his dress as much as his confidence. Toying with traditional men's clothing reveals such self-assurance, just as dressing like a lemming makes men look as though they lack it.

I doesn't have to be all or nothing. Men only need to take one risk at a time to achieve some sort of self-expression. For instance, if everything you've worn above the ankles is non-committal, python boots—if you're in a python boot sort of mood—reveal an alluring brashness.

Wear one piece of clothing with vibrant color, even if it is just a pair of socks, or a T-shirt peeking from the top of your collar.

You should own at least two white cotton ribbed tank tops. This is the only way a standard-issue shirt and tie can look sexy to a woman-with that hint of "A Streetcar Named Desire" soul beneath it all. (And all men have decent shoulders.)

If the silhouette is daring, buy it in black or navy. If the cut is classic, you can get away with an outrageous color.

Athletic garb is always sexy. Get some football or baseball pants. Trade khakis for tennis shorts. Choose cricket sweaters instead of crew necks, driving gloves instead of mittens. Real tweed riding jackets are irresistible. Of course, these clothes are especially intriguing—jodhpurs and hacking jackets in particular—if you have just finished participating in the sport of choice. A horse is a sexier accessory than a motorcycle. But not by a lot.

Any piece of clothing having its roots in history is defendable and should be embraced. If the Duke of Windsor, Gene Kelly, James Dean or Cary Grant wore it, you probably can, too.

Every male siren owns a black cashmere turtleneck.

Finally, although a tuxedo is not the only way to appear to women as a Dream, it rarely fails when the occasion demands. And there couldn't be a worse path to self-revelation than a novelty tie, especially one printed with kidneys.

Which leads to novelty tuxedos.

Slam.

DISCUSSION QUESTIONS

Men in Uniformity

1. Give examples of how the author feels men are burdened by issues of conformity in both busienss and casual dress.

2. Why would men feel the need to conceal aspects of their identity through dress even more than women?

 ## 27 Drag Queens, Transvestites, Transsexuals: Stepping Across the Accepted Boundaries of Gender

Jane E. Hegland
New Mexico State University

A common thread which seems to run through virtually all known societies is that females and males have been visually differentiated by gender-appropriate dress; males in masculine dress and females in feminine dress. The socialization process toward gender-appropriate behavior and appearance begins at birth. Eicher and Roach-Higgins (1992) indicate that at the birth of a child:

...adult caretakers (kin or surrogate kin who come to the aid of the child) act as purveyors of culture by providing gender-symbolic dress that encourages others to attribute masculine or feminine gender and to act on the basis of

Original for this text.

these attributions when interacting with the child. (p. 17)

Concepts of femininity and masculinity are historically and culturally defined, and are revealed through such observable features as clothing, accessories to the clothing, accessories to the body, hairstyle, facial features, body shape, mannerisms, voice, and gestures.

Rarely do we pause to wonder if an individual is male or female. Rather, perception is immediate and simple because, although we have no direct knowledge of a person's genital sex, we know what a woman or man is *supposed to* look like. In other words, we do not require locker-room proof as to whether a person is male or female. In short, dress and appearance are key factors in social communication. An initial nonverbal encounter with an individual reveals numerous personality characteristics. Similarly, dress can indicate occupation, religious affiliation, social status, and gender.

This article focuses on what happens when culturally prescribed and proscribed gender norms—manifested by dress and appearance—are challenged through social interaction. What occurs when individuals step across the social boundaries of gender-appropriate dress and appearance by cross-dressing? What if we cannot immediately establish the gender of an individual? What if something doesn't seem quite right? How does the public respond when confronted with an incongruous or unfamiliar image?

For a number of reasons, including the emancipation of women, practicality in the workplace, personal safety, physical comfort, and trends in fashions, women in cosmopolitan[1] societies have adopted and adapted almost every characteristic of "masculine" dress. Because of this, it has often been suggested that there are no female cross-dressers in cosmopolitan societies because women can easily wear "men's" clothing. While this does—at least superficially—seem plausible, as an explanation, it is bound by time and place. It is only in the recent past that women have been allowed to don masculine forms of dress. Although there are historical accounts of women who dressed as men, and even convinced others they were men, this was either to facilitate their participation in activities open only to men, such as being a soldier, or a sailor; to escape from a situation safely—disguised as a man, they were less apt to be approached or sexually harassed; or to connote sexual orientation, as numbers of homosexual women have traditionally rejected the feminine image, and worn masculine dress (Dekker & van de Pol, 1989; Devor, 1989; Maitland, 1986; Wheelwright, 1989).

The adoption and adaptation of mens' dress by women is acceptable, so long as women do not attempt to disguise their biological sex.[2] But the reverse has not held true. Men who adopt *any* feminine forms of dress are viewed—at best—as humorous or peculiar, and—at worst—as an abomination that should be locked up. Generally, males who cross-dress will experience immediate stigmatization if they are exposed, as their discrediting attribute is their incongruous appearance. Evans and Thornton (1989) have attached the concept of stigma to the act of cross-dressing:

> There is less threat in women's cross-dressing; it is a sign of aspiration, moving up the patriarchal hierarchy. The powerful taboo is against male [cross-dressing], partly because of entrenched homophobia, partly because it is a step down the social ladder. (p. 44)

In this article, I examine the visual presentations of males within American and European cultures[3] who don feminine forms of dress. Three types of male-to-female cross-dressers considered are the transsexual, the transvestite, and the drag queen.[4] The act of cross-dressing challenges the accepted boundaries of gender. Existing literature indicates that various types of cross-dressers cross-dress for different reasons (Ackroyd, 1979; Allen, 1989; Benjamin, 1953, 1966; Brierley, 1979; Bullough & Bullough, 1993; Cauldwell, 1956; Dekker & van de Pol, 1989; Docter, 1988; Feinbloom, 1976; Garber, 1992; Gilbert, 1926; Kirk & Heath, 1984; Lynn, [no date]; Newton, 1972; Prince, 1981; Raynor, 1966; Rudd, 1990; Stevens, 1990; Woodhouse, 1989). I have pushed the concept further, and propose that different *reasons* for cross-dressing result in significantly different visual presentations, which ultimately result in varying responses from the cross-dressers' audience.

FIGURE 5.4 *A cross dresser.*

DEFINING CROSS-DRESSING: DEVELOPING A VISUAL TYPOLOGY

I define *cross-dressing* as those occasions when a male puts on feminine dress or a female adopts masculine dress for whatever purpose or to whatever effect. However, beyond the visual transformation from male to female or female to male through body modifications and body supplements, there is also a change in the individual's body movements, posture, gestures, facial expressions, eye contact, and often vocal intonation.

Aside from the obvious growth of facial and body hair, there are a number of other visual cues which could expose the biological sex of the most convincing cross-dresser. Foot and hand size tend to be proportionally larger on males than on females. Also, men typically have a stronger

squarer jaw line than women. Makeup can disguise this feature to some extent, but it is difficult to completely hide. The most conspicuous feature cross-dressed males have to contend with is their prominent Adam's apple. If left uncovered, it will certainly reveal their biological sex.[5]

The phenomenon of cross-dressing can be divided into three general categories: the transsexual, the transvestite, and the drag queen (Lynn, no date). Within each category, the male cross-dresser modifies and supplements his biological package to create what he conceives of as a feminine image. Kirk and Heath (1984) concluded from their pictorial study of men who cross-dress that the dividing lines are often blurred, and that self-definition of *what* one is can change over time. By suggesting that an individual's motivations for cross-dressing can change with time, Kirk and Heath have alluded to a range of reasons for cross-dressing. Although the existing literature has acknowledged the three types of male cross-dressers, the possibility that each type creates a distinct feminine image has not been addressed.

In the next section of this paper, the visual differences between each of the three types of cross-dressers are considered. First, I define the parameters of each type. Second, I include a detailed description of a prototype of the cross-dresser in order to provide a sense of the visual image created by each type. Third, I discuss how the cross-dresser alters his appearance.[6] Finally, I address the possible audience responses to each type's transformed appearance.

THE TRANSSEXUAL

The transsexual has a complete psychological identification with one sex, but the reproductive organs of the other. The male transsexual conceives of himself as both female and feminine. In essence, he feels "trapped" in the wrong body. The adoption of feminine dress seems quite natural for this individual.

There are two general types of transsexuals: preoperative and postoperative. It is within the preoperative stage that I consider the transsexual to be a cross-dresser. If the male transsexual is physically changed into a biological female, *she* dresses in the manner appropriate to her newly acquired sex. Consequently, my definition of a cross-dresser is no longer applicable.

Transsexuals' visual presentations are as varied as the images of biological females. They exist in all shapes and sizes. They can be tall or short, thin or heavy; they have pronounced or nondescript facial features; they wear their hair long or short; they wear masculine or feminine styles of dress.

In the process of becoming female in appearance, the transsexual extensively modifies his body and tends to be meticulous about his transformed appearance, as he is convincing others of his "true" gender identity. All telltale body hair is removed, leaving the hair on his head, which is often grown into a feminine hairstyle.

The transsexual may also choose to modify his appearance through hormone treatments, which tend to stunt the growth of body hair and increase the growth of hair on the head. These treatments also increase breast size and expand hip width, making the transsexual's silhouette even more feminine. If hormone treatments are not taken, the transsexual will likely create the illusion of breasts and hips through padding. Makeup is expertly applied. Fingernails and toenails are apt to be buffed and polished. Ears are often pierced and adorned with earrings, and other jewelry—such as necklaces, bracelets, and finger rings—may decorate the body.

As for supplements to the body, the range of appearances of transsexuals is as great as the range of the appearances of biological females. However, in contrast to the transvestite and the drag queen, the transsexual will often wear trousers and other more casual forms of dress. The transsexual is typically not exhibitionistic in nature, and will tend to wear whatever is considered to be fashionable among women. Great care is taken to create as convincing an image as possible.

If every aspect of the transsexual's dress is carefully attended to, *she* will convince her audience that she is indeed female. Inconcealable characteristics, such as foot size or a prominent Adam's apple, will likely be overlooked. Therefore, the transsexual's presentation will be positively reviewed by her audience. In other words, the public will probably assume the transsexual is a biological female. However, if the transsexual is "read"—or found out—she will endure a stigmatized status because her presentation will have been challenged.

Because the male transsexual believes he is female in every way—except for the annoying fact that he was born with the wrong genitalia—it is essential for him to create an appearance that is unquestionably female. Consequently, in the event that the transsexual's presentation is challenged, the individual will make the appropriate adjustments to be certain it does not happen again.

THE TRANSVESTITE

The population of transvestites is quite diverse, and therefore not easily categorized. Most male transvestites are heterosexual, married with children, and cross-dressing tends to be linked with sexual activity (Ackroyd, 1979; Allen, 1989; Bullough & Bullough, 1993; Docter, 1988; Prince, 1981; Woodhouse, 1989). However, a transvestite may be homosexual or bisexual, single or divorced, an occasional or frequent cross-dresser, and the activity may not be connected to sexual arousal. Further, a transvestite's cross-dressing activities might remain invisible to the public, and be limited to the wearing of women's undergarments under men's clothing.

As a group, male transvestites differ from male transsexuals in that they are *always* aware of their male identity, and their "maleness" plays a major role in their cross-dressing activities. The male transvestite sees himself as male and masculine when in his gender-appropriate dress, and as very feminine in feminine dress. But he never forgets—and never allows his audience to forget—he is a man in feminine dress, although he does use a feminine name while cross-dressed (Ackroyd, 1979; Baker, 1968; Bullough & Bullough, 1993; Woodhouse, 1989).

Exhibitionism is a crucial factor of transvestism. Baker (1968) reinforces this point with the following statement: "All the transvestites I have spoken to...have, either blatantly or covertly, revealed a strong strain of exhibitionism. In its simplest form it is a need to go out in the street dressed as a woman" (p. 36). Yet, because of possible detrimental repercussions, transvestites generally sequester their cross-dressing activities to a private environment. Some share their activities with their wives, while others keep it to themselves. In her pictorial study of cross-dressers, Allen (1989) includes short biographies of individuals who cross-dress. One interview revealed that a banker from Oklahoma keeps a trailer for his feminine wardrobe. When he feels the urge, he visits this trailer and transforms himself into Samantha, keeping the secret from his wife.

According to Allen (1989), Stevens (1990), and Woodhouse (1989), most transvestites suffer immense anxiety from their condition, which is twofold and cyclical. First, they feel guilty when they cross-dress. Then, they experience uneasiness and depression when they try to suppress their needs or are unable to cross-dress. Many cases can be likened to a binge-and-purge eating disorder, where the transvestite goes through a period of intense cross-dressing, followed by a time period when they feel guilty and quit—often performing a ritualistic destruction of the wardrobe only to return to the shops within a few weeks to begin the cycle again.

Ackroyd (1979) divided transvestism into two broad categories: fetishistic transvestism and feminine passing. Fetishistic transvestites cross-dress in order to experience sexual arousal and generally have no interest in entering the public domain. Rather, their needs are satisfied by cross-dressing in secret, as is the case with those who limit their cross-dressing to the adoption of feminine undergarments. Because of the relative invisibility of this type of cross-dressing practices, it will be excluded from further discussion in this paper.

Transvestites who fall into the category of feminine passing move beyond the private fetishistic stage. They cease to be sexually excited by the act of cross-dressing, but instead cross-dress for exhibitionistic purposes. They dress as women for long periods of time, appear in public as such, and take seriously their aspirations of femininity. They want to prove how beautiful and desirable they can be as a woman, and their primary aim is to deceive other men. Some only want to be recognized as women

by women. Others dress in feminine attire, but do not intend to pass as women. They make a genuine attempt to behave as well as dress like women. However, unlike the transsexual, the transvestite's male identity remains firmly intact.

The transvestite tends to create a feminine image that could be characterized as "the woman next door" who is perhaps a bit old-fashioned in her style; a few curls, perhaps a string of pearls, a tweed skirt, sensible shoes, and stockings. He will usually wear conservative styles of women's clothing—concealing body curvatures, or lack thereof. The makeup may not be entirely perfect; the legs, face, and arms not properly shaved; the voice too low; the silhouette may not be convincing; the walk not quite right. Yet, another transvestite may look—in most respects—like a biological female. Although well-disguised, the visual clues to the individual's biological sex are available to the keen viewer. The transvestite will often slip up—accidentally or purposely. Because of their exhibitionistic nature, transvestites tend to enjoy the shock value of their incongruous appearance.

Transvestites will often create a feminine image that is "drab" and "old-fashioned" by contemporary standards (Ackroyd, 1979; Woodhouse, 1989). There are a few possible explanations for this inclination. First, perhaps the transvestite adopts the image of femininity derived from his earliest memories of his mother or another female relative. Or, by avoiding extravagances, the use of nondescript dress may allow the transvestite to pass unnoticed in public. Another possible explanation could be that the dress relates to the age of the transvestite. Younger transvestites may soon be dressing in the manner of contemporary women. Although this is a valid explanation, it seems doubtful, as it is difficult to express femininity and an exhibitionistic nature while in the casual dress of the modern, and often androgynous, woman. Transvestites tend to be attracted to the polarization of masculine and feminine roles *and* appearance characteristics.

All of this highlights the complexities of transvestism, along with the difficulties of visual definition. Yet, some generalizations can be made. Although the transformation of transvestites from male to female may range from extremely convincing to not believable, as a rule, they will adhere to the prevailing gender and social codes. Further, they attempt to create at least the illusion of femininity, whether or not they pass as women in public.

Because there is such a broad range of presentations created by transvestites, there is also an array of perceptions by their audience. While some transvestites will never be "read"—others will endure exposure every time they venture out to public places. Those transvestites who pass as women experience a positive response to their presentation by their audience, while those who are read—are challenged and stigmatized. If their goal is to pass, transvestites will strive to create a more believable image. However, for some transvestites, part of the excitement (including risk and danger) of cross-dressing and appearing in public is being found out. They report to enjoy the deviance involved (Ackroyd, 1979; Bullough & Bullough, 1993; Kirk & Heath, 1984). Consequently, it seems that some transvestites *aspire* to a challenge of their presentation.

THE DRAG QUEEN

Webster's Dictionary carries this simple definition for drag: slang: woman's dress when worn by a man (Gove, 1993, p. 684). *The American Thesaurus of Slang* states that drag is the female costume of a male homosexual (Berrey & van den Bark, 1953, p. 85). *The Oxford English Dictionary* defines drag as feminine attire worn by a man; also, a party or dance attended by men wearing feminine attire (1989, p. 1010). Partridge (1984), in *The Dictionary of Slang and Unconventional English*, defines drag as the petticoat or skirt used by actors when playing female roles. He suggests that the word derived from "the drag of the dress as distinct from the nondragginess of the trousers" (p. 338). One source proposes that the term drag was coined by Shakespeare as an acronym meaning DRessed As Girls (Lynn, no date, p. 5).

The ability to *do drag* is concentrated and widespread within the homosexual community. Many social events include or focus on drag— drag balls, drag shows. At these events, cross-dressed males parade in the spirit of satire, imitating female models and celebrities. *Queen* is a descriptive term used within the homosexual community, and is usually reserved for the especially effeminate male. Therefore, a drag queen is often defined as a homosexual male who cross-dresses in the spirit of satire. Although drag queens are almost exclusively homosexual, not all homosexual cross-dressers are drag queens.[7]

Drag queens are generally considered to be a subculture within the homosexual community. While creating a semblance of femininity, the drag queen relies on the fact that his audience is aware of his true sexual identity. In contrast to the transvestite, who usually adheres to the prevailing social and gender codes of behavior while in feminine dress, the drag queen tends to flout and break the rules. Also unlike the transvestite, the drag queen maintains that he does not cross-dress for fetishistic or sexual purposes. Rather, he views dressing in drag as a means of entertainment, and as a mask which allows him an entirely different view of the world.

Drag is a vehicle for satire; it parodies and mocks the ideals of feminine beauty. Ackroyd (1979) suggests that "it is misogynistic both in origin and intent" (p. 14). However, some drag queens who attach themselves to the feminist movement claim to satirize and exaggerate what seems to attract heterosexual men. Others insist their drag routine is a political act of defiance against rigidly stereotyped male and female images and ideals (Kirk & Heath, 1984).

The visual image of the drag queen is quite different from the other categories of cross-dressers, although he will modify and supplement his body in much the same manner as the transsexual and the transvestite. The drag queen creates an appearance that is comparable to that of a showgirl or a prostitute. Men in drag go "way over the top" (Kirk & Heath, 1984, p. 61), with spiked heels, a sequined dress, and a bouffant hairstyle. Body curvatures tend to be well-defined. The hair, makeup, and breasts are exaggerated. The clothing is generally quite slinky and provocative, emphasizing legs, curves, and cleavage. Extreme gestures, carriage, and vocal intonation complete the presentation.

Drag queens' satire on femininity renders an image that typically will not allow them to pass as

interesting

females (Ackroyd, 1979; Kirk & Heath, 1984; Phillips, Shapiro, & Joseph, 1980; Robinson, 1988; Woodhouse, 1989). Alternative explanations emerged in the following excerpts of interviews from Kirk and Heath's (1984) pictorial survey of males who dress in drag. Reported justifications range from a glorification of the feminine ideal, to a rejection of the restrictive masculine role in Western culture:

> Does he ever feel that, in drag, he is satirizing women? "Perhaps that's how women see it, but for me the opposite is true. For me it's a way of glorifying women. I think with drag people get confused sometimes, but it is not my confusion. Drag is a denial of politics. It takes the reality away, questions the reality of things." (p. 88)
>
> One of the reasons Colin likes to frock up is to go against the whole gay establishment which is so dull…"I like the elegance myself and my image is hopefully the latest over-the-top thing you've seen on the Paris catwalk…That's what it's all about—outrage! Entertainment for everyone." (p. 122)
>
> Whether a queen started wearing drag because he enjoyed doing it or for political reasons—it was usually a combination of the two—it soon became a symbol of separation, a political act of defiance against the stereotyped male image. It was a badge saying you disagreed with "male" values and wanted nothing more to do with them. (p. 100)

Although justifications for dressing in drag seem quite diverse, the images created by all remain relatively constant. During my fieldwork, I observed drag queens—both on and off stage—flouting and breaking prevailing gender and social codes. For example, a performer may appear on stage and work through an extremely delicate routine. In the end, an unexpected crotch gesture will break the spell *she* has cast on her audience. Another common style of performance which emphasizes the incongruence focuses on the interplay between dress and movement. When the spotlight is turned on and a stunning entertainer stands poised at center stage, the irony is soon realized when she begins to move about in a very aggressive—and typically mascu-

line—manner. Both styles of performance are calculated, as the drag queen relies on the fact that the audience is aware that *she* is actually a *he*.

The acceptance or rejection of the female image created by the drag queen is context-bound. Within the walls of gay clubs, men in drag are everywhere, and their presentations are generally appreciated by other customers. However, closing time signifies the ending of the environment that readily accepts cross-dressers. When it came time to go home, there were several occasions when bunches of people were milling around on the sidewalk and street in front of each establishment I visited. At this time, the cross-dressers endured all sorts of verbal abuse from the "outside world." So, a short time after these individuals received positive responses for their appearance, they experienced verbal and sometimes physical abuse.

There is indication from my fieldwork, as well as the research of others, that those males who dress in drag do so in defiance of established gender and sexual codes. They are fully aware of how their appearance is reviewed by members of the public. However, the stigma attached to cross-dressers by the outside world seems to be offset by the rewards received in an accepting and appreciative environment. Perhaps the presence of difference is desirable for the drag queen. Males who cross-dress in the spirit of entertainment conspicuously defy the deeply ingrained taboo of crossing the lines of rigidly ascribed gender roles. The very act of cross-dressing draws attention to itself and incurs the wrath of a society that has been known to react hysterically to any challenge of nonconformists. By overdoing their appearance, drag queens have opened themselves to the possibility of a negative response from their audience. This makes a certain amount of sense when one realizes they are mocking the prescribed and proscribed boundaries of gender within an essentially heterocentric culture.

UNDERSTANDING CROSS-DRESSING

In developing this visual typology of male-to-female cross-dressers, I have emphasized what visually distinguishes each of the cross-dressing types from the others. In summary, the transsexual becomes female, taking on the acceptable feminine image. The transvestite desires to emulate his conception of femininity, often creating the illusion of the unremarkable woman next door. The drag queen tends to go to the extreme in his transformation, which results in a flamboyant and exotic caricature of the female image.

By placing cross-dressers into these three categories, I have greatly simplified an extremely complex subject. Each of the three types of cross-dressers could have their own continuum, with variances in occurrence and visual success. However, as I indicate in my analysis, the three types create three distinct appearances, which result in three different types of responses through social interaction.

Transsexuals take on a feminine appearance that looks appropriate to the viewer. Femininity is achieved through a modest ensemble of dress, where the body is only subtly defined. Hair is an important framing device. Makeup and jewelry are consistent—but understated—modifications of their appearance. Transvestites tend to look anywhere from incongruous to inappropriate to the viewer. Some will pass as females, while others will not. They generally are conservative in their appearance, wearing clothing styles that may be slightly out-of-date, accented by modest styles of makeup and jewelry. And, in most cases, it is obvious that the transvestites are wearing wigs. Males who dress in drag have been accused of satirizing the female form, resulting in a "bad-girl" look. The makeup is overdone, the jewelry is large and flashy, and hairstyles—which are primarily wigs—are props for the personae created by drag queens. The often exotic and revealing garments define and exaggerate the curves of the body, and tend to emphasize the breasts and legs. The surfaces of the garments are most often reflective; ranging from sequined fabric, to lamé, to black vinyl.

ACCEPTED BOUNDARIES OF CROSS-DRESSING

Dress is a powerful form of communication. Ideals of femininity and masculinity are deeply entrenched in our culture, and are manifested by how we modify and supplement our bodies. One only needs to look at rest room symbols in most public buildings to realize how concretely defined our images of males and females actually are: bifurcated silhouettes for the men's room and skirted silhouettes for the women's room. It is likely that most of us are not aware of the thoroughness of our gender training until we are confronted by people who cross-dress.

The primary focus of this article has been to consider what happens when culturally prescribed and proscribed gender norms—revealed through dress and appearance—are challenged through social interaction. Equally important and equally compelling are the cultural, social, and personal issues that discourage more people from cross-dressing. For we've all experienced the urge—and the opportunity—to pretend, to play "dress up." In its most innocuous form, the consumer will indulge in some cosmetic extravagance: "It will create a brighter, more beautiful you!" is the basic premise for many advertising campaigns. However, if a person uses dress as a means for disguising his or her biological sex, observers are more apt to consider the cross-dresser as inappropriate.

Although dressing and attempting to pass as the opposite sex is considered by most as inappropriate and unacceptable, as a culture we have been fascinated with the idea and the reality of cross-dressing for as long as it has been documented. Through the ages, we have been titillated, fascinated, annoyed, or frightened by the practice. And yet, cross-dressing marches through generations of people. Recent popular entertainment venues have brought the topic "out of the closet." The music and film industries have done much to publicize and legitimate cross-dressing, gender-bending, gender-blending, and androgyny—at least as entertainment. Prominent musicians such as Laurie Anderson, David Bowie, Alice Cooper, Michael Jackson, Mick Jagger, k. d. lang, Annie Lennox, (The Artist Formerly Known As) Prince, and RuPaul have used dress to challenge the visual constraints of masculinity and femininity. Recent acclaimed films, such as *The Adventures of Priscilla, Queen of the Desert* (1994), *The Birdcage* (1996), *The Crying Game* (1993), and *Paris is Burning* (1992) have introduced drag to the straight audience (many of whom haven't yet ventured into a place where drag shows are staged).

The male-to-female cross-dressers considered in this paper move through a transformation that may seem to be quite synthetic—bordering on the abnormal, in the sense that male-to-female cross-dressing is not sanctioned as normal behavior in American and European cultures. However, Kuhn (1985) reminds us of the artificial manipulation of appearances by women in the following statement:

> A good deal of the groomed beauty of the women in the glamour portraits comes from the fact that they are "made-up," in the immediate sense that cosmetics have been applied to their bodies in order to enhance their existing qualities. But they are also "made-up" in a sense that the images, rather than the women are put together, constructed, even fabricated or falsified in the sense that we might say a story is made up if it is a fiction. (p. 13)

Male-to-female cross-dressing, in light of Kuhn's comment, seems really not that peculiar—except that it is deemed inappropriate human behavior by many in mainstream society.

To make sense of the countless groupings of peoples, objects, and ideals that exist in our world, we create stereotypes or codified categories. These categories are necessary, in that they help us to organize responses to external stimuli. However, codified categories will often encourage the viewer to overlook subtle differences that may be extremely important in understanding and defining a situation. Most people—when they think about male-to-female cross-dressing—tend to clump all males who cross-dress into one category. When this occurs, the differences in appearance are overlooked. In this case, it is the differences that are closely related to the identity of each type of cross-dresser.

A transvestite I met while doing my field-work made the following comment that sums up his years of experience as a cross-dresser. In the statement, he also emphasized the meanings people attach to dress and appearance:

> People will act and react toward you, and treat you in a certain way—according to your dress and appearance; but when they discover that you are not what they thought you were, the meaning of your appearance changes drastically for them. (Hegland, 1991, p. 183)

Those who cross-dress—whether they fit neatly into the three categories discussed here, or fall somewhere in between—force us to face issues which tend to make us feel uncomfortable. The accepted gender boundaries are so intricately woven into daily life, that to encounter one who crosses the line by dressing as the opposite sex often causes many of us to recommit ourselves—with steadfastness and vigor—to the dualities of the prevailing gender ideals; to the pairing of femaleness with femininity and maleness with masculinity, in whatever ways those concepts are defined within the contexts of time and space. For others, the act of cross-dressing is a compelling phenomenon that functions as a catalyst, and forces us to look more critically at culturally constructed gender roles and ideals of appearance.

Notes

1. In 1912, Crawley proposed that *cosmopolitan* be used as an adjective to describe the dress of industrialized (or "Westernized") parts of the world, as *Western* tends to be Eurocentric and pejorative. Baizerman, Eicher and Cerny (1993) suggest the terms *urban* or *cosmopolitan* instead of *Western* in the search for terms which designate "dress of the other." I agree with these arguments, and use the term *cosmopolitan* in this paper.

2. When females attempt to disguise their biological sex, I consider them to be "cross-dressers" as well. At this point, they are stigmatized in much the same way as male cross-dressers (Devor, 1989; Strega, 1985).

3. This paper focuses on the current phenomenon of male-to-female cross-dressing within American and European cultures. However, the phenomenon is not exclusive to any time or place. Cross-dressing has occurred for as long as humans have been dressing their bodies, or at least to approximately 4000 BC,

when the Hebrew prohibition against cross-dressing was alleged to have been written: "Women shall not wear that which pertains to a man, nor shall a man put on a woman's garment, for all that do are an abomination to the Lord God" (The Bible; Deuteronomy 22:5).

Cross-dressing exists in various religious and mythological traditions. A cross-dressed individual has often been considered a sign of an extraordinary destiny. The dualistic symbolism of men who dressed as women were often given divine authority within a community, and were regarded as sorcerers or visionaries. Oddly enough, it is almost exclusively within the religious realm where these men–women, or androgynous figures have been accepted without reservation. There is an androgynous, or at least bisexual, nature in the deities worshiped in the various creation myths (Ackroyd, 1979; Hauser, 1990; Katz, 1976; Levy, 1971; Wikan, 1977).

Detailed documentation of many tribal traditions describe males who cross-dressed (Ackroyd, 1979; Hauser, 1990; Karlen, 1971; Levy, 1971; Lindholm & Lindholm, 1982; Whitam & Mathy, 1986; Wikan, 1977; Williams, 1986). Native Americans have *berdaches*, who are males who wear women's clothing, engage in culturally defined feminine activities, and are given the status of the third sex. Among the Cocopa Indians, males who displayed feminine characteristics were dressed as women and labeled *e L ha*. In Tahiti, males who cross-dressed were know as *cudinas*, among the California Indians as *i-wa-musp*, among the Aztecs and Incas as *bardages*, and in coastal Oman as *xanith*.

Perhaps the most overt occurrences of cross-dressing can be found through an historical review of the theatre. Female impersonation is one of the oldest Thespian traditions, practiced by the Elizabethans, the Chinese, the Japanese, and the ancient Greeks. It seems that whenever and wherever the history of dramaturgy began, it was automatically the man's business to play the female roles (Baker, 1968; Gilbert, 1926).

The act of cross-dressing may be nearly as old as the act of dressing itself. From this, the implication is that—early on—humans developed a strong emotional attachment to the idea that females should appear feminine and males should appear masculine within a specific time and place. As far back as 6000 years, laws were written which admonished cross-dressing; yet, it has been practiced continuously, both covertly and overtly, to the present day.

4. I use these categories with some reservation. We all have been exposed to these labels, but even the most objective among us may experience an unsavory response to the three categories. I do not apologize for that. However, I do encourage the reader to attempt to break away from all the complex preconceptions that surround the issue. Dialogue with numerous faculty, graduate students, and personal acquaintances reinforce and highlight the stigma attached to each of these labels. Further, there seems to be consistent misunderstanding as to how each term is actually defined. I provide a brief definition of each category here, and include a more thorough explanation later in the body of the paper.

The *male transsexual* is a male with the genitalia of one sex and the psychosocial identity of the other. A preoperative male transsexual identifies with femaleness in every way, yet he has male reproductive organs. When he cross-dresses, the male transsexual becomes female.

The *male transvestite* is a male who dresses in feminine attire ranging from women's underwear worn underneath a business suit to a complete transformation. When cross-dressed, the male transvestite emulates the female form, but never forgets that he is male.

The *drag queen* is a male—often homosexual—who cross-dresses in the spirit of parody and satire.

5. In the film *Victor/Victoria* (1982), Julie Andrews plays a down-and-out singer who becomes a hit musical star by portraying a man who does female impersonations on the stage in the 1930s. While in her role as a man and a female impersonator, she is care-

ful to hide the fact that she does not have a protruding Adam's apple. If discovered, this would give away her true biological sex. In the same way, males who cross-dress are careful to hide their protruding Adam's apple.

6. While doing my fieldwork, I quickly learned how to address cross-dressed males. The general rule is to simply look at their appearance. Whether they are convincing or not, if you do not want to offend male-to-female cross-dressers, you refer to them with feminine pronouns when they are in feminine dress. In this paper, I use feminine pronouns to reflect the male's change in appearance.

7. Newton (1972) states that "the homosexual term for a transvestite is a drag queen" (p. 3). In my opinion, the issue of male-to-female cross-dressing is significantly more complex than Newton's statement would have us believe. Additional sources such as Ackroyd (1979) and Kirk and Heath (1984) support the notion that drag queens are almost exclusively homosexual males. These sources also imply that all homosexual male cross-dressers are not necessarily drag queens.

Contingent on his intent and visual transformation, the homosexual male cross-dresser could fit into either of the previously delineated categories of transsexualism or transvestism. Similarly, it is possible for a self-defined drag queen to be heterosexual, although I did not come across any in the literature or in my fieldwork. So, the term drag queen is apparently reserved for a homosexual male who cross-dresses in the spirit of satire.

References

Ackroyd, P. (1979). *Dressing up: Transvestism and drag, the history of an obsession*. New York: Simon & Schuster.

The Adventures of Priscilla, Queen of the Desert [Film]. (1994). R. Penfold-Russell (Executive Producer); A. Clark & M. Hamlyn (Producers); S. Elliott (Director & Writer). Australia: Polygram & Latent Image Productions.

Allen, M. P. (1989). *Transformations: Cross-dressers and those who love them*. New York: E. P. Dutton.

Baizerman, S., Eicher, J. B., & Cerny, C. (1993). Eurocentrism in the study of ethnic dress. *Dress, 20*, 9–32.

Baker, R. (1968). *Drag: A history of female impersonators on the stage*. London: Triton Books.

Benjamin, H. (1953). Transvestism and transsexualism. *International Journal of Sexology, 7*, 12–14.

Benjamin, H. (1966). *The transsexual phenomenon*. New York: Julian Press.

Berrey, L. V., & van de Bark, M. (1953). *American thesaurus of slang: A complete reference book of colloquial speech* (2nd ed.). New York: Crowell.

The Bible: Revised Standard Version.

The Birdcage. [Film]. (1996). N. Machlis & M. Danon (Executive Producers); M. Nichols (Director & Producer). USA: MGM & United Artists.

Brierley, H. (1979). *Transvestism: A handbook with case studies for psychologists, psychiatrists, and counsellors*. Oxford, England: Pergamon Press.

Bullough, V. L., & Bullough, B. (1993). *Cross dressing, sex, and gender*. Philadelphia: University of Pennsylvania Press.

Cauldwell, D. O. (1956). *Transvestism: Men in female dress*. New York: Sexology Corporation.

Crawley, A. E. (1912). Dress. In Hastings (Ed.), *Encyclopedia of religion and ethics* (Vol. V, pp. 40–72). New York: Charles Scribner's Sons.

The Crying Game [Film]. (1993). S. Woolley (Producer); N. Jordan (Director & Writer). United Kingdom: Palace Pictures & Miramax.

Dekker, R. M., & van de Pol, L. C. (1989). *The tradition of female transvestism in early modern Europe*. New York: St. Martin's Press.

Devor, H. (1989). *Gender blending: Confronting the limits of duality*. Bloomington: Indiana University Press.

Docter, R. F. (1988). *Transvestites and transsexuals: Toward a theory of cross-gender behavior.* New York: Plenum Press.

Eicher, J. B., & Roach-Higgins, M. E. (1992). Definition and classification of dress: Implications for analysis of gender roles. In R. Barnes, & J. B. Eicher, (Eds.), *Dress and gender: Making and meaning* (pp. 8–28). Oxford, England and New York: Berg.

Feinbloom, D. F. (1976). *Transvestites and transsexuals.* USA: Delacorte Press.

Garber, M. (1992). *Vested interests: Cross-dressing and cultural anxiety.* New York & London: Routledge.

Gilbert, O. P. (1926). *Men in women's guise: Some historical instances of female impersonation.* New York: Brentano's.

Hauser, R. E. (1990). The Berdache and the Illinois Indian tribe during the last half of the seventeenth century. *Ethnohistory,* 37(1), 45–65.

Hegland, J. E. (1991). *Drag queens, transvestites, transsexuals: A visual typology and analysis of male-to-female cross-dressing.* Unpublished Master's Thesis, University of Minnesota, St. Paul.

Katz, J. N. (1976). *Gay American history: Lesbians and gay men in the USA.* New York: Thomas Y. Crowell.

Kirk, K., & Heath, E. (1984). *Men in frocks.* London: Gay Men's Press.

Kuhn, A. (1985). *The power of the image: Essays in representation and sexuality.* London: Routledge & Kegan Paul.

Levy, R. I. (1971). The community function of Tahitian male transvestitism: A hypothesis. *Anthropological Quarterly,* 44(1), 12–21.

Lindholm, C., & Lindholm, C. (1982, September). The erotic sorcerers. *Science Digest,* pp. 78–80.

Lynn, M. S. (No Date). Definitions of terms commonly used in the transvestite-transsexual community. Compiled for the International Foundation for Gender Education's Educational Resources Committee (I.F.G.E.), P.O. Box 367, Wayland MA, 01778.

Maitland, S. (1986). *Vesta Tilley.* London: Virago.

Newton, E. (1972). *Mother camp: Female impersonators in America.* NJ: Prentice-Hall.

Oxford English Dictionary (2nd ed.). (1989). Oxford: Clarendon Press.

Paris is Burning [Film: Documentary]. (1992). D. Lacy & N. Finch (Executive Producers); J. Livingston & C. Goodman (Producers); J. Livingston (Director). USA: Offwhite Productions & Prestige Films.

Partridge, E. (1984). *A dictionary of slang and unconventional English: Colloquialisms and catch-phrases, solecisms and catachreses, nicknames, and vulgarisms* (8th ed.). New York: Macmillan.

Phillips, M., Shapiro, B., & Joseph, M. (1980). *Forbidden fantasies: Men who dare to dress in drag.* New York: Macmillan.

Prince, V. (1981). *Understanding cross dressing.* Tulare, CA: Chevalier.

Raynor, D. G. (1966). *A year among the girls.* New York: Lyle Stuart.

Robinson, J. (1988). *Body packaging: A guide to human sexual display.* Los Angeles: ELYSIUM Growth Press.

Rudd, P. J. (1990). *Crossdressing with dignity: The case for transcending gender lines.* Katy, TX: PM.

Stevens, J. A. (1990). *From masculine to feminine and all points in between: A practical guide for transvestites, cross-dressers, transgenderists, transsexuals, and others who choose to develop a more feminine image…And for the curious and concerned.* Cambridge, MA: Different Paths Press.

Strega, L. (1985). The big sell-out: Lesbian femininity. *Lesbian Ethics,* 1(3), 73–84.

Victor/Victoria [Film]. (1982). B. Edwards & T. Adams (Producers); B. Edwards (Director & Writer). Great Britain: MGM, Peerford, & Ladbroke Entertainment.

Wheelwright, J. (1989). *Amazons and military maids: Women who dressed as men in pursuit of life, liberty, and happiness.* Great Britain: Pandora Press.

Whitam, F. L., & Mathy, R. M. (1986). *Male homosexuality in four societies: Brazil, Guatemala, the Philippines, and the U.S.* NY: Praeger.

Wikan, U. (1977). Man becomes woman: Transsexualism in Oman as a key to gender roles. *Man: The Journal of the Royal Anthropological Institute, 12*(2), 304–319.

Williams, W. L. (1986). *The spirit and the flesh: Sexual diversity in American Indian culture.* Boston: Beacon Press.

Woodhouse, A. (1989). *Fantastic women: Sex, gender, and transvestism.* New Brunswick, NJ: Rutgers University Press.

DISCUSSION QUESTIONS

Drag Queens, Transvestites, Transsexuals: Stepping Across the Accepted Boundaries of Gender

1. In American culture, why do you think the practice of cross-dressing is generally associated more with male to female cross-dressing than female to male? What are some of the physical cues that could expose even the most convincing cross-dresser?

2. According to the author of the article, why is the term cross-dressing not accurate for transsexuals?

3. What is the nature of being a drag queen and why is it hard for him to "pass" as a biological female?

CHAPTER 6

Standing Out from The Crowd

Kimberly A. Miller

AFTER YOU HAVE READ THIS CHAPTER YOU WILL UNDERSTAND:

- Conformity and individuality in dress at individual, group, societal and cultural levels.

- The benefits and risks associated with being a nonconformist in dress.

- Why individuality and conformity in dress are not mutually exclusive.

- The many issues tied to school uniforms.

- Cultural issues of collectivism and individualism as they apply to dress.

In Chapter 2 we discussed the fact that it is human nature to improve on what we are born with physically. We could call that phenomenon a **cultural universal**, that is, all cultures (and hence, all humans) exhibit the characteristic of wanting to "improve" the human body. In this chapter, we will add to this idea another cultural universal. All humans have a dilemma related to dress and appearance: How can I fit in with others and still be an individual? In other words, how can I be dressed like one of the gang (i.e., conformity) and still stand out from the crowd (i.e., individuality)? In this chapter, we will see that the tension or pull between dressing to fit in and dressing to be unique is balanced very differently in diverse cultures (i.e., Korea and the United States) and groups within U.S. culture (i.e., sororities, popular culture icons, homo-punks, and convicted criminals.)

Conformity and individuality are complicated concepts that are not mutually exclusive, at least not in dress. The tension between dressing to fit in and dressing to be unique escalates when an individual wants to follow fashion—a conforming behavior—while also wanting to appear as an original person. The desire to fit in while appearing as an individual has implications for those interested in fashion careers. A basic understanding of the social and psychological needs individuals of related to dress is fundamental to fashion merchandising and design. Awareness of human needs and the ability to meet those needs through sales will lead to success in the fashion business. Commissioned sales associates and personal shoppers face the challenge of helping their customers find dress that will meet their individual needs by resolving the tension between fitting in and being unique. The more sales associates and personal shoppers understand this challenge, the more likely they will enjoy career success.

The readings in this chapter will provide many examples of this complex nature of fashion. Beginning with a focus on the individual, these readings will demonstrate the effect conformity and nonconformity can have on a person's life. At the group level, a sorority may encourage a specific type of dress to achieve a group identity. Also, at the group level, are workplace examples of dress (see Chapter 7). At the societal level, school uniforms ignite strong feelings about issues of conformity and individuality. Lastly, we examine the effect one's culture has on conformity in dress. We will see that the tension or pull between dressing to fit in and dressing to be unique is balanced very differently in diverse cultures and subcultures.

INDIVIDUAL LEVEL: CONFORMITY AND INDIVIDUALITY

Few of us, as individuals, can survive without the acceptance of others. As social creatures we need others to like us and compliment us so that we feel integrated. Within the social psychological study of conformity, scholars "examine the pressures on individuals to conform to the expectations of a group, society, organization or leader" (Marshall, 1994, p. 83). Because most people want to be part of a group in order to feel accepted, they often willingly conform to the group's expectations. **Conformity** may be defined as a change in an individual's behavior or attitude in order to achieve consistency based on real or imagined group pressure (Kiesler & Kiesler, 1970). "Conformity in dress" is defined by Horn (1965) as the acceptance of or adherence to a clothing norm, that is, dressing in accordance with the norm of a specified group (p. 146). **Individualism** is any set of ideas emphasizing the importance of the individual and the individual's interests (Marshall, 1994, p. 239). "Individuality in dress" refers to an awareness of the norm and a desire to set one's self apart from it (Horn, 1965).

Whether a person expresses individuality or conformity in her or his dress may depend on such qualities as other-directedness or inner-directedness. **Other-directedness** is when a person is sensitive to the expectations and references of others (Riesman, 1953). An other-directed person is apt to conform with respect to dress. In contrast, **inner-directedness** is the inclination of having strong and internalized standards that enable the individual to resist pressure from others (Riesman, 1953). An inner-directed person is apt to be a nonconformist in dress, a follower of a subcultural style, or a fashion leader. Individuals vary in their desire to be unique from others; a quality captured under the **uniqueness theory** (Snyder & Fromkin, 1980). This theory would explain in part why some people feel the need to dress *very* differently from others while other people feel the need to dress only a *little* differently from others.

Whether a person is other-directed or inner-directed may have implications for the fashion adoption/diffusion process (discussed in greater detail in Chapter 11). Because other-directed individuals are sensitive to the expectations of others, they may adopt fashions in an effort to conform to others in their dress (known as fashion followers). Inner-directed individuals may be nonconformists and choose not to adopt a fashion at all, thereby creating a new fashion (known as a fashion innovator). Clothing researchers hypothesize relationships between customer behavior and theories in an effort to predict consumer behavior, thereby increasing sales. Fashion merchandising and design students will discover many proposed theories directed at identifying a target market or consumer.

Conformity in dress has several benefits. Clothing researchers have studied the relationship between appearance and social participation, popularity, and peer acceptance among adolescents (Kelley & Eicher, 1970; Kelley et al., 1974; Smucker & Creekmore, 1972). An adolescent's dress can mean the difference between social acceptance and social ostracism. That acceptance, or lack of acceptance, can have profound effects on an adolescent's feelings of self-worth.

Dressing as an individual also has its benefits but requires high levels of self-esteem and support from significant others. Especially during adolescence, high self-esteem may be difficult to maintain while dressing as an individual and ignoring the expectations of peers. However, throughout this book, there are many examples of people who have risked being a nonconforming individual. For instance, Andrew Martinez (a.k.a., "The Naked Guy") was a student at the University of California at Berkeley in 1992 and was certainly considered to be an individual. He regularly attended class nude (see Figure 6.1).

FIGURE 6.1 *Andrew Martinez is an example of a nonconformist in dress. He was a student at University of California-Berkeley in 1992, where he was eventually banned from campus.*

INDIVIDUAL LEVEL: NON-CONFORMITY

Because dress offers countless possibilities for individual expression, it is fun to experiment with different symbols and combinations. Some people are more willing than others to take risks and will try "far-out" or unusual combinations. At an individual level, conforming versus nonconforming can affect self-esteem, social acceptance, and ultimately, success. Nonconformists are typically considered to be eccentric and unconventional. Three readings in this chapter present examples of nonconformists as well as the risks and payoffs of nonconforming.

"Dennis Rodman, Bad Boy as Man of the Moment," is an excellent example of nonconformity in dress at the individual level. As a result of wearing pink fingernail polish and women's clothes while also playing for the National Basketball Association (NBA), Rodman was catapulted to a household name during the 1990s (see Figure 6.2). The juxtaposition of the male macho-ism of the basketball arena with cross-dressing off the court is a good example of postmodern questioning of rules and blurring of boundaries. Although Rodman may receive high marks for individual expression, it does not come without a price. Not everyone can withstand the scrutiny and criticism Rodman endures.

Rodman expresses a unique and multifaceted identity whether on or off the court, with his multicolored hair and unusually matched accessories. Some high-profile individuals use nonconformity as a strategy to gain publicity and Rodman is no exception. He has taken the limelight of public criticism and turned it into an opportunity to explain himself. A quote from his book, *Bad As I Wanna Be*, reveals his thinking regarding dress:

> I don't think painting my fingernails is a big deal. It's not like I'm sitting home by myself, trying on lingerie. That's not my style. I don't do lingerie. I think cross-dressing, the way I do it, is more accepted than people think....It wasn't that long ago that everyone freaked out when they saw a man wearing an earring...When I cross-dress now, it's just another way I can show all the sides of Dennis Rodman. I'm giving you the whole package. I'm becoming the all-purpose person. I'm like the running back that can break one to the outside and also go over the middle to catch a pass. (p. 222)

Rodman obviously sees a big difference between painted fingernails and wearing women's lingerie. He goes on to explain, in his book, that dressing only as a macho NBA player would reveal only one dimension of himself. Of course, if Rodman were not a talented athlete fewer people would be interested in his views on cross-dressing.

Another nonconformist, Todd Bennett, is described in the newspaper article "Non-Conformist Immune to Criticism." Bennett was a student at Iowa State University whose identity as a homo-punk in the early 1990s drew verbal abuse at times. Bennett's mohawk hairstyle is reminiscent of punk hairstyles of the 1970s and 1980s. Despite the criticism Bennett received, he appeared to be happily resigned to following his own inner voice. This article is interesting because it gives the reader a real-life account of the consequences of nonconformity at the individual level.

Being a nonconformist does have its benefits, however. It can be financially rewarding to be a nonconforming NBA player (as in Rodman's case) or it can be psychologically rewarding to know that your dress truly expresses who you are regardless of what others might think (as in Bennett's case). Rodman's popular culture status means that he can publish books and make movies about his personal life and benefit financially. Bennett gets the satisfaction of being true to himself and not give in to pressures to conform to a mainstream way of living that he feels he does not fit into.

An accused criminal is an extreme example of nonconformity, as societal expectations have not been met if an individual is accused of a crime. Criminals can (and often do) take advantage of the superficial nature of dress; because identities are visible, they are also transportable. For example, a police officer's uniform (or a near version of one) is easily attainable, as are the lights that can be installed in one's car that resemble police car lights. This type of setup can enable a criminal to successfully pose as a police officer and stop women who drive alone at night. Another example of this transportable nature of identity is the subject of "Saving Face."

As described in "Saving Face," dress becomes an important tool for lawyers who hope to make jurors identify with a defendant. Lawyers often give their clients advice on what to wear during a trial or they may hire trial consultants to confer with clients. The object is to make the client look similar to the members of the jury. Changing an accused's identity from "not one of us" to "one of us" is a challenging task, but if successful it can pay off for both the client and attorney. Lawyers understand that the more jurors can identify with a defendant, the more difficult it is for jurors to convict the accused. Dress can help make this transition possible.

Turning an accused criminal into a conformist during a trial is not only difficult, it can be considered unethical. The news article, "Saving Face," reminds us of how easily appearances can be manipulated to one's advantage. Although a case of individual dress, society often condones these manipulations. The common practice of manipulating the appearances of accused criminals raises ethical concerns. How far should lawyers and trial consultants go to ensure that their clients appear to be the person next door?

GROUP LEVEL: DRESS AND GROUP IDENTITY

Conformity in dress has its advantages and disadvantages. For instance, clothing researchers have learned that accomplished women athletes often adhere carefully to uniform codes to appear credible in sports dominated by men (Casselman-Dickson & Damhorst, 1993). Therefore, women find it advantageous to conform to the uniform of male athletes. Conforming to clothing norms can also enhance one's credibility in other settings. At work (covered in Chapter 7), people spend a considerable amount of time and energy on dress to ensure that they look the part. Conformity in dress may be disadvantageous when a person feels stifled or constrained in their ability to express their individual identity.

The dilemma of "fitting in" versus "standing out" becomes salient when groups develop a particular style of dress. Following a subcultural style of dress may, on the surface, appear to be individual nonconformity. But subcultural style has been defined as **counter-conformity** (Horn, 1965). In other words, those who conform to a subculture (or counterculture) reject prevailing societal dress by conforming to the dictates of a subculture's dress.

Although not commonly thought of as subcultures, we will look at two groups that illustrate how dress is used to create a group identity. One reading demonstrates how sorority members talk about identity within a college setting. A second group, the "plain people," will show how a high degree of uniformity in dress creates a particular group identity.

Sororities and fraternities and other societal organizations are found on many college campuses. In "It's all Greek to Me: Sorority Members and Identity Talk," college women talk about judgements based on dress and appearance. Researchers Miller and Hunt approached the study under the assumption that students give up part of their individual identity to assume a collective one when they join a sorority. It is a commonly held stereotype that those who join sororities have to conform to the overall appearance of that sorority. Not entirely so, said sorority women who were interviewed during the spring of 1993. Miller and Hunt asked members a number of questions regarding appearance, including: Is there a uniform appearance for a specific sorority? The researchers discovered that sorority members placed more emphasis on personality, culture, and circumstances than on a standard appearance for all members. Sorority members indicate that they see more variety among their dress than outsiders do.

In contrast to the individual variety in dress among sorority members, there are groups that demonstrate a high degree of uniformity in dress. For example, Stephen Scott (1986) discusses dress of the "plain people" in the United States, including Christian religious groups (e.g., Amish, Mennonites, Hutterites, and so forth) who live separately from mainstream society. People in these religious groups sacrifice individual expression to devote themselves to living according to their group's religious principles. The uniformity of dress expresses commitment to the group:

> They have adopted a kind of uniform but since they are never "off duty," most wear it constantly. They need no special festivities to reveal their identity and heritage. They wish to be reminded of it every day. They observe no sacred vestments in their worship; their clergy's appearance is little different from the layperson's. They have no special religious orders, but both men and women wear a religious garb. There are no formal dress or elaborate costumes used only for rare occasions. They avoid all ostentation and keep competition at a minimum by insisting on a uniform simple dress. (p. 5)
>
> Their clothing represents their identification with the body of believers and its total belief and value system. (p. 7)

The two groups discussed above are revealing examples of the complex nature of conformity and individuality. Sororities typically have a consistent outward image (i.e., conformity) but allow for individuality among group members to a greater extent than do the "plain people" that Scott described. "Plain people" also have a consistent outward image, but may have less variation in dress among members than sororities.

We might stereotype these groups and conclude that sororities are individualistic and "plain people" are conformists. However, situations and human behavior are rarely that simple. It would be inaccurate to assume that all people are either individualists or conformists. Judgments regarding a person's individuality or conformity are perhaps more accurately discussed in terms of *degree* rather than assuming that the presence of one (i.e., conformity) automatically prohibits the presence of the other (i.e., individuality). More probable, most people exhibit varying degrees of individuality and conformity and the degree of each depends on such factors as individual personality, group influence, situational context, and cultural bias. For example, it may be more accurate to say that sororities and "plain people" exhibit both individuality and conformity but to different degrees. Sororities may exhibit a higher degree of individuality and a smaller degree of conformity when compared to the "plain people." Similarly, the "plain people," when compared to sorority group dress, may exhibit a higher degree of conformity and a smaller degree of individuality.

Moreover, all observations of dress must be framed within the context of who the observer is and who is being observed. Let's use a male skateboarder as an example. From their perspective, he and other skateboarders are "cool" because they are dressed differently from the majority of adults and adolescents in the skateboarder's community. Therefore, a skateboarder considers himself and other skateboarders as individualists. However, from the perspective of an outside observer (i.e., a business man) all skateboarders look alike. Therefore the business man considers skateboarders to be conformists. Because the skateboarder is aware of the subtle nuances of skateboarder attire, he recognizes the individuality expressed among skateboarders. Because the business man is not aware of the subtle differences among skateboarder attire, he only recognizes the similarity among skateboarding dress. Consequently, who is regarded an individualist and who is regarded a conformist depend upon the perspective of the observer.

SOCIETAL LEVEL: SCHOOL UNIFORMS

An insightful example of the tension between conformity and individuality can be found in school uniforms. The present-day debate on school uniforms includes such questions as: Should students dress alike to emphasize learning and achievement? Do uniforms inhibit creativity and self-expression? President Clinton made school uniforms a national topic when he proposed uniforms in all public schools as a way to reduce violence (State of the Union Address, January 23, 1996).

Clothing researcher O'Neal (1997) has documented news reports about clothing-related violence. However, there are still many unanswered questions about the proposed connection between reducing violence and wearing school uniforms. Several clothing researchers have tried to make connections between dress and behavior, but proving those connections is difficult and rare and heavily dependent on a specific situation. School uniforms serve as an excellent example of the difficulty in proving that dress affects behavior. Very often, schools implement several policies all at once, making it difficult to pinpoint a cause-effect relationship between dress and behavior. School officials, in an attempt to rid their schools of violence, may institute a school-uniform policy, a strict attendance policy, tutoring services, and increased security on school grounds at the same time, making it difficult to credit school uniforms for reduced violence in schools. Similarly, in other research settings, it is difficult to prove that dress affects behavior.

A school uniform may be a symbol of studiousness, politeness, and conscientiousness. Dress has the potential for communicating messages about the self to others as well as communicating messages about the self to the self. For instance, a schoolgirl's uniform may convey the message that she is serious about her studies. Moreover, her uniform (as well as the uniforms of her classmates around her) may communicate to her that schooltime is for contemplation and play will come later. **Self-perception** is the process by which individuals come to think about and know themselves (Marshall, 1994). This process of self-perception may explain why students behave differently when dressed in uniforms compared to when they are dressed in street clothes. More research is needed to tell us more about students' behavior when dressed in different types of clothes.

Appearances may often create a **self-fulfilling prophecy**, that is, when people define situations as real, they become real in their consequences (Marshall, 1994, p. 471). For example, an adult may see a child in a school uniform and assume that the child is hardworking and goal-oriented. These assumptions are known as a **halo effect**, a network (or stereotype) of positive inferences resulting from favorable judgments based on appearance. A self-fulfilling prophecy occurs when the adult interacts with the child as though he or she is hardworking and goal-oriented. The child may believe that assessment and continue to work hard and set goals. Hence, the positive halo effect stereotype comes true and the self-fulfilling prophecy becomes real. These cognitive leaps are often erroneous, however, and reveal the power of appearances, especially in cases of falsely manipulated ones as in the article, "Saving Face."

Three readings in this chapter address school uniforms. In the first reading, "Do School Uniforms Make the Grade?" the authors point out that current information about the effects of school uniforms is either not available or inconclusive. More research studies must to be conducted before launching the entire country on a school-uniform parade. The article lists pros and cons of school uniforms to date and provides a good example of issues of conformity and individuality at the societal level.

In the second reading, "Students' Rights Not as Broad as Those of Public" raises questions regarding the rights of students. Students, in most cases, cannot write, wear, and say things that those in the general public are free to write, wear, and say. However, this issue is not clear-cut; several students, with support from parents and grandparents, are pursuing the matter in court.

The third reading on school uniforms, "The School Uniform as Fashion Statement," covers the many ways students individualize their school uniforms. This individualization indicates that students will inevitably bend any dress code that is imposed on them. Because students are so creative and resourceful, they find ways to stay within the bounds of the dress code while presenting themselves as individuals. Such ingenuity in bending the rules is often called bricolage. **Bricolage** is the process of finding solutions to problems by examining, using, and combining cultural signs in ways that were not initially intended (Kaiser, 1997, p. 468). Students add accessories to their uniforms to individualize their "look" and solve the problem of having to adhere to a dress code. This article on school uniforms is a good example of the dual nature of dress regarding conformity and individuality.

In "The School Uniform as Fashion Statement" students are quoted regarding their personal opinions about having to wear a uniform to school. Not surprisingly, there are wide-ranging opinions among students regarding school uniforms. Some students appreciate the uniform because it prevents long discussions and confusion each morning about what to wear to school. Other students think a school uniform makes them feel as though they are a low-paid employee (i.e., "I hate the vests...I feel like I work at McDonald's"). On a societal level, school uniforms are obviously an important topic because you can rarely find someone who does not have an opinion about them.

CULTURAL LEVEL: COLLECTIVISM AND INDIVIDUALISM

At the cultural level, collectivism and individualism are philosophies or ideas that frame a culture's thinking and defines what is valuable. **Collectivism** is a philosophy that considers the collective good paramount to the individual good (Marshall, 1994, p. 239). Individualism in the United States is often associated with such characteristics as creativity, ability to think independently, and high initiative. From a U.S. perspective, collectivism is often associated with characteristics that are the opposite of individuality (i.e., unimaginative, dependent on others for ideas, and sluggishness) and usually carries a negative stigma. As people from the United States examine collectivist behaviors from other cultures (e.g., dress), they need to be especially aware of their own cultural bias toward individualism. For instance, Kaiser (1997) explores issues of individuality and conformity in Japan. Kaiser finds that both individuality and conformity are alive and well in Japan and must be viewed within their distinctive cultural context. Conformity in Japan is expressed within the group context demonstrating loyalty of group members (Mouer & Sugimoto, 1986). Individuality in Japan is expressed through an integration of appearance and behavior styles (Kaiser, 1997, p. 474) in which it is unnecessary for one to dress and act according to a logic that everyone else can understand (Mouer & Sugimoto, 1986, p. 195). Because the philosophy of individuality is so ingrained, U. S. residents will often find it difficult to view collective behaviors objectively or positively.

Additionally, an individual's culture impacts their buying behavior. Generally, U. S. consumers are considered to be individualists if they purchase products to meet their personal needs. Korea, on the other hand, is a society that emphasizes collectivist values more than the United States does. Korean consumers, in general, more strongly consider acceptance of society at large as well as individual expression when selecting clothing purchases. For example, prestige and a well-known clothing brand are often fairly important to Korean consumers. Individual Korean consumers' appearance looks unique, however. Cross-cultural research reported by Wickliffe in the article "Culture and Consumer Behavior" illustrates one example of the impact culture has on buying behavior.

Summary

This chapter covers a broad range of issues related to conformity and individuality in dress. Conformity and individuality affect and reflect individuals, groups, societies, and cultures. A school uniform is one example of dress that illustrates how conformity and individuality can coexist and are not necessarily mutually exclusive. This is because fashion offers so many choices that individuals can dress to conform while also dressing to assert their individuality. Fashion merchandisers and designers must be aware of these conflicting needs and assist individuals in resolving the conflict through purchase of clothing. Cross-culturally, the concepts of individuality and conformity must be considered within the context of a specific culture.

Suggested Readings

Forney, J. C., & Forney, W. S. (1995, Winter). Gangs or fashion: Influences on junior high student dress, *Journal of Family and Consumer Sciences* 87(4), 26–32.

Hebdige, D. (1979). *Subculture: The meaning of style*. London: Methuen.

Hethorn, J. (1997). *A street guide to gang identity*. [online]. Available: http//gangid. ucdavis.edu

McVeigh, B. (1997). Wearing ideology: How uniforms discipline minds and bodies in Japan. *Fashion Theory*, 1(2), 189–213.

Mechling, J. (1987). Dress right, dress: The boy scout uniform as a folk costume. *Semiotica, 64*, (3/4), 319–333.

LEARNING ACTIVITY

School Uniforms and Dress Codes—Pros and Cons

Objective: To consider the pros and cons of school uniforms and dress codes from a multitude of viewpoints.

Procedure

First, make a list of all of the advantages of school uniforms you can think of. When making your list, consider viewpoints of students, parents, teachers, school administrators, designers, manufacturers, retailers, and society at large.

BOX 1
Southern Middle School Dress Standards 1997–98

1. Students may not wear garments with obscenities, vulgarities, profane language, double meaning, alcohol or cigarette advertisements, ethnic or racially offensive stereotypical language or pictures.

2. Students may not wear garments that expose their midriff.

3. Students may not wear pants or skirts that sag below the waist, and no part of any undergarment may be revealed as a result of fashion or style. If necessary, belts or drawstrings must be worn. Long shirts or sweaters will not alter this requirement.

4. Students may not wear any clothing that is deemed too revealing by teacher or principal. (Example: short skirts or dresses, tight shirts or pants, plunge cut dresses or shirts, tank tops, or mesh tops). Skirts and/or dresses, shorts and/or skorts must be finger tip length or longer.

5. Students may not wear chains attached to wallets, belts, or pants.

6. Students may not carry or wear bookbags or backpacks. (Bookbags and backpacks must be placed in lockers before first hour.)

7. Students may not wear heavy coats, hats, bandannas or sunglasses while inside the building. (Coats should be placed in lockers before first hour.)

8. Students may not wear facial jewelry, except for in the ear.

9. Students may not wear hair color or styles that are distracting.

10. Combs that pose a safety hazard, rakes, and rollers may not be worn in the hair.

11. All clothing must be clean, safe, and appropriate.

12. Students may not wear clothing with rips or tears.

13. The Principal and Associate Principal will have the final decision regarding dress standards.

Corrective and Disciplinary Actions that Will Occur When Students are Not in Compliance

1. If a teacher has questions about the appropriateness of a student's dress, they will send them to the office with a note explaining what is in question.

2. There will be two people designated by the Principal in charge of determining appropriateness.

3. If the dress is judged to be inappropriate, the student would call a parent informing them of their dress violation, then change clothes into what the school has provided. The parent has the option to bring their child a change of clothing, but until they come the student will wear the school's clothes and return to class.

4. If the dress is judged to be appropriate, the student will return to class with a note stating such.

5. If a student refuses to take corrective actions and/or follow the dress standards, the student will be sent home on a suspension.

6. The student will be held accountable for returning the school's clothes. Upon returning the clothes, the student will be given their clothes.

Reprinted by permission. *George Rogers Jr.*, Principal, S.M.S.

Next, make another list. This list should contain all of the disadvantages of school uniforms you can think of. When making your list, consider viewpoints of students, parents, teachers, school administrators, designers, manufacturers, retailers, and society at large.

HSB Reliability Technologies
Dress Code

DATE: May 1, 1998

TO: All HSBRT Consultant employees

CC: Richard Swindell

FROM: David Reynolds

RE: HSBRT Shirts

This memo will clarify the company policy on the wearing and issuing of the HSBRT logo shirts.

The shirts are intended to enhance our professional image and promote name recognition. To that end, it is expected that the shirts are worn and displayed in a professional manner. Minimum expectations are that the oxford shirts are pressed and the polo shirts are wrinkle free. All shirts should be free of stains, tears or fraying.

Each consulting employee will initially receive 4 (four) long sleeve shirts (1 blue oxford, 1 white oxford, 2 twill sportshirts), and two short sleeve polo shirts (color of your choice). Most existing employees have received this initial issue. All new employees will receive this issue after the completion of their 90 day trial period.

Two new shirts will be issued to each employee in good standing at the end of their annual review. The type and style of the shirts is the choice of the employee but should be compatible with the working environment they typically find themselves in. Long sleeve shirts are more appropriate business attire, particularly in refineries and chemical plants. Any employee can order and purchase additional shirts at any time. All orders should be placed with Kathy in the Houston office. Cleaning and pressing of the shirts is still the responsibility of each individual employee. The company laundry policy is still in effect. Laundry will only be reimbursed by the company if the employee is away from home on company business for more than 6 consecutive days.

Reprinted by permission. Dave Reynolds, Business Operations Manager.

Group Discussion

Break into small groups and compare your lists of advantages and disadvantages to the lists of your classmates.

Discuss with your group: Pretend that you have been charged with the responsibility of creating a policy for all of the public schools in the United States regarding dress codes and/or uniforms. What would your policy include? Remember to include a policy that will be agreeable to all constituencies (i.e., students, parents, school administrators, and so forth).

Using the dress code examples in Box 1 and Box 2, compare school dress codes to work dress codes. How are the two similar? How are they different? Is there anything missing from either the school or work example? Is there too much detail in either the school or work example? How might school dress codes assist the individual in making a transition from school to work?

WRITING ACTIVITIES

School Uniforms and Dress Codes

Write a personal reflection statement (two or three paragraphs) about your experience of having to wear a school uniform or having to adhere to a dress code policy. Do you have a specific memory related to your school dress?

Ethics of Appearance Manipulation

Write two or three paragraphs about the ethics of changing the appearances of convicted criminals for the courtroom. How far is too far? Should there be restrictions on this type of activity or is everything allowable?

References

Address Before a Joint Session of the Congress on the State of the Union. (January 23, 1996). *Weekly Compilation of Presidential Documents 32:* 4 (Jan. 29, 1996), pp. 90–98.

Casselman-Dickson, M. A., & Damhorst, M. L. (1993). Female bicyclists and interest in dress: Validation with multiple measures. *Clothing and Textiles Research Journal, 11,* (4), 7–17.

Horn, M. (1965). *The second skin.* Boston: Houghton-Mifflin.

Kaiser, S. B. (1997). *The social psychology of clothing* (ed. revised). New York: Fairchild.

Kelley, E. A., Daigle, C. W., LaFleur, R. S., & Wilson, L. J. (1974). Adolescent dress and social participation. *Home Economics Research Journal, 2,* (3), 167–175.

Kelley, E. A., & Eicher, J. B. (1970). A longitudinal analysis of popularity, group membership, and dress. *Journal of Home Economics, 62,* 240–250.

Kiesler, C. A., & Kiesler, S. B. (1970). *Conformity.* Reading: Addison-Wesley.

Marshall, G. (Ed.). (1994). *The concise Oxford dictionary of sociology.* Oxford, England: Oxford University Press.

Mouer, R., & Sugimoto, Y. (1986). *Images in Japanese society.* London: KPI.

O'Neal, G. S. (1997). Clothes to kill for: An analysis of primary and secondary claims-making in print media. *Sociological Inquiry, 67,* 336–349.

Riesman, D. (1953). *The lonely crowd: A study of the changing American character.* Garden City, NY: Doubleday.

Rodman, D. (1996). *Bad as I wanna be.* New York: Dell Publishing.

Scott, S. (1986). *Why do they dress that way?* Intercourse, PA: Good Books.

Smucker, B., & Creekmore, A. M. (1972). Adolescents' clothing conformity, awareness, and peer acceptance. *Home Economics Research Journal, 1,* 92–97.

Snyder, C. R., & Fromkin, H. L. (1980). *Uniqueness: The human pursuit of difference.* New York: Plenum Press.

28 Dennis Rodman, Bad Boy As Man of the Moment

Margo Jefferson

Now that America is no longer in the forefront when it comes to industrial and mechanical invention, its job is to produce new cultural types. Today, this is being done largely on the popular culture front. It is here that performers splice myths and roles together in what we might call feats of stylistic engineering.

On these grounds, Dennis Rodman, the Chicago Bulls' forward, has made a genuine contribution to popular culture, and there must be many people across the nation who fervently hope he will get his act together by getting control of his more unruly impulses on the basketball court.

In the latest incident, he kicked a cameraman during a basketball game. Male athletes, rock stars and celebrities are regularly observed and occasionally punished for attacking photographers, fans, fellow players, umpires, referees and women in bars, cars and hotel rooms. Few of them are reprimanded quite as sternly or smugly as Mr. Rodman has been. They are called brats and bullies; once in a while they are called rapists. Mr. Rodman has been called a brat and a bully for years now. But only since he began talking about bisexuality and dressing up in campy costumes, only since his book, *Bad as I Wanna Be*, came out in 1996, only since then, have people been predicting imminent nervous breakdowns or tossing around words like "psychopath."

What *Bad as I Wanna Be* really shows is that Dennis Rodman is squarely in the American tradition of the aggressive class clown and cutup. This is a role also being played by other canny, nerve-racking performers like Howard Stern and Roseanne.

But would there be so many armchair psychiatrists if Mr. Rodman's on-court bullying weren't accompanied by all that off-court crossdressing and bisexual teasing (those transgressive acts of gender-bending, as academics like to say)?

Athletes still carry the culture's dreams of mega-masculinity on their game-ready, gym-worked shoulders. As an athlete, Mr. Rodman totes his share of this load. But as a celebrity, a pop culture star, he gets away with a lot of sexual nose-thumbing: yes, he talks (and talks) about his affairs with women, but he also talks about being attracted to men and about the eros that can fill the most heterosexual locker rooms; he does pinup-boy photography spreads for magazines, kisses RuPaul on television and is interviewed in the gay journal *The Advocate*.

In choosing his wardrobe, Mr. Rodman gives a fresh spin to the classic modernist dictum that form must follow function. For sports-linked interviews or mainstream talk shows like Jay Leno's, where the host and guest are like the leading men in a buddy film, he dons strict guy garb: T-shirts and sensible shoes. And hats too— not just the all-American baseball cap but the leather cap, the full-crowned apple cap and the fake fur Stetson: a walking history of headgear for the black street man.

For more spectacular artistic events (music award shows, book signings) he chooses a Las Vegas showgirl look: that's when we see the leather skirts or short-shorts, the wafer-thin sleeveless shirts (flagrantly displayed pectorals do for men what cleavage does for women), the boas and the voluminous bridal gown. Mr. Rodman is the first star athlete to successfully wed heterosexual macho to drag queen chutzpah. This is a genuine stylistic innovation.

As for the various hair colors, I think he looks best as a blond. The multicolored dye jobs with vaguely tribal designs do not set off the face or the red, white and black Chicago Bulls uniform very well. But as fashion's greatest grande dame, Diana Vreeland, used to say: bad taste is better than safe taste or no taste at all.

Furthermore, Mr. Rodman has brought some fresh touches to the somewhat dated notion of the White Negro. According to Norman Mailer's 1950's definition, the White Negro was a white man, a hipster who had studied and absorbed certain crucial, daring elements of black style. But by the 1970's a different kind of White Negro had emerged. He was a black man this time around, a rock-and-roller who had studied and absorbed certain crucial, daring elements of white style. Think Jimi Hendrix, Sly Stone and George Clinton. The artist we still refer to as Prince is this kind of White Negro. And so is Dennis Rodman.

It also seems that he is both a self-made man and a self-invented diva. And it is this balance that he has had such trouble maintaining. On the one hand, Mr. Rodman is the quintessential kid from the slums, skinny and short for years, determined to flaunt the chip on his shoulder, aggressively defending his every action, unwilling to admit he has ever been wrong about anything, anytime or anywhere. In short, he is a macho stereotype. On the other hand, he is the self-consciously flamboyant performer, determined to excite the public with his craft onstage and thrill them with his high jinks offstage.

Now that the National Basketball Association has ordered him to see a counselor, he might take yet another tip from the culture of femininity and divadom. When it comes to emotions men are still expected not to lose face. But women are seen as on the edge to begin with, therefore having no face to lose. Female celebrities are permitted to admit to stress, neurosis or temporary crackups, to admit they are not constantly in control or in the right and that they might just be acting out when they can't stop acting up. They are permitted to seek and find help on their own terms, and to talk about it if they wish. Often, we come to see it all as the mark and cost of their daring. And this can work to their advantage.

Why doesn't Mr. Rodman try to make it work for him? He could announce that hence-

FIGURE 6.2 *Dennis Rodman, dressed as a bride, is a good example of postmodern individuality.*

forth he will see a psychiatrist of his own choosing, and then make that fact and admission part of his mystique, just as he did his once belittled gift for rebounding and his need to shock people.

A few more incidents like the kicking of the cameraman, and the culture he has played such entertaining games with, from the sports establishment to the game-watching, book-buying public, may be all too ready to turn on him. For now, anyway, his success as a cross-dressing tease and rebel still depends on his success as a world-class (he has won three championship rings) basketball player.

Which is to say, he must play the good boy on the court if he wants to get away with playing the butch boy and the bad girl once the game is over.

DISCUSSION QUESTIONS

1. In Rodman's book, *Bad As I Wanna Be*, he states that it wasn't that long ago that men who wore earrings were considered unusual. Do you foresee any lasting impact on men's appearance as a result of Rodman's eclectic style of dress?

2. Do you agree or disagree that America is now producing "new cultural types" to compensate for a lack of producing mechanical and industrial objects?

3. Do you think Rodman is able to be who he is because of the current cultural moment? Or can you identify a Rodman equivalent during several decades of the 20th century? If you can identify other Rodman equivalents in the past, what does this do to Rodman's individuality? Give specific examples to support your position.

29 Bennett: A Non-Conformist Immune to Criticism

Jennifer Janeczko

Todd Bennett is most recognizable by his mohawk hairstyle.

He says it's comparable to the "erectile crest" of a cockatoo. It's backcombed until it stands six inches straight up and is plastered into a stiff curve with White Rain, an environmentally safe hair spray.

Bennett is similar to the unusual bird in many ways. He is certainly a bird of his own feather, and he doesn't flock with any group.

Bennett is a self-proclaimed non-conformist and considers himself a "campus activist" at Iowa State.

Bennett is openly homosexual, and he is probably the only self-acknowledged "homopunk" in the state of Iowa, he said. But being different doesn't bother him. In fact, he thrives on it.

"I like to have fun, and typical things bore me," he said. "I've never been governed by my peers."

Bennett was a student at ISU for two years in fisheries and wildlife biology, but he is no longer enrolled because he was disillusioned with the curriculum.

"I'm a student of life if nothing else," he said.

He is still an active figure in campus organizations, such as the Lesbian/Gay/Bisexual Alliance.

He is also involved in People for the Ethical Treatment of Animals, the Humane Society, Anti-Racist Action, which is an alternative movement of skinheads combating racism, and an environmental group.

He hopes to someday be employed at a zoo or a museum because he loves the idea of working with strange and unusual creatures.

Bennett stands out from the typical ISU student in many ways, aside from his alternative hair-do.

From his appearance, attitudes and musical tastes to his sexual preference and religious beliefs, Bennett is his own person.

Being "typical" is a far cry from being "normal," he said.

"I'm a very normal person. I'm just not typical."

His appearance is one of the main ways he expresses himself and is a method of activism in itself. His eyes are lined with black make-up, his fingernails are long and he wears black boots and tight black jeans.

"I simply find that frills, like hair and accessories, are a fun expression of myself. I don't dress this way because I'm gay."

Bennett feels many ISU students are conformists, but he recognizes that conformity is the majority anywhere you go, he said.

"There will always be conformity, even to a certain subculture. Conformity is not necessarily bad. I appreciate conservatives—they make a wonderful contrast."

He is sometimes approached by people who are struggling with their own identities, he said.

"I could ruin the lives of some very prominent athletes on this campus," he said.

But he wishes more people would talk to him about his alternative way of life.

Bennett said many people on campus seem frightened of him. And many homosexuals won't speak to him because he is "too outspoken." Other people who live alternative lifestyles also refuse to talk to him because he is gay, he said.

He said he understands how people feel about being gay and that can bring misery or suicide.

"I hate sexual oppression," he said. "Sex is a wonderful thing. It's not something to be embarrassed about. I refuse to accept limits society puts on me as a man—no sexual barriers for me."

Bennett said that many people in the Midwest have a rabid fear of homosexuality.

Stereotypes of gays as deviants who will molest or sell drugs to their children are ridiculous, he said, although most stereotypes contain a grain of truth that have been twisted.

Although people may have the wrong idea about him, he is a harmless and friendly guy, he said.

"I will accept anybody as a friend. Fat, thin, black, white, old or young."

He has gotten flak for being different since he was a child, but he doesn't let it ruffle his feathers. His desire for the bizarre is an "inner creative urge," he said, that had been with him ever since he can remember.

"There's a peacock in my body, screaming to get out," he said.

Bennett said he fits in better at ISU than he did in his hometown of Mason City. But some people at ISU refuse to accept him. He was involved in Story County's first hate crime in Campustown on Nov. 8. His attacker plea bargained and was sentenced to 4 days in jail and 30 days of community service, which was "disappointing," said Bennett.

He is often verbally harassed, many times by people passing by in moving vehicles, he said.

"As long as people don't touch me I could care less. I'm pretty much immune to criticism. If people don't like the way I look, they'll have to cover their eyes when I'm around.

"Life is too short not to express yourself. I could never conform to society no matter how much trouble I get," he said. "I just like fun and enjoy life. Is it really so strange?"

DISCUSSION QUESTIONS

Bennett: A Non-Conformist Immune to Criticism

1. What, according to Bennett, are the risks associated with being a nonconformist in dress? Can you think of other risks not mentioned by Bennett? What are the benefits of being a nonconformist mentioned by Bennett as well as other benefits not mentioned?

2. Even though Bennett was presented in this chapter as an example of nonconformity, can you identify aspects of his appearance that are conformist?

3. Can you explain the following statement made by Bennett: "I...find...that hair and accessories are a fun expression of myself. I don't dress this way because I'm gay."

30 Saving Face: Here's How It's Done
Dan Eggen

Some might say it's a crime to look this good.

When Dennis Gress was arrested for pumping 16 bullets into his ex-girlfriend and her beau, his long hair was straggly and his clothes were a mess.

By the time Gress appeared in front of a Polk County jury earlier this year, he was a changed man (see Figures 6.3a and 6.3b).

Hair shorn and face shaven, the 38-year-old double-murder defendant wore a red sweater, gray slacks and a tie.

The transformation was hardly accidental. Making the accused look good is a seldom-discussed but vital part of any defense.

"It's important not to necessarily look your best but to look comfortable in front of a jury," said Alfredo Parrish, a Des Moines defense attorney who has written an entire chapter called "Dressing for Court" in his book "Know Your Rights."

"You want your clients to put their best foot forward when they're accused of a serious crime. You don't want things like their clothes to get in the way of the evidence."

It didn't help Gress much: He was convicted of two counts of first-degree murder and imprisoned for life.

But many defense attorneys say appearance can be crucial to whether a client is convicted or acquitted by fickle juries, particularly in close cases.

Thus violent gangsters and gun-toting bikers become the boys next door, sporting crisp khakis, fuzzy sweaters and tasseled loafers (see Figures 6.3c and 6.3d). Female defendants are urged to wear minimal makeup and simple skirts or dresses.

Attorneys and trial consultants vary in their opinions of just how important such tactics can be. John Wellman, the chief public defender for Polk County, keeps a closet in his Des Moines office stuffed with secondhand clothes for defendants.

Wellman acknowledges the importance of appearance but also warns against overdoing it.

"Jurors makes assessments on guilt or innocence to a great extent on what a person looks like, their position in society," Wellman said. "When people look as though they're different, it's easier to convict them. They're not one of us."

"But you can't take an uneducated, unattractive client and turn them into Robert Redford," he continued. "Any attempts to do so usually backfire. It's a balancing act."

Parrish, who wrote the book chapter on the subject, is almost fanatical about client fashions.

Before every trial, Parrish says he hauls his client into his office with the client's intended wardrobe. If it's not good enough, he requires the client to make changes.

Parrish's opinions are exact. For example, he favors pink or light blue oxford shirts, tie-up shoes rather than loafers and cuffed pants for male defendants.

And then there are the sweaters. One of Parrish's law partners, Maggi Moss, traces the rise of sweater-clad suspects to the famed Menendez brothers trial in Los Angeles, where a jury couldn't decide whether to convict the two young men in the brutal slayings of their parents.

But even before the Menendez case, Parrish said sweaters did wonders for one of his clients—acquitted of first-degree murder. A nice cardigan or wool pullover strikes a balance for suspects who would look out of place in a suit and tie, experts said. "Sweaters are important," Parrish said. "It gives you a warm and fuzzy feeling, so to speak."

The goal in all this primping and preening is to put jurors at ease with defendants—many of whom are accused of ghastly, violent crimes.

"I really don t want to give the impression that we're pulling a facade or something over on the court," Moss said. "Depending on what they're charged with, everyone has a good side. If you hate a defendant who looks really mean and somebody they'd be scared of, that would not help. It's going to taint the jury's impression of the case itself."

Some attorneys—including both Moss and Parrish—often use trial consultants to help dress defendants, not to mention aid in picking jurors

Eggen, Dan, "Saving Face: Here's How It's Done," *Des Moines Register* November 7, 1995, pp. 1T-2T. Copyright 1995, reprinted with permission by *The Des Moines Register*.

a   b   c   d

FIGURE 6.3 *Dennis Gress (a) when he was arrested in September 1994 for killing two people and (b) when he appeared in court in March 1995 and was convicted and sentenced to life imprisonment. Montez Shortridge (c) when he as arrested in June 1994 for vehicular homicide and (d) in February 1995 when he was convicted and later sentenced to up to 12 years imprisonment.*

and other strategic decisions. Such consultants have steadily gained favor in courts during the last two decades: Consider O.J. Simpson's reliance on them.

A leader in the field is V. Hale Starr, who runs West Des Moines-based Starr Litigation Service, Inc. The key, Starr said, is to eliminate characteristics that people rightly or wrongly associate with dishonesty. "We have a belief in our society that nice people look like nice people, mean people look like mean people, and murderers look like murderers," Starr said from her branch office in Phoenix.

"The question that we have is, should people be judged by their appearance? No. Do we judge people by their appearance? Absolutely."

Starr and other experts are acutely aware of the criticisms of their work—that they are altering reality or "coaching" clients. It's no different, she says, than when police officers testify in their best dress uniforms.

"Do you clean up before you go to church?" Starr asked. "Of course we do. Is that bad? No. Do we clean up before going to court? Of course we do. Is that bad? Yes, most people think it is. The question is how far you can go. It's one you struggle with every time you work with a witness."

But sometimes, there's little hope.

Wellman, the Polk County public defender, has a long list of horror stories. He tells of one client who, when told to wear his Sunday best, showed up at trial in a new Harley Davidson T-shirt—giving the jury a nice view of his full-body tattoos. "I had another client that had Harley Davidson wings tattooed across his forehead," Wellman said. "There's not much you can do in that situation."

"Lawyers would like everyone to look like Mr. and Mrs. Cleaver, or at least a friend of Wally and Beaver's," he said. "But in real life, you can't change people to any great degree. It's an attempt to make the best possible world with what you've got."

DISCUSSION QUESTIONS

Saving Face

1. Is there an unspoken rule in the United States that people should appear to be who they truly are? Is there an unspoken "ethic of appearance"?

2. Do you believe there should be restrictions on trial lawyers when it comes to dressing their clients for court appearances? Why or why not?

31 It's All Greek to Me: Sorority Members and Identity Talk

Kimberly A. Miller
Scott A. Hunt
University of Kentucky

This article examines how identities are developed and maintained through talk about dress and appearance. In 1965, the sociologist Gregory Stone indicated that dress was equally as important as speech to the task of establishing and maintaining one's identity. More recently, Boynton-Arthur (1992) and Holloman (1990) have studied the use of dress in Greek (i.e., fraternities and sororities) organizations.

We approached our task by analyzing the identity talk of sorority women from a single university in the southeastern United States.[1] In 1993, sixteen campus sorority presidents were contacted about the study. When sorority presidents agreed to announce the study at their next chapter meeting, some members volunteered to participate because of interest, while others participated in order to meet a community service requirement.

The information in this article is based on eight in-depth interviews with eighteen sorority members. All interviews were held in sorority houses in semiprivate meeting rooms. The interviews were open-ended, question-and-response sessions that lasted 45 to 75 minutes each. An analysis of the interviews revealed that many of our questions asked respondents to "evaluate" their appearances as well as the appearances of others. The responses indicate that evaluating appearances is a complex task with many possibilities. Therefore, the interview data reflected respondents' efforts to explain the rules of appearance evaluation to naive outsiders.

THE INTERVIEWS

An important theme that occurred again and again in the interviews with sorority members was that of respect for individual identity. Suggestions of an "ideal" appearance were rejected by respondents, and factors such as personality, culture, and circumstances were emphasized. To illustrate, when asked about paying attention to appearances, one respondent stated:

> I guess if you look presentable—but who's to say what's presentable, you know? One person might pay attention a lot to their appearance and think that they look really good, and someone else might [not].

The sorority members we interviewed often questioned the "legitimacy" of an ideal that would govern dress and appearance—for example, "who's to say what's presentable?"

Responses from sorority members indicated a high tolerance of different "personalities" or "cultures." This tolerance was revealed in an interview with four sorority members who were asked about their views on the existence of an "ideal" appearance:

> First Respondent: I think there is a difference between a person who likes to dress preppy and a person who likes to dress all in black....I think it depends on your personality.
>
> Second Respondent: I think it depends on your organization or what group you want to surround yourself with....They have different ideas of what is beautiful or what is in style for your group.
>
> Third Respondent: Your culture too. I have a friend in Europe now and she dresses sexy now. So I think it depends on where you grow up.
>
> Second Respondent: I don't think there is really an ideal way to look....I don't think there is an ideal. I think it varies from person to person.

Original for this text.

Fourth Respondent: I don't think there is an ideal person. I think it's whether they are happy with the way they want to look. [If they are], then that's all that really matters. You can't say they are wrong because they are not wearing the same things you are.

In another interview, a different sorority member made similar comments:

I think a lot of it [dress and appearance expectations] is regional. I went home last year and I wore bows, but nobody had bows [there]. I think that's [wearing bows] more [common in local college town]. People will say why do these people [sorority members] have ribbons around their waist and bows in their hair. I have never seen it [bow wearing] but here in [local college town]. Last year I went to Alabama for a talent contest with sorority women from the Southeast. It's so funny when people say that [bow wearing] is the sorority look. When you see some girls from sororities you are totally shocked. It went from extremes. Girls wore boots and high heels and all done up from head to toe. All the way down to girls who looked like they just rolled out of bed, hair was a mess, and no makeup.

Another respondent made a similar point:

...if you had big hair and a lot of makeup and slutty-looking clothes, to us that are in the middle class, then you were lower income [sic]. A lot of stuff I wear you wouldn't dream of wearing, because you would think it was the slutty-looking female. Where I'm from, it's perfectly acceptable.

According to the above statements, a person's dress and appearance were viewed as a reflection of an individual's "personality" or "culture." In addition, the respondents generally agreed that it would be "inappropriate" to assume certain kinds of personalities or cultures were superior to others.

Another aspect of tolerance was respect and understanding of the situation and surrounding circumstances. One respondent commented on this view by comparing summer camp to everyday life on a college campus:

At summer camp nobody cared [about appearances] because we were out in the middle of the woods, but here we have our shirts tucked, belts with the little thing over here on the side.

Another respondent indicated that situations were heavily influenced by the individuals within a given situation and that dress and appearance were affected by these interactions with others:

Every day you go to high school. I cared more there than I do now, because on campus you don't [sic] hardly see anybody you know. If you go back to high school, you're still going to look good because you don't want them to think you gained a few pounds and they don't think you look as good....When you go out to the bars you want to look attractive because there are guys there. You want to look attractive when you come to meetings because you want to keep up a nice image....I don't try to impress my parents or my family. That [appearance] doesn't matter. They are family.

In addition to personality, cultural, and situational circumstances, the respondents suggested that set expectations were not possible because images given are not always identical to images given off (Goffman, 1959). One respondent gave this example:

If you should wear, like, those warm-up suits, like, you know, jogging suits or something you wear after you play tennis, exercise, people might think, "Oh, they're into sports and fitness," but really it's kind of more of a fashion statement.

Later in the same interview, this respondent also said:

Like with the example of the exercise suit, I mean I think the way dress...definitely can be a big reflection of your personality, but in a situation like that it can definitely not be....if you're just looking at a person and all you have to go by is what they have on, then you can judge them by that, but so often it ends up that the way they dress is not [a reflection of their real personality].

To summarize, the sorority members we interviewed communicated a commitment to respect for individual identity. Their interpretations of individuals' dress and appearance depended on understanding a variety of factors (i.e., personality, culture, and situation).

While there was general disagreement regarding an ideal appearance, sorority members did agree that "minimal" standards were expected. These expectations revolved around "minimal" hygiene and grooming. For example, in one interview, two respondents articulated minimal expectations:

> First Respondent: Keeping up with general maintenance of personal appearance [means] keeping up with a haircut, clean fingernails. Just keeping up with your appearance on a general basis. Have your shirttail tucked in and things of that sort.
>
> Second Respondent: Have your hair cut regularly and things like that.
>
> Interviewer: How can you tell if someone is not paying attention to their appearance?
>
> Second Respondent: Just the opposite. Sloppy hair, dirty face, shoes untied, nails are not filed, neck can be dirty.

In a different interview, another sorority member said that those with "offensive" body odor were violating a fundamental, universal standard. She said:

> Body odor. I know people will say that other people from foreign countries smell bad, but this is just part of our culture. More than 95% of the people are opposed to body odor and that has become a symbol of uncleanliness. That's something I find to be very uncomfortable and difficult to work next to someone. You can't concentrate.

Almost all of the respondents suggested that "appropriate" appearance included bathing on a regular basis, washing and combing one's hair, brushing one's teeth, and practicing "basic" hygiene. One sorority member said, "People tend to not socialize with people that are obviously offensively dirty." Several respondents admitted being annoyed when people appeared to have "just rolled out of bed" without making any effort at minimal hygiene. However, as we shall see below, the sorority members also suggested that there are "exceptions" for occasions when minimal hygiene is not met. Sorority members indicated that there were times when the lack of minimal hygiene was necessary but it really did not cause "any great harm." For example, one respondent denied that her lack of attention to her appearance caused her personal identity any harm:

> Today I was late for my eight o'clock class. I put on a pair of sweats and a T-shirt. I really didn't care because I really don't know anybody in class.

This quote suggests that because the respondent did not "really know" anyone in her class, her appearance did not cause any permanent damage to her personal identity. Along similar lines, another respondent offered this statement:

> My friends I have in class that I feel close to, I don't think they are going to dislike me if I walk into class one day looking bad or not having paid much attention to try to look nice.

Again it was denied that a single bad day would cause significant harm to personal identity. Several individuals also denied that their "deviant" appearances injured their sororities' collective identities, because they would not wear their sororities' letters on such occasions.

Condemnation of the condemners (Sykes & Matza, 1957) allows the "offender" to shift "…the focus of attention from [his/her] own deviant acts to the motives and behavior of those who disapprove of his violations." One sorority member spoke for herself and her friend on this matter:

> If people aren't going to, you know, like you because you don't look nice, then neither one of us want to hang out with people like that.

Most often, respondents referred to physical comfort to neutralize a "dressed down" look. For instance, one sorority member claimed that "…there are times when I just want to be comfortable and just wear some T-shirts or something." Physical comfort, as the following quote implies, goes beyond comfortable clothes:

When people just go on what I look like, I have been termed granola [i.e., natural look]. People say, "There goes that granola girl over there." I'll tend to look at girls who always have the bow in their hair, makeup on, always fixed up, and I can't understand why somebody would get up at seven in the morning every day to make themselves look like that. I guess that is more of a lifestyle choice. I enjoy sleeping.

This respondent believed that comfort (i.e., sleep) has a higher priority and therefore justified her "granola" look.

Psychological comfort, in addition to physical comfort, was mentioned by several sorority members. One respondent explained her typical dress and appearance this way:

I guess some women feel they need makeup and a nice outfit. It is part of their self-confidence, and if they don't have that then they don't feel like a whole person. You can feel comfortable with yourself and have to put on makeup and wear fancy outfits. I guess I'm comfortable with myself the way I look so I don't feel I have to go through this big ritual to be ready to face the world.

However, explanations that emphasized psychological comfort tended to justify why individuals "dressed up." For example, one sorority woman explained the rings that she usually wore:

If I leave and forget to put on my rings, no one else will notice. But I feel I notice if it is not there....There is some degree of personal comfort there. If I feel comfortable then I feel that I am acting comfortable and other people are going to get along with me more.

Making a similar claim, another sorority member reported:

I feel, in classes, the nicer I look, the better I feel. That goes for every day, not just when I go to class. The better I look, I feel better about myself. Especially in class, I pay more attention. Things go smoother if I look nicer. You carry yourself better around campus maybe when you look better and hold your head up high and just carry yourself better

than you would if you didn't have time to do all you wanted to do in the morning because you wanted to sleep that extra 15 minutes.

However, another sorority member gave an opposite opinion, citing school obligations (i.e., a test) as more important than appearance. She said:

Sometimes if I have a big test, and I have been up late, or I get up early to study, and the shower comes later and stuff like that.

In summary, sorority members used comfort (i.e., personal, physical, and psychological) to rationalize a variety of looks, from "natural" to "dressed up."

Conclusion

Our findings suggest a belief held by sorority members that one should respect individual identities and tolerate differences in personalities. Perhaps this belief is a practical one because those who live in sorority houses live in close proximity to one another, and tolerance enables the house to function smoothly. To support this claim, sorority women interviewed repeatedly mentioned that gossiping about another member was a bad trait for a sorority sister to have. This respect for others, however, seemed to extend only as far as one's own sorority, as it was mentioned in every interview that "our sorority has all kinds [of people]" but respondents were quick to stereotype other campus sororities. These stereotypes invariably included comments about what the typical dress of another sorority member might be.

Notes

1. This study is part of a larger project that includes surveys of: a) sorority rush participants, and b) non-Greek male and female students at the same southeastern university. The survey data are not analyzed here. An expanded version of this article was published in *Symbolic Interaction*, volume 20, in 1997.

References

Boynton-Arthur, L. (1992). *Idealized images: Appearance and the construction of femininities in two exclusive organizations.* Unpublished doctoral dissertation, University of California–Davis.

Goffman, E.(1959). *The presentation of self in everyday life.* Garden City, NY: Doubleday.

Holloman, L. O. (1990). Clothing symbolism in African American Greek letter organizations. In B. Starke & L. Holloman (Eds.), *African American dress and adornment.* Dubuque, IA: Kendall/Hunt.

Stone, G. P. (1965). Appearance and the self. In M. E. Roach & J. B. Eicher (Eds.), *Dress, adornment and the social order* (pp. 216–245). New York: John Wiley & Sons.

Sykes, G., & Matza, D. (1957). Techniques of neutralization: A theory of delinquency. *American Sociological Review 22,* 664–670.

DISCUSSION QUESTIONS

It's All Greek To Me: Sorority Members and Identity Talk

1. How would you describe sorority members in terms of other-directedness or inner directedness? Why?

2. Give several examples of situations in which dress may affect the self-perception of sorority members.

3. Why do you think the sorority members interviewed rejected suggestions of an "ideal" appearance? Is that a typical response of other college students as well?

4. Individual identity was stressed by sorority members who were interviewed. Why do you think stereotypes of sorority members as women who "all look alike" continue?

32 Do School Uniforms Make the Grade?

Charlotte Coffman and Amaliya Jurta

Whether to adopt school uniforms is being debated in classrooms and by boardrooms across the US. A national consensus eludes us but, in general, the idea is gaining support. Many schools are tightening dress codes, and schools in at least ten states have implemented mandatory or voluntary school uniform policies. In his State of the Union address, President Clinton supported school uniform policies if they deter violence.

The seven benefits historically cited by proponents of school uniforms are:

*   improved discipline

*   increased respect for teachers and students

*   higher academic standards and achievement

*   decreased emphasis on socioeconomic differences

Coffman, Charlotte, and Jurta, Amaliya, "Do School Uniforms Make the Grade?" *Textiles and Apparel News* (Dec. 1996). Textile & Apparel, Cornell University, Ithaca, NY.

- enhanced group spirit
- decreased clothing expenditures
- increased visibility of campus intruders

Given today's headlines about gang activity, robberies, and violence on school campuses, improved disciplinary and school safety have become primary goals. Ray Bennett, founder and head of the Public School Uniform Project in Baltimore, MD, admits that fights over leather jackets and sneakers led to the introduction of school uniforms in 1986 (6). Today, uniforms are worn in all of Baltimore's elementary schools. Administrators are convinced that uniforms have a positive effect on behavior. When Baltimore principals tried a "free-dress day," the number of students given misconduct referrals increased 300 percent (6).

Other schools have followed suit. In the autumn of 1994, students from the 56 elementary and 14 middle schools in the Long Beach Unified School District in California answered the class bell wearing the newly required school uniform (3, 6). School representatives assert that incidents of assault and battery decreased from 319 to 212, fighting decreased from 1,135 to 554, and robbery decreased from 29 to 10. Dr. Lorraine Monroe, principal of Frederick Douglass Academy in New York City (NYC), explained in a 1995 news quote, "Having uniforms differentiates school from the street. It says that street behavior, street attitudes are not acceptable here." (6).

Most news reports focus on reducing "crimes of fashion," but many schools are reporting improvement in other areas as well (3, 6). Whittier Elementary School in Long Beach has seen a tremendous improvement in school attendance. Whittier is located in an area with many transient and immigrant families. Some children reportedly did not attend school because they were embarrassed by their lack of stylish clothing. The use of uniforms decreases the emphasis on socio-economic differences and allows children to be judged by their ideas and achievements.

Scholastic achievement also seems to improve when the student body is uniformly dressed. The reasons for this are unclear. Do teachers pre-judge a child's performance based on his/her appearance and then teach and assess that child accordingly? Do children become more involved in their studies when their dress signifies the seriousness of their role? Are students simply more focused on classwork when clothing is no longer a distraction? Perhaps all of these factors are involved.

Research indicates that physical appearance is an important variable in the judgment of another's character or abilities. A 1978 study (4) found that by second grade, 75% of the sampled students believed that clothing communicated something about the wearer (4). In recent studies at private and public secondary schools (1, 2), teachers and peers predicted higher grades, greater academic ability, and greater leadership potential for male and female models who wore suits, blazers, or "preppy" outfits than for those who wore torn jeans and T-shirts.

Students whose clothes provide this "halo effect" may be encouraged to work harder to justify the faith of their peers and teachers, but self-perception is also a factor. Ronald Stephens, director of the National School Safety Center at Pepperdine University in Malibu, CA says, "Kids tend to behave the way they dress" (3). Miles away, a NYC principal agrees that uniforms are a "signifier" and that wearing a uniform signifies responsibility, possibility, maturity and hope (6).

Many parents favor school uniforms and cite reduced clothing expenditures, decreased shopping and maintenance time, and fewer morning hassles. A typical girl's uniform of pants, shirt, and tie costs $15–25. A typical boy's uniform of pants, shirt, sweater, and tie costs $31–$42. All parents know that one item at the mall can cost as much as an entire uniform. Most uniforms are easy-care fabrics such as acrylic, cotton, polyester, or cotton/polyester blends. The are available in a variety of styles, colors and fabric weights, and in a range of sizes including "chubby" (girls) and "husky" (boys).

Despite convincing arguments for wearing school uniforms, even the most ardent supporter cautions against seeing a change of clothes as a permanent makeover. Firstly, most studies involved small numbers and did not compare attitudes among diverse populations and geographical locations. Secondly, schools adopting uniforms have done so as a part of a larger program aimed at modifying student behavior. It is difficult, for example, to differentiate the effects of additional tutoring, new textbooks, and school uniforms when all were initiated at the same time.

Some argue that requiring students to wear school uniforms infringes on their constitutional right of freedom of expression. In 1969, the Supreme (Court [sic]) ruled that students in an academic setting have the right to express themselves freely, including the way they dress and wear their hair, as long as their actions do not interfere with the rights of others. Nonetheless, in 1994 the California legislature passed a law granting school districts the right to require uniforms if the parents agreed and were notified six months in advance (6). The American Civil Liberties Union has declined to challenge that law because most schools protect themselves with an opt-out clause for reluctant parents (6).

Ironically, the main inhibitor to uniform adoption may be money. Some parents in Long Beach have brought suit against the school district to force it to provide free uniforms (3), an expense that the district is unable to meet. This problem has been solved in other communities by local business donations, school fundraisers, and charity grants. One New York parochial school holds an annual uniform exchange day (5). Used uniforms are exchanged for larger sizes, sold at reduced cost, or donated.

Administrators from the same school noted that the uniform distributor comes to the school to size the children and to accept orders. Other schools work with companies through catalogs and mailings. Information is also available on the world-wide web.

Resources

1. Behling, D. School Uniforms and Person Perception. *Perceptual and Motor Skills*. 79: 723–729. 1994.

2. Behling, D. and E. Williams. Influence of Dress in Perception of Intelligence and Scholastic Achievement in Urban Schools with Minority Populations. *Clothing and Textiles Research Journal* 9: 1–7. 1991.

3. Cornwell, T. True Colours of Uniformity. *Times Educational Supplement* 4137: 18. October 13, 1995.

4. Parr, J.L. and M.S. Halperin. *Children's Impression of the Social Meaning of Clothing*. University of Delaware, Department of Educational Foundations, Newark, NJ. 1978.

5. Personal communication. Immaculate Conception School, Ithaca, NY. 1996.

6. Pushkar, K. Dressed for Success. *Village Voice* 4(3): SS12. January 17, 1995.

DISCUSSION QUESTIONS
Do School Uniforms Make the Grade?

1. If you were to conduct the next research study on school uniforms, what information would you be interested in learning? Consider information that was not covered by Coffman and Jurta. How would you approach students for the study? Would you go to the mall or to schools? Would you interview students, show a video with several choices of school uniforms, or hand out a written questionnaire? What incentives would you provide for participation in your study? Or would incentives be necessary? What steps could you take to minimize your personal bias?

2. Consider the five frameworks introduced in Chapter 2 for viewing the body. Which framework or frameworks seem most applicable to the study of school uniforms? Why?

33 Students' Rights Not as Broad as Those of Public

Lucy May

Lexington's Morton Middle School had its own version of the infamous Pike County girl with black lipstick.

She came to school last week, mouth painted black, hoping to rile teachers. She even stuck her face in the face of the assistant principal, hoping to get noticed.

When everyone continued to ignore the girl's licorice-colored lips, she said something "really terrible" to one of her teachers and ultimately got into trouble for that, said Morton Principal Jack Lyons.

The case illustrates that schools all over Kentucky deal with students and their fashion statements every day. The situations that steal the headlines, though, are the ones where schools and students clash.

- Tessa Wilson, the 13-year-old Pulaski County girl suspended Oct. 23 for wearing a lip ring to Somerset's Meece Middle School, has since taken out the lip ring. But she and her mom, Janie Wilson, have a Somerset lawyer who is still pursuing the situation with school officials.

- Siddell Jones, the Louisville 18-year-old who was suspended Nov. 15 by Butler Traditional High School Principal Kenneth Frick after refusing to unbraid his hair, unbraided it and went back to school on Wednesday. But his grandmother, a Louisville civil rights activist, has said she won't drop the matter.

- And Karla Chapman, the Pike County 13-year-old sent home from Runyon Elementary School on Nov. 13 when she refused to remove her black lipstick, has vowed to stay out of school in protest. Her parents said they'll take her case to the state Supreme Court if necessary to stand up for her rights.

But children's rights in public schools aren't as broad as most people think, said Wayne Young, a lawyer and executive director of the Kentucky Association School Administrators.

The U.S. Supreme Court ruled in two cases in the 1980s that students can't say or write things in a public school that they might be allowed to say or write on the public streets of America, Young said.

The Supreme Court hasn't really ruled on the whole notion of dress codes, said Everett Hoffman, executive director of the American Civil Liberties Union of Kentucky. The U.S. Sixth Circuit Court of Appeals, which covers Kentucky, has been very supportive of allowing schools to set dress codes, he said.

Even so, Hoffman said that there are limits to what schools can do. A school can't impose a dress code that singles out students based on their ethnicity or race; that is so arbitrary that students are denied "due process"; or that violates students' free speech or free expression, he said.

But Young argues that not every fashion statement is "free speech" or "free expression."

Free speech is any message conveyed by any means by which a message can be conveyed, he said. But the recipient of the message must be able to clearly understand what it means, Young said.

"What am I expressing when I'm wearing black lipstick?" he said. "People want to say anything you wish to wear or look like is protected by the Constitution, and it's not. That means to me that principals can use common sense to regulate that."

Hoffman thinks that's where some of the schools in these recent cases have failed. He also

May, Lucy, "Students' Rights Not as Broad as Those of Public," *Lexington Herald-Leader* (Nov. 22, 1996) Reprinted by permission of *the Lexington Herald-Leader.*

thinks some of the dress codes—like the one in Karla Chapman's case—are so vague as to be arbitrary.

"I think there does need to be order in the schools. I just don't think whether an eighth-grade girl wears black lipstick has anything to do with order," Hoffman said. "I do think schools need to be more tolerant of young people's rights."

Morton's Lyons, for one, thinks the best way to handle teens and their fashion fads is to ignore them.

"Last year, we had a fellow that had blue hair, and it didn't shock us, so he tried orange," Lyons said. "If I put all the people in this school out who changed their hair color, I'd have to suspend 80 percent of the staff."

DISCUSSION QUESTIONS

Students' Rights Not as Broad as Those of Public

1. What are the advantages of limiting students' rights to be less broad than those of the general public? What would the disadvantages be?

2. Visit the web site "A street guide to gang identity" at http//gangid.ucdavis.edu. What

type of information is available at this web site? How does the information assist in your understanding of counter-conformity?

34 The School Uniform as Fashion Statement: How Students Crack the Dress Code

William L. Hamilton

Paris, Milan, Seventh Avenue and Mayor Rudolf W. Guiliani, please take note.

"It's how you *want* to look," said Nicole Adu, a senior at Frederick Douglass Academy in Harlem, in discussing her outfit. Ms. Adu and her colleagues, grades 7 through 12, are required to wear a school uniform: white blouse and navy skirt or slacks for girls, white shirt and navy pants for boys.

Ms. Adu was dressed to code one morning last week, but she was anything but uniform.

"I have my skirt right here," she said, indicating a precise point just above the knee. "Last year I used to wear short skirts. This year I decided to go

a little longer." Ms. Adu turned to indicate shoulder seaming sewn on a bias at the back of her navy vest. "I have this vest that you will not see any other girls in this school wearing," she said. "I know how other girls are coming in, and I try to look different. I have my own style."

At the School of the Incarnation on West 175th Street, Xiofranys Garib, a sixth grader, pointed to her regulation red cardigan sweater, which was held closed at the top with a single button.

"I'm the weird one," Ms. Garib explained of her sweater. "I'm just totally different." Two friends, standing at her side, cardigan fronts fully buttoned, nodded their heads in agreement.

A proposal last week by William C. Thompson, the president of the Board of Education, to require uniforms in all public elementary schools in the fall of 1999—with the possibility of including older students in the future—has prompted a fresh debate among students and parents about the merits of cool versus school, individuality versus assembly, comfort versus conduct.

Proponents argue that uniforms can instill a sense of pride and discipline, save parents money and spare students the distraction and potential danger of competition over clothing. But visits to several public, private and parochial schools in the city that already require uniforms made it clear that for most students, the dress code is a challenge, not a mandate. The goal: to bend and stretch the rules with sartorial statements as subtle as the codes are strict.

"Everybody finds their own different way to get around the rules," said Taylor Spearnak, a 15-year-old 10th grader at the Convent of the Sacred Heart School in Manhattan. "They know you're not going to totally conform, because half the time you don't want to be in perfect uniform."

This year's corridor runway news: boots, big heels, suede shoes, wide collar, French-tail blouses, bagged at the waistband for women. Open top buttons, neckties that sag like utility wires in the summer, boots, metal belts and baggy trousers for the men. Uniform-color-coordinated contact lens for both men and women.

"French cuffs," said Jannel Lee, a 17-year-old senior at Frederick Douglass Academy, a public school. "Where you turn up your cuffs like this so either they'll be long or to the mid-hand—kind of like the old England style."

Yandielle Smith, also a student at Frederick Douglass, had managed to marshal her uniform to a sense of fashion as much as it had marshaled her to code.

"A little white Gap shirt under my blouse," she said. "I have my collar up. Since this is a

FIGURE 6.4 *James Ward, student at the Frederick Douglass Academy, likes to add some droop to his standard navy pants.*

baby-doll shirt underneath, I have a baby-doll kind of hairdo: a baby-girl 'Spice Girl' look. Blue hair clips to match the navy uniform."

"I have on short sleeves, so I wore a watch," she added. "Usually I don't wear watches." And the fingernails? "White nail polish to go with my white shirt," Ms. Smith explained, adding: "I love the uniform. There are no hour-long decisions in the morning."

In fact, many students interviewed approved of the uniform policies, citing the same savings in time, money and self-esteem sought by parents and school officials. But like students of fashion everywhere, students without fashion are pushing the envelope with color, shape and materials.

"Cream we can get away with," said Ms. Spearnak, whose uniform specifies a white shirt.

"You make your pants baggy," said Oscar Rodriguez, a 12-year-old seventh grader at the School of the Incarnation in Washington Heights. "You put them down low, and you put your shirt over it so they don't see your boxers or anything."

"Then you tie like a belt around it to hold your pants up," he said, but added, "You get into trouble anyway."

Some uniforms are too well designed to defy.

"I hate the vests," said Michelle O'Connor, a 14-year-old eighth grader at St. Francis Cabrini on 21 Bay 11th Street in Brooklyn. "I feel like I work at McDonald's."

The level of enforcement of the dress codes varies widely from school to school. Dr. Gregory Hodge, principal of Frederick Douglass Academy, posted himself at the school's entrance at 7:30 A.M. to greet his students and personally check the uniforms. Four full-length mirrors line the vestibule.

Dr. Hodge, with the sharp choreography of a traffic officer, directed any and all code-cracking style statements to the mirrors. He has been known on occasion to examine everyone so thoroughly that students are backed up to the subway station next to the school.

At the School of the Incarnation, the dog-ate-my-homework, my-navy-pants-are-in-the-wash variety of excuse is absolved with a writing assignment. Though there is no morning entrance check, there is an informal inspection at lunch, which produces backups in the bathrooms after recess, among students reinstituting corrected offenses.

In the quest to stand out even in uniform, accessories are important allies.

"I just add on stuff that I like, like earrings," said Latisha Lawrence, a 13-year-old eighth grader at St. Angela Merici School on East 163rd Street in the Bronx. "I have three holes and I put more than one earring in a hole."

Ms. Lawrence's most distinct fashion look was in her eyes. "Contact lens," she said. "They're misty gray; they bring out my cranberry uniform."

Dustin Bowden, a 13-year-old eighth grader, was wearing a diamond earring, which Mr. Kelly, atypically among uniform-policy administrations, allows.

"It's a statement," said Mr. Bowden, who also wears his necktie with an exaggerated droop, like his trousers (see Figure 6.4). Mr. Bowden favors regular gray pants over school-uniform supply-company pants. As students citywide have discovered, Tommy Hilfiger and Eddie Bauer also work in navy and gray.

Mr. Bowden's colleague Edwin Velasquez, a 14-year-old eighth grader, was less sanguine about the possibilities of style.

"The uniform is *lame*," he said, interviewed at lunch recess in the school cafeteria. "If you go outside and you see a pretty girl, she doesn't want to see you in a uniform."

Kevin Sime, a 13-year-old eighth grader at School of the Incarnation, disagreed. For Mr. Sime, the uniform *is* style.

"The girls love the uniform," he said. Mr. Sime was wearing his favorite blue necktie, as per code, with a repeating motif of the Tasmanian devil on it.

Who pushes the limit the most on the uniform rules?

"Boys—but they get caught," says Ms. Smith at Frederick Douglass Academy.

"The girls—they like to wear the skirts really, really, short," said Edwin Velasquez at St. Angela Merici School. "We like it, too."

For most girls, the tradition of raising a skirt's hem by rolling the waistband is as honorable as the institution of the school uniform.

"I think everybody rolls up their skirt at least once; mine would be down to here," said Ms. Spearnak of Convent of the Sacred Heart School, pointing to the ground. Upon request, Ms. Spearnak displayed one roll beneath her coat.

"Some of my friends do four or five rolls," Ms. Spearnak said. Two colleagues passed as they left the school, plaid pleats barely visible beneath their waist-length parkas. "You can *so* tell," she said.

The School Uniform as Fashion Statement

1. Because students often make attempts to individualize their school uniforms, where should school administrators (principals and teachers) "draw the line"? What is acceptable individualization? What constitutes unacceptable individualization?

2. Because students have such varied opinions regarding school uniforms, how can policies be developed to keep everyone happy? Would it help to have several uniform styles that students can choose from? Why or why not?

3. Describe the examples of individualization of uniforms from the article according to your understanding of postmodernism (see Chapter 3).

35 Culture and Consumer Behavior

Vanessa P. Wickliffe
University of Kentucky

Koreans are collectivists and behave in a way that is good for the group. Americans are individualists and behave in a way that is good for the individual. Although many still believe in and use this collectivism/individualism model as a method to describe cultural differences, recent research indicates that things may not be that clear-cut. Members of a collectivist society accept the beliefs, views, needs, and goals of the "ingroup" rather than themselves individually. (Wagner, 1995). In contrast, individualist consumers are "those who define the self independently of groups, and exist solely as individuals" (Hui, 1988).

Although Koreans generally are collectivists and purchase such goods as dress that will meet with societal approval, there are signs that Korean individualism is more prevalent than we think. We find that although cultural affiliation is important, perhaps a consumer's buying practices may not be completely influenced by their culture. Recent research indicates that the importance of ingroup association may influence a consumer's buying practices.

While a consumer may exhibit individualistic characteristics, some buying practices may reflect their concern for continued affiliation with their culture or group. An individual identifies with their ingroup, which is usually characterized by similarities among the members. Individuals have a sense of common fate with members of the ingroup (Triandis, 1995). In some cultures the main ingroup is the family. Depending on the culture, other group affiliations may be that of race, tribe, caste, language, or location. Still other group affiliations may consist of friends, social classes, religious groups, athletic groups, and economic groups.

In many instances ingroup acceptance may influence the selection and purchase of clothing based on friendship. Gangs, sororities, and fraternities are examples of ingroups based on friendship. The clothing selections indicate ingroup acceptance and affiliation. Some of the current and traditional clothing worn by male gang members may include: white oversized T-shirts creased in the center front, and black, gray or brown oversized Dickie brand or khaki-beige work pants. Other types of sports clothing worn by male gang members are black "Kings" and "Raiders" jackets, sweatshirts, jerseys, pinstriped

Original for this text.

imitation baseball-style oversized shirts, and black woven crosses worn around the neck. Female gang members also use clothing as a method of ingroup identification. Examples of clothing worn by female members include: dark Dickie brand work pants, tank tops, black or dark clothing and shoes, unfastened overalls, and oversized, plaid dark wool Pendleton-type shirts (Office of Prevention, Texas Youth Commission, 1998).

Within American society, most consumers are considered individualistic, and therefore they are expected to select clothing that is specific to their needs, and not those of the ingroup. Americans tend to dress to please themselves, and thus satisfy their own personal needs. Clothing therefore reflects American personalities, work roles, and financial status. Both Jacqueline Kennedy Onassis and Cher dressed in a manner which reflected their personalities and work roles. When dressing for a particular event, many will select clothing to reflect themselves, and not follow the rules established by society. For example, movie stars may wear jeans and a tuxedo jacket to a formal affair instead of an outfit that is expected by society (e.g., after-five wear for a wedding or the Emmy Awards).

Other American consumers portray their individuality, although they are affiliated with an ingroup. Athlete Dennis Rodman, a professional basketball player, is obviously a member of an athletic team. As a member of this ingroup, he must follow all of the rules set forth by the group. However, Rodman uses his dress and body adornment as an indication of his individuality. His multicolored hair, body piercing, and tattoos reflect his individuality. He further portrays his personality in his appearance on the *Oprah Winfrey Show* with no shoes. Similarly, Madonna, Cindy Lauper, and Erika Badu are all members of the music industry. Although they are all members of a particular group—in this case, the music industry—their personal choice of dress and body adornment also reflect their personalities. Erika Badu wears extremely high headwraps and a great deal of jewelry, both of which are reflective of her ties to African culture, and the clothing styles worn in the early 1970s.

Let's turn our attention to the example given earlier regarding the comparisons between Koreans and Americans. One may assume that Koreans are *only* collectivists and Americans are *only* individualists. Historically, that may have been true. From my research comparing the two cultures (Wickliffe, 1998), I have discovered that Koreans are showing signs of individualism. In samples of Korean consumer groups, I found that while a large portion were collectivists, many others were also individualists (Wickliffe, 1998). These changes in Korean consumers' level of individualism/collectivism could be the result of an increase in wages, which has created more disposable income; the emergence of a larger population of younger consumers; accelerated urbanization; and product quality improvements (Ekvall, 1990; Flake, 1995). Because of these new developments, Korean consumers have adopted clothing items associated with western culture. In 1998, we find that westernized dress has become the norm for everyday dress for Korean men and women. Traditional dress is now worn only on special occasions by women and more rarely by men (Geum & Delong, 1992).

Korean consumer buying practices have changed over the past few decades. Earlier, I indicated that there has been an emergence of a young consumer group. Questions to consider for future research are:

- How much buying power does this group have?

- How many of their buying practices are still tied to the past?

- Are there certain groups in which the consumers are more collectivist than individualist (coworkers, kin, family, etc.)?

- Are older consumers tied more to the collective identity of the culture than younger consumers?

When individuals purchase clothing, they reflect on product characteristics, such as brand or price. These reflections might include such questions as: Will this brand of clothing be received favorably by my coworkers or friends?

Clothing and technological equipment often reflect an individual's social status; therefore, these products have high consumption rates in most countries—Korea and the United States are no exceptions. My research indicates that when Korean and American consumers purchase a television (technology) or a sweater (clothing) they are concerned about brand name, price, and country of manufacture. Given that every social situation requires specific clothing needs as individuals interact with coworkers, family, or friends, future research needs to address whether or not the association with a particular group influences clothing purchases.

Retailers and manufacturers are continuously seeking new market arenas to develop and expand their product lines. Because of the changes in the demographic makeup of the world and increased technological advancement, more questions and areas need to be researched. Today, there are more older consumers in the United States and Korea, and they continue to become more and more technologically advanced. With changes in demographics, can we continue to assume that Americans are still more individualist than collectivist, and Koreans more collectivist than individualist? Will Koreans lose their past traditions completely by becoming individualistic?

References

Hui, C. H. (1988). Measurement of individualism-collectivism. *Journal of Research in Personality*, 22, 7–36.

Ekvall, D. (August, 1990). Quality beyond the 90s: The pacific rim. *Quality*, 29(8), 16–18.

Flake, L. G. (1995). South Korea: Business associations and the economic miracle. *Business Korea*, pp. 7–9.

Geum, K. S., & DeLong, M. R. (1992). Dress as an expression of heritage: Exploring Korean culture. *Dress*, 19, 57–68.

Office of Prevention, Texas Youth Commission (1998). Gang related clothing. In *The Prevention, yellow pages*.

Triandis, H. C. (1995). *Individualism and collectivism*. Boulder, CO: Westview Press.

Wagner, J. A. (1995). Studies of individualism-collectivism: Effects on cooperation in groups. *Academy of Management Journal*, 38(1), 152–172.

Wickliffe, V. P. (August, 1998). A cross-cultural analysis of the relationship between decision making styles, consumer demographics, and product characteristics. Unpublished doctoral dissertation: Michigan State University.

DISCUSSION QUESTIONS

Culture and Consumer Behavior

1. Wickliffe makes the case that contemporary Americans and Koreans are more similar with regard to consumer behavior than they are different. Use the items that you dressed in today and identify those that were bought with the individualist in mind and those that were bought with the collectivist in mind. You can use all the clothes in your wardrobe for this exercise.

2. What do you believe the consequences to be of collectivist cultures (such as Korea) becoming more Euro-American (Western) in their consumer behavior? Are the consequences favorable or unfavorable? To whom?

CHAPTER 7

Dress in the Workplace

Kimberly A. Miller

AFTER YOU HAVE READ THIS CHAPTER, YOU WILL UNDERSTAND:

- How dress facilitates or hinders human interaction in the work place.

- How dress affects and reflects specific jobs in academia, service professions, and business.

- Why dress helps individuals acquire, learn, and perform job roles.

- How casual dress in the workplace reflects societal characteristics.

- The casual business dress phenomenon from multiple perspectives.

Working takes up a large portion of adult life. Spending 40 to 60 hours a week at work, in addition to commuting time and getting ready for work (including getting dressed) make our time spent on work-related activities substantial. Work dress becomes one of the most frequently used parts of the wardrobe, and for many individuals, is the part of the wardrobe on which they spend the most money. Because work provides money for family and self support, work tends to be highly valued by most individuals. In addition, many people prepare for careers through long years of education, training, and building a professional reputation and accomplishments. For many adults, work roles define much of self-identity.

The purpose of this chapter is to describe how dress affects relationships at work. Dress is a powerful communicator and especially so when people interact at work.

Clothing researchers have attempted to unravel the role that dress plays in the work environment, but more research is needed to fully understand this phenomenon. For instance, Johnson and Roach-Higgins (1987) have studied the effect women's dress and appearance has during job interviews. More recently, clothing researchers have examined the effect of masculine dress (Johnson, Crutsinger & Workman, 1994); body type (Thurston, Lennon & Clayton, 1990); and the ideal business image (Kimle & Damhorst, 1997) on a woman's success in the workplace. Several articles in this chapter will address women's dress at work, but all readings will demonstrate the importance of appropriateness of work dress.

In the late 1990s, casual dress is receiving attention from business executives and clothing scholars. The casual dress trend is interesting from several perspectives. One explanation for casual dress is that following the turbulent late 1980s/early 1990s when downsizing in business was so prevalent, employers wanted to give employees a perk, especially one that did not cost employers money. So casual dress days became a cost-effective way to raise morale among apprehensive employees. Several readings in this chapter will discuss casual dress and offer explanations for its occurrence at the close of the 20th century.

DRESS AND HUMAN INTERACTION AT WORK

In Chapter 1 we learned that roles are positions that people occupy in a group or society. Work roles typically require a specific type of dress. For example, a farmer needs overalls, a lawyer needs a business suit, and a judge needs a robe. To a large extent, if one looks the part through appropriate dress, she or he can be confident that others will assume that he or she legitimately holds the position they claim. Because dress is such a powerful communicator, appropriate work dress conveys that individuals not only understand their work roles but can perform them effectively.

Roles within a society can be either achieved or ascribed. **Achieved roles** are those that we work to earn. College degrees, work skills, even marriages, are roles that individuals must strive to attain. A wedding band and an academic robe are examples of achieved roles expressed through dress. An **ascribed role** is a position that people acquire through no fault or virtue of their own. Age, gender, skin color, and birth order are examples of ascribed roles. Ascribed roles have an immense impact on individuals because they are so visible and, with the exception of gender, they can rarely be changed. Age, gender, and skin color are difficult to hide in everyday interactions with others, therefore their impact is very great. Both achieved and ascribed roles are expressed through dress at work.

If roles are the special tasks that a person performs in a society, **status** or **prestige** is the social stratification in which groups and individuals are ranked and organized by legal, political, and cultural criteria (Marshall, 1994, p. 510). In addition, a status hierarchy reflects the value society places on certain roles or groups of roles (Storm, 1987). The presence (or absence) of a status symbol is one way that perceptions regarding status are formed. A Rolex watch, for example, is a major status symbol in U.S. culture. If a doctor or lawyer wears a Rolex watch, others may assume that he not only has the financial means to purchase such an item, but the skills required to achieve occupational success in his field. Height in men is an example of a status symbol. Tall men are judged to be more attractive than short men, and since attractiveness equates to higher prestige, tall men are afforded more status than their short counterparts. As an example, see "Short Guys Finish Last" in Chapter 2. For example, adding a hat to a policeman's uniform not only adds inches to his or her height, but can enhance perceptions of authority and status (Volpp & Lennon, 1988). Dress at work functions to visually express status distinctions in the workplace.

Social class is a concept that is related to, and greatly defined by, one's occupation. Although social class distinctions are blurry, generally in the United States, individuals are divided into three classes: upper, middle, and lower. Social class is a complex issue involving a person's social background, education, and occupation, (see Chapter 10). When social class and dress become a concern in the workplace, it is typically because an individual does not adopt dress appropriate to their position. For example, when a woman is promoted to management, but continues to wear dress similar to what secretaries wear in her firm, she may hit the "glass ceiling" preventing further promotion or even causing demotion (cf. Form & Stone, 1957). An employee is expected to look the part that he or she plays, and when that does not occur, that person may be labeled as someone who does not have the right image and therefore, the right qualifications for the job. Social class expressed through dress at work can create problems when an employee's social class does not correspond to the job they hold.

The terms **white collar dress** and **blue collar dress**, refer to types of occupations. These terms imply the social classes historically associated with white collar and blue collar occupations. Management and labor jobs were symbolized by dress typically worn for these roles: a man's white dress shirt worn with a suit for a management role and denim and a darker-colored shirt or uniform worn by a laborer (see Figure 7.1). Some presidential candidates have borrowed the traditional symbolism of blue collar and white collar dress. These candidates have worn a blue shirt while campaigning in parts of the country that have organized labor unions. The message of the blue shirt is, "I may be running for President, but I know what it means to physically work hard." The purpose of wearing a blue shirt is to establish connections with constituents and gain voter support. Conversely, the candidate will adopt a white shirt for general campaigning and official duties. Wearers of white collar dress are perceived as professional, conservative, and credible. Awareness of different environments and expected dress is often half the battle when dressing for work. One way to ensure appropriate work dress is to observe others at work and adopt their dress codes.

FIGURE 7.1 *Carhartt manufactures apparel for those who work and play outdoors and identify their primary market as blue-collar males, age 18-55. Carhartt is often referred to as the "Cadillac" of workmen's clothing.*

RESEARCH ON DRESS IN THE WORKPLACE

People often make judgments about others in just a few seconds. **Person perception** refers to the way we learn and think about others, their characteristics, intentions, and inner states (Taguiri & Petrullo, 1958). Forming a first impression is the first step in person perception. A job interview is one situation in which a first impression can determine one's future earning capacity; therefore appropriate dress for an interview is crucial. Not surprisingly, clothing researchers have studied the effect of dress during a job interview (Rucker, Taber & Harrison, 1981; Damhorst & Pinaire Reed, 1986).

Physical attractiveness has also been studied in relation to job interviews. In general, we know from research studies that attractive people have several advantages over those who are perceived as unattractive. Attractive people have advantages over unattractive people in the classroom, the courtroom, and in asking for and obtaining help (see Kaiser, 1997, for a summary of research on physical attractiveness). In a job interview setting, attractiveness is an advantage for men, however women who are moderately attractive have advantages over women who are unattractive or highly attractive (Heilman & Saruwatari, 1979).

Susan Watkins (1984) studies and designs clothing for specific needs, that is, a bulletproof vest for a police officer, protective clothing for an agricultural worker who sprays chemicals, and clothing that is easily donned and doffed for physically handicapped individuals. As jobs become more specialized and as the population grows older, clothing for specific needs becomes important. A hockey player needs a specialized type of dress to protect him from injury while engaging in a physically demanding occupation just as a construction worker needs specialized dress items that enable him to work on rooftops efficiently and without injury. With the advancement of technology, some workers are required to wear clothing that protects the product (e.g., sensitive computer equipment, electronics) from the worker (e.g., hair, lint, tobacco smoke). And as baby boomers approach retirement age, their needs must be addressed by the clothing industry. By now it should be obvious that dress at work is multifaceted. Next, we will look at some specific examples of work dress.

Dress and Ascribed Roles

In order to successfully perform one's job, the appropriate dress is mandatory. It is often difficult to meet the requirements for work dress while simultaneously meeting physical comfort needs. For example, pregnancy (discussed in Chapter 2) challenges female employees who want to meet both their professional and comfort needs. Many women in the 1980s and 1990s have worked to establish themselves in a career prior to having children. After becoming established professionally and financially, some women start to have families. Maternity career apparel (see Figure 2.4) is a specific type of dress that allows a pregnant woman to successfully fill her work role while meeting her changing physical needs (see Belleau, Miller, Elliot & Church, 1990). Maternity career apparel can also help a pregnant woman battle the stereotype that she will no longer be productive or will be less interested in her work after she has a child. Specialized clothing can assist individuals in meeting their work expectations, especially when a person's gender (i.e., being female and pregnant) might work against them.

Earlier in this chapter, we discussed the ascribed roles of age, skin color, and gender. Another example of the impact an ascribed role can have is the exclusion of a person from a position because of their skin color. In "Fine-Tuning Your Corporate Image," Anne Russell addresses how African Americans aspiring to middle and upper management positions in corporate America can use dress to their advantage. Professional dress inspires confidence and communicates authority. African Americans, who in the past were barred from success in white corporate America, use business dress symbols to help them overcome prejudicial stereotypes about their abilities. Another example is "Business Casual Dress: An African American Male Perspective" by Harriet McLeod. To record their feelings about casual dress, McLeod interviewed 15 African American business men.

Age, another example of an ascribed role, might hinder promotability if an individual looks younger than the amount of job experience he or she holds. A college professor might be mistaken for a teaching assistant if he or she looks particularly youthful. Dress can often help in creating a mature, professional appearance that instills credibility. Several examples of this are shown in "Frumpy or Chic? Tweed or Kente? Sometimes Clothes Make the Professor" by Alison Schneider.

Dress and Specific Occupations

Whereas it might be difficult to describe the dress of a mother in U.S. society (a role that has undergone significant changes), most people have a clear picture of what a policeman should be wearing. A police uniform is an example of **role-related dress**, that is, dress that has become inextricably tied to a particular occupation. Legitimacy, power, and authority are characteristics communicated by police uniforms. Research confirms that such clothing as uniforms can legitimize and convey power (Bickman, 1974). In order for police officers to successfully do their job, they must be perceived as legitimate and authoritative. The appropriate clothing symbols make this perception possible.

In "Sharper Image: The N.Y.P.D. Dresses for Success," author George James effectively connects public perception of the New York Police Department (NYPD) to the color and style of their uniforms. Police uniforms that included light-colored fabric, a baseball cap, and a service repairman appearance were perceived by the public as approachable. Unfortunately, the image of approachability undermines a policeman's authority, and authority is a necessary element to be an effective police officer. Changes to NYPD uniforms include darker-colored fabric, formal hats, and military-style details. After these changes, police officers were perceived by the public as authoritative and intimidating. Included in this article is a brief history of NYPD uniforms (1843–1994) and how the changes in the uniforms over time has affected public perception. This article is an excellent example of role-relatedness and how societal expectations can affect occupational dress.

In "Frumpy or Chic? Tweed or Kente? Sometimes Clothes Make the Professor," Schneider focuses on dress and academia. Have you ever noticed how the dress of professors differs depending on their field of study? A business professor may have a very businesslike appearance, while the mathematics or biology professor may have a very casual, even disheveled appearance. Because the academic profession is about generating ideas, clothes should reflect the mind of the wearer, the image of a competent and serious intellectual is paramount, but appearing overly interested in appearance may indicate that the individual is not serious enough for the job. This can leave professors wondering what to do about practical matters such as dress. Topics also included in this article are: job interviews and first impressions, institutional and regional context, minority professors, and young female professors. This reading will be especially entertaining to any past or present college student.

"Fine-Tuning Your Corporate Image" is an article that addresses individuals typically in the minority in the business world, that is, African Americans. "Fine-Tuning Your Corporate Image" advises African American managers (but the advice applies to all) to pay special attention to dress, speech, and body language. Presentation skills are extremely important to upward mobility in corporate America and individuals cannot present ideas effectively if they do not reflect the visual image of the corporation through appropriate dress. Image consultants offer professional advice on clothing and presentation skills to enhance career advancement. Although written specifically for African American managers, this article offers advice for anyone who wants to ensure that their appearance does not limit their career opportunities.

SOCIETAL IMPLICATIONS OF CASUAL DRESS

Work dress codes can be simply implied or they can be explicitly spelled out for employees. As written dress codes tend to be rare, often dress expectations are assumed and never openly discussed with employees. The assumption on the part of many employers is that the new employee will take note of what others are wearing and dress accordingly.

In "Saturn Corporation: A Casual Businesswear Case Study," casual dress in the workplace is addressed. The Saturn philosophy is reflected in employees' dress. It was important to those who created the Saturn Corporation that status distinctions be minimized. Therefore, Saturn wanted dress to reflect this philosophy and serve as a visual reminder to all employees that they work as a team. Although Saturn does not have a written dress code their policy is fairly explicit. If visitors arrive in formal business suits, their neckties will be snipped off!

Saturn Corporation is somewhat unique in that employees can dress casually every day. Designating one day of the week or month as casual day is more common in U.S. businesses. For instance, businesses that traditionally required employees to dress in suits and dress clothes five days a week are designating Friday (usually) as the casual dress day of the week.

Another interesting aspect of casual dress days is the new market it has created for manufacturers and retailers. Buying an entirely new wardrobe just for Fridays has much appeal to clothing manufacturers and retailers who hope to improve their bottom line. Because casual dress falls somewhere in between a business suit and active sportswear, some employees anguish over what to wear on casual days. Actually, male employees seem to be more confused over what to wear on casual dress days than female employees (see Negotiations @ Work: The Casual Businesswear Trend). There is evidence that women have numerous skills when it comes to negotiating dress at work (Rafaeli, Dutton, Harquali & Mackie-Lewis, 1997), and perhaps those skills are better honed in women than in men.

Casual Dress from Multiple Perspectives

Casual dress is examined from several different perspectives in six short essays. This multidisciplinary approach to casual dress includes perspectives from history, popular culture, feminism, sociology, gender studies, minority studies, marketing and economics. Ideas are proposed as to why casual dress has occurred at this particular time (i.e., 1990s) and what the implications for society might be. Why has casual dress become so popular in the 1990s? Many thought-provoking explanations are proposed by the authors of these essays. Almost all authors mention the aging baby boomers and the effect that group is having on the casual dress trend. Looking back through history, Jane Farrell-Beck in "Not So New: Casual Dress in the Office" asserts that in many instances casual dress styles eventually evolve into formal dress.

Abby Lillethun is especially provocative in "An Interpretation of Negative Press Coverage of Casual Dress" where she proposes that men fear the feminization of the workplace that casual dress represents. Lillethun raises some interesting ideas that you may want to consider when forming opinions about why casual dress is happening at this point in history. Janus et al. also raise interesting questions in their article entitled "Negotiations @ Work: The Casual Businesswear Trend" about the new negotiations over meanings of role identity that must occur at work as a result of casual dress days. As companies move from hierarchical structures to teams, dress can facilitate this change, but casual dress can also confuse employees regarding everyday interactions among colleagues.

Whereas Janus et al. focused primarily on men, Kimle and Damhorst chose to focus on women in the workplace in the article "Women's Images in Corporate Culture: The Case of Casual Day." Given that women still have a minority status in the workplace, how will the move to casual dress affect their status? Will casual dress further minimize their status, or will women achieve new status because of their more practiced skills in managing dress choices? Similar questions have also been raised about minority ethnicity in the business sector in the article by Harriet McLeod.

Lastly, Margaret Rucker covers the economic issues related to casual dress. How has casual dress affected the market for textiles and apparel? Has the general trend toward casualness over the past several decades prepared those in the apparel industry for the casual dress phenomenon? Do social trends influence economics of the marketplace? This article provides a broad view of casual dress by surveying the economics of the textiles and apparel industry.

What is important about this collection of essays is that a single topic (i.e., casual dress) is addressed from multiple perspectives. Such trends as casual dress in the office, offer an opportunity for rich reflection of societal changes. Input from many disciplines is needed in order to understand complex social phenomena such as causal dress.

Summary

Dress in the workplace is important because most working people spend 40 to 60 hours a week at their job. That is a lot of time and a lot of human interaction to consider. Appropriate dress can make the difference in receiving a job offer, appearing effective in a job role, and receiving a promotion. Understanding how dress can facilitate or hinder human interaction in the workplace can give employees a head start on making favorable impressions at work. Casual dress in the workplace, as the single biggest change in 20th century work dress, reflects such societal characteristics as aging baby boomers and relaxing formal dress codes. Considered from such diverse perspectives as history, feminism, and economics, the casual business dress phenomenon takes on broader implications than just a workplace trend. Most importantly, however, dress is a powerful communicator—especially in the workplace.

Suggested Readings

Kimle, P. A., & Damhorst, M. L. (1997). A grounded theory model of the ideal business image for women. *Symbolic Interaction, 20,* 45–68.

Scott, M. (1996, July/August). Casual day casualties: Getting uptight about dressing down. *Utne Reader, 18,* 20.

Warren, S. (1998, January 27). Updating a classic: "The man in the gray spandex suit." *The Wall Street Journal,* p. A2.

Interview a Professional

Objective: To observe and interview a professional about their work dress including casual dress policies and personal preferences. To form an opinion about dress in the workplace based on an interview with a professional in a field of personal interest.

Procedure

Choose a profession in which you have an interest. Talk to a professional in that field for a minimum of 20 minutes about his or her dress for work. Ask the person if you can meet him or her at work, so you can see that person in a professional setting.

Ask as many of the following questions as time allows:

1. Does your company have a dress code? Formal or informal? If so, what is it?
2. What do you wear to work on most days? Do you vary your dress according to activities you have planned that day?
3. How much time and energy do you spend on dress for work?
4. Does your company allow casual dress? If so, why? If not, why not?
5. Is casual dress allowed every day or just certain days of the week or month?
6. How do you feel about the company's casual dress policy? Do you like it? Why or why not?
7. How do you prefer to dress at work?
8. Have you seen a difference in your performance when dressed in formal dress versus casual dress?

Discussion Questions

What did you learn about dress at work that surprised you? Are you still interested in this profession after completing this assignment? If so, why? If not, why not? How do you want to dress when you begin a career?

WRITING ACTIVITY

Write two or three paragraphs about your thoughts on the dress policy at Saturn Corporation. Do you agree with their philosophy? Why or why not? Do you believe that team work in business is here to stay? If team work is a passing fad in business, do you think casual dress days are also a passing fad? Why or why not?

References

Belleau, B. D., Miller, K. A., Elliot, P., & Church, G. E. (1990). Apparel preferences of pregnant employed women. *Journal of Consumer Studies and Home Economics, 14,* 291–301.

Bickman, L. (1974). The social power of a uniform. *Journal of Applied Social Psychology, 4,* 47–61.

Damhorst, M. L., & Pinaire Reed, J. A. (1986). Clothing color value and facial expression: Effects on evaluations of female job applicants. *Social Behavior and Personality, 14*, 89–98.

Form, W. H., & Stone, G. P. (1957). *The social significance of clothing in occupational life* (Technical Bulletin 262). East Lansing, Michigan: Michigan State University Agricultural Experiment Station.

Heilman, M. E., & Saruwatari, L. R. (1979). When beauty is beastly: The effects of appearance and sex on evaluations of job applicants for managerial and nonmanagerial jobs. *Organizational Behavior and Human Performance, 23*, 360–372.

Johnson, K., Crutsinger, C., & Workman, J. (1994). Can professional women appear too masculine? The case of the necktie. *Clothing and Textiles Research Journal, 12*, 27–31.

Johnson, K., & Roach-Higgins, M. E. (1987). Dress and physical attractiveness of women in job interviews. *Clothing and Textiles Research Journal, 5*, 1–8.

Kaiser, S. B. (1997). *The social psychology of clothing: Symbolic appearances in context*, (2nd ed. revised). New York: Fairchild.

Kimle, P. A., & Damhorst, M. L. (1997). A grounded theory model of the ideal business image for women. *Symbolic Interaction, 20*(1), 45–68.

Marshall, G. (Ed.). (1994). *The concise Oxford dictionary of sociology*. Oxford, England: Oxford University Press.

Rafaeli, A., Dutton, J., Harquali, C. V., & Mackie-Lewis, S. (1997). Navigating by attire: The use of dress by female administrative employees. *Academy of Management Journal, 40*, 9–45.

Rucker, M., Taber, D., & Harrison, A. (1981). The effect of clothing variation on first impressions of female job applicants: What to wear when. *Social Behavior and Personality, 9*, 53–64.

Storm, P. (1987). *Functions of dress: Tool of culture and the individual*. Englewood Cliffs, NJ: Prentice-Hall.

Taguiri, R., & Petrullo, L. (1958). *Person perception and interpersonal behavior*. Stanford, CA: Stanford University Press.

Thurston, J., Lennon, S., & Clayton, R. (1990). Influence of age, body type, fashion and garment type on women's professional image. *Home Economics Research Journal, 19*, 139–150.

Volpp, J. M., & Lennon, S. J. (1988). Perceived police authority as a function of uniform hat and sex. *Perceptual and Motor Skills, 67*, 815–824.

36　Fine-Tuning Your Corporate Image
Anne Russell

Think about it. Who do you know that always looks terrific, whose voice commands attention and who never seems flustered, no matter how important the presentation may be? Sure, some of us seem to be born with style and polish, but if you're like most professionals, a little help from an image professional can go a very long way in helping advance your career.

As businesses continue to shrink staff size and compress layers of management, companies are catapulting administrative and technical professionals into positions of increased responsibility and exposure, often with little or no formal preparation. For these newly minted managers, gaining access to the executive suite is only half the challenge. In this highly competitive environment, staying there is getting harder every day. Face it, doing a good job is not enough. Today, you've got to look and act the part—exuding style, competence and authority—to ensure that your meteoric ascent up the corporate ladder doesn't end in a crash landing.

Corporations and nonprofit agencies have a vested interest in having polished executives represent the organization in the marketplace, on the fundraising trail and in the media. That's why enhancing the image of managers is viewed as a bottom-line investment. Corporate leaders must command attention and respect from colleagues and clients. The millions that corporations spend each year for management training and development, career seminars, tuition reimbursement and fitness training demonstrates the value corporate America places on prepared, articulate and well-groomed executives.

WHY YOUR CORPORATE IMAGE COUNTS

"Your image is like the weather," observes Marily Mondejar, founder and executive director of the San Francisco-based Image Industry Council

International (IICI), a 4-year-old trade association of nearly 1,000 image development enterprises, with aggregate annual sales of $500 million. "People notice when it is extremely good or extremely bad." Mondejar, also president of Mondejar Associates & Image Consultants in the same city, counts Apple Computer, Security Pacific National Bank and Hartford Insurance Co. among her clients.

Your image is your reputation and is a reflection of how you are perceived by others, either through your conversation, appearance or written words. When the image you project is in sync with your firm's corporate culture, you'll find yourself standing on much surer footing. However, a persona not in keeping with protocol reflects poorly on you, your superiors and ultimately your company.

A positive public image encompasses a lot more than just knowing not to wear brown shoes with a blue suit. Indeed, it is a way of life in which your wardrobe style, voice intonation, grooming habits, etiquette, office decor, body language and business presentations, oral and written, denote a style of performance commensurate with success.

"People use image as a gauge of how well you've adapted to the corporate culture and how well you understand the philosophy and values of the company," explains Joyce E. A. Russell, Ph.D., an associate professor of management at the College of Business at the University of Tennessee in Knoxville, who specializes in organizational behavior and human resources management. "If you don't look and act the part, you will probably be denied opportunities."

A myriad of interpersonal skills factor into an individual's corporate image. Proper etiquette, whether on the telephone, at dinner or when introducing colleagues is extremely important in business and social settings. While generally not an issue for professionals firmly entrenched in their careers, it is often the lack of these skills that impedes the progress of aspiring middle managers and may result in career derailment.

Accomplished executives have long known the merits of enlisting the aid of image consultants. Helping professionals refine their style is what the business of image consulting is all about. It is not, its proponents emphasize, about making you into something you're not. Rather, a good consultant will teach you how to feel comfortable with your inner self and to project confidence and authority. "A consultant analyzes a client's needs by examining his or her lifestyle, occupation and daily schedule," says consultant Cynthia Moody, president of Personal Expressions Inc., an image consulting firm in New York City. "Individuals need to feel comfortable with their image in order to project it in the right way."

The image consulting industry is a small, but lucrative one, says Jennifer Maxwell Morris, the 37-year-old president of Look Consulting International and founding president of the Association of Image Consultants International (AICI), both based in New York City. AICI's estimated 700 members command salaries ranging from $25 to $500 per hour, with prices adjusted by the services rendered, status of the client and experience of the consultant. Beyond the normal wardrobe consultation, consultants can provide a variety of other services, including personal shopping, grooming and cosmetic advice, coaching on speech, and presentation skills, and media training. Some consultants, like Rhonda Peterson, even offer nutrition and fitness counseling, "so you project a look-good, feel-good attitude." The 31-year-oid president of New York City-based Nouveau Image Consultants Inc. has serviced members of the National Black MBA Association, among others.

WHEN IT'S TIME TO CALL IN THE PROS

Colleagues are rarely willing to advise one another on personal appearance or inappropriate manners. So, how are you to know if your image needs sprucing up? Armelda Byrd, a Chicago image consultant, who is president and creative director of a firm bearing her name advises: "One tip-off that you don't have the right image is being excluded from high-profile meetings, even when you know your performance is up to par, and you should have been included."

"As you move into positions of increased authority you become very aware of how you present yourself," says Zeila Edwards-Elizenberry, a program manager in the artificial intelligence area at the Maynard, Mass.-based Digital Equipment Corp. Now in her early 40s, Edwards-Elizenberry sought out consultants' services early on in her career and has subsequently advanced through a series of technical positions, each with higher degrees of managerial responsibility. "An astute individual takes notice of how other people prepare for and communicate at meetings and presentations," adds Edwards-Elizenberry. In fact, she explains, part of your strategy should be to closely monitor those in your company who have the type of position you want. Watch what they wear and note their communication style. Then, if you feel comfortable doing so, seek to emulate, but not imitate them.

"Having the right look won't close the deal, but it can win the opening argument," says Cheryl Blackwell Bryson, a partner at the Chicago offices of Rivkin, Radler & Kremer law firm. Bryson initially sought out the services of image consultant Armelda Byrd in 1986, after the birth of her second child. "I'd decided that I wasn't going to buy another garment that wouldn't make me look at least 10 pounds thinner," recalls the 39-year-old labor and employment attorney. "That's when I knew I needed professional help."

Bryson was so pleased with the results that she encouraged her husband, James, a 44-year-old physical engineer and section manager at Inland Steel to consult Byrd for a much-needed wardrobe consultation and personal shopping assistance. "He recently was promoted," says his wife, "and I think the consultation had something to do with it. His colleagues now have more of a sense that he's in charge."

Maisha Bennett, Ph.D., president and executive director of Hamilton Behavioral

Healthcare Ltd. in Chicago, first used an image consultant back in 1985. Then Chicago's deputy commissioner of health, Bennett was asked to be spokesperson for a new media health campaign, but was cautioned by an associate to hire an image consultant first. "I was initially insulted because I thought I looked and presented myself just fine," she says in retrospect. However, Bennett, 43, took her friend's advice, since television interviews and formal presentations would now be an integral aspect of her job. After the success of that campaign, Bennett admits to now relying solely on her image consultant for all her personal appearance and shopping needs.

Given the standard five seconds it takes a person to make a visual first assessment of you, most experts agree that your appearance exudes a powerful message. Jean E. Patton, a 44-year-old president of New York-based Second Skin Color and Cosmetics and coauthor of *Color to Color: The Black Woman's Guide to a Rainbow of Fashion and Beauty* (Simon & Schuster, New York, $13) notes that black managers face enough barriers to upward mobility without having to contend with their appearance being one of them. "Make the effort to look the way any successful executive looks — effective!" she advises.

SIGNING ON TO THE TEAM

As tough as it may be, putting together the right look is often the easiest part of the image enhancement process. "The hardest part is mastering the communication skills, which will ultimately have more impact on your promotability," says John W. Aldrich, 52, president of Aldrich Associates, a training and development firm in Shelton, Conn.

Employees who are slow to pick up on their company's culture will soon begin to pay the price, warns Aldrich, who estimates that he has worked with over 2,000 executives on organizational and managerial effectiveness through his three-day *Workshop for Black Managers*. "An indication of trouble is when people stop inviting you to meetings or they won't cooperate with you," he says. "You may find you're not getting much feedback from your boss or not getting meaningful assignments. Organizations have their own ways of communicating that you're not fitting in."

Many a frustrated manager has learned that confidence in their ability and respect for their authority is not a natural byproduct of a job title. Rather, they are rewards that must be earned and then reinforced through the ongoing upgrading of your personal presentation. Chicago image consultant Armelda Byrd, 38, who counts the Miller Brewing Co. and McDonald's Corp. among her clients, recommends that executives periodically evaluate their career progress, while measuring the caliber of their personal effectiveness against that action plan. "Being self-assured in your appearance and execution can get you through the rough spots in many stressful situations," she advises.

But what if you're coming across as cocky when you mean to seem confident? You'll figure that out fairly quickly, says Byrd. "Overconfidence will invite hostile responses," she warns. "Learn to distinguish between a take-charge and a takeover mentality."

Monitoring the behavior of office veterans can also provide clues to acceptable behavior within your corporation, counsels management consultant John Aldrich. "Do people call each other by their first names? Do they tell jokes? Picking up on their style can serve as a guide," he says.

Murvin Lackey, vice president of purchasing at Digital Equipment Corp. in Maynard, Mass. has been promoted seven times during his 12 years with the company and acknowledges having taken numerous personal development courses throughout his career. Now in his late 40s, Lackey notes that the importance vested in a manager's ability to inspire trust and respect escalates as he ascends the corporate ladder. He also warns African-American managers that they may be held to a higher level of scrutiny than their white counterparts: "Blacks have to prove themselves for admission to the inner circles of corporate America. Whites have to *disprove* themselves to be kicked out."

Some aspects of corporate protocol can be particularly sensitive and bear watching. "Physically touching someone can be dangerous behavior for both women and older men," cautions the IICI's Marily Mondejar. A woman stroking a male colleague's arm may be interpreted as a sexual advance, while a similar gesture from an older man can be perceived as being aggressive or condescending. And considering the multicultural nature of today's work force and the heightened awareness of sexual harassment issues, it's best that most physical contact with business associates be restricted to a firm, quick handshake.

ROUNDING OUT THE IMAGE PACKAGE

The right clothes, presentation and attitude go a long way to ensure that most of your first impressions will be great ones. However, innocuous details, though easily overlooked, can sabotage what would otherwise be considered an impressive image package.

It goes without saying that good grooming habits (proper hygiene, styled hair, shined shoes, manicured nails) are requisite. Other image tips:

- Put the same confidence, conviction and authority you've placed in your presentation into the voice that will convey it. Mumbling, whispering, stuttering or bellowing your point will distract attention from the message and from the effectiveness of the messenger.

- Invest in classic, quality accessories such as a briefcase, trench coat/overcoat, watch, pen and daily planner. These items suffer considerable wear and tear, so they should be purchased with longevity in mind.

- Like your home, your office (or desk) décor reflects your style and level of professionalism. Personal items and decorating touches provide clues to aspects of your personality and lifestyle. And contrary to a popular school of thought, consistent clutter is not an indication of a busy executive—it's just an indication of clutter.

- Clunky jewelry, garish makeup and overpowering cologne speak volumes without your ever saying a word. Moderation is the key in these areas.

DISCUSSION QUESTIONS

Fine-Tuning Your Corporate Image

1. This article includes several suggestions to ensure that an individual is dressed in a way that accurately reflects their company's culture. What steps could a new employee take to ensure they are "in sync" with their corporate culture?

2. Given that image consultants can be expensive resources, when do you know it is time to use a consultant's services? What criteria would you use to determine the time to hire an image consultant?

37 Frumpy or Chic? Tweed or Kente? Sometimes Clothes Make the Professor

Alison Schneider

There was just one problem with the English department's job candidate: his pants.

They were polyester, green polyester, and the members of the hiring committee considered that a serious offense. For 10 minutes they ranted about the cut, the color, the cloth. Then and only then did they move on to weightier matters.

He did not get the job.

Neither did a woman lugging an oversized tote bag (too working-class). Or a man sporting a jaunty sweater and scarf (too flaky). Or a woman in a red-taffeta dress and cowboy boots (too—well, too much).

In the world of academe, where the life of the mind prevails, does it really matter if a scholar wears Gucci, gabardine, or grunge? What about good looks? Can such things tip the scales in a job interview, weaken a bid for tenure, or keep you off the A list on the conference circuit? Many professors say they can, although there is quibbling over the reasons why.

Talk about appearances might seem unjustified given the profession's showing in the arena of good looks and good taste. "Academics are still the worst-dressed middle-class occupational group in America," says Valerie Steele, chief curator at the museum of the Fashion Institute of Technology and editor of *Fashion Theory: The Journal of Body, Dress & Culture.*

A FETISH FOR FASHION

But despite their threadbare reputation, scholars spend a lot of time thinking, talking, and writing about appearances. Last month, Elaine Showalter, an English professor at Princeton University, came out of the closet, so to speak, and admitted in *Vogue* magazine that she has a fetish for fashion. She waxed eloquent about her Cossack minidress and turquoise boots from Bologna. "For years," she wrote, "I've been trying to make the life of the mind coexist with the day at the mall."

She is not alone. Scholars squirm when the topic of appearance arises, but a growing number agree that even in the ivory tower, image and intellect are hopelessly intertwined.

"I absolutely judge what people wear," says Wayne Koestenbaum, an English professor at the City University of New York's Graduate School and University Center, who dabs on specific perfumes to pay homage to particular writers. (He declined to provide an example. "It's much too personal," he says.) But "there are people who are excited as I am by certain ideas, certain artistic movements. There are semiotic codes of dress, makeup, and hair that say things about your allegiances."

He should know. He dyed his hair red when he entered graduate school. "It was intimately connected to my intellectual advancement and my movement into feminist and gay theory."

That sounds like self-conscious gobbledygook to some professors. When it comes to appearances, academe breaks down into two camps: pro-frumpy and pro-fashion. Fans of frumpiness insist that if you want to prove you're intellectually a cut above the competition, think twice before parading around in an Italian-cut blazer.

"If it's a choice between being chic or frumpy, I think it benefits academics more to be frumpy," says Emily Toth, a professor of English and women's studies at Louisiana State University. "If you look like you spend too much time on your clothes, there are people who will assume that you haven't put enough energy into your mind." Dr. Toth, who doubles in her off-

FIGURE 7.2 *Karla F.C. Holloway, Duke University Director of African and African-American Studies, notes that "casualness has never been a part of minority professors' professional demeanor."*

hours as Ms. Mentor—the Miss Manners of academe—has dished out pithy advice for years, first in a column for *Concerns*, the journal of the Women's Caucus of the Modern Language Association, and now in a book, *Ms. Mentors Impeccable Advice for Women in Academia.*

As for the taffeta dress and cowboy boots—which Ms. Mentor saw for herself—such an outfit may signal that a scholar doesn't grasp the right professional priorities, she says in an interview. "If you don't know how to dress, then what else don't you know? Do you know how to advise students or grade papers? The clothes *are* part of the judgment of the mind."

Clothes also help determine if someone will fit into a particular institution. Ask around, and you'll hear professors talk about regional norms for acedemics: The Midwest dresses down, the South dresses up. Tailored but casual wins the day in the Northeast, and anything goes in California—as long as it looks good. Not to mention the fact that individual universities have their own idiosyncratic norms, which professors ignore at their peril.

"A lot depends on institutional context," explains Catherine R. Stimpson, dean of the graduate school of arts and sciences at New York University. "At a small, fraught department, where everybody is out to get everybody else, they'd use anything—they could even use a little Liz Claiborne—as a sign of overreaching."

Perhaps the biggest liability of looking too good is that colleagues and students may spend more time thinking about what a professor wears than what he or she says. When clothes become a distraction, the frumpiness faction contends, they do a disservice to young scholars who are trying to establish themselves in their field.

Men occasionally take flak for putting too much of a premium on their own appearance. People still talk about what Andrew Ross, the ultra-hip director of the American-studies program at N.Y.U., wore to the M.L.A.'s 1991 meeting: a yellow Comme des Garçons blazer, a Japanese hand-painted tie, and wedge-heeled suede shoes. Back then, Mr. Ross told *The New York Times* that the jacket was "a sendup of the academic male convention of yellow polyester," but these days he doesn't care to comment. Little wonder. The outfit made him a legend in some eyes and a laughingstock in others.

Still, he says, "I don't think it's a bad thing that academics think more about their appearance right now, when the profession is under siege. It translates into a perception that they're not otherworldly, that they don't live in ivory towers, that they meet people where they are rather then tell them where they ought to be." His only fashion regret: removing his earrings when he went on the market. It didn't even land him a job.

'THE BAR IS NOT THAT HIGH'

"Dressing fashionably in academia is like clearing the four-foot high jump. The bar is not that high," says Michael Bérubé, an English professor at the University of Illinois at Urbana-Champaign. "Anything with some cut or color draws derision—and admiration—because the sartorial requirements of the business are so low."

Mr. Bérubé may know whereof he speaks. He showed up at last month's M.L.A. meeting sporting an electric-blue suit of 100-per-cent polyester. He loves the outfit: "It's an amazing color, and it never loses its crease!"

A man may be able to pull off an electric blue suit without raising eyebrows, but what about a woman? "I still think there's a predisposition to take men more seriously," says Domna C. Stanton, a professor of French and women's studies at the University of Michigan. Junior-faculty women face a particularly difficult quandary, she says. "How do they convey professional seriousness without looking like a man in drag?"

Here's the short list of Ms. Mentor's do's and don'ts: For starters, younger women should play down their sexuality. Skirts should be knee-length or below. Pants are never appropriate for interviews. Steer clear of high-heeled shoes. Choose dark colors over light ones. Ms. Mentor recommends dark purple: "it looks good on everyone."

But some people think playing by the rules is the riskiest move of all. "I don't think frumpy gets you anywhere except forgotten," says Jane Gallop, a professor of English and comparative literature at the University of Wisconsin at Milwaukee. She's made strong fashion statements for years. She wore velvet jeans and a sweater when she went on the job market; donned a now-legendary skirt made of men's ties when she lectured on psychoanalytic theory and the phallus; and slipped into suede fringed pants and cowboy boots to talk about Western civilization.

She hasn't toned down her look much, since her junior-professor days. "I teach in torn T-shirts that I have actually torn myself," she says. And she still defends using clothing as conceptual art: "There's a stupid impression that a lack of style signifies seriousness, but anyone who comes from a literary sense of things knows that style is often the best way to convey complicated things. You should use everything you have to make people think."

Dr. Showalter agrees: "Teaching is performance. We use everything we've got, and costume is part of it. Thats not to say that you dress up like Emma Bovary, but a little liveliness it desirable."

"Give me a break," replies Camille Paglia, a humanities professor at the University of the Arts. "Yes, teaching is a performance art. But when the teacher hijacks the classroom for self-display—of fashion or mannerism or cult of personality—we have a corruption of education. Professors think, 'They're here because of me, because of my wonderful whimsy, my wonderful way of doing things.' It makes me want to throw up!" Ms. Paglia favors pantsuits for public lectures—she's especially fond of her flowing, Donna Karan tuxedo suit—but sticks to simple slacks, a plain jacket, and rubber-soled shoes in the classroom.

'A DISPLACEMENT OF THE REAL ISSUE'

What does all this sartorial sniping mean for scholars going on the job market and the people who are grooming them? Professors spend an inordinate amount of time fine-tuning not only what their protégés will say at interviews but also how they will look when they say it. Mentors criticize everything from the studs in the jobseekers' ears to the shoes on their feet.

The result: Scholars hunting for jobs are expected to look far better than those who have one, says Nancy K. Miller, an English professor at CUNY's graduate school. "I wonder if the emphasis on appearance at the hiring level isn't a displacement of the real issue: that these students aren't going to get jobs. We focus on their clothing as if the perfect suit or haircut, or the toning down of extravagant styles, will guarantee them a job." Alas, she says, it won't.

'A SPECIAL TURN OF THE KNIFE'

The deconstruction of dress weighs particularly heavily upon minority professors (see Figure 7.2).

"There is a special turn of the knife for racial and ethnic women," says Nell Painter, a black historian at Princeton. "There are prejudices against people who look too Jewish, too working-class, too Italian, too black, or too much of anything different." She adds, however, that "if you look too WASPish, that's probably all right."

The stakes are high for blacks, Ms. Painter says, because nothing they do is neutral. "If you wear a pair of classic trousers and no kente cloth, that makes a statement. And if you wear kente cloth, *that* makes a statement."

"My difficulty with that," says Karla F.C. Holloway, director of African and African-American studies at Duke University, "is that it makes the other parts of you invisible—your scholarship, your intellect, your seriousness." That's why she favors formality. She doesn't repress her African–American roots—she wears ethnic prints and wraps her hair in a braid, like her grandmother did—but she steers clear of casual couture. "Casualness has never been part of our professional demeanor," she says. "Maybe because we can't afford to make it part of our professional demeanor."

The most glaring exception may be Robin D.G. Kelley, a historian at N.Y.U. He does have some designer suits in his closet, but most days he pulls on a pair of black jeans, black combat boots, and a "contemporary"—meaning '50s-looking—shirt or sweater.

Students think he's hip and approachable. But looking cool has its cost. "At every stage in my career, youth and informality—in dress, in appearance, in presentation—have been the bane of my existence. Professors take me less seriously."

Fortunately, Dr. Kelley says he has found that "the one thing that speaks louder than dress is the work that you do."

Hair, however, is something else entirely. "People lose their jobs over how they style their hair," he says. A big Afro is associated with late-'60s radicalism, while straightened hair signals that you're a "serious sell-out white wannabe." Braids, dreadlocks, and shaved heads give the impression that you've got a chip on your shoul-der. "When I had my hair short, I was a safe Negro," Dr. Kelley says. Now he's growing dreadlocks, a decision that's cramping his style when it comes to his current work, a book about Thelonious Monk. He'd like to don the kind of funky hats that the jazz pianist wore, but he can't until his hair finishes "locking," he says. "It's really messing up my vibe."

GOOD LOOKS

Things are complicated in other ways for those professors—men or women, white or black—graced with exceptionally good looks. In academe, beauty is a double-edged sword. Scholars, like everybody else, sometimes assume that a sound mind isn't likely to be accompanied by a sexy body.

Bennett Link, a physicist at Montana State University at Bozeman, posed bare-chested last year in the "Studmuffins of Science" calendar, a tongue-in-cheek tribute to good-looking geeks. The attention over his appearance as "Dr. April" has died down, but he admits that when the calendar came out, he wanted to keep it quiet.

"The way a person looks doesn't play much of a role in the sciences," he says. In fact, he adds, it's a matter of pride among scientists to dress down. But image is critical. "It's important to appear smart and competent. I wasn't sure if the calendar would hurt my chances for tenure." (He went along with the idea after his girlfriend at the time had sent in the photos.)

Most people think good looks don't hurt. "Generally, looking attractive helps you get a job," Ms. Gallop says. "It's not supposed to be true—and it's nothing that ever gets said—but prejudices operate against people who are seriously overweight or have bad skin or are really unattractive. It produces a kind of discomfort."

As Ms. Mentor puts it, if A is the cream of the academic crop when it comes to looks, and F is "wolf man," then "wolf man does not get a job." Fortunately, she says, most scholars fall somewhere between B + and D + . But then, she's grading on a curve.

Frumpy or Chic? Tweed or Kente? Sometimes Clothes Make the Professor

1. University dress codes are widely interpreted by faculty. From your observations, do you believe that a professor's dress corresponds to their teaching or lecturing style? Do you believe that a professor's dress should correspond to their teaching style? Why or why not?

2. Academia presents a dilemma about dress for its faculty. If you pay too much attention to dress you'll be considered too frivolous for the job. On the other hand, if you don't give your dress some attention you'll appear detached. From your observations of college professors, how do you see this dilemma being resolved or going unresolved?

38 Sharper Image: The N.Y.P.D. Dresses for Success

George James

Arriving from Boston last January to become the New York City Police Commissioner, William J. Bratton looked at his 31,000 officers, their two-tone uniforms, 25 pounds of equipment dangling from drooping gun belts, and saw service repairmen.

As a result, the New York City Police Department will no longer look as approachable as it has for the last 22 years. It will soon look like the Los Angeles Police Department. Less Mr. Goodwrench, more Terminator 2. By next October the N.Y.P.D. will abandon its medium-blue shirt, putting on navy to match the trousers. The dark style creates a more militaristic and, yes, more intimidating appearance. Thus does N.Y.P.D. blue become L.A.P.D. blue (bare bottoms optional).

Since standard military uniforms evolved in the 17th century to prevent armies from shooting their own soldiers, uniforms have been designed to send a clear message. In the case of police, the message to the public is one of authority. (We're cops and you're not—get behind that barricade!") and to fellow officers one of esprit de corps ("We're cops and they're not. Let's go for doughnuts.")

In choosing a uniform, says Michael Solomon, a psychologist and chairman of the marketing department in the business school at Rutgers University, "You're letting everyone know that this is something that matters. You want to avoid sloppiness because it reflects on the organization." (See Figure 7.3.)

Mr. Bratton, hired to overhaul the nation's largest department and reduce crime and the fear of it, formed a dozen "re-engineering" committees. One focusing on appearance found that many officers looked like slobs—and were proud of it.

The result, the committee reported, is "a culture of slovenliness," in which putting on the uniform is "wearing the bag." Rookies trying to appear like veterans achieve a "hair bag" look by weathering their uniform and leather belt. While the department might pride itself as the finest in the country, it said, "the corporate culture of the uniform does not value a well-

FIGURE 7.3 *The NYPD uniform has changed many times over the past decades to correspond with social trends and public perception.*

Association of Uniform Manufacturers and Distributors, a trade organization. "There's a school of thought that the darker the uniform the more authoritative and conservative the police appear," she said. "Would you like to see police officers in a pink uniform?"

In many rustic and suburban areas, she said, the officers wear the color of the land, dark brown or green.

Military-like hash marks indicating years of service will be worn on the new long-sleeve shirts in New York City; on short sleeves, a bar over the breast pocket serves the same purpose. The insignia will help commanders arriving at the scene of an emergency to identify experienced officers.

Prior to 1972, the police department wore a monochromatic dark blue uniform. But after riots in New York and other cities erupted in the 1960's and the Knapp Commission began exposing widespread corruption in the early 1970's, the uniform became synonymous with the force's oppressive image. A more approachable image was sought, and "New York City blue" became regulation wear.

ENOUGH TOUCHY-FEELY

But then, for more than a century and a half the police have been touchy about uniform fashions and statements they make. The city's first effort to put its officers into uniform around 1843 failed. The men thought the blue, double-breasted frock coat make them look like British bobbies, said John R. Podracky, curator of the New York City Police Museum. "And there was much anti-British sentiment," he said.

In 1845, officers adopted a vestige of that uniform, an eight-pointed star badge. Around 1853, they agreed to wear a single-breasted frock coat with a round cap, Mr. Podracky said. In the 1880's the department adopted a domed felt helmet—the Keystone Cop look.

Today, a remnant of that eight-pointed badge is seen in the eight-pointed cap, which has become a standard for other departments as well. Many county law enforcement departments choose an equally authoritative and intimidating chapeau, the Smokey Bear hat

groomed appearance," and public confidence suffers.

Mr. Bratton, whose well-groomed appearance includes a seemingly inexhaustible supply of suits and Hermès neckties with small animals on them, said the new uniform offers a more professional and authoritative appearance.

The look also creates a leaner, if necessarily meaner look. "It makes us look a lot slimmer, which a lot of us need," said Lieut. Richard Greene, who headed the uniform committee.

Other departments, from Mr. Bratton's native Boston to Fresno, share the city's new look, and more are adopting it, said Jackie Rosselli, a spokeswoman for the National favored by state troopers. At the other extreme is the baseball cap that many departments, including New York City, adopted in the mid-1980's to look more user-friendly. These were later dropped because they were deemed to add an unprofessional air to policing, Ms. Rosselli said. Mr. Bratton's predecessor, Raymond W. Kelly, a spit-and-polish Marine reserve colonel, reintroduced the caps, emblazoned with "N.Y.P.D.," for special units like the narcotics division who, when going on a raid, need to be quickly identified as the good guys.

Mr. Kelly did much to spiff up the uniform, introducing navy turtlenecks (a favorite of the troops), jackets to identify plainclothes officers on a crime scene and patent-leather dress shoes.

Since Mr. Kelly approved the 9-millimeter semi-automatic pistols to give officers the psychological lift of having firepower parity with the hard guys on the streets, the gun belt has become neater, higher and thicker, better able to bear the gun, flashlight, handcuffs, notebook and pepper spray.

Psychologically, "the uniform provides a shield," said Mr. Solomon of Rutgers. "People are less likely to mess with you if you're an intimidating presence."

"I think it's a backlash to the touchy-feely approach that drove many departments to make themselves less intimidating," he said. "Now it's swinging back the other way because there is the feeling it didn't work."

DISCUSSION QUESTIONS

Sharper Image: The N.Y.P.D. Dresses for Success

1. This article is an interesting case study of perceptions based on appearance. Color of police uniforms and styling details can elicit a range of perceptions from "user-friendly" to "intimidating." Can you think of other professions that have gone through changes in dress (uniform or nonuniform) to change the perceptions of others?

2. Can you identify societal changes/issues that correspond with police uniform changes?

39 Saturn Corporation: A Casual Businesswear Case Study

Levi Strauss & Co.

When adopting casual businesswear in the workplace, many companies move slowly from a traditional business dress code to more relaxed options. Not so at Saturn, the innovative division of General Motors founded 10 years ago to market vehicles developed and manufactured in the United States. The Saturn staff has dressed casually since the company's inception.

Saturn was established in 1983 when parent company General Motors picked 99 people from all levels throughout the GM organization and sent them around the world to study other

Article courtesy of Levi Strauss & Co.

successful companies. This research drove development of a plan for the creation of Saturn.

When laying the groundwork for the new company, it was important that everyone be viewed equally in the work environment. Accordingly, the research team's vision included innovations that were noteworthy not only for an auto maker, but for any manufacturer. For example, there are no time clocks at Saturn—every employee is on salary. Executive perks, including assigned parking and special cafeterias, were eliminated.

To further enhance equality in the workplace everyone at Saturn dresses similarly, in casual clothing. Even the president can be spotted wearing casual slacks and a golf shirt on most days.

"When executives are dressed in suits, it separates them from the people on the line," says Jennifer Graham, community relations representative. "Teamwork is a very important element of our philosophy, and dressing casually helps promote the Saturn team spirit."

Saturn has no written dress guidelines for its casual dress policy. Employees are trusted to dress appropriately and this, too, is a reflection of the Saturn philosophy. "When you let people have responsibility, they do the right thing," says Graham.

The casual dress policy extends beyond the workplace—Saturn executives often wear their casual work clothes when they leave the Spring Hill, Tenn., complex to attend meetings or give speeches.

Do Saturn employees really think that dressing casually has made a difference in their corporate culture? "Yes," says Graham. "It really changes your attitude to be completely comfortable at work all of the time."

The company believed so much in what they were creating that, back in 1986 when suit-clad visitors from GM arrived at the Tennessee headquarters and plant, they were greeted rather unceremoniously. The visitors had their ties snipped off.

DISCUSSION QUESTIONS

Saturn Corporation: A Casual Businesswear Case Study

1. What is your opinion about Saturn Corporation's casual dress policy? Do you think Saturn has gone too far by allowing casual dress every day?

2. Because role-related dress, such as a police uniform, can be critical at a crime scene by allowing all players to be identified, wouldn't the same premise hold true at a corporation such as Saturn? In other words, wouldn't the work day move more efficiently and effectively if people in different roles dressed differently rather than having everyone dressed alike? Why or why not?

Casual Day and Everyday

Casual dress in the office is examined from six different perspectives in this collection of short essays. This multidisciplinary approach to casual dress includes perspectives from history, popular culture, feminism, sociology, gender studies, minority studies, marketing, and economics. Ideas are proposed as to why casual dress has occurred at this particular time (i.e., the 1990s) and what the implications for society might be. The papers were developed from presentations delivered during a special conference session held at the International Textile and Apparel Association annual meeting in Banff, Alberta, Canada, in August of 1996.

40   Not So New: Casual Dress in the Office

Jane Farrell-Beck
Iowa State University

Casual clothing in the office, which seems like a 1990s phenomenon, really had its roots in the 1600s. When Charles II became King of England in 1660, men in his court wore full-cut silk breeches and short doublets, enhanced by enormous quantities of ribbon and set off by shirts with costly lace collars and cuffs. Charles wanted his courtiers to adopt a different style, one that would show independence from these French fashions and would use fine woolen fabrics, which were (and are) important to the English economy. In 1666, Charles decreed that a wool coat, "cassocke" (or vest), and breeches replace the fancier styles. This was the forerunner of the three-piece suit. Although the new styles copied some of the lines of Turkish garments (Jirousek, 1992), they also drew upon informal fashions popular with English country gentry (Kuchta, 1990). Thus the suit was an informal fashion transplanted to London and worn in business places as well as at court (see Figure 7.4).

Suit styles changed with the years. Coats became slimmer, breeches longer, and waistcoats (vests) shorter. Coat cuffs shrank and their collars became deeper. By the latter 1700s, cutaway coats were the rage for horseback riding, which was both a necessity for daily travel and a sport for the rich. Short vests, boots, and top hats

were worn with the tailcoats for comfort and safety. By 1800, styles identical to those worn for the sport of horseback riding had entered the business offices of England. This illustrates a principle expressed by several costume historians: Styles originally designed for active sports gradually evolve into businesswear and then into formal clothing (Laver, 1968; Waugh, 1964). Consider where tailcoats and top hats are worn today—only for the *most* formal weddings and parties!

In the late 1780s, upper-class men wore knee breeches; long pants were suitable only for men doing heavy labor and for small boys. By 1800, however, this utilitarian style began to win favor among fashionable young men, perhaps as an outgrowth of their experience wearing long pants as young boys. Gradually, knee breeches were relegated to the wardrobes of "old fogies," and long pants took over the business office and the ballroom. Changes in pants didn't end there. Men working outdoors in muddy fields, in mines, and at construction sites turned up the bottoms of their pants. This purely utilitarian trick of the 1860s had become part of a dapper gent's daytime clothes by about 1900. So, too, did the creases in pants, which resulted from storing the pants in a clothes press. Men liked the flattering effect of slim-looking legs, so they

FIGURE 7.4 *This is one of the earliest known images of the three-piece suit.*

began to incorporate a crease in the routine pressing of their trousers.

Suit coats varied from the tailcoat of the early 1800s to the flared "frock coat" of the 1830s through the 1850s. Both of these styles had nipped-in waistlines, which were snug and rather uncomfortable for all-day wear. When the city businessman went to the country to hunt or fish he wore a "sack" coat, cut straight with no waistline indentation. This roomy garment, often made in rough tweedy wool, so impressed its wearers that they began to want business suit coats of similar cut, in smooth town wools. Gradually, beginning in the 1870s and more often in the 1880s, men's daytime suits featured sack coats. Today's single and double-breasted suit coats are

descendants of this 1860s tweedy sack coat. So, too, is the "tux" or tuxedo coat, which was introduced in the 1880s in Tuxedo Park, New York, as a semiformal jacket with sack styling (Payne, Winakor, Farrell-Beck, 1992). In the 1990s, a tux is about the most formal jacket any man wears.

Speaking of double-breasted jackets: They began life as blazers for dress-up wear by sports teams, such as rowing crews. Today, the double- or single-breasted blazer is a cornerstone of business clothing, except in the most conservative offices. Double-breasted styling appears everywhere, including pinstriped suits for upper-level executives.

The root of the word "sweater" is "sweat," and the humble sweaters of the late 1800s and early 1900s were used during or after active sports, so that the sweaty athlete wouldn't become chilled. Between 1920 and 1940, fashionable and glamorous movie stars wore sweater vests with their slacks and jackets; sporty college students wore sweaters to classes with full-cut Oxford Bag trousers (forerunners of skateboarders' oversized styles of the 1990s). Young men even wore sweaters with knickers for spectator sports. By the 1940s, the sweater vest was often teamed with a suit coat and trousers, partly because of the World War II prohibition against three-piece suits of woven wool. (Wool was being conserved for military uniforms). In some business offices of the 1990s, sweater vests form an acceptable third layer and even pullovers and cardigans may appear on casual days.

What will the future bring? Will today's sweatsuits displace suits or tailored jackets and slacks in the workplace? When soft clothing of jersey or fleece rules the corporate roost, what will "casual" clothing be made of? How will it look? Perhaps *you* will design or discover the next step in the evolution of styles from sport field to ballroom.

References

Jirousek, C. (1992). More than oriental splendor: Western dress and the Levant. In: L. Wehrle, (Ed.). *The costume society of America annual meeting and symposium abstracts.* Earleville, MD: Costume Society of America.

Kuchta, D. (1990). "Graceful, virile, and useful;" The origins of the three-piece suit. *Dress, 17*, 18–26.

Laver, J. (1968). *Dandies*. London: Weidenfeld and Nicolson.

Payne, B., Winakor, G., & Farrell-Beck, J. (1992). *The history of costume*. New York: HarperCollins.

Waugh, N. 1964. *The cut of men's clothes 1600–1900*. London, England: Faber.

DISCUSSION QUESTIONS

Not So New: Casual Dress in the Office

1. What principle from a historic perspective does Farrell-Beck give regarding the evolution of businesswear? Can you give two examples of this principle?

2. From which garment did the tuxedo coat originate?

41 An Interpretation of Negative Press Coverage of Casual Dress

Abby Lillethun
Ohio State University graduate student

The trend in American fashion toward casual dress in the 1980s and 1990s resulted in coverage in the popular press. Most of this coverage treated the fashion in relatively unbiased accounts. But once the casual trend, or dressing down, began to take hold in the workplace, negative or adversarial articles appeared. This dissenting tone clashed with the position of most coverage as well as with the fast growing acceptance of the trend by the public.

This article presents a case study of popular press articles that were negative toward the trend in casual dress. An interpretation is made of selected articles that presents the view that negative press of the casual trend was motivated by a fear of feminization of the workplace. Three main issues support this interpretation. First, men wear less clothing in casual dress than they do in business attire and less dress equates to feminine rather than to masculine stereotypes in American culture. Second, in casual dress men have more expressive options in their clothing selection than in traditional business dress. Thus, men are moving from a restricted dress code to a more elaborated dress code, which is the type of dress code that has been the norm for feminine dress in America. Third, casual dress is perceived by the press as an indication of the wearer's lack of self-control. The lack of self-control equates to childish behavior which is traditionally viewed as feminine rather than masculine behavior.

To become familiar with the popular press coverage of the trend, I initially searched the following electronic databases for articles: *Article First-Daily, Newspaper Abstracts, The Periodicals Index, The Readers Guide*, and *The Wall Street Journal*. An overview of the notions of the press concerning the phenomenon and its operation in American culture was provided by 39 articles in 26 magazines published from 1983 through 1994 (e.g., *Business World, Glamour, New York Times Magazine, Vogue*). In 1995, the frequency of press coverage increased, coinciding with an increase in the adoption of the style in the workplace. To evaluate the extent and type of coverage that was occurring, database searches were performed for the period beginning 1995 to mid-1996. For example, a search was made of Lexus/Nexus in the Current News/Magazine library, restricted to articles published after January 1, 1995 and before June 15, 1996 with the key phrases "dressing down" or "casual dress." The use of the word "sloppy" or "messy" was then added, which limited search results to articles with a negative descriptor. There were many more articles that covered or mentioned the new fashion trend (5,471) as compared to those that were negative, or that covered negative reactions (191).

In general, the press understands that various cultural qualities and shifts are signaled by the adoption of casual dress. The ascendance of baby boomers to economic power, adjustments in attitudes toward materialism, adjustments in attitudes toward meeting physical comfort needs, and a visual leveling of the classed and gendered society are among the cultural themes credited for the adoption of casual dress. Positive aspects of the trend in the workplace that are reported include that it: 1) improves morale, 2) provides a perceived benefit, 3) helps employees to save money on clothing expenses, 4) attracts new employees, and 5) boosts productivity. Some of the positive descriptions of the qualities of the wearers are "creative," "substance," and "honesty."

Five articles received in-depth analysis. They were selected to provide a range of attitudes representing varying levels of negativity, to represent regional and national press, to include articles with a variety of visual presentations, and to represent a variety of perspectives, from fashion magazine to national newspaper front page story. Adler's (1995) "Have we become a nation of slobs?" (see article in Chapter 13) stands out as the most negative, lengthy, and extensively illustrated reaction to the casual dress trend. It appeared as the cover story of *Newsweek*, an internationally circulated weekly magazine. Belcove's (1996) "Fixing Mr. Gates," from the fashion magazine W, gives unsolicited appearance advice to Bill Gates. Gellers (1995), also writing in W, addresses workplace casual dress from the fashion perspective. Bragg's (1994)

"Nowadays, Workers Enjoy Dressing Down for the Job" from *The New York Times*, precedes the mushrooming of the press coverage, represents a minimally negative press article, and includes a single photographic image. Goldberg's (1995) "This Fad Deserves a Dressing Down" from the business-oriented *Wall Street Journal* gives analysis of the trend in the corporate workplace.

How does the adoption of casual dress affect the perception of men and women? The notion that casual dress works to expose the male body was found in Adler (1995) and Bragg (1994). Bragg's (1994) news article examined specific changes in appearance in the workplace. For men, the primary change is not wearing the tie, longstanding symbol of male corporate power. The article's single photo image is a close-up of a man's open buttondown shirt collar and his exposed neck and throat. The article implies an equivalence between women not wearing pantyhose or tights to men not wearing the tie and opening their shirt collars. But, not wearing pantyhose or tights often results in women wearing pants to work instead of skirted clothes, and, thus, there is less leg exposure. Therefore, in the corporate workplace with casual dress, female bodies are more covered (in pants) and, thus, are more masculine while men's bodies are less covered (by open-necked shirts) and, thus, are more feminine than when the older business dress standards are practiced.

In Adler's *Newsweek* (1995) cover story, an undercurrent of fatherly masculine control is heard in the accusatory phrases "You're going out in that?..." and "Have We Become a Nation of Slobs?" (Adler, 1995). In addition, the article's images present a disproportionate number of 70 male figures to 31 female figures, suggesting a preoccupation with male over female presentation in casual dress. For example, in the entire article there are two images of females with an undue degree of exposed flesh, and both are of women in performance situations: Madonna flexes her muscles in a stylized corset and tights costume and Charlotte Moorman wears a bra top and panties as she plays her cello. But, male images with lots of exposed flesh are common in the article. President Clinton is shown twice in leg-exposing jogging shorts, several well-known male personalities are shown with exposed chests or legs, and a photograph of baseball fans on a hot day shows ten of the 13 male fans wearing no shirt. The article emphasizes the newly increased exposure of male skin as a result of the casual dress trend. Yet, traditionally, it is the female body that is more exposed than the male. Linked to the traditionally more-exposed female body is the male-centered world view in which the female is the "object" of male sexual satisfaction. In casual dress the male body is found to be in a condition of increased physical exposure and is thus cast in the traditionally feminine role. Perhaps this process of redefining objectification, as shown in casual dress—where more nearly equivalent types of dress and degree of body exposure for men and women are practiced—indicates changes in gender roles in the culture. Adler (1995) reflects his apprehension of the future of the dressing down trend and his fear of changes in society indicated by it in his closing phrase "…better not to think about it."

What or how is the process of selecting and wearing the new casual dress different from other dress? Primarily it is in the change from a restricted appearance code to a more elaborated dress code. In Euro-American societies, historically men have used a "restricted" appearance code and women have used an "elaborated" code (Davis, 1992). This can be observed in the slow changes in men's fashions in which styles are few as compared to changes in women's fashions, which have more variety in colors, textiles, and trims. Business dress practices have been particularly conservative and limited, but corporate casual dress involves wearing a more elaborated wardrobe of colors, textures, and garments. Because women have already used an elaborated code, it is the men's practice that is becoming more like the women's practice.

Peter Schwadel, a suit manufacturer, explains that casual dress "is all about self-expression, variations, and changes" (Gellers, 1995). But casual dress, not Schwadel's product—the suit—is the type of dress that allows for the broader range of expression and variations for men. The result of the expression of a more elaborated dress code is that increasing self-expression, or the process of individuation, confuses the meaning and reading of appearance symbols. The meanings associated with an old established social order no longer hold. The loss of the familiar appearance codes causes some people to experience confusion as

they adapt to the new code. It is this discomfort that negative critics use to claim that changing dress codes and practices in the workplace reflect a degeneration of the overall culture. Adler (1995), stringent in his condemnation of the trend, links dressing down to lost values. In his article, three image and text boxes treat the church, the corporation, and the academy. In the three comparisons, the gender- and class-conscious restricted dress codes of the 1950s are contrasted with modern casual styles practiced in these places. It is clear that the editorial perspective prefers the older, more rigid and, therefore, more easily read codes of the past. Belcove (1996), in an ironic twist, implores the casual-dressing, self-expressing Bill Gates to undertake vanity plastic surgery on his face. Yet, since this practice is more common for women than for men, Belcove links Gates's self-expression to historically feminine practices. The link of casual dress with increased expressiveness through a more elaborate dress code threatens the business status quo and reveals an underlying fear of feminization of the workplace.

Lastly, critics of casual dress propose that casual business dress wearers demonstrate a lack of self-control. Goldberg (1995) characterizes casual dress as "playclothes," showing that he interprets casual dress wearers as childish. This article attempts to merge corporate casual dress with feminine behaviors. Qualities of expressiveness, through dress and other means of communication, are linked to historically patriarchal views of women as lower in status and power (i.e., playful children).

Several issues are raised by examining the negative press of dressing down. They include trends toward androgynous dress, trends to increase individuation, efforts to decipher social clothing codes, and changing gender roles and dress. The shift to a more androgynous style of dress may reflect cultural adjustment to less stereotyped conceptions of masculine and feminine gender roles. Perhaps it is to protest these changes in the fabric of corporate life that criticism has been directed at casual dress. The extension of self-expression and assistance to the blurring or loss of class and gender codes caused by casual dress has resulted in critics' attacks on the style. Yet, the critics do not directly address their fear that the fashion trend is feminizing the workplace.

References

Adler, J. (1995, February 20). Have we become a nation of slobs? *Newsweek*, pp. 56–62.

Belcove, J. (1996, April). Fixing Mr. Gates. W , p. 60, supplement.

Bragg, R. (1994, July 15). Nowadays, workers enjoy dressing down for the job. *New York Times*, pp. A1, A8.

Davis, F. (1992). *Fashion, culture, and identity.* Chicago, IL: The University of Chicago Press.

Gellers, S. (1995, October 26). Executive Fridaywear teams suits with knits. *Daily News Record*, pp. 1, 5.

Goldberg, R. (1995, January 16). Manager's journal: This fad deserves a dressing down. *The Wall Street Journal*, p. A14.

DISCUSSION QUESTIONS

An Interpretation of Negative Press Coverage of Casual Dress

1. Lillethun presents one interpretation of negative press coverage of casual dress. Why do you think casual dress was negatively reviewed by some members of the press?

2. If you had to pick one factor that was the most influential for the development of casual dress, what would it be? Why?

42 Negotiations @ Work: The Casual Businesswear Trend

Teresa Janus
Susan B. Kaiser
University of California–Davis

Gordon Gray

In the black—Futures are always risky, but you'd bet the bank on one thing—dress-down will once again sweep the workweek. Today's dramatic tip: a softly constructed, two-button black blazer that practically oozes confidence (quietly so). Superb blend of 70% wool, 20% nylon and 10% cashmere slips over sweaters and tees; tapered seaming makes it fine over a dress shirt. Padded shoulders; acetate lining. Also in Tan. Imported for even sizes 38–46. Dry clean. $159.00. (Coldwater Creek, 1997, p. 58)

I call it my inventory problem...I have ten suits, and I have twenty-five button-down shirts and I've got a slew of nice ties. I'm not gonna just stop wearing those, because I work at a place that does casual. And then also, I'd have that same stressful situation Monday through Friday that I now have on Fridays, 'cause I don't know how to put the stuff together...[My wife] hates Friday mornings, because I'm always begging her: "What should I wear? What should I wear?" And she tells me what to wear. But it's like...I don't always remember...something about lights and darks. I hate casual Fridays. [Other days?] Easy; I've done this [have worn suits] for, you know, over ten years....(White male vice president in a large bank's corporate office, 33 years old)

For some professionals, at least, the idea of "dressing down" may not exactly ooze a sense of confidence. For others, what has become hailed by many analysts as a sea change in professional wear may offer a welcome shift from more traditional ways of doing business. In mapping the trend toward casual businesswear, perhaps one can at least "bet the bank" on the idea that there are profits to be made in some segments of the apparel industry—especially in menswear. The acceptance of casualwear for men has modified the working wardrobe, with a range of jackets, slacks, and shirts challenging the dominance of the formal suit, business shirt, and tie. A few more suits and ties may move to the back of the closet as they are replaced by new separates and as a fundamental change in workplace fashion seems to be sweeping many companies. This trend toward casual businesswear began with high-tech firms and has moved to such companies as Ford and Procter & Gamble. In some firms, casual Fridays have extended to everyday casual (Mannix, 1997). Companies appear to be adapting to a changing business climate by exploring new ways of doing business: negotiated ways that inevitably touch on issues of gender and race/ethnicity (as more women and minorities have a visual impact on business culture); generation (as more baby boomers—known for being casual—obtain positions of authority); and general profitability (as employers devise "perks" other than salary increases for employees). The apparel and retail industries, of course, are pleased to comply with the trend toward casual businesswear and, in many ways, shape its course by influencing not only consumers, but also companies through publicity campaigns aimed at casualizing the work force. Levi Strauss, for example, offers human resource managers information about the casual businesswear trend, including videos, a newsletter, a "portfolio," and phone consultation. On the one hand, the trend toward casual dress offers employees, as consumers, possibilities for creatively negotiating new looks through the mixing and matching of

casual separates into new business looks. On the other hand, consumers shoulder much of the economic responsibility for the trend, and some may lack the financial or creative resources to pull the trend off with ease. In addition to costs at the retail cash registers, some employees are required to contribute modest amounts to charitable causes in order to dress casually.

We use a "negotiations @ work" perspective in an attempt to understand the interplay among company, industry, and consumer contributions to the trend. In many ways, developments in casual businesswear provide a unique opportunity to study a fashion process that is occurring right now. Here we are especially interested in the following two questions: What kinds of negotiations are at work? What do these negotiations have to say about the fashioning of everyday identities and organizational cultures?

To explore these questions, we draw on an analysis of three sources: 1) the popular and business literature on changes in organizational culture; 2) industry trends and advertising/publicity appeals; and 3) a larger study based on in-depth interviews with 31 college-educated professionals, ranging in age from 27 to 60 years. Twenty-five men and six women were interviewed. The major focus of this study was menswear, but because we believe gender negotiations at work to be one of the vital factors in the casual businesswear trend, we were also very interested in women's perspectives and clothing choices. One third of the professionals were nonwhite, representing African American, Chinese American, Filipino American, Iranian American, and Mexican American cultural backgrounds. The interviews were usually conducted in the work setting, with both the private and the public sectors represented in three California locations: the Silicon Valley, San Francisco and Sacramento. In popular accounts (e.g., Walsh, 1994), California is described as leading the casual businesswear phenomenon, based in part on the informal culture of high-tech organizations, large apparel companies focusing on separates (e.g., Levi Strauss, GAP, Esprit), and a relatively casual consumer lifestyle.

The clothes people wear to work provide clues on shifts in organizational culture. Some analysts suggest that there has been a "loosening of ties" between individuals and the organizations for which they work. A high frequency of mergers and acquisitions has contributed to a declining commitment of employees to organizations, resulting in a central need for companies to manage organizational culture and diversity among employees (Alvesson & Berg, 1992). Most companies have historically been hierarchical, with multiple layers of management. They have had strong boundaries between management and staff, with clothes to match a worker's level of status and with a relatively high degree of conformity within each classification. Decisions have been centralized and tightly controlled. As a departure from these structures, team cultures have been emerging in some organizations, especially in high-tech companies requiring multiple approaches to problem-solving. Firms with team cultures are described as "flatter" or matrixed, and as having fewer managerial demarcations and hierarchical boundaries. Status is said to come from the ability to master problems and situations—across boundaries. Decision-making is described as decentralized and more widespread. In a team environment, boundaries become fuzzier and structure is more nebulous. The safety net of hierarchy is supposed to be lost (Sherriton & Stern, 1997). But is hierarchy truly gone? Some critics would argue that it is folks at the "top" who are still managing organizational culture and diversity in the workplace. A male professional describes the top echelon of a company he has been auditing:

> The very top floor is where their chief executive officer and their corporate lawyers are. And the vice president. So all their bigwig offices are on the sixth floor. Now that floor has a different atmosphere than any of the other buildings or any of the other floors in this building....They do predominantely wear suits, white shirts, sometimes striped. I haven't seen color up there. Dark suits. Dark ties.

For some executives and some companies, as another professional notes, "it's that simple rule; rotate the suits." A vice president at a large computer firm, in his 40s, who now dresses down on Fridays, comments that many people "haven't really quite figured" out what it means to mix-and-match casual separates in a business context:

> It's what you get used to. I mean, after 18 or 19 years, I guess I am comfortable in a suit....I did not catch on ten years ago onto this Friday casual thing....The CEO of the company [where he used to work] had to, you know, sort of...good humoredly reprimand me a couple times. And then I started moving to the point where I'd have slacks and a blazer, and I'd keep my tie in my, you know, pocket, just in case, you know, I might get called to go to San Francisco. (He goes on to share a story about going with casually dressed colleagues to a restaurant in San Francisco with a tie-only dress code. One of his colleagues had to borrow a tie from the restaurant, and it didn't work very well with his casual shirt.)

Some successful younger men may resist the trend toward casualwear, feeling that they have worked hard and want their clothes to reflect their status, or that it is more of a hassle to mix-and-match separates. The banker quoted at the beginning of this article is a good example.

A 57-year-old white female attorney comments that most men in her firm are "still in the suit schtick," but that there has been a shift toward more variety in style:

> Through the 80s and into the 90s, it was blue suit city around here. But now, now we're getting a lot more variety in the colors and the fabrics that they wear. But they're still wearing the pants and dress shirts and ties and jackets...except for the last Friday in the month.

An African American male attorney working for another firm notes some changes, as well: "It used to be much, much more formal, or if not formal, maybe formulaic is the way to say it."

Some critics of the casual businesswear trend note that going casual does not do away with hierarchy. In some firms, top management continues to wear suits; in others, "it might as well be a suit," as one top executive points out, because the separates worn by colleagues at his level are very expensive. He indicates that "we're all slowly adjusting [to casualwear], you know, and buying a little bit better…sports coats instead of the next suit." Brand consciousness is high, with Polo, Armani, Rolex watches, and other symbols (e.g., Porsches) continuing to convey status and wealth. The professionals use terms like "casually nice" and "high-end casual" to describe their new separates. One notes that "actually, this stuff on the weekend is more expensive than work stuff."

Much of the expense for consumers comes from the immersion into mixing and matching. One writer argues that although casual Fridays were supposed to be about men rejecting the uniformity of the suit, in reality, "that's backward":

> Men started wearing khakis to work because Dockers and Haggar made it sound as if khakis were going to be even easier than a suit. The khaki-makers realized that men didn't want to get rid of uniforms; they just wanted a better uniform. The irony, of course, is that this idea of nonfashion—of khakis as the choice that diminishes, rather than enhances, the demands of fashion—turned out to be a white lie. Once you buy even the plainest pair of khakis, you invariably also buy a sports jacket and a belt and a whole series of shirts to go with it…and before long your closet is thick with just the kinds of details and options that you thought you were avoiding.…[K]hakis, even as they have simplified the bottom half of the male wardrobe, have forced a steady revision of the top. (Gladwell, 1997)

Most professionals agree that there are more colors, textures, and styles in the workplace. Some of this variety can be attributed to increasing gender and ethnic diversity. Although many of the hierarchies remain intact, this diversity influences the visual negotiations at work. A 30-year-old Filipino American male auditor notes:

> The women—they wear so many different things…And I think that kind of interplay between men and women—it's going to change attitudes that men have about how they dress themselves. Like, for example, some of the ties that I wear are—I would say—are on the cutting edge of what you would want to wear in a business environment. They're

things that you wouldn't think of wearing them, but if you do you kind of say, "Oh yeah; I guess that's okay; that's kind of neat actually." And some of the women in the office…would compliment us [he and his male colleagues] on the tie or the design on our tie. And that has helped me define what kind of other ties I may buy in the future.

The process of creating looks every day through a mixing and matching of separates is probably more familiar to women and to professionals in minority cultures (e.g., African American culture, gay male culture; see Kaiser, 1997). Individuals and communities who traditionally have had less power seem to use style as a visual resource for expressing identity, community values, and resistance to dominant culture (Barnard, 1997; Freitas et al., 1997; Kaiser, 1997; O'Neal, 1998). To some, the ongoing process of coordinating separates may symbolize change or even assurance.

A 31-year-old Chinese American woman who works for a transportation company notes that she has always thought about "mix-and-match" as a way of making people "think you're always looking different." She also indicates that if people feel comfortable, "maybe they feel that they're more productive and happier and stuff like that.… Sometimes, like when I'm in my jeans, I like really…enjoy going, oh, Friday, I don't have to put my suit on…I'm like all psyched."

Yet some critics argue that those who have traditionally had less power cannot afford to abandon traditional business symbols in favor of casualwear. In some ways, they are the ones who have the least to gain from the casual business-wear trend, because unless status hierarchies can be truly broken down, this trend may serve to "keep them in their place" and reinforce the glass ceiling. For many companies, there is an increasing goal toward the appearance of power becoming diffused throughout the culture of the organization, with increased motives for productivity and consensus rather than conflict. Diversity management, some argue, seems to reflect a genuine attention to and sophisticated analysis of identity differences in the workplace. Yet it can also have the effect of cultural difference becoming absorbed into the culture of the organization, without truly doing away with hierarchy. The distinction between at-home appearances and those in the workplace become "managed" in the workplace in a way that keeps workers "comfortable." As one 27-year-old Chinese American male software engineer comments, [the company] "keep[s] you like a family member, I guess."

Among all of the complexities involved in unraveling the casual businesswear trend, at least one thing appears to be certain: the need for more daily negotiations at work. Several professionals comment on the influence of clothes on business interactions and organizational culture. For example, if one is not wearing a suit, the other party has to understand why that is so and "sort of make peace with that" to maintain the business interaction. Additionally, it is important "that clothes won't be a barrier." In State government, where the profit motivation is not as intense as it is in the private business sector, casual businesswear is described as "casual economy." The status symbolism may not be as intense as it is in the private sector, but status and power relations still need to be communicated and understood.

These questions remain: Is the casual businesswear trend part of a huge makeover of the workplace? Who is shaping the trend, and who wants it to occur? Who stands most to profit—to end up "in the black"? Are hierarchies truly breaking down, and if so, who will benefit, in the long run? Clearly, further study is needed to understand this trend in terms of its implications for individuals and communities who have traditionally had less power. Hearing the voices of individuals in a wide variety of geographic locations nationally and internationally can contribute to a broader understanding of the complex interplay among organizational culture, the apparel industry, and what it means to be a consumer and a worker in contemporary society. Some kind of blurring of traditional boundaries seems to be underway; yet many new questions emerge in the context of a global economy where it remains to be seen who will gain from new ways of doing business, new consumer markets, and new strategies for understanding identity and difference.

References

Alvesson, M., & Berg, P. O. (1992). *Corporate culture and organizational symbolism*. New York: Walter de Gruyter.

Barnard, M. (1997). *Fashion as communication*. London and New York: Routledge.

Coldwater Creek: Milepost four—Clothing for men. (1997, Autumn).

Freitas, A. J., Kaiser, S. B., Chandler, J. L., Hall, C. L., Kim, J-W., & Hammidi, T. N. (1997). Appearance management as border construction: Least favorite clothing, group distancing, and identity...not! *Sociological Inquiry, 67*(3), 323–335.

Gladwell, M. (1997, July 28). Listening to khakis: What America's most popular pants tell us about the way guys think. *The New Yorker, 73*(21), 54–65.

Kaiser, S. B. (1997). *The social psychology of clothing: Symbolic appearances in context (2nd edition, revised)*. New York, NY: Fairchild.

Mannix, M. (1997, August 4). Casual Friday, five days a week. *U. S. News and World Report*.

O'Neal, G. (1998). African American aesthetic of dress: Current manifestations.

Clothing and Textiles Research Journal, 16(4), pp. 167–175.

Sherriton J. C., & Stern, J. L. (1997). *Corporate culture, team culture: Removing the hidden barriers to team success*. New York: Amacom/American Management Association.

Walsh, P. (1994, May 23). How to wear FridayWear in and around the boardroom. *Daily News Record*.

Negotiations @ Work: The Casual Businesswear Trend

1. Janus, Kaiser, and Gray cite several ways that the transition to casual dress has been a difficult one. Identifying the structural changes that have been affected by casual dress would indicate some of the sources of confusion behind the dress changes. What have the changes in dress signified?

2. Given the confusion that casual business dress has created for its wearers (especially men) at the onset of casual dress days, where do you think this trend is headed in the future? Will casual dress days become the norm, will they disappear completely, or will we have a new type of business dress that is in between all casual and all formal business dress? Give reasons supporting your position.

43 Women's Images in Corporate Culture: The Case of Casual Day

Patricia A. Kimle
Mary Lynn Damhorst
Iowa State University

"Casual day" is a recent phenomenon during which businesses suspend more formal dress codes, written and unwritten, on one day or week and encourage employees to wear more casual clothing to work. Casual day is becoming a widespread practice among businesses of all types and sizes.

We wanted to explore business women's attitudes toward and experiences with casual days. For this study 24 female managers and executives in the Des Moines, Iowa, business community were interviewed during 1994. These findings were part of a larger study that explored images of women in business careers (Kimle, 1994; Kimle & Damhorst, 1997). Women are still a minority in upper ranks of most U.S. business organizations and have not yet become an entrenched part of the hegemonic ruling class. We wondered if their minority status influenced their feelings about casual days.

Although business dress formality is suspended for casual days, rules still apply, and a new set of rules is emerging. Casual days require conformity to a new standard, which in many cases has yet to be clearly defined. As a result, some employees approach casual days with uncertainty. The women in this study reported they were generally comfortable with the concept of casual day, but, in their opinion, the men they worked with often were not. One middle manager for an international agricultural products firm described responses of her male and female employees to an invitation to wear casual dress to a business meeting:

> On the last [meeting] agenda I put out, I said, "Wear casual business attire." I almost just said "casual," but I didn't want people to come dressed in jeans. But I also didn't need the tie or the hose for women. I got a couple of phone calls from men asking, "What the heck is casual business attire?" I didn't hear from any of the women. Men seem to be having a terrible time negotiating what to do on a casual

day. Some of them just wear the dress slacks and the shirt, and leave off the tie. They walk around and you can tell they are completely uncomfortable.

Women may be more comfortable with the shift in rules on casual day because they are familiar with the processes of "constructing" themselves via dress for various contexts. They are socialized to spend time on appearance and are, therefore, highly attuned to the capabilities of clothing to send messages and influence interactions. Men are socialized to focus more on their clothing as an indicator of past accomplishments in certain situations (Kaiser, Freeman, & Chandler, 1993). But casual dress is intended to foster equality, similarity, and camaraderie among employees and deemphasize status differences. For some men, the vague rules for casual dress and lack of obvious visual expression of accomplishment and status in the workplace require a new way of thinking about dressing for work.

Business dress, by emphasizing conformity and similarity among group members, can create a variety of organizational dynamics. Dress contributes to the image of the organization (Rafaeli & Pratt, 1993), and casual dress emphasizes group cohesion. Dress also helps employees identify with work and the organization. An organization that allows casual days says to its employees that it is okay to relax and be themselves rather than appear in the corporate, self-masking uniform at all times.

The participants in this study recognized an inherent risk in relaxing the standards of business dress for casual day. The risk is that workers will appear to be less professional, less businesslike, and less competent. This risk is allegedly neutralized when everyone in a group participates in casual day. However, casual day was often a source of stress among group members when someone elected not to participate for some reason. The middle manager we heard from earlier describes such an incident:

It seems to be a way to build staff morale now. Once in a while, we have a casual day on a Friday. Then if everyone does it, it's more acceptable than if just you are at work in a sweatshirt and everyone else has suits on. You would feel very uncomfortable....When we have had casual days and for some reason I had an appointment that day and dressed up...then either I'm uncomfortable or I have made other staff uncomfortable. They say: "Well, are you really going to dress casual tomorrow, or are you just saying that you are?" Comments like that make you realize that it bothers them that they took the risk of coming in casual and you didn't....I think it's that perception about skill and ability and credibility. Those are not there if you're wearing jeans.

An executive in a banking industry association described the distancing among employees caused by a "deviant" who refused to go along with casual day:

There's one person in our office who will still dress up in a very nice dress or suit even on casual day. She is trying to portray the image of professionalism; she doesn't believe in the casualwear thing. I think she likes the image of being up above. It separates her from other people. Its almost like she's too good to dress down like everyone else.

On the other hand, casual day is often considered subordinate to normal business activities. The women interviewed expected that casual day should be suspended when there was something special going on in the office, such as a visit from a client or an important presentation to give. A communications specialist relates such an incident:

Once a month, we have a casual day. I never really pay much attention to it, because usually, we have something going on. For example, this last Friday, a colleague and I were presenting a new program idea to our CEO. He came dressed in just a sweater. Clearly he was observing casual day. It didn't occur to us to dress casually at all. I don't care that it's casual day, I'm presenting an important idea. And actually, his dressing that way made me uncomfortable. But you see, he's above us, so that must go without saying.

Uniform acceptance of casual day seemed to foster *esprit de corps* among coworkers (Joseph & Alex, 1972). If not uniformly adopted, commitment of all workers to harmonious group interaction and collaboration came into question. The women seemed to enjoy casual days, but only if others went along with the practice. Perhaps women's minority status in upper management and executive ranks makes them uneasy about the risk of losing "face" when all do not comply with casual norms. Casual day can disrupt the flow of established relationships in the business office, if hierarchical differences are normally expressed. The women we interviewed overall viewed "dressing down" and eliminating some of the barriers to personal expression on casual day as a valuable benefit of working in some organizations.

References

Joseph, N., & Alex, N. 1972. The uniform: A sociological perspective. *American Journal of Sociology, 77,* 719–730.

Kaiser, S. B., Freeman, C. M., & Chandler, J. M. (1993). Favorite clothes and gendered subjectivities: Multiple readings. *Studies in symbolic interaction, 15,* 27–50.

Kimle, P. A. (1994). *Business women's appearance management, career development, and sexual harassment.* Doctoral dissertation, Ames: Iowa State University.

Kimle, P. A., & Damhorst, M. L. (1997). A grounded theory model of the ideal business image for women. *Symbolic Interaction, 20,* 45–68.

Rafaeli, A., & Pratt, M. G. (1993). Tailored meanings: On the meaning and impact of organizational dress. *Academy of Management Review, 18*(1), 32–55.

DISCUSSION QUESTIONS

Women's Images in Corporate Culture: The Case of Casual Day

1. Why do you think that women are more comfortable with casual dress days than men?

2. What happens when casual dress days are not observed uniformly by everyone in the office setting? What dynamics come into play when someone chooses not to observe casual dress day?

44 Business Casual Dress: An African American Male Perspective

Harriet McLeod
Iowa State University

This article is part of a larger study that examined African American business men's dress in a major Midwest city. Very little research has focused on how African American executives or managers expressed themselves through their business attire, their perception of the impression they made with their dress to different audiences, and their assessment of the usefulness of their appearance in maintaining and furthering their careers. In talking with these informants about the above issues, the phenomenon of casual day dressing at work was discussed. The following comments, including the researcher's analysis, represent the major themes that emerged from those discussions.

Fifteen African American male executives, managers, professionals, and administrators in Des Moines, Iowa, were interviewed about their participation in casual days at work. A number of informants were employers or employees at businesses that practiced dress down/casual day, similar to a trend in 1995 that was practiced at 70 percent of major U.S. corporations (Longo, 1995) or by 90 percent of U.S. workers (Dressing in America, 1995). Only five (33 percent) of the men in this study wore items they considered casual clothing to work. Casual attire included open-neck shirts, either plaid wovens or knitted sports, with Dockers or khaki pants. Nine (60 percent) of the informants wore a more dressy "corporate casual" attire, which included blazers or sport coats with ties and slacks on designated casual days or when the informants selected (see Figure 7.5).

One last informant, a facilities manager, explained he always wore a suit because as manager he was ultimately responsible for operations at that location. His job involved a high level of involvement with the public at his office location, as well as the possibility for impromptu meetings away from his office.

...you may not plan to go out of the office that particular day, but sometimes you get called out and you may have to go, and one should dress appropriately at all times. (#5 — Facilities Manager)

Similarly, the men who wore corporate casual dress also sensed the need to be dressed professionally at all times in the event of a

FIGURE 7.5 *African-American males have a dressier version of "corporate casual" attire because of the possibility of negative perceptions by others.*

chance meeting with a client or customer. Furthermore, casual dress was not adopted on a limited or regular basis by all companies that the informants interacted with and could create dissonance during business meetings.

> I think it is kind of cumbersome, particularly when you are dealing with external customers, and if they are not necessarily involved or accustomed to casual dress, then it puts you in an awkward situation. I know that I have had luncheon meetings and taken people, my guests, to our executive dining room and there were people walking around with blue jeans on. So it is kind of awkward in some instances because I don't think everyone appreciates the nature of it. (#7—Legal Coordinator)

Some of the informants maintained that their executive or managerial roles required them to "look in charge" at all times. Casual attire did not identify them in that capacity.

> I will not go into a plant location, I say, wearing jeans and a sweat shirt, but I will go in a very casual way, but not to that extent…[I] still want to be in a place (style of dress) so that I am not confused with the people working in the plant. (#13—Director of Human Resources)

Popular literature is replete with articles debating the merits of casual dress. One opinion is "…if you look sharp, you're more likely to act sharp" (Falconi, 1996). A contrasting point of view is that formal dress, (i.e., a traditional business suit) "impedes communication" (Verespej, 1994). Some of the informants felt that dress that is too casual could affect their sense of professionalism or productivity.

> I think that if you are in business you should dress professional every day, but that is my own personal opinion.…I don't feel that I'm at work a lot of times if I'm not dressed professional. (#3—Sales Analyst)
>
> Well, I'd rather have a shirt and tie on for the week. Now one day casual is fine. It doesn't affect my work, but image-wise you project a better image [when you wear a shirt and tie] (#2—Credit Analyst)

> You know when you wear a suit and tie…versus dressing with a casual shirt and pair of jeans, I think people do respond to you more so. In fact I know that people will respond to you more readily or quickly when you wear a suit and tie. (#15—Investigative Agent)

In addition to how casual dress influenced their self-image as professionals, the informants also believed that casual dress could affect how professional they appeared to others.

Several of the men commented on the future of casual dress at work:

> It won't last. It is a trend. The dress down, it won't last. The consumer—and we all in this world are trying to make contact with a consumer—a consumer expects certain standards. A consumer is going to expect certain levels that are uniform. A consumer expects certain consistencies, some predictability. If you get to the point that you lost that, then you are going to lose the [consumer's confidence] because along with that product comes the person who serves and represents that product. (#1—Insurance Agent)

The majority of men felt casual dressing at work was a trend. However, one informant whose company was engaged in diversity training believed as businesses became more tolerant of diversity in their environments, their attitudes about what is appropriate for business dress would change also.

> I can see how even some dress standards may be even more relaxed in years to come if we continue to move in this direction that I see us going in the company…Our company, represents the good old Midwestern value, hard work, very conservative, very traditional in thinking, everybody in the company looked the same, even the black folks were an exception to the rule. That is very different now. In the last three years we have seen the racial composition, the ethnic composition of our company change. (#7—Legal Coordinator)

For the majority of these men, casual dress was not viewed as a welcomed escape from the traditional dress code of the business environment. Wearing casual clothing, albeit corporate casual, affected the men's feeling of professionalism and could influence how they were perceived by others. The possibility of a negative perception from others was a major reason why some of the men declined to wear casual dress. As one African American scholar asserted, "the same rules that apply to whites do not apply to African Americans in U.S. society" (O'Neal, 1996). O'Neal's conclusion may be an explanation as to why these men did not feel comfortable dressing too casually at work.

One informant remarked that his professional dress as well as his attitude about business dress may differ from his white coworkers:

> A lot of them (white males) like to be casual everyday....When they go on trips, they typically go somewhere and go casual. They might not have a shirt and tie on when they go into a dealership, but that's them. I'm the only one that is me. So I look at it totally different. Business is business, I don't take it casually or lightly. You have to treat it as business. (#2—Credit Analyst)

Casual dress may be seen by some African Americans as a rule or dress code practiced in white corporate America, but it does not apply to them. Ethnic identity was a more powerful influence for the men when they were confronted with issues related to casual dress at work. As one informant stated:

> I do know that I truly believe that people of color and women are held to a different standard. And I never forget that, and that could be probably more my paranoia/neurosis than truth. It doesn't matter, it is my perception....No, I would never come in here on a work day with an open collar, and I don't care who else would do it. (#12—Director of Human Resources)

References

Dressing in America. (1995, March). *Bobbin, 36*, 114.

Falconi, R. R. (1996, January/February). If you want to move up, don't dress down. *Financial Executive, 12*, 13–14.

Longo, D. (1995, June 5). On casual days, Antonini didn't get it either. *Discount Store News, 34*, 15.

O'Neal, G. (1996, August 2). Personal communication.

Verespej, M. A. (1994, March 21). Goodbye, status—Hello, communication. *Industry Week, 243*, 9.

DISCUSSION QUESTIONS

Business Casual Dress: An African American Male Perspective

1. Why do you think that some of the African American business men interviewed in the study regarded casual dress days as a dress code practiced more by white corporate America than by African Americans?

2. Several African American men see casual dressing at work as a trend that will not last, especially if the casual dress trend affects consumer confidence. Others think that casual dressing is not here to stay but it will have a lasting effect on appropriate business dress in the future. With which viewpoint do you agree? Or do you see another outcome of casual dressing?

45   Economic Impacts of Casual Business Attire on the Market for Textiles and Apparel

Margaret Rucker
University of California, Davis

Although researchers have been interested in the role of clothing in the workplace for a number of years (cf., Form & Stone, 1955), this topic has received heightened attention in the last few years as a result of changes in business dress codes. As employees have been permitted or actually encouraged to "dress down," questions have been raised about just what constitutes appropriate dress under the new rules. Both academic and popular sources have attempted to provide some answers (e.g., Omelianuc, 1996; Woodard, 1997). In addition to investigating what types of items are acceptable in today's workplace, researchers have also asked how employees, as well as their supervisors and their clients, have been affected by changes in business dress codes (Giddings & Bellinger, 1997; Kwon & Hillery-Johnson, 1997; McCleod, 1996; Rucker, Anderson, & Kangas, in press; also see "Negotiations @ Work: The Casual Businesswear Trend, p. 264).

The impacts of changing business dress codes are not limited to the employees who wear the clothing, however. The changes have also affected all sectors of the textile and apparel industries, from fiber producers to retailers of apparel. The effects on each sector will be discussed below.

FIBERS

Cotton's share of the apparel market has increased substantially from the mid-1980s to the mid-1990s (from 38 percent to 65 percent). This increase has been attributed at least in part to the trend toward corporate casual (Anson, 1995; Brown, 1994). Cotton's core business is in commodity items such as jeans, T-shirts, and sweaters. Sales of these items have been increasing as more dress-down codes are including them on the list of garments that are acceptable

in the workplace. Rayon is another fiber that has benefited from the casual trend. Printed rayon shirts have become a popular component of the corporate casual look, thereby boosting the demand for that fiber. In contrast, wool's share of the apparel market has remained relatively stable during the past decade. Fewer men have been wearing wool suits to the office on a regular basis. However, The Wool Bureau has responded by promoting wool for casual business dress (Brown, 1994; Rudie, 1995.)

FIBERS, DYES, AND FINISHES

The trend toward more casual workwear has affected mills in several ways. One important issue has been how to ensure that customers will feel they are getting an appropriate return on their investments in casual business attire. Two main ways in which mills have tackled this problem include providing more interesting and varied textures and cutting costs. Brown (1994) cites Burlington Industries as an example of the former strategy. In ten years, Burlington went from producing only a few weaves for this men's market to making "thousands" of weaves. The other approach, cutting cost, has led to increases in the production of fabrics that blend less expensive fibers with those that are more expensive and relatively lightweight versions of some of the traditionally heavier fabrics such as denim (Rudie, 1995, 1996).

Corporate casual has also brought about a change in linings for apparel. One way to signal a change from a traditional sport coat to a casual jacket is to go from plain to fancy linings, and manufacturers have been doing just that. The distinction between solids and prints is also important for the tie market. Last year, tie compa-

Rucker, M. (1999). Economic Impacts of Casual Business Attire on the Market for Textiles and Apparel. In M.L. Damhorst, K.A. Miller and S.O Michelman's (Eds.)*The Meanings of Dress.* Fairchild Publications: New York

nies tried to be players in corporate casual by creating ties in casual (rough and rugged) materials such as denim. According to interviews with tie manufacturers, this approach generally was not successful. As one executive stated, if employees in casual attire wear a tie at all, they wear a novelty. The relationship of plain to dress-up and print to dress-down is considered so strong, in fact, that the industry is looking at purchases of solid ties as an indicator of a shift in attitude back to a more serious and dressed-up climate in many offices.

With respect to finishes, the shift to casual has been given credit for the popularity of wrinkle-resistant finishes. As an executive from Dan River Inc. pointed out in an interview with Abend (1996a), men are apt to send fine dress shirts to commercial dry cleaners but to subject casual clothing to home care.

Sales of dyes may also be affected by nuances in the new corporate dress codes. For example, the fact that some dress codes list black jeans as acceptable—while blue jeans are not acceptable—may increase the sales of dyes for the former and decrease it for the latter.

In addition to affecting the production of fabrics, the shift in dress codes is also having an influence on the marketing of fabrics. For example, Première Vision, a major European fabric show, has just added an Activewear Forum. Friday wear was mentioned by the show's organizers as a guiding force behind the reorganization (Maycumber, 1997).

APPAREL

Perhaps the most obvious impact of casual business dress on the apparel industry has been on the sales of tailored clothing versus sportswear. According to Edmondson (1996), there was a 37 percent drop in spending on men's suits from 1990 to 1994. Abend (1996b) noted that the middle-range manufacturers of tailored clothing have been especially hard hit by the trend toward casual; a number have gone out of business including such former stalwarts as L. Greif, Kuppenheimer, and Eagle. Other tailored clothing makers have tried to survive the trend by entering the casualwear business themselves. To capitalize on the concern for comfort, such tra-

ditional suitmakers as Brooks Brothers have produced lines of businesswear with a looser, baggier appearance (Brown, 1994).

On the other hand, as noted by Brown (1994), many companies and designers who have always specialized in sportswear have benefited from the redefinition of acceptable business attire. Those cited by Brown as being particularly successful in capitalizing on a casual image include Ralph Lauren, Tommy Hilfiger, Nautica and the Docker's division of Levi Strauss. Furthermore, companies that were once typed as sports outfitters are now being classified as mainstream clothing companies. Success stories here include Eddie Bauer and Timberland.

The loosening of business dress codes has also created winners and losers in the hosiery and shoe industries. In hosiery, both men and women have often switched to casual socks as opposed to dress socks or pantyhose. Tights have also proved to be a strong alternative to sheer pantyhose for working women (Abend, 1995; Rabon, 1995). As for shoes, sales of men's dress shoes and athletic shoes have slowed while sales of hiking shoes, boots and sandals have risen, according to Brown (1994). Walsh (1994) also commented on the popularity of sandals as a complement to casual linen outfits.

Changing fashion rules in the workplace have resulted in sluggish sales for neckwear. Such casual shirt styles as the banded collar have contributed to the decline of interest in ties, according to Hart (1994).

Similar to mills, apparel manufacturers have been concerned about price resistance among customers for casual work clothing. In addition to looking to mills for more blends and lighter-weight fabrics, manufacturers of businesswear have been moving production to lower-wage countries to cut their costs (Abend, 1995).

Marketing of apparel has also changed in response to the trend toward casual clothing in the workplace. For example, Haggar Clothing Co. boosted its marketing budget 35 percent in 1994 to fuel its casual dressing campaign (Haggar Clothing Co., 1995). Buying offices have also felt the need to spend time and money to conduct clinics on "Friday wear" for retailers in need of guidance (Kaplan, 1994).

RETAILING

Sales of suits and suit separates have declined appreciably from the 1980s to the 1990s. For example, Webb (1994) cited statistics from the NPD Group market research company indicating that sales of suits and suit separates fell from $4.2 billion in 1988 to $3.8 billion in 1992. Moreover, retailers have reported a drop in dress shirt sales paralleling the drop in the suit business. This latter drop has caused concern about inventory control. To reduce the inventory of dress shirts, there has been some pressure applied to manufacturers to supply this product in small, medium, large, and extra large, rather than the more traditional sizing system that had each of a number of neck sizes paired with a series of sleeve lengths.

On the other hand, retailers of sportswear, as with manufacturers of sportswear, have done well as a result of the casual business climate. Sportswear companies that have been especially successful include the Gap, Lands' End, and L. L. Bean (Brown, 1994).

Individual items that have seen increases in sales thanks to the move to a more casual workplace include sweaters and golf/rugby shirts. Abend (1995) cited data collected by the NPD Group showing a four percent retail volume increase from 1991 to 1993 in sales of women's sweaters and also in sales of golf/rugby shirts. For men, there was an eight percent retail volume increase in golf/rugby shirts during the same time period. More recently, Homan (1997) noted that the persistence of the casual trend in the workplace has been reflected in the continued popularity of sweaters.

EFFECTS OF THE ECONOMY ON ACCEPTANCE OF CASUAL BUSINESS ATTIRE

In examining the trend toward casual dress in the workplace, one should consider economic causes as well as economic effects. For example, economists for the textile and apparel industries have noted for some time that whenever there is an economic downturn, consumers reduce spending on big ticket merchandise, which is mostly tailored clothing. Men's suits seem to be particularly sensitive to recessions (Priestland, 1972). Therefore, what we may have in the corporate casual trend is a social movement taking advantage of an economic cycle. At the very least, this possibility deserves further exploration.

References

Abend, J. (1995). Capitalizing on casual. *Bobbin*, 36(7),112–116.

Abend, J. (1996a). Hand, styling drive wrinkle-resistant apparel. *Bobbin*, 37(5), 62–66.

Abend, J. (1996b). Makers pursue market niches, mixes. *Bobbin*, 37(7), 64–68.

Anson, R. (1995). U.S. cotton: A growing market. *Textile Horizons*, 15(4), 49–50.

Brown, C. (1994). Dressing down. *Forbes*, 154(13), 155–160.

Edmondson, B. (1996, January). The latest in spending. *American Demographics*, p. 2.

Form, W. H., & Stone, G. P. (1955). *The social significance of clothing in occupational life* (Technical Bulletin 247). East Lansing, MI: State College Agricultural Experiment Station.

Giddings, V. L., & Bellinger, V. (1997, November). An investigation of male and female employees' attitudes toward dressing down. Poster session presented at the annual meeting of ITAA, Knoxville, TN.

Haggar Clothing Co. (1995). *Bobbin*, 37(4), pp. 35–36.

Hart, E. (1994, August 5). Stores hot on casual looks in neckwear for Spring. *Daily News Record*, pp. 1, 5.

Homan, B. (1997, December 31). Comfort clothes: Designers cash in on the popularity of snuggy sweaters. *Entertainment Star*, p 1.

Kaplan, D. (1994, September 8). Buying offices to conduct clinics at MAGIC. *Daily News Record*, p 5.

Kwon, Y. H., & Hillery-Johnson, J. (1997, November). Perceptions of occupational attributes as determined by formality of business attire. Poster session presented at the annual meeting of ITAA, Knoxville, TN.

Maycumber, S. G. (1997, September 22). Premiere Vision creates new activewear section. *Daily News Record*, pp. 10, 12.

Omelianuc, J. S. (1996). *Work clothes*. New York: Alfred A. Knopf.

Priestland, C. (1972, April). Life-style, fashion, and the economy. *Apparel Manufacturer*. Reprinted in J. A. Jarnow, & B. Judelle (1974). Inside the fashion business (2nd ed.). New York: Wiley.

Rabon, L. (1995). Makers target new benchmarks. *Bobbin*, 37(4), 60–62.

Rucker, M., Anderson, E., & Kangas, A. (in press). Clothing, power and the workplace. In K. Johnson & S. Lennon (Eds.), *Appearance and power*. Oxford, England: Berg Publications.

Rudie, R. (1995). American mills take an elegant approach to dressing down. *Bobbin*, 37(2), 46–50.

Rudie, R. (1996). Denim does Spring. *Bobbin*, 37(8), 34–37.

Walsh, P. (1994, March 30). It's Spring, it's sportswear, it's linen. *Daily News Record*, pp. 1, 5.

Webb, B. (1994). Dressing down is up. *Bobbin*, 35(11), 4.

Woodard, G. (1997, November). *Casual apparel in the workplace: What's in and what's out.* Poster session presented at the annual meeting of the ITAA, Knoxville, TN.

DISCUSSION QUESTIONS

Economic Impacts of Casual Business Attire on the Market for Textiles and Apparel

1. Do you agree with Rucker's suggestion that the casual dress phenomenon coincided with an economic downturn? Why or why not?

2. Rucker notes that the casual dress trend is good for sportswear companies (e.g., L.L. Bean, Lands' End, Gap) and not so good for middle-range manufacturers of tailored clothing (e.g., Kuppenheimer and Eagle). If you were planning to enter the apparel and textile business within the next 12 to 18 months, which direction would you take? Why?

CHAPTER 8

Dress from Infancy to Adolescence

Mary Lynn Damhorst

AFTER YOU HAVE READ THIS CHAPTER, YOU WILL COMPREHEND:

- The many ways in which dress and appearance are an important part of childhood and adolescence.

- Physical, cognitive, emotional, and social aspects of dress and human development.

- How both the family and society invest identities in children through dress.

- How conformity and similarity in appearance can be positive experiences during childhood and adolescent development.

As we age, human lifespan stages shape the types of roles we take on in society. At each stage, important developments occur in physical characteristics, thinking and knowledge, and social skills. Cognitive, social, emotional, and physical developments at each stage also influence needs for dress and how the individual becomes involved with appearance. We will take a quick tour through the lifespan stages in the next two chapters. In this chapter we look at childhood through adolescent stages of life. Chapter 9 considers adult life stages through the elder years. Our focus tends to be on individuals in U. S. society because of limited comparable information from other cultures.

CHILDHOOD

Dress and appearance are pertinent components in child development. We will consider how involvement with dress progresses at each major developmental stage. Approximate age divisions or "stages" within which major physical, cognitive, and socialization changes occur help to map development in relation to dress. The age divisions for major developmental changes vary by authority and focus of analysis; we will consider the following:

- **Infancy** from birth to six months.
- **Toddler stage** from six months to two years.
- **Early childhood** from two to six years.
- **Middle childhood** from six to ten years.

All children go through developmental stages in the order given, but the exact age at which each event happens varies (Flavell, 1977). Disabilities, of course, may prevent some individuals from reaching all stages. We will trace some of the major features of a child's developmental changes during all stages.

Physical Coordination

Infants are constantly moving when awake, though their movements have a small range as infants cannot yet walk or crawl. Clothing should not be too binding so as to allow small motor movements that facilitate an infant's exploration of the surrounding environment and development of such skills as reaching and grasping. During the toddler stage, large motor coordination progresses as the toddler learns to crawl and walk. The fit of clothing (i.e., loose but not too bulky) should not impede these activities and thus becomes more vital at this stage (Ryan, 1966; Stone & Sternweis, 1994). The transition from diapers to training pants usually begins during the toddler stage; this is an important step toward building a feeling of independence in the child.

Skills at physical activities increase as muscular coordination advances during early childhood. Fit, flexibility of materials, and comfort continue to be crucial for the child. Durability and safety (e.g., flame retardance, no swallowable or removable objects) of clothing and materials become increasingly important to anyone who purchases clothing for the child. Fine motor skill coordination also develops during early childhood. Clothing, dolls, and toys with large buttons, zippers, laces, and other fasteners can help children practice dressing skills (see Figure 8.1). During the early childhood years, many dressing skills are mastered, giving the child a sense of independence (Allen & Marotz, 1999). However, it may take until age nine or later that the child can handle more complex hair care and other grooming regimens.

The elementary schoolchild may enjoy sports activities, including the prestige that comes from accomplishments and involvement in sports. The child may like clothing that represents those sports (e.g., a soccer shirt or Nike brand clothing) or that associates the wearer with well-known sports figures (e.g., Air Jordan shoes).

Cognitive Development and Symbol Usage

During the infant months, sensory skills and memory structures develop. Clothing and blankets are part of the infant's tactile and visible environment. Textures and colors may be interesting and stimulating to an infant.

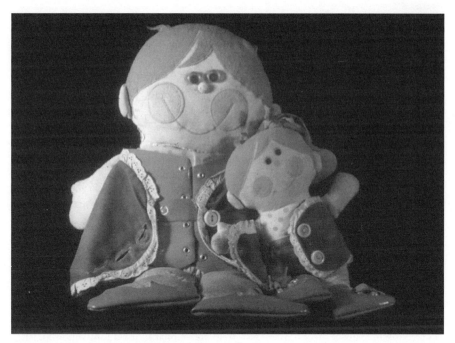

FIGURE 8.1 *Dressy Bessy teaching dolls by Playskool, circa 1970. Their buttons, laces, zippers, snaps, and buckles encouraged practice for little hands.*

By the toddler stage, the child recognizes people and objects and begins to develop a sense of ownership of clothing items (Allen & Marotz, 1999). Verbal skills also emerge during the toddler years. The child often learns names of colors, garment pieces, and recognizable figures in prints and embroidery, making clothing one of many tools in the process of learning how to talk.

By the end of early childhood the child moves into what Piaget called **concrete operations**, the stage during which the child develops, among other skills, basic math reasoning and ability to generalize (Schickedanz et al., 1998). Children can learn some cultural stereotypes, many triggered by appearance stigmas such as obesity, physical unattractiveness, and old age (Brylinsky & Moore, 1994). This is an important time for parents to be aware that peer groups and media may introduce negative and limiting stereotypes; parents need to talk openly with children about these stereotypes and their dangers.

Depending upon peer and family purchase patterns, apparel brand names and logos may become familiar symbols during early and middle childhood and may be highly desired by the child (Mayer & Belk, 1985). Brands are symbols that can develop meanings of acceptance and prestige and may help the child feel associated with a particular group or admired person. Berner in "Now Even Toddlers Are Dressing to the Nines" describes how children's apparel brands purchased by some families are challenging our sense of what should be spent on children's clothing. However, many children do not own the kind of wardrobes described by Berner; about 23% of children under the age of 6 and 18% of 6- to 17-year olds live in poverty in the United States today (Young Children Still Live in Poverty, 1993).

Socialization

Taking on the role of the other, that is, imagining how another person thinks, requires advanced cognitive development. Imagining the other's perspective is a crucial foundation for communication and socialization into society. Children start developing **role-taking** skills at an early age (Schickedanz et al., 1998). During the early childhood years, it is not unusual for children to **play with dress** to help them "put on a role" and experiment with identities, whether it be the identity of Wonder Woman, Darth Vadar, a mother, or an elephant (Stone, 1962). During middle childhood, play with dress and enjoyment of fantasy through Halloween and other costumes continues (see Figure 8.2). Toni Wood in "The Magic of Dress-Up" describes the benefits of play with dress for children.

During middle childhood, dressing for games also becomes common. Gregory Stone (1962) defined **game dress** as uniforms and team emblems that help the child identify and take on roles of self and other players in a game. Taking on the role of multiple others in a game is a complex cognitive task; game activity helps the child develop skills at thinking about perspectives of multiple others.

Throughout childhood, parents and guardians are continually dressing their children to conform to socioeconomic, gender, religious, and other role expectations. In addition, conformity in appearance becomes increasingly important to the child as she or he ages (Schickedanz et al., 1998). The toddler frequently mimics dress of others and begins to learn meanings of dress through adults' often bemused responses to imitations (Cahill, 1989). During early childhood, a garment similar to that of an admired parent, adult, or older sibling may make the child feel grown-up and similar to the admired person. Also, dressing like friends in preschool and in the neighborhood becomes increasingly important, and by middle childhood, fitting in with neighborhood friends and at school is highly important (Ryan, 1966). Conformity fosters a feeling of belonging; similarity helps the child feel socially comfortable. Uniforms may be well liked by a child, especially if the uniform links the child to a desired group such as a sports team or other youth groups such as the Boy Scouts. Even school uniforms may be liked if the child likes school.

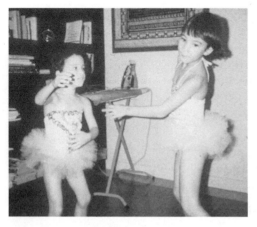

FIGURE 8.2 *A four- and a six-year-old put on the role of ballerina as they play in their tutus.*

Gender is learned through socialization and is expressed through dress as well as other behaviors. Infants and toddlers do not make independent choices for apparel, so purchase agents such as parents play a dominant role in "investing" gender in the child through selection of gender-specific apparel (Stone, 1962). Cahill (1989) noticed that day-care personnel and parents tend to reward both boys and girls for appearing in gender-specific clothing. By early childhood, play with dress also helps the child learn gender roles. Cahill described how preschool children up through age three seem quite comfortable playing with opposite gender roles. Play with clothing and makeup may be encouraged more among girls who are being socialized to develop greater interest in dress and the hedonic aspects of appearance. But around age four, boys in particular start to become increasingly sensitive to teasing and criticism from peers if they stray from the restricted code of menswear. As we saw in "Day-Care Dress Up Not

Amusing to Boy's Dad" (in Chapter 5), some parents are disturbed to see cross-dressing in their children. However, there is no evidence that cross-dressing during childhood necessarily leads to transvestism or homosexuality in adult life. By middle childhood, codes for gender appropriateness of dress are well learned (Kaiser, 1989), and are often believed more rigidly than apparent from the way the child actually dresses (Allen & Marotz, 1999).

Appearance Concerns

Engaging in dressing activities can be fun, and the gaudier and frillier the dress, the more fun it can be for many toddlers (Ryan, 1966). The toddler also learns that cute or new garments and clothing patterned with well-known cartoon characters and logos can generate positive responses from adults. The link of appearance to social rewards is established early in life. The intriguing world of beauty pageants for young girls in the United States is described in "Tots Grow Up Fast in Pageant World." This article questions whether extreme engrossment in appearance as an "occupation" for children ultimately puts too much emphasis on appearance in society. In addition, children are not immune to ideal images of thinness as attractive. Researchers are finding girls as young as four years old who express concerns about their weight and who mimic dieting behaviors and restrict their food intake (e.g., Smolek & Levine, 1994). Many girls in middle childhood talk about their need to diet, indicating that socialization to weight control is well learned at an early age.

By age nine or earlier in the United States, children become independent purchasers of some clothing and grooming products and are becoming socialized to shopping skills. In a Youth Monitor study of children as consumers conducted in the 1980s, researchers were surprised to find the degree to which children were involved in shopping (Greene & Greene, 1990). Over half of girls ages nine to 11 were buying hair conditioner, nail polish, and deodorant and about a third bought their own perfume. About one-fifth were purchasing various types of makeup. Almost half of boys ages nine to 11 purchased deodorant for themselves, and about one-fourth were buying various hair care products and cologne.

Some businesses look at children as a lucrative target market, while critics have questioned whether the independence children have in selecting and purchasing adult grooming products is appropriate. In agreement with this concern, Smith, in "The Changing Image of Childhood," wonders if styles offered in girls' clothing encourage them to look too similar to adult women and if present-day marketing approaches overemphasize sexuality in girls at too early an age. Are children growing up too fast? Do children's appearances reflect more maturity than they can handle during childhood? These are questions that, at present, have no clear-cut answers. In an era when some children begin sexual activity around age 12, sexual abuse of children is constantly in the news, and teen pregnancy is at a record high level in the United States, it is no surprise that many adults question the push to sexualize and "adultize" children at younger and younger ages.

ADOLESCENCE

Adolescence is often divided into the following two periods:

Early adolescence—11 to 14 years for girls and 12 to 15 years for boys.

Late adolescence—15 or 16 to 20 years.

Physical, cognitive, and social developments continue throughout adolescence. Many of these changes influence adolescent interests and needs in regard to dress.

Physical Changes

Dramatic changes occur in the body during adolescence. Adult height is reached during these years, and growth spurts may cause some adolescents to go through phases of being physically awkward. Complexion problems are not uncommon among teens, leading to purchases of an array of products designed to control and camouflage pimples and acne.

Primary and secondary sex characteristics develop, further increasing body awareness. Boys and girls reach sexual maturity, and concern about sexual attractiveness and defining sexuality also increases. Because of growing interest in looking like an adult, both boys and girls start to prefer styles that, to them, do not look too childish. Increasing conflicts between adolescents and parents are common as their offspring, who seemed to be children "just yesterday," attempt to experiment with adult appearances. Girls in particular are given cultural encouragement through media images, fashion trends, and certain peer groups to dress in a sexually provocative manner, often despite the objections of protective parents. Of course, individual differences abound. Some mothers register concern that their daughters do not spend much time on their appearance and do not use makeup as soon as other teens do.

Body satisfaction tends to increase slightly in later adolescence, probably resulting from greater satisfaction with the body as it more fully matures and develops (Damhorst, Littrell, & Littrell, 1987). As boys mature they may become more involved in body-building to develop upper body muscles for a culturally ideal male physique (see Chapter 2). Emphasis on priming the body for various sport activities may also occur. Recent deaths among adolescent boys who are starving themselves and exercising excessively to reach weight goals for wrestling raised questions about the pressures put on young men training for sports (Naughton, 1998). Boys, and increasingly girls, are often encouraged by coaches, family members, and peers to endanger personal health and safety through extremes of weight management and drug abuse for the sake of sports achievements.

Girls in the United States are culturally encouraged to diet and exercise to pursue a thin body. Parker and colleagues in "Body Image and Weight Concerns Among African American and White Adolescent Females" give an excellent review of body image research. Their findings demonstrate that ethnic backgrounds can shape how the adolescent feels about her body. African American girls grow up in a cultural tradition that encourages making the best of one's appearance and openly praising others for looking good, regardless of physical size or shape. In contrast, white girls seem to feel there is only one option for attractiveness—thinness. The Caucasian girls in this study described substantial dissatisfaction with appearance and extensive criticism of themselves and others in measuring up to thinness standards. The obsession with thinness and weight control has made white adolescent females in the United States a population at risk for poor nutritional status and unhealthful eating behaviors (Adams & Shafer, 1988).

Cognitive and Socioemotional Development

In addition to body changes, cognitive changes lead many adolescents to feel that everyone notices everything about how they look. The adolescent still has some of the concreteness in thinking and egocentrism of childhood while moving on to development of more complex hypothetical thinking skills of **formal operations** (Schickedanz et al., 1998). The adolescent becomes increasingly adept at taking on the role of the other, but sometimes over-interprets and over-imagines reviews from others.

Adolescents who are overweight or have appearance impairments truly suffer during this phase of development. In "Pony Party," Lucy Grealy describes the burdens of living with substantial facial disfigurement caused by cancer when she was nine. Continual procedures of facial reconstruction surgery failed to repair her appearance. She describes feeling like a "freak" during adolescence as she witnessed young children staring at her in amazement and adults turning away and trying not to notice. Her distorted face became the center of her identity.

Creekmore (1980) found that high school students strongly believed that the most popular students are apt to be attractive and well dressed. They tend to believe they can judge people on the basis of appearance. Many teens become preoccupied with appearance in their search for identity. They use dress as one of many tactics to achieve belonging in peer groups and success in dating relationships. These social supports may help to ratify the self and strengthen self-esteem (Daters, 1990).

Conformity through appearance may be more common in adolescence, particularly early adolescence, than at any other stage in life. Rather than passive acquiescence to others, adolescents use conformity for actively trying out identities. Many teenagers seem almost to "graze" through new looks in a very dynamic search of self-identity (Kaiser & Damhorst, 1995). In "Goin' Gangsta" (Chapter 10) white girls in Los Angeles adopt clothing styles and mannerisms of Mexican American girls, seemingly to try on ethnic identity.

Shopping becomes an enjoyable socializing activity for many teenagers. Now that so many parents are working outside the home, adolescents are often allowed more independence in shopping (Walsh, 1985). Adolescent boys also are more involved in shopping for their own clothes than in prior generations. Teens prefer to shop with friends; they need the social consensus of help in making purchase decisions. Early adolescents are particularly interested in and comfortable with conforming to appearance norms of peers.

Teens today are also more skilled at using computer technology than were prior generations. Retailers popular with adolescents, such as Delia's Inc., have been able to reach a broad market through their online catalogs ("For Clueless Grown-Ups," 1998). Website stores offer instantaneous access to latest trend ideas, regardless of where the teenager lives. As Web access continues to increase in households across the United States and around the world, adolescents may increasingly use the Internet as a source of fashion information and product access.

Adolescents also use media imagery to learn about possibilities for self-expression and self-image. Kaiser and Damhorst (1995) found that early adolescents are highly attracted to MTV and other media performers who are fashion leaders. Some performers are perceived by adolescents as "powerful" in that they attract attention and inspire others to follow them. Early adolescents seem to use media to learn about adult life, even though they may realize that many of the appearances they see are not appropriate for themselves during early adolescence. One of the ideal role models for many adolescents is the fashion model. The article, "James Is a Girl" by Jennifer Egan, looks at the life of a teen model who left school for a life of work that removed her from normal adolescence. The article examines how James' identity became based on her appearance as she was living the "ideal" life for young women.

Summary

Dress and appearance are critical components of child and adolescent development. Physical skills and coordination increase throughout childhood, allowing the child to increase independence and mastery over the physical actions involved in dressing. Sport dress facilitates participation in physical activities during childhood and adolescence.

By early and middle childhood, cognitive and social developments lead to skills that may result in stereotypical thinking triggered by appearance cues. Children use dress to form impressions of others, and by adolescence may move to more complex and hypothetical thinking about appearances and what they mean. Adolescents may become convinced that appropriate and attractive dress and appearance are crucial to popularity and successful dating relationships.

Conformity to peers begins to become important by early childhood and increases in importance through early adolescence. Dress plays an important role in helping the individual feel a sense of belonging and acceptance and to help in searching for self-identity. Shopping for dress also increases as a social activity for many individuals during middle childhood and adolescence. Learning to dress and manage appearance are key components of socialization to societal norms.

Suggested Readings

Brumberg, J. J. (1997). *The body project: An intimate history of American girls.* New York: Random House.

Cahill, S. E. (1989). Fashioning males and females: Appearance management and the social reproduction of gender. *Symbolic Interaction, 12,* 281–298.

Grealy, L. (1994). *Autobiography of a face.* Boston: Houghton Mifflin.

Rudd, N. A., & Lennon, S. (1995). Body image: Eating, substance abuse, and appearance disorders. In *Invest in youth: Build the future* (pp. 41–57). Alexandria, VA: American Association of Family and Consumer Sciences.

Roach, M. E. (1969). Adolescent dress. *Journal of Home Economics, 61*(9), 693–697.

LEARNING ACTIVITY

Those Embarrassing Moments of Childhood

Objective: Recalling your own childhood incidents of embarrassments and mistakes related to dress helps understanding of the importance of dress during child development.

Background

Childhood is a time of learning and exploring, so it is no wonder that many children make gaffs and goofs related to appearance along the way. Learning to dress is as complicated a process as any, demanding physical, mental, and social coordination. And sometimes the body just doesn't cooperate and grow in a socially desirable way. Most men and women seem to be able to recall in painful but amusing detail something about dress or the body that caused them embarrassment while they were growing up. These childhood *faux pas* in appearance could be caused by one's own error, the whims of a parent or relative, or the wrath of nature.

For example, Conti, the *San Francisco Chronicle* "Question Man," used to go out on the streets each day and ask people simple questions. Back on June 2, 1989, he asked, "What were you ashamed of growing up?" (Conti, 1989). Six of the seven embarrassments reported in the column related to appearance—things such as big feet, being too tall as a girl, and hair that was too curly. A 35-year-old graphic designer, Dale Hoover, recalled:

> When we first got a TV, I was afraid to dress in front of it. I thought the TV personalities could see me. I was very ashamed when I realized that I was so stupid.

Chuck O'Brien, a 33-year-old systems analyst suffered on account of his mom:

> My brothers and I fought over socks. My mom resolved it by putting big initials on everything with a marking pen. The kids would say things like, "Can't you remember your name?"

When I ask students in class to relate childhood dress embarrassments, a number of common themes emerge. Many remember being out of fashion or showing "bad taste," such as lack of color coordination. A few students recall incidents when they felt immodest, such as ripped pants that exposed underwear on the playground. Some were embarrassed by body features (e.g., hair, nose, height) or slowness in sexual development. Some recall being upset because they couldn't be like others—one girl was ashamed that she couldn't have a Forenza sweater. Moms were the cause of many embarrassments. Moms make kids wear goofy things (like Moon Boots when no one else wears them anymore), force kids to wear hand-me-downs or garage-sale clothes, or do things like put noticeable patches on knees. Other kids make what might be a minor error a horrible experience through teasing, taunting, and snubbing. And many students recall that even though they weren't embarrassed by dress as a child, they now look at old photos and cringe that they were ever allowed to wear such hideous things!

Write and Discuss

Write down your own childhood recollection of an embarrassment related to dress or appearance. Then share your account with a small group of class members or the entire class. As a group, think about why the things you remember caused embarrassment. What did the incident reflect about child development?

- Was it a mistake you make on your own because you didn't know the rules or "in" thing to do?
- Were you uncomfortable because you didn't fit in with friends or peers?
- Did you make a mistake because of lack of physical coordination or clumsiness?
- Was your physical development slow or too fast in comparison to that of other kids?
- How was the embarrassment related to taking (or not taking) on the role of the other? Did you over-interpret others' responses?
- Did someone else make you wear something that embarrassed you? Who? And why did you have to go along with their wishes?
- Did responses from others make the situation worse? Better?
- Did you grow beyond that embarrassment, or does it still bother you today?

References

Adams, L. B., & Shafer, M. B. (1988). Early manifestations of eating disorders in adolescents: Defining those at risk. *Journal of Nutrition Education, 20*(6), 307–313.

Allen, K.E., & Marotz, L.R. (1999). *Developmental profiles* (3rd ed.). Albany, NY: Delmar Publishers.

Brylinsky, J., & Moore, J. (1994). The identification of body build stereotypes in young children. *Journal of Research in Personality, 28,* 170–181.

Cahill, S. E. (1989). Fashioning males and females: Appearance management and the social reproduction of gender. *Symbolic Interaction, 12,* 281–298.

Conti. (1989, June 2). Question man. *The San Francisco Chronicle,* p. A30.

Creekmore, A. M. (1980). Clothing and personal attractiveness of adolescents related to conformity to clothing mode, peer acceptance, and leadership potential. *Home Economics Research Journal, 8,* 203–215.

Damhorst, M. L., Littrell, J. M., & Littrell, M. A. (1987). Age differences in adolescent body satisfaction. *Journal of Psychology, 121,* 553–562.

Daters, C. M. (1990). Importance of clothing and self esteem among adolescents. *Clothing and Textiles Research Journal, 8*(3), 45–50.

Flavell, J. H. (1975). *The development of role-taking and communication skills in children.* Huntington, NY: Robert E. Krieger.

Flavell, J. H. (1977). *Cognitive development.* Englewood Cliffs, NJ: Prentice-Hall.

For clueless grown-ups: A retailing field guide. (1998, December 9). *The Wall Street Journal,* p. B1.

Greene, K., & Greene, R. (1990, March). The shocking statistics. *Redbook, 174,* 93.

Kaiser, S. B. (1989). Clothing and the social organization of gender perception: A developmental approach. *Clothing and Textiles Research Journal, 7*(2), 46–56.

Kaiser, S. B., & Damhorst, M. L. (1995). Youth and media culture: Research and policy issues. In *Invest in youth: Build the future* (pp.153–169). Alexandria, VA: American Association of Family and Consumer Sciences.

Mayer, R. N., & Belk, R. W. (1985). Fashion and impression formation among children. In M. R. Solomon (Ed.), *The psychology of fashion* (pp. 293–308). Lexington, MA: Lexington Books.

Naughton, J. (1998, March 18). The weighting game: High schools taking action for wrestlers. *Des Moines Register,* pp. 1S, 5S.

Ryan, M. S. (1966). *Clothing: A study in human behavior.* New York: Holt, Rinehart and Winston.

Schickedanz, J. A., Schickedanz, D. I., Forsyth, P. D., & Forsyth, G. A. (1998). *Understanding children and adolescents* (3rd ed.). Boston, MA: Allyn and Bacon.

Smolek, L., & Levine, M. (1994). Toward an empirical basis for primary prevention of eating problems with elementary school children. *Eating Disorders, 2*(4), 293–307.

Stone, G. (1962). Appearance and the self. In A. Rose (Ed.), *Human behavior and social processes* (pp. 86–118). Boston, MA: Houghton Mifflin.

Stone, J., & Sternweis, L. (1994, September). *Consumer choices: Selecting clothes for toddlers, ages 1 to 3.* University Extension Bulletin Pm-1105. Ames: Cooperative Extension Service, Iowa State University.

Walsh, D. L. (1985, February). Targeting teens. *American Demographics,* pp. 21–25, 41.

Young children still live in poverty—Despite parental employment. (1993). *Child Poverty News and Issues, 3*(1). cpmcnet.columbia.edu/news/childpov/newi0008.html#top.

46　Now Even Toddlers Are Dressing to the Nines

Robert Berner

Judith Kelly spent $20,000 last year on designer clothes she never wore. Her two-year-old daughter did.

"I can afford it, so why not?" asks Mrs. Kelly, a home maker in Short Hills, N.J., whose husband is a Wall Street junk-bond trader.

And she's not alone: Today, many of Versace's best customers are sporting Pampers underneath.

Sales of children's clothes are growing faster than all other apparel categories—largely because the number of newborns skyrocketed in recent years. And because the parents are older and richer than in previous generations, the labels in the baby's room aren't just Gap and OshKosh B'Gosh anymore.

In fact, Mrs. Kelly's daughter has so many designer outfits in her closet that she's worn many of them only once. "I have pecking orders of people waiting for her hand-me-downs," says Mrs. Kelly, 36 years old.

Children's designer clothing is well outpacing the sluggish designer market for women. Sales of kids' clothing are up 8% this year at Barneys New York and they've nearly doubled at Infinity, another trendy children's store on New York's Upper East Side. The phenomenon isn't limited to Manhattan: sales are up 20% at LePapillon in Los Angeles and Kidz in Miami, both fashionable children's outfitters.

Among designers, two big beneficiaries are Versace and Moschino, which have sold children's apparel in the U.S. for several years. But others are scrambling to join the market, including Sonia Rykiel, Hermes and Kenzo of France; Missoni, Enrico Coveri and Laura Biagiotti of Italy; Paul Smith of England, Dries Van Noten of Belgium and Nicole Miller of the U.S.

Giorgio Armani, who dropped his children's line two years ago, is considering a comeback. "There is renewed interest and bigger demand," says Linda Grant, the Italian designer's U.S. spokesperson.

Most designers recreate the styles and colors of their adult clothing in their children's lines. Sonia Rykiel, for example, does most of her girl's outfits in her signature black palette, using the same body-hugging velours on dresses, tops and bottoms, which range from $150 to $400. Moschino continues his bold colors in boy's and girl's denim jacket-and-pant sets in yellow, orange and green ($329) and a girl's short dress with a bright, abstract pattern ($189).

Where would kids wear, say, a $250 Versace black motorcycle jacket or a $150 Nicole Miller cocktail dress? Parents say they buy the clothes for special occasions, such as parties, plays, bar mitzvahs and bas mitzvahs. Some kids wear them to church and out to dinner. Babies and toddlers go to parties, too, and they tend to balk less at being dressed up than, say, 13-year-old boys who'd prefer jeans and T-shirts.

Miami resident Sheryl Alonso says her three children—ages seven, nine, and 11—sometimes wear their Versace, Moschino, and Sonia Rykiel clothes to school. "They just think they have more fun clothes than some of their friends," says Ms. Alonso, 41. "And I like them to look very nice. Your apparel is part of the way you carry yourself."

That sentiment isn't limited to the wealthy. At Karl's, a children's store in the inner city of Philadelphia, sales of designer clothes are up 30% this year, says owner Adam Richman.

As a cleaner of houses, 25-year-old William Brunson earns only $700 a week. But on a recent day, he steps up to the counter at Karl's to buy a $329 Moschino jacket and $99 pair of jeans for his four-year-old daughter. He adds in a pair of $139 Versace shoes to complete the outfit. "I want her to look as good as the rest of them or better," he says.

Nearby, another customer, Dawn Evans, guffaws at the $325 price tag on a girl's lime green skirt-and-jacket set from Versace. "It's teaching people to judge people by what they have on their back," says Ms. Evans, a 29-year-old phone-company administrator who is in the store to buy pantyhose.

Curiously, many parents who buy designer outfits for their kids are not in the Versace set themselves. Ms. Alonso says she not really sure why she spends more on her children's clothes than on her own—other than she likes them to look nice. "I guess I am obsessive about it," she says.

"It's a parent's way of wanting to do better for their children," says 33-year-old Dale Zimmer of Wilmington, N.C., who dresses her daughters, ages seven and nine, and her five-year-old son in Missoni, Versace and Moschino. "I just don't want them to become so label conscious that they can't appreciate things for what they are."

To be sure, some educators find the trend troubling. "It used to be cars and jewelry—today children have become symbols of conspicuous consumption," says David Elkind, a Tufts University child-development professor. As for children, he says, "it gives them a feeling of entitlement, a sense that they are to the manner born and that everything is due them."

Even some designers are disturbed. "To dress children in a status manner is very wrong,"

says women's designer Todd Oldham. "That's a hideous conception."

Yet often, the desire for designer names comes from the kids themselves. "They love those Moschino purses," Susan Gliedman, a Manhattan housewife, says of her nine- and 12-year-old daughters. "I tell them they are not for kids. I don't want my children validated by a designer label."

Parents who acquiesce say it can be hard to know where to draw the line. Kathryn Bregman, a part-time real estate broker in Manhattan, buys some high-end clothing for her 12-year-old daughter at Infinity. But at Dalton, the expensive private school her daughter attends, there are always girls who have more. "It causes tensions," says Ms. Bregman.

The emphasis on clothes "is very disturbing," says Ellen Stein, director of the lower grades at Dalton. "There should be other values we want to impart to our children rather than what they are wearing."

Yet other parents have no qualms—or apologies—for wanting their children to have the best. Beth Jaffe, a 51-year-old lawyer in Bayonne, N.J., says "I have more money at my disposal" than many other parents and than she herself did earlier in her career. And she likes to spend it dressing her four-year-old daughter in Versace and Moschino outfits.

"It's an extension of the way I like to dress," says Mrs. Jaffe, "and I like to think I dress well."

DISCUSSION QUESTIONS

Now Even Toddlers Are Dressing to the Nines

1. How do parents who dress their children in expensive designer clothes explain these consumer choices?

2. What do some child development experts and others suggest are potential problems that could result from dressing children in extremely expensive clothes?

47 The Magic of Dress-Up
Toni Wood

Our family planned a party not long ago that was to include both adults and preschoolers. Several days before it took place, I swept through the local thrift store, looking for eye-catching items costing less than two dollars. I brought home a fur vest, bright scarves, a pair of gold slippers, Mexican-style cotton dresses, and many other treasures. Then, just before the party started, I put the box of dress-up items in the back bedroom, near full-length mirrors, and directed the children into the room as they arrived.

Left to their own devices, the kids came up with outlandish getups that made them—and us adults—howl with laughter. From that evening we got two spontaneous plays and one pricelessly silly group picture.

The only grim moment in the party came when the parents said that it was time to go: several girls cried over not getting to wear what I considered the pièce de résistance of my thrift-shop excursion: a hot-pink lace-and-satin dressing gown.

The success of the party only demonstrated, once again, that preschoolers—for whom the boundaries between reality and fantasy are still wonderfully blurred—find the world of dress-up pure magic. Just by pulling on Mom's beads and high heels, or by wearing Dad's sports jacket that falls to their ankles, children enter into a form of dramatic play that offers them a wonderful chance to gain control, to "minimize the problems of being little," says Peggy Jenkins, an early-childhood educator and author of *The Joyful Child* (Harbinger House).

DRESS-UP IS AN IMPORTANT LEARNING TOOL

Pretend play can also help preschoolers try out and develop important new skills, such as working and sharing with other children, and learning how to express their emotions appropriately.

From the first year of life, children watch and imitate the words, movements, and attitudes of people around them. But as children enter the preschool years, their observe-and-copy behavior becomes more sophisticated. Now they are no longer content to talk like Mommy; they also want to look like Mommy. Or the baby-sitter. Or the mail carrier.

"In the adult world, preschoolers feel so small and helpless," Jenkins says. "But during dramatic play, they can take on adult roles. They can say no to the baby, they can be the daddy, they can go to the store and drive a car."

PRETEND PLAY CAN HELP KIDS VENT FEELINGS OF ANGER

Dress-up play, with its borrowed identities, allows children to act out their own frightening or inappropriate feelings, the ones that might lead to a time-out if they expressed them otherwise. A docile little girl with a few props can often transform herself into a fierce, tooth-baring tiger, or a mommy who "accidentally" bounces her baby doll on its head. "The play can be rough and tough or angry and mean," says Jenkins, "but it's all pretend."

And when preschoolers get together for a session of dress-up play, they can learn about taking turns ("Who will be the prince?"), helping one another ("This robe keeps falling off—can somebody tie it for me?"), and solving problems ("What can we use to make the crown?").

Although you can expect a tea party consisting of two- and three-year-olds to be chaotic, children of four and five will mount a more sophisticated production—planning, using dialogue, and making props an integral part of play. "Young children only need a towel across their backs to turn into a superhero," says Jeri Robinson, early-childhood program director at the The Children's Museum, in Boston. "Older kids are much more particular about having all the appropriate parts of the costume. They're the ones who have to have the badge to dress up like a sheriff."

Encouraging dress-up play can be as simple as allowing a child to poke through Mom and Dad's closet, or at least a special dress-up drawer or trunk. Few adventures are quite so delicious for children this age. They breathe in the special scent that closets have, rummage around, and usually discover some unexpected marvel—partly because they're so easily delighted. Probably the best way to encourage dramatic play is simply to make dress-up props available, set guidelines so that the children take turns and don't hurt one another, and then let them take the lead.

When adding to your child's dress-up collection, think of what will stimulate the senses. Furry, leathery, and silky textures and bright, rich colors are especially delightful to children. You might even let your child help with the shopping, and go along with what inspires them.

You should avoid jumping in to assign roles or to show children the "right" way to put together an outfit, however. "Parents should be careful not to be too intrusive," advises Jerlean Daniel, Ph.D., assistant professor of child development at the University of Pittsburgh. "What you want is the child's imagination to take hold. It doesn't need to be tended by adults—in fact, that can take the fun out of what kids are doing."

Instead, compliment all of the children's creations, even if one participant is sporting a particularly interesting mix of props—cowboy boots, a purse, and gloves, for example. You can gush to your young movie star, "You look mahvelous, dahling!" Or tell your pirate how mean he looks with his eye patch.

DON'T WORRY MUCH ABOUT GENDER-APPROPRIATE DRESS

Both boys and girls should have the chance to try on feminine and masculine items and to explore the textures, materials, and fantasies attached to those objects. "If a little boy picks up a feather boa, parents shouldn't assign much significance

BOX 1
"Mommy, You Be the Little Girl!"

Sometimes your child wants you either to participate in or to watch dress-up play. Says Jonathon Bloomberg, M.D., a child psychiatrist at Rockford Memorial Hospital, in Illinois. "It's an invitation you should try to honor because it tells her that you want to be involved in her world."

Here are several ways to take part:

Let Your Child Make the Rules. If you're tapped for a role in a pretend scenario, "accept that you're a bit player and that the child is the star, director, and producer," says Bloomberg. "Parents sometimes say things like, 'If we're in a car, we can't fly through the air.' To a preschooler, though, limitless possibilities matter more than correct details."

Have the Children Put on a Play. Many children enjoy putting on theater productions for grown-ups. The scripts and acting may be a little ramshackle, and the acting more charming than polished, but these playlets are lots of fun for both parents and children.

Play "Stump the Parents." One great dress-up game that doesn't require parents to change wardrobes is to have children dress as a specific character and then to have parents try to guess who they are.

—William McCoy

to it," Daniel says. "The same is true if a girl wants to try on one of Grandpa's old flannel shirts."

Parents who want to add to their prop collection needn't feel obliged to make or buy full costumes. In fact, experts say that doing so discourages children from putting together their own creations. A Superman outfit from a catalog allows a child to turn into…well, Superman. But a swatch of red fabric allows a child to become a vampire, Little Red Riding Hood, Superman, or a dozen other characters.

Dress-up treasures can turn up in all kinds of places. The back of your closet is a logical starting point. Pull out those prom dresses and bell-bottoms. One mother I know resurrected a 1970's fringed leather jacket that her children have since used to become frontiersmen, Indians, and hippies. Thrift shops are excellent sources of flamboyant clothes and jewelry. (Look for clothing items that can be easily washed or sanitized.)

According to Daniel, flexibility and variety should be your prime considerations in looking for dress-up materials. "That way," she says, "when a child's mood changes—boom! They can change. They're something else immediately, and that's a lot more fun."

DISCUSSION QUESTIONS

The Magic of Dress-Up

1. Toni Wood outlines the benefits that play with dress has for child development. What does play with dress facilitate for children?

2. Do you remember playing with dress when you were a child? If not, did you ever wear costumes for Halloween or other events? What did you wear for play and Halloween? How did the costumes and play dress make you feel?

48   Tots Grow Up Fast in Pageant World

Yonkers, N.Y. (AP)—As her mother tucked her into bed one night, little Gabrielle Citrino laid it on the line: "I don't want to do it anymore."

For nearly five years, she's been traveling from state to state dolled up in rhinestones, feather boas and lipstick. She's been tap dancing, singing "Bye Bye Baby" and turning on the charm for countless judges. Finally, just shy of her sixth birthday, she's burned out.

"Pageants are hard and you try to remember all those steps," says Gabrielle, who has been on the beauty pageant circuit since she was 11 months old. "Sometimes they give me crowns that are hard to balance."

"It's her decision," says her mother, Ann Diantonio. "She's 5. She has a mouth. She knows what she wants to do."

Murder has suddenly thrust the world of children's beauty pageants into the spotlight. Since 6-year-old JonBenet Ramsey was found strangled in her Boulder, Colo., basement last month, national magazines and TV shows have run photographs and videotapes of the dyed-blonde woman-child vamping across stages in showgirl costumes and heavy makeup.

There are thousands of children like JonBenet. Charles Dunn, publisher of Pageantry magazine, estimates that, every year, beauty pageants show off 100,000 children under the age of 12.

It's a subculture of bleached hair, blue contact lenses and false eyelashes. Little girls sashay in sequined gowns and swimsuits, sometimes adding a touch of striptease by removing wrap-around skirts.

ENTRY FEES, GOWNS

Parents pay entry fees of up to $500 and buy thousand-dollar gowns so their girls can compete for 10-inch crowns, 6-foot trophies and $10,000 savings bonds. Some of the children travel with an entourage of makeup artists, hairdressers and talent coaches.

It pays to start young. Jo-Ann Guerin, director of All Star Kids U.S.A. Pageants, once got two entry forms from a woman with only one child. When Guerin asked why, the woman explained she was pregnant.

Babies too young to walk are paraded down pageant runways, their mothers holding the confused children out in front of them to display their chubby cheeks.

CAN FOSTER POISE

Pageant life isn't for everyone, industry organizers acknowledge. But for youngsters and parents who can handle wins and losses with aplomb, pageantry can foster poise and self-confidence, they say.

"I've never said that this is the greatest thing in the world for your child," says Guerin, who runs All Star Kids from her home in Yonkers. "Are there mothers that are nuts? Absolutely. But there are hardworking people who are devoted and want their kids to enjoy it."

Others are more critical.

FIGURE 8.3 *JonBenet Ramsey became nationally known as a child beauty pageant contestant when she was found murdered in her home.*

If parents keep pageantry from consuming a child's life, it can be a positive experience, says William Pinsof, a clinical psychologist and president of the Family Institute at Northwestern University.

However, he says, "being a little Barbie doll says your body has to be certain way and your hair has to be certain way. In girls particularly, this can unleash a whole complex of destructive self-experiences that can lead to eating disorders and all kinds of body distortions in terms of body image."

LOCAL, NATIONAL LEVELS

For many parents, pageantry starts when they see an ad for a local pageant. Usually, all it costs is a $20 entry fee and the price of a party dress. But when the winners move up to state and national pageants, the costs escalate.

"You can go $10,000," says Noreen Williams, the mother of a beauty contestant in Yulan. "Some mothers get loans out for the pageants. Those are the ones that get angry at their girls when they lose."

Guerin got started with beauty pageants when her daughter, Genevieve, won a few pageants in New York as a pre-teen several years ago. With Genevieve's godmother, they set out for a huge pageant in Dallas. They coordinated their outfits for each day of the weeklong competition.

"If she was in pink, we were in pink. Of course, I thought I was bringing home a national winner," Guerin says. "We weren't in the lobby for 10 seconds when we thought, 'What are we doing here?' The Southern girls had it all—the coaches, the makeup artists, the clothes. My daughter did not win anything at that pageant."

Some mothers lie about their daughters' ages so they can appear more poised and mature compared to younger girls, Guerin says. For her pageant, she now requires birth certificates with entry forms.

Sometimes mothers accuse each other of trying to buy influence by spending upwards of $250 a page for advertising in pageant directories.

"Let's face it, they'll cut your throat in a minute," says Williams whose daughter—a beauty contestant since age 4—was runner-up in the Miss New York Teen U.S.A. pageant last spring.

But for the most part, she says, it's healthy competition. Her 16-year-old daughter, Dorothy, has been taking part in pageants for 12 years. She gets good grades and has a fledgling career as a model.

One day she hopes to win a place in the Miss America Pageant.

"It's a little girl dream," Dorothy says. Dreams have to start somewhere."

DISCUSSION QUESTIONS

Tots Grow Up Fast in Pageant World

1. Why is the competition of young children in beauty pageants a concern to some adults?

2. There are no clear answers as to whether these competitions have a negative effect on children. Do you feel that beauty pageants are positive, negative, or mixed experiences for young children and their development? Why?

49   The Changing Image of Childhood
Lynn Smith

They look like caricatures of grown-ups—sexy grown-ups; rich, sophisticated grown-ups; silly grown-ups on vacation in Waikiki. But really, they're just kids promoting J.C. Penney's spring and summer "retro-chic" children's line.

They're cute, in that twisted sort of way that has come to pervade the marketing of clothing and cosmetics and triggers an insidious merging of childhood and adulthood—especially for girls.

FIGURE 8.4 *Child model in adult-like outfit.*

In this case, the boys pose in baggy T-shirts, while the girls wear bathing suits and pose in S-shaped curves. A girl toddler strikes a cheesecake pose while a boy toddler takes her picture.

According to Penney publicist Robbie Ellis, the ads are nothing more than kids dressing up. "Didn't you play dress up when you were young?" she asked.

When I was young, childhood was a different experience altogether. Children were considered separate from adults. No one I knew had sex in the seventh grade. No one had heard of designer jeans or blow-dryers.

The concept of childhood came into existence slowly after the Middle Ages, a time when children dressed like adults. Over the past few decades, the pendulum has started to swing back.

"We've come full circle, back to children being pictured as little adults," said Mary Pipher, an anthropologist and psychologist who, in her popular book "Reviving Ophelia," describes how mass culture has affected the mental health of young girls.

J.C. Penney is not Calvin Klein, but any blurring of the distinction between children and adults can be a dangerous contribution to the trend, she said.

"One of the sad things about this is the message it sends to parents and young girls that what's important about a 7- or 10-year-old girl is her appearance, how expensive her clothes are, how attractive and sexy she is. I think it a dead wrong message to send. What's important is, in fact, everything else. Her character, her interests, her talents."

In her research, Pipher has found girls as young as 5 who are preoccupied with dieting. By sixth grade, she said, 79 percent of girls say they want to be thinner.

One of the problems with ads such as Penney's, said Seattle sociologist Pepper Schwartz, is that young girls start early on to compare themselves to adult standards of attractiveness and worthiness far removed from their own physical development. Schwartz has an 11-year-old daughter who wants to wear sexy tube tops. The girl is old enough to know why it's cool. But, Schwartz said, "She doesn't understand the consequences of masquerading like an older girl."

One of the consequences is that girls who dress like adults attract boys or men who mistakenly think young girls are in the ballpark as companions.

Schwartz said she asked her daugher, "Do you want little boys to grab and kiss you?

"She said, 'Oh, mother.'"

Schwartz urged parents to just say no when their children beg for clothes that are too old for them.

Pipher advised parents to boycott products that are advertised in ways that are harmful to children.

Corporations can use alternative images to sell their products, and some do. Nike commercials stress what girls can achieve if they are allowed to participate in sports. Timberland boot ads show the contributions of ordinary young men and women.

In addition, Pipher said, consumer protection legislation could prohibit certain kinds of marketing to young children.

"I'd like to restack the deck so advertisers give children a decent set of guidelines about what's heroic and what's important," she said.

1. Smith examines the adult appearances fostered for children through some advertisements. What problems for children does she foresee as a result of this "adultizing" and, in some cases, sexualization of children in mainstream marketing campaigns?

2. Do you agree or disagree that these ads have negative effects for children?

3. What does Smith suggest this trend reflects about society?

50 Body Image and Weight Concerns among African American and White Adolescent Females: Differences that Make a Difference

Sheila Parker
Mimi Nichter
Mark Nichter
Nancy Vuckovic
Colette Sims
Cheryl Ritenbaugh

Dissatisfaction with weight and inappropriate dieting behaviors are reported to be pervasive among adolescent Caucasian females. Survey research has suggested that there is an "epidemic" of dieting among White adolescent females (Rosen and Gross 1987) with estimates that as many as 60–80% of girls are dieting at any given time (Berg 1992). By contrast, research on African American adolescents suggests that these girls are less dissatisfied with their body weight and are far less likely to engage in weight reducing efforts than their White peers (Casper and Offer 1990; MMWR 1991). Explanations of such ethnic differences typically revolve around the statement that "cultural factors" are somehow implicated (Rosen and Gross 1987).

Utilizing data collected from a multi-ethnic study of adolescent females, this paper explores cultural factors which have an impact on weight perception, body image, beauty, and style. African American perceptions of beauty, charac-terized by informants as flexible and fluid, will be contrasted with White images which tend to be more rigid and fixed. Ramifications of this difference will be broadly considered.

ETHNIC DIFFERENCES IN PERCEPTIONS OF WEIGHT AND DIETING

Weight has been identified as an important health concern, source of psychological stress, and measure of self-esteem among White females (Attie and Brooks-Gunn 1987; Moses *et*

Parker, Sheila, "Body Image and Weight Concerns among African American and White Adolescent Females: Differences that Make a Difference." *Human Organization*, Vol. 54, No. 2, 1995. Copyright © Society for Applied Anthropology.

al. 1989). Numerous surveys have documented the pervasiveness of dieting and body dissatisfaction among White adolescent females (Desmond *et al.* 1986; Greenfield *et al.* 1987; Koff and Rierdan 1991). In one study among White high school students, 80% of girls surveyed felt they were above the weight at which they would be happiest and 43% said they would like to weigh at least 10 pounds less (Fisher *et al.* 1991). Storz and Greene (1983) found that 83% of White adolescent girls they surveyed wanted to lose weight, though 62% were in the normal weight range for their height and gender.

Results of recent nationwide surveys have revealed that White and Hispanic girls perceived themselves to be overweight even when their weight for height fell within "normal" parameters as established by the National Center for Health Statistics. By comparison, African American adolescent females were found to be less likely to perceive themselves as overweight (MMWR 1991). Desmond, Price, Hallinan, and Smith (1989) contend that both African American and White adolescents maintain distorted perceptions of their body weight, but in opposite directions. Their study suggests that African American adolescents of normal and heavy weight tend to perceive themselves as thinner than they actually are, while White adolescents of thin and normal weight perceive themselves as heavier than they actually are. Such studies call attention to differences in standards of acceptable weight and their variability across cultures.

A study conducted by Casper and Offer (1990) found that African American female adolescents were less preoccupied with weight and dieting concerns than White adolescent females. In an item by item comparison, African American adolescents had fewer thoughts about dieting, were less fearful of weight gain, and had a less negative valuation of overeating. Rosen and Gross (1987) concluded that African American girls were more likely to be engaged in weight gaining than weight loss efforts when compared to their White and Hispanic counterparts.

Differences in cultural standards for acceptable weights have been reported both among adult women as well as among adolescent females. Using a structured interview technique, Rand and Kuldau (1990) assessed the prevalence of obesity and self-defined weight problems in a large sample (n=2,115) of African American and White women. Almost half (46%) of African American women in their study (n=306) were overweight by an average of 25 pounds, an amount which exceeded the average of all other groups. Significant differences emerged when acceptable weights by race and age were considered. Younger White women (aged 18–34) who considered themselves to have "no weight problem" were thin and were an average of 6–14 pounds under the lower limit of the "ideal weight range." African American women of the same age category who reported "no weight problem" had an average (rather than thin) body weight. Acceptable weights for this group fell within the recommended weight range, but acceptance of "overweight" became more pronounced as women became older. At older ages (55–74), African American women who reported "no weight problem" were on average 17–20 pounds overweight. Kumanyika (1987) has noted that "controlling for socioeconomic status does not eliminate the obesity prevalence differences between Black women and White women" (1987:34).

Allen (1989), in a study of weight management activities among African American women, reported that although most of her informants had been overweight for years by biomedical standards, they did not perceive themselves to be overweight. Awareness of being overweight came from outside the immediate family—a social or health encounter. As Allen notes, these women had not evaluated their body size "in relation to the White ideal in the media but in comparison to other African American women who on the average are heavier than white women" (1989:17). Most informants did not define overweight as unhealthy. These findings are corroborated in a National Health Interview Survey (NHIS) which found that fewer African American women than White women considered themselves overweight, even when they were by actual weight.

Kumanyika, Wilson, and Guilford-Davenport (1993), drawing from a sample of 25-

to 64-year-old African American women (n=500), found that about 40% of the women in the overweight categories (based on BMI) considered their figures attractive or very attractive. Almost all of these women recognized that they were overweight by biomedical standards. Furthermore, only half of the women who were moderately or severely overweight reported that their husband or boyfriend was supportive of their dieting efforts. Almost unanimously, overweight women reported that their body size had not been the source of difficulties in their personal or family relationships.

Anorexia and bulimia are estimated to affect 2–3% of the White population. To date, few cases of anorexia and bulimia among African American females have been reported in the literature. A comparative study of bulimia among African American and White college women found that fewer African American women experienced a sense of fear and discouragement concerning food and weight control than did their White counterparts (Gray et al. 1987). Researchers have suggested that the cultural milieu of African Americans offers "protective factors" against the development of eating disorders. Such factors include family and community appreciation of a fuller and physiologically healthier body size and less emphasis on physical appearance as measured solely by one's weight (Root 1989). There has been some concern, however, that increased affluence and acculturation of African Americans into White culture may result in higher incidence of eating disorders as African Americans seek to emulate White middle class ideals (Hsu 1987). Silber (1986) has suggested that professionals misdiagnose eating disorders among African Americans due to stereotypical ideas that such problems are restricted to White women.

Beyond considerations of weight, several researchers have noted that women of color are compelled, at various points in their lives, to compare their appearance to the dominant White ideal. Such comparisons extend beyond body shape to hair and skin color (Gillespie 1993; Lakoff and Scherr 1984; Okazawa-Rey et al. 1987). Okazawa-Rey, Robinson and Ward (1987) have argued that the African American women are twice victimized and in "double

jeopardy" because they must respond to the desires and expectations of African American men and to White cultural values and norms.

Research conducted up until the last decade tended to highlight the self-contempt some African Americans feel about their appearance as a result of the hegemony of the White beauty ideal. Researchers have recently pointed to the manner in which African American women are supportive and appreciative of one another's efforts to fashion a positive identity in a proactive and aggressive manner (Cross 1991; Okazawa-Rey et al. 1987). Little research has focused on the lived experience of African American adolescent females and the extent to which conflict about appearance affects their lives in various social interactional settings.

Survey research suggests that there is greater satisfaction with body weight and less dieting among African American than among White adolescent populations. This does not mean that African American adolescent females are less concerned about their appearance than are their White counterparts. At issue here is: *what type of self presentation is culturally valued by African American females, in what context, and for what reasons.*

To date, little research has focused on African American females although issues relating to self presentation of males has been discussed. Research on African American males suggests that one coping strategy adopted to deal with oppression and marginality has been "cool pose" (Majors and Billson 1992). Animation marks African American style expressed verbally, non-verbally, at the site of the body, and through a wide range of performance (Fordham 1993). Cool pose is a "ritualized form of masculinity that entails behaviors, scripts, physical posturing that deliver a single, critical message: pride, strength and control" (Majors and Billson 1992:4). According to these authors, cool pose empowers black males in their daily lives by helping them stay in control of their psychological and social space. "Styling" provides an individual voice for males who might otherwise go silent and unnoticed.

While Majors and Billson (1992) do not specifically discuss African American women, other researchers (Fordham 1993) have noted the importance of styling and *ad hoc* construction of a gendered self in an environment where style is both valued and commented upon. The existing literature does not address how African American adolescent girls negotiate their identities and relate to their bodies in a variety of settings. Toward this end, the present study examines African American perceptions of weight and beauty in a Southwestern city marked by ethnic diversity and as geographically diffuse as distinct from centralized African American population. African American and White adolescent females' attitudes about appropriate body size and dieting are contrasted to highlight important differences between these groups.

METHODOLOGY

Data for our analysis are drawn from a three-year longitudinal study (the Teen Lifestyle Project) on dieting, smoking, and body image among adolescent girls. Two hundred fifty girls were recruited into the study while they were in the 8th grade (junior high) and 9th grade (senior high school). Informants were 75% White, 16% Mexican American, and 9% Asian Americans. In the final year of the project, a second sample of 46 African American adolescent girls, drawn from grades 9–12 and other community groups in the same city was added to the study. Both the White and African American participants in the study were from a range of lower middle to middle class families.

Data collection during the study took place primarily in four schools and community organizations. Each girl in the study participated in one in-depth semi-structured interview each year. Each interview took about 45 minutes and was conducted in the school. In addition to individual interviews, focus groups were also conducted with groups of four to five girls on issues regarding perceptions of beauty, ideal body shape, and dieting practices.

Each participant in the study completed a survey questionnaire each year on a range of issues including body image, eating, and dieting behaviors. Height and weight were measured at the time of each survey.

Our study of African American adolescent girls utilized both ethnographic interview and survey methods. Ten focus group discussions with 4–5 girls per group were conducted by African American researchers in order to identify the perceptions and concerns that African American girls held about their weight, body image, dieting, and other broader health and lifestyle factors. These discussions were followed by individual interviews with several key informants. Two surveys were administered to the African American participants. The first survey was the same as that given to the larger multi-ethnic sample. The second survey was designed specifically for African American girls based on issues generated in interviews.

RESULTS
Teen Lifestyle Project Survey Results

In this section a comparison will be drawn between responses to the Teen Lifestyle Project survey (year 3) collected from the sample of White, Hispanic, and Asian-American girls (n=211) and African American girls (n=46). Responses show distinct differences with regard to the issue of satisfaction with weight. In response to the question, "How satisfied are you with your weight?'" 70% of the African American informants responded that they were satisfied or very satisfied with their current weight. While 82% of these girls were at or below the normal weight for height range for African American girls of their age, 18% were significantly overweight (above the 85th percentile). Only 12% of girls who were normal weight expressed dissatisfaction with their present weight (see Table 1).

Among Whites, results of a survey question about satisfaction with body shape revealed that almost 90% of these informants expressed some degree of negative concern about their body shape. Dissatisfaction with body weight and shape among White girls, even when their weight/height ratio is normal, has been continually confirmed in the literature (Fisher *et al.* 1991; Storz and Greene 1983).

Despite the differences in body satisfaction expressed by African American and White girls,

TABLE 1

How Satisfied Are You with Your Present Weight? Responses of African American girls, age 14–18 (n=44)

BMI	Very dissatisfied	Dissatisfied	Satisfied	Very satisfied	Total
Low*	25%	25%	25%	25%	10%
Mid**	4%	11%	71%	14%	72%
High***	14%	57%	29%	—	18%

* Low BMI indicates girls below the 15th percentile of BMI.

** Mid BMI indicates girls who were above the 15th and below the 85th percentile.

*** High BMI indicates girls above the 85th percentile.

responses to survey questions on weight control behaviors reveal few significant differences between the two groups. This was initially puzzling for the researchers. In response to the question "How often have you tried to lose weight during the past year?" 48% of African American girls stated that they had not tried to lose weight, as compared to 39% of White girls. Approximately 30% of girls in both ethnic groups had tried to lose weight one or two times in the past year. In both groups, 11% said that they always dieted. No significant differences between White and African American girls emerged (see Table 2).

In response to the question "Are you trying to change your weight now?" 54% of African American girls said they were trying to lose weight as compared to 44% of White girls. No significant differences emerged between ethnic group responses (see Table 3).

Data derived from this survey seemed contradictory. While African American informants seemed similar to White informants with regard to dieting practices, they expressed much greater satisfaction with their weight than White girls. Why did these African American girls report trying to lose weight if they were satisfied with how much they weighed?

Being Perfect: Beauty Ideals among White Adolescents

Females, particularly those who are White and middle class, are socialized through a host of influences from the media to fantasy play with Barbie dolls to believe that slenderness is essential for attractiveness and is a key component for interpersonal success (Freedman 1984; Hawkins and Clement, 1980). Many adolescent females strive for the bodily perfection depicted in the

TABLE 2

How Often Have You Tried to Lose Weight During the Past Year?

	Haven't tried	1–2 times	4–6 times	Once a month or more	Always trying
White (n=211)	39%	28%	14%	9%	11%
Black (n=46)	48%	30%	6%	4%	11%

TABLE 3

Are You Trying to Change Your Weight Now?

	No to gain	Yes, I'm trying to lose	Yes, I'm trying
White (n=211)	51%	5%	44%
Black (n=46)	39%	7%	54%

media, believing that they are somehow inadequate in comparison to the American ideal. As Freedman (1989) has noted, the adolescent search for a personal identity has been distorted into a search for a packaged image.

The ideal, "perfect" girl was often described by our White informants as being 5'7" tall and between 100 and 110 pounds. She was usually a blonde and her hair was long and flowing, "the kind you could throw over your shoulder." Descriptions mirrored those of fashion models: "I think of her as tall—5'7", 5'8", long legs, naturally pretty, like a model's face with high cheekbones." To many informants, the ideal girl was a living manifestation of the Barbie doll. The researchers were continually struck by the uniformity of descriptions of the ideal girl, regardless of what the speaker herself looked like. This led us to conclude that there was a prototypic, ascribed standard of beauty that girls struggle to achieve. The attributes of the ideal girl were encapsulated by the word "perfect." This sense of beauty was fixed: fixed on the pages of magazines, fixed on the airbrushed faces of models, and fixed in the minds of our adolescent informants.

For the vast majority of girls, "being perfect" was an unattainable dream which led to a devaluing of their own looks and a sense of personal dissatisfaction and frustration. This was particularly striking when informants were in junior high school and their bodies were undergoing rapid change. Some girls described their practices of bodily concealment in an effort to hide their bodies. As one girl explained:

> I just want to look like one of those models in the swimming suits when they walk on the beach—like a flat stomach, little hips, little

waist, and skinny thighs, so you don't, like me, have to put on the shorts and the shirt and the sunglasses.

In focus group interviews, girls were asked to describe what kind of attributes made another girl's life seem perfect. One girl answered, "I don't know. Their friends and their attitude, their looks and their weight." Another girl in the group elaborated on the weight issue:

> Well, they're not like malnutritioned or anything, I mean they look healthy. I mean, you don't look at them and say, 'Oh my God, they're too skinny' or 'Oh my God they're too fat.' They're just perfect.

Interviews revealed that the right weight was often perceived as a ticket to the perfect life. The girl with the perfect body who can "eat and eat and eat and not gain anything" was described as being "perfect in every way." By extension, the girl with the perfect body has a perfect life: She gets the boy of every girl's dreams.

> Most girls buy *Seventeen* magazine and see all the models and they're really, really skinny and they see all these girls in real life that look like that. They have the cutest guy in the school and they seem to have life so perfect...

Girls, particularly in junior high school, described how being thin was a prerequisite for popularity. Girls equated being thin with being "totally happy" and noted "how being skinny makes you fit in more." Many girls thought that boys wanted them to be thin. As one girl said "Guys always say they don't want big chunky girls, they want skinny, slim girls."

Dieting among White Adolescent Females: An Attempt to Achieve Perfection

To many White adolescents, achieving the thin body ideal was viewed as the key which opens the door to success, popularity, and romance. In group discussions, girls talked about wanting to lose weight. They spoke of dieting not just as a way to become thinner, but as a way to gain control of other aspects of their lives. This logic was explained succinctly by one high school girl:

> ...if I went on a diet, I'd feel like it was a way of getting control...like a way to make myself thinner, and make my appearance, and my social life better. So it would be like getting control over lots at different things I guess.

Dieting, a mode of producing a more perfect thin body, held the promise of control over one's present and future. A thin body constituted symbolic capital having exchange value for popularity. As one girl noted:

> I think the reason that I would diet would be to gain self-confidence...but also that self-confidence I would want to use· to like get a boyfriend. Do you know what I mean? It seems like that's the only way that I would be able to...to be accepted.

For many White girls, talking about body dissatisfaction and the need to lose weight is a strategy for establishing group affiliation. It reproduces a model of, as well as a plan for, achieving a more perfect life. Drawing on focus group and individual interview data from the Teen Lifestyle Project, Nichter and Vuckovic (1994) explored the commonality of the expression "I'm so fat" among adolescent girls. This discourse, which they term "fat talk," was commonly used among White informants to express dissatisfaction with themselves as well as a broad range of other negative feelings. "Fat talk" was also used to maintain group affiliation and served as a leveling device: in order to be part of a group, a girl had to express some degree of dissatisfaction with herself. Calling attention to one's physical imperfections afforded girls a sense of belonging with those who shared similar concerns.

Analysis of interview and survey data revealed that although talk about body dissatisfaction and the need to diet is pervasive, this does not always result in actual sustained dieting behavior among White adolescent females. Quantitative data analysis confirmed that more girls engaged in "watching what they ate" as a strategy to maintain their weight and to be healthier than were actually dieting (Nichter *et al.* 1994). "Watching what you eat" was usually deemed as "eating right, like eating a lot of fruits and vegetables and avoiding junk foods." A thin, toned body was clearly identified as a symbol of being healthy by White adolescent informants.

Competition among White Girls

Ironically, White girls who were closest to the image of the ideal girl were admired, but at the same time were the object of envy and dislike. The perfect girl provokes frustration for other girls, sometimes to the point where these girls feel their own efforts are futile:

> You just see all these older girls, like when you go to the mall, and there's like, it's like, "why was I born?" because they're so perfect.

Despite the desire to be perfect, a White female who is extremely attractive may find herself shunned by her female peers, as she represents all that her peers are not and aspire to be. Adolescent girls as well as boys scrutinize and evaluate her "reified parts" and envy is gained at the cost of self-alienation (Goldman 1992). Some informants noted that when they saw a beautiful girl at school, in the mall, or even on television, they would label her a "bitch." Since the perfect girl's flaw is not visible, it is assumed to exist in her personality. As one girl noted:

> Girls, they completely stare at another girl. If a new girl would walk in I would like notice every single flaw and then I'd wait for her to make me happy—I mean show me that she is really okay and then I kind of blow off her flaw, but until then I'm like "god do you see that big thing between her teeth...do you see

how much makeup she's wearing?," I like have to know everything…If she is really pretty, then I want to see her flaw…all of it. All of it. I want to know every single part of her flaw.

Not uncommonly, girls would state that they hated this girl, despite the fact that they didn't know her. Some girls remarked "I want to hurt her" or "I feel like killing her."

Comparing themselves to other girls and failing to measure up to self-imposed standards of beauty made some girls feel bad about themselves. As one girl noted, "A lot of times I envy other people and then I start to feel bad… that I'm ugly or something." Rather than accentuate the positive aspects of their looks, many White girls expressed a desire to alter their perceived imperfections in order to achieve the ideal.

Using What You've Got: Body Image and Beauty among African American Adolescents

African American perceptions of beauty are markedly different than White perceptions despite frequent media images of African American models and dancers who depict White beauty ideals. In focus groups, African American girls were asked to describe their sense of an ideal girl. Commonly, girls responded with a request for clarification: Were we asking about an African American ideal girl or a White one? This response signaled to the researchers that the girls were keenly aware of differences in ideals of beauty between the African American and the dominant White culture.

This was confirmed in the second survey administered to African American girls in which they were asked whether there was a difference between their ideal of beauty and that of White girls. Sixty three percent of the girls agreed that there was, while the rest reported that there was little difference. In response to the open-ended question "If yes, what is the difference?" girls wrote comments such as: "White girls have to look like Barbie dolls and Cindy Crawford to be beautiful," and "White girls want to be perfect." African American girls noted that "their attitudes

and the way they wear their clothes is different" and that White girls "want to be tall, be thin and have long hair."

When the researchers asked African American girls for their description of an ideal African American girl, their response often began with a list of personality traits rather than physical attributes. The ideal African American girl was smart, friendly, not conceited, easy to talk to, fun to be with, and had a good sense of humor. Many girls noted that their ideal girl did not have to be "pretty," just "well-kept" (i.e., well-groomed). In terms of physical attributes, girls tended to respond by calling attention to an ideal girl having it "going on." This indexed making what they had work for them: long nails, pretty eyes, big lips, nice thighs, a big butt— whatever. The skin color of the "ideal girl" was described as dark, medium, or light depending on the skin color of the respondent.

What was particularly striking in African American girls' descriptions, when compared to those of white adolescents, was the deemphasis on external beauty as a prerequisite for popularity. As one girl noted:

> There's a difference between being just fine or being just pretty…because I know a lot of girls who aren't just drop-dead fine but they are pretty, and they're funny, all those things come in and that makes the person beautiful. There are a lot of bad-looking (physically beautiful) girls out there, but you can't stand being around them.

Girls were aware that African American boys had more specific physical criteria for an "ideal girl" than they had themselves. They commented that boys liked girls who were shapely, "thick" and who had "nice thighs." One girl noted that "guys would be talkin' about the butt…it be big." Another girl explained:

> I think pretty matters more to guys than to me. I don't care. Just real easy to talk to, that would be the ideal girl for me, but the ideal girl from the guy's perspective would be merely different. They want them to be fine, you know what guys like, shapely. Black guys like black girls who are thick—full figured (laughs).

African American girls were notably less concerned with standards for an "ideal girl" depicted in the media. What emerged from interviews was a sense of self esteem which led several girls to describe the ideal girl in terms of themselves—not somebody "out there" to be emulated. As one girl noted:

> ...the ideal girl? That's me. I don't know. I'm happy with the way I am. My friends like me the way that I am and they don't think that I should change and neither do I.

Beauty was not described in relation to a particular size or set of body statistics. Girls noted that beauty was not merely a question of shape. It was important to be beautiful on the inside as well as on the outside, and to be beautiful a girl had to "know her culture." One girl explained that "African American girls have inner beauty in themselves that they carry with them—their sense of pride." This sense of pride was commonly described as a legacy they received from their mothers.

We asked girls to describe what kinds of qualities they admired in a Black woman. Girls noted that they admired a woman who "keeps her self up and acts like herself" and "is strong on the inside, knows what she wants, and looks good on the outside and inside." One girl explained that a beautiful Black woman is "a woman who accepts who she is but yet can stand up for herself, and a woman who truly believes in herself, works hard and doesn't accept negative things in her life that will bring her down." Having a positive attitude and "not worrying about your looks too much" were important components of a beautiful woman. Attitude eclipsed body parts as a measure of value.

In focus group interviews we asked girls if they heard or engaged in much talk about being fat with their friends.

> I don't hear that a lot. I hang out with black people and they don't care—we don't worry if we're fat because we'd all be drawn away from that. We want to talk about what's going on, you know, about where we're going for lunch. We're not concerned with that.

We asked girls what they would do if a friend did complain about being fat. One girl responded in the following manner: "I'd tell her 'Don't think negative. People who think negative aren't gonna get nowhere'."

Standards for body image and beauty among these African American adolescents can be summed up in what these girls term "looking good." "Looking good" or "got it goin' on" entails making what you've got work for you, by creating and presenting a sense of style. In a recent article on body size values among White and African American women, Allan *et al.* (1993) similarly report that "looking good" among African American women is related to public image and overall attractiveness rather than to weight. Adolescent informants explained that regardless of a girl's body size or shape, height, weight, skin color, hairstyle, etc., if you can clothe and groom yourself and have the personality to carry off your personal style, you are "looking good." "Looking good" had to do with projecting one's self image and confidence—having "tude" (i.e. attitude), and "flavor." "Throwing your attitude" entails establishing one's presence, creating a "certain air about yourself," being in control of your image and "things around you," being able to improvise effectively, and maintaining poise under pressure. "Flavor" refers to the sensual dimension of one's presence beyond gross physical appearance.

African American perceptions of beauty are flexible: they include, and go beyond, physical characteristics. In the second survey administered to African American girls, they were asked to select one of several possible answers to complete the statement "In my opinion, beauty is....Almost two thirds (63%) of these girls responded that beauty is "having the right kind of attitude and personality when you deal with others." Thirty five percent of girls responded that beauty is "making what you got work for you in your own way." Only 2% of our sample noted that beauty is "making yourself look as close as possible to an ideal body shape and face."

Another theme which emerged in discussions with African American informants was that beauty is fluid rather than static. Beauty is judged on the basis of "how one moves" rather than on what one weighs. Participant observation with African American girls and women trying on clothes and looking in the mirror revealed a greater tendency for these women to move with the clothes being tried on than to strike a series of static poses, a behavior more typical of White women. The importance of movement and body language has likewise been noted with reference to Black English. Speicher and McMahon (1992:391) discuss how their informants described style in conversation as a means of projecting self. As one woman noted, "When you're trying to get your point across, there's style, there's movement, there's a lot of moving." Another informant described Black English as a "very interactive form of language" noting that "it has to do with eliciting an audience's response, not just an audience's listening and understanding, but very much a visceral response, a physical response." The emphasis was as much on how you moved and the sense of style that was projected, as what was actually said.

Style among African American Girls: Using What You've Got

Style is appreciated and commented upon by peer group members. "Putting it together" entails creating style that not only fits one's person, but projects an attitude. African American girls in the study were far less likely to purchase ready made "looks" off a rack or to derive identity from wearing the label of a particular brand. The wearing of brand name clothes and recognizable styles was a major identity issue among adolescent White girls, especially in junior high school. Economics, as well as the cut of clothing (most ready made clothes are fit for a Caucasian body), affected African American girls' efforts to create a style. While brand names continued to be recognized as a sign of status, brands did not dominate African American girls' fashion statement. Style demanded that resources once marshaled be tailored, adapted, and appropriated. Brands did not create distinction in and of themselves.

Creation of a style "which works" involves making a personal statement and projecting a unique presence. This presence reflects not only on one's person, but on the African American community at large. As Taylor (1982:61) notes, style is a domain of life strongly linked to ethnic pride:

Black style is our culture. It's our collective response to the world. Our style is rooted in our history and in knowledge of our inner power—our power as a people. Black style is the opposite of conformity. It's what others conform to. In fact, quiet as it's kept, our style is envied and emulated throughout the world.

Beginning in early adolescence, an African American girl is encouraged to develop a look which "works" given her own physical endowments and her social and economic environment. In a context in which the beauty standards of the larger society are often the antithesis of African American physical attributes (facial features, body shape, body size, and hair), positive feedback from other members of the African American community is important. This feedback is essential given the constant barrage of ideal standards from the dominant White culture and negative stereotypes generated about African Americans (Gillespie 1993:75):

For who among us has not at some point in time succumbed to the propaganda, looked in a mirror felt ourselves to be wanting? Wanting because our skin is too dark, or our noses too wide or our hips too large, or because our hair wouldn't grow and never blew in the wind, or just because we never seemed to measure up.

How an African American female is valued within her family and community will determine whether she does or does not succumb to this constant assault on her person.

African American girls in the study reported routinely receiving compliments from other African Americans of both genders for "looking good" and "having it going on." Compliments were received from people of close as well as casual acquaintance, in public as well as in private, as a matter of course without any offense taken. Interview data strongly suggested that African American girls received far more positive feedback about how they look from their families and friends than negative feedback. At the same time, however, they are taught to maintain their composure in verbal battles (such as playing the dozens) in which one's opponents attempt to exploit areas of potential sensibility and vulnerability. All in all, however, African American girls reported receiving far more positive feedback for creating their own style around their given attributes than did White girls who received support for altering their looks to fit established beauty ideals. Support for dieting was commonly articulated by White girls but rarely mentioned by African American girls. Allan *et al.* (1993) confirm these findings and note that African American adult women in their sample were influenced by friends and family to maintain a larger body size.

Positive Feedback among African American Girls

Juxtaposed to the envy and competitiveness which mark White girls' comments of others whom they perceive to be attractive, African American girls described themselves as being supportive of each other. In focus groups, girls talked about receiving positive feedback from family members, friends, and community members about "looking good." This is consistent with Collins (1989:762) who noted that in traditional African American communities, Black women "share knowledge of what it takes to be self-defined Black women with their younger, less experienced sisters." Collins further contends that there is a sisterhood among Black women in their extended families, in the church, and in the community-at-large.

On the survey designed for African Americans. we asked girls what their response was when they saw a girl "who's got it going on"—a girl who has put her personal resources and attributes together. Almost 60% of our informants noted that they would "tell her she's looking good," while another 20% of girls noted that they "would admire her but wouldn't say anything." Only 11% of girls noted that they "would be jealous of her." These findings stand in stark contrast to the earlier discussion about competition among White girls.

A girl's peer group serves an important function in her socialization among African Americans. Being the same age as other group members is not as necessary a prerequisite for group membership as it is among White girls.

Broader based group membership and support contributes to flexibility in the way beauty and style is perceived and accepted. Groups do engage in surveillance, however, and hold members accountable for how they look, how they carry themselves, and whether or not they are "taking care of business." As one girl noted:

> Other people, our peers like when they don't like what you have on they will tell you and if they like it they will say so ('that's fresh')…the white girls, oh whatever, they say 'that's nice' even if it's not, they will say it anyway.

Beauty and Aging

Another difference between White and African American perceptions of beauty involves the manner in which age is represented. Age is represented as physical deterioration in the dominant White culture. Age is an enemy to be fought with vigilance through the use of wrinkle creams, dieting, and exercise programs and when all else fails cosmetic surgery. Wolf (1991), citing interviews with editors of women's magazines, notes that the airbrushing of age from women's faces is routine. Wolf contends that to airbrush age off a woman's face is to erase her identity, individuality, power, and history. With regard to adolescence, the lack of portrayal of adult White women as beautiful adds an increasing tension to achieve the beauty ideal during the teenage years.

Among African Americans less emphasis is placed on being young as a criteria for being beautiful. This theme emerged during focus groups and was queried on the African American survey. In response to the question "As women get older, what will happen to them in terms of how they look?" 65% of girls said that they would get more beautiful and 22% said they would stay the same. Only 13% of girls thought women would lose their looks as they became older.

For African American girls, beauty is not associated with a short window of opportunity as it is in dominant White culture. It may be achieved, maintained, and enhanced as one grows older and more sure of herself. The number of African American girls who spoke of their mothers as "beautiful" far exceeded White girls who tended to speak of their mothers either in terms of their youth ("when she was young..."), or as "alright for a mother," implying that as one became older, the possibilities of being beautiful were reduced.

Attitudes toward Dieting among African American Adolescents

Beauty work is closely tied to dieting in dominant White culture. Among African Americans, dieting carried less significance. On the African American survey we asked girls to complete the statement "For your health, is it better to be...." Responses included "a little overweight" or "a little underweight." Sixty four percent of the girls thought it was better to be "a little overweight," while the remaining 36% chose being "a little underweight" as a response. In the same survey, girls were asked to respond to the question "For people who are normal weight or underweight, I think dieting is...." Responses indicate that 40% of girls thought it was "okay if you want to do it" while 42% thought dieting was "harmful to your body." Only twelve percent of girls thought it was "good because it puts you in control of your life."

During interviews with African American girls, most agreed that dieting was appropriate for someone who was "very overweight." "Very overweight" was defined in focus group interviews as "someone who takes up two seats on the bus." Some girls noted that harming the body through dieting was a sin in as much as one's body was God given. Notably, informants who reported dieting behavior on surveys, articulated a different set of cultural values related to dieting and body image in focus groups and individual interviews.

Self Esteem

In addition to one's peer group, the African American family and community are sources of positive feedback that serve to enhance self-esteem and supplant negative comments directed against individuals from outside (Barnes 1980). African American children, especially those in lower socioeconomic groups, are taught

by their parents to function in and deal with an oppressive and hostile society in which they are expected to survive and excel (Ladner 1971). Children are raised with the knowledge of "how it is." Parents teach their children that resources may not be available to them, but they can succeed if they learn to "make what they got work for them."

During focus groups, African American girls expressed a greater acceptance of their physical bodies than did White girls as well as a sense of self and style based on making what they had work. Rather than reaching for an abstract ideal, these girls talked about achieving their own personal ideal. As one girl noted:

> I think that Black people, Black kids, we're all brought up and taught to be realistic about life and we don't look at things the way you want them to be, or how you wish them to be. You look at them the way they are.

Acceptance of self is also a message girls take home from the church. African American parents must prepare their children to understand and live in two cultures. W.E.B. Dubois wrote in the early 1900s about the idea of a double consciousness: "Blacks have to guard their sense of blackness while accepting the rules of the game and cultural consciousness of the dominant white culture" (1903). To achieve the former, children are raised to be part of an African American community as well as a member of an African American family. For many African American women, this entails developing a spiritual self which becomes "the greenhouse in which a woman can nurse her self-image and build her self-esteem" (Lewis 1988:64). In Christian spiritual belief, one's body is conceptualized as the temple of the holy spirit. In many communities, the church is one of the places where one's sense of style is displayed and appreciated.

Conclusion

Existing studies have identified cultural differences in body image and weight control behavior among adolescents of different ethnic groups. They have not, however, explored reasons underlying such differences. In this article, the authors point out differences in the conceptualization of beauty and style which influence how White and African American adolescent girls perceive themselves and relate to others around them. Two distinct ideologies have been contrasted that are articulated at the site of the body. While these ideologies coexist, they have an impact on White and African American women in different ways.

The ideology of advanced capitalist society is reproduced at the site of the body through the mode of working toward bodily perfection. This task engages the imagination if not the lives of a majority of young White women in America. This ideology has promoted critical assessment leading to dissatisfaction with one's physical attributes, fostered competition and envy among women, and encouraged the pursuit of goals impossible to obtain/maintain (Nichter and Nichter 1991; Goldman 1992). In a multicultural nation, the idealized beauty of White culture has been valorized and a multitude of products made available to women of color promising "melting pot" success in the form of products which help one pass/blend in mainstream America.

A second ideology, propagated within African American culture, is built around egalitarian ideals, the principle of reciprocity, and the recognition of strength and balance in diversity (Fordham 1993). Fostered is an approach to life where improvisation is valued and identity is constructed through creativity and style. Writing about the ways in which knowledge is transmitted between mothers and daughters in an African American community, Carothers (1990:239) notes:

> Daughters learn competency through a sense of aesthetics, an appreciation for work done beautifully…This aesthetic quality becomes one of the measures of competently done work as judged by the women themselves and by other members of their community.

African American girls learn from their mothers and through interactions with their peer group and community that they can project an image and attitude of power through the way they dress and carry themselves. Competency is required in knowing how to present oneself in bicultural contexts ranging from the school and street to the church and job market. In focus groups, girls continually noted the importance of style not only to project an image of themselves as individuals, but in their role as representatives of the family and African American community.

One way in which lessons about freedom, competency, and community are learned is through aesthetic appreciation in African American culture. Beauty is defined less in relation to static images and more in terms of performative competence in a multicultural world marked by conflict as well as egalitarian ideals. In contrast to a more static image of beauty as bodily perfection, a more fluid, flexible image of beauty prevails. Instead of competition which fosters envy and alienation, an egalitarian ethos is promoted, marked by mutual appreciation, cooperation, and approval of someone "whose got it going on."

Several researchers (e.g., Collins 1990; Stack 1974; Valentine 1978) have noted that American racial-ethnic communities have developed collective social strategies that contrast with the individuation of the dominant culture. Among African Americans, creating one's own style as an individual statement is important, but equally important is a positive presentation of one's community. An egalitarian ethos does not imply the absence of hierarchy nor the absence of historical tensions and interpersonal power struggles that form part of daily existence (Fordham 1993). What it does imply is that individuality, while respected in the form of personal style, attitude, and improvisation, is also encompassed by sociocentric values.

Okazawa-Rey, Robinson, and Ward (1990:100) contend that African American women are becoming increasingly proactive in their negotiation of identity:

> Rising above externally sanctioned characterizations of womanhood, some black women are fashioning their identities based upon an analysis and understanding of their own struggles and successes. Further, Black woman have united to support one another's efforts in the creation of newly defined roles and identi-

ties. Within this dynamic of self-determination, the black woman is proactive rather than reactive, aggressive rather than passive, and assertive rather than receptive.

As Root (1989) has noted, increased opportunities are available to women of color, particularly those who can operate in ways that conform to the norms of the dominant White culture. Middle class African American women may be more likely to deemphasize their black identities in order to get ahead, and may be particularly vulnerable to the message of dominant White society that "thin is everything" (Villarosa 1994). For example, Bordo (1993) claims that African American women are as likely to have disturbed relationships with food as all other women. For evidence of this, she points to African American magazines which have an increased number of articles on weight, dieting, and exercise issues. The extent to which hegemonic values articulated in popular magazines are ignored and/or resisted by individuals or groups of women bears consideration. Entering the mainstream job market may increase pressure for women of color to be "perfect" in order to counteract negative racial stereotypes. Will this translate into body discipline in the form of dieting to obtain a thin body by girls who aspire to make it, or will preexisting and/or postmodern sensibilities alter the way in which beauty and success are perceived in this community?

A final note on project methodology is in order. The initial Teen Lifestyle Project survey administered to a multi-ethnic, but largely White, population of adolescents did not reveal pronounced differences in perceptions of beauty, body image, or weight management between White and African American girls. These differences only emerged when a culturally sensitive survey was constructed following ethnographic research and administered by African American researchers. Two lessons were learned. First, survey instruments on body image and weight control designed largely for White populations mask important differences that exist between African American and White girls. Second, performance on such surveys by African American youth attending predominantly White schools reveals more about their bicultural competency than the way in which they think about beauty and body image. Because questions asked in the initial Teen Lifestyle Project survey did not address issues relevant to African American girls and because the survey was administered in a space associated with dominant White cultural ideals, responses tended to conform to those expected of the dominant population.

Follow-up research in the African American community of a sprawling Southwestern city revealed that adolescents expend considerable time and energy negotiating a sense of style in contexts where they are on display to their peers. The dominant White beauty ideal was clearly recognized, but did not play an influential role in negotiating identity. Similar studies need to be carried out in other regions and "school cultures" within America to ascertain the degree to which the findings of the present study are generalizable.

About the Authors

Sheila Parker is in the Division of Environmental and Community Health; Mimi Nichter, Mark Nichter, Nancy Vuckovic, and Colette Sims are with the Department of Anthropology; and Cheryl Ritenbaugh is with the Department of Family and Community Medicine at the University of Arizona, Tucson, Arizona 85721. This longitudinal study and a minority supplement grant were funded by the National Institute of Child Health and Human Development, grant HD24727.

References

Allan, Janet D., 1989. *Weight Management Activities Among Black Women*. Presented at the Annual Meeting of the American Anthropological Association, Washington D.C., November 15–19, 1989.

Allan, Janet D., Kelly Mayo, and Yvonne Michel, 1993. "Body Size Values of White and Black Women." *Research in Nursing and Health* 16:323–333.

Attie, Ilana and Jeanne Brooks-Gunn, 1987 "Weight Concerns as Chronic Stressors in Women." In Rosalind Barnett, Lois Biener and Grace Baruch, eds., *Gender and Stress*. New York: Free Press.

Barnes, Edward J., 1980. "The Black Community as the Source of Positive Self Concept for Black Children: A Theoretical Perspective." In Reginald Jones, ed., *Black Psychology*, pp.106–130. New York: Harper and Row.

Berg, Frances, 1992. "Harmful Weight Loss Practices are Widespread among Adolescents." *Obesity and Health* July/Aug:69–72.

Bordo, Susan, 1993. *Unbearable Weight: Feminism, Western Culture and the Body.* Berkeley: University of California Press.

Carothers, Suzanne C.,1990. Catching Sense: Learning from Our Mothers to be Black and Female. In Faye Ginsberg and Anna Lowenhaupt Tsung, eds., *Uncertain Terms: Negotiating Gender in American Culture.* Boston: Beacon Press.

Casper, Regina C. and Daniel Offer, 1990. "Weight and Dieting Concerns in Adolescents: Fashion or Symptom?" *Pediatrics* 86(3):384–390.

Collins, Patricia Hill, 1989. "The Social Construction of Black Feminist Thought." *Journal of Women in Culture and Society* 14(4):745–761.

——, 1990. *Black Feminist Thought: Knowledge, Consciousness and the Politics of Empowerment.* Boston: Routledge.

Cross, William E. Jr.,1991. *Shades of Black: Diversity in African-American Identity.* Philadelphia: Temple University Press.

Desmond, Sharon, James Price, Christopher Hallinan, and Daisy Smith, 1989. "Black and White Adolescents' Perceptions of Their Weight." *Journal of School Health* 59:353–358.

Desmond, Sharon. James Price, Nancy Gray and Janelle K. O'Connel, 1986. "The Etiology of Adolescents' Perception of Their Weight." *Journal of Youth and Adolescence* 15:461–474.

Dubois, William Edward Burghardt, 1903 [1961] *The Souls of Black Folk.* Greenwich, Conn: Fawcett Publications.

Fisher, Martin, Marcie Schneider, Cynthia Pegler, and Barbara Napolitano, 1991. "Eating Attitudes, Health-risk Behaviors, Self-esteem, and Anxiety Among Adolescent Females in a Suburban High School." *Journal of Adolescent Health* 12:377–384.

Fordham, Signithia,1993. " 'Those Loud Black Girls' ": (Black) Women, Silence, and Gender 'Passing' in the Academy." *Anthropology and Education Quarterly* 24(1):3–32.

Freedman, Rita, 1984. "Reflections on Beauty as It Relates to Health in Adolescent Females." *Women's Health* 9:29–45.

——, 1989. *Bodylove: Learning to Like Our Looks—and Ourselves.* New York: Harper and Row.

Gillespie, Marcia Ann, 1993. "Mirror Mirror." *Essence*, January 1993, pp. 73–79.

Goldman, Robert, 1992. *Reading Ads Socially.* London: Routledge.

Gray, James, Kathryn Ford, and Lily M. Kelly, 1987. "The Prevalence of Bulimia in a Black College Population." *International Journal of Eating Disorders* 6: 733–740.

Greenfield, David, Donald M. Quinlan, Pamela Harding, Elaine Glass, and Anne Bliss, 1987. "Eating Behavior in an Adolescent Population." *International Journal of Eating Disorders* 6(1):99–111.

Hawkins, Raymond C. and P. F. Clement, 1980. "Development and Construct Validation of a Self-report Measure of Binge Eating Tendencies." *Addictive Behaviors* 5:219–226.

Hsu, George, 1987. "Are Eating Disorders Becoming More Common among Blacks?" *International Journal of Eating Disorders* 6:113–124.

Koff, Elissa, and Jill Rierdan, 1991. "Perceptions of Weight and Attitudes toward Eating in Early Adolescent Girls." *Journal of Adolescent Health* 12:307–312.

Kumanyika, Shiriki, 1987. "Obesity in Black Women." *Epidemiologic Reviews* 9:31–50.

Kumanyika, Shiriki, Judy Wilson, and Marsha Guilford-Davenport, 1993. "Weight-related Attitudes and Behaviors of Black Women." *Journal of the American Dietetic Association* 93(4):416–422.

Ladner, Joyce, 1971. *Tomorrow's Tomorrow.* New York: Doubleday.

Lakoff, Robin, and Raquel Scherr, 1984. *Face Value: The Politics of Beauty.* Boston: Routledge Kegan Paul.

Lewis, Mary C., 1988. *Herstory: Black Female Rites of Passage*. Chicago: African American Images.

Majors, Richard, and Janet Mancini Billson, 1992. *Cool Pose: The Dilemmas of Black Manhood in America*. New York: Lexington Books.

Moses, Nancy, Mansour-Max Banilivy, and Fima Lifshitz, 1989. "Fear of Obesity among Adolescent Girls." *Pediatrics* 83(3):393–398.

Morbidity and Mortality Weekly Report (MMWR), 1991. "Body Weight Perceptions and Selected Weight Management Goals and Practices of High School Students—United States, 1990." *Morbidity and Mortality Weekly Review* 40:741–750.

Nichter, Mark, and Mimi Nichter, 1991. "Hype and Weight." *Medical Anthropology* 13:249–284.

Nichter, Mimi, and Nancy Vuckovic, 1994. "Fat Talk: Body Image among Adolescent Females." In. N. Sault, ed., *Mirror, Mirror: Body Image and Social Relations*. New Brunswick, NJ: Rutgers University Press.

Nichter, Mimi, Cheryl Ritenbaugh, Mark Richter, Nancy Vuckovic, and Mikel Aickin, 1995. "Dieting and 'Watching' Behaviors among Adolescent Females: Report of a Multi-method Study." *Journal of Adolescent Health, in press*.

Okazawa-Rey, Margo, Tracy Robinson, and Jamie Victoria Ward, 1987. "Black Women and the Politics of Skin Color and Hair." *Women and Therapy* 6(1/2):89–102.

Rand, Colleen, and John Kuldau, 1990. "The Epidemiology of Obesity and Self-defined Weight Problem in the General Population: Gender, Race, Age and Social Class." *International Journal of Eating Disorders* 9:329–343.

Root, Maria, 1989. "Treating the Victimized Bulimic: The Functions of Binge-purge Behavior." *Journal of Interpersonal Violence* 4:90–100.

Rosen, James C., and Janet Gross, 1987. "Prevalence of Weight Reducing and Weight Gaining in Adolescent Girls and Boys." *Health Psychology* 6:131–147.

Schiele, Jerome H., 1990. "Organizational Theory from an Africentric Perspective." *Journal of Black Studies* 21(2):145–161.

Silber, Tomas, 1986. "Anorexia Nervosa in Blacks and Hispanics." *International Journal of Eating Disorders* 5:121–128.

Speicher, Barbara, and Seane McMahon, 1992. "Some African-American Perspectives on Black English Vernacular." *Language in Society* 21:383–407.

Stack, Carol, 1974. *All Our Kin*. New York: Harper and Row.

Stortz, Nancy, and Walter H. Greene, 1983. "Body Weight, Body Image, and Perceptions of Fad Diets in Adolescent Girls." *Journal of Nutrition Education* 15:15–19.

Taylor, Susan L., 1982. "In the Spirit: Cherishing Black Style." *Essence*, October 1982, p. 61.

Valentine, Bettylou, 1978. *Hustling and Other Hard Work*. New York: Macmillan.

Villarosa, Linda, 1994. "Dangerous Eating." *Essence*, January 1994. p. 19.

Wolf, Naomi, 1991. *The Beauty Myth: How Images of Beauty Are Used against Women*. New York: William Morrow and Company.

Body Image and Weight Concerns Among African American and White Adolescent Females

1. The authors summarize prior research on body satisfaction of adolescents. Outline the key findings from this prior research.

2. How did the African American and white girls differ in body satisfaction?

3. How did the two groups differ in what they thought about other young women who are very attractive?

4. What are characteristics of African American culture that might help many African American women feel better about their bodies?

5. How are the body and dress important means of expression among African Americans?

6. Does minority status and discrimination against African Americans have any relationship to body satisfaction of African Americans?

---

51 Pony Party

Lucy Grealy

I had finished chemotherapy only a few months before I started looking in the Yellow Pages for stables where I might work. Just fourteen and still unclear about the exact details of my surgery, I made my way down the listings. It was the July Fourth weekend, and Mrs. Daniels, typically overbooked, said I had called at exactly the right moment. Overjoyed, I went into the kitchen to tell my mother I had a job at a stable. She looked at me dubiously.

"Did you tell them about yourself?"

I hesitated, and lied. "Yes, of course I did."

"Are you sure they know you were sick? Will you be up for this?"

"Of *course* I am," I replied in my most petulant adolescent tone.

In actuality it hadn't even occurred to me to mention cancer, or my face, to Mrs. Daniels. I was still blissfully unaware, somehow believing that the only reason people stared at me was because my hair was still growing in. So my mother obligingly drove all sixty-odd pounds of me down to Diamond D, where my pale and misshapen face seemed to surprise all of us. They let me water a few horses, imagining I wouldn't last more than a day. I stayed for four years.

That first day I walked a small pinto in circle after circle, practically drunk with the aroma of the horses. But with each circle, each new child lifted into the tiny saddle, I became more and more uncomfortable, and with each circuit my head dropped just a little bit further in shame. With time I became adept at handling the horses, and even more adept at avoiding the direct stares of the children.

When our trailer pulled into the driveway for a pony party, I would briefly remember my own excitement at being around ponies for the first time. But I also knew that these children

---

lived apart from me. Through them I learned the language of paranoia: every whisper I heard was a comment about the way I looked, every laugh a joke at my expense.

Partly I was honing my self-consciousness into a torture device, sharp and efficient enough to last me the rest of my life. Partly I was right: they *were* staring at me, laughing at me. The cruelty of children is immense, almost startling in its precision. The kids at the parties were fairly young and, surrounded by adults, they rarely made cruel remarks outright. But their open, uncensored stares were more painful than the deliberate taunts of my peers at school, where insecurities drove everything and everyone like some looming, evil presence in a haunted machine. But in those back yards, where the grass was mown so short and sharp it would have hurt to walk on it, there was only the fact of me, my face, my ugliness.

This singularity of meaning—I *was* my face, I *was* ugliness—though sometimes unbearable, also offered a possible point of escape. It became the launching pad from which to lift off, the one immediately recognizable place to point to when asked what was wrong with my life. Everything led to it, everything receded from it—my face as personal vanishing point. The pain these children brought with their stares engulfed every other pain in my life. Yet occasionally, just as that vast ocean threatened to swallow me whole, some greater force would lift me out and enable me to walk among them easily and carelessly, as alien as the pony that trotted beside me, his tail held high in excitement, his nostrils wide in anticipation of a brief encounter with a world beyond his comprehension.

The parents would trail behind the kids, iced drinks clinking, making their own, more practical comments about the fresh horse manure in their driveway. If Stephen and I liked their looks (all our judgments were instantaneous), we'd shovel it up; if not, we'd tell them cleanup wasn't included in the fee. Stephen came from a large, all-American family, but for me these grownups provided a secret fascination. The mothers had frosted lipstick and long bright fingernails; the fathers sported gold watches and smelled of too much aftershave.

This was the late seventies, and a number of corporate headquarters had sprung up across the border in New Jersey. Complete with duck ponds and fountains, these "industrial parks" looked more like fancy hotels than office buildings. The newly planted suburban lawns I found myself parading ponies on were a direct result of their proliferation.

My feelings of being an outsider were strengthened by the reminder of what my own family didn't have: money. We *should* have had money: this was true in practical terms, for my father was a successful journalist, and it was also true within my family mythology, which conjured up images of Fallen Aristocracy. We were displaced foreigners, Europeans newly arrived in an alien landscape. If we had had the money we felt entitled to, we would never have spent it on anything as mundane as a house in Spring Valley or as silly and trivial as a pony party.

Unfortunately, the mythologically endowed money didn't materialize. Despite my father's good job with a major television network, we were barraged by collection agencies, and our house was falling apart around us. Either unwilling or unable, I'm not sure which, to spend money on plumbers and electricians and general handymen, my father kept our house barely together by a complex system of odd bits of wire, duct tape, and putty, which he applied rather haphazardly and good-naturedly on weekend afternoons. He sang when he worked. Bits of opera, slapped together jauntily with the current top forty and ancient ditties from his childhood, were periodically interrupted as he patiently explained his work to the dog, who always listened attentively.

Anything my father fixed usually did not stay fixed for more than a few months. Flushing our toilets when it rained required coaxing with a Zenlike ritual of jiggles to avoid spilling the entire contents of the septic tank onto the basement floor. One walked by the oven door with a sense of near reverence, lest it fall open with an operatic crash. Pantheism ruled.

Similarly, when dealing with my mother, one always had to act in a delicate and prescribed way, though the exact rules of protocol seemed to shift frequently and without advance notice. One day, running out of milk was a problem easily dealt with, but on the next it was a symbol of her children's selfishness, our father's failure, and her tragic, wasted life. Lack of money, it was driven into us, was the root of all our unhappiness. So as Stephen and I drove through those "bourgeois" suburbs (my radical older brothers had taught me to identify them as such), I genuinely believed that if our family were as well-off as those families, the extra carton of milk would not have been an issue, and my mother would have been more than delighted to buy gallon after gallon until the house fairly spilled over with fresh milk.

Though our whole family shared the burdens of my mother's anger, in my heart I suspected that part of it was my fault and my fault alone. Cancer is an obscenely expensive illness; I saw the bills, I heard their fights. There was no doubt that I was personally responsible for a great deal of my family's money problems: ergo, I was responsible for my mother's unhappy life. During my parents' many fights over money, I would sit in the kitchen in silence, unable to move even after my brothers and sisters had fled to their bedrooms. I sat listening as some kind of penance.

The parents who presided over the pony parties never fought, or at least not about anything significant, of this I felt sure. Resentment made me scorn them, their gauche houses, their spoiled children. These feelings might have been purely political, like those of my left-wing brothers (whose philosophies I understood very little of), if it weren't for the painfully personal detail of my face.

"What's wrong with her face?"

The mothers bent down to hear this question and, still bent over, they'd look over at me, their glances refracting away as quickly and predictably as light through a prism. I couldn't always hear their response, but I knew from experience that vague pleas for politeness would hardly satisfy a child's curiosity.

While the eyes of these perfectly formed children swiftly and deftly bored into the deepest part of me, the glances from their parents provided me with an exotic sense of power as I watched them inexpertly pretend not to notice

me. After I passed the swing sets and looped around to pick up the next child waiting near the picnic table littered with cake plates, juice bottles, and party favors, I'd pause confrontationally, like some Dickensian ghost, imagining that my presence served as an uneasy reminder of what might be. What had happened to me was any parent's nightmare, and I allowed myself to believe that I was dangerous to them. The parents obliged me in this: they brushed past me, around me, sometimes even smiled at me. But not once in the three or so years that I worked pony parties did anyone ask me directly what had happened.

They were uncomfortable because of my face. I ignored the deep hurt by allowing the side of me that was desperate for any kind of definition to staunchly act out, if not exactly relish, this macabre status.

Zoom lenses, fancy flash systems, perfect focus—these cameras probably were worth more than the ponies instigating the pictures. A physical sense of dread came over me as soon as I spotted the thickly padded case, heard the sound of the zipper, noted the ridiculous, almost surgical protection provided by the fitted foam compartment. I'd automatically hold the pony's halter, careful to keep his head tight and high in case he suddenly decided to pull down for a bite of lawn. I'd expertly turn my own head away, pretending I was only just then aware of something more important off to the side. I'd tilt away at exactly the same angle each time, my hair falling in a perfect sheet of camouflage between me and the camera.

I stood there perfectly still, just as I had sat for countless medical photographs: full face, turn to the left, the right, now a three-quarter shot to the left. I took a certain pride in knowing the routine so well. I've even seen some of these medical photographs in publications. Curiously, those sterile, bright photos are easy for me to look at. For one thing, I know that only doctors look at them, and perhaps I'm even slightly proud that I'm such an interesting case, worthy of documentation. Or maybe I do not really think it is me sitting there, *Case 3, figure 6-A*.

Once, when my doctor left me waiting too long in his examining room, I leafed through my file, which I knew was strictly off-limits. I was thrilled to find a whole section of slides housed in a clear plastic folder. Removing one, I lifted it up to the fluorescent light, stared for a moment, then carefully, calmly replaced it. It was a photograph taken of me on the operating table. Most of the skin of the right side of my face had been pulled over and back, exposing something with the general shape of a face and neck but with the color and consistency of raw steak. A clamp gleamed off to the side, holding something unidentifiable in place. I wasn't particularly bothered; I've always had a fascination with gore, and had it been someone else I'd have stared endlessly. But I simply put the slide in its slot and made a mental note not to look at slides from my file again, ever.

With the same numbed yet cavalier stance, I waited for a father to click the shutter. At least these were photographs I'd never have to see, though to this day I fantasize about meeting someone who eventually shows me their photo album and there, inexplicably, in the middle of a page, is me holding a pony. I have seen one pony party photo of me. In it I'm holding on to a small dark bay pony whose name I don't remember. I look frail and thin and certainly peculiar, but I

don't look anywhere near as repulsive as I then believed I did. There's a gaggle of children around me, waiting for their turn on the pony. My stomach was always in knots then, surrounded by so many children, but I can tell by my expression that I'm convincing myself I don't care as I point to the back of the line. The children look older than most of the kids at the backyard parties: some of them are even older than nine, the age I was when I got sick. I'm probably thinking about this, too, as I order them into line.

I can still hear the rubbery, metallic thud of hooves on the trailer's ramp as we loaded the ponies back into the hot and smelly box for the ride back to Diamond D. Fifteen years later, when I see that photo, I am filled with questions I rarely allow myself, such as, how do we go about turning into the people we are meant to be? What relation do the human beings in that picture have to the people they are now? How is it that all of us were caught together in that brief moment of time, me standing there pretending I wasn't hurt by a single thing in this world while they lined up for their turn on the pony, some of them excited and some of them scared, but all of them neatly, at my insistence, one in front of the other, like all the days ahead.

Pony Party DISCUSSION QUESTIONS

1. How did Lucy Grealy's facial disfigurement as a result of cancer influence her relationships with others?

2. How did her face affect her self-identity?

52 James Is a Girl

Jennifer Egan

An October morning in Paris. James King, her hair pulled back into a ponytail, bounds from an elevator into the lobby of the Hôtel de la Trémoille, not far from the Arc de Triomphe, where she has been staying for the past week. "How do I look—what do you think?" she asks the 20-year-old Julia Samersova, who used to work at Company Management, the modeling agency that began representing James nearly two years ago, when she was still known as Jaime. (Company Management already represented Jaime Rishar, a top model. "James" was already Jaime King's nickname.) Samersova is now James's best friend and occasional chaperone. Seated at a breakfast table squeezing lemons into a bottle of Evian, she looks up at James, who gestures nervously at her black pants and long-sleeved black shirt. "Do you think this is proper? Do you think it's fierce yet subtle?" ("Fierce" is the superlative du jour this fall among the fashion crowd.)

"Yes," Samersova says, nodding. "Yes."

She has enormous dark eyes and braces on her teeth, and will tell anyone who asks that her father is a Russian mobster. Motherly beyond her years, she has taken a break from her studies in fashion-business merchandising at the Fashion Institute of Technology in New York to accompany James to this fall's ready-to-wear shows in Europe, which began the first week in October in Milan.

"Banana Republic rocks, I'm sorry," James says.

It is the morning of the John Galliano show, one of the most anticipated of the collections being shown in Paris, and James has been cast in it—a triumph for any model, not to speak of one having her first season in Paris. James has just finished her third season in Milan (fall, spring, fall), but because of French law, any model under 16 is prohibited from appearing in the Paris collections. James turned 16 in April.

When James has finished her breakfast— tea, a small pain au chocolat and a chain of Marlboros—I walk with her and Samersova to the Théâtre des Champs-Élysées, where the Galliano show is to take place. Despite the balmy weather, Paris has been a mess—a general strike and the resulting gridlock have filled the air with a throat-scorching smog; the proliferation of terrorist bombs in subways and garbage cans has led to a heavy police presence on the streets. Yet the fashion world feels eerily removed from all this. At the backstage entrance to the Galliano show, the most pressing question is who will get in and who won't. Fashion shows used to be sedate affairs catering mostly to magazine editors and department-store buyers. Now that models have become icons, the shows have about them an air of exquisite urgency: they're cultural high-low events, like a Stones concert in the 1970's.

Though the show isn't scheduled to start until 6:30 P.M., models like James who aren't yet stars are summoned hours ahead to have their hair and makeup done, so that the top models can arrive last and enjoy the full attention of the staff members. In a windowless backstage area, time drifts by on a languorous haze of smoke and hair spray and blow-dryer heat. A dance beat throbs unnoticed, like a pulse. James sips a can of Heineken and smokes. She picked up a horrible cough in Milan and developed shingles on her back from stress—a wide brush stroke of tiny purple blisters that she takes obvious glee in showing people. Samersova nags at her to take her medicine.

James likes to tell people that she and Samersova are Tauruses. "I mean she is the second me," James says. "That's why I bring her here, because I know that when I'm too frazzled to make a rational decision I can trust her

FIGURE 8.5 *James as she might appear off the runway.*

which looks freshly minted in its innocence yet, somehow, knowing.

Galliano is famous for his lush romantic details, and by 3 in the afternoon, James's hair has been wrapped around coils of wire to resemble branches of a tree. Makeup is next; then she huddles with the other younger models, wiling away the remaining time before the show. At one point they talk among themselves about how distant they feel from their old lives. "The hardest thing is when you go home and you realize you've grown up 10 years in 2 days," James says. "My sister is in college, earning $5.50 an hour working part time, and she's like, 'You make so much more money than I do, and I'm 20 years old.'" After a moment, James adds: "She has a 3.9 grade-point average. That's almost 4.0."

Having been pegged early on as a potential star, James opted to leave high school more than a year ago and pursue modeling full time, a route the industry publicly frowns upon but is not all that uncommon. The supermodel Bridget Hall, who even now is only 18, is said to have left school at 15. Like Hall and a number of other teen-age models, James is enrolled in a home-study program, but she admits that she has little time or inclination for schoolwork. Still, there is an intellectual hunger about her: she asks lots of questions (not always the case with teen-age models), keeps voluminous journals and usually has a book buried in her bag; today it's a contemporary Japanese novel, "The Hard-Boiled Wonderland and the End of the World," by Haruki Murakami.

Shortly after 4, the supermodels begin to show up: Kate Moss and Amber Valetta, Naomi Campbell, Shalom. Some rhythm backstage instantly quickens. One well-known model arrives in a long navy blue skirt and turtleneck. ("Fake boobs," a younger girl whispers.) In the imaginations of younger models and would-be models, each supermodel seems to stand for something: Linda Evangelista for hard work; Campbell for bad behavior; Moss for imperfect beauty that triumphed. Within minutes of the supermodels' arrival, the room is saturated with camera flashes and television crews, everyone tripping over wires and elbowing one another

because we think exactly the same. I mean she's like a boyfriend but not."

James seems quite childlike at times—she's easily distracted, prone to slouching and staring into space, then snapping to attention in a fit of enthusiasm. She's physically affectionate in a sweet, unself-conscious way, always hugging people and leaning against them. She can be insecure, like the time she accused a Company Management driver of preferring to drive another model rather than herself, then stalked away, looking as if she might cry. Yet other moments she seems much older than 16, so jaded as to be unshockable. She has a pierced nipple, a large tattoo of a winged fairy on her lower back, refers to people in their 20's as "kids" and frequently invokes her "whole life," as if this were an endless expanse of time. These contradictions are all present, somehow, in her face, aside to get at those famously beautiful faces. The media runoff falls to the newer, lesser-known models, who are already inured to the giant cameras clocking their every move, often only inches from their faces.

By now, outside the theater, an impatient, well-heeled crowd surges against the waist-high metal barriers cordoning off the doors. Everyone is brandishing crumpled invitations and wailing the name of Galliano's gatekeeper, a young bespectacled Englishman named Mesh. "Mesh! Mesh!" He paces frantically before them, occasionally waving his arms and consulting with the security guards. Now and then, a shaken-looking fashion editor makes herself heard and is pried from the crush. "I'm so sorry!" Mesh murmurs in soothing tones while delivering her into the theater. "I had no idea you were there." Inside, seating is assigned in direct accordance with status, and Galliano has sharpened the hierarchy at this show by seating his most important guests right on the stage.

Eventually the show opens to sound bites from the *Pulp Fiction* soundtrack. It's a convoluted spectacle, no simple runway viewing. Campbell saunters about the stage like a high priestess, several choirboys trotting in her wake; Shalom, barelegged in a tutu, pirouettes around the perimeter of the balcony. James appears in a white dress, her hair full of leaves. As she darts to and fro, following Galliano's wordless pretentious script with complete sincerity, she brings to mind nothing so much as a girl starring in the school play.

In the fashion world, models are always "girls." Successful models are "big girls." Stars like Moss and Campbell and Evangelista are "huge girls." Diminutive though the term may sound for a 30-year-old like Evangelista, who has made millions during her career, "girl" captures the peculiar role played by a model of any age. Backstage at a show or at a shooting in a loft, "girl" suggests, as it is meant to, someone more beautiful and less complicated than a woman.

In recent years, America has become obsessed with "girls," and the fashion world has a theory about why: actresses have lost their glamour by turning into real people, and models

have replaced them as the stars of our time. Certainly models are this decade's contribution to our already crowded celebrity pantheon. They are what rock stars were to the 70's and visual artists were to the 80's. The rise of models has less to do with the fashion industry, whose business has slumped since the 80's, than with the potent blend of cultural preoccupations they embody: youth, beauty and, perhaps most of all, media exposure. Models are perfectly suited to a culture obsessed with fame for its own sake. Appearing in the media is their job—their images are their stock in trade. They *are* famous for being famous.

In the fashion world, there is a feeling that models have changed. "Today, you're not looking for perfection anymore," says Michael Flutie, the owner of Company Management, one of several new modeling agencies that have been founded in New York in the last decade. What matters more than any particular look is a model's *attitude*, her ability to project an inner life for the camera: the inner life of someone whose surface fascinates us.

To "find a girl" is to discover a teen-ager with potential. The career arc of a model requires that she start young, and the preternatural beauty of very young girls (along with their quite genuine girlishness) makes them un-models of a sort. Even a face 21 years old doesn't look quite as fresh, and I've had models in their 20's admit that they're a few years older than they say, and tell me how hard it was to adjust to metabolic changes. For years now, and in summertime especially, Manhattan has teemed with schoolgirls, some as young as 12 or 13, who are building up their modeling portfolios during vacation. The ones with real potential almost always get magazine work before they graduate high school. The paradox of the outcry over Calvin Klein's recent advertisements for his jeans is that most of his young models were shown to look their real ages.

But if models have always been young, they have not always been media celebrities, and nowadays, teen-agers like James must contend with a level of attention—and the pressures that come with it—that wasn't there the early 80's, when I modeled briefly. The media presence is greater now, and the world has shrunk: a 16-year-old model might be offered jobs in Paris one week and Prague the next. She is part of a globalized industry

To "make a girl" is to put her on the map. Flutie began making James two years ago. James is big today, and there are people in the fashion world who believe that she could be huge. She has long, straight blond hair and a heartbreaking face—sexy and sorrowful. She has an endearing snaggletoothed smile and the luminous skin of a child. She is a slender girl and a voluptuous woman. She is growing up before our eyes, and she is growing very, very fast.

On the day Flutie arrives in Paris from Milan, Company Management holds dinner for its models at Natacha, a restaurant popular this fall with the fashion crowd. (Fashion people tend to surround themselves with one another, wherever they are.) In a downstairs room bathed in gold light, the models and their guests sprawl around several tables and wait for Flutie. There's Jicky Schnee, a bleached blonde whose modeling career took off when she had the good fortune to share an elevator one day with the fashion photographer Steven Meisel, whom she didn't recognize but whose dog she patted. There is Suzy Richards, from London, who recently cut off her long brown hair and bleached it white, and Lesli Holecek who recently cut off her long blond hair and dyed it blue-black (and, more recently, back to blond). The models share gossip from Milan— Evangelista looked fat, the runways were full of blondes, some models aren't coming to Paris because of the nuclear testing in Tahiti.

Joi Tyler, a black model, is having a miserable time in Paris. The designers are using few black models this season, and she has heard it's because Romeo Gigli used mostly black models in his spring '95 show and the line wasn't a commercial hit. Tyler turns to Andreea Radutoiu, a cinnamon-haired model with strong Eastern European features. "I never want to come back here," she says, almost close to tears.

Finally, Flutie arrives with James and Samersova. James looks exhausted. Flutie, who has bleached-blond hair and eyebrows and is wearing black leather pants (as he almost always does), sits down near Radutoiu, looking pained. He has bad news: a mix-up has occurred between the organizers of the Comme des Garçons show and the French bureaucrats who issue work permits, and Radutoiu, a new model who is having her first season, has been canceled from her biggest show. "But I was just there for the rehearsal," Radutoiu says in a near whisper, "and they didn't say anything." She has a sweet, unpretentious air—once, having run out of moisturizer, she rubbed Mazola oil on her face for a couple of days. She has just turned 19, and spent her adolescence struggling with the rest of her Romanian family as they all settled in Chicago. She looks stunned.

James, who was canceled from the Comme des Garçons show for the same reason as Radutoiu, bellows from her end of the table: "They can [expletive]. I have more important shows to do!" (Later, I heard she was in tears when she first found out.) After venting his frustration with Comme des Garçons, Flutie sips red wine. Among his models, he tends to assume a half-listening stance, like a distracted father whose mind is still at the office. Radutoiu broods. Her book is full of tear sheets from magazines, but in her first year she'll probably earn less than $30,000, more than half of which will go to repay the agency (on top of a 20 percent commission) for money advanced to her for the many expenses she incurred in the development process: haircuts, air fare, messenger fees, laser prints for her book, multiple copies of each magazine she appears in and even food. The model pays for everything, and it adds up. James, whose Corn Belt blond hair and blue eyes are more naturally the stuff of catalogues—a good source of income for models—will make an estimated $150,000 in this, her second year. But she, too, will have a commission and expenses to pay. The rest will go to her parents, who invest it and provide her with a weekly allowance.

Striking a balance among editorial, advertising and catalogue work is crucial to the success of any model who, like Radutoiu or James, is shooting for the top. Editorial work—that is, posing for the photographs that appear in the fashion pages of magazines—is low paying ($150 per day on average), but highly prestigious and a valuable source of tear sheets and exposure. Catalogues pay much better (day rates start at $750 and can go as high as $10,000 or more, for a star), but are useless in forwarding a career. To be perceived as a mere catalogue girl is to lose the hope of editorial work, without which a model has little chance at grasping for the real prizes of her business: campaigns, or seasonal advertising for designers, which can pay as much as $20,000 per day; and most desired of all, contracts, in which a model becomes a representative for a company's products or apparel lines (Moss for Calvin Klein, Claudia Schiffer for Revlon). A contract model may earn sums in the millions.

There is an upright piano at Natacha, and James begins fooling around on it. She has a charisma that draws others to her, and soon a group is gathered at the piano. Watching her, I find myself thinking of her description of her first meeting with Flutie, when she was 14: "Michael asked me a question. He's like, 'Why do you want to do this?' And I said, 'Because I want to be a star.' It didn't mean that I want to be famous. It didn't mean that I wanted everyone to know me, it just meant that I want to be a star to myself. That I wanted to be successful to myself, that I wanted to go somewhere with my life and I wanted it then, I wanted it now."

James is from Omaha. "I grew up in the suburbs," she tells me, "very normal family, like Mom, Dad, that kind of thing." She has an older sister and a younger brother. Her parents separated more than a year ago (something James never mentions), but the split is amicable and they still work together in Omaha, renting out mostly low-income apartments "When I was 12 or 13," James says, "that's when I started looking at magazines, and I became literally obsessed with designers and models. Like, I would stay up till 3 o'clock in the morning slicing the best pictures out of *Harper's Bazaar* and *Vogue* and making collages and posting them up on my door, like the fiercest pictures that I saw, like of Gaultier and Galliano and whatever. I knew every model, I knew who Steven Meisel was."

In the minds of a great many young American girls, modeling has replaced Hollywood as the locus for fantasies of stardom. Kelly Stewart, a 14-year-old high-school freshman who has been with the Click agency for two years, says she became obsessed at age 8. A room plastered with pages from *Vogue* has become as emblematic of American girlhood as Barbie has, and the assiduous merchandising of models in books, magazines and cable-television shows is no doubt fueling this surge of interest.

"When I was in junior high, I had a lot of problems with people," James says. "I started getting my breasts earlier than everyone, I had my period earlier, and people really made fun of me." Radutoiu, who spoke no English when she arrived from Romania with her family at 13, says that she, too, found solace in fashion magazines. Like fantasies of Hollywood stardom, modeling contains the archetypal elements of discovery, transformation and escape from an imperfect life into a world of riches and fame. But here's the twist: while few 14-year-olds find their way to Hollywood, a 14-year-old with even the slimmest prospects for a modeling career is more than likely to come to the attention of someone in the fashion world. A vast apparatus exists solely to ferret her out: traveling conventions like Pro Scout and Model Search America, where thousands of girls (and boys) pay to be seen by agents from New York and elsewhere; and countless modeling schools, ranging from the well known, like John Casablancas and Barbizon, to regional schools like Nancy Bounds's Studios in Omaha. That was where James asked her parents to let her go, and where Flutie, who routinely travels to small markets in search of new talent, spotted her in November 1993 at her graduation fashion show and invited her to New York.

James visited the city with her mother for several days in March 1994, when she was a high-school freshman. She saw photographers, did some test pictures (meaning that both model and photographer work for free, or that the model pays a small amount) and received enthusiastic responses. She returned to New York in July 1994, shortly after her 15th birthday, and did work for *Vogue*, *Mademoiselle*, *Allure* and *Seventeen*. She also shot an ad for Abercrombie & Fitch, with photographs by Bruce Weber. She made a splash.

"I went home after that first summer and I tried to go back to school," she says. "I went four days and that's when the work started kicking in. I had to choose whether I wanted to do my career or go to school. And you know what? I'm sorry, but you will learn so much more traveling around the world than you ever will sitting in a classroom with 25 people reading a history book. What they teach you in French class about France is bull. You will not know anything about French culture until you come and experience it, just like everything else they teach you."

James's mother, Nancy King, describes her daughter as the sort of child who scored high on aptitude tests but was apathetic in school and hard to control at home. "She was different from the beginning," says King, who is 43 and clearly the source of her daughter's beauty and blondness. "She would sit around the house and do nothing. We tried to screw her window shut so she wouldn't sneak out at night—didn't work. My husband and I were separating and I thought, How am I going to handle her alone? And then the modeling thing came up...everything happens for a reason." King sees modeling as providing direction for James now and financial security for her future, which she hopes will include college.

Flutie says he doesn't encourage early departures from school, like James's. "The modeling had nothing to do with her not being in school," he says. He mentions that another of his models, Ramsay Jones, 16, just signed an exclusive contract with Galliano for the House of Givenchy, but that the deal will allow her to remain in high school full time. (James is enrolled in a home-study program run by the University of Nebraska in Lincoln.)

James spent the fall of 1994 and much of the following spring commuting between Omaha and New York, where she lived either with Samersova and her mother in their home near Brighton Beach in Brooklyn; in an apartment Company Management rents in lower Manhattan to temporarily house its models, or at Flutie's apartment in Greenwich Village. When she traveled for work (especially common in winter, when shoots often take place in warmer cities like Miami, Los Angeles, and San Francisco), a family member, usually her mother, went with her. Her career continued to

flourish: she worked with top photographers like Ellen von Unwerth, Francesco Scavullo and Arthur Elgort, did a Benetton advertisement with Mario Sorrenti, and appeared on the cover of Italian Glamour and in the fashion pages of Italian Vogue, Harper's Bazaar, Spanish Vogue, British Elle, and other magazines.

But while the transformation from Omaha schoolgirl to New York fashion model was, at first, fairly smooth, the return trip was not. James recalls: "I'd come back and visit people. I would sit and watch them at the cafeteria table gossiping...and realize: It's so hard for me to relate to these kids because I have different priorities. All they know is who's going out with who, what test they have to take and how they're gonna steal the test to get the answers, and on my mind is, O.K., what job I have to do, when I have to be there— how I'm gonna balance it out."

Being in New York and working, however, created other anxieties. "I was like: I'm gonna miss the prom. I'm not gonna be able to look back and say that I went to the high-school football games. I was sitting around listening to my friends talk about all the cool things they did last summer, and I didn't have anything to say. I started feeling really isolated." She began turning down jobs—including a 10-day booking in Thailand for French Elle, where she would have shot 30 pages and had 10 cover tries—simply because she was in Omaha and didn't want to get on a plane.

James took a break from modeling and spent part of this past summer at home. "I finally felt close to my friends again," she says. "Driving around, going to movies, hanging out, gossiping, sleeping until 4 o'clock in the afternoon. I took my mom on a vacation to St. Lucia with the money I'd made from a job. We stayed at a spa for two weeks, totally chilled out. And then I realized after two months I was so bored of sleeping until 4 o'clock in the afternoon. I was so bored of sitting at people's houses watching them get plastered, drinking kegs of beer like everybody does in high school. My friends had already gone back to school at that point, and I had nothing to do during the day...and I decided, you know what? This is my time, and if I don't do it now, then I'm never gonna get the chance." In a sense, the decision was already made, her childhood ended the moment it became hers to choose or to leave behind.

Teen-age models new to New York face an array of temptations. Trendy nightclubs need models, and if they happen to be 15 or 16—well, they don't look it. Consequently, the downtown restaurant and nightclub scene, which for most mortals signifies difficult-to-get reservations and humiliating waits in line outside club doors, presents to models nothing but the best tables and free admission. Mark Baker, one of the best-known club and restaurant promoters in town, admits that an enormous amount of his time is spent keeping track of models, whose presence en masse is crucial to the success of the events he orchestrates. "Three-hundred phone calls a day—around the world," he says.

A model with the slightest interest in night life will soon find herself dining lavishly among large groups of models at restaurants that everyone admits pay all or part of the bill in exchange for a beautiful crowd, though no restaurateur will admit to doing this himself. Afterward, the models are ushered to nightclubs and whisked past the velvet ropes into V.I.P. sections, which are usually visible but inaccessible to the rest of the clubgoers. Needless to say, the collective desire to enter these roped-off areas is generally quite keen, which is exactly the point—"girls" draw paying customers, namely men. "In the 80's, 18-year-old models were going out to chase the celebrities," says Howard Stein, the former owner of Xenon and now the owner of System, a popular new nightclub. "Now it's all reversed. You find celebrities wanting to know where the model party is that night. And that draws playboys and would-be playboys, every little schlepper from Brooklyn thinking he's going to take home next year's Claudia Schiffer."

While most promoters, like Baker, have a protective attitude toward the models they entertain (and a desire to stay in their agents' good graces), a teen-ager with a taste for night life, and all that it might entail, will have no difficulty finding it. That first summer in New York, when she was 15, James got into drugs.

"When you first go to New York after living in Omaha your whole life, you realize how shel-

tered you are," she says. "And so I went out and I partied, and I got myself into a little trouble. I came to a point where they were getting ready to send me home. I was missing planes, I was screwing up jobs.

"But I think every girl who comes to New York needs to go through that stage. You know why? Because you get to the lowest point when you're so exhausted and so done from partying...and you're so depressed, and that's when you make a choice whether you're gonna let yourself sink or you're gonna swim, and I decided I was gonna swim. And you see girls who just give up hope, and then they deteriorate. But the successful girls do not do that."

Suddenly she is passionate. "I guarantee you...if you walk into a shoot drugged up, they will not put up with it," she says. She insists she no longer uses drugs. "I know when I was doing drugs, that people knew, and people told my agency, and they were like, I'm not gonna work with this girl...and so I cleaned myself up."

Recalling that first summer, James seems acutely aware that modeling in New York has exposed her to an awful lot for someone her age. "I remember the times where I was so alone," she says, "bawling and bawling, thinking: God, I'm never gonna be able to be a kid. God, I don't know what to do. To the point where I was so low and had no faith in anything. I could look back and say, 'Oh my God, I went through too much at such a young age,' like I saw too much, I shouldn't have to go through this pain at such a young age. I could feel sorry for myself."

She pauses and then adds: "But looking back on that, you know what? It made me nothing but stronger."

"I was so scared," James is saying the day after the Galliano show in Paris. "It was, like, acting. My heart was pounding." She is at a fitting for Jean Colonna, whose show will be held the following day near the Place Pigalle. In Colonna's vast warehouse-like loft, James puts on the red vinyl skirt and top she'll be wearing on the runway and holds still while an assistant pins it. "Look at her," Samersova says, "her body rocks in a big way." Like all models, James is used to changing clothes in front of people who are dressed. Though critical of her own body, she moves and stands in a way that is both unself-conscious and picturesque. If there is an art to modeling, this is it.

Samersova turns up her nose at the vinyl outfit. "What I think is sexy," she says, "is James when she first wakes up in the morning and has no makeup on, and she's coughing her guts out, but she still looks so beautiful."

James is coughing a lot today, and running a fever. When she's sick, her jaded side emerges. "I'm so sick of this business," she mutters as we leave the fitting. Outside, she cannot find the car and wanders into a sleepy Parisian neighbor-hood. A man walking toward us can't take his eyes off her, and I'm struck, as I often am, by how remarkable she looks—with her heart-shaped face and pale satin top with spaghetti straps, sunlight flashing off her hair; how other-worldly, compared with the rest of us.

James glances up, sees the man watching her and yells, "I'm a gangsta!" startling him. "I love [expletive] off the French," she adds with delight.

Having found the car, she is overwhelmed by gratitude toward her driver. 'You're dope, can I just tell you I that?" she says with feeling. "You're awesome."

"*Pardon?*" the driver asks.

As we ride to her next fitting, at Karl Lagerfeld, she talks eagerly about getting back to New York and seeing her mother and her boyfriend, Kyle, whom she met back in Omaha last winter. Both of them will arrive in New York shortly after she does and stay for Fashion Week, during which ready-to-wear collections are shown, for the most part, in two large tents in Bryant Park. Later, her father and brother will visit. "My brother is so amazing," she says. "He's only 13, but he acts, like, my age. He says 'I love you' every time we say goodbye."

Lagerfeld's studio is saturated with the dance beat that seems to reach every cranny of the fashion world, as if pumped from a single underground source. Lagerfeld himself is behind a desk in the fitting room. An amiable, ponytailed presence in a dark suit, he seems unperturbed by the fact that he will be showing three collections within four days. While James's outfits are being prepared—Jackie-esque suits in gold and pale blue—she leans against Samersova on a couch and reflects on her chaotic living arrangements. "I'm starting all over every time I go home," she says, "and I'm starting all over every time I come to New York. I think that's the hardest part for me of this job— I'm so unsettled. I need to be surrounded by peo-ple I love and care about, and who love and care about me." She stops, overcome by a coughing fit so wrenching it makes her gag. Finally it ends, leaving her red-faced. She closes her eyes.

"If I could have my Omaha house in New York, I'd be so happy," she says. "If there's one thing I could ask for, I'd ask for that."

It is Indian summer in New York, and thick, slanted light pours in columns down the avenues. The garment district is full of models— running to castings, congregating on street cor-ners. With their colorful clothing and long spiky legs, they look like a species altogether different from the men on the sidewalks pushing reams of fabric on trolleys or pulling racks of clothes in plastic. In New York, you feel the odd collision of worlds that combine to create the fashion business. In lofts of every description, models hand over their portfolios and walk for strangers. Sewing machines, usually operated by Asians, are often humming unobtrusively in a corner. For a new model to get even three shows during Fashion Week is considered an achievement; a particularly "hot" model might end up with 30.

A couple of days into Fashion Week, Michael Flutie and his boyfriend, Patrick Abbey, a painter, hold a party at Jerry's restaurant in SoHo. James's mother arrives before James does. She looks fashionably Middle Western in a bright red jacket that stands out amid the char-coal tones of SoHo. Like James, Nancy King has a ready smile and is forthcoming in conversation though she seems less worldly than her daugh-ter. "It took us all by surprise," she says of James's success. "We thought she'd live in Omaha, go back once or twice a month for jobs. Last year, we were just floundering. Now I've learned how to travel with her and also have my life at home." King's friend Jean Schroeder has come with her to New York from Omaha, and the two plan to go to Broadway shows and restaurants as well as to James's fashion shows. "People ask me, 'What about her education?'" King says. "But this is an education."

James arrives in a fuzzy long-sleeved turquoise sweater. Kyle is with her: an affable, unprepossessing youth in jeans and a T-shirt. He works as a cook in Omaha. James perches on a tall stool beside Jean and asks what she and her mom have been up to. Kyle stays close to James. "She needs one person wherever she is," her mother explains. "She's so much calmer when Kyle is around."

Both James and Kyle are staying with Flutie in his Greenwich Village apartment. James's mother laughs about permitting this arrangement. "Her older sister is 20," she says, "and I still don't let her sleep with her boyfriend in the house. Now her younger brother's saying, 'What about Jaime?' and I say, 'You have the same rules as your older sister. I can't explain it!'"

"Jaime," she suddenly says, turning to her daughter. "I don't like that new picture in your book."

"Which picture?"

"In the bath. We don't do that."

"My nipples are covered," James points out.

"It's pornographic," her mother says, half-teasing. "I'm going to talk to the agency."

"Mom! That picture is by Ellen von Unwerth!"

But both of them are smiling. "Guess what!" James says, changing the subject. "Someone saw my card at Calvin Klein on the 'confirmed' board." (In the end, she was not cast in Klein's show.)

James wanders away to talk to Jacques and Pascal, surname-less partners of Haitian descent who have just begun publishing Crème and Sugar, a racy magazine that caters to the fashion crowd. Pascal who has bleached-blond hair and a black eye patch and wears brightly hued 70's-style polyester clothes, tells James that he knows of a cooking job Kyle might be able to get. James calls Kyle over excitedly; she's dying for him to move here. But back at the table, Kyle says he's not interested in cooking in New York.

"Why not?" James asks, stung.

He shrugs. "I don't know. I'm just not."

Later, he mentions missing the friendliness of their hometown, the way everyone knows everyone else. "Sometimes I wonder, What am I doing here?" he says, glancing around him. Still, he's excited about the fact that a respected photographer, Dah Len, approached him at one of James's fashion shows and wants to photograph him. The shoot is set for later in November, and Kyle mentions it several times, as if hoping it will lead to something else.

One of Company Management's bookers breaks the news to James that she must go to a fitting for one of tomorrow's shows either late tonight or first thing in the morning. "I was there an hour and a half, and they didn't have it together—they were too busy getting drunk," James rails good-naturedly, but soon relents. "I'll do it in the morning. Tell them they can [expletive]."

"She has a mouth," her mother says.

The next day is Halloween, and James has five shows in Bryant Park—the first at noon; the last at 8 P.M. Generally, Nancy King says, she goes backstage with her daughter and then slips into the tent about a half-hour before the show to vie for a seat. At Richard Tyler, one of James's biggest shows, she snags one near the front. James wears three outfits that are all transparent from the waist up, so that her breasts are fully visible. Like the other models, she saunters to the end of the runway and pauses, gazing with an empty expression into a wall of photographers and video cameras. The photographers, by contrast, are a rowdy, familiar bunch, cajoling and heckling—"Come on, Kirsty, turn around!"—as if the models were their exasperating younger sisters. James's walk has a sweet bounce to it, but her expression is wary and unsmiling. Her mother leans forward in her seat, snapping pictures with an Instamatic.

Later that day, backstage at the Magaschoni show in the Celeste Bartos Forum at the New York Public Library, models pick at Kisses and Snickers from a Halloween assortment. Champagne is flowing. James has developed pinkeye from the constant application and removal of makeup, and it makes her look like she has been crying. Her skin is raw, and too little sleep has left shadows under her eyes. Kyle, who comes to all of her shows, is with her.

On the runway she appears in a gold bikini. ("Eat your heart out," mutters the woman next to me.) The minute the show is over, James is back in street clothes and being rushed through the rain, past flashing cameras and autograph seekers in Bryant Park to the Josephine Pavilion, where the Ghost fashion show is about to start. The minute she arrives, hair and makeup people set upon her like emergency-room personnel.

There are sandwiches and more Champagne. The room is dense with photographers, many of whom are in pursuit of Carolyn Murphy, a pixie-faced 22-year-old with short caramel-colored hair who is reportedly negotiating an exclusive Prada contract. Interviewers approach her ceaselessly, asking how it feels to be the next supermodel. A woman from a cable-television show wants to shoot her "real life" next week. 'We'll do shopping or something," she suggests. "We'll do you wandering through the city. We'll do…." Murphy, clearly exhausted, just keeps nodding.

"Looks like she'd rather do sleeping," someone says.

Later, Murphy rejects the idea of becoming, as she puts it, an "old-school supermodel." "The prima donna attitude is out," she says. "It's been out for a while. You have to be thankful. I want to do my job, do it well and also have my own life." Having come from a working-class Florida family, she is not one to take riches for granted. "It could end tomorrow," she says. (The Prada deal eventually fell through.)

James has removed her long-sleeved shirt and tied it over her black bra, so she won't have to disturb the gigantic cloud of teased hair that now hovers above her face. She cuddles with Kyle. "Did I look bad in the bikini?" she frets. "Did I look like I had cellulite?" She catches herself slouching and forces herself to sit up straight. "My [expletive] posture," she says. "I've gotta fix it…. Mommy!"

Her mother has just come from a matinee. "Oh, I love your hair," she says, touching her daughter's cotton-candy tease. Ghost will be the host of a Halloween party later tonight, and King seems more eager to go than James. "We had a great time at the Versace party," she says. "We danced until 3 in the morning!" Someone suggests setting her up on a date, and James whirls around, adamant. "No!" she cries. "Set her up on a date with Dad!"

"First outfits," someone calls.

James kisses Kyle on the lips. "I gotta go get dressed," she says.

It is easy to see how, after two years as a fashion model, James finds it hard to envision resuming her old life as a high-school student. At home she's a celebrity; even if she chose to go back, it would never be the same. And given a choice, what teen-ager could resist this fantasy—complete with glamour, money and the prospect of fame? So teen-age girls simulate an adulthood they have yet to experience, for the consumption of adult women who then feel dogged by standards of youth and beauty they will never meet. Welcome to image culture's hall of mirrors.

"I have James living in my house," Flutie says, "and often I have to come home and say: 'You know what? Mike is not gonna pick up after you and neither is the maid, and go clean your room and clean it now.' Now, I know that sounds like—what? An agent doing that? But you have to see the bigger picture. At a modeling agency, you're dealing with 15, 16, 17-year-old girls who are setting up their own shop. And they're asked to take care of their home, cook, travel, clean, manage a bank account and pay for their expenses on their own. I think that's a pretty big responsibility.

"You really pour your whole life into not only teaching a girl what is a good picture or a bad picture but, like, how to sit at a dinner table and really behave. I think education and having a modeling agency are very, very parallel in a lot of ways, because you have to have a sense of commitment and integrity to young people. In a way, a doctor or a nurse has similar psychological needs. Why does someone become a priest or a rabbi? The modeling world, the fashion industry and the entertainment industry have become a great place to really sort of give yourself."

Flutie is serious. And for those who find the notion of the entertainment industry being filled with would-be nurses and priests looking for ways to give of themselves, or of modeling agencies as educational institutions, a bit hard to swallow, we can only hope that he and others will live by this loopy idealism. For one thing we can be certain of: in a culture where "being someone" means "being someone people can see," where fame and fortune are held up as the highest possible achievements in any life, modeling will remain irresistible to children and even some parents. James King's precocious career is the fulfillment of a set of cultural desires she herself was in the grip of—before she was propelled into the very kinds of pictures that once mesmerized her. And that's what it's all about: getting to the other side of that equation. "I want little girls to want to be me," says Kelly Stewart, the 14-year-old model, in a moment of endearing tautology, as if becoming the object of her own desire will finally satisfy it.

At the end of Fashion Week, James and seemingly every other model in New York are at Bowery Bar. Crammed under its twirling ceiling fans, a gorgeous fashion crowd kisses hello on both cheeks and then hollers spearmint-gum-scented prattle over the dance beat. James sits next to Kyle, smoking and barely touching a Caesar salad. "I got 18 shows," she says. "That's more than any other girl at the agency." Yet her excitement seems fleeting, and she's quick to say that successes like these don't really matter.

Farther down the same table, Radutoiu is still basking in satisfaction over her last show, Marithé and François Girbaud, which took place this afternoon. "I want to go back to today," she sighs draining her Coke. "I want to do Girbaud again." She ended up with four shows each in New York and in Paris—a respectable first season.

James has brought her journal along to the restaurant. As the night goes on, she begins writing furiously in a fancy, looping script. When asked, she reads a few sentences aloud that describe, in rhyme, how uncomfortable she feels in this place where everyone watches everyone else.

She will go back to Omaha for the holidays. She and Kyle will break up—though there's no hint of that now. Come early March, she will be settled again in New York where, before long, the spring shows will begin. This time she hopes she'll have the pick of the lot.

By the time she is 20, she will very likely have made it to superstardom or have moved on. When James is finished modeling she wants to be a writer, she says, or maybe a photographer. Amid the chaos of Bowery Bar, James is using her straw to chase a cherry through her Shirley Temple and talking not of her future but her past.

"Should I have stayed a kid?" she asks, not looking up. "I think that's a question I'll always wonder about."

DISCUSSION QUESTIONS

James Is a Girl

1. In what way did James have the "ideal life" of a female adolescent?

2. Did her success as a model have any negative impacts on her development as an adolescent?

CHAPTER 9

Dressing throughout Adulthood

Mary Lynn Damhorst

AFTER YOU HAVE READ THIS CHAPTER, YOU WILL COMPREHEND:

- The many ways in which dress and appearance are an important part of adulthood.

- The physical and social aspects of dress and adult development.

- How identity and appearance continually change throughout adult life.

- How personal history is reflected in dress and the body.

If we were trying to describe adulthood back before the 1960s, we would find greater regularities and predictability of lifespan trends across age categories. But today, trends linked to adult ages are blurring in the United States. For example, in the first half of the 20th century during peacetime periods, most people tended to marry and begin families by their early 20s. Now, many individuals experience first marriage during their 30s and 40s. Levinson (1986) suggested that adults go through similar sequences of developmental stages, but individuals may experience those sequences at varying ages. Order of major life events is becoming less predictable. The impact of this variety of consumer lifestyles upon needs and preferences for apparel and other appearance-related products is substantial.

Three general stages of adulthood, which have been defined by Levinson (1986), are:

- **Early adulthood**, ages 17 to 45 years.
- **Middle adulthood**, ages 45 to 64 years.
- **Late adulthood**, ages 65 and older.

EARLY ADULTHOOD (17 TO 45 YEARS)

Almost 42% of the U. S. population is currently in the broad age group of early adulthood (Kiplinger Washington Letter, 1995). Tremendous **variety** characterizes the lives of early adults. Some individuals marry and have children soon after high school. They begin adult lives while still in adolescence. Others continue with education all the way through graduate school. Still others vacillate through periods of working and college education that result in a complex patchwork of roles throughout much of early adulthood. The span between the ages 17 and 45 is a time of important decisions about marriage, divorce, home life, occupational life, and personal life. Important experiences related to family formation, occupational success, love, definition of sexuality, and realization of life goals occur for many individuals during this age span (Levinson, 1986). Clothing and appearance certainly mirror these experiences in life.

At some time during early adulthood many individuals marry and begin to have children. Most individuals also begin careers during this age span. Because more women are working outside the home than ever before (over 70% in this age group according to Vandeventer, 1993) and a great number of single-parent households occur, overall family members have less time to shop. These trends are resulting in more traditionally "male" shopping patterns among adult women who are frustrated by the inefficiencies of retailers that do not cater to their time-poor lives (Vandeventer, 1993). More consumers now opt for mail-order and Internet purchases of apparel, or shop only with a limited number of retailers who give service and styles they can depend upon. Some adults harried by time demands simply buy a reduced amount of goods. Shopping is an enjoyable leisure-time activity for fewer and fewer adults in the 1990s (Vandeventer, 1993).

Aging of the body begins during this time of life, though many individuals still look relatively young. Great variety occurs among individuals as to when they will start noticing changes in hair, skin, and weight. Mithers in "A New Look at Beauty, Aging, and Power" describes a general fear that many women in early adulthood have about aging. With a **double standard** still in force in society—that as men age they develop an attractive "patina," while women who age lose attractiveness—many women feel that their worth as women deteriorates with aging of the body. Mithers found that some women felt great terror and self-repulsion at the first signs of aging, others experienced a feeling of power in work roles and sexual relationships as they began to look older, and still other women talked of how they were beginning to redefine beauty among older women. Individuals certainly approach aging in a variety of ways. Giesen (1989) found that single adult women were less apt than married women to define their attractiveness and sexual appeal on the basis of physical characteristics. Perhaps marital status and experiences influence how one thinks about the aging body.

And what about men? Researchers have found that men are more positively biased toward youthful appearances in others (Kogan & Mills, 1992). How do men feel about themselves as they begin to age? More research would be helpful in understanding men (and women) in early adulthood.

MIDDLE ADULTHOOD (45 TO 64 YEARS)

About 20% of the U. S. population today is 45 to 64 years old, and by the year 2020 the age group will comprise 25% of the United States (Kiplinger Washington Letter, 1995). During middle age, adults tend to reach their **peak income earning years** in addition to the highest career levels they will experience (Vandeventer, 1993). That gives this group substantial consumer power in society, not to mention political and economic clout. They are more apt to take leadership roles in their professions and communities and serve as mentors for younger adults at earlier stages of development. Middle agers also are likely to need appropriate work clothing. Because of career and income accomplishments, they may be willing to spend more for quality in apparel than they were at earlier lifespan stages.

Life hardly settles into a routine of sameness for all persons in middle age. Some individuals decide during this time to redefine career and self through shifts in responsibilities, such as moving into higher-level administrative roles in their organizations or professions or pursuing totally new careers. New job roles often require new wardrobes. Family roles change, too. Some individuals are involved in raising young families as a result of late starts on having children, while many others finally experience the **"empty nest syndrome,"** when children leave home and become self-supporting and parents

FIGURE 9.1 *A middle-aged model appeared in a 1997 Vanity Fair™ ad.*

have more money and time to spend on themselves. Apparel for travel and leisure pursuits may become more a part of purchase patterns for empty nest couples. During middle age, many women begin careers, start new businesses, or go back to college—pursuits delayed because of child care roles earlier in adulthood. Divorce also throws many men and women into the singles' scene, with renewed concerns about managing appearance to attract a mate. Also during middle age, adults increasingly need to take on caretaker roles for their aging parents, a role that often changes living situations, time expenditures, and income expenditures. Overall, a variety of changes in lifestyle experiences and consequent clothing needs of middle age individuals happen during these years.

The body also changes during middle age. During their 40s, if not sooner, men are apt to experience loss and thinning of hair if they are genetically inclined toward baldness. Graying of hair also becomes more noticeable during middle age. Interest in hair color products increases among both men and women. A decline in basal metabolism occurs in the 40s for most men and women, resulting in weight gain if substantially more exercise and much less food intake are not undertaken (see "The 1997 Body Image Survey Results," Chapter 2). Most people cannot sustain their thinner early adult body size, in many cases because of lack of time and an unwillingness to go hungry all the time. Wrinkles and facial lines start to appear, making the market for moisturizers increase for this age group. Tanning, if still pursued, takes an ever greater toll on skin texture and dryness. In essence, aging and its effects on the body become more apparent during middle age.

North America, in particular, is a **culture obsessed with youthfulness**. Signs of aging do not fit with cultural ideals for attractiveness. Victoria Secunda (1984) suggests that the United States is so obsessed with the physical self that we feel that as aging deteriorates the body, the self also degrades and "depreciates." The fear of physical obsolescence associated with aging leads increasing numbers of men and women during middle age to resort to body modifications that restore youthfulness or delay the appearance of aging. Most middle age individuals want to look younger and increasingly feel that it is acceptable to try to look younger (Harris, 1994). Alan Farnham in "You're So Vain" describes the vast array of hair, skin, and cosmetic surgery treatments that an increasing number of middle age men are considering and pursuing.

We should expect in a youth-oriented society that many men and women would experiment with a variety of products and processes to deal with their aging bodies. It could also be logically deduced that body dissatisfaction during middle aging should increase at substantial rates. Surprisingly, studies do not find a substantial increase in body dissatisfaction among middle age men and women in comparison to younger age groups (see "1997 Body Image Survey Results" in Chapter 2). Perhaps as the individual ages, new standards for attractiveness are personally devised, and impossibly young media images are rejected as role models. Or maybe by middle age the importance of appearance begins to decrease as individuals find themselves engrossed in work, family, and personal accomplishments that they feel are more important indicators of the self. Further research is needed to uncover the strategies middle age individuals use to psychologically cope with the aging body.

By middle age, individuals have lived and dressed themselves through decades of fashion changes. It seems intuitively logical that many would have defined and settled into a personal style by this age (cf. Eckman, 1997). This phenomenon deserves further research. The fashion industry seems to hold the general stereotype that middle age individuals are boring and uninterested in fashion, and that fashion is really defined and led by the young. If fashion is only what is new, hot, and cutting-edge, perhaps the industry should focus only on the young. But recall our definition of fashion in Chapter 1: Fashion is a collectivity, that is, what is seen as appropriate and attractive within a group. With middle agers so numerous in the population and with greater spending power than at prior stages of life, firms who listen carefully to market segments in this age group could do very well in profits (Waldrop, 1990). With so many individuals above the age of 40, does a relentless emphasis on youthfulness and thinness in fashion make good business sense? Lynn Darling in "Age, Beauty, and Truth" discusses the limited attention that image industries give to aging women and the diverse ways in which women adapt to and reject that treatment by image industries. The *Vanity Fair* advertisement in Figure 9.1 shows a recent effort to target the middle age baby boomer market segment.

LATE ADULTHOOD (65 YEARS AND OLDER)

It is difficult to know what label to use when discussing late adulthood. Such terms as elderly, elder, mature, and older are somehow imprecise or laden with negative connotations. Perhaps only in a culture so youth-obsessed as is the United States do we find ourselves in such a quandary to use politically correct terms when referring to the aging population. The aging American knows far too well, however, that the appearance of old age can serve as a **stigma**. The media often stereotype the elderly as fragile, helpless, incompetent, ugly, unproductive, and even silly (Kaiser & Chandler, 1985). And many institutions and individuals act as if they believe the stereotype is generally true. Cynthia Rich in "Ageism" discusses the revulsion we have toward the aging body. With about 13% of the U. S. population in this age group now and a projected 16% or more of the population in late adulthood by 2020, can we afford to pigeonhole so many people so narrowly and negatively?

As among other adult age stages, individuals in late adulthood lead quite varied lives and place different importance on appearance and fashion, as shown in "The Fashion-Conscious Elderly" by Alan Greco. George Moschis (1996) found that state of **health** and degree of interest in **social activity** were major variables distinguishing older consumer segments. He divided older consumers into four market segments: 1) healthy indulgers; 2) ailing outgoers; 3) healthy hermits; and 4) frail recluses. These segments, although oversimplified, give some sense of diversity among this age group. An individual may move in and out of more than one of these segments during the elder years.

The "healthy indulgers" segment are retired individuals who focus on enjoying life and doing things they always wanted to do when they were younger, such as travel, attending community events, and socializing with friends and extended family. This group tends to be in good health and are financially better off than many middle agers. They need clothing for active lifestyles, but may shift their expenditures to leisure rather than work-related apparel (Lee et al., 1997). "Ailing outgoers" are also a socially active group. Despite having experienced major health problems, they want to get the most out of life and keep as active as possible. This group is interested in looking socially acceptable, but are a prime segment for mail-order purchases probably resulting from the physical demands of in-store shopping. This group also expresses a desire for functional clothing with easy dressing features.

Not all of the elderly are quite so outgoing. Moschis found a sizeable number of "healthy hermits," individuals whose health is good but who withdraw psychologically and socially to some extent. Many in this segment have experienced challenging life events such as the loss of a spouse. Despite their more limited socializing, healthy hermits emphasize conformity in clothing and will pay more for well-known brands that give confidence in quality and acceptability.

"Frail recluses" have experienced greater levels of physical decline, which reduces their ability to go out and be socially active. They are more apt to accept old age status. The numbers of individuals with serious health problems become greater as their age increases. This is, in part, why expenditures for apparel tend to peak around age 68 and steadily decrease with increasing age (Lee et al., 1997). Other possible reasons for decreasing expenditures include such factors as reduced wear and tear put on clothing as activity decreases, reduced interest in buying clothing as concerns about limits of retirement income increase, and less need for more expensive work and formal clothing.

As aging progresses, all individuals are apt to experience many common physical changes, as illustrated for aging women in Figure 9.2. Tierney (1987) describes changes in the aging body. Both men and women lose an inch or more in height as a result of wearing down of cartilage between the bones. Gravity takes its toll via sagging and wrinkling of skin, and aging spots and other pigmentation problems will probably also occur. Clothing designs that hide wrinkled and discolored areas are often preferred by this age segment. Although weight gains tend to slow down after age 60, gravity resettles body weight downward. The waist thickens in men and women, and chest muscles and bustlines tend to sag. As muscles weaken, many individuals stand less erect. Loss of muscle control for urinary elimination requires some older people to use adult diapers, an embarrassing adjustment for some individuals (Dychtwald & Flower, 1989).

Joint and skeletal problems become more common, in some cases requiring special fitting of clothing to adjust to curvature of the spine. Arthritis is more common in late adulthood and can reduce a person's ability to reach and to manipulate fingers; easy dressing features such as front zippers and larger buttons may be helpful. The skin thins and dries out as it grows older, making aging individuals more sensitive to rough textures, heat, and cold. Further decline in basal metabolism also increases cooling of the body (Dychtwald & Flower, 1989). Layering of clothing can give flexibility in dealing with sensitivity to temperature. Need for

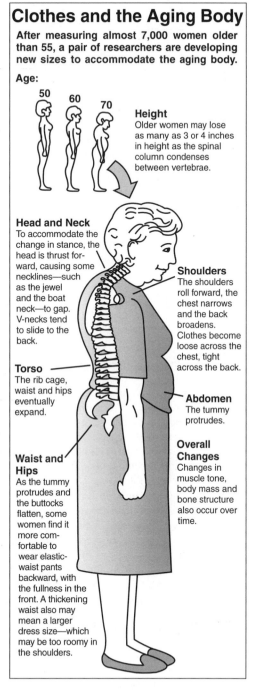

Clothes and the Aging Body

After measuring almost 7,000 women older than 55, a pair of researchers are developing new sizes to accommodate the aging body.

Age:

50 60 70

Height
Older women may lose as many as 3 or 4 inches in height as the spinal column condenses between vertebrae.

Head and Neck
To accommodate the change in stance, the head is thrust forward, causing some necklines—such as the jewel and the boat neck—to gap. V-necks tend to slide to the back.

Shoulders
The shoulders roll forward, the chest narrows and the back broadens. Clothes become loose across the chest, tight across the back.

Torso
The rib cage, waist and hips eventually expand.

Abdomen
The tummy protrudes.

Overall Changes
Changes in muscle tone, body mass and bone structure also occur over time.

Waist and Hips
As the tummy protrudes and the buttocks flatten, some women find it more comfortable to wear elastic-waist pants backward, with the fullness in the front. A thickening waist also may mean a larger dress size—which may be too roomy in the shoulders.

FIGURE 9.2 *Many changes occur as the body ages.*

moisturizers, skin care products, and protection from the sun increases. Sallow skin and gray hair may change an individual's choice of color in garments and other forms of dress.

Despite all of the probable body changes, aging adults have not been found to have lower levels of body satisfaction than individuals in younger adult groups (see "1997 Body Image Survey Results" in Chapter 2). As among middle agers, the elderly may readjust their standards for what is satisfactory. Kaiser and Chandler (1985) found that men who were judged attractive by older adults were neat and well-dressed. Appearing healthy also may have high importance in assessments of attractiveness among the elderly. In addition, more emphasis may be put on attractiveness of men among older married couples. Peterson and Miller (1980) found that couples who thought that the husband was attractive tended to have more positive marital relationships. The wife's level of attractiveness was not a factor in marital satisfaction. Do older couples simply ignore the wife's appearance because of the societal notion that older women cannot be attractive? That is a frightening thought!

Marital status also has an influence on expenditures for dress among the elderly. Single women in this age group spend more on clothing (Lee et al., 1997), possibly as a result of independence in spending patterns but also in part because of renewed interest in dating and attracting a new mate after losing a spouse. Romance does not necessarily end with retirement.

THE FLOW OF SELF-HISTORY

Adulthood, just as childhood and adolescence, is a time of continuing changes and developments (Secunda, 1984). Dress and feelings about the body reflect the **dynamic lifespan process** at any age. Two articles in this chapter round out our sense of the variety of ways that dress and appearance are important parts of adult life.

Clothing and the body have **histories**—histories that remind us of critical and valuable moments and experiences in life. In "Saving Grace," Jackie White reports on the collections of old clothing and accessories that many adult consumers save over time. These items of dress serve as mementos of old times, treasures that store personal histories.

Our bodies also have histories that very much shape our identities. The way we look in childhood and adolescence perhaps never fully leaves our sense of self. Hanan Al-Shaykh ("Inside a Moroccan Bath") tells the cross-cultural history of her body. As a young woman in Beruit, she experienced great disappointment and constant taunting by others that she was too thin. Women in Arabic cultures are perceived as more attractive if they have fuller, rounded bodies. Her adult life spent in Europe helped her to redefine her thinness as attractive because of the Western preference for thinness. She is surprised, however, to have feelings of deficiency flood back on herself when she visits an Arabic culture later in her adulthood.

Our identities are shaped by responses from others. Even through adulthood, appearance expresses our identity, and responses from others toward appearance help us to assess who we are among others. We compare ourselves to others throughout life in the fluid process that is the self.

Summary

In this chapter, we examine three general life stages—early, middle, and late adulthood. During each stage, a variety of life experiences occur, and individuals experience these in varied orders. However, general trends in life stages create dress needs and consumer wants at each stage. For example, in early and middle adulthood, career and work dress needs are stronger. Older consumers are more apt to need special adjustments in clothing because of the physical changes of aging. The aging body becomes increasingly evident as the stages progress. Our youth-oriented culture may be influencing a greater number of middle age men and women to get cosmetic surgery as they try to maintain younger appearances. Surprisingly, body satisfaction does not substantially decrease as the signs of aging increase. More research is needed on how individuals cope with the aging body.

Suggested Readings

Foster, P. (Ed.) (1994). *Minding the body: Women writers on body and soul.* New York: Bantam Doubleday Dell Publishing Group.

Harris, M. B. (1994). Growing old gracefully: Age concealment and gender. *Journal of Gerontology, 49*(4), 149–158.

Melinkoff, E. (1984). *What we wore: An offbeat social history of women's clothing, 1950 to 1980.* New York: Quill.

Moschis, G. P. (1996, September). Life stages of the mature market. *American Demographics*, 44–47, 50.

Secunda, V. (1984). *By youth possessed: The denial of age in America.* Indianapolis, IN: Bobbs-Merrill.

LEARNING ACTIVITY
Life Histories in Dress

"Integral to a sense of who we are is a sense of our past " (Belk, 1988, p. 148). In our possessions we store memories of our past, memories that define identities past and shape identity in the present. In old age, people often treasure possessions such as photographs and other mementos (Csikszentmihalyi & Rochberg-Halton, 1981). Dress is part of the past and may remain as part of our possessions. Even if an individual has not saved any items of clothing, photographs often record how a person looked and what a person wore. Photos and saved items of dress can serve as windows to the history of the self.

Objective: Talking with an older individual about old photos and saved clothing items can provide a wealth of information about the individual as well as times past. This activity will help you explore how dress reflects the lifespan of an individual.

Procedure

Read Jackie White's article, "Saving Grace," in this chapter. Then arrange to interview an older man or woman, preferably someone 70 years or older. Before the interview, ask the person to get out old photographs of him or herself and items of dress that they have saved since their childhood through younger adult years. Tell your interviewee that you want to talk with him or her about these mementos of the past to find out about how he or she dressed and appeared when he or she was younger. If possible, record the interview on audio or video tape, but be sure to ask your interviewee if it is all right to record. If not, be prepared to take extensive notes.

At the beginning of the interview, remind the person why you are there. Then ask the individual about each item of dress and each photograph. Ask things such as:

- What was happening when the picture was taken?
- What did you wear this for? Did you wear it often? Just once?
- How did you acquire the item? Where was it purchased? Did someone make it? Was it expensive? Was it a gift; if so, who gave it to you?
- Did you like the clothing/hairstyle/accessory? Why or why not?
- Was the item/hairstyle/look fashionable at the time? Or was it your own personal look?
- Does the photo/item remind you of other people you knew? In what way?

People often save items that trigger positive memories (Belk, 1988). Do not be surprised if the person tells rather happy stories about each picture and item. Some things, of course, may trigger sad memories or memories of people lost through death or distances. These recollections are all a valuable part of self-history and social history. The stories will inform you about life in the past. Let your interviewee talk at length. Many older persons will enjoy talking about their mementos and will love the attention you are giving them.

Hopefully, you will find your interview a rewarding and interesting experience. You will learn how dress is a window to the self and the past and how dress reflects the life-span of the individual. The interview might make you start thinking about items you want to save for your own future collection.

References

Belk, R.W. (1988). Possessions and the extended self. *Journal of Consumer Research, 15*, 139–168.

Csikszentmihalyi, M., & Rochberg-Halton, E. (1981). *The meaning of things: Domestic symbols and the self.* Cambridge, MA: Cambridge University Press.

Dychtwald, K., & Flower, J. (1989). *Age wave: The challenges and opportunities of an aging America.* Los Angeles: Jeremy P. Tarcher, Inc.

Eckman, M. (1997). Attractiveness of men's suits: The effect of aesthetic attributes and consumer characteristics. *Clothing and Textiles Research Journal, 15*(4), 193–202.

Giesen, C. B. (1989). Aging and attractiveness: Marriage makes a difference. *International Journal of Aging and Human Development, 29*(2), 83–94.

Harris, M. B. (1994). Growing old gracefully: Age concealment and gender. *Journal of Gerontology, 49*(4), 149–158.

Kaiser, S. B., & Chandler, J. L. (1985). Older consumers' use of media for fashion information. *Journal of Broadcasting & Electronic Media, 29*, 201–207.

The Kiplinger Washington Letter. (1995, Dec. 22.) 2000 *and beyond.* Washington, DC: The Kiplinger Washington Editors.

Kogan, N., & Mills, M. (1992). Gender influences on age cognitions and preferences: Sociocultural or sociobiological? *Psychology and Aging, 4*, 73–78.

Lee, J., Hanna, S. D., Mok, C. F. J., & Wang, H. (1997). Apparel expenditure patterns of elderly consumers: A life-cycle consumption model. *Family and Consumer Sciences Research Journal, 26,* 109–140.

Levinson, D. J. (1986). A conception of adult development. *American Psychologist, 41,* 3–13.

Moschis, G. P. (1996, September). Life stages of the mature market. *American Demographics,* 44–47, 50.

Peterson, J. L., & Miller, C. (1980). Physical attractiveness and marriage adjustment in older American couples. *The Journal of Psychology, 105,* 247–252.

Secunda, V. (1984). *By youth possessed: The denial of age in America.* Indianapolis, IN: Bobbs-Merrill.

Tierney, J. (1987). The aging body. In H. Cox (Ed.). *Aging* (5th ed., pp. 42–47). Sluice Dock, CT: Dushkin Publishing Group.

Vandeventer, E. (1993, March 18). Demographics drive buying trends. *Standard & Poor's Industry Surveys, 161*(11, Sec. 1), T61–T65.

Waldrop, J. (1990, August). The fashion harvest. *American Demographics,* p. 4.

53　A New Look at Beauty, Aging and Power
Carol Lynn Mithers

I laughed when I found my first gray hair. I was 26 and mourning the end of a relationship with a man of 38 who had often told me I was too young for him. The well-timed appearance of that silver strand was like my body making an inside joke.

A few more years went by and the hairs slowly but relentlessly multiplied. I stopped laughing and started experimenting with hair dyes. Then I started worrying about wrinkles. The last summer I got a tan I found tiny white marks under my eyes and realized with astonishment that these were under-eye creases that the sun couldn't reach. After that, I noticed deep brackets growing around my mouth. The amused, almost incredulous response I'd had to that first touch of gray—look! on me!—gave way to a muted panic: Something was happening that I was entirely powerless to stop. On the afternoon of my thirty-fifth birthday, I had what can only be described as a tantrum. My lover of many years was taking me to dinner, and I spent hours in front of the mirror frantically trying on and rejecting clothes, for none of them turned my reflection into the one I wanted to see. "Nothing looks good!" I whimpered over and over. "My hair, my face, these pants....Nothing looks right."

My lover watched, upset and perplexed. "What exactly is going on here?" he asked. The answer, of course, was that I was terrified. The first time you find it impossible to deny that you're aging—whether the evidence is the appearance of a wrinkle or the arrival of a particular birthday—is the first time you confront the melancholy fact of your own mortality. And if you're female, it is also the first time you face the truth that before long you will be an "older" woman. That the former frightened me seemed perfectly natural; that the latter did just as much was embarrassing.

As a child I'd learned not to ask the age of my mother's friends, for apparently the question was one that shamed any woman over 29. But

that had been a different time, one in which a woman's main source of power was her physical appeal, and her main job the bearing and raising of children—which meant that she was "used up" by her forties, when the kids left home, or her fifties, when she entered menopause. By the time of my thirty-fifth birthday, everything had changed. Women had a choice of professions, of when and whether to bear children; they held a real measure of political and economic clout. Even the look of female maturity I recalled from childhood—"sensible" short hair, a thick body with a shelf-like bosom clothed in a frumpy pastel housedress—was nowhere to be seen. Instead, even women in their sixties and beyond were as trim, fit and vibrantly stylish as their much younger sisters. My feelings seemed so hopelessly retro that I felt stupid just for having them. At a time when there was no shortage of older female "role models"—including, soon, a sleekly confident 45-year-old who would redefine the role of first lady—surely no one but me faced the idea of aging with such confusion and terror.

Wrong. Women are obsessed, as we are about nothing else—except, perhaps, weight—with the physical fact of growing older; our feelings are a contradictory tangle of reason and blind emotion, exhilaration and despair, old and new beliefs. In 1900, the average female life expectancy was 48. Today it is 79, which means many of us will be "older" women almost half our lives. All of us are wrestling with that fact, struggling to define what it means to age—how we want to act, look and be seen, how aging makes us feel.

Intellectually, every woman knows that she'll eventually get—and look and feel—old. Emotionally, no one believes it. So when the first real sign of aging appears, usually around the late twenties, it creates a shock so intense that women remember it in vivid detail long afterward. "Last year, I looked at pictures of myself at 22 or 23 and saw that then I'd had round cheeks and soft-looking skin and now I didn't," says Ariel*, 30, an editor. "Suddenly my face looked very thin to me, angular in a way it hadn't before. A little drawn. There seemed to be some sort of freshness of life that was missing. Suddenly I realized I didn't look young anymore."

A very few women—often those raised in places or cultures that hold elderly people in high esteem—can accept such a realization with relative ease. "I grew up in Santa Fe, New Mexico, when it was a city of only around 45,000 people and everyone had known each other's families for generations," recalls Carmella Garcia, 30, an insurance broker. "Good looks were nice, but looks didn't define who you were. I live in L.A. now and most of my friends are really neurotic about aging—they're always talking about their wrinkles and sagging knees. My mother raised 13 children and I never heard her complain about getting older. She's 69 and has these wrinkles that are really lovely—crow's-feet around her eyes and smile wrinkles on her cheeks. She has wonderful salt-and-pepper hair. I wouldn't mind looking like that."

Other women's responses are more stereotypical, with all the denial and hysteria of a "Not Another Birthday!" card. Faced with a body that no longer burns off burgers and chocolate milk shakes, Georgia, a 31-year-old bank teller, rises at five to go running, swims in the evening and does aerobics on her lunch hour. Jean, a 35-year-old store manager, is fixated on her incipient crow's-feet, cutting out every magazine article about face-lifts, collagen shots and chemical peels; "By 40, I'm going to do something serious about my skin," she swears. At 30, Hayley, an accountant, so mourns the loss of her youthful looks that it casts a pall over her life. "I wish I'd never lain out in the sun," she says. "I have wrinkles everywhere, from my hands to my face. I hate being this old. Women in their twenties have the world in their hands. Men of any age

like them. They like themselves. In your thirties, you're at the mercy of society. There's a desperate feeling, like time's running out."

Certainly such extreme responses are most common among those who have always received attention for their looks. But large numbers of average-looking women also find themselves thrown badly by the first signs of age. "All of a sudden," says one otherwise pragmatic 27-year-old, "I'm spending big money on creams that I know are just triumphs of packaging." At one level, such reactions are a predictable human response to the essential strangeness of physical alteration. We do so much growing and changing through childhood and adolescence that reaching adulthood feels like arrival: What we look like in our early twenties—how we feel and what we can do—is who we *are*. When that reality shifts—when a face that was full becomes thin, when a customary evening cup of coffee suddenly causes insomnia—it feels strange, wrong. "It's as if you don't know your own body anymore," says Ella, 31, a reporter.

In addition, the truth is that many physical changes associated with aging aren't improvements. Eyes that start to need reading glasses or once-tireless legs that now turn stiff after a single day of skiing are undeniable evidence that one's body is weakening, a warning that the coming years may impose genuine limitations—of physical ability, of choice. "I've had this self-protective attitude that people can be fit when they get older if they want to be," says Marla, 33, a graphic artist. "But this year, my grandmother, who's in her eighties and has always been very active, didn't make it to my wedding because she felt too sick. It made me think that maybe having a good attitude isn't going to save me. I'm no longer so sure that you can be terrific until you drop dead. And I've started to get some early arthritis symptoms in my knees. Sometimes in the morning I have trouble walking. It's frightening, and it's made me focus intensely on physical fragility. And *that's* brought up the question of what I'm doing with my life. There's a part of me that feels I haven't pursued things closest to my heart. I've always dreamed of being a serious painter, traveling and living in foreign cities, and my body's changes made me realize that if I really want to do that, I don't have forever. If I become a semicripple, I can't decide to suddenly change careers and go all over the world."

But human fears of mortality and physical breakdown are only part of the story. It's their changing appearance that causes many women to face aging with at best ambivalence and at worst dread. Despite the broadening of women's roles (and despite reassurances from individual men), a double standard about aging remains very much alive. In our culture, men may be considered attractive whatever their age—wrinkles make their faces "interesting"; gray hair makes them "distinguished." The attributes that make women attractive are invariably youthful qualities such as a "fresh" face and "taut" body; in fact, female attractiveness and youth are so linked that descriptions of a nonyouthful appearance almost invariably involve negative adjectives. Older breasts aren't soft, they're "sagging"; an older female face isn't just thin but, as Ariel put it, "drawn."

As a result, most women feel deep in their being that getting older makes them less desirable. Debra, a 36-year-old social worker whose clients are elderly, erupts in protest whenever she hears a remark she considers ageist—yet she admits that she finds it difficult to accept aging in herself. "There's a difference between thinking someone else is an attractive older woman and seeing your own aging as attractive," she says. "I'm obsessed with my wrinkles. I don't see them as a sign that I'm washed up, but they mean not being as pretty." Feeling "not as pretty" is no small matter: Because looks and desirability have traditionally been the foundation of a woman's power, such a change threatens a loss of status and influence.

The equation between aging and loss of power is one that many women have learned from their own mothers. Susan, a 27-year-old broker, says she first began to worry about growing older when she was 22 and her mother reached her early fifties. "She started quietly making disparaging noises about how old she was looking," Susan remembers. "One time while we were shopping I noticed that when she was trying on an outfit she was pulling on her face in an unconscious effort to make it look

younger. I found that such a sad gesture. It was the first time it struck me that aging was a tough process to deal with—that it had obviously snagged my mother and it would probably get to me as well. Looking good has been important most of my life; I credit a certain amount of the attention I've gotten to my appearance. When I expect to feel worst is that middle time—you're not yet old, but you're no longer young. My 80-year-old grandmother seems very beautiful to me. Where you see the struggle between youth and age is in the faces of *middle-age* women."

There's nothing new about the double standard in aging, or about how deeply women internalize it and how bad it makes them feel. What *is* new, however, is that these feelings, once accepted with sad or bitter resignation, now evoke overt rebellion. "I feel what I feel," Susan says fiercely. "But I'm fighting it every step of the way." It's a fight that takes several forms. As they look toward the future, women are reaching out, in a kind of hunger, for a new, more appealing image of older women. Some have embraced the ideal of the woman whose face and body actively deny her age—the woman who works out, dyes her hair, lifts her face, and looks, at 45 or 55, as conventionally attractive as someone years younger. Others vehemently object to this equation of artificial youth with attractiveness. Mary, a 41-year-old nurse, derides "women I see at my gym—50- and 60-year-olds with too much makeup, lifted faces and thong leotards." Her wish is for an expanded standard of female beauty, so that a woman who looks her age can still be considered appealing. "I want to look sexy no matter how old I am," Mary says. "But I'm not sure how a sexy 41-year-old looks. I don't want to make a fool of myself."

A few others, like Anne, 40, an educational programs analyst, argue against both positions. Either way, she says, women are judged too much on their appearance. Emphasizing that women can—or should—look great at any age denies the reality and circumstances of many women's lives. "My weight has become a big deal between my husband and me," she says. "There's this notion that women should remain thin and sexy and gorgeous forever, but when you're working, raising a child and running a house, you can't always pull it off. I can't look like a little tootsie—and I don't even want to—I'm not one."

Fortunately, many women are finding that their most negative reactions to getting older are challenged by the actual experience of aging. Age is not, they say, simply about loss. Judith, a 37-year-old teacher who reports being raised on "stories of women who get old and used up and then their husbands dump them for younger women," learned during a yearlong affair with a 26-year-old man that age could bring an unexpected sexual power. "It was great," she says. "Yes, in part I enjoyed it for the wrong reason—because I felt like if a younger man wanted me, it must mean I was still OK. But it wasn't just that. He looked up to me because I was older, and he was always a little worried about whether I'd find him interesting. Having someone worry about keeping *my* interest rather than the other way around was an amazing experience. It made me feel intellectually powerful in a way I never had before in a relationship. I wasn't afraid to let loose with what I thought. And I wasn't afraid to let loose sexually, either. You know all the publicity about how women reach their sexual capacity in their thirties? That's how he saw me—as the incarnation of this erotic, multiorgasmic creature. It was very exciting."

Thirty-six-year-old Debra acknowledges that despite her "obsession" with her wrinkles, her new face has brought her a professional respect she never enjoyed before. "When I first started working, I was 23, probably looked 19, and everyone around me was much older," she says. "They treated me like a cute little girl rather than a professional. I had to just go quietly about my job until they saw I could do it—I later had people tell me they never expected me to be competent. I once had a run-in with a colleague who was in her late thirties, and afterward she remarked to someone, 'Go tell the little girl....' Those things don't happen anymore. I don't have to struggle to get people to believe I know what I'm doing. I can be more relaxed in how I act at work, even in how I dress." It's not, she points out, that gaining professional respect cancels out her sadness at feeling she looks "less pretty"; none of the women I spoke to said that job success completely overshadowed their concerns about aging. "How I want to get treated at work and how I want to look are two separate things," Debra says. "But at least I have the chance to trade one strength for another."

Similarly, many women reported that having a good love relationship eased, but did not eradicate, their fear of growing older. "There's no respect for age in my business," says Linda, 42, who works in the film industry. "But I'm happily married and still in love, and my husband still thinks I'm beautiful and desirable. Because of him, it's harder to make me feel I'm getting fat or used up. I never lie to people in my profession about my age."

Sharon, 34, a homemaker, points out that motherhood can make the signs of aging seem less important. "My rear end is floppy, and there's not much nice that I can say about it. The minute I heard you could use Retin A to make stretch marks disappear, I meant to go out and get some. But I haven't. I guess I figure that if you let yourself get obsessed about these things, they'll take over your life. Besides, I have two wonderful kids to show for those marks. Would you want to go through something as life-changing as pregnancy without having it show?"

Forty-two-year-old Marty, who owns a temporary-employment agency, points out—as did a number of women in their forties—that being forced to face the physical imperfections that come with age can, ironically, lead to feeling at ease with one's body for the first time. "Since I was 35 I've worked out almost every day, and I'm very proud of how I feel and look," she says. "In college, I could barely make it around the track—I'm far stronger now than I was. And I'm happier with what I have. I've never had what you'd call a great body, and it really used to grieve me. But now when I see some perfect creature, I don't feel bad anymore. It's because I've had to let that wish go. I know I'm never going to look like that—I'm too old, it's impossible. In some ways that's a little sad. But it also frees me from the old envy and compulsion."

"I wish I were less tired and more fit, but in general, I like the way I look now," says Leslie Spanier-Wyant, 42, an executive at a child-care-management company and mother of a-five-year-old. "Ten years ago, whether or not I looked perfect was always at the forefront of my mind. But who has time for that anymore? Besides, it turns out that it doesn't matter. It doesn't matter in terms of doing well at my job, it doesn't matter to my daughter, it doesn't even matter to my husband. In everything that's important to me, perfect looks just don't matter."

What one hears most in women's voices is that a rebellion against negative images of the "older woman" and a discovery of the gains that come with age have begun to alter the way we feel about getting older. There are signs that the old cultural double standard may be crumbling a bit, too. It's no longer taboo to talk about menopause, for example, and here and there one hears the adjective "beautiful" applied to a woman in her fifties or sixties—and not just a Gloria Steinem or a Jacqueline Onassis. For the first time ever, photos of over-40 models in sexy, glamorous poses are appearing in major magazines—a step forward even when you acknowledge the inevitable airbrushing. Last year, sultry, sensual photos of Hillary Rodham Clinton were published in *Vogue*. The photos acknowledged something revolutionary: A woman who was not conventionally beautiful could become physically alluring through her power. Increasing female visibility in business and government has brought nearer the advent of the woman whose appeal is ageless because it is based on her strength and ability. "You don't look at Janet Reno or Pat Schroeder and think 'Gee, they're looking old,'" says Karen, a 31-year-old union organizer. "These are women of substance."

Full change will require more. Women, insists 27-year-old Susan, must learn to be kinder to each other. "Some of this we do to ourselves," she says. "We go to reunions with nothing more pressing on our minds than seeing who'll look ten years older and who won't. I've heard the pleasure in my mother's voice when she talks about how old her sister looks. Even if those words aren't aimed at you, you feel their brutality. We make each other feel diminished, and we've got to stop it."

A deep transformation of culture is needed too. It's unrealistic to expect that we'll ever lose our profound attraction to youthful beauty, for such beauty symbolizes a time in life when everything is new and full of promise. But in large part we have prized youth in women because the qualities we most valued in women *were* those of youth: innocence, guilelessness, malleability. As that changes, and as more and more women occupy positions of importance, prestige, power, and respect, the chances increase that women, like men, may be considered beautiful by virtue of our sophistication, wit, talent, and accomplishments, for who we are and what we have done rather than how old we happen to be. We may finally understand that we can praise "taut" faces and bodies and also celebrate those that are "ripe," "plush," or "soft," that enjoying images of young women doesn't mean that we can't also enjoy the beauty of older women—a beauty that is unlifted, unretouched, *real*.

DISCUSSION QUESTIONS

A New Look at Beauty, Aging and Power

1. What were the various images and ideas that women in their 20s and early 30s had about getting older?

2. How do the negative fears that some women had about aging reflect current U.S. societal myths about aging?

3. Are the positive images of getting older that some women had rare and unrepresentative? Or do the positive images foretell a changing societal notion of women, aging, and beauty?

4. How do you feel about becoming middle aged and then elderly?

54 You're So Vain: I Bet You Think This Story's About You

Alan Farnham

"Saddam Hussein has a hairy back," reads an ad for depilatories in *Muscle & Fitness* magazine, "but you don't have to!" Indeed not. No man need suffer any longer the indignities inflicted on him by a whimsical creator: furry back, nose hair, ear hair, gray hair, thinning hair, no hair; big gut; little weenie; raccoon eyes. Science has joined hands with cosmetology to give men new and potent weapons against ugliness. An older generation had styptic pencils and elevator shoes, and counted itself lucky. Today's men have lasers and alpha-hydroxy acid. With these they are blasting every wad of gum and speck of lint off the alabaster loveliness of Self—some men purely out of vanity, others to hang on to marriages and jobs.

Chris Reitano, 45, a customer service executive with Siemens, spent around $4,000 in December to have his eyelids lifted by Dr. Richard Dolsky, a Philadelphia plastic surgeon. Why? Reitano felt his droopy lids sent co-workers the wrong message: "I looked tired, puffy—not very alert." So pleased is he with the change that he says he'd now consider getting a face-lift.

Gary Tombs, 41, a Manhattan commodities trader, periodically drops in at the beauty parlor to get himself a facial. Why? It's pleasant. "They clean your face really well with exfoliants. Then they massage it, dig out the blackheads, put on different creams. First time I ever had one I was on a golf outing at La Costa with a bunch of other guys. I said, 'Hey, I'm getting a facial.' It was no big deal." (Maybe so, but like several other men quoted in this story, he asked that his name be changed.)

Gary gets pedicures. He gets his back waxed to remove fur. Doesn't that hurt? "Only a little less than being hit with a cane." For a long time he wondered if he'd keep getting it waxed once he got married. "Then one day I realized, I'm doing this for me."

Vain males aren't confined to the Atlantic or Pacific coasts. Nor do all of them conform to stereotype.

Peter Farnham (no relation to your author), a salesman in Dallas, says he met a UPS driver who'd had implants to improve the contour of his butt. "I said to him, 'You've got to be kidding.' He was serious. Then he says, 'And for Christmas, my parents are giving me the money to have my smile lines removed.' The guy's a UPS driver, for God's sake. In Texas!"

The circulation of *Men's Health* magazine, a kind of male *Cosmo*, has since 1986 rocketed from zero to 1.3 million. Sneak a peek inside the medicine chest of just about any guy you know, and you'll find exotic unguents he'd be delighted you didn't find. So many rare-earth masks, eye creams, and miscellaneous goos did *Fortune* find with a little snooping that we put together a composite Vain Man's Chest. Male grooming products, depending on how that category is defined, now rake in as much as $3.3 billion in sales. Conservative estimates call for spending to grow 11% in three years.

If retailers are upbeat, surgeons are actually doing a little jig. Men now account for almost one in four cosmetic surgeries. In 1994 (the last year for which statistics are available), men had nips, tucks, and other procedures in the following numbers: hair transplants and/or restorations, 197,276; liposuctions, 37,743; chemical peels (e.g., of the face) 36,290; rhinoplasties, 22,204; and eyelifts, 18,350. That's according to the American Academy of Cosmetic Surgery. (The hair jobs alone amount to $789 million.) Another 12,318 men had their own fat reinjected into them (for instance, had their thigh fat injected into their cheeks). Of that subject, more later.

Nonsurgical hair replacement is booming. There are an estimated 40 million bald men in the U.S., and they don't take their light-hairedness lightly. Pharmacia & Upjohn, maker of Rogaine, estimates that U.S. men are spending over $67 million a year on minoxidil (the hair-growing ingredient in Rogaine), $400 million on wigs and toupees, and another $100 million on what the company is too polite to call quack remedies (elixirs, teas, horse-hoof ointments, etc.).

Sales of men's hair dye have tripled in the past ten years, according to Jim Kelly, director of marketing for Combe Inc., makers of Grecian Formula and Just for Men. He estimates annual sales of all men's hair coloring at about $100 million.

Then there's girdles.

Girdles?

Girdles.

Last year a company called Bodyslimmer introduced three new foundation garments for men: the AbFab Cincher tank top, the Double Agent boxer (which flattens the gut and hips), and the Man Band (which constrains love handles). These garments, say company founder Nancy Ganz, "will be very liberating for men. They will no longer have to pretend they don't care about vanity." Thanks, Nancy.

Another company, Rush Industries, has introduced Super Shaper briefs that "give you eye-catching buttocks instantly!" Rush's marketing director, Barbara Baron, cites surveys showing that many women (and men) quickly zero in on the butt when assessing a man's attractiveness. Cost: $24.95. For $5 more the customer gets an "endowment pad" up front. How are sales? "We're a private company, but I can tell you this: We're running the factory on two shifts."

Marketers, a-drool, ask themselves: What won't these vain guys buy? A few limits do constrain the market, but these, as we'll discover, are far from obvious. On the surface, men seem willing to try any gimmick, pay any price. Ike Wilkins, 31, a vitamin salesman, estimates that his custom-made toupee set him back $5,000. "It's not a matter of money," he says. "If this hair had cost me three times that amount, I'd gladly have paid it."

How come?

Whatever a man's cosmetic shortcoming, it's apt to be a career liability.

The business world is prejudiced against the ugly. True, you can be a burn victim and do just fine (Sumner Redstone did). You can have a ruined arm and run for president. But there's no denying one's upward path is more likely to be lily strewn if one is pretty. Recent studies (see next story) suggest that even the most successful men might be more so, were they better buffed.

We had trouble thinking of any line of work where being pretty holds you back. Cowhand, maybe? We asked cowboy-poet Waddie Mitchell to play around with the idea of a cowboy who flirts with cosmetic. Mitchell's opinion? A man's good looks are largely wasted on cattle.

In other vocations, however, being handsome has become a near requirement. A businesswoman who'd prefer to remain nameless says, "Any guy who goes into consulting has to be attractive. It struck me one day. Every time I met a good-looking guy and asked him, 'So, little boy, what do you do?' he was a consultant. The ugly ones are accountants."

Too many employers think old faces mean old ideas. In a time of wholesale layoffs, a man is a fool not to pinch his cheeks to make himself look livelier.

Dress-down Fridays have exposed things that might better have been left covered up. "You know," says a female executive cattily, "those Brooks Brothers suits you men wore really hid a lot."

Remember the Arrow Shirt man? The message of his ads was clear: A guy could meet 90% of his obligation to be beautiful just by going out and buying an Arrow Shirt. Did the Shirt man have great pecs? Who knew? Who cared? He was wearing a shirt. Now comes Marky Mark—chiseled, protuberant, pretty much buck-naked—leering out from ads as if to taunt men, "Hey, pal—buy *this*." A man has to do more than buy new undies to look like Marky Mark. He has to do 200,000 sit-ups.

Back when bad bodies were the norm, money distinguished male from male. Now muscles have devalued money. "Any woman with a job can take herself out to dinner," says Edward Jackowski, founder of Exude, a New York City company providing personal trainers. "They don't need to be wined and dined." A faraway look comes into Jackowski's eyes. "It used to be two dates at Lutèce, and she'd give herself up." Five years ago males represented only 20% of Jackowski's clientele. Now: 50%.

There's divorce. Plastic surgeon Robert Cattani, who operates on a lot of ex-husbands, says, "Men who divorce in their late 40s do a lot of things when they start dating again. Right off, they lose 15 pounds. They stop drinking half a quart of vodka a day and switch to Evian." If Cattani's lucky, they also get a face-lift.

Are you a man curious to know where your own vanity puts you in this new pantheon? Begin by taking this simple word association test: When I say "free radicals," is your first thought "Eugene Debs"? If so, your vanity likely falls below today's norm. Being a somewhat older man, you probably made peace years ago with your big gut and luxuriant nasal hair. Vanity appears to diminish with age. Scientists call this the "Ah to hell with it" effect.

Film producer David Brown, 80, says that for a while, earlier in life, he flirted with using hair dye. Then one day he gave it up. "I didn't like the way I looked," he says. Plastic surgery? Brown wouldn't dream of having it now: "I don't want to look like a mummy." (His 1987 book on aging, *Brown's Guide to Growing Gray*, is a masterpiece of wit, restraint, and elegance.)

Fortune does not mean to belittle, of course, the older man's cosmetic afflictions. Enlarged breasts, for example, are now a common enough problem in older (and some younger) men that an episode of *Seinfeld* was devoted to dreaming up an undergarment to keep these breasts in check—the "mansiere." According to the American Academy of Cosmetic Surgery, 5,654 men had breast reduction surgery in 1994, compared with 8,527 women.

Today's vainest are not the old-old. They're men on the cusp of middle age—men still fairly young. And dammit, they mean to stay so. Their patron saint is Clarence Bass, an Albuquerque lawyer who started bodybuilding at the age of 40 and now, at 58, looks great in his bikini posing briefs. He's not just muscular, he's "ripped" (a term Bass popularized meaning chiseled). His series of three instructional books (*Ripped*, *Ripped* 2, and *Ripped* 3) describes him as "the ageless master of perpetual leanness." The ageless part is true. "I actually am younger," he says. Tests show Bass has the heart rate of a 30-year-old. He's predominantly bald (you can't have everything), but his remaining hair contains no gray. "It's the 40-year-old guy," says Bass, "who's the guy most interested in me."

Aren't there holdouts against perpetual leanness? Sure. It's still possible, here and there, to find men who clench unmanicured fingers into fists of defiance. But in a day when UPS drivers are getting butt implants, you've got to wonder how many there really are.

I put the question to a roomful of female executives: Of all the men currently in their lives—husbands, fathers, sons, boyfriends—how many men had what we might term the John Wayne attitude? How many men felt proud to bear the marks of life—the scars and bumps and little dings and leathery skin that show a man has been around? How many men put "moisturizing" at the low end of their priority list? The ladies thought this over, and their answer was, "Not one." No man of their acquaintance had this attitude.

I asked them how they'd felt on occasions when they had caught their men being vain. "Amused" was the consensus. One woman, speaking anonymously about her boss, said, "All of a sudden one day, he came in and his hair was black. It had been gray. He'd gotten some of that Grecian Formula. I was amused. I still think very highly of him, but I was amused."

"Gloating" is more like it. Women, having suffered the torments of vanity for centuries, are delighted to see men coloring their hair, struggling into girdles, and getting fur waxed painfully off their backs. It's nice to see men suffer. It strikes women as the height of fair play.

Men aren't any too eager to discuss their beauty regimens, fearing (correctly) that exposure will make them look ludicrous and vulnerable. Even while doing 50 extra pushups, men feign nonchalance. Press them, however, and the truth leaks out, one detail at a time:

"Me? Oh, I don't do anything at all, really. Shave, of course. After that—just good old soap and water." Really, Jim? That's remarkable. You look great. You don't use anything else? "Oh, at the beach, I guess, I use a moisturizer." Uh-huh.

Ever had a facial? "A facial? As a matter of fact, I did. Buddy of mine recommended it, and now I find I like them quite a lot." What else do you get done when you get the facial? "Every other Thursday, I get a pedicure. I get waxed sometimes. Say, have you ever had that thing where they use live steam and a loofa bat and they reach up under your…?"

Viewed up close, male vanity appears to be an individual thing—a matter of Jim's getting his steam, Gary his wax, Chris his eyelift—or of a muscular 58-year-old, late at night, hand-washing his posing briefs. But step back, and a wider tableau opens up, something out of Bosch, or from the movie *Network*: a huge edifice crammed with some 93 million adult males, all yelling—as lightning flashes overhead—"I'm pretty as hell, and I'm not going to wrinkle anymore!" as they hurl tubes of Sensidyne and bottles of Mylanta II onto the street below.

Let's step inside that edifice right now. Let's visit Vain's World.

Our first stop, a classic: the face-lift. We shall see it performed for us today not in some fancy-schmancy Fifth Avenue salon but in digs far homier and intimate: the Pavilion for Cosmetic Surgery on Staten Island. The Pavilion is a converted one-family, Colonial-style residence. Trans Ams and Crown Victorias fill adjacent driveways.

The Pavilion's founder and only physician, Dr. Robert Cattani, greets us, resplendent in black Armani suit and pocket handkerchief. He is a board-certified cosmetic surgeon, a member of the American Society of Liposuction Surgery, vice chairman of the American Society of Hair Restoration Surgery—and himself a patient, having had both liposuction and a hair transplant.

Cattani, who divides his practice between the Pavilion and an office in Manhattan, says about 30% of his patients are men, and the percentage is rising: "Excess skin over the eyes or a saggy neck makes a man look less energetic. It's a competitive market, with people changing positions. People are taking better care of themselves now."

His first patient today is not Ron Perelman. It's Don Perelman, 42, a supervisor for the transit authority and something of an exercise fanatic. Don has already had one face-lift, but since having it he lost considerable weight. Now he's back for a slack-reducing yank. This will cost him about $8,000. As is the case with most cosmetic procedures, insurance picks up none of it. Don also will be having liposuction of his belly today, at an additional cost of $3,000.

Surgery starts at 9:13. Before it's over, Don's head will have been peeled like a grape.

"This is very, very invasive surgery," says Dr. Cattani, making an incision forward of the right ear, cauterizing as he goes. The skin is peeled toward the face, the flap held open by a rake retractor. Skin aft of the ear is peeled toward the back of the head. Soon, only the ear itself is left unskinned—a white island in a red lake.

Watching Don be skinned, I find I have involuntarily drawn my hand up to my breast, the way heroines in cheap novels do when shocked. To see a man's face cut is painful—perhaps because the face is such a scrapbook of emotion. That spot, there, behind Don's ear—might not some granny once have planted a kiss on it to heal a boo-boo? Oh, if she could see it now!

Dr. Cattani snips off a band of skin about three-fourths of an inch wide, then he sutures the incisions shut. As he switches over to begin work on Don's left side, I attempt a conversation gambit: "So…ever find anything you didn't expect to, under a patient's skin?"

Yes, he says, he did find something once: a rear-view mirror. The patient had been in a terrible auto accident, her head thrown forward through a windshield. A hunk of the mirror had somehow become lodged so deeply in her face that it went undetected until Dr. Cattani was called in to perform plastic reconstruction. Human skin, he notes, is wonderfully forgiving—stronger and more elastic than we imagine.

He finishes Don's face 40 minutes after starting, then moves on down the hall to see his next patient.

This is James, 39, in for a hair transplant. En route, Dr. Cattani warns that James is very nervous: Hair is just a damn strange thing. It exerts a power over baldies far in excess of what the hirsute might suppose. Men feel about hair the way women feel about their breasts—touchy. They will go to almost any lengths to get it back.

"I have to be careful what postoperative instructions I give them," he says. "If I told them to stand on their heads every other hour, they'd do it."

James is to have micrografts of hair (each graft containing three or four hair follicles) planted on his thinning pate. Where to get them?

Dr. Cattani picks up what looks to be a tiny, sharp, three-disk rototiller and runs it laterally across the back of James's head, slicing off two strips of hairy scalp. These, when minced, will provide better than a hundred grafts. The wound is sutured shut.

Now for the holes in which to plant the grafts. Asks James, kidding gamely: "If you finish on me early, Doc, can you maybe do under my eyes?" Then plaintively: "Next time I get married, I'm going to marry an older woman instead of one who's ten years younger. Let her worry about this."

Dr. Cattani starts drilling holes in James's head. Each time the drill goes in, out comes a spiral whorl—exactly as if Edgar Bergen were drilling holes in Charlie. James's whorls, of course, are flesh, not wood. An assistant keeps track of how many have been drilled by clicking off each one with a ticket-taker's counter. "This drilling part I like," says James, exuding false good humor.

Nibs of flesh go flying. When the head looks like a bloody pincushion and the counter reads 103, the doctor stops. He will return to finish James's transplant later, once his assistant has minced 103 grafts.

Now, back to Don.

Liposuction is a wonderful thing. So tiny are the incisions required that the procedure, after a man heals, usually goes undetected. In the case of Don's belly, just two incisions need be made—one on each side of the abdomen— each no longer than a quarter of an inch.

Into first one, then the other, Dr. Cattani sticks a long, thin, wandlike nozzle called a cannula. Through it, he sucks out fat. That's it. There's not a lot more to it. The noise made is like custard being sucked off a plate.

"You see the tedium involved?" asks Dr. Cattani, moving the cannula back and forth, in a motion that suggests chipping paint with an ice pick. Bored, he lapses into history: Fat removal

was pioneered with great success by a Frenchman in the 1920s. One day his instrument slipped, and the patient—a prima ballerina—was left crippled. "That set liposuction back 50 years," he says gravely. Now the bugs have been worked out, and liposuction ranks next to hair transplantation as men's favorite cosmetic procedure.

How much fat can be removed at one time? "We've had cases where we've filled up five of those," he says, gesturing toward the ultimate repository of Don's fat—a cylindrical two-quart canister connected to the cannula by a long hose.

We have now witnessed three procedures that have been, to say the least, invasive. Feeling queasy? Tired? More resigned than ever to growing fat, wrinkled, and bald? Don't be. There are remedies more modest. Let's go peeling!

Dr. Lewis Feder, whose Fifth Avenue office fronts on Central Park, says he counts seven billionaires among his clients. Seeing his office, one can believe it. Modern art covers walls that are themselves padded in light blue silk. On one hangs a life-size portrait of Dr. Feder. Behind the receptionist's counter, watching every move, sits Dr. Feder's mother.

The doctor's long-running cable TV show, *Here's Looking at You!*, airs twice weekly in Manhattan. He sells his own line of cosmetic products, which includes (but is by no means limited to) Dr. Feder's Natural Repair Complex, Dr. Feder's Glycoderm With Glycolic, Dr. Feder's Cleansing Emulsion, Dr. Feder's Retinoid Facial Therapy, Dr. Feder's Thigh Toning and Firming Cream, Dr. Feder's Super Peel, Dr. Feder's Dual Action Blem Erase, and Dr. Feder's Fade-away (recommended for old soldiers).

And now, without further ado, Dr. Feder:

"I think I'd like for you to quote me here: You must look at the face as if it were a balloon." When a balloon loses air and sags, do you stretch it? No. You reinflate it. And so with Dr. Feder's patients, into whose faces he injects their own fat. "I have more than 800 patients' fat in my freezer now," he says.

Fat stored by just anybody would quickly die. But Dr. Feder has figured out a way to keep it living longer by giving it "a little picnic basket" of nourishment. He defrosts the fat, then uses it for "liposculpture" touch-ups, injecting it beneath wrinkles and lines and then molding it by hand into permanent position.

I was not surprised to learn he had inflated his own features. His cheeks seem eager to meet you. The overall impression conveyed by his face is of a man whose tire pressure is perhaps a pound or two higher than the one the factory recommends.

"There are," he says, "so many ways I can rejuvenate you without cutting you." Ever game, I decide to try one: a mild, mild, mild as springtime "luncheon peel"—so called because although it removes several layers of aging skin, the result is so unobtrusive that a man can have it done on his lunch hour and return immediately to work, good as new. Such peels have become the third-most popular cosmetic procedure for men, after transplants and liposuction.

Mine began with a thorough cleansing, followed by an up-close inspection by Dr. Feder. "Did you have acne?" (Once, for about 12 years.) Surveying my skin, he claims to see broken capillaries, irregular coloration, and enlarged pores. There follows, in quick succession, the application of two acids, the first milder than the second. This phase of the procedure takes less than three minutes. Afterwards, my face feels as if it had spent a day at the beach—prickly, windburned.

Cost: $405. I had been peeled indeed.

Strolling back to work, I noticed I was getting looks from passers-by. A momentary fear passed through my mind: Had my peel dislodged my hairpiece?

Did I mention I was wearing a hairpiece? Sorry, it must have slipped my mind. A few days before visiting Dr. Feder, I had had $2,500 worth of hair glued to my predominantly bald head. This step I took as an experiment on behalf of bald men everywhere, and in the best tradition of participatory journalism: With hair, would I get kissed more by my wife? Would I get a raise? And would it all be worth it, considering the grief I'd probably get from friends and colleagues?

This particular adventure began by visiting a clinic called MHN, a Manhattan clinic that makes what owner Michelle Cipriano calls a "hair-replacement system." The system com-bines real human hair (picked to match the owner's own in color and texture) with a skullcap of fine synthetic mesh, to which the hair is rooted. The perimeter of the cap then is glued to the client's bald spot with surgical adhesive. MHN can remove it; the customer cannot—at least not easily. You shower with it, sleep in it, rumba in it. As a different company's ads used to say, "You can be towed underwater by it!"

I wasn't sure I wanted to be towed underwater. But I was curious to know why—in a day of minoxidil and transplant surgery—men are spending $400 million a year on hair prostheses.

The answer? Simple: Minoxidil does not grow hair on everybody, and what hair it does produce is often thin and wispy. Surgery, on the other hand, scares a lot of men. They want hair, they just don't want to be cut to get it. Solution: the prosthesis, or wig, which gives plenty of hair with lots of body.

Inauthentic hair carries with it, however, a terrifying possibility: detection. Were its fakeness to be discovered, two awful secrets would be exposed at once: The man is vain; worse he's deceitful. That hair's not really his!

Women, long inured to such flimflammery may laugh, but with men the fear is absolute and electric. To display false goods is have broken an 11th commandment, to be exposed as a wearer of Super briefs is to have one's entire credibility as a man called into question (and without the enhancement pad). The advertising should apply: Buffing and tweaking what God gave you is fine. Outright fraud is not.

MHN and companies like it easily charge $2,500 and up for persuasive hair. And then there's upkeep. Wearers who want to keep their fake hair credible bring it in for periodic maintenance: a trim of their remaining real hair, plus a refitting of their piece every six weeks at say, at $65 a pop, in perpetuity.

Further, to escape detection men can wear a piece with a receding hairline. Sound incongruous? Think about it: How convincing would an 18-year-old's hairline look on a 50-year-old guy? Marketers take note: Possibility of detection constitutes the single restraint on the male vanity market—not just on hairpieces but on the whole testicular enchilada. So significant are its commercial implications that this fear perhaps deserves a little further inquiry. For starters:

Detection by whom?

Not women. The vain heterosexual man takes a gamble. He risks a highly uncertain upside (women's finding him more attractive) against a downside both sure and visible: Other guys will poke fun at him if they discover what he's up to. For whatever reason, guys just love to stick their fingers in other guys' sorest spots.

The only thing worse, probably, than getting caught wearing fake hair is getting caught wearing "bad" cosmetics. I say "bad" because some cosmetics fall within parameters that render them acceptable to men. Understanding these parameters is Job One for the cosmetics industry, which now looks to men for its sales growth.

The men's market now is only two-thirds the size of the women's. But while the women's market is mature, men's spending should grow 11% in the next three years, according to Packaged Facts. Tom Bonoma, CEO of Renaissance Cosmetics, points out that male customers are more loyal to brands than females. Hook 'em once, and you have them for life.

How to hook them into buying $3 billion more? The following strategies all work:

➤ Describe the new dingus as an extension (however tenuous) of the one cosmetic ritual familiar to all men: shaving. Aramis did it with an alpha-hydroxy cream, Lift Off! introduced in 1994. (Such creams offer an over-the-counter version of the peel I got from Dr. Feder.) Aramis told men that by exfoliating regularly with the product, they could reduce their shaving time by one-third. Men have bought it eagerly ever since.

➤ Stress the product's undetectability. Hair colorings have made great strides in just the past few years. As Bobby Ray Mastrangelo, manager of the Ray Beauty Supply company in midtown Manhattan, explains: "Years ago, there was only one shoe-polish shade: black. Now there are gradations of color." Example: Just for Men, a coloring for sideburns and beards, comes in eight shades, including Natural Ash Brown and Natural Sandy Blond ($5.99 each).

➤ Get a female to give him the product as a gift. Tom Bonoma says that more than 80% of males attribute their first use of a fragrance to

their being given it as a gift from a mother, sister, or some other female.

As plenty of disgruntled women can attest, men don't always wait to get a gift: They filch cosmetics from wives and girlfriends. BeautiControl, a Texas direct-sales company, heard in 1993 from female customers that men were filching one of its products—Regeneration (an alpha-hydroxy cream). The company capitalized on its discovery, repackaging the cream in a dignified gray box. Dubbed Regeneration for Men, it has sold briskly ever since.

Prospects for selling men "serious" makeup—liquid or powder concealers to hide, say, dark circles under the eyes—look, for now, dim. You won't be seeing a combination Skoal-and-mascara compact anytime soon. Again, discovery is the issue. If truly undetectable makeup ever did become available, Mike Lafavore, editor of *Men's Health* magazine, thinks men would buy it. "There's a tremendous opportunity there—millions to be made—if it were impossible to detect." At the moment, bronzers are about as far as most men will go.

But not, of course, me.

After being made up in $180 worth of cosmetics by professional makeup artist Alexis Kelley, I decided to go in and show the boss— fake tan, fake hair, and all.

The boss seemed less than entirely comfortable having me in his office—not exactly as if I'd had the flu, but something like that. I asked him to critique my look. "Dead," was his first reaction. "Nobody has that smooth a skin." Then he seemed to warm a little. "You look as if you're from the leisure class—you look rich, like a rich playboy." (This didn't seem to augur well for my getting a raise.)

If makeup represents the worst possible cosmetic combo (fake and detectable), muscles represent the best (obvious and real). So compulsory a fashion accessory have muscles become that writer Sam Fussell calls them "a dress code made flesh." Fussell, in a 1991 book about his bodybuilding career, *Muscle* (sort of a *roman à cleft*), and in a subsequent essay, describes the advent of a new male subspecies: the muscle fop.

Until quite recently, a demonstrated affection for one's musculature was the surest way to lose an election for scoutmaster. Yet in a few short years muscles have become a kind of public holy grail. "From totally geek to totally chic—and in one decade!" marvels Fussell. In suburbia, he says, leather weightlifting belts have become as ubiquitous a weekend fashion accessory as the pager.

For the fop too lazy to lift weights, there's the California Muscle Machine ($325) and devices like it. These do for the stomach what the state of New Jersey did so memorably to Bruno Richard Hauptmann in 1936. The user attaches electrodes from the Machine to his abdomen (or to any other muscle group he wishes to exercise), throws a switch, and—*voila!*—he twitches away involuntarily, able to watch movies (or shake martinis) at the same time.

With such tools at his disposal, is it any wonder modern man is overreaching? And isn't overreaching at the very heart of vanity? So, at least, thinks Mike Lafavore of *Men's Health*. "Vanity," he says, "is when you try too hard and it looks unnatural." His poster boy? "Burt Reynolds."

Yet men insist on rushing in even where better-looking angels might fear to tread.

Wouldn't you have thought, for instance, that John Wayne Bobbitt would have been happy just to have all his genitalia back safely in one place? No. A year or so ago he asked a Southern California plastic surgeon, Dr. Melvyn Rosenstein, to enlarge his member. This Dr. Rosenstein did—sort of. You can judge for yourself how successful the procedure was, since Bobbitt's enlarged organ has a starring role (and Dr. Rosenstein a cameo) in Bobbitt's new adult video, *Frankenpenis*, in stores now.

Nationwide, an estimated 10,000 enlargements have been performed. Typically, shaft length is increased by cutting ligaments inside the groin, allowing the shaft to extend farther from the body. To increase girth, fat is injected. (Paging Dr. Feder!) The fat can migrate, forming lumps. Patients have reported mixed results. So mixed, in fact, that Dr. Rosenstein has been asked by his medical brethren in California to knock it off. With their wish he has complied, there being some 100 malpractice suits outstanding against him already.

We may be witnessing the birth of a new thing: the Silly Putty self—a self so bent on being bigger, stronger, hairier (or less hairy) that it will push and pull its poor old flesh through just about any wringer.

But though the flesh is willing—eager, even—the wringer still is weak. Today's beautifying gizmos, however much they'd dazzle Grandpa, still can't deliver what the vain man really wants: perfection. Oh, it's coming—via genetic engineering—but not in time to do any ugly man alive much good.

For now, the vain hang suspended somewhere in between John Wayne and John Wayne Bobbitt. They've completely repudiated stoicism, but they haven't yet found a technology that can bring them total satisfaction. Halfway measures are their bane. Figuratively, they are stuck wearing a penis hat.

The hat is my name for a serious product, called by its Canadian manufacturer the Manhood—a genital beanie worn by men unhappy to have been circumcised. It evokes, as nothing else quite does, the plight of *Vainus americanus*, circa 1996: He's fighting his cosmetic battle on all fronts, with every weapon at his disposal, however blunt, whatever the cost to his own dignity.

Maybe it's not a bad thing men can't yet win total victory—that they can't, by throwing a single switch, remake themselves entirely. For when they can do that, how will they know where to stop? Freed of all his physical moorings, a man might have a little trouble remembering who he is. Or as Saint Mark might have asked, on visiting Dr. Feder: What profiteth it a man to gain smaller pores but lose his soul?

I thought about this the day Alexis Kelley put makeup on me. "If you put enough on, she said, not kidding, "you can disappear." When the hubbub of the workday had subsided and I knew I wouldn't be discovered, I strolled into an empty men's room, leaned on the sink, and for the first time surveyed myself carefully: makeup, fake tan, facial peel, someone else's hair—the works. You know, I really did look good. I exuded a kind of Cary Grant bonhomie. Then the words of a friend came back to me—a colleague who had seen me both before makeup and after: "It looks nice, Alan," she said. "But I miss you."

You're So Vain

1. What does Alan Farnham suggest are the various reasons for the increasing use of cosmetics, weight training, and other body modifications by men?

2. What does increasing use of cosmetic surgery, hair replacement, and other body modifications by men tell us about changing gender identity in the U. S.?

3. Do you think that as you age you will make use of hair dyes, cosmetic surgery, or baldness treatments? What procedures might you be willing to use? Which do you think you will never adopt?

55 Age, Beauty and Truth

Lynn Darling

One by one the women face the camera.

"I would never want to be less than 40," says an unidentified 44-year-old. "It's so much more fun now."

A woman who gives her age as 79 says: "Age to me is nothing. This nonsense about being old is nothing."

The film, produced by Maysles Films, is called "Real People Face Aging," and it is part of a current Clinique sales campaign.

Not all the women in the film are quite so optimistic about aging, but all of them look beautiful. They make you realize how rare such images are: barely made up, and unadorned, filmed in black and white, with no music and no florid images to fancy up faces that for one bear all the traces of time. When the last of their images fades away, the screen goes black, and a single sentence appears in stark white letters: "Beauty isn't about looking young."

O.K., so it's not $E=mc^2$ or even Newton's apple. But coming as it does from a top cosmetics company, it does represent an attitude readjustment that makes Saul's change of heart on the road to Damascus look like a passing fancy.

Clinique, a division of Estée Lauder Inc., is not the only company to figure out that there is life after 20. Lately, the commercial crocuses, the harbingers of what is yet to come, have been popping up all over the cultural landscape, enough to make women old enough to remember Woodstock almost giddy. A new Nike magazine advertisement features a middle-aged woman complete with crow's feet and a supremely confident smile. She is 50, the ad says. And that, she adds, is the "the age of elegance."

The copy next to Lauren Hutton's picture in a current Revlon advertisement reads: "This is our prime time. Let's make the most of it." Ms. Hutton certainly is: since she turned 50, she's been on the cover of just about everything except Soldier of Fortune.

Age, and it's attendant traumas, is a hot publishing subject: Betty Friedan celebrates the second half of life in "The Fountain of Age." Two sisters, both over 100 years old, have their say on the best-seller lists. Books on menopause have become their own genre.

The entrepreneurs of aging spout dollars and demographics faster than you can say Mick-Jagger-is-50, which is the very first thing every one of them says.

"The 18-to-34-year-old segment of the population, which has really dominated, is shrinking, crashing," said Ken Dykewald, a 43-year-old gerontologist who has formed Age Wave, a consulting and marketing company in Emeryville, Calif., that advises corporate clients about how to cash in on an older clientele. "The 50-plus generation is growing by 12 million people in this decade alone. And they're recession-proof. In this decade alone they're going to have over $300 billion in spending power."

Coming up right behind them, according to the Census Bureau's figures for 1990, are almost 16 million women between ages 40 and 49, an increase of 36 percent over 1980. Which is enough to induce a few signs of penitence in the beauty industry for its long adoration of the dewy and the doe-eyed.

"We felt that we had walked away from that more mature skin," said Dan Brestle, Clinique's chief executive. Already, Mr. Brestle said, the company has excised the word "young," used as a positive adjective, from the advertising copy. Clinique's sales force in the department stores is even receiving "special training to interact sensitivity with people of every age," he added.

Dorothy Schefer, the deputy editor for beauty at Mirabella magazine, said: "We've all been guilty of promoting the youth culture. We've erred in photographing too many young women in too many static ways. They don't look like they have lives or bodies or characters."

Could it be? Is it finally permissible to grow older in this youth-sodden culture? Have the baby boomers finally done to age what they did to rock-and-roll and sex and health food? In exchange for the punishment of having lived long enough to hear a Muzak version of "Satisfaction" in the supermarket, can you really be proud of your wrinkles, or rather, "expression lines"?

Women old enough to know better know better.

"It's complicated," said Cynthia Gorney, 40, a writer in San Francisco. "I love Lauren Hutton, and I love what she's doing. But I don't see very much of that. When you look through a magazine, about one out of every hundred faces is old enough to drink. The waif thing made me crazy. It was so anti-grown-up woman, as if we were afraid of being grown-ups."

Maureen Garrett, 45, of New York, an actress who appears on the "The Guiding Light," also identifies with Ms. Hutton. "I love it," she said. "It's like we're all comrades. I love her attitude. I love seeing it in the older newscasters. My mother was resigned at this age, but we're still fighting. There's so much to look forward to."

On "The Guiding Light" set, Ms. Garrett said, a good percentage of the actresses are over 40, and she likes the way the plot lines for older characters have changed since she first appeared on the show 20 years ago. Then, 40-year-old characters were mostly worrying about their children's problems. "Now," she said, "we're involved in love stories." In fact, her character, Holly Lindsey, is again involved in a triangle with two men 20 years after they were first involved with her. In the soaps, not even the older characters learn from experience.

Other women have simply stopped trying to find their reflection in the mirror of popular culture. "Lauren Hutton doesn't speak to me," said Lisa Jackson, 43, a film maker in New York. "I see myself in my friends and in the people I work with, not on Madison Avenue, and certainly not in the movies. I look at my friends as we all crumble gracefully and find joy and power in that."

Dr. Debby Then, a scholar at the Center for the Study of Women at the University of California at Los Angeles, doesn't see much change in the old double standard: a man of 45 looks distinguished, but a woman of the same age is over the hill. As evidence, she offered what she described as a popular joke: "What's 10, 9, 8, 7?" The answer: "Bo Derek getting older."

Dr. Then said, "Women in their 40's are feeling better than ever about themselves, but unfortunately, that's when they become invisible to society."

Dr. Then first realized the negative impact of age when she turned 30. "This man I was seeing said, 'Now you're 30, and soon you'll be 35 and then 40,'" she remembers. "People categorize you accordingly, and that's unfortunate."

And how old is Dr. Then?

"I'm in my 30's," she said.

Isn't that the sort of answer that perpetuates the idea that there is something shameful about getting older?

"Right," she said. "And I choose to accommodate the system."

Despite the recent glaze of interest in older women, "I really do think that we live in a culture that rejects us for our looks just as we have more to offer," said Patricia Bosworth, a former model and the author of "Diane Arbus: A Biography" (Avon, 1985).

"The age thing is real scary," said Ms. Bosworth, who declined to reveal her own age. "Most of my women friends are terrified."

E. Jean Carroll, a New York writer, said she knows exactly why women are so afraid. In fact, she has come up with an over-the-top, hyper-Darwinian theory: "The only reason men have been put on earth is to shoot sperm at women," she said. "And because men are programmed this way, it's killing us. We have to stay tight, juicy and succulent because after we lose our eggs, no one is going to look at us. That's it. It's over. Forget it."

What about the admittedly small number of men who say they find women over 40 attractive? "They're liars," said Ms. Carroll, who recently celebrated ("because I was told to celebrate it") her 50th birthday. "It's not O.K. to be older. We should just all blow our brains out."

Ms. Carroll, who writes an advice column filled with the same kind of cheeky hyperbole for Elle magazine, hears from a lot of women between ages 40 and 50. The letters, she said, are often filled with the desperation that comes from losing one's looks, when looks are still considered a woman's leading asset. "They ask," she continued, "'What the hell have I done with my life?' The future has closed down; there's nothing left."

Dr. Myra Dinnerstein, the research professor of women's studies at the University of Arizona and author of a book about women in midlife, "Women Between Two Worlds" (Temple University Press, 1992), said, "Research has shown that the more women have relied on appearance, the harder it is to get older."

Dr. Dinnerstein, 59, concedes that the use of older models signals a nascent recognition of older women. But she added: "These models present images that real people can't meet. What we don't have is a model of aging that is not unrealistic."

But presenting a realistic image of age isn't that easy, given the air-brushing many people give themselves every time they look in the mirror. According to a yearly survey conducted by Cadwell Davis Partners (USA), a New York advertising agency, men and women over 50 now say that they feel 14 years younger than their actual ages and that they look 6 years younger. Maybe they do, given more healthful habits and more active lives. Nevertheless, said Frankie Cadwell, the agency's president, "there's still a certain amount of denial."

All of this makes for tricky advertising terrain. Except for Clinique's, most of the messages are aimed at stopping the clock, not accepting its handiwork. For instance, Revlon promises that the product Lauren Hutton is hawking will produce "skin that acts and looks younger in just three weeks or get your money back!"

The paradox here is that the best part of getting older has little to do with the temptations of a consumer-driven culture. For all the talk of energetic 50-year-olds eager to spend their money on hip-hop and helicopter skiing, the real satisfaction of age is the freedom to abandon the kinds of commercial camouflage that the insecurities of youth demanded.

"It is perhaps only in old age, certainly past 50, that women can stop being female impersonators, can grasp the opportunity to reverse their most cherished principles of femininity," wrote Dr. Carolyn G. Heilbrun a professor emerita at Columbia University and the author of "Writing a Woman's Life" (Norton, 1988).

"What the culture says is: 'Stay young, buy drugs, impersonate youth,'" Dr. Heilbrun, 67, said. "Nobody ever made money saying: 'If you just want to gain weight, do it. If you just want to let your hair go gray and wear it in a bun, do it.'"

But life after 50, she said, is "a totally different kind of life: when you are not looked at, you are looking."

Dr. Heilbrun's model for how to grow old was the anthropologist Margaret Mead. "She was about 5 feet and weighed 180 pounds or so and carried a shepherd's crook," she said. "I remember having lunch with my aunt, who was asking me, 'Why don't you do something with yourself?' I looked over at Margaret Mead, who was surrounded by people, including young men. I figured I'd settle for that."

It may be a while before the beauty industry figures out how to market that attitude. For the moment, it seems, the extent to which the culture is ready to embrace aging women remains painfully limited.

Two years ago, said Ms. Schefer, the Mirabella editor, the magazine was the first to put Patti Hansen, a supermodel in the 70's, on its cover.

Of course, the photograph was retouched, as virtually all fashion magazine cover photographs are. "We're talking about a 36-year-old woman here," Ms. Schefer said. "We don't want to be cruel."

DISCUSSION QUESTIONS

Age, Beauty, and Truth

1. Up to the present, how has the image industry attended to the middle age market?

2. Why is it a loss for the cosmetics and apparel industries that they have ignored middle age women to a great extent?

56   Ageism and the Politics of Beauty
Cynthia Rich

If you are a younger woman, try to imagine what everything in society tells you not to imagine: that you are a woman in your seventies, eighties, nineties, or older, and yet you are still you. Even your body is yours. It is not, however, in the language of the embalmers, "well-preserved," and though the male world gives you troubles for it, you like it that way. Apart from those troubles, you find sometimes a mysterious integrity, a deep connection to life, that comes to you from having belonged to a body that has been large and small, thin and fat, with breasts and hips of many different sizes and shapes, and skin of different textures.

In your fifties and sixties when your eyebrows and pubic hair and the hair on your head began to thin, it bothered you at first. But then you remembered times when you tweezed your eyebrows, shaved your pubic hair and legs and underarms, or took thinning shears to your head. "Too much" hair, "too little" hair—now you know that both are male messages.

One day you pick up a book that you find rich and nourishing—for example, *Getting Home Alive* by Aurelia and Rosario Morales, published by a feminist press. It is a political book and a sensuous book, and you like the way

"Ageism and the Politics of Beauty," Cynthia Rich in *Look Me in the Eye*, by Barbara Macdonald with Cynthia Rich. San Francisco: Spinsters Ink: 1983. Available from Spinsters Ink, 32 East First Street #330, Duluth, Minnesota 55802. Reprinted by permission.

its politics and its sensuality seem merged. One of the authors, Rosario, is a younger woman, in her fifties, with a warmth of connection to other people, especially women. It is when you come to a section about aging that abruptly the connection—with you—is broken. You find the poet writing with dread and loathing at the thought that one day she must live inside the body of a woman who looks like you:

> Stop!
> I don't want my scalp
> shining through a few thin hairs.
> Don't want my neck skin to hang—
> neglected cobweb—in the corner of my chin.
> Stop!

It shouldn't take this guided tour for any of us to recognize that an old woman must find it insulting, painful, personally humiliating, to be told in print that other women in her community find her body disgusting.

What you—the old woman—find especially painful is that the feminist newspaper where this excerpt was first printed, the feminist publisher, the poet herself, would surely protest if Jewish features, Black features, or the feature of any other marginalized group were described—whether in the form of the outsider's contempt or the insider's self-hatred—with this kind of revulsion. They would not think of their protest as censorship of literary expression. They would know that such attitudes do deep damage to a work artistically, as well as humanly and politically.

Yet clearly they are not the same standards when speaking with disgust about the bodies of old women. So the message has a double sting. The "ugliness" of your physical being is not a cruel opinion but an accepted fact; you have not even have the right to be insulted. How is it that you, the old woman, find yourself in this place?

I believe the revulsion toward old bodies is only in part a fear of death, as the poet suggests—she ends the poem, "No quiero morir." (Of course there is no reason why women over 60 should have to hear such insults whether they remind us of death or not.) Or else everybody would find soldiers going to battle repugnant,

young women with leukemia disgusting, the tubercular Violetta in *La Traviata* loathsome. This is a death-obsessed and death-fearing society, that's true enough. But the dying young woman has always been a turn-on.

No, there is another more deeply anti-woman source for this disgust. Once again it is men who have defined our consciousness and, as Susan Sontag noted ten years ago, in aging as in so much else a double standard reigns. Time, old men who are quite powerless are sometimes viewed by younger men as if they were old women. But older men routinely seek out much younger women for exotic companions and usually find them. In white Western society, the older woman is distasteful to men because she is such a long way from their ideal of flattering virginal inexperience. But also she outlives them, persists in living when she no longer serves them as wife and mother, and if they cannot make her into Grandma, she is—like the lesbian—that monstrous woman who has her own private reasons for living apart from pleasing men. On the one hand she is a throwaway, on the other a threat.

White men have provided the world with little literature, sculpture, or painting in which the old woman's body is seen through the eyes of desire, admiration, love, wonder, playfulness, tenderness. Instead they have filled our minds with an extensive literature and imagery of disgust, which includes a kind of voyeuristic fascination with what they see as the obscurity of female aging. Men's disgust for old women's bodies, with its language of contempt (shriveled, sagging, drooping, wizened, ravaged, liver spots, crow's feet, old bag, etc.) is so familiar to us that it feels like home.

Still, if this were all, how is it that twenty years of ground-breaking feminism have not led us to rise up to challenge such a transparent, gross form of woman-hating? An honest answer to that question is painful but essential, and Barbara Macdonald has named the key to our resistance. Younger women can no longer afford to ignore the fact that we learned early on to pride ourselves on our distance from, and our superiority to, old women.

While I was thinking about this article, the picture of an old woman caught my eye from the comic pages. The three frames of "The Wizard of Id" show an old woman with thin hair pulled to a tiny topknot on her head, her breasts and hips a single balloon. The wizard, her jaunty old husband, hand debonairly on hip, legs crossed with a flair, has bragged: "The king and I are judging a beauty contest tonight." She wags her finger. "That's degrading!" she exclaims through her down-turned toothless mouth. "My lady friends and I will picket!" The Wizard gets in the last word, which of course leaves her speechless: "That'll make a nice contrast."

This slice of mainstream media is jammed with political messages. Old women are ugly. Their view of things can be dismissed as just a way of venting their envy of young women. The old men, who have status and power, and therefore are the judges who matter, prize the young women's beauty and judge old women's bodies to be contemptible. The old woman has no defense since she, too, knows old women are ugly. And: the young woman's body in fact gains in value when set beside that of an old woman.

Images like this accustom younger women to unthinkingly adopting an ageist stance and woman-hating language from men. But also the old woman's low currency temporarily drives up our own. Just as the "plain" white woman is at least not Black, the "plainest" younger woman is at least not old. The system gives us a vested interest in maintaining the politics of beauty and in joining in the oppression of old women.

The principal source of the distaste for old women's bodies should be perfectly familiar. It is very similar to the distaste anti-Semites feel toward Jews, homophobes feel toward lesbians and gays, racists toward Blacks—the drawing back of the oppressor from the physical being of the oppressed. This physical revulsion travels deep; it is like fear. It feels entirely "natural" to the oppressor; he/she believes that everybody who claims to feel differently is simply hiding it out of politeness or cowardice.

When I was twelve, I had an argument with my grandmother. (Because of ageism, I feel a need to point out that she was no more racist than most white Baltimoreans of all ages in the 1940s.) It was probably my first political argument, and I felt both shaky and strong. Buttressed by a book on what in the '40s was called "tolerance," I didn't see why little Black girls couldn't go to my school. I can still remember her voice as she bypassed the intelligence argument. "But just think—would you want one to come to your house and spend the night!" Yes, *but would you want to marry one?* Physical revulsion is an ideal tool for maintaining oppressive systems, an instant check whenever reason or simple fairness starts to lead us onto more liberal paths.

To treat old women's minds as inconsequential or unstable is in one sense more serious, more dangerous, than disgust for their bodies. But most women find that the more our bodies are perceived as old, the more our minds are dismissed as irrelevant. And if we are more than our bodies (whatever that means), we also are our bodies. If you find my body disgusting, no promises that you admire or love my mind can assure me that I can trust you.

No, the issue of "beauty" and "ugliness" is not frivolous. I think of two white women who are in their sixties. One, a lesbian psychologist from a working-class, radical home, has written about the compelling urge she felt to have a facelift—until she became aware that what she was dealing with was not her own ugliness but the ugly projections of others, and became instead an activist against ageism. The other, a former airplane pilot and now a powerful photographer, has made a series of self-portraits that document, mercilessly, the bruises and scars of her own facelift. These are not conforming Nancy Reagans. These are creative, independent, gutsy women, and they heard the message of society quite accurately: the pain of an operation for passing is less than the pain of enduring other people's withdrawal.

One example of how the danger increases when an old woman's body is seen as less valuable than a younger woman's is that the old woman is unlikely to receive equal treatment from medical practitioners, male or female. Old women attest to this fact. Recent research agrees:

a UCLA study confirms that old women with breast cancer are treated less thoroughly than younger women, so that their lives are "needlessly shortened."

In her pamphlet, *Ageism in the Lesbian Community* (Crossing Press), Baba Copper points to the daily erosions of "ugly." She observes that the withdrawal of eroticism between women "which takes place after middle age (or at the point when a woman no longer passes for young) *includes withdrawal of the emotional work which women do to keep the flow of social interaction going:* teasing, touching, remembering details, checking back, supporting" (emphasis mine).

I hear a voice, "All of this may be true. But aren't you trying to place the heavy boot of political correctness on the mysteries of attraction?" No. But obviously the fewer women we can be drawn to because they are "too" Jewish or fat or Asian or old, the more impoverished our lives. And also: if we can never feel that mysterious attraction bubbling up towards an old woman, a disabled woman, an Hispanic woman, we can pretty well suspect that we are oppressive to such women in other ways.

Sometimes I sense a presumption that the fact that each of us is growing older gives us all license to speak of old women's bodies in insulting and degrading ways—or even makes this particular form of woman-hating somehow admirable and honest. Yet the fact that one of us may well in the next twenty years become disabled or fat doesn't make feminist editors eager to hear the details of any "honest" loathing we may feel for the bodies of disabled or fat women.

It does not surprise me that ageism is still with us, since eradicating oppressive attitudes is hard, ongoing, embarrassing, painful, gut work. But as a movement feminism has developed many sensitivities that are at least well beyond those of the mainstream. And we are quite familiar by now with the basic dynamics that almost all oppressions have in common (most of which we learned from the insights of the civil rights movement and applied to feminism and other liberation movements). Erasure. Stereotyping. Internalized self-hatred including passing when possible. The attempt to prove the oppression is "natural." Impugning of the mental and emotional capacities. Blame-the-victim. Patronizing. Tokenizing. Segregation. Contempt mingled with fear. And physical revulsion. So it seems almost incredible that we have not learned to identify these most flagrant signals of ageism.

How can we begin to change? We—especially those of us in our forties and fifties—can stop the trend of examining in public how disgusted we are at the thought of the bodily changes of growing old. Such examinations do not display our moral courage. They reveal our insensitivity to old women who have to hear once more that we think their bodies are the pits. We can recognize that ideas of beauty are socialized into us and that yes, Virginia, we *can* begin to move in the direction of re-socializing ourselves. We can work for ourselves and for any revolution we might imagine, to develop a deeper and more resonant—dare I say more *mature?*—concept of beauty.

I am looking at two photographs. One is of Septima Clark, on the back of the book she wrote in her late eighties about her early and ongoing work in the civil rights movement. The other is a postcard of Georgia O'Keeffe from a photo taken twenty years before her death. The hairs on their scalps are no longer a mass, but stand out singly. O'Keeffe's nose is "too" strong, Clark's is "too" broad. O'Keeffe's skin is "wizened," Clark's is "too" dark. Our task is to learn not to look insultingly beyond these features to souls we can celebrate, but instead to take in these bodies as part of these souls—exciting, individual, beautiful.

Note

1. The poem excerpted here is "Old," by Rosario Morales, from *Getting Home Alive* by Auora Leviris Morales and Rosario Moreles (Firebrand Books, 141 The Commons, Ithaca, NY 14850, 1986), p. 186.

DISCUSSION QUESTIONS

Ageism

1. What is ageism?

2. How is appearance a central part of fear and hatred of the aging process?

3. Do you agree that society is more ageist toward women than men? Why or why not?

57   The Fashion-Conscious Elderly: A Viable, But Neglected Market Segment

Alan J. Greco

For many years the senior citizen market has been eclipsed by the youth market. This has been especially true in the market for apparel. While manufacturers, such as Levi Strauss, have offered fuller-cut clothing and jeans for the mature consumer, a void still exists in the fashion clothing market for older Americans.

Some retailers, however, have taken a closer look at the market potential of older consumers and have recognized the importance of serving this market. Sears, Roebuck is attempting to get older consumers back into their stores by offering memberships in their Mature Outlook Club, an organization aimed at increasing the elderly's awareness of the stores' merchandise and service offerings designed to appeal to older people. May's Department Stores have established the Oasis Club for persons over 60 years of age; members obtain a 10 percent discount on certain days and also are provided with club meeting rooms along with scheduled cultural and educational programs. The May Company has reported that Oasis Club members represent a lucrative market and account for an important volume of sales.

THE POTENTIAL MARKET SEGMENT

Despite these efforts to appeal to the older consumer market, many retailers and manufacturers seem to think that age alone dictates singular buying patterns and purchasing motives. It is often forgotten that age is only one dimension for classifying consumers. When a person reaches 60 or 65, he or she does not automatically become part of a specialized segment which is uninterested in clothing or fashion. On the contrary, research suggests that 25 to 30 percent of persons over 65 are fashion conscious and are fashion innovators and opinion leaders.[9] When one considers that there are over 25 million Americans aged 65 and older today, it becomes evident that at least 6.3 million are being neglected by apparel manufacturers and retailers. Since the number of senior citizens

Greco, A. (1986). The Fashion-Conscious Elderly: A Viable, But Neglected Market Segment. *The Journal of Consumer Marketing*(3) 4, pp. 71–74.

will reach more than 50 million in the next 50 years (or over 20 percent of the total population), the need to recognize the existence of fashion-conscious subsegments of the elderly market becomes even more compelling.

Beyond the sheer numbers of elderly consumers, at least two other factors account for the attractiveness of the elderly apparel market. First, the majority of the elderly are not poor. Census data for 1980 indicate that this segment of the population has an after-tax per capita income that is $335 higher than the national average. Second, the active, noninstitutionalized elderly are relatively heavy spenders for clothing as compared with durable goods.[14]

Given the elderly market's size, growth, disposable income, and willingness to spend on apparel, how can practitioners identify and cultivate those who are fashion conscious? First, the members of this subsegment must be identified and profiled. When such information is obtained, an appropriate marketing strategy can be developed.

Recent research utilizing a national probability sample of 373 men and women aged 65 and over indicates that active, fashion-conscious respondents are demographically similar to those who are uninvolved in fashion.[9] This finding highlights the need for marketers to look beyond traditional demographic profiles and to expand their market analyses to include activity and lifestyle dimensions.

Independent investigations of elderly apparel shoppers have provided the following shopping, lifestyle, and pre-purchase information source profiles.[7, 9, 12] Fashion-conscious elderly consumers are both socially active and active in the community.[7, 9] They are fashion opinion leaders and exchange relevant information with their friends. For these groups. shopping is a pleasant activity. These consumers spend more on clothing than the elderly who are not involved in fashion.[9] Store reputation is more important to these shoppers than label or brand.[10, 12]

The more important sources of information for the elderly fashion consumer include newspapers, friends, salespersons, and point-of-purchase displays.[9] Little significance is attached to the broadcast media. Department stores and specialty shops are the most preferred types of stores for apparel purchases for both fashion and non-fashion-conscious elderly shoppers.[3, 10]

The Marketing Mix

The recognition of lifestyle and behavioral differences among elderly clothing shoppers is a necessary, but not a sufficient, condition for successfully appealing to the fashion-conscious subsegment of this market. This knowledge must be used to formulate actionable marketing strategies. Once the decision is made to evaluate the possibility of targeting the fashion-conscious segment, then product, distribution, promotion, and pricing decisions must be made. The following approach is recommended:

1. Product. It is a mistake for clothing designers, manufacturers, and retailers to assume that today's older consumers are content with a geriatric look. Levi Strauss's "Action Slacks" for men and "Bend Over" slacks for women illustrate fashionable product refinements with the older shopper in mind.

    While many apparel manufacturers lack a marketing orientation, the Marx and Newman Company, the distributor for Liz Claiborne shoes and apparel, has taken the time to research and segment their markets on the basis of lifestyle and product design.[11] Focus groups can be used to gain insight into older persons' perceptions of problems and preferences for apparel. On the basis of the results of this qualitative research, several styles of clothing can be developed for further consideration by a larger probability sample of elderly persons. These subjects can be asked to examine drawings, pictures, or samples of several styles and to rank them according to likelihood of purchase.[13, 15] The more popular styles can then be correlated to the known characteristics of the fashion-conscious elderly such as opinion leadership, social activity, community involvement, and so on to yield an array of styles preferred by the fashion conscious subsegment.

2. Distribution. Since store reputation has been found to be more important to the elderly than brand or label, it is important that manufacturers or designers get distribution through department stores and specialty shops.[4, 10] As was noted earlier, Sears, Roebuck and the May Company have established clubs and fashion shows designed to appeal to older shoppers. Bloomingdale's, Marshall Field's, and Bonwit Teller are major department stores which carry Janet Sartin and other cosmetics aimed at older women. These product lines could be extended to include fashionable apparel directed to the same market. Other organizations opening stores featuring larger-sized fashionable apparel directed to older shoppers include Allied Stores Corporation and The Limited.

To capture a share of the fashion-conscious elderly market, a "push" strategy on the part of the manufacturer or distributor is warranted since the customers tend to choose the retailer first and the brand second. Intrachannel promotion, built around the research findings of Marx and Newman, would play a dominant role in getting preferred styles into the appropriate retail outlets.

Research has indicated that older shoppers would like to be treated with more courtesy, dignity, and patience.[8] Moreover, 56 percent of the elderly respondents in a Houston study said they would pay a little more to shop in a store that went after the business of retirement-age people.[5] According to these findings, retailers can strive to develop a consumer franchise among older consumers by providing friendly and better trained salespeople.

Because many elderly persons pride themselves on their independence and life experience, a consultative style of interaction with older customers is likely to be successful in satisfying their personal needs and desires. Sales personnel for example, may offer advice on style and fit if this is asked for by the customer.[12] Courteous treatment by salespersons is especially important to the older shopper, who may feel that store personnel are not happy to see them come in.[5, 8]

3. Promotion. Promotional appeals must be designed to reach the active, fashion-oriented subsegment of the elderly population. With the knowledge gained from lifestyle and product research described earlier, a manufacturer should work with an advertising agency to develop a plan that reaches members of this audience with messages that are congruent with their self-image and reference groups.[11] Advertising agencies that have set up task forces to study the maturity market include Ogilvy & Mather, Young & Rubicam, Dancer Fitzgerald Sample, and Cadwell Davis Partners.

Studies conducted by Cadwell Davis Partners and other groups indicate that older, fashion-conscious consumers often see themselves as 10 to 15 years younger than their chronological age and therefore identify themselves with the middle-aged.[1, 2, 12] This younger self-image is most common among the elderly in good health and in the higher-income brackets. In 1984, Macy's ran a newspaper ad showing a sophisticated model with the headline "Forty and Fabulous!" A similar tack could be taken to reach the elderly fashion shoppers by using 50-year-old models to whom these consumers can relate.

Since the fashion-conscious elderly tend to engage in community and other social activities, it is likely that fashion shows and the sponsorship of refreshments at Senior Center meetings would reach this audience and at the same time might instill a greater degree of fashion awareness among other members of these organizations. An alternative approach, similar to that organized by May Department Stores, would be special in-store fashion shows which would appeal to the fashion-conscious opinion leaders, who, through word-of-mouth communication, could disseminate the news about the sponsoring retailer's apparel offerings.

Retailers can also direct more attention to point-of-purchase displays. A transgenerational approach incorporating mannequins outfitted in fashions appropriate to this target market as well as other age groups would be useful for gaining attention and at the same time would be less likely to offend older shoppers. This approach could also be used in conjunction with in-store portrayals of older celebrities.

4. Price. The identification of price points perceived to be acceptable to the fashion-conscious elderly could be identified through the Marx and Newman research process described in step 1. This variable seems to be important, since older shoppers tend to adhere to predetermined price limits for apparel to a greater extent than do younger shoppers.[12]

At the retail level, special discounts for older shoppers could be used as an additional means of attracting new customers. The May Company, Sears, Roebuck, and other retailers have offered such discounts to their older customers. To minimize the risk of offending older shoppers, salespersons could indicate that there is an older shopper discount and rely on word-of-mouth to disseminate this information. The discount approach should be used with caution, however, because it has been found that store reputation and store loyalty are often more important to senior citizens than a store's participation in a discount program.[5]

Conclusion

The successful adoption of the above approach requires the cooperation of clothing designers, producers, and retailers as part of a channel system. Research results and sales feedback regarding popular styles and price points must be communicated among channel members. This control function should be part of an ongoing information flow to monitor the success of these marketing efforts.

Above all, it must be remembered that the senior citizen market for apparel is not homogeneous. Grouping all elderly consumers into one age-based category can cause and has caused marketers to overlook important subsegments of this large and growing market.

End Notes

1. Albin, Len, "Big Money Is Changing How Madison Avenue Views the Maturity Market," *50 Plus, 25* (April 1985), 17–18

2. Barak, Benny, and Barbara Stern, "Fantastic at Forty! The New Young Woman Consumer," *The Journal of Consumer Marketing, 2* (Spring 1985), 41–54.

3. Bernhardt, Kenneth L., and Thomas C. Kinnear, "Profiling the Senior Citizen Market," in *Advances in Consumer Research, Vol. III*, B. B. Anderson. (Ed.) Urbana, Ill.: Association for Consumer Research, 1976, pp. 449–452.

4. Dove, Rhonda W., "Retail Store Selection and the Older Shopper," in *Marketing Comes of Age*, ed. D. M. Klein and A. E. Smith. Boca Raton, Fla.: Southern Marketing Association, 1984, pp. 75–77.

5. Gelb, Betsy D., "Exploring the Gray Market Segment," *MSU Business Topics, 26* (Spring 1978). 41–46.

6. Gillett, Peter L., and Robert L. Schneider, "Community-Wide Discount Programs for Older Persons: A Review and Evaluation," *Journal of Consumer Affairs, 12* (Winter 1978), 309–322.

7. Greco, Alan J., "A Profile of Fashion-Conscious Elderly Women," in *Proceedings*, eds. J. O. Smith, Jr., and C. W. Gooding. New Orleans: Southeast American Institute for Decision Sciences, 1985, pp. 234–236.

8. Lambert, Zarrel V., "An Investigation of Older Consumers' Unmet Needs and Wants at the Retail Level," *Journal of Retailing, 55* (Winter 1979), 35–57.

9. Lumpkin, James R., "Shopping Orientation Segmentation of the Elderly Consumer," *Journal of the Academy of Marketing Science, 13* (Winter/Spring 1985), 271–289.

10. Lumpkin, James R., and Barnett A. Greenberg, "Apparel Shopping Patterns of the Elderly Consumer," *Journal of Retailing, 58* (Winter 1982), 68–69.

11. *Marketing News,* "Apparel Manufacturers Face Extinction Because of Their Failure to Assume a Marketing Orientation, Consultant Says," 19 (January 18, 1985), 1, 3.

12. Martin, Claude R., Jr. "A Transgenerational Comparison—The Elderly Fashion Consumer," in *Advances in Consumer Research, Vol. III,* ed. B. B. Anderson, Urbana, Ill.: Association for Consumer Research, 453–56.

13. Richards, Mary Lynne, "The Clothing Preferences and Problems of Elderly Female Consumers," *The Gerontologist, 21* (June 1981), 263–267.

14. Tongren, Hale N., "Retailing to Older Consumers," in *Progress in Marketing Theory and Practice,* eds. R. D. Taylor, J. H. Summey, and B. J. Bergiel. Carbondale. Ill.: Southern Marketing Association, 1981, pp. 93–96.

15. Young, Shirley, Leland Ott, and Barbara Feigin, "Some Practical Considerations in Market Segmentation," *Journal of Marketing Research,15,* (August, 1978), pp. 405–412.

DISCUSSION QUESTIONS

The Fashion-conscious Elderly

1. For people past the age of 65, does age alone shape their clothing needs and preferences?

2. What characteristics do fashion-conscious older consumers have?

3. What marketing strategies might more effectively serve fashion conscious elderly?

58 Saving Grace
Jackie White

Some people might be pressed to remember what they wore one night in the early '80s to a high school reunion. Not Marilyn Nicholson of Lee's Summit. She can even show you.

She has carefully kept the lipstick red ruffled Diane von Furstenberg wrap dress and, if pressured, she can still slip into it. The same goes for a blue one-shoulder gown she wore to the BOTAR ball in 1976.

Nicholson, a stress management teacher and counselor, is one of a legion of women who save clothes.

In basements, attics and backs of closets they have the prom dresses, the Girl Scout uniforms the high school jeans, the vintage lace inherited from an aunt, the college cashmeres, the dress they wore on the first date after a divorce and the wedding dresses.

Fashion may indeed be a come-and-go kind of thing, but clothes can become like old treasured photographs or pressed corsages that trigger warm memories and sentimental feelings.

Also, there is always the chance they may come back in style. Or, as Kansas City singer

White, Jackie, "Saving Grace," *Kansas City Star* (June 15, 1997). Reprinted by permission of the Kansas City Star, © 1997.

Angela Hagenbach says of some wide M.C. Hammer '80s vintage pants, they "just look good on me."

Terri Reynolds, the sportswear buyer for Halls specialty store in Kansas City, says friends and relatives frequently call her in to help cull their wardrobes because they are too emotionally attached to discard the clothing easily.

"They felt great wearing the clothes," she says, and they want to hold on to those feelings.

Terry Richardson, an owner of Revue and Garage vintage clothing store, says she has seen many sentimental savers.

"Clothing makes memories of the event," she says, adding that elderly women often are reluctant to give things up. So are "Depression babies who were taught never to throw anything away."

SAVINGS SYSTEMS

Susie Brown, a personal fitness trainer, categorizes her clothing collection under headings: "Vintage" clothes include old pieces from her grandmother such as an extraordinary lace dress with "spider web" weave. Her "sentimental" group refers to denims from high school and a tapestry skirt she wore "all the time," during her hippie phase in the 1970s. "I keep the jeans because, well, they still fit," she says.

And she calls another group of classics "forevers," clothes so timeless they will always work. She also has her "funky hip fashion" and others.

Shirley Schoettlin, a manager of a Country Club Plaza high-rise apartment building, has boxes of gloves, hats and handkerchiefs, because she enjoys remembering a more elegant era of dress.

"I liked the way we felt when we were dressed up," she says.

Hat boxes containing long-savored picture hats and cloches are used as decor in a guest room of her home. She keeps vintage handkerchiefs clean, starched and pressed and, on frequent occasions, tucks one into her bag.

"I remember being told as a child, no matter where you had to put it, you always had a clean handkerchief." she says.

Lina Stephens, who moved to Kansas City from Detroit last year to work on the 18th & Vine project, admits to being a saver. "I figure I can always make it into a quilt or give it to someone I love."

She brought with her a pair of bright yellow blousey Girbaud knickers purchased in Spain in 1984. "I just like them," she says.

She'll recycle a zipper-trimmed leather jacket given to her in 1984 as soon as she has the lining repaired. Then there is the dark green Ellen Tracy jacket bought on sale for $25 in 1984 and worn with a much-loved mustard skirt. She keeps the jacket now because "I remember the outfit looked so perfect." And back in Detroit, she has stored a "Christmas tree green" lace dress she inherited from her aunt a decade ago. She is hoping to wear it for a Christmas card photograph.

"It fits me perfectly," she says.

Kansas City artist Shea Gordon Festof still treasures a pale green terry-cloth bathrobe her mother sent her more than 30 years ago when she was in college. "I feel like a Roman Princess in it."

She also has her first riding pants, her mother's vintage fox cape and a kimono jacket she still wears.

"You like the style...You think may come back in," she explains. "You hate to throw things out if they may be of value. And you have memories of the way something was beautifully draped."

SIGNIFICANT TIMES

Marcie Cecil, a Kansas City events planner, has a significant clothing collection, including antique laces as well as more recent contemporary styles.

Among her own favorites, she cites a Halston red pinafore dress with a jacket—"very Jackie Kennedyish"—she wore with high black boots in the late 1960s. And she still has her Pan American stewardess uniform of '60s vintage.

Another woman, who asked that her name not be used, has proudly kept packed away a hot pink terry-cloth jumpsuit ('70s) and the Diane von Furstenberg dress she only wore on her first date after her divorce. "It was very freeing," she says of the event.

Clothing "represents certain periods, segments, in my life," she says. "…You associate it with those periods."

Sherryl Cossey of Merriam has her Brownie uniform, recital outfits and some prom dresses from the 1974–1975 years, that "are good for a chuckle."

And some women routinely save most clothing because it's just worth saving. The late Anna Marie Gray (Mrs. Ralph L. Gray) kept her designer clothes beginning mostly in the 1950s and up, says her daughter Gayle Gill of Kansas City.

"The things she had just didn't go out of style. They were so finely made," Gill says.

When she died in late 1995, her daughter was left with the challenge of sorting through them. The Kansas City Museum, which maintains a costume collection, took several pieces. And even now, Gill says she can't part with some of the most special outfits—the dress her mother wore for her 90th birthday party or her 50th wedding anniversary celebration.

Saving Grace

1. What kinds of meanings are "stored" in clothing saved for many years?

2. Do you save clothing, jewelry, and accessories that you no longer use? Why?

59   Inside a Moroccan Bath
Hanan al-Shaykh

The steam rises. It ascends like clouds drifting upward from the earth to the sky, brushing the naked bodies as gently as butterflies or eyelashes closing in sleep. But it spoils eye makeup, robs hair of its shine, dissolves the red on lips and cheeks, and erases penciled eyebrows. I'd be glad if it engulfed me completely and turned me into a ghost. I am hesitant, embarrassed, unsure of myself. I want to rush and hide away in a corner, or just leave altogether.

I didn't expect to react like this. When I undressed and entered the baths, the throb of noise and heaving female flesh took me completely by surprise. What's happening to me, the emancipated woman who writes about frustration, passion, lust, ecstasy, and describes thighs and breasts in minute detail? Why am I staring as if I've never seen a woman's body before, overwhelmed by the sight of them all, even those I know, and shyly clasp my arms across my front, clutching my armpits as if I'm desperate to hide my breasts? This means I'm still suffering from the same complex I always had about my body, which I thought was dead and buried once I dared to wear a two-piece bathing suit, fell in love, married, had children, lived in the West.

The steam increases, rising from the tiles, soapy, sweaty, smelling of henna and perfume, bearing the gossip exchanged by the bathers in

al-Shaykh, Hanan, "Inside a Moroccan Bath." From: Foster, Patricia (ed.), *Minding the Body*, New York: Anchor Books, 1994 spite of the shrieking and yelling of the children. The baths are for washing but also for caring for the body on a grand scale. Bodies that are not laid aside after fulfilling their functions in marriage, sex, and childbirth to become merely factories swallowing and excreting food can continue to expect this fate. I see women descending on their bodies like furies, flaying them with loofahs and stones as if they want to exchange their existing skins for new ones. I've never seen a shop in Europe with half the bath products that they have on offer here: country-style soap, cleansing mud the color of petrol, dried rose petals ground to a powder, ghassoul for the hair, artificial loofahs with bristles that look as if they're for washing the dishes or sweeping the floor, natural loofahs, pumice stones, manufactured stones. Bathing and massaging the body is supposed to be the main point of visiting the public baths, even though most houses have their own bathrooms. From what I've seen of these small, cold rooms, they are mainly used for washing the clothes, while here the women are dotted about the vast space singly and in clumps, intent on pulling and pummeling their flesh, pouring water over themselves, rinsing their hair, embracing the steam as it enters every pore, and sitting in silence from time to time. It's as if the desire to be alone with their bodies as they wait for the heat to strike them has killed the wish to talk with the others. So all this activity is for the sake of being alone with the body released from its prison of constricting undergarments, thick outer garments, headcover and shoes, and cleansed from the dust of the streets, the clinging smells of food, and the sweat running under the arms, between the breasts, and down the forehead with the effort of scrubbing tiles in dim rooms, washing children's heads, rubbing chickens with lemon and cumin.

I look at the women sitting, standing, bending, squatting, stretching, some silent, some shouting and laughing. I gaze at their plump, plump bodies, their hanging breasts, the numerous folds of skin on their stomachs, the fat that makes the flesh around their thighs pucker into circles like fans. And there are bodies disfigured by burn marks, scars, surgery, old age. However, it seems to me as I watch them move gracefully

around the baths, floating, ethereal, that they are preparing to make love to freedom and will soon be in ecstasy. I stand here totally confused in the heat. I am in Shoufshawen in Morocco with my Moroccan friend, who has begun scrubbing a patch of the tiled floor with her loofah and soap, muttering to herself for forgetting the extra towels to sit on, then raising her voice to a shrill cry to answer back to an old woman who's accused her of stealing her place.

I would like to sit down in the heart of the muggy warmth and close my eyes so that all I can hear is the slop and smack of the water as it rinses bodies clean of the dust of the outside world, but I can't bring myself to. I am still shocked by my discovery that I am not completely at ease with the shape of my body, having thought I'd gone beyond that stage long ago. It doesn't help when the masseuse remarks laughingly to my friend that she will only charge me half price since she is only going to have to massage half a body.

From the time I first began to have a mental picture of my face and figure without needing to look in a mirror, I understood that I was suffering from an incurable illness: the disease of thinness, with its accompanying symptoms of pallor and weakness. No, I didn't discover this for myself. I heard it constantly on the lips of others, adults and children, and saw it in the way they looked at me. They not only made comments and throwaway remarks, confirming what I already knew, but were out to criticize and reproach me. "Why are you so thin?" "Why are you letting yourself fade away?" Some went to great lengths to stress the defect they had been kind enough to draw my attention to, and I was known as the skinny girl, kibbeh on a stick (i.e., my head was the kibbeh and my body the stick), bamboo cane, cornstalk. They would put their thumbs and forefingers round my forearm and if they met (and they always did) there would be roars of laughter and a general feeling of satisfaction that the magic test had worked. When the teacher wanted to describe the backbone in nature study, she made me take off my overall and turn my back so that she could point with her ruler to each vertebra.

Being thin meant that I was branded as sickly and physically weak, and so I was never encouraged in sports periods or picked for teams. Instead they would call out, "Hey, skinny! If they rolled you up in the gym mat no one would notice!" So the idea that I was different from my peers began to preoccupy me and make me keep to myself, unsmiling and with none of a child's spontaneity. I think now that my reluctance to concentrate in class might have been a product of this feeling of terror that overcame me every time I thought I might have to leave my cozy lair and stand up by the board in front of the whole class.

As soon as I was old enough to know what I was doing, I began to take cod liver oil capsules and make my family buy fresh milk, for I had made up my mind to gain weight by any means possible. When my efforts came to nothing I forced myself to get used to my bony shoulders and my protruding collarbone, which formed a necklace each time I raised my shoulders, although I don't suppose anyone was entertained by this but me.

I used to envy the ripe, round cheeks of the other girls, and their chubby arms and legs. I was jealous of the fattest girl in our class, with her many chins, thick forearms, and her huge bottom that shook at the tiniest movement. I envied swellings of any kind: swollen eyes, cheeks inflamed with toothache, thighs that were red and angry following injections. I welcomed anything that would allow me to enjoy an increase in flesh, to prove that I was not a barren wasteland, had a normal body that reacted to illnesses and external influences. I was so envious, and I withdrew from my fellows and drew pictures of myself looking like a balloon on a couple of matchsticks. I was jealous, jealous and turned inward, convincing myself that I was different. I pretended not to enjoy belly dancing like the rest of the girls because it was old-fashioned, and so I sat out at weddings, my jealous eye observing the swaying breasts and buttocks of the girls who were dancing, and the perfect control they had over their waists and stomachs so that their whole bodies writhed and coiled like serpents in venomous harmony. My other eye tried to pretend it wasn't there, terrified that it would meet the eyes of the dancers and they would insist that I join them on the floor, as was the custom, whereupon I would fall into the snares of shame

and humiliation. I was quite certain that if I danced and tried to twist and sway I would bend stiffly like a wooden plank and if I squirmed sensuously I would look as if I'd suffered an electric shock.

I kept apart, in mixed gatherings as well as all-female occasions, persuaded that I was different because of my passion for words and stories, and that I was going to be a writer. I used to retire into a corner with pen and paper, and pretend to be writing poetry, off in another world far removed from my companions' ephemeral preoccupations, knowing in advance with absolute conviction that nobody would ever ask me to dance, or marry me, and that I would never have children. My periods didn't come because I was so thin, and the proof was that I was almost fourteen and therefore well past the age when they should have arrived. So as soon as I saw the long-awaited brownish spots in my knickers, I flew to announce it to the women of the house, then rushed to the neighbors to give them the news, or rather to make them acknowledge that I was normal. However, reaching puberty did nothing to alleviate my anxiety about my scrawny shoulders, the nonexistence of my chest and bottom, and my thin wrists and arms. I used to shut my eyes attempting to push away the recurring image of a boy holding me in his arms, because a schoolfriend had said I was like a soup made of bones when she embraced me one day, and after that I had always imagined that as soon as a boy touched me my bones would stick into him so sharply that this would be his abiding image of the encounter.

I created an image of pure fantasy for myself, a girl sitting staring distractedly at the horizon or up into the sky, alone day and night, a girl who had abandoned her body and become a specter, or a spirit, pale and solemn like one of Dracula's victims. I convinced myself that I had been made of different clay from those plump, fleshy girls who won the hearts of boys with humdrum tastes and greedy appetites. God had created me without bumps or curves to flutter gracefully through life like a butterfly. To my surprise, this self-made persona attracted a boy who used to call me the Virgin Mary, or the nun, and who got out of dancing with me by saying he was afraid I'd break or be contaminated. He sent me Khalil Gibran's books and pictures of sunrises and sunsets.

I did nothing to change my image until I saw a poster of Audrey Hepburn that stuck in my mind. I felt she had come to take revenge on Brigitte Bardot for me.

I saw her closing her eyes and yielding to a kiss. I saw her encircled by two strong arms. I saw her, and I saw myself for the first time: long neck, pale skin, dark eyes, black hair and eyebrows. I bought a copy of *Breakfast at Tiffany's* and a pair of dark glasses with round frames, and borrowed a long black cigarette holder. I followed her news on and off screen. Was she in love? Married? Did she have any children? Was she planning to? I went to see all her films two or three times to observe and register everything that passed between her and the hero and try to detect whether he really wanted to kiss her even though she was so thin. Did he hold her fragile body as if she was any other actress, or was he scared that he would break one of her ribs? Would he reach out to feel her breast or deliberately ignore it to avoid causing embarrassment? I gazed at the relevant scenes to learn by heart the position of her arms and the manner of her response, and eventually made the discovery that with her thin body she had exploded preconceived notions of what a woman ought to be like. I remember writing after I'd seen one of her films, "She isn't the woman everyone falls in love with, or a flirt, or a woman with problems. She's a child, personifying innocence. She's untamed love, a fragrant fruit, graceful as a willow. Her face talks, laughs, cries, lives, captivating the hero and the audience and leaving them satisfied."

By imitating Audrey Hepburn and her hairstyle when I was seventeen, I attracted the attention of assorted poets, journalists, and cinema buffs of the opposite sex in my city, Beirut. First I had prepared the ground and redirected their ideas and enthusiasms along a particular course, feeding them with the notion that I belonged to a new breed of women who were attractive in a special, different way, by virtue of being thin and delicate in contrast to the male's brute strength. As this new-style woman was discussed and the

connection made between me and her, I began to gain in confidence and self-esteem, although I put myself in a special category, which separated me from conventional femininity. A poet who was responsible for the cultural page of a daily newspaper began contacting me every time he came across a news item relating to Audrey Hepburn or a photo of her. I felt he was flirting with me via her, especially when he got his hands on the first photos of her in a bathing suit. He said she was like a swan or Lolita. Hope grew in me that I would become an object of desire even if it meant copying Audrey Hepburn's style. I pictured that anyone sitting across a table from me would be enchanted by my slender body and my innocent, childlike gestures, until one day I was sitting in a café with the poet just as she would have sat, confused and lost in the bustle and smoke and loneliness. I inhabited a different world from my family. I had been born and brought up in the heart of a noisy city in a house where they preferred the call to prayer and the sound of the Quran to singing and music. The clash between the city, with the clamor of its cinemas and cafés and universities, and my restricted home environment with my family's subdued voices and monotonous daily routine was almost killing me. Uncertain where I stood, I longed to retreat into a corner and write of the sorrow and despair that gripped me whenever I thought about death and loneliness, or about getting away from home and re-creating myself on my own terms. So I cried tears of bewilderment in front of the poet, wondering what it was I wanted. I cried like Audrey Hepburn when she stood in the rain calling her cat: "Cat! Cat!" The poet reached out a hand to me, squeezed my arm, and patted me on the shoulder. I knew he couldn't take me in his arms like the hero when he was trying to ease Audrey Hepburn's loneliness and confusion in the face of the turbulent world. I was reassured by the warmth of his touch even though I was worried that people would notice. I clung to his hand as if it was my temporary life line, a compass that would help me find my way to the ends of the earth. Within me I carried this image of woman as fragile, delicate, and passionate beside man's overwhelming strength. Then the poet spoke hesitantly, full of sympathy and understanding: "I know what your problem is. It's because you're thin. That's what's responsible for all this grief. This uncertainty. You have to put on weight. A few kilos and you'll see, you'll be a different person. I used to have exactly the same problem."

After this episode I was no longer surprised by the way others viewed me, or how their ideas and perceptions regarding my thinness acted upon each other. I attached myself to an imaginary raft and rode the waves, rising and falling but never losing my grip. When I went to Egypt to study I wrote to a journalist friend who had his own arts and gossip page in a magazine, describing my experiences abroad and enclosing a recent photograph, and I was only mildly annoyed when a poem by him appeared in the magazine a few weeks later that included the line "My love's put on about two kilos and I love her almost twice as much." While I was in Egypt an Egyptian student used to follow me around the university saying "You're pretty. I love you. If only you weren't so skinny. Try and put on a bit of weight. You'd be a really beautiful woman. I'll tell you how to make me fall in love with you. If you do as I say you'll become like a big ripe peach. You have to eat macaroni. Blancmange. Rice. Beef marrow." And I wasn't really hurt when they told me that his girlfriend didn't care when she saw him pursuing me because she was sure that he couldn't fall in love with a woman whose arms and legs were practically nonexistent. Meanwhile his mother took pity on me, totally convinced that being away from my family and my country had affected my health and reduced me to this weakened state.

The poet's words, which had robbed me of my confidence and happiness, made me able, eventually, to stick my tongue out in response to a remark I heard as I walked proudly past a café: "What a pity! That face and a body like a sparrow!" They also made me tolerant with the dressmaker when she suggested putting a double lining in my dress especially at the shoulders and hips. I blocked my ears and remained attached to my imaginary raft, swinging between the heights and the depths, but never falling off. I calmed down and took a hold of myself, reminding myself that I hadn't come to Egypt because I

was desperate to find love, but for the sense of freedom I could enjoy there. I remembered the mother of one of my friends back in Lebanon. She weighed over two hundred kilos, and how her eyes had sparkled when she found out I was going to Cairo! Her hand had flown to her throat in a thoroughly feminine gesture. "You're so lucky! Cairo! Only in Cairo do I feel that I'm really beautiful." Meanwhile her husband, who was a gynecologist, remarked that I should massage my breasts with olive oil every day to make them grow.

The steam rises from my body and the bodies around me. I realize why I am sad. The moment I entered the baths I saw myself as thin again, imperfect next to the plump ripeness of the other women. I am filled with sadness for the years that should have been like Aladdin's lamp or a magic carpet, transporting me away to discover the color of music or the heart of an ant, while instead I had been crammed into a rigid, gloomy mold with only a tiny chink to breathe through. Now I am demanding of myself, of the steam, of the women, why I had been denied this kernel of joy and security, this chance to explore, all because of a handful of flesh that wasn't there. I'd felt poverty-stricken and embarrassed hearing people say all the time that I was thin because I hadn't been fed properly. I'd stopped having the heart to look for emotional attachments, and felt inhibited when I moved and spoke. Sometimes I would rush into the café limping, pretending I'd hurt my foot to distract attention from my thin legs, and also just to confuse things. In my attempts to convince myself that I was desirable, I would be drawn into playing games with men, even those I didn't care about at all. For the sake of this absent flesh I had begun hiding my body under yards of material so that I looked like a cabbage with a human head, and inhabiting dark chambers of anxiety, fearful that I would never be able to have children. A neighbor of mine used to encourage her daughters to eat up food they didn't like by saying "Look at Hanan! If you don't eat up, you'll get like her!" And when one of them shouted, "I like Hanan! I want to be like her!" her mother said, to shut her up, "But Hanan will live all by herself. She'll never have children and nobody will ever call her Mama." How could I carry a child? Would the fetus have room, or would it be squashed up against my pelvis? How would it get its nourishment, seeing that the food I ate didn't seem to put any flesh on me?

I feel that the bodies around me, the hills and mountains of flesh observing me, have themselves nailed the conditions of entry over the door to happiness, by setting the standards of strength and beauty and decreeing what is acceptable and desirable. For these women still stick to the rule that says that the male eye is the only mirror where they can see their true reflection.

In the past, mothers, grandmothers, aunts, and neighbors were equipped with microscopic eyes for seeking out and examining future brides for the sons of the family in the public baths. They preferred to make their inspection there because the steam removed penciled eyebrows, made fine hair cling limply to the scalp, revealed whether the woman's body was firm or not. It had to be rounded, even if this meant there was no waist to speak of, have broad hips and a gently curved stomach sloping down to the thighs, uninterrupted by any bony protrusions. A woman's body was for bearing children, providing them with nourishment, giving them all the milk they wanted, and keeping them warm in the folds of its flesh. It was also for feeding and satisfying man's greedy lust. This is why the famous poets of the pre-Islamic era did not sing about thin women. Their poems about love and beauty are always concerned with curvaceous bodies, and even modern literature glorifies solid, voluptuous flesh and connects it with sexual desire.

But do the standards of the past still apply? Have Arab women not been affected by the West, where the revolutions not just against fat but any surplus flesh have resulted in illnesses, the coining of terms like anorexia and bulimia to designate them, and widespread recourse to cosmetic surgery, sometimes with unfortunate or even disastrous results?

Although it's hard to generalize, I think thinness is still considered undesirable in the Arab world, even among young women and adolescents. By this I don't mean they'd choose to be fat these days, but they like a shapely, athletic figure, combining grace and energy with femininity: prominent bust, slender waist, flat stomach, then curving buttocks and nicely rounded but firm bottom and thighs. They have a keen sense of what men find attractive, but at the same time have their own clearly defined criteria of what is desirable in a man: an athletic, well-proportioned body, "someone who fills his clothes," as they say, for a thin man, according to the conventional wisdom, is weak, has low self-esteem, and lacks personality, the exact opposite of what a woman wants in a man.

Inside the bath, the women's eyes never leave me and I am certain they are wondering where I am from. It must be the color of my skin. Am I from Fez, where the women delight in white skin and black hair? From the way they look I guess they approve of my fair skin, apparently still desirable because the dominant skin color in the Arab world is brown. Nevertheless, brown skin features in all the popular songs, but when I remarked on this to my mother, who was lamenting over the way my skin had changed color that summer, she replied, "Don't let these songs fool you. They're purely to reassure brown-skinned women."

It's my white skin that saves me now. It is a mark of femininity and fragility because it contrasts with the darker skin of men. It inspires poetic comparisons like "pearly white," "white as snow," "white as the surface of a jug of milk." But even whiteness has its conditions: There must be a tinge of crimson on the cheeks, otherwise it represents purity, chastity, and coldness.

The looks and whispers are giving way to laughter, or barely suppressed sniggers. I have the uneasy feeling this time that they are thinking about my thinness in connection with sex, trying to picture me with a man. I'm used to provoking such reactions in other women fatter than me. Several years ago an elderly relation had picked me up and lifted me high in the air, exclaiming "You poor thing! You're as light as a feather! Does your husband squash you flat?" A friend asked me where my bottom had gone, and there are people who commiserate with my husband, saying there's nothing for him to hold on to.

I return their stares, wishing they knew what I am thinking: They will leave here buried under mounds of cloth to protect themselves from the shock of the cool air outside and perhaps also from the wounding glances of men, but when they reach home they will throw it all off and prance and sway before their husbands. Some will dress up in belly dancers' costumes, like a woman I know, or in underwear so clearly designed to be crudely seductive that it ends up with a surreal quality: I once saw a pair of battery-powered panties with a light that flashed on and off at the crotch. I know these women are scared of their husbands being prey to other women and want to keep them at home at any price, so they attract them at the level of lust and purely physical satisfaction, discounting the idea, on behalf of both themselves and their men, that love is also the desire to possess and delight in beauty.

I am boiling hot and move into one of the baths' cool rooms. Suddenly I think of my daughter, who is eighteen, and feel myself returning to normal. I see her slender figure in my mind's eye, and people complimenting her

on being so tall and slim. I recall a photo of myself in my adolescence and decide that my thinness wasn't sickly but attractive: I look exactly like my daughter in it, except that I am seven centimeters shorter than her. I laugh involuntarily at the memory of another photo taken around the same time of me with my stomach sticking out. I used to take deep breaths and inflate it so that I looked fatter, even though I knew it gave me a distorted shape.

I retreat into myself. I will try to give this quietness to the one I love. I am perfectly content to be leaving and going back to the European city where I live, where people compliment me on keeping my figure. But I am still weighed down by these old-new feelings, which bring back to me a picture of my friend's father, the gynecologist, stamping on his brakes in the middle of a Beirut street indifferent to the stream of cars behind him, and shouting through the window as if there was no one else for miles around, "Hanan al Shaykh! So you're married at last! Are your tits any bigger these days?"

DISCUSSION QUESTIONS

Inside a Moroccan Bath

1. How did Hanan al-Shaykh feel about her body when she was a young woman?

2. What kind of reviews shaped her feelings about her body? Who gave her feedback?

3. What change in her life brought her a marked change in body satisfaction?

4. Why does she return to adolescent feelings about her body in the Moroccan baths?

CHAPTER 10
Race, Ethnicity, and Class

Susan O. Michelman

AFTER YOU HAVE READ THIS CHAPTER, YOU WILL COMPREHEND:

- That people have culturally constructed categories of race, ethnicity, and class affecting social issues and problems regarding appearance.

- The relationship of race, ethnicity, and class—particularly as they impact issues of appearance—to gain an appreciation for the experience of those in the minority in American society.

- How issues of race, ethnicity, and class impact American consumer culture.

In this chapter, we will consider how race, ethnicity, and class affect issues of dress and appearance. Although these concepts will be considered and discussed individually, it is important to understand that these issues have an impact on appearance and must be considered collectively as they intersect and interact with one another within every society.

RACE AND APPEARANCE

Race is a term that refers to certain visible and distinctive characteristics that are determined by biology. Along with gender, it is the first thing we notice about another person. The challenge, however, lies in identifying the physical traits that distinguish one race from another. By convention, people are assigned to one of three racial categories—Caucasoid, Mongoloid, or Negroid. Many of the world's population of 5.6 billion people do not fit neatly into one racial category in which there are sharp dividing lines distinguished by features such as black skin versus white or curly hair versus straight (Ferrante, 1994). For example, most Australian Aboriginals have black skin and Negroid facial features, but also may have blond, wavy hair (Newman, 1995) (see Figure 10.1).

Race is a social construction. The physical characteristics that distinguish one group from another are determined less by physical characteristics than by what a particular culture defines as socially significant. Consider the diversity of being "black" in the following statement.

> Brazil historically has not had a rigid conception of race and thus has a variety of "intermediate" races. In fact, the designation of race is so fluid that parents, children, brothers, and sisters are sometimes accepted as representatives of very different races (Harris, 1964).

> In South Africa there are four legally defined races—black, white, colored, and Indian—but in Great Britain the term *black* is used to refer to all people who are not white. An African American visiting Tanzania is likely to be considered white by the African blacks there (Newman, 1995).

In American society we tend to see race in categorical terms: black or white, red or yellow, brown or black. Even when there are mixed-race children, we still tend to place them in categories.

The United States still adheres to the **one-drop rule** for blacks but not for any other racial group. The term comes from a common law in the South during slavery that a "single drop of black blood" made a person black. According to the U.S. Census, to be considered black one only needs to have any known African black ancestry. Anthropologists call this a hypodescent rule, meaning that racially mixed people are always assigned the status of the subordinate group. Hence, a person with seven out of eight great-grandparents who are white and only one who is black is still considered black. (Davis, 1991)

People have created categories of race, and therein lies the source of some of the social issues and problems regarding appearance that will be addressed in articles in this chapter. For example, Richard Rodriguez in "Complexion," reflects on the personal and social meaning of his "tawny" skin color as it relates to issues of race, ethnicity, and social class.

Racial injustices have their basis in equating the social value of individuals with their physical appearance. **Racism** is a belief that something in the biological makeup of an ethnic

FIGURE 10.1 *Physique and dress of this gentleman of 1860 are indicators of his status in society.*

or racial group explains and justifies its subordinate or superior status (Ferrante, 1994). A hundred years ago in the United States there were churches that "had a pinewood slab on the outside door...and a fine-tooth comb hanging on a string..." (Angelou, 1987). You could attend the church if your skin was no darker than the pinewood and if you could comb your hair without any snags. In the past in South Africa, a state board oversaw the racial classification of everyone in the country. One test was to place a pencil in a person's hair; if it fell out, the person was classified as white (Finnegan, 1986). Other readings in this chapter will challenge you to examine social constructions of race as they relate to issues of appearance.

ETHNICITY AND APPEARANCE

Ethnicity is a learned cultural heritage shared by a category of people that can include a common national origin, ancestry, style of dress, language, dietary habits, and ideology to name a few characteristics. Race and ethnicity are separate concepts, yet are frequently used incorrectly as interchangeable in meaning. For example, Chinese Americans are quite different ethnically from Chinese people born in China, although their racial background may be identical. One's ethnicity plays a major role in others' perceptions of a person's appearance. The sociologist Paul Starr (1982) found that in the absence of a distinctive skin color and other physical characteristics, ethnicity is judged by others on the basis of many imprecise attributes such as language, residence, type of jewelry, tattoos or other body markings, and, of course, dress.

Racial and ethnic classification schemes may contain false assumptions that specific abilities (e.g., athletic talent, intelligence), social traits (e.g., criminal tendencies, aggressiveness), and cultural practices (e.g., dress, language) are transmitted genetically. Therefore, the experience of being a minority person in a predominantly white culture such as the United States is one where individuals may be denied access to important resources such as education, health care, and higher levels of income based on the false assumption that their race or ethnicity is inferior. In the article "Black, Hip, and Primed (To Shop)" by Christy Fisher, American blacks state that they choose to shop in stores where they are given respect. Consumer research groups has confirmed that blacks often speak of being watched too closely, or, on the other extreme, ignored in retail settings. This is a good example of how a behavior of minority groups may be stereotyped on the basis of race and ethnicity.

Ethnic dress and ethnicity are linked to each other (Eicher, 1995). Much has been written about both the history and present-day practice of the meaning of ethnic dress. It remains a tangible and visible way that many hold on to their own backgrounds within the context of rapid social change and shifting identities. In the article "African American Women's Professional Dress as Expression of Ethnicity," author Gwen O'Neal interviews professional women regarding use of cultural dress to construct identities based on knowledge and appreciation of their cultural heritage. O'Neal makes the point that these women have chosen to "quietly but visibly take control of the definition of self and to implement an agenda to debunk the myth of African Americans as only a race."

Frequently, ethnic clothing, by its symbolic nature, has become the piece of material culture that remains part of the unwritten history of certain groups. For example, some Hmong quilts made by women who experienced the Cambodian conflict in the 1960s are a pictorial history of their lives before, during, and after the war that was infrequently recorded in words. In Chapter 13, author Annette Lynch explores similar issues in the article "Hmong American New Year's Dress: The Display of Ethnicity."

Currently, changing demographics, particularly in urban areas, have created a new interest in what it means to be a member of an ethnic minority, particularly if the person is white and from the dominant culture. Many popular clothing styles are **trickling up** from the media, street culture, and styles formerly reserved for ethnic minorities. Consequently, what was "out" in terms of ethnic dress style in the past may be very "in" today, particularly for adolescents. This concept is discussed in the article, "Going Gangsta." In this reading by Neil Bernstein, for adolescents, having an attitude and looking rebellious is discussed as being more of a style than a way of life, whereas to appear too mainstream (i.e., white middle class) is considered boring and therefore unstylish. The article "Common Threads" examines adolescent style and social class issues from a slightly different perspective. By affecting the style of another class, adolescents can play or experiment with issues of social and class identity through dress and appearance.

SOCIAL CLASS AND APPEARANCE

Social inequality exists in all societies through a structured system of stratification. **Stratification** is a ranking of groups of people that perpetuates unequal rewards and life chances in a society (Newman, 1995). In some societies today, such as India and Pakistan, stratification is created by a **caste system.** One's caste, which determines a person's lifestyle, prestige, and occupational choices, is determined at birth and cannot be changed. Cultural rules in the caste system specify that a person should take the occupation of the parent and must marry within his or her caste (Weber, 1970).

In most industrialized societies, including the United States, stratification of society is based on social class. **Social class** refers to any group of people who share a similar economic position in society based on their wealth and income (Newman, 1995). Closely related to the concept of social class is social status. **Social status** is defined as the prestige, honor, respect, and lifestyle associated with different positions or groups in society (Weber, 1970). Social status is closely associated with wealth and income but can also be derived from such **achieved characteristics** as educational attainment and job prestige or **ascribed characteristics** such as race, ethnicity, gender, and family social standing. In the article "The Cool Cat Lifestyle," Majors and Billson express that in a society such as ours, blacks have been kept invisible and use flamboyant clothing to heighten their social visibility.

Social mobility refers to movement from one class to another. **Vertical mobility** is a change in class status that amounts to a gain or loss in social rank or prestige. An example of a change in **upward mobility** is when a college student graduates and lands a good job. This transition might be symbolized through dress by the person changing from wearing jeans and sweatshirts to a business suit. In contrast, an example of **downward mobility** would be when someone loses his or her job and is forced to apply for unemployment. An extreme example of this would be how the disheveled appearance of most homeless individuals prevents them from having normal human interactions, particularly with strangers. In the article "You Become What You Wear" by Kathleen Carlin, the students who posed as street people or homeless quickly found that they became social outcasts based on their appearance.

How issues of class in American society affect people's lifestyles and in turn how this relates to dress and appearance issues raises interesting questions. Do all Americans have equal access to social mobility? In theory under the U. S. constitution, yes, but the reality for many individuals follows a clear pattern of economic inequality, and coming out of the vicious cycle of poverty is not easy. Many people are not connected to family values and orientation that emphasize education, economic opportunity, and social background that facilitate access to upward social mobility.

Prior to the 20th century, fashionable clothing (carefully constructed by hand, not machine) was regarded as a **status symbol** that announced the class membership of the individual. It was also during this period that having a slightly corpulent physique (for both men and women) was regarded by others as an indicator of high status. To take up more space physically was a symbolic indicator of one's place in society. Susan Bordo points out in the article "Slenderness and the Inner State of the Self" that being fat as a status symbol went out of vogue around the turn of the century. Today, it is popular to think that issues of willpower and personal discipline are demonstrated by one's ability to control what one eats. Bordo points out that American culture is literally obsessed with issues of being fit and thin, particularly for women. Fitness and thinness have become signs of higher socioeconomic status.

The Industrial Revolution of the 19th century, with the subsequent mass marketing of clothing, helped diminish class distinctions reinforced by a person's appearance through the introduction of many models that were more quickly manufactured, cost less money, and were readily available. Therefore, although upper-class fashion leaders undoubtedly played important roles in establishing fashion precedents, their present role in stimulating the fashion process has diminished as people look to other sources such as the media and the street scene.

Summary

By examining the relationship of race, ethnicity, and class, particularly as they impact issues of appearance, we can gain an appreciation for the experience of those in the minority in American society. The articles presented in this chapter will challenge critical thinking skills that relate to the multiple realities and perspectives of "appearing" in the minority. This is helpful in order to develop a framework to evaluate our social system, to question it, and to understand how a person's perspectives, life chances, options, and opportunities, as well as those of others, are shaped by it.

Suggested Readings

Holloman, L. (1990). Clothing symbolism in African American Greek letter organizations. B. Starke, L. Holloman, & B. Nordquist (Eds.) *African American dress and adornment: A cultural perspective*, pp. 140–150. Dubuque, IA: Kendal Hunt Publishing Co.

hooks, bell. (1992). *Black looks: Race and representation*. Boston: South End Press.

Mercer, K. (1991). Black hair/style politics. In *Out there: Marginalization and contemporary cultures*, pp. 247–264. Cambridge, MA: MIT Press.

Thieme, O., & J. Eicher. (1985). The study of African dress. In *African dress II: A select and annotated bibliography*, pp. 1–16. Lansing, MI: African Studies Center.

Thompson, R. F. (1988). Recapturing heaven's glamour: Afro-Caribbean festivalizing arts. In *Caribbean festival arts: Each and every bit of difference*, pp. 112–140. Seattle: University of Washington Press.

Turner, T. (1980). The social skin. In *Not work alone: A cross-cultural view of activities superfluous to society*, pp. 112–140. London: Temple Smith.

Weiner, A.& J. Schneider. (1989). *Cloth and human experience*. Washington, D. C.: Smithsonian Press.

References

Angelou, M. (1987). Intra-racism. Interview on the Oprah Winfrey Show. *Journal Graphics* transcript #W172:2.

Davis, F. J. (1991). *Who is black?* University Park: Pennsylvania State University Press.

Eicher, J. (1995). Dress as expression of ethnic identity. In J. Eicher (Ed.) *Dress and ethnicity*. Oxford, England: Berg Publishers.

Ferrante, J. (1994). *Sociology: A global perspective*. Belmont, CA: Wadsworth Publishing Co.

Finnegan, W. (1986). *Crossing the line: A year in the land of apartheid*. New York: Harper & Row.

Harris, M. (1964). *Patterns of race in the Americas*. New York: Norton.

Mercer, K. (1991). Black hair/style politics. In *Out there: Marginalization and contemporary cultures*. Cambridge, MA: MIT Press.

Newman, D. (1995). *Sociology: Exploring the architecture of everyday life*. Thousand Oaks, CA: Pine Forge Press.

Sproles, G., & Burns, L. (1994) *Changing appearances: Understanding dress in contemporary society*. New York: Fairchild.

Starr, P. (1982). *The social transformation of American medicine*. New York: Basic Books.

Weber, M. (1970). In H.H. Gerth & C. W. Mills (Eds.), *From Max Weber: Essays in sociology*. New York: Oxford University Press.

LEARNING ACTIVITY

Ethnic Stereotypes and Their Consequences

Mary Lynn Damhorst, Harriet McLeod, and Cassie Moon
Iowa State University

Objective

This exercise is a challenging in-class group activity that helps participants dissect a stereotype, consider the relationships of component parts of a multifaceted phenomenon, and understand consequences of labeling minority groups in the United States.

A stereotype is a classification or typing of a group of people that results in applying a set of generalized characteristics to people labeled with the stereotype. Even though the stereotype usually does not completely fit any individual, all members of the group are typed the same. In this exercise, each student in class will be asked to verbalize a stereotype in society. Do not be afraid to "speak the unspeakable," and list highly controversial ideas. You are not saying that you hold this stereotype, but that these ideas are held by some people in the United States. We will examine the dangers of stereotypical thinking as we move through the exercise.

Procedure

Form groups of four to seven people.

Think of a group of Americans (i.e., Native, Asian, African, or Hispanic) that is stereotyped in United States society. List the label given to the group.

Next, work as a group to write down a list of characteristics commonly assigned to that group when stereotyped. As you list items, put a star next to those that relate to appearance.

Next, identify those parts of the stereotype that are either negative or positive.

Ground Rules

Some essential ground rules when working on this exercise are:

1. It is okay to feel uncomfortable about writing down a stereotype; we all can learn valuable lessons from the discomfort.

2. It is okay to write socially and politically incorrect thoughts and words during this exercise. You will need to verbalize and understand the components of a stereotype that may seem ugly or even absurd. Laughing about the stereotypes is permissible, as this helps relieve tensions about the stereotypes.

3. It is important that no one gets angry at stereotypes that other groups construct; no one in class should be accused of actually holding the verbalized stereotypes. This is a learning exercise, not a statement of personal beliefs. An atmosphere of tolerance and openness is essential for learning.

Discussion

When class groups are through recording the stereotypes and noting positive and negative components, each group should:

1. Read the stereotype their group devised to the whole class.

2. Consider whether the appearance components of the stereotype help to trigger the labeling.

3. Read what they think is negative about the stereotype and think about what consequences those negative components may have for the people to whom the stereotype is applied.

4. Read what they think is positive about the stereotype and think of what consequences those positive components may have for the people so labeled.

Discuss whether any two or more individuals can have all the components of any of the stereotypes. Is it fair to apply the stereotype before knowing a person, even if the stereotype fits somewhat?

60 Complexion

Richard Rodriguez

Visiting the East Coast or the gray capitals of Europe during the long months of winter, I often meet people at deluxe hotels who comment on my complexion. (In such hotels it appears nowadays a mark of leisure and wealth to have a complexion like mine.) Have I been skiing? In the Swiss Alps? Have I just returned from a Caribbean vacation? No. I say no softly but in a firm voice that intends to explain: My complexion is dark. (My skin is brown. More exactly, terra-cotta in sunlight, tawny in shade. I do not redden in sunlight. Instead, my skin becomes progressively dark; the sun singes the flesh.)

When I was a boy the white summer sun of Sacramento would darken me so, my T-shirt would seem bleached against my slender dark arms. My mother would see me come up the front steps. She'd wait for the screen door to slam at my back. "You look like a *negrito*," she'd say, angry, sorry to be angry, frustrated almost to laughing, scorn. "You know how important looks are in this country. With *los gringos* looks are all that they judge on. But you! Look at you! You're so careless!" Then she'd start in all over again. "You won't be satisfied till you end up looking like *los pobres* who work in the fields, *los braceros*."

(*Los braceros*: Those men who work with their *brazos*, their arms: Mexican nationals who were licensed to work for American farmers in the 1950s. They worked very hard for very little money, my father would tell me. And what money they earned they sent back to Mexico to support their families, my mother would add. *Los pobres*—the poor, the pitiful, the powerless ones. But paradoxically also powerful men. They were the men with brown-muscled arms I stared at in awe on Saturday mornings when they showed up downtown like gypsies to shop at Woolworth's or Penney's. On Monday nights they would gather hours early on the steps of the Memorial Auditorium for the wrestling matches. Passing by on my bicycle in summer, I would spy them there, clustered in small groups, talking—frightening and fascinating men—some wearing Texas *sombreros* and T-shirts which shone fluorescent in the twilight. I would sit forward in the back seat of our family's '48 Chevy to see them, working alongside Valley highways: dark men on an even horizon, loading a truck amid rows of straight green. Powerful, powerless men. Their fascinating darkness—like mine—to be feared.)

"You'll end up looking just like them." Regarding my family, I see faces that do not closely resemble my own. Like some other Mexican families, my family suggests Mexico's confused colonial past. Gathered around a table, we appear to be from separate continents. My father's face recalls faces I have seen in France. His complexion is white—he does not tan; he does not burn. Over the years, his dark wavy hair has grayed handsomely. But with time his face has sagged to a perpetual sigh. My mother, whose surname is inexplicably Irish—Moran—has an olive complexion. People have frequently wondered if, perhaps, she is Italian or Portuguese. And, in fact, she looks as though she could be from southern Europe. My mother's face has not aged as quickly as the rest of her body; it remains smooth and glowing—a cool tan—which her gray hair cleanly accentuates. My older brother has inherited her good looks. When he was a boy people would tell him that he looked like Mario Lanza, and hearing it he would smile with dimpled assurance. He would come home from high school with girl friends who seemed to me glamorous (because they were) blondes. And during those years I envied him his skin that burned red and peeled like the skin of the *gringos*. His complexion never darkened like mine. My youngest sister is exotically pale, almost ashen. She is delicately featured, Near Eastern, people have said. Only my older sister has a complexion as dark as mine, though her facial features are much less

From *Hunger of Memory* by Richard Rodriguez. Reprinted by permission of DAVID R. GODINE, PUBLISHER, INC. Copyright © 1982 by Richard Rodriguez.

harshly defined than my own. To many people meeting her, she seems (they say) Polynesian. I am the only one in the family whose face is severely cut to the line of ancient Indian ancestors. My face is mournfully long, in the classical Indian manner; my profile suggests one of those beak-nosed Mayan sculptures—the eaglelike face upturned, open-mouthed, against the deserted, primitive sky.

"We are Mexicans," my mother and father would say, and taught their four children to say whenever we (often) were asked about our ancestry. My mother and father scorned those "white" Mexican-Americans who tried to pass themselves off as Spanish. My parents would never have thought of denying their ancestry. I never denied it: My ancestry is Mexican, I told strangers mechanically. But I never forgot that only my older sister's complexion was as dark as mine.

My older sister never spoke to me about her complexion when she was a girl. But I guessed that she found her dark skin a burden. I knew that she suffered for being a "nigger." As she came home from grammar school, little boys came up behind her and pushed her down to the sidewalk. In high school, she struggled in the adolescent competition for boyfriends in a world of football games and proms, a world where her looks were plainly uncommon. In college, she was afraid and scornful when dark-skinned foreign students from countries like Turkey and India found her attractive. She revealed her fear of dark skin to me only in adulthood when, regarding her own three children, she quietly admitted relief that they were all light.

That is the kind of remark women in my family have often made before. As a boy, I'd stay in the kitchen (never seeming to attract any notice), listening while my aunts spoke of their pleasure at having light children. (The men, some of whom were dark-skinned from years of working out of doors, would be in another part of the house.) It was the woman's spoken concern: the fear of having a dark-skinned son or daughter. Remedies were exchanged. One aunt prescribed to her sisters the elixir of large doses of castor oil during the last weeks of pregnancy. (The remedy risked an abortion.) Children born dark grew up to have their faces treated regularly with a mixture of egg white and lemon juice concentrate.

(In my case, the solution never would take.) One Mexican-American friend of my mother's, who regarded it a special blessing that she had a measure of English blood, spoke disparagingly of her husband, a construction worker, for being so dark. "He doesn't take care of himself," she complained. But the remark, I noticed, annoyed my mother, who sat tracing an invisible design with her finger on the tablecloth.

There was affection too and a kind of humor about these matters. With daring tenderness, one of my uncles would refer to his wife as *mi negra*. An aunt regularly called her dark child *mi feito* (my little ugly one), her smile only partially hidden as she bent down to dig her mouth under his ticklish chin. And at times relatives spoke scornfully of pale, white skin. A *gringo's* skin resembled *masa*—baker's dough—someone remarked. Everyone laughed. Voices chuckled over the fact that the *gringos* spent so many hours in summer sunning themselves. ("They need to get sun because they look like *los muertos*.")

I heard the laughing but remembered what the women had said, with unsmiling voices, concerning dark skin. Nothing I heard outside the house, regarding my skin, was so impressive to me.

In public I occasionally heard racial slurs. Complete strangers would yell out at me. A teenager drove past, shouting, "Hey, Greaser! Hey, Pancho!" Over his shoulder I saw the giggling face of his girl friend. A boy pedaled by and announced matter-of-factly, "I pee on dirty Mexicans." Such remarks would be said so casually that I wouldn't quickly realize that they were being addressed to me. When I did, I would be paralyzed with embarrassment, unable to return the insult. (Those times I happened to be with white grammar school friends, *they* shouted back. Imbued with the mysterious kindness of children, my friends would never ask later why I hadn't yelled out in my own defense.)

In all, there could not have been more than a dozen incidents of name-calling. That there were so few suggests that I was not a primary victim of racial abuse. But that, even today, I can clearly remember particular incidents is proof of their impact. Because of such incidents, I listened when my parents remarked that Mexicans were often mistreated in California border towns. And in Texas. I listened carefully when I heard that two of my cousins had been refused admittance to an "all-white" swimming pool. And that an uncle had been told by some man to go back to Africa. I followed the progress of the southern black civil rights movement, which was gaining prominent notice in Sacramento's afternoon newspaper. But what most intrigued me was the connection between dark skin and poverty. Because I heard my mother speak so often about the relegation of dark people to menial labor, I considered the great victims of racism to be those who were poor and forced to do menial work. People like the farmworkers whose skin was dark from the sun.

After meeting a black grammar school friend of my sister's, I remember thinking that she wasn't really "black." What interested me was the fact that she wasn't poor. (Her well-dressed parents would come by after work to pick her up in a shiny green Oldsmobile.) By contrast, the garbage men who appeared every Friday morning seemed to me unmistakably black. (I didn't bother to ask my parents why Sacramento garbage men always were black. I thought I knew.) One morning I was in the backyard when a man opened the gate. He was an ugly, square-faced black man with popping red eyes, a pail slung over his shoulder. As he approached, I stood up. And in a voice that seemed to me very weak, I piped, "Hi." But the man paid me no heed. He strode past to the can by the garage. In a single broad movement, he overturned its contents into his larger pail. Our can came crashing down as he turned and left me watching, in awe.

"Pobres negros," my mother remarked when she'd notice a headline in the paper about a civil rights demonstration in the South. "How the gringos mistreat them." In the same tone of voice she'd tell me about the mistreatment her brother endured years before. (After my grandfather's death, my grandmother had come to America with her son and five daughters.) "My sisters, we were still all just teenagers. And since mi pápa was dead, my brother had to be the head of the family. He had to support us, to find work. But what skills did he have! Twenty years old. Pobre. He was tall, like your grandfather. And strong.

He did construction work. 'Construction!' The gringos kept him digging all day, doing the dirtiest jobs. And they would pay him next to nothing. Sometimes they promised him one salary and paid him less when he finished. But what could he do? Report them? We weren't citizens then. He didn't even know English. And he was dark. What chances could he have? As soon as we sisters got older, he went right back to Mexico. He hated this country. He looked so tired when he left. Already with a hunchback. Still in his twenties. But old-looking. No life for him here. Pobre."

Dark skin was for my mother the most important symbol of a life of oppressive labor and poverty. But both my parents recognized other symbols as well.

My father noticed the feel of every hand he shook. (He'd smile sometimes—marvel more than scorn—remembering a man he'd met who had soft, uncalloused hands.)

My mother would grab a towel in the kitchen and rub my oily face sore when I came in from playing outside. "Clean the graza off your face!" (Greaser!)

Symbols: When my older sister, then in high school, asked my mother if she could do light housework in the afternoons for a rich lady we knew, my mother was frightened by the idea. For several weeks she troubled over it before granting conditional permission: "Just remember, you're not a maid. I don't want you wearing a uniform." My father echoed the same warning. Walking with him past a hotel, I watched as he stared at a doorman dressed like a Beefeater. "How can anyone let himself be dressed up like that? Like a clown. Don't you ever get a job where you have to put on a uniform." In summertime neighbors would ask me if I wanted to earn extra money by mowing their lawns. Again and again my mother worried: "Why did they ask you? Can't you find anything better?" Inevitably, she'd relent. She knew I needed the money. But I was instructed to work after dinner. ("When the sun's not so hot.") Even then, I'd have to wear a hat. Un sombrero de baseball.

(Sombrero. Watching gray cowboy movies, I'd brood over the meaning of the broad-rimmed hat—that troubling symbol—which comically distinguished a Mexican cowboy from real cowboys.)

From my father came no warnings concerning the sun. His fear was of dark factory jobs. He remembered too well his first jobs when he came to this country, not intending to stay, just to earn money enough to sail on to Australia. (In Mexico he had heard too many stories of discrimination in *Los Estados Unidos*. So it was Australia, that distant island-continent, that loomed in his imagination as his "America.") The work my father found in San Francisco was work for the unskilled. A factory job. Then a cannery job. (He'd remember the noise and the heat.) Then a job at a warehouse. (He'd remember the dark stench of old urine.) At one place there were fistfights; at another a supervisor who hated Chinese and Mexicans. Nowhere a union.

His memory of himself in those years is held by those jobs. Never making money enough for passage to Australia; slowly giving up the plan of returning to school to resume his third grade education—to become an engineer. My memory of him in those years, however, is lifted from photographs in the family album which show him on his honeymoon with my mother—the woman who had convinced him to stay in America. I have studied their photographs often, seeking to find in those figures some clear resemblance to the man and the woman I've known as my parents. But the youthful faces in the photos remain, behind dark glasses, shadowy figures anticipating my mother and father.

They are pictured on the grounds of the Coronado Hotel near San Diego, standing in the pale light of a winter afternoon. She is wearing slacks. Her hair falls seductively over one side of her face. He appears wearing a double-breasted suit, an unneeded raincoat draped over his arm. Another shows them standing together, solemnly staring ahead. Their shoulders barely are touching. There is to their pose an aristocratic formality, an elegant Latin hauteur.

The man in those pictures is the same man who was fascinated by Italian grand opera. I have never known just what my father saw in the spectacle, but he has told me that he would take my mother to the Opera House every Friday night—if he had money enough for orchestra seats.

("Why go to sit in the balcony?") On Sundays he'd don Italian silk scarves and a camel's hair coat to take his new wife to the polo matches in Golden Gate Park. But one weekend my father stopped going to the opera and polo matches. He would blame the change in his life on one job—a warehouse job, working for a large corporation which today advertises its products with the smiling faces of children. "They made me an old man before my time," he'd say to me many years later. Afterward, jobs got easier and cleaner. Eventually, in middle age, he got a job making false teeth. But his youth was spent at the warehouse. "Everything changed," his wife remembers. The dapper young man in the old photographs yielded to the man I saw after dinner: haggard, asleep on the sofa. During "The Ed Sullivan Show" on Sunday nights, when Roberta Peters or Licia Albanese would appear on the tiny blue screen, his head would jerk up alert. He'd sit forward while the notes of Puccini sounded before him. ("Un bel dí.")

By the time they had a family, my parents no longer dressed in very fine clothes. Those symbols of great wealth and the reality of their lives too noisily clashed. No longer did they try to fit themselves, like paper-doll figures, behind trappings so foreign to their actual lives. My father no longer wore silk scarves or expensive wool suits. He sold his tuxedo to a second-hand store for five dollars. My mother sold her rabbit fur coat to the wife of a Spanish radio station disc jockey. ("It looks better on you than it does on me," she kept telling the lady until the sale was completed.) I was six years old at the time, but I recall watching the transaction with complete understanding. The woman I knew as my mother was already physically unlike the woman in her honeymoon photos. My mother's hair was short. Her shoulders were thick from carrying children. Her fingers were swollen red, toughened by housecleaning. Already my mother would admit to foreseeing herself in her own mother, a woman grown old, bald and bowlegged, after a hard lifetime of working.

In their manner, both my parents continued to respect the symbols of what they considered to be upper-class life. Very early, they taught me the *propria* way of eating *como los ricos*. And I was carefully taught elaborate formulas of polite greeting and parting. The dark little boy would be invited by classmates to the rich houses on Forty-fourth and Forty-fifth streets. "How do you do?" or "I am very pleased to meet you," I would say, bowing slightly to the amused mothers of classmates. "Thank you very much for the dinner; it was very delicious."

I made an impression. I intended to make an impression, to be invited back. (I soon realized that the trick was to get the mother or father to notice me.) From those early days began my association with rich people, my fascination with their secret. My mother worried. She warned me not to come home expecting to have the things my friends possessed. But she needn't have said anything. When I went to the big houses, I remembered that I was, at best, a visitor to the world I saw there. For that reason, I was an especially watchful guest. I was my parents' child. Things most middle-class children wouldn't trouble to notice, I studied. Remembered to see: the starched black and white uniform worn by the maid who opened the door; the Mexican gardeners—their complexions as dark as my own. (One gardener's face, glassed by sweat, looked up to see me going inside.)

"Take Richard upstairs and show him your electric train," the mother said. But it was really the vast polished dining room table I'd come to appraise. Those nights when I was invited to stay for dinner, I'd notice that my friend's mother rang a small silver bell to tell the black woman when to bring in the food. The father, at his end of the table, ate while wearing his tie. When I was not required to speak, I'd skate the icy cut of crystal with my eye; my gaze would follow the golden threads etched onto the rim of china. With my mother's eyes I'd see my hostess's manicured nails and judge them to be marks of her leisure. Later, when my schoolmate's father would bid me goodnight, I would feel his soft fingers and palm when we shook hands. And turning to leave, I'd see my dark self, lit by chandelier light, in a tall hallway mirror.

DISCUSSION QUESTIONS

Complexion

1. Why was Richard Rodriguez's mother so adamant that her son not spend too much time tanning in the sun? What did this symbolize to her?

2. How did the author learn to relate to his cultural/ethnic identity? How did he address his own issues of skin color as they relate to social class?

3. Why does skin color remain a powerful signifier of social class?

61   Black, Hip, and Primed (To Shop)

Christy Fisher

E. Jean Lee likes to shop. On most weekends, Lee can be found with her sister-in-law or a friend at one of her favorite shopping malls in the Washington, D.C., area in search of a bargain. She prefers to shop at department stores-like Hecht's, Macy's East, and Nordstrom Inc. But she also likes Sam's Wholesale Club.

She rarely wraps up a shopping excursion with nothing to show for it, resulting in closets that are bursting at the seams. "I like everything," says the 29-year-old magazine production coordinator. "I have several closets at home that I have to clean out because I can't fit anything more in them. I just gave away a bunch of old shoes to make room."

Erwin Brown, another Washington-area shopper, visits his favorite stores about four times a month. Despite living in Prince George's County, one of the most affluent counties in the U.S., he must travel across town to the Tysons Corner mall in northern Virginia to shop at Hecht's, Lord & Taylor, and Britches Great Outdoors. He is partial to designers Perry Ellis, Tommy Hilfiger, and Bill Blass. "I buy whatever looks good," says Brown, a senior research services specialist in his mid-30s. "I look for quality stuff."

Lee and Brown should be dream customers in the eyes of retailers and marketers. But as black consumers, they are often judged a market too small and with too little spending power to be worth wooing. New data from Yankelovich Partners and the Consumer Expenditure Survey show that companies who ignore blacks may be missing a significant opportunity.

Non-Hispanic blacks are a relatively small share of the U.S. population, at 12 percent in 1996. Yet their numbers are expected to grow faster than average into the next century. The Census Bureau projects the non-Hispanic black population may increase 23 percent by 2015, to 39.5 million. That's slightly faster than the 17 percent growth expected for the U.S. as a whole. Between 2015 and 2050, the non-Hispanic black

population may increase almost 36 percent, to 53.6 million, compared with U.S. population growth of 27 percent.

Blacks make up large shares of the population in several major metropolitan areas. More than four in ten residents of the Memphis metro are black. And more than three in ten residents of the New York metropolitan area are black, according to estimates from Woods & Poole Economics, Inc., of Washington, D.C. Richmond-Petersburg, Norfolk-Virginia Beach-Newport News, New Orleans, Baltimore, Atlanta, and Washington all have populations that are more than one-fourth black.

One reason why most companies don't invest heavily in targeting black consumers is their low median household income. At $21,000 in 1994, it is well below the median of $32,300 for all U.S. households. Consequently, black households spend less than average on many things, from food away from home to charitable contributions. But millions of middle-class and upper-class black households have discretionary money to spend, and the choices they make boost black household expenditures above average for numerous goods and services.

SPENDING TO LOOK GOOD

Black adults care about their appearance, and they show it in their spending on personal-care services. More than six in ten black householders spent something on such services in 1994, including hair styling, massage, and manicures. The average annual household expenditure for those who spent anything was $530, 34 percent more than the U.S. average of $349. Black households spend 41 percent more than average on personal-care services for women, at $532 a year, and 24 percent more on services for men, at $212 a year.

Looking good means more than having a smart hair style and tidy nails. Black households that spend anything also spend more than average on hosiery, women's accessories, jewelry, and even home electronic equipment. However, their spending is significantly lower than average for housing, including owned and rented dwellings, as well as appliances, furnishings, and home maintenance, repairs, and insurance, among others.

"It is still difficult for African Americans to buy the house of their choice, in the neighborhood of their choice, and send their children to college," says Byron Lewis, chairman and chief executive officer of UniWorld Group, a New York City advertising agency specializing in multicultural marketing. Many blacks who can't acquire the home they want divert their spending to other things, he says. "We have more money, or disposable income, for attainable status symbols. It is how we acquire the American dream."

STILL SHOP 'TIL YOU DROP

Retailers who believe the recreational shopping trend of the 1980s has long since departed should notice black shoppers. They're hitting the mall to enhance their personal appearance and image, and also to have fun. The supermarket holds appeal for these shoppers, as well. Six in ten blacks say it's "fun and exciting" to shop for clothes, according to a 1995 survey of 1,000 blacks and 4,000 whites aged 16 and older by Yankelovich Partners. Sixty-five percent describe food shopping the same way. The shares are smaller for white Americans, at 35 percent and 54 percent, respectively.

In addition, the share of blacks who describe clothes and food shopping as "fun and exciting" increased over the three years since Yankelovich's last survey. The share who enjoyed clothes shopping increased 5 percentage points from 1992, and the share who say food shopping is fun jumped 10 percentage points.

One reason for these growing shares is that blacks are making shopping a social event. "Blacks go shopping with friends and family. It is seen very much as a social experience and less of a hassle," says Alvin Styles, vice president and director of research for Burrell Communications Group, a Chicago advertising agency specializing in the black consumer market. "Shop 'til you drop still applies to the African-American market."

Discount department stores are the most popular retail outlets for virtually all Americans, including blacks. Yet blacks are a little less likely than their white counterparts to say they shop at stores like Wal-Mart and Kmart at least once a month. Seven in ten white Americans aged 16 and older say they go to a discount store at least once a month, compared with six in ten blacks.

One probable reason for the difference is that many blacks patronize discounters' upscale competitors. Blacks are significantly more likely than whites to say they shop at department and specialty stores once a month or more, at 41 percent and 30 percent, respectively. In contrast, 32 percent of whites say they frequent department stores, and 19 percent often shop in specialty stores.

The propensity of blacks to favor department and specialty stores isn't lost on some retailers, including J.C. Penney Company, Sears Roebuck & Company, and Nordstrom Inc. "We recognize that our customers come from every community, and it is important that we serve all the communities where we do business," says Paula Stanley, public affairs coordinator for Seattle-based Nordstrom, which has 81 stores in 16 states. "It's part of our corporate commitment to diversity." That commitment includes increasing minority representation in employment and management, and doing business with women and minority vendors. "Also, one-third of the models we use represent ethnic diversity, and we regularly advertise in minority-owned media and do community outreach projects," Stanley says.

Offering products specifically designed for blacks helps, too. Spiegel Inc., the giant mail-order company, and *Ebony* magazine have successfully targeted blacks with *E Style*, a quarterly fashion, accessories, and home-decor catalog for black women. *E Style* went to 2.7 million women in spring 1996, up from 1 million at its launch in fall 1993. "We conducted focus groups and found that a lot of fashions do not meet African-American women's need in style and fit," says Lori Scott, associate merchandise manager for *E Style* in Downers Grove, Illinois. "We saw that as an opportunity."

Sara Lee Hosiery, the Winston-Salem, North Carolina-based marketer of the Hanes and L'eggs brands, discovered that black women buy more hosiery and buy better quality hosiery. "The ultrasheer (category), which is a more dressed up look, is particularly well developed," says Leila Meresman, public relations director for Sara Lee Hosiery in New York. "Our research also shows that black women are less likely to wear casual clothes for work, and overall they have fewer casual days, or bare-leg occasions." Consumer Expenditure Survey data bear out this observation. Black households that spend anything on hosiery spent an average of $108 in 1994, 13 percent more than the average for all U.S. households that bought hosiery.

A LITTLE RESPECT, PLEASE

Wanting a put-together appearance doesn't mean the blacks will settle for anything in their shopping experience as long as it yields stylish goods. In some ways, blacks are more discriminating than whites in their retail interactions. Price matters to both groups, but a smaller share of blacks than whites say reasonable prices are most important to them in deciding where to shop, 72 percent and 83 percent respectively.

With those shares, reasonable pricing is the number-one deciding factor for both blacks and whites. But from there, the top-five factors diverge significantly for the two groups. The second most important factor for whites in deciding where to shop is the availability of quality merchandise. But for blacks, it's respect. More than six in ten say one of their most important reasons for choosing a store is that it treats customers with respect.

"Respect is so important," says Pepper Miller, president of The Hunter-Miller Group, a Chicago research and planning firm. "So many African Americans do not feel welcome. In research groups, they constantly talk about being watched or being ignored."

Automatically suspecting black customers of wrongdoing or ignoring them has lost companies not only customers, but big bucks in legal fees and settlements. In 1995, two black Maryland teenagers filed a lawsuit against Eddie Bauer, Inc., and two white police officers acting as store security guards. The guards ordered one of the boys to take off his shirt because the officers suspected it was stolen. The incident caused enough of a flap among the company's black customers that its president, Rick Fersch, traveled from Seattle to Washington, D.C., to meet with community groups and apologize for the incident.

The Los-Angeles-based Denny's restaurant chain also found itself in hot water following two 1993 lawsuits. A California lawsuit alleged that 32 black customers were ordered to prepay for meals or pay a cover charge, neither of which were required of white customers. A second case was brought in Maryland by six U.S. Secret Service agents who alleged they were denied service at a Denny's restaurant. Both were settled about a year later for a total of $54 million.

Feeling respected as customers is key to black shoppers, and it is consistent with their use of shopping for recreation. It's hard to have fun when you feel put down or mistreated. Blacks want more than a good price and a nice frock— they're looking for a pleasant shopping experience. A pleasant store atmosphere ranks fourth among blacks as an important factor in deciding where to shop, at 58 percent. Atmosphere is less important to whites, ranking 13th at 48 percent.

Geography plays an important role for blacks, too. Locating retail outlets near places where blacks live and work is a good move for companies wanting to woo them. Fifty-six percent of blacks aged 16 and older say a store's location near home or work is very important in their shopping decision. The share of whites who say so is slightly less, at 52 percent.

NOTHING BUT THE BEST

Retailers that make blacks feel welcome and comfortable in their stores are on their way to enjoying the patronage of customers who don't mind spending money to get the best-quality merchandise available. Blacks aren't compulsively brand-oriented. More than six in ten say that all brands are about the same. Yet they recognize that some brands stand out from the crowd. And for those, blacks will gladly pay.

Almost two-thirds of blacks say they are willing to pay more to get "the best," even if that brand or product isn't widely recognized. Whites are less likely to feel this way, at 51 percent. For many blacks, discerning what brands are worth buying over others is important to enhancing one's personal image. Four in ten blacks say they like to buy brands that make them feel they've made it, compared with 33 percent of whites. For 30 percent of blacks, buying brand-name goods also signals their success to others. Blacks are twice as likely as whites to say they buy brands that let others know they've made it, at 30 percent.

"It's all about image. We will buy a $500 suit and $200 shoes, and drink premium liquor," says Miller of The Hunter-Miller Group. "We buy fancy cars and clothes." A big motivator for many blacks is quality, not quantity, adds Styles of Burrell Communications Group. "If I can't get a lot of things, I can get some things most people recognize as being top-quality stuff," he says.

The blacks who can least afford premium goods are the ones for whom "the best" matters most—those aged 16 to 24. Seventy percent of young blacks say they are willing to spend more to get the best; 51 percent say they buy brands "that make me feel I've made it"; and 43 percent say they buy brands "that let other people know I've made it." The propensity to shop for status decreases to age 49, then rises slightly for those aged 50 and older. However, the shares who say brands convey status are still below those for young blacks.

Blacks aged 50 and older have higher incomes than young adults, so they are better able to afford name brands. But their reasons are different, says Styles of Burrell Communications Group. "For older blacks, brand is more quality assurance," he says. "Among the younger generation, brand also is image. It is a statement of how cool or how hip you are, if you are a leader or a follower."

Companies with hot brands have good reasons to eye black consumers in the next century. The blacks who are most likely to say they buy the best, buy brands that make them feel they've made it, and agree that brands signal success to others, are in the age groups projected to grow the fastest in the next decade, according to the Census Bureau. The numbers of non-Hispanic blacks aged 14 to 17 and 18 to 24 are projected to increase 16 percent and 15 percent, respectively, between 1996 and 2006. That's faster than the average of 12 percent for all non-Hispanic blacks. The U.S. could have 2.6 million non-Hispanic blacks aged 14 to 17 by then, and 4 million aged 18 to 24.

The number of non-Hispanic blacks in the brand-loving 50s-and-older group is expected to grow even faster. The U.S may have more than 4.7 million non-Hispanic blacks aged 45 to 54 in 2006, a 46 percent increase from 1996. The number aged 55 to 64 may grow 45 percent to almost 3 million. The number aged 66 and older will grow at an average pace.

TARGETING AND TUNING IN

There are dozens of black-oriented media available to companies wanting to tout their products to black Americans. But one of the best is a mass medium—television. Black households watch an average of 73 hours and 30 minutes of television each week, according to March 1994 data from Nielsen Media Research in New York City. That's well above the national average of 48 hours and 25 minutes for all households.

Yet choosing which shows to advertise around is key in reaching black audiences and age groups within the black population, says Doug Alligood, senior vice president, special markets, for the New York City-based advertising agency BBDO New York. The top-ten rated shows for black households and all U.S. households diverge dramatically, according to BBDO's analysis of Nielsen data from September 1995 to December 1995. The two groups shared only one top-ten preference—"NFL Monday Night Football." The top-20 rated shows for both blacks and U.S. TV households as a whole included two additional mutual pleasers in "Monday Night Movie" and "E.R."

What makes shows appeal to black audiences? All programs on the black viewership top-ten list last fall featured a black performer in a starring or major-supporting role, says BBDO. The top-five were "New York Undercover," "Living Single," "The Crew," "In The House," and "Fresh Prince of Bel Air." The top-rated shows among all households were "E.R." "Seinfeld," "Friends," "Caroline in the City," and "NFL Monday Night Football."

There are two crossover audiences of blacks and whites—viewers aged 12 to 17 and aged 50 and older. Both black and white teens like many of the same shows. Eleven of the top-20 shows for all viewers aged 12 to 17 are also in the top-20 for black teens. That's more than three times the crossover for all viewers. "I think it reflects on society. Teenagers have more crossover in their experience than those of us who are older," Alligood says. "Teens share more music. They share more outings, and more sports."

That shared interest declines in middle age, though. Racial commonality in television viewing generally decreases to age 50, then picks up again. The top-20 lists for blacks and whites over age 50 at the end of 1995 shared six common shows, including "Walker, Texas Ranger," "60 Minutes," "NYPD Blue," and "20/20." "Shows featuring black performers and strong family values, such as 'Family Matters' and 'Fresh Prince of Bel Air,' continue to pull older black viewers," Alligood says. "But many of the successful shows featuring black comedians, such as 'Martin' and 'The Wayans Brothers,' have an irreverent brand of humor, which has less appeal for older blacks."

Blacks are a relatively small market nationally, but they are a key group in many large urban areas and in the Southeast. Many who can't afford some of the trappings of the successful life, such as owned homes, show their good taste by spending on high fashions and name brands. While mass retail markets are crying for value, many blacks want quality and name brands. And that spells opportunity for many companies.

DISCUSSION QUESTIONS

Black, Hip, and Primed to Shop

1. According to the article, what steps could a retailer take to attract more African American customers?

2. For African Americans, how is shopping for brand names associated with signaling success to others? How does the meaning of buying brand names vary for African American shoppers in their 20s and those over 50?

62 African American Women's Professional Dress as Expression of Ethnicity

Gwendolyn S. O'Neal

Ethnicity is "among the most complicated, volatile, and emotionally charged words and ideas in the lexicon of social science" (Nash, 1989, p. 1). The concept of ethnicity refers to a socially defined group based on cultural criteria (Landrine & Klonoff, 1996; Littlefield, Liebermann, & Reynolds, 1982; van den Berghe, 1978). Eicher (1995) observed:

> The ideas behind ethnicity connect to the preservation of an identity for individuals that links to a meaningful heritage...discussions of ethnicity have focused on self-definitions as opposed to definition by others...(p. 4)

Dress is used today in establishing and preserving an identity. In addition, to actively construct and reconstruct the self, dress is often used in efforts to influence or control a situation (Craik, 1994; Finkelstein, 1991; Kaiser, 1990). The purpose of this article is to examine the use of "cultural dress" by some African American professional women. Cultural dress includes traditionally styled garments and accessories imported from various African countries, made of fabrics and other materials constructed and finished in those countries, or replicas of such. In addition, styles and forms of adornment are noticeably of African influence. For purposes of this research, "dress" is considered as a gestalt that includes the body and all modifications (e.g., painting and piercing) and supplements (e.g., garments and accessories) added to it (Eicher & Roach-Higgins, 1992). The use of the word "traditional" here is not intended to suggest the lack of change. Instead, it is more related to identifying with that which comes from Africa. Eicher (1995) states, "The body modifications and supplements that mark the ethnic identity of an individual are ethnic dress." (p. 1)

RATIONALE

Individuals and groups use dress to create meaning and to position themselves in society. Fox-Genovese (1987) suggested that dress has always served political functions. Its visual symbols establish codes of domination and subordination that link distributions of resources, opportunities, and respect in the society. As objects of material culture, dress is used to express symbolically cultural and philosophical orientations of the group that sanctioned it. The field of dress codes, according to Ash and Wilson (1992), has become a site of struggle for control of the power to define the situation and the self.

During the civil rights era of the 1960s and 1970s, much media attention was given to the dress of African Americans as both males and females allowed their hair to "go natural" and wore other symbols of their West African heritage, such as bright colored kaftans. Men donned the kofi hat, and some women wore headwraps. These items became linked to the civil rights revolution and for some they symbolized rebellion. African Americans, both men and women, adopted more subtle forms (e.g., a short version of the afro or braids) to express their ethnicity. Still others, albeit small in number, continued to wear "traditional" African dress.

The use of dress for ethnic group differentiation appears to be universal. Such usage of dress serves as a link between identity and one's heritage. The problem, however, is the lack of knowledge in general of a meaningful cultural heritage traceable through generations of descendants of West Africans with which African Americans might identify. Because of the negative stereotypes associated with the African American "race," education and acculturation are viewed as keys to acceptance by the dominant culture.

Gwendolyn S. O'Neal, *Journal of Family and Consumer Sciences* Spring 1998, pp. 28–33, copyright © 1998 by Sage Publications, Inc. Reprinted by permission.

Using dress to establish an identity linked to ethnicity stands in opposition to the norm of acculturation. Such behavior carries the risk of possibly being perceived as deviant in the dominant culture where fairly well defined rules concerning professional dress exist. Wearing symbols representing an African heritage might elicit perceptions ranging from eccentric to adversarial with the potential to impede positive interactions, thus negatively affecting one's career. With these possible negative reactions, the question then arises, "Why the use of cultural dress as professional attire?" To further clarify the rationale for seeking to *understand* the use of cultural dress by some African American professional women, a discussion of race, ethnicity, and acculturation is warranted.

Race and Ethnicity

As recently as 1963, Glazer and Moynihan wrote, "The Negro is only an American and nothing else. He has no values and culture to guard and protect" (p. 53). The notion was that any culture enslaved Africans might have had was destroyed during slavery (Jones, 1991). Noble (1991) argues that segregation and Jim Crow laws served to preserve aspects of African culture by forcing enslaved Africans and later Negroes and Black Americans to remain isolated, thus insulating some cultural orientations. In addition, many domestic slaves overtly adopted European manners while covertly retaining their African cultural roots (Bush, 1986; Genovese, 1972). Nevertheless, African Americans historically have been defined as a race and not as an ethnic group. Race and ethnicity represent different paradigms for understanding. Race refers to groups that are socially defined on the basis of physical criteria, while ethnicity refers to groups that are socially defined on the basis of cultural criteria (Landrine & Klonoff, 1996).

Despite the fact that, for almost a half century, researchers (see for example Gayle, 1971; Herskovits, 1958; Holloway, 1990; Semmes, 1992; Sieber, 1972) have documented links between African American cultural aesthetics and West African countries, such knowledge is given cursory attention, at best, in curricular offerings at all levels of American educational systems. Its absence continuously perpetuates the notion of African Americans as a race without a culture. Works by Gould (1981), Cyril Burt (as cited in Kamin, 1974), Rushton (1992, 1994), and *The Bell Curve* (Herrnstein & Murray, 1994) have continued to denigrate, degrade, and perpetuate the myths of a subordinate Black race. Features of African Americans that are clearly African are placed in opposition to White and therefore considered negative. Such positioning has created a negative social identity for African Americans.

Nash (1989) delineates "boundary markers" of ethnic group differentiation (p. 11). Dress serves as a surface pointer that makes recognition of group affiliation possible at a distance. The book *Dress and Ethnicity* (Eicher, 1995) consists of works in which dress is analyzed as an aspect of ethnicity. Research about ethnic groups and dress from five continents is included. In one chapter Griebel (1995) discusses the use of the headwrap among African American women. She concludes, "The headwrap serves African Americans as the fundamental symbol of self in relation to ethnic identity" (p. 225). The implication is that African Americans constitute an ethnic group. While the academic literature in Black/African American history and aesthetics implies ethnicity, the dominant culture gives no formal recognition of such. Thus, for some African Americans the solution is acculturation (Landrine & Klonoff, 1996; Lott, 1992).

Acculturation

Landrine and Klonoff (1996) define acculturation as the extent to which ethnic cultural minorities participate in the cultural traditions, values, beliefs, and practices of their own culture versus those of the dominant society. They view the concept as a means of providing a rudimentary theory of the relationship between culture and behavior. Thus ethnic differences can be understood as a manifestation of an individual's level of acculturation. While measures of acculturation have long been developed for Americans of Chinese, Japanese, Cuban, and Mexican descent as well as some Native American tribes, prior to the work by Landrine and Klonoff no such measure had been developed for African Americans. They attribute this lack to the viewing of African Americans as a race and not as an ethnic group.

However, as more and more African Americans received formal education and sought to leave behind the negative social identity by exiting the community and when possible, the group, varying levels of acculturation resulted. Landrine and Klonoff (1996) describe three levels of acculturation: *traditional*—one is immersed in the culture of origin; *bicultural*—one is immersed in both the culture of origin and in the dominant culture; and *acculturated*—one is immersed mostly in the dominant culture. Also, some members of minority groups are considered "marginal" as either rejecting (or never acquiring) the beliefs and practices of their own culture or of the dominant culture. The result is great disparity among African Americans in terms of how they relate to the dominant culture and their emphasis on a cultural heritage rooted in Africa. Therefore, it is important to understand why professional women, i.e., educated African Americans who have obtained the knowledge to become fully acculturated, would choose to assume risks that might be avoided by conforming to the dominant culture's norm of professional dress.

METHOD

Subjects

I had observed each of 15 women wearing cultural dress at various times in the workplace, church, and/or during social and cultural functions other than special African American celebrations during Black History month. All had completed education earning at least a bachelor's degree, with one third having earned a doctorate. All were employed in professional positions in fields such as education, government, and human services.

Data Collection

I conducted an in-depth interview with each of the 15 women using semistructured questions concerning their use of cultural dress. The interviews were audiotape-recorded and transcribed. Each interview lasted approximately one hour.

My goal was to construct an interpretation that allowed the voices of the women to be heard. After constructing the interpretation, I shared the narrative with five of the informants to assess the faithfulness of the interpretation to the context and individuals it is supposed to represent. They concurred with the interpretation.

FINDINGS
Definition of Self

In defining the self, informants chose to construct identities that clearly establish, through dress, cultural boundaries that express cultural aesthetics as well as a cultural context of self/other relationships. Statements such as, "It is an expression of who I am," suggest that cultural dress provides a constructed discourse that can be interpreted as expressing membership in a group with a common history, symbol system, and geography. Although different and distinct from that of the dominant culture this symbol system serves as an expression of pride in one's heritage. These elements can be seen in the following excerpts:

> It is a personal statement...I feel that I am expressing a part of my own culture, and the fact that it is different from someone else's doesn't bother me at all.

> ...it has become more of a statement. Not to say who I am, because that is very physically evident, but it makes a statement in terms of my preferences in...adornment...It is different. It sets me apart to a certain degree....It helps me let the majority know that I am proud of who I am and where I come from....

> I think it is very important for African Americans to make that statement because where we have come from...has been so shrouded in darkness and negativeness that it is time for us to...say, in spite of the terms that have been used to describe who we may have been or where I may have come from, I am still proud of me and proud of my heritage.

While cultural dress is used to define the self as ethnic, express pride in the ethnic self, and identify with the cultural heritage of West Africa, at a more personal level it serves to help balance the tension created by the dual self. There is a sense of being neither fully American nor fully African. The struggle is as DuBois

(1903) described: "two souls, two thoughts, two unreconciled strivings; two warring ideals in one dark body…" (p. 45). One informant described the use of cultural dress as completing

> …the whole picture of who I am and where I'm from and all of that…and that's inclusive of my American dress as well as my return to African dress…I think it's a part of what represents who I am: a combination of an African woman and a woman who was born in America.

Another person described the use of cultural dress to help alleviate this tension as follows:

> The principal reason I dress this way is to recognize my ancestors…at the same time it's not practical that I would go totally into the dress of my ancestors. So I try to pull them together. And the things I continue to purchase as well as the things that I have had in my wardrobe before, I began to integrate. I am a woman of African descent, born in America. That is who I am.…

These statements indicate these women have chosen to establish a definition of self based on their heritage. It is not relevant whether appearance always conforms to the dominant ideals of fashion, but that the self is rooted in a culture they understand and with which they can identify. This action suggests that the dominant culture's definition of appropriate professional dress is less relevant than self definition. It includes an element of resistance to institutional norms of appropriateness that hinders self definition.

Educating Others

Another use of cultural dress is the education of others about African and African American culture. Most of the women take a proactive posture in correcting the prescribed ignorance resulting from an educational system dominated by Eurocentric ideals. As seen in the following excerpts, they use dress as a catalyst in stimulating conversation about their culture. Such conversation is purposeful with the aim of educating.

> …it's good to be who you are, and it's good to be proud of that…so you reflect it…in your dress.…So I guess I'm trying to educate and as

well to feel good about it…and…I think I am contributing to someone else's knowledge base by sharing with them, whether they ask a question about it or not.

> When people are interested enough to ask, I feel that that's an opportunity to educate. When someone say [sic], "Oh that is beautiful," I say, "Oh that came from Nigeria."

> I see it [cultural dress] as an opportunity to educate people.

Link to Heritage

Dress is used as tangible evidence of the geographic place of their cultural heritage. In addition to bringing about equilibrium between the "two selves," dress serves as a link to the geographic place of origin as well as to ancestral relationships. From the perspective of West African metaphysics, such connecting is not unusual in that there is an inter-relatedness and interconnection between humans, objects, and the universe, which is not bounded by time or space. This link is seen in the following excerpts:

> You know how when children are adopted they still want to know who their biological parents are, no matter how well they're loved. I think that inside of each African American who has been told the stories of Western enslavement…there is this piece that always wanted to go back and embrace that African piece.…

> There is a group of us who really do have a genuine desire, as well as the money, to purchase these things, and to recreate those connections.…It's a sense of who you are, and where you come from.…Knowing who your mom and dad really are.

> It speaks to an ongoing process of a search for self…and how I want others to see me, and how I have come to terms with the way in which a Eurocentric position or an Afrocentric position jive or a lack thereof…I guess I am trying to attach that connection to ancestors.…It is sort of my own way of connecting.

The shift toward wearing cultural dress by the participants in this study evolved as appreciation for Africa and African heritage developed. For some, this happened during the civil rights era of the 1960s, while for others it was more recent. Informants frequently established the link between wearing cultural dress and an understanding of one's cultural heritage. One informant's explanation of this process follows:

> It was a whole evolutionary process for me…as I came to learn more about myself and became able to accept myself for who I am. That increased my self-esteem. Then when I began to accept myself more I began to embrace more things within my culture….As I accepted myself as an African American and as a Christian, that enhanced it even more because I understood that God made me this way.

Another person stated:

> I think because most middle-income African Americans are more educated in terms of their history. Many…have traveled to Africa, West Africa in particular….I think that whole idea of understanding,…being around other African people, having visited the country, helped them to recognize the beauty there is in being African. It has opened up to the middle-class African American in a way that it has not done…the lower-income African American.

Suggested in the above excerpt is the notion that the construction of an ethnic identity based on the valuing of one's culture may be constrained by economics. Since the study of African and African American culture is not the norm in educational systems in these United States, the exposure to such knowledge might be hampered where resources are limited.

DISCUSSION AND IMPLICATIONS

The professional women interviewed for this study use cultural dress to construct identities based on knowledge and appreciation of their cultural heritage. In addition, instead of abandoning dress of the dominant culture, choices are often made in terms of expediency, suggesting that these informants share a level of acculturation best described as bicultural. They understand and embrace elements of both the dominant culture and their own as deemed nec-

essary. However, tension is noted in the need to reconcile the two selves.

The women have chosen to quietly but visibly take control of the definition of self and to implement an agenda to debunk the myth of African Americans as only a race. As interactions ensue, they articulate their history and cultural heritage with passion and expertise. The passion with which the women talk about educating others suggests they might serve as resources for Family and Consumer Sciences professionals, such as teachers, extension agents, and administrators, as they incorporate multicultural concepts and issues into the curriculum.

The inclusion of ethnic characteristics in dress of African Americans in curricular offerings will serve to inform Americans about characteristics of dress common to African Americans that are often viewed as deviant. Such understanding aids in alleviating negative stereotypes and fears associated with the unknown. For example, knowledge of the fact that West Africans and African Americans share a common interest in adorning the head in elaborate ways might lead to interpreting elaborate hairstyles as the expression of a cultural aesthetic rather than as a deviant act.

For some of the women, self-esteem was enhanced as knowledge of their heritage increased. Family and Consumer Sciences professionals concerned with the well-being of individuals and families might note the implied relationship between high self-esteem and knowledge and appreciation of one's culture. An additional implication is that of a relationship between achieving knowledge about one's history and culture and economic resources. Low self-esteem and poverty are two factors often used to explain violence in schools and in the larger society. It is possible that the understanding and appreciation of one's cultural heritage may serve to reduce violence if it also enhances self-esteem. However, knowledge and appreciation must not be contingent upon one's economic resources.

Since learning about their heritage, the women do not wish to live as if they are simply American. They share common "building blocks of ethnicity" (Nash, 1989)—physical characteristics, language patterns, history, and ways of relating to the supernatural that can be linked to their geographic area of origin. Dress serves as the visual expression of that ethnicity.

References

Ash, J., & Wilson, E., 1992. Chic Thrills: A Fashion Reader. Berkeley: University of California Press.

Bush, B., 1986. " 'The family tree is not cut': Women and cultural resistance in slave family life in the British Caribbean." In G.Y. Okihiro, (ed.), In Resistance: Studies in African, Caribbean, and Afro-American History, pp. 117–132. Amherst: University of Massachusetts Press.

Craik, J., 1994. The Face of Fashion: Cultural Studies in Fashion. New York: Routledge.

DuBois, W.E.B., 1903/1969. The Souls of Black folk. New York: The New American Library.

Eicher, J.B., 1995. Dress and Ethnicity. Oxford and Washington, DC: Berg.

Eicher, J.B., & Roach-Higgins, M.E., 1972. Definition and classification of dress. In R. Barnes and J.B. Eicher (eds.), Dress and Gender: Making and Meaning in Cultural Context, pp. 8–20. New York: Berg.

Finkelstein, J., 1991. The Fashioned Self. Cambridge, UK: Polity Press.

Fox-Genovese, E., 1987. "The empress's new clothes: The politics of fashion." Socialist Review, 17(1), 7–32.

Gayle, A., Jr., 1971. The Black Aesthetic. Garden City, NY: Doubleday.

Genovese, E.D., 1972. Roll, Jordan, Roll: The World the Slaves Made. New York: Pantheon Books.

Glazer, N., & Moynihan, D.P., 1963. Beyond the Melting Pot. Cambridge, MA: MIT Press.

Griebel, H.B., 1995. "The West African origin of the African American headwrap." In J.B. Eicher (ed.), Dress and Ethnicity, pp. 207–226. Oxford and Washington, D.C.: Berg.

Gould, S.J., 1981. The Mismeasure of Man. New York: Norton.

Herrnstein, R.J., & Murray, C., 1994. The Bell Curve: Intelligence and Class Structure in American Life. New York: Free Press.

Herskovits, M.J., 1958. The Myth of the Negro Past. Boston: Beacon Press.

Holloway, J.E., 1990. "The origin of African American culture." In J.E. Holloway (ed.), Africanisms in American Culture, pp. 1–18. Bloomington: Indiana University Press.

Jones, J.M., 1991. "The politics of personality: Being black in America." In R.L. Jones (ed.), Black Psychology, pp. 305–318. Hampton, VA: Cobb & Henry.

Kaiser, S.B., 1990. The Social Psychology of Clothing, 2nd ed. New York: Macmillan.

Kamin, L.J., 1974. The Science and Politics of IQ. Potomac, MD: Lawrence Erlbaum.

Landrine, H., & Klonoff, E.A., 1996. African American Acculturation: Deconstructing Race and Reviving Culture. Thousand Oaks, CA: Sage Publications.

Littlefield, A., Liebermann, L., & Reynolds, L.T., 1982. "Redefining race: The potential demise of a concept in physical anthropology." Current Anthropology, 23, 641–655.

Lott, T., 1992. "Marooned in America: Black urban youth culture and social pathology." In B.E. Lawson (ed.), The Underclass Question, pp. 71–89. Philadelphia: Temple University Press.

Nash, M., 1989. The Cauldron of Ethnicity in the Modern World. Chicago: University of Chicago Press.

Nobles, W.W., 1991. "African philosophy: Foundations for Black psychology." In L.R. Jones (ed.), Black Psychology, pp. 47–63. Hampton, VA: Cobb & Henry.

Rushton, J.P., 1992. "Cranial capacity related to sex, rank, and race." Intelligence, 16, 401–413.

Rushton, J.P., 1994. "Sex and race differences in cranial capacity from International Labour Office data." Intelligence, 19, 281–294.

Semmes, C.E., 1992. Cultural Hegemony anal African American Development. Westport, CT: Praeger.

Sieber, R., 1972. African Textiles and the Decorative Arts. New York: Museum of Modern Art.

van den Berghe, P.L., 1978. Race and Racism: A Comparative Approach. New York: Wiley.

1. Can you think of other examples of ways ethnicity is expressed by other cultural groups in settings such as the office or other work environments?

2. How does the author think that ethnic dress helps contradict the myth that African Americans are only a race?

63   Goin' Gangsta

Neil Bernstein

Her lipstick is dark, the lip liner even darker, nearly black. In baggy pants, a blue plaid Pendleton, her bangs pulled back tight off her forehead, 15-year-old April is a perfect cholita, a Mexican gangsta girl.

But April Miller is anglo. "And I don't like it!" she complains. "I'd rather be Mexican."

April's father wanders into the family room of their home in San Leandro, California, a suburb near Oakland. "Hey, cholita," he teases. "Go get a suntan. We'll put you in a barrio and see how much you like it."

A large, sandy-haired man with "April" tattooed on one arm and "Kelly"—the name of his older daughter—on the other, Miller spent 21 years working in a San Leandro glass factory that shut down and moved to Mexico a couple of years ago. He recently got a job in another factory, but he expects NAFTA to swallow that one, too.

"Sooner or later we'll all get nailed," he says. "Just another stab in the back of the American middle class."

Later, April gets her revenge. "Hey, Mr. White Man's Last Stand," she teases. "Wait till you see how well I manage my welfare check. You'll be asking me for money."

A once almost exclusively white, now increasingly Latin and black working-class suburb, San Leandro borders on predominantly black East Oakland. For decades, the boundary was strictly policed and practically imperme-

able. In 1970 April Miller's hometown was 97 percent white. By 1990 San Leandro was 65 percent white, 6 percent black, 15 percent Hispanic, and 13 percent Asian or Pacific Islander. With minorities moving into the suburbs in growing numbers and cities becoming ever more diverse, the boundary between city and suburb is dissolving, and suburban teenagers are changing with the times.

In April's bedroom, her past and present selves lie in layers, the pink walls of girlhood almost obscured, Guns N' Roses and Pearl Jam posters overlaid by rappers Paris and Ice Cube. "I don't have a big enough attitude to be a black girl," says April, explaining her current choice of ethnic identification.

What matters is that she thinks the choice is hers. For April and her friends, identity is not a matter of where you come from, what you were born into, what color your skin is. It's what you wear, the music you listen to, the words you use—everything to which you pledge allegiance, no matter how fleetingly.

The hybridization of American teens has become talk show fodder, with "wiggers"—white kids who dress and talk "black"—appearing on TV in full gangsta regalia. In Indiana a group of

Reprinted with permission of Knight-Ridder/Tribune Information Services white high school girls raised a national stir when they triggered an imitation race war at their virtually all white high school last fall simply by dressing "black."

In many parts of the country, it's television and radio, not neighbors, that introduce teens to the allure of ethnic difference. But in California, which demographers predict will be the first state with no racial minority by the year 2000, the influences are more immediate. The California public schools are the most diverse in the country: 42 percent white, 36 percent Hispanic, 9 percent black, 8 percent Asian.

Sometimes young people fight over their differences. Students at virtually any school in the Bay Area can recount the details of at least one "race riot" in which a conflict between individuals escalated into a battle between their clans. More often, though, teens would rather join than fight. Adolescence, after all, is the period when you're most inclined to mimic the power closest at hand, from stealing your older sister's clothes to copying the ruling clique at school.

White skaters and Mexican would-be gang-bangers listen to gangsta rap and call each other "nigga" as a term of endearment; white girls sometimes affect Spanish accents; blond cheer-leaders claim Cherokee ancestors.

"Claiming" is the central concept here. A Vietnamese teen in Hayward, another Oakland suburb, "claims" Oakland—and by implication blackness—because he lived there as a child. A law-abiding white kid "claims" a Mexican gang he says he hangs with. A brown-skinned girl with a Mexican father and a white mother "claims" her Mexican side, while her fair-skinned sister "claims" white. The word comes up over and over, as if identity were territory, the self a kind of turf.

At a restaurant in a minimall in Hayward, Nicole Huffstutler, 13, sits with her friends and describes herself as "Indian, German, French, Welsh, and um...American": "If somebody says anything like 'Yeah, you're just a peckerwood,' I'll walk up and I'll say 'white pride!' 'Cause I'm proud of my race, and wouldn't wanna be any other race."

"Claiming" white has become a matter of principle for Heather, too, who says she's "sick of

the majority looking at us like we're less than them." (Hayward schools were 51 percent white in 1990, down from 77 percent in 1980, and whites are now the minority in many schools.)

Asked if she knows that nonwhites have not traditionally been referred to as "the majority" in America, Heather gets exasperated: "I hear that all the time, every day. They say, 'Well, you guys controlled us for many years, and it's time for us to control you.' Every day."

When Jennifer Vargas—a small, brown-skinned girl in purple jeans who quietly eats her salad while Heather talks—softly announces that she's "mostly Mexican," she gets in trouble with her friends.

"No, you're not!" scolds Heather.

"I'm mostly Indian and Mexican," Jennifer continues flatly. "I'm very little...I'm mostly..."

"Your mom's white!" Nicole reminds her sharply. "She has blond hair."

"That's what I mean," Nicole adds. "People think that white is a bad thing. They think that white is a bad race. So she's trying to claim more Mexican than white."

"I have very little white in me," Jennifer repeats. "I have mostly my dad's side, 'cause I look like him and stuff. And most of my friends think that me and my brother and sister aren't related, 'cause they look more like my mom."

"But you guys are all the same race, you just look different," Nicole insists. She stops eating and frowns. "OK, you're half and half each what your parents have. So you're equal as your brother and sister, you just look different. And you should be proud of what you are—every little piece and bit of what you are. Even if you were Afghan or whatever, you should be proud of it."

Will Mosely, Heather's 17-year-old brother, says he and his friends listen to rap groups like Compton's Most Wanted, NWA, and Above the Law because they "sing about life"—that is, what happens in Oakland, Los Angeles, anyplace but where Will is sitting today, an empty Round Table Pizza in a minimall.

"No matter what race you are," Will says, "if you live like we do, then that's the kind of music you like."

And how do they live?

"We don't live bad or anything," Will admits. "We live in a pretty good neighborhood, there's no violence or crime. I was just…we're city people, I guess."

Will and his friend Adolfo Garcia, 16, say they've outgrown trying to be something they're not. "When I was 11 or 12," Will says, "I thought I was becoming a big gangsta and stuff. Because I liked that music, and thought it was the coolest, and I wanted to become that. I wore big clothes, like you wear in jail. But then I kind of woke up. I looked at myself and thought, 'Who am I trying to be?'"

They may have outgrown blatant mimicry, but Will and his friends remain convinced that they can live in a suburban tract house with a well-kept lawn on a tree-lined street in "not a bad neighborhood" and still call themselves "city" people on the basis of musical tastes. "City" for these young people means crime, graffiti, drugs. The kids are law-abiding, but these activities connote what Will admiringly calls "action." With pride in his voice, Will predicts that "in a couple of years, Hayward will be like Oakland. It's starting to get more known, because of crime and things. I think it'll be bigger, more things happening, more crime, more graffiti, stealing cars."

"That's good," chimes in 15-year-old Matt Jenkins, whose new beeper—an item that once connoted gangsta chic but now means little more than an active social life—goes off periodically. "More fun."

The three young men imagine with disdain life in a gangsta-free zone. "Too bland, too boring," Adolfo says. "You have to have something going on. You can't just have everyday life."

"Mowing your lawn," Matt sneers.

"Like Beaver Cleaver's house," Adolfo adds. "It's too clean out here."

Not only white kids believe that identity is a matter of choice or taste, or that the power of "claiming" can transcend ethnicity. The Manor Park Locos—a group of mostly Mexican-Americans who hang out in San Leandro's Manor Park—say they descend from the Manor Lords, tough white guys who ruled the neighborhood a generation ago.

They "are like our…uncles and dads, the older generation," says Jesse Martinez, 14. "We're

what they were when they were around, except we're Mexican."

"There's three generations," says Oso, Jesse's younger brother. "There's Manor Lords, Manor Park Locos, and Manor Park Pee Wees." The Pee Wees consist mainly of the Locos' younger brothers, eager kids who circle the older boys on bikes and brag about "punking people."

Unlike Will Mosely, the Locos find little glamour in city life. They survey the changing suburban landscape and see not "action" or "more fun" but frightening decline. Though most of them are not yet 18, the Locos are already nostalgic, longing for a Beaver Cleaver past that white kids who mimic them would scoff at.

Walking through nearly empty Manor Park, with its eucalyptus stands, its softball diamond and tennis courts, Jesse's friend Alex, the only Asian in the group, waves his arms in a gesture of futility. "A few years ago, every bench was filled," he says. "Now no one comes here. I guess it's because of everything that's going on. My parents paid a lot for this house, and I want it to be nice for them. I just hope this doesn't turn into Oakland."

Glancing across the park at April Miller's street, Jesse says he knows what the white cholitas are about. "It's not a racial thing," he explains. "It's just all the most popular people out here are Mexican. We're just the gangstas that everyone knows. I guess those girls wanna be known."

Not every young Californian embraces the new racial hybridism. Andrea Jones, 20, an African-American who grew up in the Bay Area suburbs of Union City and Hayward, is unimpressed by what she sees mainly as shallow mimicry. "It's full of posers out here," she says. "When *Boys N the Hood* came out on video, it was sold out for weeks. The boys all wanna be black, the girls all wanna be Mexican. It's the glamour."

Driving down the quiet, shaded streets of her old neighborhood in Union City, Andrea spots two white preteen boys in Raiders jackets and hugely baggy pants strutting erratically down the empty sidewalk. "Look at them," she says. "Dislocated."

She knows why. "In a lot of these schools out here, it's hard being white," she says. "I don't think these kids were prepared for the backlash that is going on, all the pride now in people of color's ethnicity, and our boldness with it. They

dislocated

have nothing like that, no identity, nothing they can say they're proud of.

"So they latch onto their great-grandmother who's a Cherokee, or they take on the most stereotypical aspects of being black or Mexican. It's beautiful to appreciate different aspects of others people's culture—that's like the dream of what the 21st century should be. But to garnish yourself with pop culture stereotypes just to blend—that's really sad."

Roland Krevocheza, 18, graduated last year from Arroyo High School in San Leandro. He is Mexican on his mother's side. Eastern European on his father's. In the new hierarchies, it may be mixed kids like Roland who have the hardest time finding their place, even as their numbers grow. (One in five marriages in California is between people of different races.) They can always be called "wannabes," no matter what they claim.

"I'll state all my nationalities," Roland says. But he takes greater interest in his father's side, his Ukrainian, Romanian, and Czech ancestors. "It's more unique," he explains. "Mexican culture is all around me. We eat Mexican food all the time, I hear stories from my grandmother. I see the low-riders and stuff. I'm already part of it. I'm not trying to be; I am."

His darker-skinned brother "says he's not proud to be white," Roland adds. "He calls me 'Mr. Nazi.'" In the room the two share, the American flags and the reproduction of the Bill of Rights are Roland's; the Public Enemy poster belongs to his brother.

Roland has good reason to mistrust gangsta attitudes. In his junior year in high school, he was one of several Arroyo students who were beaten up outside the school at lunchtime by a group of Samoans who came in cars from Oakland. Roland wound up with a split lip, a concussion, and a broken tailbone. Later he was told that the assault was "gang-related"—that the Samoans were beating up anyone wearing red.

"Rappers, I don't like them," Roland says. "I think they're a bad influence on kids. It makes kids think they're all tough and bad."

Those who, like Roland, dismiss the gangsta and cholo styles as affectations can point to the fact that several companies market overpriced knockoffs of "ghetto wear" targeted at teens.

But there's also something going on out here that transcends adolescent faddishness and pop culture exoticism. When white kids call their parents "racist" for nagging them about their baggy pants; when they learn Spanish to talk to their boyfriends; when Mexican-American boys feel themselves descended in spirit from white "uncles"; when children of mixed marriages insist that they are whatever race they say they are, all of them are more than just confused.

They're inching toward what Andrea Jones calls "the dream of what the 21st century should be." In the ever more diverse communities of Northern California, they're also facing the complicated reality of what they 21st century will be.

Meanwhile, in the living room of the Miller family's San Leandro home, the argument continues unabated. "You don't know what you are," April's father has told her more than once. But she just keeps on telling him he doesn't know what time it is.

DISCUSSION QUESTIONS

Goin' Gangsta

1. What social and economic forces contribute to the kind of fluidity of identity discussed in this article?

2. Explain why some white students might have a difficult time feeling satisfied with their own racial and ethnic identity in light of the prevailing multicultural environment in many schools.

3. Examine how the phrase "cultural hybridization" might apply to this article. Give some examples of how it can be symbolically displayed through dress and appearance.

64 Common Threads
Michiko Kakutani

Central Park West. A cold, sunny day. In front of the Museum of Natural History, there's a motley crowd of folks milling about: a busload of tourists here to show their kids the dinosaurs, a group of homeboys on their way somewhere and some bored-looking private-school kids lounging on the steps waiting for someone or something. The odd thing is that everyone is dressed almost exactly alike—lots of puffy ski jackets, lots of polo shirts, lots of Gore-Tex and polar fleece. Designer logos (DKNY, Nautica, Ralph Lauren, North Face, Tommy Hilfiger) are de rigueur, as are bright Crayola colors. Industrial-strength sneakers and high-tech hiking boots are big; so are baseball caps and ski hats. The whole scene looks suspiciously like a tailgate party at an Ivy League football game.

What's going on here? Not so long ago, it was hard to imagine hip young kids—black or white—even deigning to look at the sort of clothes that soccer moms and their golfer husbands wear to the country club or ski slopes. For Panthers, hippies and punks alike, subversive dressing that sneered at bourgeois notions of class and taste was the rule: tattered jeans, worn leather coats, combat boots, military fatigues, tie-dyed T-shirts.

So what's behind this new preppy revolution? Well, a few years back, rappers and hip-hop kids got rid of their gold chains and urban commando gear and started dressing…well, suburban, wearing classic sportswear straight from the "Leave It to Beaver" era: rugby shirts, khakis, Windbreakers. Black and camouflage green gave way to primary colors and racing stripes, and the vogue for athletic gear expanded from designer sweat suits to two-tone varsity jackets, E.M.S. ski jackets, fishing vests and Polartec pants. The rap impresario Russell Simmons opened a classy SoHo boutique called Phat Farm, selling sportswear with a rural motif (T-shirts emblazoned with log cabins and cows), and a Georgia designer named Charles Walker Jr. began marketing a line of clothing described as "Afrocentric preppy" (its slogan: "We Don't Play Polo").

Part of this development is simply a testament to hip-hop's post-modernist esthetic. In much the same way that rap music appropriates disco and funk, as well as street noise and sound bites, hip-hop's sampling of preppy styles is a way of reinventing—or, as academics would say, recontextualizing—the past. This appropriation comes with a kind of spin. Just as some rap songs play upon popular caricatures of blacks—exaggerating stereotypes of sexual prowess and lawlessness—so "badd" becomes good and "nigga" a word of empowerment. Hip-hop prep similarly winks at mainstream culture. The clothes, after all, aren't worn the way white-bread suburbanites wear them. They're worn more than a couple of sizes too big, pants pulled down prison-style on the hips, shirts hanging to the knees. They're mixed and matched in a wild cacophony of styles—ski clothes paired with basketball sneakers, golf togs paired with hiking boots. All in all, a sly cartoon of upscale dressing.

Hip-hop prep, however, isn't meant simply as an ironic comment on the good life; it also represents an earnest yearning after the American dream. In Russell Simmons's words: "Ghetto kids want to escape, so they wear things that represent success." More and more rap videos these days purvey sleek images of material success. Forget the Panthers' attacks on capitalism. Forget gangsta rap put-downs of bourgeois Huxtable blacks. Dr. Dre's latest video, "Been There, Done That," depicts a ballroom full of elegant couples doing the tango, while LL Cool J's new video, "Ain't Nobody," shows cheerfully attired rappers playing golf and snowmobiling.

Yet for the white kids known as wiggers, who spurn the moneyed life of their parents, being black means being hip and rebellious. Like Norman Mailer and Carl Van Vechten before them, these cultural tourists romanticize the very ghetto life that so many black kids want to escape. Instead of the terrible mortality rate for young black males, they see the glamour of violence. Instead of the frustration of people denied jobs and hope and respect, they see the verbal defiance of that frustration. Perhaps this is why the most violent of gangsta rap has found its largest audience among white suburban males. Such music not only commodifies the worst of black stereotypes but at the same time enables white teen-agers to co-opt black rage as a metaphor for their own adolescent angst.

Rap started out as a kind of reportage, a means of testifying to the reality of life on the streets, but as promoters and producers began to realize its marketability, something began to change. Some performers were packaged as gangsters for the voyeuristic consumption of honkies; others were promoted as avatars of a new domesticated brand of rap, offering the beat and pulse of the original with none of its grittiness or threat.

Meanwhile, slick magazines like Vibe—started by Time Warner and Quincy Jones—tried to turn hip-hop into a life style, an attitude, a look that could be acquired through the right clothes. Hence, the white kids from Chapin and Dalton hanging out on Central Park West, outfitted in their Hilfiger jeans, their DKNY oversize parkas, their $150 Nikes, speaking fluent ebonics and doing their best to be young black teenagers, even as their role models, the homeboys from uptown, don the same clothes as a talisman of the better life they wish they had.

At an age when nearly all kids feel powerless, the class war becomes a kind of looking-glass world. Rich white kids, guilty about their privileged lives and fearful of being wimps, equate power—and authenticity—with the streetsmart, badman swagger of the homeboys, while poor black kids, facing dead-end jobs and unemployment lines, equate power with money and bourgeois comforts. Everyone looks in the mirror and covets what the other side has—or, at least, the clothes the other side is wearing.

DISCUSSION QUESTIONS

Common Threads

1. Do you agree with the author about the "looking-glass world" of dress as it relates to social class? Can you think of some contradictions to this point of view? Name some designers who have appealed to this "looking-glass" market.

2. "Hip-hop's sampling of preppy styles is a way of reinventing—or, as academics would say, recontextualizing—the past." What does this mean? How is this done?

65 The Cool Cat Life-Style

Richard Majors
Janet Mancini Billson

The cat seeks through a harmonious combination of charm…the proper dedication to his "kick" and unrestrained generosity to make of his day to day life itself a gracious work of art.[1]

For many African-American males, the character that best exemplifies the expressive life-style is the cool cat. Like other forms of cool pose, being a cool cat provides a way to accentuate the self. The cool cat is an exceptional artist of expressiveness and flamboyant style. He creates his unique identity by artfully dipping into a colorful palette of clothes and hairstyles that set him apart from the ordinary. His nonverbal gestures—his walk and handshakes, for example—are mixed with high verbal agility. He can be found "rapping it down to a woman" with a flair and virtuosity that others envy. He does not simply drive a car—he "leans" (drives with one arm) and sets his neighbors talking about his self-assured risk-taking. The cool cat is the consummate actor. His performance may also be characterized by deftly manipulative and deceptive strategies.

Black males put great emphasis on style and acting cool. Appearing suave, urbane, and charming is at the heart of being a cool cat. The black male is supremely skilled at utilizing cultural symbols in a way that stamps his personal mark on all encounters. This allows him to elevate his sense of pride and control. He can broadcast strength and masculinity or shore up flagging status and dignity.

PORTRAIT OF THE COOL CAT

The portrait of the typical cool cat is usually that of a young black male found on the streets of American cities. He is probably unemployed, may be involved in drugs or alcohol, and has limited education. He is involved in some kind of hustling activity and is probably from a low-income, beleaguered family. Some embrace values of education and work and are marked by self-assurance. For example, in *Strategic Styles*, Mancini describes Hank as a "together guy" who exudes confidence and autonomy, as well as flamboyance; he states simply, "I got my own way in everything. I don't copy nothing from nobody."[2]

McCord and his colleagues in *Life Styles in the Black Ghetto* characterize the cool cat as a young man who spends his time on street corners, in pool halls, or in "running some type of racket." He has a distinctive style. Firestone defines the cool cat as a man who combines charm, dedication to his "kick," and unusual generosity to make everyday life balanced and a "gracious work of art" that contributes in some way to a pleasant, aesthetic life-style. The cool cat is unruffled, self-assured, and eminently cool in the face of emergencies.

CLOTHES AND THE COOL CAT

Few African-American males now wear the *dashikis* of the Black Revolution, but clothes are still used to make fashion and status statements. Clothes help the black male attract attention and enhance his self-image. After all, in a society that has kept blacks invisible, it is not surprising that seemingly flamboyant clothes might be worn to heighten visibility.

Clothes can also contribute to violence and fighting, even death, among young black males. For example, some gangs use baseball caps or colors to symbolize gang membership. Gangs have been known to kill youths for wearing the wrong colors or clothes. They have also fought, occasionally to death, over brand name clothes (such as Georgio and Gucci items), basketball sneakers, or gold chains. Black fraternities often use jackets to indicate membership and solidarity.

Majors, R., & Billson, J. M. (1992) *Cool Pose: Dilemmas of Black Manhood in America*. New York: Lexington Books.

To style is the ultimate way hustlers attempt to act cool. Clothes are a portable and creative expression of styling. The interest in colorful male plumage begins in the early teens when attention-getting costumes earn the young cat his place on center stage. He begins to establish his own personal signature in dress, hairstyle, and language. To "style," "front off," friend," "high sign," or "funk" all mean to show off or upstage others in a highly competitive war of masculine self-presentation. A young black woman describes how she compliments the cool cats in her life: "You all dressed up and you have your apple hat on, your flairs, and your boots and you walkin' down the street lookin' at all d' people, so you goin' style wid the lookin' good. Be more less flamboyant....He's decked to kill! Da's what we [young women] tell 'em."[3]

Getting "clean" and dressing with style is an important way to get over in the world. Some teens see the world as a constant stage—a series of personal performances. They earn street applause for being clean and having style. Folb notes that because how you dress says so much about who you are, black males often resent wearing work-related uniforms. The uniform de-styles them. Folb quotes a youth who is contemplating quitting his job as groundskeeper aide for the County of Los Angeles: "I like to get clean and stay sharp."[4]

Hudson calls the attire of the hustler flashy and flamboyant and stresses that clothing is a central part of a hustler's front. In order to make money, he must look like he already has money (somewhat akin to the Madison Avenue grey flannel suit or recent evocations for yuppies to "dress for success"). He cannot expect to "take off some fat suckers" if he looks like a "greaseball."

When a hustler starts making money, he immediately puts his wardrobe together in order to establish prestige with his audience. A monologue by well-known black recording artist Lou Rawls describes a popular young hustler on the South Side of Chicago who epitomizes the cool cat style:

Every Friday evening about 4:30 he would be standing there because his girlfriend works at Walgreen's...and on Friday, the eagle flies. He was wearing the very popular silk mohair wool worsted—continental to the bone—$250 hustler's suit...a pair of highly shined hustler's alligator shoes...white on white tab collar shirt, a very thin hustler's necktie...a very large artificial diamond stick pin in place...a hustler's hairdo...a process...hustler's shades on, cigarette in hand, a very broad smile on his face...staring hard and elated at what he saw...his automobile parked at the curb...white on white on white. The hustlers call them hogs, the trade name is Cadillac...(As the hustler is standing on the corner, he sees his wife approaching with a razor in her hand, screaming at him): You no good jiving farmer...the rent's not paid and the baby is hungry and needs shoes and you're out here hustling and carrying on...(He says): Baby, you can have this car and anything you want. Just don't cut my new suit. I just got it out of the pawn shop and I've got to have my front so I can keep on making my game.[5]

COOL WHEELS

Cars also underscore the significance of style and feature heavily in "making the game." Hustlers and others in the ghetto value and treasure their automobiles. The more expensive the automobile, the more valid is the hustler's claims to have made it. As the expression goes, "he is doing good in this town."

From an early age, black teens see cars as a status symbol. Many learn to pop the ignition so they can take joyrides—preparation perhaps for organized car theft later in life. Cars allow visible, conspicuous display of status—a perfect way for the cool cat to stage his performance literally throughout the community.

One stylized type of physical posturing noted by Folb is "leaning" or "low-riding," in which the driver (and sometimes the passenger) sits so low in his seat that only the top of his head is visible and his eyes peer out over the steering wheel. Low-riding is designed to draw attention to both driver and car—a performance that may be specifically directed toward females. Folb quotes a young woman's perception of these performances:

Leanin' that when a dude be leanin' so hard like he layin' down in d' car. Da's what they do in their cars. Lean like, "I'm jus' the man. But guys in low-ridin' cars lean and low ride 'cause they know they gotta be funky and they say, "Well, the car be lookin' good, I gotta look good."[6]

For the cool cat, driving a Cadillac (or any luxury car) is important for more than just transportation. Cadillac-type cars epitomize class because of their reputation and because they take up a great deal of physical space. They symbolize being seen—a critical experience for those who have been invisible in this country for so long. The cool cat feels, "If I can drive a stylish car like this, it proves to myself and others that I am as important as anyone else. I haven't given up. I am going to make it." The cool cat often sacrifices other economic goods in his life or his family's life to have a big luxury car as a way to make such a statement.

LAME TO THE BONE

If style is the ultimate way to act cool, cool cats must have definite beliefs as to what represents nonstylistic behavior. Being called "lame to the bone" or "uncool" is the ultimate insult in black teenage vernacular. Being lame means to be socially incompetent, disabled, or crippled—a sissy. The "lame brand" does not even know how to talk to females; he may appear frightened of them. Folb reports:

> Dudes be talkin' to d' young lady, he run aroun', shootin' marbles. Not too situated…Dumb sucker have no girls, don't know where everything is!…stone SUCKER! Sissy boy, hangin' 'round his momma all the time. Dedicated to d' home front. He don't know what's happ'nin'. He like a school book chump…stupid, ignorant, hide in d' book all d' time—like a bookworm. He square to d' wood!…Don't get high, don't smoke no weed. Show 'im a reefer, he wouldn't even know what it is!…Uncoordinated. He cain't fight or nothin'. Like he followin' you everplace you go…wanna be wid everybody but don't do nothin'…They can't catch on to what's happ'nin'.[7]

For those who are lame, there is probably no hope of rehabilitation.

Half-stepping means to do something halfway and is a form of being lame or uncool. A person who is not appropriately dressed for an occasion is not mounting the correct performance. If he is giving a party, he should not dress the way he would for school or work, in off-brand tennis shoes or Levis, or wrinkled clothing: "Don't come half-steppin', come fiendish, righteously dap to a tee, silk to the bone. Or like a date. Like you dress yo'self up—some bad-boy bell bottom, nice shirt. Don't half-step. Get yo'self together brother."[8]

WHY IS STYLE SO IMPORTANT?

We might ask why style is so important to cool cats. Styling helps cool cats draw attention to the self and communicates creativity. The African-American man in this country has been "nobody" for generations. The purpose of styling, then, is to paint a self-portrait in colorful, vivid strokes that makes the black male "somebody."

The extravagant, flashy clothes often worn by cool cats, the blaring ghettoblasters playing earsplitting music as they walk or drive down the street, signify their need to be seen and heard. Styling is an antidote to invisibility and silence, a hope in a hopeless world, a defense against multiple attacks on cultural and personal integrity. It is proactive rather than defensive. Styling lets the black male show others that he is alive, and reminds himself as well.

The cool cat styles for the cosmetic effect (how he looks) and to symbolize the messages he wants to portray: "No matter how poor I am or what has happened to me in the past, this shows that I can still make it…and with class."

Irrespective of race or class, it is not enough to survive or just live from day to day in a social vacuum. Rather, individuals have a genuine need to know that they can make a contribution to their own welfare and personal growth and that they have control over their own destiny. That they can be noticed and can better their lives.

Perkins writes that black children internalize the roles that will allow them to perform on the only stage they know: the black ghetto colony. The cool cat and similar roles are adopted because they have great survival value, not just because they elicit applause from the immediate audience. Black children learn how to be cool under the most extenuating circumstances because being cool is a clear advantage. Perkins adds that when a situation is fraught with danger or anxiety (becomes "uptight"), the most sophisticated response is being cool, "hip," or "together." Cool stabilizes the situation and either minimizes or ignores threats that cannot be easily dealt with in other ways.

Firestone see the "idea cat" as a person who is adequate to any situation. He adopts a cool image in order to deal with status and identity problems in a society that denies equal access. Foster hypothesizes that as the black man's drive for middle-class status in the North was thwarted by racism, a cool street-corner life-style evolved. White racism in urban areas both stimulates and perpetuates street-corner behavior. Whereas other ethnic groups have been allowed to assimilate after a period of initial bigotry, doors have remained impermeable to African-Americans. (Foster notes that where the doors have been opened for black males, a highly organized street life-style is not as likely to develop.) In most places in America, those doors remain at least partially closed.

The cool cat life-style has long functioned as a means to enhance the black male's ability to survive the harsh effects of racism and social oppression. Because of a lack of resources, services, goods, information, and jobs, lower-income blacks often have hours of free time on their hands. The cool cat life-style provides a kind of stimulation and entertainment. Something is always going on or being contemplated. Those who live in the ghetto often view cool cats as fashionable, hip, cool, and chic. This glamorized life-style helps the black male to achieve balance—entertainment and stimulation counter frustration and boredom.

Being a cool cat is one route toward creative masculinity, toward recognition. It helps black males to survive, to style and act cool, to show disdain for the white man and the Protestant work ethic, and to show pride and dignity. It enhances manhood, commands respect, vents bitterness and anger, establishes a sense of control, expresses artistry, accentuates the self, and provides a form of amusement.

Notes

1. Firestone 1957, 5.
2. Mancini 1981, 164.
3. Folb 1980, 109–10; see also Knapp 1978 and Majors 1987, 1991.
4. Ibid.
5. Dworkin and Dworkin, 2–3.
6. Folb 1980, 112, 115.
7. Folb 1980, 38.
8. Folb 1980, 42.

References

Dworkin, B., and S. Dworkin. *Cool: Young adults in the Negro ghetto.* Unpublished manuscript, Washington University, St. Louis, MO.

Firestone, H. 1957. Cats, kicks and color. *Social Problems* 5:3–13.

Folb, E. 1980. *Runnin' down some lines: The language and culture of black teenagers.* Cambridge, MA: Harvard University Press.

Knapp, M. L. 1978. The field of nonverbal communication: An overview. In *On speech communication: An anthology of contemporary writings and messages,* ed. C. J. Stewart and B. Kendall. New York: Holt, Rinehart & Winston.

Majors, R. 1987. Cool pose: A new approach toward a systematic understanding and studying of black male behavior. Unpublished Ph.D. diss., University of Illinois, Urbana, IL.

— .1991. Nonverbal behavior and communication styles among African Americans. In R. Jones, ed., *Black psychology,* 3rd ed. Berkeley, CA: Cobb and Henry.

Mancini, J. K. 1981. *Strategic styles: Coping in the inner city.* Hanover, NH: University Press of New England.

DISCUSSION QUESTIONS

The Cool Cat Lifestyle

1. What do you think the meaning of "cool" clothes are to the young African American male?

2. Why does the author of this article think that uniforms are particularly difficult for some African American males to wear?

66 You Become What You Wear

Kathleen Carlin

A standard criticism of sociological research projects is that they go to great lengths to prove what most people with common sense already know. Without exactly taking sides for or against that criticism, I want to describe a sociological exercise that might seem to validate it—except that, for me and a classmate (and maybe for some who read this account), the experience made a truism come alive.

What we did: During spring break from a local college, my friend and I went downtown to shop. First, however, we made ourselves virtually unrecognizable to our friends and even to our families. We wore clothing slightly inappropriate for the weather, clean but wrinkled, clearly out of sync with the styles worn by most visitors to the area. We carried plastic bags of nameless possessions. Both of us were slightly unkempt. My friend wore a faded flannel shirt and T-shirt, a wrinkled skirt over sweat pants. I wore a wool hat that concealed my hair, an unfashionable coat and scarf, and glasses with clip-on sun shades.

The aim was to look like street people, and to observe what difference that made in the way other people responded to us; whether the appearance of poverty would place a stigma on us. We were also prepared to act out some mildly unusual behaviors that might speak of some emotional disabilities, without appearing seriously disturbed or dangerous. As it turned out, there was no need for histrionics; people turned us off or tuned us out on the basis of appearance alone.

Our first stop (after parking our cars near the railroad tracks) was in the bargain store of a local charity, where we politely asked access to a bathroom, and were refused. Next we entered the lobby of a large hotel, where we asked for a coffee shop and a bathroom. The bellhop said, "You must go to the twentieth floor." We weren't up to trying our gig at an exclusive restaurant, so we wandered around the first floor and left. From there we went to a pawnshop, where we more or less blended with the patrons, and then on to the upperscale stores and coffee shops during the lunch hour.

It was stigma time. Some of the children we encountered stared, pointed, and laughed; adults gave us long, incredulous looks. Clerks in stores followed us around to watch our every move. In a lunchroom a second assistant hurried to the side of the cashier, where they took my $2 check without asking for an ID; it seemed worth that price to have us out the door. At one doorway a clerk physically blocked the entrance, apparently to discourage our entry.

We had money to cover small purchases, and, apart from wearing downscale clothing, we did nothing in any of these settings to draw attention to ourselves; we merely shopped quietly in our accustomed manner. At one establishment we did blow our cover when we ordered croissants with a latté and an espresso; that may have been too far out of character for "bag ladies." Elsewhere we encountered derision, mockery, distrust, and rude stares.

So what did we learn? Mostly what we expected, what everybody knows: People judge by appearances. Just looking poor brings with it a stigma, accompanied by the withdrawal of much of the social civility most of us take for granted. Lacking the culturally acceptable symbols of belonging in this milieu, we became, to a degree, "objects," with less inherent dignity as persons.

There was, however, one surprise; more accurately, a shock. It came clear most strongly at the shop I mentioned earlier, the one where a clerk conspicuously positioned herself in the entryway on seeing us. I had just noticed the place and had turned to my companion, saying, "I've never seen this store. Let's go in." She looked at me with dismay: "You're not really going in there, are you?"

I knew what she meant and shared her feeling. The place felt out of bounds for us. In a very few hours, we found ourselves accepting and internalizing the superficial and biased judgments of ourselves that prevailed among the people we met; we stigmatized ourselves. It's a good lesson to learn, maybe especially for sociologists.

DISCUSSION QUESTIONS

You Become What You Wear

1. Explain this phrase: "Just looking poor brings with it a stigma." What does stigma mean and how does it relate to appearance?

2. Give some suggestions how homeless people could be helped within the commu-

nity to face less stigma regarding their appearance.

3. How could the experience of homeless people in the community be similar to those with physical handicaps?

67   Slenderness and the Inner State of the Self
Susan Bordo

The moral—and, as we shall see, economic—coding of the fat/slender body in terms of its capacity for self-containment and the control of impulse and desire represents the culmination of a developing historical change in the social symbolism of body weight and size. Until the late nineteenth century, the central discriminations marked were those of class, race, and gender; the body indicated social identity and "place." So, for example, the bulging stomachs of successful mid-nineteenth-century businessmen and politicians were a symbol of bourgeois success, an outward manifestation of their accumulated wealth. By contrast, the gracefully slender body announced aristocratic status; disdainful of the bourgeois need to display wealth and power ostentatiously, it commanded social space invisibly rather than aggressively, seemingly above the commerce in appetite or the need to eat. Subsequently, this ideal began to be appropriated by the status-seeking middle class, as slender wives became the showpieces of their husbands' success.[1]

Corpulence went out of middle-class vogue at the end of the century (even William Howard Taft, who had weighed over three hundred

pounds while in office, went on a reducing diet). Social power had come to be less dependent on the sheer accumulation of material wealth and more connected to the ability to control and manage the labor and resources of others. At the same time, excess body weight came to be seen as reflecting moral or personal inadequacy, or lack of will. These associations are possible only in a culture of overabundance—that is, in a society in which those who control the production of "culture" have more than enough to eat. The moral requirement to diet depends on the material preconditions that make the choice to diet an option and the possibility of personal "excess" a reality. Although slenderness continues to retain some of its traditional class associations ("a woman can never be too rich or too thin"), the importance of this equation has eroded consid-

FIGURE 10.2 *A graceful slender body displays wealth and power.*

status, and they have often been suffused with racial meaning as well (as in numerous film representations of sweating, glistening bodies belonging to black slaves and prizefighters). Under the racial and class biases of our culture, muscles thus have been associated with the insensitive, unintelligent, and animalistic (recall the well-developed Marlon Brando as the emotionally primitive, physically abusive Stanley Kowalski in A *Streetcar Named Desire*). Moreover, as the body itself is dominantly imagined within the West as belonging to the "nature" side of a nature/culture duality, the *more* body one has had, the more uncultured and uncivilized one has been expected to be.

Today, however, the well-muscled body has become a cultural icon; "working out" is a glamorized and sexualized yuppie activity. No longer signifying inferior status (except when developed to extremes, at which point the old association of muscles with brute, unconscious materiality surfaces once more), the firm, developed body has become a symbol of correct *attitude*; it means that one "cares" about oneself and how one appears to others, suggesting willpower, energy, control over infantile impulse, the ability to "shape your life." "You exercise, you diet," says Heather Locklear, promoting Bally Matrix Fitness Centre on television, "and you can do anything you want." Muscles express sexuality, but controlled, managed sexuality that is not about to erupt in unwanted and embarrassing display.[14]

To the degree that the question of class still operates in all this, it relates to the category of social mobility (or lack of it) rather than class *location* So, for example, when associations of fat and lower-class status exist, they are usually mediated by moral qualities—fat being perceived as indicative of laziness, lack of discipline, unwillingness to conform, and absence of all those "managerial" abilities that, according to the dominant ideology, confer upward mobility. Correspondingly, in popular teen movies such as *Flashdance* and *Vision Quest*, the ability of the (working-class) heroine and hero to pare, prune, tighten, and master the body operates as a clear symbol of successful upward aspiration, of the penetrability of class boundaries to those who have "the right stuff." These movies (as one title makes explicit) are contemporary "quest myths"; like their prototype, *Rocky*, they follow the struggle of an individual to attain a

erably since the 1970s. Increasingly, the size and shape of the body have come to operate as a market of personal, internal order (or disorder)—as a symbol for the emotional, moral, or spiritual state of the individual.

Consider one particularly clear example, that of changes in the meaning of the muscled body. Muscularity has had a variety of cultural meanings that have prevented the well-developed body from playing a major role in middle-class conceptions of attractiveness. Of course, muscles have chiefly symbolized and continue to symbolize masculine power as physical strength, frequently operating as a means of coding the "naturalness" of sexual difference. But at the same time, they have been associated with manual labor and proletarian personal grail, against all odds and through numerous trials. But unlike the film quests of a previous era (which sent Mr. Smith to Washington and Mr. Deeds to town to battle the respective social evils of corrupt government and big business) *Flashdance* and *Vision Quest* render the hero's and heroine's commitment, will and spiritual integrity through the metaphors of weight loss, exercise, and tolerance of and ability to conquer physical pain and exhaustion. (In *Vision Quest*, for example, the audience is encouraged to admire the young wrestler's perseverance when he ignores the fainting spells and nosebleeds caused by his rigorous training and dieting.)

Not surprisingly, young people with eating disorders often thematize their own experience in similar terms, as in the following excerpt from an interview with a young woman runner:

> Well, I had the willpower, I could train for competition, and I could turn down food any time. I remember feeling like I was on a constant high. And the pain? Sure, there was pain. It was incredible. Between the hunger and the muscle pain from the constant workouts? I can't tell you how much I hurt.
>
> You may think I was crazy to put myself through constant, intense pain. But you have to remember, I was fighting a battle. And when you get hurt in a battle, you're proud of it. Sure, you may scream inside, but if you're brave and really good, then you take it quietly, because you know it's the price you pay for winning. And I needed to win. I really felt that if I didn't win, I would die...all these enemy troops were coming at me, and I had to outsmart them. If I could discipline myself enough—if I could keep myself lean and strong—then I could win. The pain was just a natural thing I had to deal with.

As in *Vision Quest*, the external context is training for an athletic event. But here, too, that goal becomes subordinated to an internal one. The real battle, ultimately, is with the self. At this point, the limitations of the brief history presented in the opening paragraph of this essay are revealed. In that paragraph, the contemporary preoccupation with diet is contrasted to historical projects of body management that were suffused with moral meaning. In this section, however, I have suggested that examination of even the most shallow representations (teen movies) discloses a moral ideology—one, in fact, seemingly close to the aristocratic Greek ideal described by Foucault in *The Use of Pleasure*. The central element of that ideal, as Foucault describes it, is "an agonistic relation with the self"—aimed, not at the extirpation of desire and hunger in the interests of "purity" (as in the Christian strain of dualism), but at a "virile" mastery of desire through constant "spiritual combat."

For the Greeks, however, the "virile" mastery of desire took place in a culture that valorized moderation. The culture of contemporary body-management, struggling to manage desire in a system dedicated to the proliferation of desirable commodities, is very different. In cultural fantasies such as *Vision Quest* and *Flashdance*, self-mastery is presented as an attainable and stable state; but, the reality of the contemporary agonism of the self is another matter entirely.

Notes

1. Kim Chernin, *The Obsession: Reflections on the Tyranny of Slenderness* (New York: Harper and Row, 1981), pp. 36–37.
2. Christopher Lasch, *The Culture of Narcissism* (New York: Warner Books, 1979), p. 88.
3. Michel Foucault, The History of Sexuality. Vol. 1: *An Introduction* (New York: Vintage, 1980), p. 155.

DISCUSSION QUESTIONS

Slenderness and the Inner State of the Self

1. Why do you think that in American society we tend to equate thinness with a person's moral adequacy? Why has thinness become associated with positive virtues?

2. How do we stereotype overweight and particularly obese people in terms of personal values?

3. How is the slender (and toned) body related to issues of social class?

CHAPTER 11
Fashion as Social Process

Mary Lynn Damhorst

AFTER YOU HAVE READ THIS CHAPTER, YOU WILL COMPREHEND:

- Why fashion is a social process requiring human interaction.

- The complex interaction of cultural, industry, group, and individual factors that fuel fashion change.

- No one theory explains all of the fashion change process.

- How fashion change has continual impact on meanings of styles.

- That not all styles are fashion and that some cultures, groups, and individuals opt not to participate in the larger fashion system.

Cargo pants, everywhere in 1998. Ralph Lauren cargo pants in suede—$2,295. Abercrombie & Fitch cargo pants—$58. Arizona private-label cargo pants at JC Penney—$25. For fall 1998, Old Navy corduroy overalls with cargo pockets for babies. (See Figure 11.1.)

How do trends get started and how do they spread? The *Wall Street Journal* (Ono & Bounds, 1998) credited hip hop group Goodie Mob with starting the 1998 cargo pants trend three years earlier. European kids in army-surplus cargo pants were another purported innovator, while an ad campaign by retailer Old Navy in 1997 may have

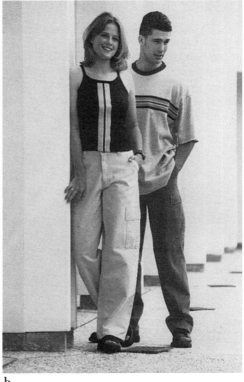

a   b

FIGURE 11.1 *Cargo pants came in many styles and prices during 1998 and 1999. Here are examples targeted for two different markets: (a) Ralph Lauren and (b) Lees.*

spread awareness of the trend in the United States (Ono & Bounds, 1998). The style was originally developed as functional wear for British military men in the early 20th century, but why is the style recycling as fashion now? Initial innovation of a trend is often impossible to trace. In this chapter, we will consider a number of cultural, social, and personal factors that can influence fashion trends. These factors shape meanings of fashion.

The term **fashion** has many meanings to many individuals. It might imply slavish conformity to some, styles that are new and exciting to others, a threat to tradition or yet another group, or merely products to sell in the open marketplace for economic gain to those in the garment or fashion industry. Although it means many things to many people, fashion is a social process. As was stated in Chapter 1, fashion is a way of behaving that is temporarily adopted by a discernible proportion of members of a social group as socially appropriate for the time and situation (Sproles, 1979). Fashion is a complex process that cannot be explained by any one theory, so we will take many perspectives to understand the process.

Jean Hamilton (1997) organized influences of fashion on a continuum from **micro-level** personal or individual factors to larger **macro-level** cultural influences (Table 11.1). Hamilton emphasized that fashion results from:

TABLE 11.1
Hamilton's Micro–Macro Continuum

Level		Influencing Factors
Macro-level		
M	**Cultural system**	• Cultural values and ideology
A		• Tradition versus change
C		• Media, arts, economy, religion, politics
R		• Generation and population trends
O		
•	**Fashion system**	• Retail buyers, fashion designers
		• Fashion media and promotions
•		• Global production system
•	**Negotiation with others**	• Conformity
		• Fashion leaders and innovators
•		• Trickle-down theory
		• Trickle-across diffusion
M		• Trickle-up theory
I		
C	**Negotiation with self**	• Individual choice, tastes
R		• Aesthetic learning
O		• Ambivalence
Micro-level		

¹Table expanded from Hamilton (1997).

- Individual action within…
- Social groups and choosing (or not choosing) products and style ideas offered by…
- The fashion industry that is, in turn, influenced by…
- Larger trends and forces of the surrounding culture.

These four levels in the continuum are interconnected in that fashion is influenced by all components of the system working together simultaneously. We will examine each level, starting with the macro-level first.

CULTURAL SYSTEM

The culture of a society will determine whether a fashion system exists. Fashion change is found most frequently in cultures that value technological progress, individual expression, and capitalistic free-market exchange (Sproles & Burns, 1994; Kaiser, Nagasawa, & Hutton, 1995). Cultures that allow youthful experimentation and search for identity are also conducive to rapid changes in fashion (Horn & Gurel, 1981). An economic situation in which notable numbers in the population have discretionary income to spend on extras is also necessary, as fashion change requires expenditure on new styles before clothing is completely worn out.

Herbert Blumer (1969) proposed that a new style is most likely to be adopted as fashion when the style fits with the **zeitgeist** or spirit of the times. Large population groups can shape lifestyles in a society and can have substantial influence on fashion changes, largely as the result of economic rewards that can be gained from catering to this huge market segment. Behling (1985) demonstrated how the baby boomer generation influenced U. S. fashions during their adolescence in the 1960s through early adulthood in the 1980s. By the late 1980s, however, it was clear that the baby boomers were losing hold on fashion trends, at least those featured in fashion media. Short skirts and narrow silhouettes became fashionable at the same time many boomers were developing middle aged bodies. Clearly, more than numbers and economic clout is required to shape fashion trends in U. S. culture where youthfulness is so adored.

As we saw in Chapter 3 a trend in the arts and popular culture, such as postmodernism, may be reflected in dress. Another present-day trend is pluralism or acceptance of diversity (see Chapter 1). Perhaps the increasing trend toward recognition of diversity in the population has encouraged the U. S. fashion industry to pay attention to more diverse markets. William Kissell in "Styles with a Sizable Difference" describes how various retailers are focusing marketing efforts on groups of ethnic consumers with tastes and fit needs not attended to in mainstream fashions. Brecca Farr in "Plus-Size Modeling" explains that possibilities for employment as a petite women's plus-size model were almost nonexistent before the early 1990s when that **target market** need was generally unrecognized by the fashion industry.

In a highly traditional culture, however, styles rich in historical meaning change slowly over time. Dressing to represent membership and role in a group, tribe, or clan is emphasized over individual expression (see Figure 11.2). This type of dress is **traditional**, and styles do not change substantially with each season or year.

FIGURE 11.2 *Cuna women of the San Blas Islands incorporate unique expressions in their reverse appliqué molas, jewelry, and waist sashes, but display an overall conformity to form and color.*

In some groups, modern fashion systems are rejected to make political or ideological statements. Brodman in "Paris or Perish: The Plight of the Latin American Indian in a Westernized World" describes how some of the Maya in Guatemala rejected modern fashion change systems and maintained their traditional native dress. Their native dress became symbolic of their rejection of other more politically powerful groups in Guatemala who were trying to destroy native ways of life and superimpose modernization.

In another example, the communist political system of the People's Republic of China systematically repressed individual expression through dress and other behaviors during the 1950s through the 1970s. The good of the many was emphasized over the individual. However, China began to relax its repressive policies and opened its doors to the outside world in the late 1970s. By 1985, political leaders declared that fashion would be good for China's textile industry and opened up markets to supply changing styles to the people of China for the first time since the communist takeover in 1949 ("Peking's Designer Diplomacy," 1985). That change in political opinion about fashion may reflect deeper changes in ideology of the Chinese communist system, as it has moved from an idealistic form of communism to a pragmatic policy of involvement in world markets and other systems (see Figure 11.3).

FASHION SYSTEM

The **fashion system** today is a globally based set of business establishments, small entrepreneurs, industry and government institutions, trade unions, and other agencies that have an impact on what products the consumer has to choose in the marketplace. Economic interests drive most fashion system decisions, though government interests (e.g., a boycott of a disfavored nation's products or raw materials) can put limits on choices too. Rita Kean (1997) pointed out that consumer choice is dramatically limited by the industry as it makes many fashion and style decisions based on such matters as cost, production feasibility, government import quotas, and gut-level guesses about what will sell. Many design features such as diamond-shaped godets and bound buttonholes rarely appear in moderately priced ready-to-wear apparel today because of the high cost of labor for sewing those details. Only in couture designer originals and custom-made apparel can these details appear, at a very high price.

No single agency or occupation has complete control over product offerings. A channel of interrelated decisions about colors, materials, and style details is made by textile manufacturers, design firms, producers, promoters, and retailers. The overall system tends to simplify the range of offerings to control complexity (Kean, 1997). For instance, simplification of offerings is reflected in sleeve stylings offered in shirts and jackets today. Very few apparel lines include anything but simple set-in and drop-shoulder sleeve cuts. Color choices are also simplified. If a U. S. consumer wanted to buy a brown sweater back in 1988, his or her search probably would have been futile. In 1998, an endless array of brown sweaters were available resulting from color trends followed by industry.

Style decisions are also substantially influenced by retail buyers. A designer who had worked for several apparel firms in New York City once told me about the many styles that firms show at market but that are never ordered by retail buyers. "We come up with many designs you would probably love to buy that never make it into stores." Design firms regularly offer a variety of styles at each market but cannot predict ahead of time exactly which styles buyers will order (personal communication, Lisa Hendrickson). Retail buyers are one type of **gatekeeper** for the fashion industry, making choices for their stores that further limit and simplify the range of style offerings.

a

b

FIGURE 11.3 *(a) Uniformity was apparent in white short-sleeved shirts and pants worn by men and women in the People's Republic of China during the summer of 1983. (b) By 1995, a greater variety of styles was available and worn in China.*

The fashion industry attempts to interpret societal trends in its merchandise to capture the *zeitgeist* and consumer dollars. "Scent of a Market" in Chapter 4 illustrates how the scent industry uses packaging, advertising, and naming of its products to create meanings that capture the attention and buying intentions of diverse consumers. Ralph Lauren is a master stylist as shown in "Ralph Lauren: The Emperor Has Clothes" by Susan Caminiti. Lauren has defined a world of refined yet casual, conservative yet stylish taste in menswear, womenswear, and household textiles and furnishings. By strategic selection of symbols in carefully controlled advertising and retailing displays, over the years Lauren has attracted a market niche of consumers who are loyal and appreciative customers.

The fashion system works simultaneously with the cultural system. Edwards in "Seinfeld and the *Real* John Peterman" gives an interesting example of how popular culture, in this case a television sitcom, has added meaning to the image of an apparel retailer. Although the Seinfeld show comically spoofed the company, the J. Peterman catalog company felt that the television exposure probably enhanced their sales through greater public exposure and free advertising. "Marketing Street Culture: Bringing Hip-Hop Culture to the Mainstream," by Marc Spiegler, describes how certain designers have profited by courting rap groups who endorse designer styles in song and performance costume; styles innovated by rap groups currently sell well to many suburban and small-town teenagers who seem to be inspired by messages of societal rejection and rebellion in rap music and lifestyle.

NEGOTIATION WITH OTHERS

Ultimately, it is consumer choice that makes a style fashion. Retail buyers and fashion designers may limit product offerings, but consumers do not buy all of what is offered. Fashion magazines feature a limited selection of designs each season, but these are fashion "proposals" that become fashions only if a substantial number of consumers adopt the new looks. The specific items featured by a company usually do not make a trend; it is that company's offerings plus many knockoffs (copies by competing brands) and similar-looking designs that, if purchased by a mass of consumers, determines the dominant styles that are popular for the season or year.

The diffusion of a style or look across a great number of consumers has been studied by many researchers (Sproles & Burns, 1994). **Diffusion** is a process of style adoption and change involving face-to-face interactions of individuals, strangers seeing each other on the street, and mass media display of styles. **Innovative consumers**, always a small proportion of a population, first sport new ideas in hairstyles, clothing, and other aspects of dress. **Early adopters** then select from the innovative looks and help to make the chosen styles visible to the wider population. If early adopters include fashion opinion leaders who are successful in making the new look acceptable or legitimate to friends and acquaintances, greater conformity and mass adoption will probably follow. As the look spreads in acceptance and use, innovators are apt to become bored by the look and move on to something new and challenging. The diffusion process shifts to new style introduction and continues to cycle onward. The older looks, unless they are classics that never go out of style, tend over time to become so familiar that they are adopted less frequently. Their use goes into decline until the style virtually disappears—until it is revived 25 or more years later as new and "cool." During the late 1990s, flared leg jeans, previously fashionable in the late 1960s and early 1970s, reappeared as fashionable.

Consumer adoption across leaders and followers involves complex processes of **negotiation** of meanings. Leaders and innovators must be individualistic and willing to take risks, as many of their choices may not be liked by others. Opinion leaders have been found to talk a lot about new trends, helping to introduce new styles to friends and discuss attractiveness and benefits of the style (Reynolds & Darden, 1972).

Much of the "negotiation" about "what is fashion" occurs through observation and not direct discussion, however. Most of us watch what others in our communities are wearing and adopt or reject accordingly. If something is seen on others around us, it is easier to get comfortable with the new look and to think of it as fashionable and attractive. If we start to notice that a style we bought a few years ago is now rarely worn by others, we begin to redefine the meaning of the old style as out-of-date or "dowdy."

A number of theories have been proposed to explain the reasons why fashion change occurs. Some of the earliest theories tended to emphasize social class emulation. The **trickle-down theory** of fashion proposed that the upper classes introduce new styles (Simmel, 1904; Veblen, 1912). Style ideas are copied, in cheaper versions, by the middle and lower classes who want to mimic the upper classes. When they see themselves copied, the upper classes move on to new styles that haven't been worn by the "un-chic" in middle and lower classes. This theory may have worked fairly well when class divisions were highly emphasized in the United States. However, it is now difficult to identify many fashion trends that start with the upper classes. Each social class in the United States may be doing its own thing or all may adopt their own versions of the same look in a sort of horizontal or **trickle-across diffusion** (King, 1963).

Some celebrities with upper class status may help to start new trends, but often they have copied their ideas from innovative groups in lower socioeconomic classes. The celebrity helps to legitimize the new idea as fashion for mainstream society but does not usually come up with the idea. This process fits what some have proposed as a **trickle-up theory** of fashion (Sproles, 1985). For example, the torn jeans and T-shirts, buzzed and freezed hairstyles, and creative use of fabrics and colors by working-class punk youth in 1970s England had a lasting influence on mainstream fashions during the 1980s and 1990s. Certain rock performers and celebrities helped to legitimize punk ideas by making them more visible to a wider proportion of society. Dick Hebdige (1979) analyzed the early years of punk style in England and traced the role of media in shaping the meanings of punk for mainstream society.

Herbert Blumer (1969) contended that social class was not the main driver of fashion change. Any group that captures the spirit of the times can have an influence on fashion. The rap groups discussed in "Marketing Street Culture" are not shaping fashion trends only on the basis of the desirability of their inner-city origins. It is a combination of the tough living situation they come from, their creative music, their rebelliousness, and their active and bold manipulation of style that gives rap groups a cachet that captures the interests of many adolescents today. Interestingly, some rap groups have not let the mainstream fashion industry profit solely from borrowing (some call it stealing) their style ideas. Some groups have started their own alternative apparel design firms.

Ted Polhemus in "Tribal Style" examines how subgroups that want to distinguish themselves from mainstream society put together unique looks to express their group identity. Conformity within groups may be substantial to show identification with the group, but deviation and differentiation from mainstream consumers is emphasized. A great deal of innovation and diversity is expressed through appearance among diverse subgroups in many societies today. Such groups may arise to express religious ideas, interests in hobbies or lifestyles (e.g., biker groups or quilting enthusiasts), or commitment to political statements or feelings of isolation from society (e.g., Grateful Dead followers). **Hybrid tribal** styles may arise when different groups interact together, such as in the rave and club scenes in urban settings. Different groups borrow style ideas from one another in a dynamic process of changing group and self-identity.

NEGOTIATION WITH SELF

Of course, an individual's unique tastes and sense of style will also shape adoption of new styles. Economic circumstances and lifestyles place limits on what consumers can afford and use. Each individual also has his or her own speed at becoming accustomed to and accepting of new aesthetic combinations and forms (Sproles, 1985).

Kaiser et al. (1995) proposed that a decision process fueled by psychological **ambivalence**—a feeling of tension or unease—moves consumers to adopt or reject new style ideas. Individuals are constantly assessing and reassessing their appearance choices every day. Is a look too young or mature, too formal or casual for a situation, too straight or too questioning of norms? We carry on inner dialogues with ourselves as we decide what to buy, what to wear, and what to discard. Ambivalence arises from uncertainty as a person considers the many style options from which to choose.

Summary

Macro-level and micro-level factors and influences help shape individual choices for dress. We look to others around us, to industry offerings, and to cultural themes and trends to help in deciding what to wear or not wear. Even an individual who decides not to fit with the mainstream uses many levels in making that decision. Fashion systems require social interaction. Individuals who are innovative and consumers who are conforming both are necessary for the process of fashion diffusion. Industry marketers or famous designers alone cannot make fashion trends happen without consumer acceptance and adoption of styles.

Characteristics of culture are reflected in the fashion trends of a society. Trends in the arts, technology, and popular culture shape style trends. Large population groups sometimes shape fashion trends because of their vast market potential. Smaller groups—such as segments of the upper class, punk rockers, or rap groups—may inspire fashion trends if they capture the spirit of the times. In order to express political, religious, or other values, some cultural groups do not engage in rapidly changing fashions. In cultures dominated by value in tradition, fashion systems may not develop. Even within fashion-oriented cultures, subcultural groups or tribes and nonconforming individuals may reject popular looks and dress to express their lack of fit with mainstream values and lifestyles. The process of fashion change and individual adoption or rejection of fashion is tremendously complex and involves all levels of a society.

Suggested Readings

Behling, D. (1985). Fashion change and demographics: A model. *Clothing and Textiles Research Journal, 4*(1), 18–24.

Hamilton, J. A. (1997). The macro-micro interface in the construction of individual fashion forms and meanings. *Clothing and Textiles Research Journal, 15*(3), 164–171.

Hebdige, D. (1979). *Subculture: The meaning of style.* London: Methuen.

Kaiser, S. B., Nagasawa, R., & Hutton, S. (1995). Construction of an SI theory of fashion part 1: Ambivalence and Change. *Clothing and Textiles Research Journal, 13*(3), 172–183.

Kean, R. C. (1997). The role of the fashion system in fashion change: A response to the Kaiser, Nagasawa and Hutton model. *Clothing and Textiles Research Journal, 15*(3), 172–177.

Sproles, G. B. (1985). Behavioral science theories of fashion. In M. R. Solomon (Ed.), *The psychology of fashion* (pp. 55–70). Lexington, MA: Lexington Books.

LEARNING ACTIVITY
Advertising Morality

Objective

Recent advertising and marketing strategies help us consider ethical responsibilities of the fashion industry. Perspectives of many groups and individuals are important in assessing ethical issues. Two examples are discussed in this learning activity.

Procedure

Problem 1: Recently, the fashion industry has been criticized by parents, newspaper columnists, and even the President of the United States. The industry's apparent agenda—that anything is okay as long as it sells clothes—is under attack. Models with heroin tracks on their arms and clothing hangtags commanding "Destroy All Girls" are condemned by some as promoting inappropriate behaviors and ways of thinking among young people (see Box 11.1, page 420). Mothers Against Drunk Driving put recently pressure on the retailer Abercrombie & Fitch to apologize for including in its *A&F Quarterly Back to School Issue* 98 mail-order catalog a page of recipes for playfully named alcoholic beverages, such as "Brain Hemorrhage," "Foreplay," and "Sex on the Beach" (Coleman, 1998). The "Drinking 101" feature encouraged college students to "...indulge in some creative drinking..." and included a colorful cutout spinner chart for drinking games. Abercrombie & Fitch was accused of connecting alcohol abuse with sex, fun, and fashions on campus. In response to attacks by the public, the retailer sent a follow-up postcard to all consumers on its mailing list claiming that the firm in no way supports underage or binge drinking. Abercrombie & Fitch also promised to address "...the responsibilities and hazards involved in alcohol use..." in future issues of its catalog.

Discussion

What do you think of the Abercrombie & Fitch alcohol recipes and other promotional campaigns described in the editorial "Bad Taste in Vogue"? Discuss the apparel promotions in a small group in class. Consider some of the following issues:

- Do the promotional campaigns described really encourage such activities as heroin use, binge drinking, and abuse of girls?

- Do most young people see the promotions as merely humorous and harmless or as "just advertising"?

- Do you see the promotions as interesting, fun, appealing, or truly dangerous?

- Would you buy garments or other products from a company that advertises in these ways?

- Why do you think Abercrombie & Fitch sent out the apologetic postcard? Do you think they needed to send the card? Will the postcard solve problems its ads might have created?

Problem 2: Examine the JNCO "Crimescene" jeans ad in Figure 11.4. The advertiser has included a great deal of ambiguity in the ad to engage viewers in the "text" or content of the ad. The product is surrounded by a number of images that may be interpreted differently by various viewers of the ad.

BOX 1
Bad Taste in Vogue[1]

If other retailers followed the lead of Galyan's Trading Co., manufacturers would soon stop putting offensive slogans and sayings on their products.

The Plainfield-based sporting goods chain recently cleared its shelves of a brand of T-shirts, sweatshirts, pants and boxer shorts carrying the message "Destroy All Girls." The order appeared on a tag giving laundering instruction.

The apparel was packed up and returned to the California firm that made it. And in order to emphasize its point, the chain also returned the firm's line of skating gear.

"We will not have that in our stores. It's counter to the culture we have at Galyan's," said Joan Hurley, director of marketing. Hurley said Galyan's was unaware of the vicious message until a customer brought it to their attention.

The maker acknowledged it had complaints from other markets as well and will discontinue the slogan but will not recall goods previously distributed. It had already made concessions, said a representative of the firm. Originally the tag was to say, "Kill Your Parents," but was changed because of objections that it was too extreme.

It was not too extreme for another manufacturer, however. A recent Mona Charen column on the cultural depravity of some rock music noted that kids lined up to hear Marilyn Manson and his band, who wore T-shirts proclaiming, "Kill Your Parents" and "This Is Your World in Which We Grow Up and We Will Grow to Hate You."

Thus has the brutishness of gangsta rap, with its admonitions to kill police and defile women, moved into the garment trade, even into the world of high fashion.

President Clinton recently blasted the fashion industry for glamorizing drug addiction in order to peddle designer clothes. The emaciated, strung-out look of models on runways and in fashion magazines, he said, was responsible in part for the rise of heroin as the drug of choice on college campuses and inner-city neighborhoods.

The president's criticism was a little late. Insiders say "heroin chic" has about run its course and will soon give way to another craze. Morality had nothing to do with the decline, according to Michael Gross, author of a book on the modeling business. Apparel manufacturing is amoral, he said. It doesn't care what messages it sends. All that counts is selling clothes.

That is where retailers like Galyan's and smart consumers come in. If customers complain about exploitative or degrading merchandise, if responsible stores refuse to carry it and thoughtful consumers refuse to buy it, manufacturers will soon get the message.

The fashion industry may be oblivious to morality but it pays careful attention to the bottom line.

---

[1]Bad taste in vogue. (1997, May 29) *Indianapolis Star*, p. A10 [editorial]

Discussion

Consider the following issues:

- What is going on in the ad? Do all students in your group interpret the ad similarly?

- What do the themes in the ad imply about the advertised JNCO jeans? Why do you think JNCO has created this theme for its product?

- Do you think that wearers of JNCO jeans are or are trying to be a certain type of person?

- Do you feel there is anything inappropriate about this ad campaign? Does your group agree or disagree on this?

FIGURE 11.4 *JNCO "Crimescene" jeans ad, 1998.*

References

Behling, D. (1985). Fashion change and demographics: A model. *Clothing and Textiles Research Journal, 4*(1), 18–24.

Blumer, H. (1969). Fashion: From class differentiation to collective selection. *Sociology Quarterly, 10*, 275–291.

Coleman, M. S. (1998, August 7). Course canceled: "Drinking 101." *Des Moines Register,* p. 11A.

Hamilton, J. A. (1997). The macro–micro interface in the construction of individual fashion forms and meanings. *Clothing and Textiles Research Journal, 15*(3), 164–171.

Hebdige, D. (1979). *Subculture: The meaning of style.* London: Methuen.

Horn, M. J., & Gurel, L. M. (1981). *The second skin* (3rd ed.). Boston: Houghton, Mifflin.

Kaiser, S. B., Nagasawa, R., & Hutton, S. (1995). Construction of an SI theory of fashion part 1: Ambivalence and change. *Clothing and Textiles Research Journal, 13*(3), 172–183.

Kean, R. C. (1997). The role of the fashion system in fashion change: A response to the Kaiser, Nagasawa and Hutton model. *Clothing and Textiles Research Journal, 15*(3), 172–177.

King, C. W. (1963). Fashion adoption: A rebuttal to the "trickle-down" theory. In S. A. Greyser (Ed.), *Toward scientific marketing* (pp. 108–125). Chicago: American Marketing Association.

Ono, Y., & Bounds, W. (1998, July 9). Army pants with pouchy pockets storm fashion world. *The Wall Street Journal,* pp. B1, B7.

Peking's designer diplomacy. (1985, May 20). *Newsweek,* p. 46.

Reynolds, F. D., & Darden, W. R. (1972). Why the midi failed. *Journal of Advertising Research, 12,* 51–62.

Simmel, G. (1904). Fashion. *International Quarterly, 10,* 130–155.

Sproles, G. B. (1979). *Fashion: Consumer behavior toward dress.* Minneapolis, MN: Burgess Publishing.

Sproles, G. B. (1985). Behavioral science theories of fashion. In M. R. Solomon (Ed.), *The psychology of fashion* (pp. 55–70). Lexington, MA: Lexington Books.

Sproles, G. B., & Burns, L. D. (1994). *Changing appearances.* New York: Fairchild.

Veblen, T. (1912). *The theory of the leisure class.* New York: Macmillan.

68   Styles with a Sizable Difference
William Kissel

National retailers have been sizing African-American shoppers lately, and not everyone is thrilled with their intentions—to use differences in body type as a marketing tool.

Last August, J.C. Penney launched a new fashion catalogue, Influences, that company officials say "caters to the clothing tastes and size needs of African-American women."

Spiegel, the Chicago-based mail-order giant, is following suit with E Style, a 64-page catalogue of clothes and accessories co-produced by Ebony magazine that will be delivered to 1.5 million African-American households in September.

While many black consumers welcome the wave of targeted marketing that promises to make finding the right clothes easier, others warn that playing up physical differences among races is a tricky, divisive business.

"We see this as an opportunity to serve a customer who isn't having her needs met currently by retailers," Spiegel spokeswoman Ann Morris says of E Style. She declined to discuss how its sizes and selection might differ from that in other catalogues, but Linda Johnson Rice, president and chief executive of Ebony's owner, Johnson Publishing, recently told the New York Times: "Spiegel has done its homework (with E Style). What they've done is taken a random selection of black women with different body types and analyzed them, so that when the clothes are manufactured, they fit the needs of black women."

Penney's used African-American fit models to come up with sizes—generally, more generous in the hips and thighs—for its Influences clothing by designer Anthony Mark Hankins. "We are building the collection with a particular set of specifications in mind," says merchandise manager Barbara Bierman, adding that some of the clothes will be available in stores this fall.

Carl Jones, co-owner of the fast-growing L.A.-based sportswear company Cross Colours, has no problem with using body type as a mar-keting tool. African-Americans—men, too—have been long neglected by retailers, he says. "We thought that the fit that was out there was a fit that catered to the African-American male body, which tends to have a smaller waist, wider hips, bigger thighs and longer arms than the average Anglo man," Jones notes. "And a lot of African-American women have very small waists but wider hips than other women."

But Lois Anderson, curator of the Black Fashion Museum of Harlem and author of "Blacks and the History of Fashion," says talk about size differences between blacks and whites is "just a bunch of malarkey."

"There is absolutely no difference in people's bodies to that extent. It sounds good," she says, "but there is no truth to it at all."

Byron Lars, a successful New York-based women's wear designer, finds the new marketing efforts blatantly offensive. "To separate African-Americans from the rest of the American population is a very dangerous thing," he says. "It's what we've worked so long and so hard to combat and this is just a slap in the face and a step backward."

Sales will ultimately decide the fate of the trend. "It's hard to make a profit without filling a need," says Bobby Glanton-Smith, sales and marketing director for Recycling Black Dollars, an Inglewood group that promotes black-owned businesses. "Business is parasitic, so I don't think it's necessarily exploitive to market to a race of people. The stores have just refined their marketing strategies to meet the needs of a specific audience. What's wrong with that?"

Robert Goldman, a sociology professor at Lewis & Clark College in Portland, Ore., and author of a new book on the social ramifications of product marketing, "Reading Ads Socially," sees the potential for misunderstanding.

"It all sort of resembles this movement toward multiculturalism," Goldman says. "And the danger with multiculturalism is this thing called identity politics, where one group sees another's benefits coming at their expense.

Certainly it will be perceived as leading to greater divisiveness (between races). While at the same time there's a kind of flattery involved that will probably prove effective."

DISCUSSION QUESTIONS

Styles with a Sizeable Difference

1. How are the recent efforts to target African American apparel consumers a positive situation for African American consumers?

2. What are some potential negative ramifications of ethnic marketing on the part of the apparel industry?

69 Plus-Size Modeling: The Industry, the Market, and Reflections as a Professional in the Image Industry

Brecca A. Farr
Doctoral Candidate
Iowa State University

"Plus-size petite model."

Say that phrase and you'll likely hear, "What's that?" "You're kidding, right?" or "That's an oxymoron like 'military intelligence'."

Plus-size petites, also known as women's petites, is an apparel size range targeted for women between 5' and 5'4" tall and a size 14 or larger.

But wait, didn't I also say *model*? Yes, at 5'2" tall and a size 18 (approximately 195 pounds), I worked as a plus-size petite model and consultant. In this article I discuss my work as a plus-size petite model and give an insider's perspective of the modeling industry, the plus-size market, and reflections on being a plus-size petite professional in the U. S. image industry.

THE MODELING INDUSTRY

Everyone in the modeling industry has their own story about how they began modeling. Many young women and men start off modeling part-time during their preteen or early teen years. Perhaps they entered a national contest and were among the winners. No one in their right mind graduates from college, works long enough in the apparel industry to advance into a well-paying job with a bright career ahead just to quit for a two week modeling gig with absolutely no

Original for this text.

guarantee of work afterward. But that's what I did. I don't recommend that as a common approach to career change. I was very lucky, literally being in the right place at the right time with the right height, size, and shape of body.

Most people don't realize that working as a model usually means you're self-employed. Being self-employed means no guaranteed salary and no benefits, such as medical insurance or a retirement plan. A few models are employed to work exclusively for one firm; often these are "fit models," and the firm attempts to create product differentiation based on the fit to that model's measurements. The vast majority of models are self-employed, however, be they free-lance or under contract with an agency.

A reputable modeling agency, such as Ford Models, Inc., acts as a professional service. When my agent accepted bookings for me, Ford ran a credit check on the client. Additionally, Ford billed and collected my hourly fees. Modeling agencies also put together books of their models. Models usually pay for their pictures to be included in these books. The cost depends upon the agency, the number of pictures to be included, and the type of book being published. A full-color book highlighting all the agency's fashion models is more expensive than a black-and-white book featuring industry fit models (see Figure 11.5). For these services I paid Ford a percentage of my fees, as is the practice in the industry.

As a model under contract with an agency, I capitalized on the reputation of my agency. Saying that I was a model with Ford initiated expectations for appearance and professionalism. When I walked into a prospective client's office, there was an expectation of attractiveness as well as knowledge about women's petites. The expectation of attractiveness included wearing stylish clothing of my own (including shoes and complete accessories), having my hair in a flattering style, and using makeup befitting my skin tone and ensemble. As do most new models, I worked with a professional makeup artist to learn how to appropriately apply my makeup when I first began to work.

There are two general types of models that I categorize as "fashion" and "closer-to-real-life." Fashion models include the supermodels, such as Cindy Crawford, Iman, or Christy Turlington,

FIGURE 11.5 *Brecca Farr as a women's petite fit model.*

and the models seen on the haute couture runways of New York, Paris, Milan, and so forth. Also, these models are featured in fashion magazines, such as *Vogue, Elle,* and *GQ.*

Fashion models represent idealized standards of beauty and attractiveness. Usually they are taller, thinner, and younger than the average woman or man. It is common for female fashion models to be over 5'10" tall and a size six or smaller. By comparison, when I worked in the New York City garment industry from the early to mid 1990s, industry statistics reported that the average woman in the United States was 5' 3.8" tall, weighed 145 pounds, and wore either a size 12 or 14 dress. Within a group of fashion models, there may also be "body parts models." These models are women and men whose specific body part or parts, such as hands, chest, or legs, represent the ideal size and shape.

Compared to fashion models, closer-to-real-life models represent one or more target markets. These models still emphasize attractiveness, but they do not differ as greatly from the average person in their target market as do fashion models. Specialty size models are closer-to-real-life models and are often identified with apparel size ranges, such as petites, talls, or plus-sizes.

Even within a group of plus-size models, there are degrees of how similar to real people a model may be. Many plus-size models featured in upscale clothing catalogs, such as *Spiegel For You*, wear sizes 12 or 14 because they are close to 5′11″ or 6′ tall. Often these models are sizes 12 or 14 because of their height, not because they are overweight. This is also true for many store or mall fashion show models who work in the plus-size range. Considering that plus-sizes range from size 14 to 24, these models are on the small side of the scale.

Regardless of the type of model a person may be, there are body expectations. These expectations not only govern how the person will walk, talk, dress, and carry the self, but will also govern what the model must do to maintain her or his body and image. Critical expectations include the key body measurements that must be maintained, such as bust or chest, waist, high and low hip, thigh, and calf. Ongoing maintenance may be more difficult during a woman's menstrual cycle, when her breasts may swell or she retains more water and her body's measurements increase 1/2″ or more.

Models constantly manipulate their bodies through a variety of methods, ranging from adjusting their caloric intake, exercising, surgery, smoking, or taking prescription or illegal drugs. The degree to which models manipulate their bodies depends on the individual, personal body chemistry, and what image or target market they are attempting to represent. Many of the models I knew had surgery—liposuction was most common.

Keeping the body in good condition may involve more than just exercising or eating healthy. Two hand models I knew wore gloves at all times to protect their hands. Dry skin or chipped nails could cost them jobs and their income. Leg models I knew never shaved their legs with razors for fear of scratches. They also had to watch what types of exercises they did; too

many repetitions on a stair master would increase the size of their calves. Any imperfections or blemishes could mean the difference between working and being unemployed.

For myself, I adjusted my diet and exercise routine to maintain the measurements I needed to work. I refused to have surgery to change my body's shape. I must state that I was never asked to have surgery. However, it was understood that if I wanted to extend the years I had to work in the industry and increase my client list, I would have to seriously considered cosmetic surgery at some point in the future.

THE PLUS-SIZE MARKET

My work as a women's petite model was only possible after the establishment of the plus-size market. I first worked as a women's petite model in 1992. It simply was not possible to earn a living as a women's petite model much before 1992 because the market didn't exist, according to the industry.

The plus-size market has been around for many years. Lane Bryant, one of the oldest plus-size retailers, has been in business for over 90 years. Traditionally, the plus-size market targeted older women, offering them dresses shaped like tents and bullet-proof polyester pants. Only within the last ten to 15 years has the apparel industry taken hold and pushed the boundaries of the plus-size market toward a more youthful and fashion-forward customer.

Why are these markets important? Estimates state that approximately 40 to 60 percent of all U.S. women are petite, specifically 5′4″ and shorter (Shim & Kotsiopulos, 1990). In addition, 60 percent of U.S. women wear a size 12 or larger, and 31 percent of U.S. women wear size 16 or larger (Daria, 1993; "Why Is Size 8…," 1994). Table 1 presents the percent of the population classified as overweight. Erring on the conservative side, approximately 45 to 60 million U.S. women are represented in this special size market.

The women's apparel industry has been experiencing lackluster sales for the past several years. Retailers finally realized that opportunities for growth and increased sales were available in the plus-size market (Darnton, 1991; Feldman, 1992;

TABLE 1

*Percentage of the U.S. Population that is Overweight**

Age Range	1976–1980		1988–1991	
	Men	Women	Men	Women
20–34	17.3	16.8	22.8	24.5
35–44	28.9	27.0	35.7	35.1
45–54	31.0	32.5	35.5	39.8
55–64	28.1	37.0	40.5	48.7
65–74	25.2	38.4	42.2	39.7
75 and older	n/a	n/a	26.0	31.5

n/a = DATA NOT AVAILABLE

*Overweight is defined for men as body mass index (BMI) greater than or equal to 27.8 kilograms per meter squared, and for women as BMI greater than or equal to 27.3 kilograms per meter squared. These points were used because they represent sex-specific 85th percentiles for persons 20 to 29 years of age in the *1976–1980 National Health and Nutrition Examination Survey* (NHANES). Data are based on physical examinations of a sample of the civilian non-institutional population in the NHANES. Pregnant women are also excluded (U.S. Bureau of the Census, 1997).

Gill, 1991; Owens, 1997; "Sales of Women's Plus Sizes...", 1995; "Sizing Up Women's Apparel," 1994). One research organization stated that from June 1990 to June 1995, the plus-size apparel market increased 42 percent compared to a 23 percent increase of total women's apparel during the same five years ("Sales of Women's Plus Sizes...", 1995). Many apparel retailers and manufacturers anticipate continued growth for this market. "The reason there's so much growth in this part of the industry is simple: there's a lot of money to be made" (Stiven, 1989). Phrased another way and often quoted in the market, "When looking at a firm's profit margin, there's no difference between skinny and fat dollars."

The recognition of the potential profits from the plus-size and plus-size petite markets challenged many beliefs about overweight women and men. Studies have documented a pervasive negative stereotype of large-size people[1]. Some of the attributes of the stereotype include laziness, lower socioeconomic status,

[1]Many studies have examined the stereotypes associated with overweight or obese people (e.g., Crandall, 1994; Harris, Harris & Bochner, 1982). The associated negative attributes were not found to be significantly different between overweight men versus overweight women.

weak-willed, blameworthy, dirty, slow, unintelligent, withdrawn, unattractive, and incompetent (Harris, Harris & Bochner, 1982; Harris, Walters & Waschull, 1991; Harris, Waschull & Walters, 1990; Jasper & Klassen, 1990; Millman, 1980; Tiggemann & Rothblum, 1988). Apparel merchandisers and modeling agencies were not immune to these stereotypes.

Large-size women and men are assumed to be responsible for their condition, as if they all choose to be overweight. Society in the United States sanctions overtly hostile behavior toward plus-size women and men, unlike other stigmatized groups such as African-Americans (Crandall, 1994).

Millman (1980) states that large-size women are "mythologized," that is the issue of size goes beyond the reasons "normal" people cite for being offended by a large-size woman. Her size symbolizes deviant tendencies in relation to societal norms; large-size women are somehow seen as expressing rebellion against what society deems as appropriate. The reasoning follows that if you accept the societal norm of beauty and attractiveness, you can't accept plus-size people.

Little sympathy or understanding of an individual plus-size woman's situation is accorded (Millman, 1980). She is blamed for being fat. Furthermore, plus-size women may internalize this blame, thereby believing the myths and stereotypes (Harris, Waschull & Walter, 1990). This belief may include self-fulfilling prophecies (Snyder, Tanke, & Berscheid, 1977). If a woman believes that she's unattractive, and she can't find clothing that looks good or fits well, she will likely project a message that says she doesn't care about how she looks. If people believe that she doesn't care how she looks, she'll be treated accordingly. And the cycle continues as she reacts to the way she's treated by others.

Millman (1980) puts it best when she states, "Being [a plus-size person] and the interpretations made of it wind up affecting all of a person's life, pushing the fat person into a special, marginal relationship to the world" (p. 72). This marginalization by society affects plus-size women in the way they interact with others. Withdrawing from society is not unusual for the plus-size woman (Millman, 1980), and if she withdraws, her ability to develop social skills is hampered; therefore, she withdraws further, promoting the image that she doesn't care about her appearance. This also continues to feed into the cycle of society's negative attitude and stereotype of plus-size people.

When I worked in the modeling industry, public perceptions of the mere existence of a plus-size model was still an oxymoron at times. For example, I was discussing the new plus-size holiday line of a better price-point brand with a fashion consultant. An acquaintance in the apparel industry joined our conversation, having overheard us discuss details such, "stylish," "contemporary," "greater comfort for a more shapely body without sacrificing aesthetics," "she [the consumer] can feel attractive and ready for a night out on the town." The newcomer to the conversation commented, "What are you talking about?" We replied with the name of the line and our excitement about its new offerings for the plus-size market. Her only comment was, "I never thought that company would produce clothes for fat women. I always thought they were concerned about their image."

These attitudes and stereotypes about overweight people are also prevalent when you examine the evolution of the women's plus-size market. At first, plus-sizes were recognized as only appropriate for older women. The assump-

tion was that these women, because they were older and overweight, were not concerned about their appearance. If they weren't concerned about their appearance, then they wouldn't spend a lot of money on their clothing. So, merchandise from budget-priced apparel firms comprised most of the market's offerings. Slowly, apparel firms recognized that overweight women were not just 65 years of age and older, but that there were a lot of younger women as well. Furthermore, if the women were younger, then they most likely needed clothes for work and leisure time. However, it has only been during the past 15 years that the plus-size market has begun to offer clothing for young women (under 30), as well as more contemporary styles at better to bridge price points (Wallach, 1985; Werner, 1987). Only published articles from the 1990s regularly state that plus-size consumers seek most of the same fashion trends as their smaller counterparts.

Very little scholarly research has focused on the plus-size market beyond documentation of stereotypes and potential social behaviors resulting from being overweight in the United Staes. Recent research includes a study that examined the relationship between a special-sized consumer's level of satisfaction toward her body and her level of satisfaction relating to apparel shopping and shopping behaviors (Shim & Kotsiopulos, 1990). Other research has focused on needs assessments of either the petite or the plus-size consumer (Chowdhary & Beale, 1988). No research has examined women's petites. The most consistent source of literature comes from trade press concerning recent market sales figures. Numerous articles also appear in popular periodicals, such as *Glamour, Essence,* and *The New York Times,* which discuss the difficulty plus-size consumers face when trying to find well-fitting and stylish clothing.

THE IMAGE INDUSTRY

When reflecting on my role as a professional in the image industry, three themes emerge. First is my perception that I was not a threat to other models in the industry. Second is enhancement of my self-esteem due to recognition and acceptance as an attractive woman. Third is development of plus-size markets and the fundamental challenge that development gives to the image industry.

As I mentioned earlier, many plus-size models featured in catalogs or on the runway were size 12 or 14 and very tall. Rarely were sizes 18 or larger models used, yet these sizes are closer to the midpoint of the plus-size range. If several models were hired for a particular photo shoot or modeling job, usually there was a specific look that was desired for each model. For example, if three plus-size models were to be featured, the client likely had a list of preferences—such as one blond model, one mature model, and one African American model. If a plus-size petite model was also included on the list of preferences, at the time I worked that meant she would be myself or one of three other models working in New York.

When a general call for all plus-size models went out for a show or photographic work, most of the other models were surprised to see me. I was significantly shorter and larger than they were. Subsequently, I was not perceived as a competitor for their jobs. Because I was not a competitor, most of the models were very friendly and openly discussed how they maintained their body size and shape. We also swapped tips for makeup, hair styling, fixing shoes, and numerous other ways to change image and appearance.

When I was with other models or working with clients in the plus-size market, my status as a Ford Model granted me instant acceptance. My education, professionalism, and personality were important with regard to maintaining that acceptance and earning their respect. That instant acceptance was, to me, a measure of my attractiveness; recognition and acceptance also gave me self-confidence. The Ford Modeling Agency doesn't offer contracts to unattractive women. When I worked, I played the role of a Ford model; therefore, I needed to capture some of the essence of being a model—my hair done, makeup just right, good clothes, nice shoes, and a very put together appearance. Additionally, I represented millions of women—regular women across the United States. And I wasn't the unattainable ideal standard of beauty.

The mere fact that I earned a nice living as a plus-size petite fit model and consultant validated the existence of the plus-size petite market. While Sak's Fifth Avenue, Liz Claiborne, Ellen Tracy, as well as other firms produced, marketed, sold, and emphasized the continued development of plus-size clothing, the image industry made the statement that overweight women and men are acceptable. Yet, recognition and continued development of the plus-size market challenged a fundamental belief of the image industry—that thinner is better.

Since the time I left the market, the "thinner is better" belief continues to be challenged. Fashion magazines, such *BBW* and the newly launched *Mode* ("Plus-Size 'Mode' Hits Stands," 1997), devoted to the plus-size woman and featuring models larger than a size 14, continue to gain greater visibility on retailers' shelves. *Glamour* purports that each issue will include at least one ad or feature with a plus-size model. The Body Shop introduced an advertising campaign featuring Ruby, a redheaded rubenesque "Barbie-like" doll and accompanying caption: "There are 3 billion women who don't look like supermodels and only 8 who do" (Elliott, 1997). Recent health studies have stated that it is possible to be overweight and physically fit ("Experts Challenge Assertion," 1997).

Hopefully, the continued growth and development of the plus-size market will help women and men accept themselves and their bodies. From that acceptance, I wish everyone could feel the joy that self-confidence brings. I am still amazed at how much self-confidence I gained from working as a professional in the image industry and being well-paid because of the size and shape of my body.

References

Chowdhary, U., & Beale, N. V. (1988). Plus-size women's clothing interest, satisfactions and dissatisfactions with ready-to-wear apparel. *Perceptual and Motor Skills, 66*, 783–788.

Crandall, C. S. (1994). Prejudice against fat people: Ideology and self-interest. *Journal of Personality and Social Psychology, 66*, 882–894.

Daria, I. (1993, February). Why more designers are designing large-size clothes—and why some still won't. *Glamour, 91*, 149–150.

Darnton, N. (1991, February 25). Big women, big profits. *Newsweek, 117*, 48, 50.

Elliott, S. (1997, August 26). The Body Shop's campaign offers reality, not miracles. *New York Times*, C8.

Experts challenge assertion that thinner is always better. (1997, August 12). *Washington Post*, Z13.

Feldman, A. (1992, March 16). Hello, Oprah, good-bye, Iman. *Forbes, 142*, 116–117.

Gill, P. (1991, April). 14+ niche: A perfect fit. *Stores, 73*, 44–46.

Harris, M. B., Harris, R. J., & Bochner, S. (1982). Fat, four-eyed, and female: Stereotypes of obesity, glasses, and gender. *Journal of Applied Social Psychology, 12*, 503–516.

Harris, M. B., Walters, L. C., & Waschull, S. (1991). Gender and ethnic differences in obesity-related behaviors and attitudes in a college sample. *Journal of Applied Social Psychology, 21*, 1545–1566.

Harris, M. B., Waschull, S., Walters, L. (1990). Feeling fat: Motivations, knowledge, and attitudes of overweight women and men. *Psychological Reports, 67(Part 2)*, 1191–1202.

Jasper, C. R., & Klassen, M. L. (1990). Stereotypical beliefs about appearance: Implications for retailing and consumer issues. *Percpetual and Motor Skills, 71*, 519–528.

Millman, M. (1980). *Such a pretty face: Being fat in America*. New York: W. W. Norton & Company.

Owens, J. (1997, April 30). Plus-size market is segmenting. *Women's Wear Daily, 173*, 10.

Plus-size 'Mode' hits stands. (1997, February 17). *Mediaweek, 7*, 3.

Sales of women's plus sizes outpace total apparel biz. (1995, November 6). *Discount Store News, 34*, 25.

Shim, S., & Kotsiopulos, A. (1990). Women's physical sizes, body cathexis, and shopping for apparel. *Perceptual and Motor Skills, 71*, 1031–1042.

Sizing up women's apparel. (1994, May 16). *Discount Store News, 33*, A48.

Snyder, M., Tanke, E. D., & Berscheid, E. (1977). Social perception and interpersonal behavior: On the self-fulfilling nature of social stereotypes. *Journal of Personality and Social Psychology, 35*, 656–666.

Stiven, K. (1989, April 24). Underserved market dresses up options. *Advertising Age, 60*, S-15.

Tiggemann, M., & Rothblum, E. D. (1988). Gender differences in social consequences of perceived overweight in the United States and Australia. *Sex Roles, 18*, 75–6.

U.S. Bureau of the Census. (1997). *Statistical Abstract of the United States: 1997* (117th edition). Washington, D. C.: U. S. Bureau of the Census.

Wallach, J. (1985, April). Strategies for selling large-size apparel...Who's doing it and how. *Stores, 67*, 13–23.

Werner, T. (1987, March 9). Sizing up: Conston, apparel retailer, caters to larger customers. *Barron's*, 69.

Why is size 8 the industry standard? And where does that leave the rest of us? (1994, April). *Glamour, 92*, 205–206.

1. Why was the plus-size market ignored and under-serviced until the 1990s?

2. What negative consequences does ignoring the plus-size market have for U.S. consumers?

3. How did Brecca's experience as a model affect her feelings about her body?

70 Paris or Perish: The Plight of the Latin American Indian in a Westernized World

Barbara Brodman

I crossed the border carrying dignity…

I carry the huilpil of colors for the fiesta when I return…

I will return tomorrow…

Rigoberta Menchú

Patria Abnegada

Like Mother Fashion, Paris delivers her haute couture designs to the world at large. From fashion hub to fashion hub, city to city around the world, disciples of Western fashion bow to their Parisian mecca. Yet, not all have accepted the hegemony of Paris and the West in matters of style and dress. In the Americas, for example, indigenous peoples continue to wear with pride the tribal designs that mark them as Indian. Their dress is an expression of culture as rich in history and symbolism as oral literature or other indigenous art forms. It is part of the glue that holds Indian cultures together and that safeguards them against extinction. Sadly, the price Indians pay for preserving their native fashion is social degradation, persecution, and, often, death. Adoption of Western dress is part of an ongoing process of Western colonialism that began almost five centuries ago, and it may sig-nify the demise of cultures that have existed and thrived for millennia.

In the two areas of the Americas where indigenous populations are most concentrated, the Andean region of South America and Middle America (Mexico and Central America) Indians face economic and legal discrimination, and have even become victims of blatant, sustained genocidal campaigns. Often, the Indians' choice of whether to adopt Western dress or continue to wear native designs determines whether they will live or die. In 1932, for example, after troops of the dictator Maximiliano Hernández Martínez slaughtered 30,000 Indian peasants, indigenous peoples in El Salvador stopped wearing traditional Maya garb, and Indian identity all but disappeared. In Guatemala, however, a particularly brutal conquest led to the creation of a tradition of revolt and the retention of culture. Of today's Guatemalan Indians, some 40 percent speak one of over 120 dialects of 22 Maya languages as their primary tongue and wear with pride one of hundreds of distinct costumes that not only mark them as Indian but also proclaim their village or town of origin.[1]

Considered one of the worst violators of human rights in the Western Hemisphere, Guatemala focuses its pogroms on the elimination of its indigenous people, who are considered naturally susceptible to "communist subversion." With the largest percentage of Indians in Mesoamerica—some 60 percent of the total population—Guatemala provides a fine killing field for death squads and civil patrols for whom the Guatemalan Indian wears his or her native garb like a red flag. It should come as no surprise that Indians make up a large percentage of the estimated 45,000 "disappeared" and 100,000 persons murdered in Guatemala since the mid-1960s.[2]

In Guatemala, as elsewhere in Indo-America, to dress like an Indian is to be an Indian. And to be an Indian is to be socially and economically deprived, at best, and persecuted to death, at worst. Yet, many Guatemalan Indians choose to perish rather than accept the cultural dictates—including fashion—of a world in which indigenous peoples and their cultures have become increasingly expendible.

CULTURAL SIGNIFICANCE OF DRESS

Worldwide, fashion is a clear and definitive expression of the culture from which it derives. Western fashion, for example, reflects the dynamism of modern industrial societies characterized by rapid change and innovation, by individualism coupled with an increasingly global perspective, and by a superficiality that, to some, represents a threatening uniformity. Western fashions change with the seasons and at the whim of the fashion industry.[3] By direct contrast, consistency of style and design characterizes native American dress.

Among indigenous Latin American peoples, like the Maya of Guatemala, dress reflects little of the capriciousness and superficiality of Western fashion because it is linked to cultural survival. It symbolizes a time when ancient American civilizations were among the most advanced in the world, when being Mexican or Maya, Chibcha or Inca, was a source of pride and power, not degradation. In contemporary Middle America, as elsewhere in Indo-America,

patterns of native dress reflect not only the rich symbolism that lies at the heart of Indian ritual life but the basic institutional framework of the culture. Within this context, native dress helps perpetuate divisions of labor, family systems, and hierarchical orders that have stood the test of millennia and that today are threatened.

Once the Maya were the greatest cultural force in the Americas. They left copious records of their history, cosmology, and achievements, but most of them were destroyed before or during the Spanish Conquest. Today, the splendor of those times is perpetuated mainly in an oral tradition and in the style and design of traditional Maya clothing. So linked to cultural identity and survival are the sacred symbols and colors that characterize Maya dress and textiles that their mythical origin is recounted in the *Popol Vuh, The Sacred Book of the Ancient Quiché Maya*. It explains that the great god Tohil presented the ancient Maya with the symbols and colors of their being painted on three cloths.[4] Their contemporary descendants use the same designs and colors in memory of that event. They employ the figures of the jaguar, the eagle, wasps, and bees, and the colors of the Maya cosmology: green, the royal color, signifying eternity and fertility; red, the color of the sun and of blood, signifying life; yellow, the color of death and of maize, the staple food of life and the substance of which man was made by the gods; black, the color of obsidian, symbol of war; and blue, the color of sacrifice. All remind the Maya of a time when they communed directly with the gods and produced a high culture unsurpassed in the hemisphere. Indigenous designs thus form a text of Maya origins, religions, and history and, as such, help keep alive a culture that is increasingly threatened. All the colors of the Maya cosmology can typically be seen in contemporary Guatemalan marketplaces, including the flower market in Chichicastenango. The traditionally woven fabrics worn by the flower women are elaborately brocaded and embroidered with designs and colors that reflect both ancient and modern influences. Note, however, that the flowerwoman's sweater of synthetic fabric, symbol of the encroachment of Western dress into Maya culture, mars the splendor of this display of Maya textile art.

It may be that when the Maya cease to use the ancient symbols on their clothing and textiles, their culture will have died; and they will indeed have been westernized. In the face of genocidal campaigns, planned dislocations, and forced assimilation into a hostile culture and environment, preserving these overt and material vestiges of culture becomes all important. The imposition of Western fashion, within this context, is no less than a subtle form of genocide.

But it is not just the mythical/religious symbolism reflected in Middle American textile and clothing design that renders its preservation essential if Indian cultures are to survive. The "text" of a weaving more often incorporates a broader theme: the worldview and basic institutions founded on that worldview that serve as the framework of Maya culture. Incorporated in native dress is the blueprint of an entire social system: agriculturally based, community oriented, and decidedly non-Western. Within this broader context, dress helps perpetuate divisions of labor that harken back to earlier periods of cultural development and achievement, when the Indian community offered its members— females included—a level of prosperity, security, and safety that no longer exists, except in the most remote areas.

From ancient times, a woman's life revolved around weaving. The technology and skills used in this all-important female activity were, like the designs and colors they incorporated, gifts of the gods. In ancient codices, Ix Chel, the Mother Goddess, is depicted sitting at her backstrap loom, one end tied to a tree, the other around her waist, her shuttle in hand. According to legend, Ix Chel first attracted the attentions of the sun god by her weaving, and from their union was produced a daughter, Ixchebel Yax, patroness of embroidery. Young Maya girls still pray to Ix Chel, patroness of weaving, for skill with the loom sufficient to attract them good husbands, and some continue to use the bone needle of Ixchebel Yax to create elaborately embroidered huipiles. To the Westerner, this link between industry and myth signifies a level of inefficiency and ignorance that rightfully, in accordance with the Judeo-Christian and capitalist world view, targets a people for exploita-

tion. To the Maya, however, it represents a continued bond between the people and their tribal gods that is perceived by many as their only hope and protection in an otherwise totally hostile environment. "Children, wherever you may be, do not abandon the crafts taught to you by Ixpiyacoc," the *Popol Vuh* exhorts them, "because they are crafts passed down to you from your forefathers. If you forget them, you will be betraying your lineage."[5] To sever such bonds would not only shatter the cosmic reality of the Maya but would upset the very institutions that have helped preserve them as a culture. Although the affluence of others might be enhanced by the destruction of traditional Maya ways, what hope of affluence and harmony remains for the Maya people today and in the future may well rest on their preserving certain divisions of labor and economies upon which their ancient affluent culture rested.

In ancient times, as today, women were responsible for clothing themselves and their families and for producing the exquisitely made textiles that adorned priests and temples. As mothers, they were responsible for passing their skills on to their daughters, whose status in the community rested largely on their skill as weavers. On the basis of their skill, they could, regardless of class, gain prestige and fame. The material from which they wove their cloth and the dye plants they used to color it varied from region to region, but the weaving tools and techniques they used and the style of garments they wore were fairly standardized. Thus it was the individual skill of the weaver that served to distinguish one garment from another, not innovations in style. Weaving, then, provided not only an essential economic commodity (textiles having been valuable trade items long before the Conquest) but provided as well for a degree of egalitarianism and female mobility that is impressive even by modern standards. In contrast with the extreme "machismo" and socioeconomic disequilibrium that characterize mainstream Latin American culture, such a system seems far less inefficient and born of ignorance.

The construction and tailoring of native garb has always been of the simplest kind; but the textiles of which that garb is made are the product of a complex technology, by which are woven into each piece the threads of a harmonious and affluent village economy. Through weaving and textile design the ancient American was able to perpetuate symbols and designs that reflected the Indian view of the cosmos and that clearly proclaimed the status and role of the wearer and the weaver. Although Indian dress has changed somewhat over the past half-millennium, it remains an essential expression of cultural continuity.[6]

CONTEMPORARY PATTERNS OF DRESS

Rarely, however, do modern indigenous people completely preserve the ancient style of dress. Even the primitive Lacandon of the Usumacinta River region that separates Mexico and Guatemala have eschewed their traditional bark fiber garments for tunics of cotton—which they wear with high plastic boots for trips to town. When Europeans invaded and conquered the New World, they imposed their manner of dress and customs upon the native peoples of the region. In Mesoamerica, as elsewhere in Spanish America, Spaniards replaced the native elite classes and assumed all power and access to wealth. The Indian assumed the lowest position in society, although always with the option of rising above his humble status merely by assuming the look of the Spaniard. Those who chose to retain their Indian identity paid a heavy price.

Despite this, important vestiges of ancient dress remain, particularly in the Maya heartland. These are most evident in women's dress, which more clearly reflects a pre-Colombian tradition. But they are not lost in the typical male garb. True, in all but the most conservative villages and among older Maya males, the ancient turbanlike head covering (the "tzut") has been replaced by the ubiquitous cowboy hat; and the traditional sandal, often quite elaborate if the wearer were a nobleman, has in most of the region been replaced by shoes and boots of Western design and construction (including, alas, plastic). Nonetheless, in the southern Mexican state of Chiapas, Maya males continue

to wear ribbon-strewn straw hats that serve as the post-Colombian equivalent of ancient plumed headdresses, and brightly colored textiles of assorted design continue to distinguish members of one village from another. In Guatemala, it is not unusual to see village men wearing long pants, a Western-inspired garment, made of handwoven Maya fabric and topped with an overpant that resembles the peculiar, short, "eared" trousers of ancient times, the symbols on which identify the male's age group and status in the community.

A visit to any major marketplace in the Guatemalan highlands will reveal the degree to which traditional male garb has been preserved, on the one hand, and has given way to Western influences on the other. In this scene women wear the traditional dress of their village, while the men display a mixture of Western and Maya dress. Their woven short pants and skirt reflect their village and cultural ties, but to this traditional garb they have added Western shirts and the ubiquitous cowboy hat. Some young men have clearly adopted Western dress to the exclusion of any traditional items. For them, as for many, the pressures of modern commercial relations have led to the complete abandonment of traditional dress. For others, the transition has been less complete. Despite some significant additions and modifications, most men preserve key elements of their indigenous heritage through their dress and distinguish themselves from their more Western-influenced compatriots. They are Maya first and Guatemalan second. However, since, traditionally, it has been the indigenous male who has interacted most with Spaniards and "ladinos," often against his will, it is not surprising that male dress should reflect a strong Western influence.[7]

Women's costume has changed little since ancient times. The costume of a conservative Maya woman still consists of a traditional upper garment, the huipil; a wraparound skirt, or "corte"; a woven belt; and a head covering or braid wrap. In the more conservative villages of Mexico and Guatemala, Indian women continue to produce the textiles for these garments on backstrap looms identical to those employed by their earliest ancestors. These looms are light and portable enough to allow a woman to use them when attending to other chores, like tending sheep or caring for home and family. They are also versatile. On a backstrap loom, a woman can produce intricate designs using complicated techniques impossible to replicate on commercial looms. Even a woman of the simplest means can produce a fabric of great intricacy. A textile technique known as brocade allows the Indian woman to weave designs and symbols of ancient origin into the cloth itself. From the textile emerge images of gods and animals who give fertility to the earth, protect the growth of corn, and symbolize the Maya cosmology. Women who devote their lives to brocade and become skillful in the complicated techniques and symbolism it incorporates are venerated. It is through them that ancient myths, symbols, and visions of the cosmos are preserved. To her weaving skills a woman may also add her skill in embroidery, as she embellishes the seams and borders of her simply constructed garments with traditional designs of great complexity and beauty.[8]

Although dress and class are no longer as indistinguishable as they were in ancient times, traditional village costumes still reflect slight differences in status and wealth. Officeholders generally wear elaborate costumes for ceremonial occasions, and often put themselves in debt to do so. In general, though, costume reflects not rank but village affiliation. In less conservative villages and towns, men and women alike have borrowed freely from Western fashion. In addition to garments of Western origin, one sees costumes of machine-made textiles, sometimes machine-embroidered, and incorporating designs of nonindigenous origin. In these places Indian identity is threatened.

In the more traditional villages, this is not the case. Each village has its distinctly colored and patterned costume, in which it takes great pride. Although once a means of distinguishing combatants in war, this custom serves today not only to foster pride and solidarity within villages but also to promote pride and solidarity among Indian peoples who are fighting for cultural survival. In Guatemala, where almost 300 distinctive village costumes have been identified, Maya Indian culture remains strong even under the

impress of Western religion. A woman religious practitioner in native dress may serve as a symbol of religious syncretism in the Maya heartland, where the distinction between Catholicism and indigenous ritual and religion is blurred. Note that in her role of "chuchkajau" (independent native religious practitioner) she displays more of the Indian than Western influence. Her dress is traditional Maya.

But Maya culture is severely threatened. In much of Middle America the Indian has been forced to assimilate into mixed-blood, Western-based society. Those who have chosen to preserve their ancient customs and way of life have been relegated to the lowest levels of the socioeconomic scale. Increasingly, that position alone singles them out for physical destruction.

DRESS AND CULTURAL SURVIVAL

There is no more obvious expression of Indian identity than costume. Perhaps for that reason, so many groups intent on influencing or controlling Indian peoples have attempted to alter their patterns of dress. First the missionary, intent on imposing his religion on the peoples of the New World, forced the Indian to dress like a Christian (who, by some strange coincidence, dressed like a European). Since then, land barons, armies, churches, and guerrilla rebels have attempted to do the same as part of a larger plan to change or adjust the Indians' relationship to their land.

At the heart of genocidal campaigns in Guatemala and elsewhere in this hemisphere is the threat of land reform inspired by the existence of culturally unified peoples who are tied to the land but increasingly landless. In Guatemala, some 80 percent of cultivated land is owned by 2 percent of landowners, who, aided by centuries of institutionalized racism and the ever-increasing rapaciousness of the agro-export sector, continue to rob Indians of land that they need to survive. Agro-exports have made Guatemala one of the strongest economies in Central America. Yet 74 percent of the rural population, most of whom are Maya Indians, live below the level of absolute poverty, while 85 percent of rural households are landless or possess insufficient land to satisfy the basic food needs of their families.[9] Consequently, families routinely watch their children die of malnutrition and find themselves forced to labor on the *fincas* (plantations) of the wealthy Ladinos, separated from their communities and stripped of their dignity as members of a once great and still multitudinous race. On the fincas, Indians endure an appalling deficiency of food and health care, the cruelty of overseers, and backbreaking labor for wages that are criminally inadequate. They often return to communities that are systematically ravaged by the Guatemalan military, whose fear of Maya insurgency, born of deteriorating living standards and an increasingly threatened way of life, inspires them to commit unconscionable acts of brutality. In the last decade alone, the Guatemalan army has razed hundreds of Indian villages, forced tens of thousands of Indians into "model villages" that are little better than concentration camps, and subjected thousands of rural Maya, young and old, male and female, to rape, torture, and murder, often as public spectacle. Nominally, these atrocities are aimed at deterring the growth of "communism"; in reality, they are aimed at discouraging highly justified and growing calls for reform. It is a hope of the privileged class that by "ladinizing" the Indians they can better control them and assimilate them into systems that favor the interests of the few over the many.

For Ladinos it is enough to glorify ancient Maya culture, as a means of proclaiming ethnic pride and individuality in the face of foreign domination, while denigrating modern indigenous peoples whom they revile and treat as slaves. No better evidence of this Ladino paradox exists than the national Folklore Festival held every August in Cobán. The festival culminates in the selection of an Indian beauty queen. Contestants, selected earlier by the ladino authorities of towns throughout Guatemala, parade their distinct regional costumes before a largely foreign and non-Indian audience that flocks to Cobán to participate in this widely advertised celebration of national identity. For the contestants themselves, who are required by

law to travel from their villages to the festival at their own expense, the spectacle is often a source of humiliation and impoverishment. But for the Ladinos it is an opportunity to bask in the splendor of Maya textile art—among the best in the world—and a Maya heritage that they rarely associate with modern indigenous peoples about whom they prefer to remain ignorant.

Among those who are regularly drawn to this display of exquisite indigenous fashion are buyers and representatives of designers and clothing manufacturers from around the globe. For them, the festival provides a unique opportunity to view a living catalog of masterfully woven fabrics that can be purchased at astoundingly low prices and fashioned into some of the world's most expensive designer creations. That the weavers and wearers of these incomparable textiles are being exploited, perhaps to the point where their craft will eventually disappear, seems not to occur to these entrepreneurs, for whom the people and culture that produced such beauty are of little interest. Increasingly, Indians realize that as long as they remain unable to communicate with Ladinos in their own language or understand and work within the Ladino system they will be exploited and robbed of their land, their dignity, and their lives. Although the more conservative Maya still prefer isolation from Ladino society, they cannot escape the degradation of folk festivals in which they are reluctant participants or the brutality of military and civil forces bent on eliminating the call for reformed systems by exterminating the people who would most benefit from reforms.

Growing political activism among the Maya reflects their awareness that to learn about and work within the Ladino system does not require that the Indian *become* a Ladino. Indeed, it may only be through some emergence from cultural isolation and greater dialogue with the outside world that traditional Maya culture can be preserved in the future. It is a lesson of the Conquest that the Indian cannot defeat what he or she does not understand. In the last few years, rural Maya have become active in a burgeoning network of organizations established to deal with issues of labor and land reform, human rights abuses at the hands of the government and military, and the retrieval of bodies of "disappeared" family and community members.

Many of those involved in these organizations have been forced into exile. For them to leave the communites and land in which their Maya identity is rooted is a personal tragedy. But it has allowed them to bring their struggle to the attention of international organizations without whose support they will probably be unable to counter the genocidal campaigns of the government or accomplish reforms that will improve conditions for the Indian majority. These reluctant refugees proudly continue to wear their native Maya garb in the capitals of Europe and the Americas as proof that political activism need not threaten indigenous culture but may indeed be a means of preserving it.

There are those who believe that survival of traditional societies in the twenty-first century is impossible. The better-intentioned of these individuals believe that improving the lives of indigenous peoples is more important that preserving their cultures. Others believe that cultural survival is essential at any price. It is often said that the Maya spirit was never conquered, although the Indian was subjugated to Ladino rule. It is this undaunted spirit, kept alive and venerated in oral tradition and dress, that suggests a less radical solution to the problems that confront the Maya today. Survival of Indian culture in Guatemala and elsewhere in Latin America may depend, in the future, upon the ability of indigenous peoples to balance change with tradition. In Guatemala, this balance may be achieved by focusing both on radical, long-term political and social reforms (including land reform) and on increased integration of Indians into the commercial infrastructure of the nation.

Within this context, and assuming an ever increasing role in the battle for cultural survival through commercial integration, are the Maya women who produce the native garb that helps perpetuate their culture. Perhaps because of the male-centered nature of Spanish society, Maya women have escaped some of the exigencies imposed on Maya males. Being invisible, except when it benefits ladino culture to put them on display for tourists and entrepreneurs, Maya women have been able to retain their ancient crafts and costumes, even when in fairly regular contact with Westerners. The complex and central role of women in the village life and economy of the Maya has gone largely unnoticed by members of the mainstream culture; and, thus, it is only recently that they have begun to take notice of the growing number of weavers' cooperatives and female-run commercial enterprises through which Maya women may improve their own and their families' standard of living without sacrificing their culture in the process.

Decades of civil war and state-sanctioned genocide have catapulted women into realms of political and economic activism that were formerly closed to them (and largely unnecessary within the traditional balance of power structure of the village). Sheltered (or trapped) under the umbrella of a patriarchal ideology, Maya women have traditionally, and unobtrusively, shouldered a disproportionate burden of labor within the household, serving not only as household managers and agricultural laborers but as weavers and clothers of their people as well. They are, therefore, well positioned for assuming a dominant role in preserving Maya culture while at the same time working to achieve greater integration into the national economy, for, next to agriculture, the most important economic activity of the Maya is textile production. The growing demand for Maya textiles, so popular today in the fashion industry, has led to increased use of the foot loom, a method of textile production introduced by the Spanish and, until recently, used only by men. However, the best and most valuable cloth is still that produced (only by women) on the backstrap loom. The work of producing such pieces is slow and painstaking, but thanks to the creation of weaving cooperatives, women can, for the first time, receive a fair price for their efforts.

On the other hand, cooperatives are generally viewed as politically subversive. Although eliminating ladino middlemen is often enough to increase a weaver's earnings several times over, the reaction of those disaffected may be severe. After centuries, conditions established by the Spaniards have not ameliorated. Indians who wish to prosper or, indeed, subsist in the ladino economy are forced to adapt to the mainstream culture in ways that threaten their indigenous lifestyles, while those who wish to retain key elements of their culture find it increasingly perilous to do so. Today, the Western fashion industry collaborates in a process of oppression and exploitation that goes back centuries. Perhaps it does so unwittingly: first by sanctioning the encroachment of Western dress into non-Western cultures; and next through the co-optation of native textile arts into Western fashion. Co-optation need not signify exploitation, however. If, indeed, imitation is the purest form of compliment, then isn't it also a means of preserving cultures in danger of extinction?[10]

The fashion industry is a powerful special interest. Although it may not recognize itself as actively involved in international affairs, its involvement is considerable. Take the recent case of Liz Claiborne and the "model village" of Acul, in the Guatemalan highlands. In 1983, Acul became Guatemala's first "model village," an army-controlled enclave, inspired by U.S. counterinsurgency in Vietnam, and reviled by Indian and human rights advocates for whom it and others like it are little more than concentration camps. A year ago, Guatemalan officials discovered that the residents of this particular village were skilled at crocheting. They contacted executives of Liz Claiborne in New York, with whom they developed a project that would give the Maya of Acul "a chance at a brighter future."[11] Using seed money from the Guatemalan government, Claiborne and the government-sponsored National Fund for Peace developed a project to teach Acul villagers to redirect their skills toward hand-knitting sweaters for sale in the United States, where they would sell, with Claiborne labels, for up to $200 each. The villagers were to earn up to $40 per sweater, a great deal by regional standards. After two months of knitting, however, villagers were yet to receive any pay for their work, whereas their crocheting had brought them instant earnings. In addition, the sweaters they made, but did not design, did little to perpetuate Maya culture. While Guatemalan officials optimistically billed this project as one that could produce "as many as 20,000 jobs over five years," the people of Acul remained skeptical.[12] All in all, the project promised to do little for the Maya villagers; and Liz Claiborne, however unwittingly, had helped perpetuate the traditionally exploitive relationship between Native Americans and the fashion industry.

Projects like this one can, however, benefit Indians and the fashion industry alike. They can be designed to direct profits to Indians and not to middlemen. And they can be designed to promote the preservation of traditional designs and textile-making skills on which cultural survival in part rests. In the long run, the fashion industry will benefit from preserving important sources of quality textiles and artistic inspiration. To do so, though, will require a greater and more responsible involvement of the industry in the preservation of indigenous cultures. It will, above all, require a commitment on the part of the fashion industry to turn its international lobbying powers in a new direction. First, it must sensitize itself to the practices within the industry that may contribute to the exploitation, oppression, and even extermination of indigenous peoples. It should work hand in hand with organizations already committed to the cause of human rights and cultural survival for indigenous peoples. And, certainly, it should assist directly in the protection and proliferation of weavers' cooperatives, through which women can produce and market their textiles while, at the same time, preserving and perpetuating the ancient designs and techniques that periodically "revitalize" haute couture.

The future of indigenous cultures in the Americas is by no means assured. Already, in many nations of Latin America, Indian identity has disappeared. In other nations of the region, it is severely threatened. The survival of indigenous culture depends, in great part, on the Indians' ability to preserve its essential elements, like dress, while at the same time adapting more and more to the political and economic exigencies of the times. Nothing proclaims the tenacity of Indian cultures more than their refusal to succumb to the hegemony of the West in matters of style and dress. And nowhere is that tenacity more evident than in Guatemala.

In her internationally acclaimed autobiography, Maya political activist Rigoberta Menchú states that "what hurts Indians most is that our costumes are considered beautiful, but it's as if the person wearing it didn't exist."[13] Rigoberta expresses the desire of all Indians in Latin America that they be accorded the respect and opportunity that is their right as human beings and as descendants of once-great civilizations.

After five hundred years, voices like Rigoberta's are being heard. For over a decade, Rigoberta has championed Indian rights from exile. During that time she has continued to wear the traditional dress of her Guatemalan Highlands village. Her style has been a vital part of her message. Rigoberta Menchú's receipt of the 1992 Nobel Peace Prize attests not only to her own tenacity and devotion to culture but to that of all Native Americans. Tradition tells us that when Indians stop wearing their native garb they will have lost their culture. Then they will truly not exist. But as long as they preserve the fashions of their ancestors, their culture survives—until better times.

Notes

1. For excellent historical analyses of the role and plight of Indians in Latin America generally and Middle America specifically, see E. Bradford Burns, *Latin America: A Concise Interpretive History*, 5th ed. (Englewood Cliffs, NJ.: Prentice Hall, 1990), and Benjamin Keen, *A History of Latin America*, 4th ed. (Boston: Houghton Mifflin, 1992).

2. Recent general data about Guatemala and other Indo-American nations may be obtained through any of the many international human rights organizations dedicated to the protection of indigenous peoples in the Americas and elsewhere. Always reliable sources are Amnesty International and Americas Watch.

3. On the link between Western fashion, modernity and capitalism, see Elizabeth Wilson, *Adorned in Dreams: Fashion and Modernity* (London: Virago, 1975).

4. *Popol Vuh: The Sacred Book of the Ancient Quiché Maya*, English version by Delia Goetz and Sylvanus G. Morley, from the translation of Adrián Recinos (Norman: University of Oklahoma Press, 1983).

5. Quoted in Elisabeth Burgos-Debray, ed., *I...Rigoberta Menchú: An Indian Woman in Guatemala*, trans. Ann Wright (New York: Verso, 1984), 59.

6. For excellent discussions of the cultural and social significance of Indian dress in Middle America, see Donald and Dorothy Cordy, *Mexican Indian Costumes* (Austin: University of Texas Press, 1978), and Sheldon Annis, *God and Production in a Guatemalan Town* (Austin: University of Texas Press, 1987).

7. In the narrowest sense, *ladino* refers to persons of mixed race or Indians who speak Spanish as their primary language and wear Western garb. In a broader sense, it refers to anyone who represents a system that oppresses the Indian.

8. For outstanding pictorial analyses of Maya dress, see Carmen L. Pettersen, *The Maya of Guatemala: Their Life and Dress* (Seattle: University of Washington Press, 1976), and Linda Asturias de Barrios, *Comalpa: El Traje y Su Significado* (Guatemala: Ediciones del Museo Ixchel, 1985).

9. These figures come from UNICEF, *State of the World's Children*, 1989, and the Worldwatch Institute.

10. An interesting case in point is that of artist Frida Kahlo, who wore native Indian garb as a means of discovering her own and the collective Mexican identity.

11. See Tim Johnson, "Sweater-knitting Project Giving Guatemalans Hope for Better Life," *The Miami Herald*, June 29, 1992, 8A.

12. Ibid.

13. Burgos-Debray, ed., *I...Rigoberta Menchú*, 204.

Paris or Perish

1. What political statements do the Maya of Guatemala make when they wear traditional dress and refuse to adopt modern styles?

2. How do the Mayan men and women differ in their adoption of traditional Mayan dress? What does this suggest about their roles?

71   Ralph Lauren: The Emperor Has Clothes

Susan Caminiti

On a brilliantly sunny summer afternoon, the kind of day people dream about to get them through the dreary frigid winter, we're in a Manhattan office building trying to figure out where Ralph Lauren will sit. Actually, we're in Lauren's small, all-white office on Madison Avenue, and with two large, lovely chairs and a big cushy couch laid out before us, the answer is far from obvious. Rather than chance some GIANT FAUX PAS by claiming his favorite spot as our own, we bravely put the question to him: "Mr. Lauren, is there a particular place you'd like to sit?" His response: "Wherever the light makes me look best."

That's Ralph. For nearly 30 years Lauren, 57, has earned a handsome living showing Americans (men especially) how to look good, using himself as the model. And therein lies a puzzle.

Somehow Lauren, who thinks it's fine for men to wear (as he does) black velvet slippers in the office, has become the designer of choice for guys to whom the mere *mention* of velvet slippers causes first one and then the other eyebrow to be raised. Men with no tolerance for velvet slippers in the office, at home, in the tool shed, or on the moon. Men whose feelings toward men who *do* wear velvet slippers may fairly be expressed as: Yikes!

Then consider Ralph in his Rancher guise. Does this look like any real rancher of your acquaintance? Any rancher, that is, who's willing

to break either a sweat or a few vertebrae chasing after cattle? Real cowboys have nicknames for such ranchers. Ralph's might be "Hopalong Casually."

And yet mainstream guys bought $2.7 billion in suits, shirts, ties, and other Ralph Lauren garments last year. Add in women's clothes, eyeglasses, perfume, bedsheets, dinner plates, leather couches, and the rest, and consumers around the globe spent some $5 billion on Lauren goods—making him the best-selling designer in the world. Somehow Lauren—*faux* cowboy, relentless Anglophile, exponent of yachting and polo—has come to occupy the kind of solid middle ground that Brooks Brothers did in the 1950s: He is the default fashion choice for men who don't care a whole lot about fashion but nevertheless want to look good in office clothes. "Buying Ralph is like buying a Maytag," says Hal Reiter, president of the executive search firm Herbert Mines Associates in New York, who owns six pairs of Ralph Lauren trousers and two Ralph Lauren suits. "He's an established brand that stands for reliability and quality."

Let other designers—Italians, handbag-toting Frenchmen—urge kilts and capes and corduroy plus fours upon an impressionable public. Lauren stands manfully above the fray, upholding simple, classic good looks (allowing for occasional lapses like those slippers). Risky dressing? Not for Ralph. He is the nation's leading proponent of safe slacks.

"Ralph's world is not unapproachable or scary," says Neil Kraft, former head of advertising for Calvin Klein. "Everything is done with the promise of good taste." And derivative idealism. When Lauren creates the look of an English country home, the panache of a Savile Row suit, or the luster of some Western belt belonging to an imaginary rancher, his version is always a little cleaner, a little brighter, just a touch more polished. He doesn't sell socks; he sells his very mildly fevered (98.7°) dream.

Could Martha Stewart have existed without Ralph? He blazed the trail of "lifestyle" merchandising, selling not just items but his own personal context—and at a premium price, no less—at a time when such things weren't done. He was the first fashion designer to have his own stores. He was the first to sell not only the suit you wear to work but the pajamas you wear to bed and the sheets you sleep on. And indeed, before Martha was Martha, she made gift baskets for Lauren's clientele in the 1980s. "When people buy his products, it gives them the feeling of having class and stature," she says. "They're buying a piece of his world."

The price of admission is relatively high, as befits a business with aspiration at its soul. A Polo suit might sell for $600 to $900; a woman's blazer for $1,200; a pair of socks, $11; a leather sofa, $9,000. Even so, there are enough customers to sustain 116 freestanding Polo/Ralph Lauren stores, 62 discount outlets, and some 1,300 boutiques inside department stores all over the world. A new, 45,000-square-foot store—the length of an entire city block—is scheduled to open in London, of all places, late next year.

Since 1993, Polo/Ralph Lauren's revenue—including its share of worldwide licensing income—has increased 30%, to some $900 million; operating profit has grown nearly 70%, to around $110 million. Not surprisingly, perhaps, the buzz is that Ralph is contemplating going public. Over the past year investors have been attracted to designers and department stores like lint to a sweater: Witness such high-profile IPOs as Gucci and Saks Fifth Avenue. In June, Donna Karan finally dropped the veil. Now, with the possible exception of Calvin Klein, no private company gets investment bankers' mouths watering quite like Lauren.

Lauren himself admits an IPO is "in the realm of possibility," but adds "I doubt if I'm going to do it. I like my privacy. I have no reason to do it unless I want to buy something else. And I sort of have everything I want."

Darn it, he pretty much does. His car collection includes a 1929 Blower Bentley, a 1937 Alfa Romeo, a 1938 Bugatti, and a 1962 Ferrari GTO. He has a 13,748-acre ranch in Colorado, a duplex apartment on Fifth Avenue in Manhattan, beachfront homes in Jamaica and Long Island, a 240-acre estate in Bedford, New York—and a company-owned Gulfstream II to get from one home to another. His estimated net worth? Better than $1 billion.

Lauren has Goldman Sachs largely to thank for his current comfort. Two years ago, when Polo/Ralph Lauren needed money to open new stores and overhaul older ones, it raised $135 million by selling a 28.5% stake to the investment house.

With its minority stake, Goldman doesn't get involved in the day-to-day running of the business. "They're in my hands, I'm not in theirs," Lauren says firmly. But few on Wall Street believe Goldman isn't needling Lauren for an IPO. Says Richard Friedman, the partner at Goldman who heads GS Capital Partners, the investment pool that purchased Polo: "Both Ralph Lauren and Goldman Sachs would be remiss in not looking at the possibility. But there's no pressing need to do one other than the strength of the market."

How does Lauren keep coining money? His accomplishment depends partly on magic, mostly on machinery. The magic part he expresses as a question: "Did you ever see a man or a woman walk into a room and they look great, but you don't know exactly why they do? You just know that you want to look like that?"

The machine is driven by licensing. No fewer than 26 companies pay to make, ship, and advertise Lauren's goods. Lauren provides the design and creative talent, getting in return a cut of sales (around 6%) plus minimum guaranteed payments. Polo/Ralph Lauren still manufactures its top-of-the-line men's and women's clothes, but the bulk of its profit comes from these licensing agreements. Example: Cosmair, a division of L'Oréal, which makes Lauren scents, is one of the biggest licensees; fragrance industry expert Allan Mottus figures this one license could put as much as $20 million in Lauren's pocket this year alone. He sews not much, but damn if Ralph don't reap!

Just last August, Lauren launched two big new licensing ventures, Polo jeans and a line of women's clothing called Lauren. Both are priced far below what Lauren's clothes have sold for in the past—jeans at roughly $48, women's pants and jackets mostly below $250. The idea is to reach a whole new category of customer, the ones who couldn't afford Ralph Lauren before.

Both the jeans and the Lauren line are scoring well with shoppers; the latter has retailers particularly giddy. "It's just been remarkable. Overwhelming," says LaVelle Olexa, a senior vice president at Lord & Taylor. "The clothes hit the floor, and they just go." A big part of the attraction is that consumers are in love with status brands again, especially if they can get them for under four figures. The Lauren line features Ralph's best-known styles—crested navy blazers, tartan plaid skirts, and crisp oxford shirts—but all done up in less expensive fabrics with fewer details.

Other designers have gone down the licensing road, of course, and quite a number have lurched into a ditch when they let their licensees get control of their brand. That isn't likely to happen to Lauren: His need to protect everything bearing on his company's image, and his own, is palpable, unsleeping, electric, scary. While we were shooting the studio photographs for this story, Lauren weighed in on lighting, backdrops, props—even on the height of the tripod holding the camera taking his picture. (He stands about 5 foot 6.)

More than any other designer, he grasped early the importance of protecting his brand. Back in 1967, as he struggled to build a business out of his line of wide men's ties, he refused to sell to Bloomingdale's. The retailer wanted him to make the ties narrower and take his name off the label. "We're talking a quarter of an inch. That's all they wanted," Lauren explains. "And as for my name being on them, well, no one could care less who Ralph Lauren was. But I said no. When I left the store, I thought, 'What am I, crazy?' I was dying to sell Bloomingdale's, but I didn't because I really wanted to do what I believed in." Months later, Bloomingdale's came knocking on Lauren's door. It saw how briskly his ties were selling in competitors' stores and agreed to carry the ties exactly as Lauren had designed them.

Emboldened by this early success, Lauren next designed a line of men's shirts, then turned his attention to suits, favoring wide lapels—to go along with his ties—and natural shoulders. It wasn't long before Lauren branched off into women's clothes (partly to suit the tastes of his wife, Ricky).

In 1971 he opened the first Polo/Ralph Lauren store on Rodeo Drive in Beverly Hills. More stores soon followed.

In 1983 he started his home collection of sheets, towels, flatware, and furniture. Rather than simply putting out new colors or patterns like others in the field, Lauren created products that revolved around themes, like New England Cottage and English Countryside. The recent Serape collection, for instance, features aged solid-oak tables and chests as well as distressed leather chairs and couches tooled, as the brochure points out, "in the tradition of fine leather boot making."

"I bought some Ralph Lauren sheets last year, and I just love them," says Sheri Kersch-Schultz, wife of Starbucks founder Howard Schultz, from their summer home in New York's tony East Hampton. "And he has a sleigh bed that is just to die for."

The most recent addition to the home line: paint, produced under license by Sherwin-Williams. "I was a little skeptical at first," says Bernard Marcus, CEO of Home Depot, whose stores have carried the line since early this year. "But we're happy with the progress it's making. When I first heard about it, I thought it was just paint with a big designer name on it."

That's exactly what it is.

"Look," says Mort Kaplan, head of Creative Licensing, a firm that brings together licensing partners, "I'm sure the paint is good, but azure blue is azure blue is azure blue. The difference here is that Ralph Lauren stands for something. He knows how to package it, how to set it up in stores so it conveys his image." Walk into any Home Depot, and you'll see what Kaplan means: Behind each mixing counter stands a Ralph display, all lit up. Brochures group paint hues by theme—Safari, Desert Hollywood, Santa Fe—and show not just paint swatches but evocative bits of Laurentian context: a horse, a sideboard, a pair of satin gloves. One brochure displays 32 shades of white. Don't laugh: Lauren's home furnishings business rings up retail sales of $535 million a year worldwide, vastly outselling any other designer's.

Ever since his first in-store shop opened in Bloomingdale's in 1971, Lauren has insisted that retailers sell his goods *his* way, in boutiques set up with his props and fixtures. Most of the time he gets what he wants. Says Kenneth Walker, an architect who has worked for department stores installing Polo in-store shops: "Ralph's people are hard but fair. They don't throw hissy fits, but they know exactly what they want." And they walk when they don't get it. Last year when Bergdorf Goodman's men's store in New York refused to build a Polo boutique to the company's specifications, Lauren pulled his business from the store.

Nowhere is his need for image control as evident as in his flagship store at 72nd Street and Madison Avenue in Manhattan. The store, opened in 1986 in the landmark Rhinelander Mansion, marked the first time Lauren had gathered all his goods under one (slate) roof. He oversees presentation, service, décor, even fragrance (which, the day *Fortune* visited, seemed to be a compound of patchouli, cloves, and leather-bound sets of Scott's Waverley Novels).

The store is quite simply over the top in its Englishness, lacking only an Anglican bishop, a Simpson's meat cart, and Dr. Johnson buried under the tie counter. Practically everything is for sale. If, for instance, you should find yourself humming a Ralph-sanctioned tune while shop-

ping ("Pennies From Heaven" was playing as we warmed ourselves against the air conditioning's chill, rubbing our hands beside a gas-fired hearth), $15 buys it: Ralph Lauren's *Black Tie Collection* CD from Sony.

Looking the place over, it's a wonder there's a single cricket bat left in England—or set of sculling oars, or antlers, or silver croquet trophy, or oil painting of a dog smoking a pipe. (Where does all this stuff come from? It's just as you suspected all along: Lauren has a giant warehouse in New Jersey jammed with props and antiques. A team of 75 people has traveled the world and filled the 25,000-square-foot space with antique mahogany chests, hundreds of bed frames, antique Persian rugs, a hay bale, thousands of hardcover books, golf clubs, baseballs, a lobster trap, an elk's head, polo helmets, saddles, suitcases, ship's wheels, and chunks of coral. Lauren periodically prunes the inventory: Last year a pair of tapestry-upholstered Queen Anne walnut settees, circa 1710, sold for $54,625 at Sotheby's.)

With access to a corporate attic like that, the 72nd Street flagship store makes an indelible impression—but not money. A former high-ranking Polo executive figures that what with fresh flowers, antiques, blazing gas hearths, and payments on a long-term lease, the place loses $1 million a month. "I'm not going to comment on exact numbers," says vice chairman Michael Newman. "I can tell you that it meets the budget we plan for it. When I look at it that way, the fact [the store loses money] doesn't trouble me."

The store does trouble some WASPs who see it as a rip-off of their heritage. Explains one patrician young woman: "It's like this: People who buy Ralph Lauren are trying to keep up with the Joneses. We *are* the Joneses." Among her set, Lauren will never be anything more than a parvenu. It will be easier for his camel's-hair coat to go through the eye of a needle than for Ralph to get invited to Newport (as if that mattered to him).

Which raises the question: Who is he?

Lauren was born Ralph Lifshitz in the Bronx. His father was an artist who painted houses for a living; his mother raised the kids (Ralph was the youngest of four). He played stickball, dated girls, did all the normal stuff. He didn't grow up sketching clothes, and he didn't go to fashion school. "I don't know, from the time I was 12 years old I looked cool," he explains. "My father was a painter, so maybe I got some sense of color from him. I do know that whatever I had on, other kids would say, 'Hey, where'd you get that?'"

As he got older and worked after school Lauren would use his paychecks to buy expensive clothes. "If I saved $100 to buy a suit, which in those days was a lot of money, my parents would say, 'Why didn't you go to this place? It's cheaper.' And I would say no."

Lauren pursued a business degree at City College in Manhattan, taking night classes, but dropped out after two years. He worked as a salesman for two glove companies and then for tie manufacturer A. Rivetz & Co. While working at Rivetz he started designing his wide ties, and before long he decided to go into business for himself. In 1968, Norman Hilton, a clothing company executive, took a chance on Lauren and backed him with a $50,000 loan. Lauren called his company Polo Fashions, a name that he and his brother Jerry (now executive vice president of Polo men's design) liked because it connoted money, style, and a sort of international mystique.

By the early 1970s sales were nearly $4 million, and the company was expanding too quickly. Lauren bought out Norman Hilton's stake and hired a boyhood chum as his treasurer and CFO. The friend turned out to be "somewhat in over his head," Lauren says, and the business, though booking lots of orders, was hemorrhaging money.

To save the company, Lauren poured in his life savings—$150,000—and hired one of Hilton's key executives, Peter Strom, to help run it. Strom liked Lauren and agreed to come aboard if Lauren gave him a 10% equity stake in the business. "When I joined the company, it had 800 accounts, was doing about $5 million in sales, and wasn't making a dime," recalls Strom, who retired from Polo in April 1995. "I thought we'd be lucky if we ever broke $20 million in sales," he says. "Ralph loves to remind me that I said that."

There wasn't really any breakthrough that thrust Lauren's clothing into the nation's fashion consciousness; the closest his work came to making a splash was when Diane Keaton wore his clothing in *Annie Hall*. Lauren did runway shows, but rather than make the models look like hookers from space, he dressed them in clothing you could wear to the office. From one year to the next, changes were of degree, not of kind. In retrospect, he was formulating the Ralph Doctrine: clothing that isn't shocking, just incrementally nicer, with snob appeal prominently in the weave.

That's his same m.o. today, of course, and its latest expression is his Purple Label line of "mostly handmade" suits, shirts, and ties. In the late 1980s, during the height of Giorgio Armani and the Italian power suit look, Polo's preppy garments started to look a little dull. "Polo had been the power suit back in the early 1980s," concedes Lance Isham, head of Lauren's men's wear business. "But it was difficult to hold onto that because of the influence from Italy." Lauren puts it another way: "I was selling the Madison Avenue and Wall Street guys, and Armani was selling the Hollywood agents—the Mike Ovitzes of the world."

Lauren saw that his suit business was stagnating. "I wanted something not Italian-looking, just more sophisticated." He envisioned elegant handsewn garments cut from fine fabrics, then shaped closer to the body. Lauren wanted a tasteful look for someone with a well-toned body who isn't shy about showing it off—himself, in other words.

Buttons wouldn't just be sewn onto jacket sleeves but would have real buttonholes. (We wondered: Does that really make the suit fit any better? No, admits Stanley Tucker, fashion director at Saks Fifth Avenue in New York. "It's just a little bit of snobbism. If you leave one of the buttons undone and someone notices, they'll see you have actual buttonholes. It's just very Savile Row.")

It's those incremental touches, however, that make Ralph Ralph. Some Purple Label suits, for example, sport a discreet tab on the top of their left lapel. "That's a wind tab," explained a salesman in the flagship store. A wind tab? we asked. "That's so that when you're walking home from church across the moors on a windy day, you can pull that lapel over and button it to a corresponding button on the jacket collar." Oh.

A suit like that costs an ungodly amount, of course: between $1,500 and $2,500. But like the flagship store itself, the Purple Label line is intended more to cast a long shadow of opulence than to be much of a moneymaker.

How does Lauren come up with a thing like a wind tab? In New York City and elsewhere, Lauren's scouts comb vintage clothing shops, looking for garments (or for details on garments) that they think Ralph might like. Some of them he does. After experiment and prototyping, an old green-striped broadcloth shirt from the 1930s, say, may get a new lease on life.

Ralph has had his share of duds. For more than a decade, for instance, he has been stumped by—of all things—blue jeans. His first try at that market, in partnership with the Gap in the late 1970s, bombed badly. One Gap executive says of the venture: "Every possible mistake that could have been made, was made." Over the years Lauren made other blunders: Either the jeans were cut too narrow for women of normal size (meaning those who actually possess hips) or deliveries were late or the products were not properly merchandised in the stores.

Lauren's last foray was three years ago with a line of weathered, vintage-looking jeans and shirts called Double RL, named after his ranch in Colorado (which is short for Ralph and Ricky Lauren). These clothes, aimed at the college crowd, turned out to be way overpriced. Jeans and flannel shirts cost as much as $78, and weathered leather jackets upwards of $300. "They totally misjudged the demographics," says Jerry Magnin, owner of the Polo/Ralph Lauren store in Beverly Hills.

This fall Lauren is trying again, as you may have noticed: He's got a whopping $20 million advertising budget, provided by Sun Apparel, the licensee for Polo jeans. The print ads are visually startling: They feature clean-cut, healthy-looking men and women, without tattoos or nose rings, who aren't naked, underage, or anorexic, and don't grope one another. Calvin Klein won't be making any noise about Lauren stealing his ideas. Says Lauren: "Look, I'm not anti-sex. But what's sexy to younger people may not be sexy to everyone else. It might be the right time not to cater to the kids."

Lauren surrounds himself with seasoned executives, most of whom have been with him for years—a rarity in the fashion business. They understand what Lauren wants, usually without his having to spell it out. Says Buffy Birrittella, senior vice president of women's designs and a 25-year veteran of the company: "When Ralph says he wants something white, I know what kind of white he means."

Or the kind of brown. Last year Birrittella, Lauren, and a few other executives were in Europe looking for fabrics that would be used for the fall clothes now in the stores. During this particular trip, they felt they had been seeing way too much of one color: gray. Says Birrittella: "I don't know why I said it first—sometimes Ralph will feel something first—but I just looked at him and said, 'Brown.' And he said, 'Yeah, I'm feeling brown too.' We were just both…well, just feeling brown." As we said before, it ain't all science.

A question of authenticity has dogged Lauren much of his career. Chatting with him late one sunny afternoon on the porch of his Colorado ranch house, it's clear he's weary of the charge that somehow his work, and by extension his life, are phony.

"I slept in a room with two brothers growing up," he recalls. "I couldn't wait for one of them to move out so I could have half the drawers. That molded me. But do I want to live like that today? No, I don't. I don't think it's a comfortable way to live. So is it phony, then, to say I want to live out west, or I want to live in the country? If you're born in the Bronx, does that mean you have to stay in the Bronx?

"I've tried to do things honorably in my business. I think I've added something to America. I don't rip people off. I don't downgrade children," he says getting a parting dig at Calvin Klein. "I try to give people a clean, aspirational quality, with no bullshit. Where's the negative in that?"

To which we answer: There isn't one. Our economy is kept wound by aspirations of the sort young Ralph held (hell, old Ralph holds). No wonder business people like to buy his clothing: In Lauren they recognize a brother under the skin (those velvet slippers notwithstanding).

Ralph Lauren: The Emperor Has Clothes

1. How has Ralph Lauren strategically produced the meaning of style for his customers?

2. Does Lauren dictate to his customers, or does he create style by some other process?

3. How are micro- and macro-levels involved in Ralph Lauren's marketing of style?

72 Seinfeld and the *Real* John Peterman

Don Edwards

Welcome to holiday shopping at the only store in Lexington where the owner gets an advance look at "Seinfeld" scripts because he's part of the show.

Yes, it's John Peterman, founder of the upscale image mail-order business and the fictional Elaine character's employer on "Seinfeld."

"We see our stuff on 'Seinfeld' all the time," said Mindy Keller, retail director of J. Peterman Co. "The apparel, the things in Elaine's office.

"Jerry Seinfeld and Julia Louis-Dreyfus (who plays Elaine) were both Peterman catalog customers before that (Peterman story line) began."

Cartoonist Garry Trudeau once skewered the J. Peterman catalog by calling it "J. Pretentious."

And the tone on Seinfeld is definitely satirical, with fictional Peterman catalog items such as "the urban sombrero" and a self-absorbed Peterman played by a silver-haired actor.

Even the real Peterman doesn't like the "Seinfeld" Peterman.

"He portrays John as—what were John's exact words?—'quite a jerk,'" Keller said. "But when 37 million people hear your name on TV every week, it's got to be good for business."

Peterman receives advance scripts from the "Seinfeld" producers "to see if he has any objections to anything." On one show, the fictional Peterman's mother died. The real Peterman called his mother to warn her of her coming demise, said Keller.

Some customers think that the real Peterman plays himself on the show. Keller assures them that the real Peterman is far too busy with his company to have time for acting on TV.

Even the real Seinfeld might think twice about the price of the major item in this year's Peterman holiday catalog:

A 1930 Bugatti Type 50 that sells for $525,000.

"It's created a lot of interest," Keller said of the vintage auto. "We've had many inquiries about it."

More affordable are the English racing goggles ($120) that go with it.

Or the Schwinn "deluxe cruiser chair" with real handlebar grips and a bicycle horn for $1,298.

Not to mention a $220 coat that looks like the one Lauren Bacall used to wear in old movies with Humphrey Bogart. And for $550 there's a dead ringer of the coat that Julie Christie wore in the movie *Doctor Zhivago*.

And though Peterman doesn't act, he has a daughter who does. That's how he met Broadway star Tommy Tune, who, on the day they met, was wearing a shirt that Peterman liked.

Reprinted with permission of the *Lexington Herald Leader*.

Now it's in the catalog as "The Tommy Tune Shirt" ($48). In "brown houndstooth, umber plaid or charcoal glen plaid."

For football fans, there's a "Bear Bryant Coat" ($195) that looks like something the former UK coach might have worn on the sidelines of some long-ago game.

But most of the imagery in Peterman's merchandise comes from the nostalgic, romantic side of Hollywood—old movies that gave millions of ordinary people a peek at glamour for the price of a ticket.

Keller said that Peterman's perceives its customers as "well-educated or well-traveled, who are looking for the unique or unusual and are leaders rather than followers."

Of course, there's another point of view about "image-catalog" shoppers—that such catalogs are for people who have no real style of their own, but desperately want to buy somebody else's.

No one knows for sure—Seinfeld, Peterman or even Tommy Tune.

DISCUSSION QUESTIONS

Seinfeld and the Real John Peterman

1. Why does the J. Peterman catalog retailer feel that the spoof of their founder and company on the Seinfeld show did not hurt their company?

2. How is this an example of media contributing to meaning of styles? What did the Seinfeld show contribute to these meanings?

73 Marketing Street Culture: Bringing Hip-Hop Style to the Mainstream

by Marc Spiegler

The Scene: Martha's Vineyard, Massachusetts, a bastion of the white East Coast establishment. A teenaged boy saunters down the street, his gait and attitude embodying adolescent rebellion. Baggy jeans sag atop over-designed sneakers, gold hoops adorn both ears, and a baseball cap shields his eyes. On his chest, a Tommy Hilfiger shirt sports the designer's distinctive pairing of blue, red, and white rectangles.

Four years ago, this outfit would have been unimaginable to this cool teen; only his clean-cut, country-club peers sported Hilfiger clothes. What linked the previously preppy Hilfiger to

jeans so low-slung they seem to defy gravity? To a large extent the answer lies 200 miles southwest, in the oversized personage of Brooklyn's Biggie Smalls, an admitted ex-drug dealer turned rapper.

Over the past few years, Smalls and other hip-hop stars have become a crucial part of Hilfiger's open attempt to tap into the urban youth market. In exchange for giving artists free

Reprinted with permission © 1996 American Demographics, Ithaca, New York.

FIGURE 11.6 *Rap dress style of the Alkaholiks.*

wardrobes, Hilfiger found its name mentioned in both the rhyming verses of rap songs and their "shout-out" lyrics, in which rap artists chant out thanks to friends and sponsors for their support.

For Tommy Hilfiger and other brands, the result is de facto product placement. The September 1996 issue of *Rolling Stone* magazine featured the rap group The Fugees, with the men prominently sporting the Tommy Hilfiger logo. In February 1996, Hilfiger even used a pair of rap stars as runway models: horror-core rapper Method Man and muscular bad-boy Treach of Naughty by Nature.

Threatened by Hilfiger in a market he had profited from but never embraced, it hardly seems coincidental that Ralph Lauren recently signed black male super-model Tyson to an exclusive contract. Even the patrician perfumier Esteé Lauder recently jumped on the Hilfiger bandwagon, launching a new cross-promotion series with the clothing company. The name of one of Lauder's new perfumes says it all.

"Tommy Girl" plays on both Tommy Hilfiger's name and the seminal New York hip-hop record label Tommy Boy. Hilfiger also launched a clothing line for teenaged girls in fall 1996, projected by the company to gross $100 million in its first year on retail racks.

On the surface, it seems Hilfiger and others are courting a market too small and poor to matter. The majority of true hip-hoppers live in inner cities, although not all urban youths embrace the culture. About 5 million U.S. teens aged 15 to 19 lived in central cities in 1994, or 28 percent of all people that age. Inner-city blacks aged 15 to 19 are an even smaller group. At 1.4 million, they are only 8 percent of all teens. They also have significantly lower incomes than their white suburban counterparts. The numbers of 20-to-24-year-olds and black 20-to-24-year-olds in central cities are also small, at 6.5 million and 1.6 million, respectively.

So why are companies pitching products to the hip-hop crowd? Because for most of the 1990s, hordes of suburban kids—both black and white—have followed inner-city idols in adopting everything from music to clothing to language. The most prominent examples are in evidence at suburban shopping malls across the country: licensed sports apparel, baseball caps, oversized jeans, and gangster rap music.

Scoring a hit with inner-city youths can make a product hot with the much larger and affluent white suburban market. But to take advantage of this phenomenon, you have to dig into how hip-hop culture spreads from housing projects to rural environs, understand why hip-hop is so attractive to suburban whites, and discern the process by which hip-hoppers embrace products.

HIP-HOP HITS THE MAINSTREAM

In its early years, MTV drew jeers for being too "white," for shying away even from vanilla-flavored black pop stars such as Michael Jackson. Yet most pop-culture watchers agree that the cable channel's launching "Yo! MTV Raps" in 1992 was the pivotal event in the spread of hip-hop culture. Running in a prime after-school spot, and initially hosted by graffiti artist and rapper Fab Five Freddy, the show beamed two daily hours of inner-city attitude at adolescent eyeballs even in even the most remote Iowa corn country.

"There's no question—'Yo! MTV Raps' was the window into that world for Middle America," says Janine Misdom of Sputnik, a Manhattan-based firm that tracks youth trends for clients such as Levi-Strauss, Reebok, and Pepsi. Other video-oriented media soon followed. Within a few years, an all-day viewer-controlled channel called The Box supplied a steady stream of harder-edged hip-hop to any kid within the viewing area of a major metropolis. In 1993, about a year after "Yo! MTV Raps" hit cable, more than six in ten teens aged 12 to 19 rated hip-hop music as "in" according to Teenage Research Unlimited (TRU) of Northbrook, Illinois.

Music and fashion went hand in hand, as teens adopted the looks sported by rappers. Most Americans first saw baggy jeans in music videos sagging around the hips of white rap star Marky Mark. Teens also got an eyeful of Mark's boxers-exposed backside in his beefcake ads for Calvin Klein jeans. By spring 1993, 80 percent of teens favored the style, up from two-thirds six months earlier. And the look has staying power. Seventy-eight percent of teens still say baggy clothes are "in," according to TRU's Spring 1996 survey, although the style's popularity may be waning slightly.

Today, elements of hip-hop culture appear in the mainstream media, from commercials using rapped slogans to hit films such as *Menace II Society* and *Boyz N the Hood*. Suburban record stores stock relatively extensive hip-hop sections, and with good reason. Among consumers aged 12 to 17, almost three in five (58 percent) either "like" or "strongly like" rap, according to SounData of Hartsdale, New York, which tracks sales and other trends for the music industry. The 1996 figure is equally high among 18- to 20-year-olds. And even among the solidly adult 21- to 24-year-old age group, almost two-fifths favor the genre. Not surprisingly, it has now become a music-industry maxim that for a rap record to go platinum, it must sell strongly among white youths.

What draws white teens to a culture with origins so strongly linked to the inner city, and so distant from their suburbia's sylvan lawns? Clearly rebellion is a big factor. "People resonate with the strong anti-oppression messages of rap, and the alienation of blacks," says Ivan Juzang of Motivational Educational Entertainment, a six-year-old Philadelphia firm specializing in targeting urban youth. "All young people buy into rebellion in general, as part of rebelling against parental authority."

EMBRACING FEAR

Gangster rap artists such as the late Tupac Shakur and Dr. Dre represent only the latest link in a long chain of anti-establishment American icons (Shakur was wounded in a drive-by shooting in Las Vegas in September 1996 and died a week later). American teens have always been fascinated with outsider heroes, who score money and fame without being cowed by societal strictures. Such idols run from John Dillinger and Dennis Rodman, to Marlon Brando's fictional biker in *The Wild One* to James Dean's *Rebel without a Cause*.

Yet many argue that hip-hop's attractiveness transcends mere rebellion, placing it in a different category from past teen trends. For instance, punk, with its body piercing and mohawked heads, was often rebellion for rebellion's sake. Based on the urge to shock, it constructed a new reality for its adherents outside of societal norms. In contrast, hip-hop springs from the experiences of young blacks living in cities. It's based on a real culture, giving it more permanence than earlier teen trends. People who want a part of hip-hop culture always have something new to latch onto, because the culture is always evolving.

But perhaps more important to white teens, embracing hip-hop fashion, language, and music lets them claim to be part of black, inner-city culture. "By entering into the hip-hop sphere, I felt like I was opening a whole world that was closed to me before—it gave me a basis to meet all these people I had been scared of, whose main context for me was that they stole my bikes," says white 23-year-old William "Upski" Wimsatt, author of the memoir *Bomb the Suburbs*. The book in part details his trajectory from University of Chicago faculty brat to graffiti artist and journalist covering the rap music scene.

The attraction, he says, is part admiration, part fascination, and part fear. "A lot of white kids suspect they wouldn't make it through what inner-city blacks do, so there's an embedded admiration that's almost visceral," Wimsatt says. "Fear is one of our strongest impulses, and poor black men are the greatest embodiment of that fear."

Skateboarders, snowboarders, and other practitioners of nontraditional sports were among the first white teens to adopt the accouterments of hip-hop culture. Yet they are also some of the culture's least devoted adherents. "Most of them don't really understand hip-hop," says Chicagoan Tim Haley, a Midwest sales representative for snowboarding gear. They want to come off as being bad ass, pumping their stereo around town," he says. "So you'll see a bunch of white kids in Podunk, Michigan, trying to dress 'hip-hop,' but really they're just jocks with rich parents."

GOT TO BE REAL

Turning teens like these on to hip-hop styles begins with a much smaller group—hard-core hip-hoppers. "If we develop the hardest core element, we reach middle-class blacks, and then there's a ripple effect," says Juzang of Motivational Educational Entertainment. "If you don't target the hard-core, you don't get the suburbs." For example, marketers for the 1995 Mario Van Peebles film *Panther* misfired by casting it "as *JFK* for African Americans," Juzang says. The flick bombed. Soon after, the comedy *Friday* came out, pitched as a straight-up ghetto laugh-fest, and scored big both inside and outside city borders. The lesson here: core hip-hoppers display an almost fanatical obsession with authenticity. Sanitizing any element of hip-hop culture to make it more palatable for middle-class suburban whites is likely to result in failure, because the core hip-hop audience will reject it. And other groups look to this core for their cues. This wasn't always the case. The pop-music audience was responsible for the commercial success of artists such as faux rapper Vanilla Ice and thinly disguised pop star MC Hammer. Both scored

major hits by unimaginatively sampling 1980s pop songs and rapping bland rhymes over them. But now, even peripheral hip-hop consumers have grasped the difference between real and rip-off. If white kids realize a product has been toned down in a bid to make it "cross over," they'll avoid it. Instead they go for music with a blunt, urban sensibility—the harder-edged stuff Chuck D of the rap group Public Enemy once described as "CNN for black America." Soundscan sales statistics bear this out. In 1994, three-quarters of hard-core rap albums were sold to white consumers.

THE INNER AND OUTER CIRCLES

The hip-hop market encompasses consumers with varying levels of commitment to the culture. Millions of people buy rap records, but can hardly be called hard-core. Strictly speaking, a person must do at least one of three things to qualify: rap or be a disc jockey; breakdance; or paint graffiti.

Few white teenagers meet these criteria. Some are afraid to venture into inner cities or cities at all, many are restricted by their parents, and others are content to absorb hip-hop culture through television and other media. "Lots of kids' parents won't let them cross certain borders. So they're watching videos to see how to dress, how to look, how to talk," says black urban-sportswear designer Maurice Malone. "They can visualize the inner city. But they don't go there, so they can't fully communicate with the heart of the hip-hop movement."

Wimsatt, the Chicago hip-hop writer, sees the white parts of the "hip-hop nation" as a series of concentric attitudinal rings. At the center lie those who actually know blacks and study the intricacies of hip-hop's culture. "These people tend to consider themselves the racial exception," says Wimsatt. "They have a very regimented idea of what's cool and what's not."

Next is a group that has peripheral contact with the culture through friends or relatives, but doesn't actively seek "true hip-hopper" status. They go to shows, but don't rap, spray-paint, or breakdance. "After that, you have people who play hip-hop between other types of music," Wimsatt says. "They're sort of free-floating fans." Most white suburban teens probably fall into this category, listening to accessible acts such as Tribe called Quest and De La Soul.

Finally, the people in the outermost circle are those Wimsatt documented in a controversial 1993 article for hip-hop's *Source* magazine. Touring America, he met rural "wiggers" who avoided cities, thought blacks complained too much about their societal lot, and spouted phrases such as, "We wear a lot of pro-black clothes." To Wimsatt, such kids "are pure consumers—they're really into rap, but don't know much, so they're easily manipulated."

UNLOCKING THE DOOR

As hip-hop has made its mark on the mainstream, all but the most gullible fans have spotted a flurry of laughable bids to capitalize on the trend. Anybody with a drum machine and a rhyming dictionary, it seemed, could be presented as a true hip-hopper. "The history of semi-insiders trying to exploit hip-hop is an incredible comedy of errors," Wimsatt says. "I've seen so many commercials with some sort of hip-hop theme that are just transparent. You can almost see the creatives looking around the office and saying, 'Hmm...who do we know who's black and has a teenage cousin? Maybe that cousin raps...'" If you're trying to reach the hip-hop crowd, he says, take the time to find and hire legitimate hip-hop players. Good places to start tracking down insiders include record stores, music venues, and recording studios. National magazines such as *Vibe*, *RapPages*, and *The Source* may also mention local players on their pages.

Sprite evidently did its homework. For a series of NBA-game commercials, Coca-Cola Company (makers of Sprite) hired two of hip-hop's legendary "MCs," wordsmiths KRS-One and MC Shan. Even better, they had them face off in the sort of extemporaneous "freestyle battle" seen as any rapper's truest test of verbal skills and mental agility. The spot was roundly acclaimed, both inside and outside the rap world.

In the clothing arena, it's the same game. Mainstream designers such as Hilfiger and Lauren have scored. But smaller "underground" lines can also flourish in both city and suburb, says Misdom of Sputnik. "Even in places like [Minnesota's] Mall of America, you'll see kids who dress 'hip-hop' wearing grass-roots brands like Mecca, Boss Jeans, and Phat Farm," she says. "They are embracing these brands because they are seen as 'true.'"

Not every company that wants to sell to the inner-city crowd has grasped this wisdom. Malone cites two design prototypes making the rounds recently. Both try to emulate the boxers-exposed-by-sagging-jeans look. One pair of pants sports an underwear-like band of cloth sewn directly into the jeans waist, to peek out in a risk-free risqué style. Another features two waists—the first hangs at pelvis height giving the impression of disdain for belts, the second sitting traditionally on the hips. Both models have yet to make any splash. As Malone points out mockingly, "The most successful crossovers don't try. People will cross over to you if you don't try to play to them."

AN EVER-CHANGING SCENE

There's another reason the phony jeans may have failed. In hip-hop, the baggy jeans look has started to fade, following the lead of the skateboarding subculture that abandoned drowning in denim for a "cleaner," tighter look in 1995. Baggy clothes of all kinds reached their peak in popularity in Fall 1993 and Spring 1994, when 82 percent of teens aged 12 to 19 said baggy clothes were in. That share slipped to 78 percent in spring 1996, according to Teenage Research Unlimited.

Hip-hop culture is constantly evolving, partly because of the commercial success of some of its elements. As Don DeLillo wrote in his novel *America*, "as soon as Madison Avenue breaks the code, Harlem devises a new one." But hip-hop music, language, and fashion also change because looking good and sporting the latest styles are very important to core members of the culture.

The 1995 Yankelovich African-American Monitor clusters black consumers into six segments based on attitudes and income. Its "hip-hopper" segment includes 27 percent of U.S. blacks. These single, urban blacks probably include members who are not authentic hip-hoppers. But their attitudes are telling, nonetheless. More than half of Yankelovich's hip-hoppers strongly agree that they feel the need to be fashionably dressed, compared with only 33 percent of all blacks aged 16 and older. These hip-hoppers are twice as likely as all blacks to strongly feel the need to keep up with new styles, at 42 percent.

To Sputnik's Misdom, hip-hop culture's emphasis on innovative fashion counts among its strongest selling points for teens, who demand a never-ending slew of status symbols to define them against both their peers and parents. "All the rock and grunge styles have stayed the same," she says. "But hip-hop always has a lot of styles coming out." Already her studies project a shift away from the preppier Hilfiger style toward "uptown, high-end designer labels such as DKNY, Versace, and Dolce & Gabbana." Garments bearing these labels have a sleeker, more European look than brands such as Hilfiger. They also have higher price tags.

Recent rap videos support her observations. "Roughneck" styles featuring hunting and fishing apparel are on the wane. Another emerging hot style uses high-tech fabrics and styles that resemble those worn by scientists at the South Pole and by mountain climbers. Last summer, designer Donna Karan dressed many of New York City's fashionable young in DKNY Tech. This lower-priced line of clothing featuring high-tech fabrics represents the designer's nod to the trendsetting power of urban teens.

Hip-hop culture is in some ways the next page in the decades-long book of teenagers embracing the forbidden. Yet it's also more lasting, because it is based on the day-to-day experiences of millions of inner-city teens. Targeting this relatively small group of teens may open the door to the larger, more affluent, white, suburban market. But the niche has countless pitfalls. Companies that have successfully negotiated them know a fundamental truth of hip-hop culture: For a product to appeal to a rapper in south central L.A. or a white mall crawler in Des Moines, it's got to be real.

DISCUSSION QUESTIONS

Marketing Street Culture

1. What fashion theory(ies) help in understanding the impact of rap dress on fashion?

2. How has the industry capitalized on street culture style innovation?

3. How have some rappers made use of the fashion system?

74 Tribal Styles
Ted Polhemus

The annual British Tattoo Festival in Dunstable, England. A semicircle of men in motorbike boots, jeans, T-shirts and battered, cut-off leather jackets has formed around one of the many tattooists' booths. In the centre a similarly dressed young man is acting as nonchalant as possible while the electric needle buzzes loudly over his upper arm. Why all this interest in what appears to be quite a small tattoo?

It turns out that this is a rite of passage. The guy in the chair is becoming a member of the Bracknell Chopper Club. The tattoo, an elegant pair of gold wings, is the club's insignia. Everyone watching except myself has an identical design on his left bicep. Noticing that the same insignia appears on their leather jackets, I ask the guy next to me why duplication in the form of a tattoo is necessary:

'A tattoo's for life. And so is joining the club. We're all in this for good. Understand?'

The members of the Bracknell Chopper Club and this significant event vividly demonstrate the difference between fashion and style. These men are not fashion victims. We can see this in their clothing—the most treasured items being those which are the oldest (and which look it). And any permanent body decoration like a tattoo is as anti-fashion as it is possible to get—literally making change difficult if not impossible. When one and then two years later I notice these same men at subsequent tattoo conventions they look exactly the same except for a few additional tattoos and some grey hairs.

Style isn't trendy. Quite the opposite. It's inherently conservative and traditional and it is for this reason that it often makes use of permanent body decorations. The intricate tattoos of the Maori and other peoples of the South Pacific, the scarification patterns of various African peoples, the enormous lip plugs found in parts of the Amazon and the tattooed insignia of the Bracknell Chopper Club all serve to resist change.

And to mark membership in a social group. In all probability styles of body decoration have served to distinguish 'Us' from 'Them' throughout history and we can see this important function of style at work in any of those tribal societies which survive today. Different colours of body paint, different designs, different adornments provide an immediately recognizable visual guide as to who is a member of which tribal group.

The history of streetstyle is a history of 'tribes'. Zooties, Hipsters, Beats, Rockers, Hippies, Rude Boys, Punks...right up to today's Travellers and Raggamuffins are all *subcultures* which use a distinctive style of dress and decoration to draw a line between 'Us' and 'Them'.

What's intriguing about this is the fact that such *styletribes* have blossomed and flourished at precisely that time in history when individuality and personal freedom have come to be seen as the defining features of our age. As Margaret Thatcher told us, 'Today there is no such thing as society. There are just individuals and their families.' And by and large this is something she was right about. The old groupings of class, region, religion and ethnic background have decreased in importance, leaving the individual free to pursue life as he or she personally chooses.

Why should anyone want to give up this freedom to join a group like the Bracknell Chopper Club? Or, on a larger scale, groups like Rockers, Mods, Hippies, Punks, Goths and Raggamuffins?

My view is that the tribal imperative is and always will be a fundamental part of human nature. Like our most distant ancestors we feel alienated and purposeless when we do not experience this sense of belonging and comradeship. It is no coincidence that the decline of traditional social groupings which has intensified so markedly since the Second World War precisely parallels the rise of a new type of social group, the *styletribe*. Hipsters, Teddy Boys, Mods, Rockers

FIGURE 11.7 *London punks display tribal style.*

and so forth arose to satisfy that need for a sense of community and common purpose which is so lacking in modern life.

So it comes as no surprise that these styletribes are particularly attractive to teenagers. It is during the adolescent years that a person is moving apart from his or her parental family while not yet having formed a new family. If contemporary life was made up of more than 'individuals and their families', this would not be a problem. But in our anti-society society the teenager steps out of the parental family into a social vacuum.

The simplest way to fill this vacuum is the gang—a small group with a territory (a 'home turf') and, typically, a distinctive style of dress ('colours') to set it apart from other gangs and from the mainstream. This situation is vividly portrayed in the film *The Warriors* (1979), which opens with an attempted reconciliation between some ten different New York street gangs. The Warriors themselves wear black leather waistcoats with their vivid insignia painted on the back. Another gang wears Hawaiian shirts and Panama hats. Another, baseball uniforms and blue facepaint. And still another dresses in a style reminiscent of *Clockwork Orange*, with white facepaint, top hats and braces.

Styletribes are also marked out by a distinctive appearance style but their enormous scale and national or even international boundaries indicate a uniquely modern approach to 'tribal' identity. While all the members of a gang (or, for that matter, a 'real' tribe) know and are personally involved with each other, the vast majority of the members of styletribes are complete strangers—linked together only by reports in the media, by pop music role models and by a shared style of dress and adornment.

How do styletribes form and how do they function? Let us look at one example—the

Punks. In London, in 1975 and into 1976, a small clique of young people (many known as the Bromley Set because they came from Bromley, in Kent) began to meet up in various places at the less prestigious end of the King's Road. Vivienne Westwood and Malcolm McLaren's shop SEX was one such meeting place and the unusual items of clothing on sale there (for example, fetish garments in rubber and PVC) provided a stylistic focus. The number of kids involved was small—at a guess, no more than a couple of hundred. Most were known to each other and in this sense, at this point in time, they were a gang rather than a styletribe.

When the media began to take an interest in these early proto-Punks (and especially when McLaren's rock group, the Sex Pistols, outraged the public via a notorious TV appearance), a stereotype began to form of a typical 'Punk Rocker'. Thanks to this publicity, young people throughout Britain began to imitate this style. Within a few months there were thousands of Punks spread across the UK—and, before long, hundreds of thousands of Punks as far afield as Berlin, Barcelona, Rome, New York, LA and Tokyo. These have more recently spread into Eastern Europe.

Sharing (at least at first glance) only an appearance style and an interest in a new form of rock music, thousands of Punks scattered between different cities, countries and continents would hardly seem to qualify as a subculture, let alone a 'tribe'. But this view forgets that style is a wonderfully expressive medium—capable of representing complex ideas, attitudes and values.

It is impossible fully to translate the meaning of the appearance style of Punks or any other styletribe into words. Nevertheless, when we compare, for example, the Punks' style with that of the Hippies, we immediately appreciate the extent to which these express very different worldviews. The Punks' black leather, fetishistic garments, studs and Crazy Colour hairstyles indicate a nihilism, an aggressive stance and a delight in artifice and deliberate perversity which is a complete opposite to the Hippies' new-age, love-&-peace, back-to-nature philosophy (itself perfectly expressed in the form of typical Hippy dress and adornment).

Style isn't just a superficial phenomenon. It's the visible tip of something much greater. And encoded within its iconography are all those ideas and ideals which together constitute a (sub)culture. Like-looking is like-thinking and in this sense the members of a styletribe have a great deal in common.

Nor should we forget that the decision to dress and adorn oneself in an extreme or unusual manner is no trivial matter. The Punks who dyed their hair green or even the Hippies who let their hair grow long at a time when short hair was the norm were risking a great deal—job prospects, family harmony, verbal and sometimes even physical abuse. To adopt the look of a particular styletribe is to put oneself on the firing line. But if such stylistic commitment brings a sense of group solidarity and comradeship, then, for many, it is worth it.

Like all tribes, styletribes hope that they will be timeless, unchanging. It is this wish which leads the members of many styletribes to make use of the permanent body arts like tattooing. While mainstream society attempts to dismiss such subcultures as 'just a fad', those within them want to believe that their tribe will carry on 'forever'. History, however, has frequently revealed the futility of this dream. 'Punk's Not Dead' may have been the rallying cry heard a decade after Punk first began but by that time one was more likely (at least in Britain) to encounter Punks on postcards than in real life.

It is easy to conclude, therefore, that Punk was just a passing fashion in a history of youth-culture which is more often than not typified by transience. Such a view, however, does not entirely fit the facts. Firstly, the *spirit* of Punk is very much alive, to the extent that its style and attitude have influenced other contemporary styletribes and even mainstream culture (more about which in subsequent chapters). Secondly, in countries other than the UK—from Germany to Japan, the USA to Russia—small but flourishing Punk communities continue to exist. Finally, even in Britain, where media overkill and the stigma of classification as a tourist attraction had a negative effect in the 1980s, a new generation which was not even born when 'Anarchy in the UK' first appeared is producing a tiny but enthusiastic new Punk subculture.

A similar story could be told regarding Teddy Boys, Mods, Rockers, Skinheads, Rockabillies, Hipsters, Surfers, Hippies, Rastafarians, Headbangers, Goths and many others. In traditional historical terms, it is still early days, but already it is clear that both individually and as a generic social phenomenon styletribes cannot be dismissed as something transitory. In practice as well as in hope, such groups and the appearance styles which they create to express their shared values and beliefs remain as an exception to the rule of our culture's mercurial inclinations.

DISCUSSION QUESTIONS

Tribal Styles

1. How does author Polhemus define tribes?
2. What is the difference between style and fashion according to Polhemus?
3. What types of personal, group, and societal meanings are embedded in tribal styles?

CHAPTER 12

Dress and World Religions

Kimberly A. Miller
and
Susan O. Michelman

AFTER YOU HAVE READ THIS CHAPTER, YOU WILL COMPREHEND:

- Examples of dress in different religions.

- How ideology in religion may be reflected through dress.

- The roles that modesty and sexuality play in religion as reflected through dress.

- Dress as a material artifact that mirrors change in religions.

This chapter focuses on the meaning of dress within world religions. Specifically, the articles in this chapter will consider issues of dress in the Hasidic sect of Judaism, Roman Catholic women religious (nuns), Islamic women who veil, fundamentalist Christians, and Mennonites. Membership in a religious group is not always associated with a particular style of dress. For example, in the United States many Roman Catholics or Protestants wear the equivalent of work dress to worship at church. Other religious groups use dress to differentiate and set themselves apart from others in the larger society or surrounding world. The articles have been chosen to illustrate how and why religious dress symbolizes the values and beliefs of religious organizations. Dress will be examined for its ability to promote social stability within religious organizations and resist the rapid style changes associated with the contemporary fashion process of secular society.

IDEOLOGY AND DRESS

To understand religious dress the cultural context of a religious group must be considered. Each of the major world religions included in this chapter—Islam, Judaism, Christianity—have dominant ideologies that guide decisions about dress. **Ideology** is a set of ideas that do not hold up under the rigors of scientific investigation and that support the interest of dominant groups (Ferrante, 1995). For instance, dress within Christianity is based in large part on the story of Adam and Eve in the Garden of Eden; therefore, modesty should be a goal in dress. Judaism is based on the philosophy that individuals exist to glorify God; therefore, to be well-dressed is a religious duty—not one of personal preference. Islamic philosophy (similar to Mennonite beliefs) promotes the separation of the sexes. A philosophy of male dominance dictates that women's bodies must be covered and that their movements within society be highly restricted and carefully controlled by male family members.

WHAT IS RELIGION?

Religion is a set of beliefs, symbols, and practices that is based on the idea of the sacred and unites believers in a socioreligious community (Marshall, 1994). **Sacred** refers to that which people define as extraordinary, inspiring a sense of awe and reverence. Contrasted to the sacred is the **profane** or that which is considered an ordinary element of everyday life. **Monotheism** is a belief in a single God whereas **polytheism** is a belief in many gods (Marshall, 1994). Three examples of monotheism practiced worldwide are Islam, Judaism, and Christianity.

Islam is based on the principal of submission to Allah or God. Its holy texts are the Koran and the Hadith (or sayings of the Prophet). Islam pays special attention to the status and clothing of women (Marshall, 1994). Although there are no specific injunctions or rules in the Koran regarding veiling, women are believed to have sexual powers that may tempt males (Ribeiro, 1986). Therefore, many Islamic women veil their faces and cover their heads, hair, necks, and bodies to a greater or lesser extent. Some Islamic women do not veil at all and are indistinguishable in a group of Western women. The nature and extent of veiling of women varies greatly from one Islamic nation and from one group to another, depending on the nature of their beliefs and the political context in which they live. For example, the article in this chapter by Sciolino, "The Chanel Under the Chador," examines the present-day social status and veiling practices of women in Iran. Veiling can also be associated with expressing nationalism and/or anti-Western sentiment associated with rejecting Western fashion. For example, a number of years ago under the Shah, most Iranian women did not veil and wore Western dress. When the Ayatollah Khomeni, an arch-conservative ruler who desired a totally Islamic state, took power in 1978, women were mandated to veil. Currently, veiling is still in place, but is less strictly enforced.

Judaism originated in the prophetic activities of the Jews in relation to the God Yahweh. Jewish religious knowledge is found in the Torah, the first five books of the Hebrew Bible or the Old Testament (Macionis, 1996). As with other religions, Jewish beliefs vary from liberal to highly conservative interpretation. Hayt's article "For Stylish Orthodox Women, Wigs That Aren't Wiggy" examines dress practices of orthodox Jewish women, who are part of a conservative sect of Judaism. Women who follow this tradition wear wigs in public from the time of their marriage. Covering their head with wigs ensures their modesty under Orthodox interpretation of Jewish law but helps them visually fit into mainstream U. S. culture.

Christianity, which includes sects of Catholicism, Protestantism, and the Anabaptists (which include the Amish and Mennonites), from early times handed down a code of morals, including strict rules about clothing. Early Christian teachings stress the link between the outward appearance of the body and the state of the person's soul (Ribeiro, 1986). Several articles in this chapter examine how Christian religious beliefs have strongly influenced appearance. For example, in "Clothing, Control, and Women's Agency: The Mitigation of Patriarchal Power," Linda Arthur discusses how compliance with group norms and more specifically control of women by male ministers within the community have left Mennonite women with few avenues for personal expression within the dictates of that church. The Mennonites are descendants of a 17th-century Swiss German Anabaptist sect who believed in the complete separation of church and state and asserted that contemporary society is corrupting. In all facets of Mennonite life today they strive for a simple existence including plain dress for both men and women based on 19th-century styles (Ribeiro, 1986).

Michelman's article "From Habit to Fashion: Dress of Catholic Women Religious" examines how traditional habits or uniforms of nuns made their social identities more outwardly visible than their personal identities. When women take vows of religious life, they relinquish individuality in dress for social control of their bodies by the Church.

> Dress should reveal not just a humble state of mind, but show by its simplicity that the wearer spends little time on the adornment of the body, and is thus free to devote more—time and money—to the poor. This mixture of religious and personal morality is most evidenced in the habits of religious orders; their ample, loose robes of humble, often coarse fabrics, are both unprovocative and a protection against the temptations of the world. (Ribeiro, 1986)

From the time that women religious first wore religious attire as novices, they were instructed to view themselves not as individuals, but as representatives of a group. Michelman examines the personal and social conflicts that occurred when these women shed their habits but not their social roles in the 1960s.

DRESS AND RELIGIOUS FUNDAMENTALISM

Fundamentalism is a conservative religious doctrine that opposes intellectualism and worldly accommodation in favor of restoring traditional, otherworldly religion (Macionis, 1996). Fundamentalism is a more complex phenomenon than popular conceptions would lead people to believe. First, a fundamentalist cannot be stereotyped by gender, age, race, ethnicity, social class, or political ideology. Second, fundamentalists are characterized by a belief that a relationship with God, Allah, or some other supernatural force provides answers to personal and social problems (Ferrante, 1995). Third, fundamentalists do not differentiate between the sacred and profane in their everyday lives. *All* areas of their lives, including work, family, and leisure, are governed by religious principles. Edwards in her article, "Worldly Lessons," discusses how female students at Bob Jones University, a Christian fundamentalist school, learn how to be "worldly" without denying their religious convictions.

Fourth, fundamentalists want to reverse the trend toward gender equality, which they believe is symptomatic of a declining moral order (Ferrante, 1995). Fundamentalists often believe the correct ordering of priorities in life requires subordinating women's rights to the concerns of the larger group and the well-being of the society, such as the "traditional" family.

Many of the articles in this chapter are about dress and religious fundamentalism. Why is control of dress, particularly for women, frequently a component of fundamentalist beliefs? Fundamentalist religious groups have often emerged after a perceived threat or crisis—real or imagined. Any discussion of a particular fundamentalist group must include some reference to an adversary. Dress, then, can be linked to a way of expressing group solidarity as well as indicating opposition to the general culture.

Dress acts as a visible symbol for the precepts of fundamentalism, including the fact that religious principles govern all aspects of their lives (including dress) and that women's roles are frequently more "traditional" with individual needs and beliefs relinquished to the greater good of the family and religious group. This leaves fundamentalists open to criticism by feminists regarding the oppression of women by the patriarchal nature of many fundamentalist groups. **Patriarchy** refers to cultural beliefs and values that give higher prestige to men than to women (Newman, 1995). Women's roles as wives, mothers, and supporters of the faith may be seen as important, but men are given priority or exclusive rights to govern and take power in the group. Patriarchy has been regarded as a form of social organization and has been considered, particularly by feminists, as an undifferentiated theory to explain the whole of human history (Grimshaw, 1986).

> Patriarchy is itself the prevailing religion of the entire planet...All of the so-called religions legitimating patriarchy are mere sects subsumed under its vast umbrella/canopy...All— from buddhism and hinduism to islam, judaism, christianity—to secular derivatives such as freudianism, marxism and maoism—are infrastructures of the edifice of patriarchy...Consequently, women are the objects of male terror, the projected personifications of 'the Enemy,' the real objects under attack in all the wars of patriarchy. (Daly, 1990)

Agency is a concept used by feminists to describe the resistance women use to combat patriarchy. Arthur describes in her article, "Clothing, Control and Women's Agency: The Mitigation of Patriarchal Power" the agencies (i.e., the various forms of resistance) women in one Holdeman Mennonite community use in subverting the strict dress codes dictated by male ministers and deacons. Arthur describes the daily process of subtle changes in dress that give women an opportunity to creatively express themselves. Agency can also be found in Elaine Sciolino's article about the elite Islamic women working to affect political changes more favorable to women.

DRESS, MODESTY, AND SEXUALITY

Common themes can be identified among the articles included in this chapter. One such theme is modesty. Modest dress for women includes covering the body in an attempt to obliterate body curves and covering women's hair, a sign of sexuality in some groups. Although not part of all religions, some religions hold beliefs that regard female sexuality as dangerous if left unharnessed and uncontrolled (Fernea & Fernea, 1995). This belief leads to the religious practice of prescribing modest and proper dress for female members. Quite frequently, societies in developing nations may enforce dress codes quite enthusiastically that might otherwise be ignored in Europe or the United States.

> In the west we retain the idea of a white wedding out of traditional sentimentality, for one suspects that a minority of brides are virgins on their wedding day. In Africa, however, where the outward signs of Christianity are as appreciated as its spiritual values, a great deal of importance is placed on a bride's virginity. Pregnant brides in the Roman

Catholic diocese of Lagos [Nigeria], reported in *The Times* (August 13, 1984), were forbidden to wear white on their wedding day. (Ribeiro, 1986)

Another common theme among the readings in this chapter is the practice of covering women's hair. As Hayt notes in "For Stylish Orthodox Women, Wigs That Aren't Wiggy," "...women's hair exudes sensual energy" (p. 468). For an orthodox Jewish woman to be properly dressed she must cover her hair after marriage. This practice helps the woman to avoid expressing sexuality outside her marriage. Holdeman Mennonite women must also cover their head and hair. The starched cap represents a Mennonite woman's humility to God and her resistance to worldly possessions. Submissiveness to her God, her community, and her husband is also symbolized by her head covering.

Among Iranian women, the chador covers the entire body (with the exception of the eyes). Sciolino reports in "The Chanel Under the Chador" that her informant mentioned twice that her hair was not to be described in the article. No mention of her hair color or length could be made. A description of an Islamic woman's hair is considered in that culture as "going too far."

Covering body curves appears to be somewhat less of an issue for Mennonite and orthodox Jewish women than for Islamic women. Thinness is the ideal body shape for Mennonite men and women. Their culture defines thinness as an expression of self-denial and control. Sensory enjoyment such as eating is considered sinful; therefore, a properly "dressed" Mennonite woman is one who is thin.

RELIGIOUS DRESS AND SOCIAL CHANGE

Although changes in religious dress occur with much less frequency than among those of the general population, forces of social, economic, and political change do influence sacred dress as discussed in several articles in this chapter. For example, Michelman's study of women religious demonstrates the identity struggle Catholic nuns experienced when moving from full religious habit to secular dress after the changes mandated by Vatican II in the 1960s. Susan Michelman's article "From Habit to Fashion: Dress of Catholic Women Religious" examines how difficult it was for the women to make the transition from a well-recognized and revered social identity as a Catholic nun in full habit to nonuniform, secular dress.

Sciolino's article supplies us with an excellent example of the differences between sacred and secular dress. The differences are in sharp contrast. The irony of wearing a Chanel-style suit (secular dress) under a chador (sacred dress) would prove baffling to most non-Islamics. Class differences among Islamic women were also noted by Sciolino. She describes the women she studied as the cultural elite, women who have both a Western education and growing political influence in their country. Sciolino compares the agendas of these well-educated women to those who are lower class, uneducated, and who never stopped wearing the veil before and throughout Iran's troubled political times. Education and wealth provide social agency to individuals, so limits on movement and role-taking in society may seem more problematic to women in the culutural elite than to poorer women who lack access to political and social power.

Social class issues can be expressed through religious dress. For example, Bob Jones University students aspire to move among the cultural elite of U. S. society, which is not a modest goal. Recognizing that dress can advance or retard professional goals, "safe beauty classes" prepare women for entry into professional and well-paying positions.

Style is described by church-sanctioned teachers as a woman's armor, while fashion is characterized as "letting oneself go"—a description that is a clear condemnation of the evils of worldliness.

Similarly, Orthodox Jewish women who buy custom-made wigs that closely resemble their natural hair may also be baffling to non-Jews. In Hayt's article, a rabbi states that there is a difference between immodest dress and stylish dress—and one does not necessarily preclude the other. Real hair that is covered with hair that is not the woman's own hair is perfectly modest to an Orthodox Jew. As frequently happens in cultures throughout the world, what might seem to be an illogical contradiction to outsiders may be completely sensible to an insider of the group.

Summary

This chapter covers examples of dress in different religions. In particular, we focus on dress in the Orthodox sect of Judaism, Roman Catholic women religious, Islamic women who veil, fundamentalist Christians, and Mennonites. Ideology reflects the beliefs of a culture that justify particular social arrangements (Marshall, 1994) and these beliefs are reflected in religious dress. Several themes (i.e., modesty, sexuality, patriarchy, and agency) were identified in our discussion of religious dress. Lastly, religious dress as a material artifact mirrors changes in religion that often coincide with changes in the greater society or culture. Dress within religion illustrates that the relationship between social stability and resistance to rapid style changes associated with fashion is apparent.

Suggested Readings

Dunbar, D. (1991, October 27). Everybody wants a piece of Africa now. *Los Angeles Times*, E5.

Polaneczky, R. (1995, December). You'll never guess who this woman works for. *Redbook*, 98–101, 119–120.

LEARNING ACTIVITY
Religions' Rules for Dress

Objective

To learn about dress within a religion that was previously unfamiliar.

Interview

Interview someone who believes in a religious ideology with which you are unfamiliar. Consider religions (or faiths) of which you have little or no knowledge. Use the Yellow Pages of the telephone directory in your area to determine who you could interview. Depending on your background, you may want to consider some of the following:

- Amish
- Buddhist
- Catholic priest or nun
- Greek orthodox priest
- Hindu
- Jewish rabbi (or layperson)
- Mennonite
- Mormon
- Muslim

Develop five or six questions about religion and dress for your interview. You may want to know about specific dress items that you have seen in the media but did not understand. You may want to ask general questions about how dress is used during formal ceremonies (and by whom) compared to how a religious observer might dress on a daily basis. Other possible questions include: How is dress used in rituals of the faith? How does the dress of clergy (or religious leaders/teachers) compare to the dress of the worshiper?

After conducting the interview, share your information in small groups or during a class discussion.

References

Daly, M. (1990). *Gyn/Ecology: The metaethics of radical feminism*. Boston: Beacon Press.

Fernea, E. W., & Fernea, R. A. (1995). Symbolizing roles: Behind the veil. In M. E. Roach-Higgins, J. B. Eicher, & K. K. P. Johnson (Eds.), *Dress and identity*. New York: Fairchild.

Ferrante, J. (1995). *Sociology: A global perspective*. Belmont, CA: Wadsworth Publishing Co.

Grimshaw, J. (1986). *Philosophy and feminist thinking*. Minneapolis, MN: University of Minnesota Press.

Macionis, J. J. (1996). *Society: The basics* (3rd edition). Upper Saddle River, N. J.: Prentice-Hall.

Marshall, G. (Ed.). (1994). *The concise Oxford dictionary of sociology*. Oxford, England: Oxford University Press.

Newman, D. (1995). *Sociology: Exploring the architecture of everyday life*. Thousand Oaks, CA: Pine Forge Press.

Ribeiro, A. (1986). *Dress and morality*. London, England: Batsford Press.

75   The Chanel Under the Chador

Elaine Sciolino

On a street blocked to traffic in the wealthiest section of Teheran, a white-gloved honor guard salutes a parade of women swathed in black as they hurry into an opulently furnished guest house that once belonged to the Shah.

The women remove their black floor-length chadors—garments that cover all but their faces and more than anything else symbolize the 1979 revolution that transformed Iran and returned its women to a shrouded life. Beneath their chadors, the women are clearly ready for a party, with lacquered hair, careful makeup and stylish clothes. One wears a black taffeta party dress with a plunging neckline and a big black bow at the shoulder, another, a form-fitting black suit trimmed in fake zebra.

The hostess is Fatimeh Hashemi, the 36-year-old daughter of Iran's President, Ali Akbar Hashemi Rafsanjani. She runs a women's organization associated with the Foreign Ministry, a foundation for specialized diseases and a high-tech hospital for kidney patients south of Teheran. Nevertheless, few Iranians have any idea what she—or any of the other women associated with the elite of the Islamic Republic—really looks like.

The event this evening is for women only. So Fatimeh dispenses with her chador, and her head scarf and coat as well, and stands revealed. With her perfectly tailored lime-green-and-white Chanel-style suit, pale hose and pumps and a single strand of pearls, she looks, well, modern.

Fatimeh is one of the new power women of Iran. Charming and outgoing, she is a mother of two who was married at 18 to a man chosen by her parents. She is also one of a small, elite group of women connected to the regime, loyal daughters of the revolution who have entered the fluid, mysterious maze of Iranian politics to negotiate ever so carefully for change.

Her message goes well beyond dress: that despite the Western perception of Iranian women as ignorant, backward and oppressed, she and others like her are very much of the modern world. The theme is underscored by tonight's guest of honor, Hamideh Rabbani, the daughter of Afghanistan's former President, who was ousted last year by the fundamentalist Muslims known as the Taliban. Rabbani, who now lives comfortably in Canada, spellbinds her audience with tales of horror about women under Taliban rule: how they cannot leave their homes to go to work, how they cannot send their daughters to school, how they are denied medical care in hospitals.

Fatimeh gasps, as outraged and uncomprehending as any Western feminist. It's not an act. Women in Iran make up a third of the labor force and nearly half of the university population; they drive their own cars; they go grocery shopping and run businesses, most important, they vote in elections and hold political office. Even in Western-friendly Middle Eastern nations—Saudi Arabia and Kuwait, for example—most of these things are forbidden to women.

"The image of Iranian women is so distorted around the world," Fatimeh laments. "How unfair it is."

But that's only part of the story. Fatimeh is blind, sometimes conveniently so, to the harsh restrictions imposed on women by the fundamentalist Muslim regime. Iranian women cannot shake the hand of a man who is not a close blood relative. They are forbidden from jogging or bicycling or swimming, except in sexually segregated spaces, and from exposing their heads and necks and the curves of their bodies in public. They cannot become judges or senior religious leaders. Adultery is still punished by stoning to death. Fathers control custody of the children after divorce, and girls are allowed to marry as soon as they reach puberty. And, as in Iran under the Shah, women cannot leave the country without the written permission of their

FIGURE 12.1 *This photograph illustrates the separation of the sexes in Iran. First, the chador (a body covering that leaves only the eyes exposed) hides the female form from male view. Secondly, a male professor is separated from female students by a screen.*

husbands, rape is more often than not blamed on the woman and a woman's testimony in court has half the weight of a man's.

And yet women are using their growing political clout to press for more rights, more important jobs in government, the same pay, work benefits and promotions as men. They want to have the right to participate in competitive sports, to avoid beatings by their husbands, to divorce and get custody of their children. The women leading the charge are not the familiar secular professional women who have struggled on the fringes of society all these years to reclaim the rights the mullahs took away from them. These new power women are a product of the revolution, and they are pursuing a women's agenda—albeit within the confines of Islam.

They want something much more fundamental than sisterhood. "They want power," says Haleh Esfandiari, author of the forthcoming book "Reconstructed Lives: Women and Iran's Islamic Revolution." "The regime women go after power and use power to affect legislation and policies. They want to project an image of women that is progressive but within Islamic law and rituals. Nobody can accuse them of being Western puppets."

So over caviar and grilled fish at the dinner with Fatimeh, the table talk moves to less weighty matters: the sleep patterns of toddlers, the problems of Teheran traffic and the value of a good tailor. When I ask what gifts I should buy for my two daughters, one American-educated aide to Fatimeh laughs and says, "Barbie dolls."

I have no idea whether she is joking. Last year, a hard-line newspaper here branded the all-American creations as "Satanic and perverse," and Iran has begun to market Islamically correct versions of Barbie and her boyfriend, Ken—Sara, who wears long flowing clothing and a veil on her head, and Dara her brother, who wears the cloak and turban of a cleric. Still, imported Barbies are the preferred toys of Teheran. It is just one more ambiguity on this night.

At the evening's end, the women say affectionate goodbyes, with kisses on both cheeks, wrapping themselves again in black to re-enter the public space of men.

To the outside world, the unveiling by Fatimeh—and later by her mother and her better-known sister, Faezeh—in front of a foreign journalist may seem insignificant. But I saw it differently—as part of a mission by women who now have the connections and the skills to reclaim their place in society.

The role of women has become one of the most vexing issues of Islam today. Just as race has been the great dilemma for American democracy, gender is the fault line of the Islamic world, as women struggle at different stages and at different speeds to push beyond the confines of the veil. Nowhere is that struggle being fought with more passion, tension and guile than in Iran.

I first came to Iran in 1979 on a chartered plane from Paris with Ayatollah Ruhollah Khomeini as he ended a long exile to lead his country into revolution. And in many trips since, the black clad women of Iran had all seemed the same: scary, unsmiling servants of the ayatollahs.

But I decided to take another look after Faezeh announced during her successful campaign for Parliament last year that there was no reason under Iran's Constitution why a woman could not become President. Her offhand remark fueled a national debate that is still unresolved. Just last month, Azam Taleghani, 50, daughter of the late Ayatollah Mamoud Taleghani, one of Iran's most prominent clerics during the revolution, announced her candidacy for President precisely to clarify the situation.

So what has changed in the 18 years since turbaned clerics occupied palaces of kings?

Iran's clerics, first of all. They may cling to the revolutionary oratory that once drove a nation into the streets, but they dearly understand their people want prosperity more than Islamic guidance. They have moved in contradictory directions. To keep the system strong enough to govern but supple enough to survive, they have both imposed strict limits and allowed some room for maneuver—as long as it poses no threat to their authority. There is, for example,

harsh repression of intellectuals and politicians at home and the deliberate use of terrorism against enemies abroad; but there is also enough disorganization and corruption for people to find ways around the system.

The clerics want to present Iran as a modern, powerful state and to counter the Clinton Administration's characterization of Iran as an "international outlaw." Given the harsh treatment of women in much of the Islamic world, it is understandable that the mullahs would try to rehabilitate their image by celebrating the centrality of women.

But it isn't just the mullahs, or the priorities, that have changed. Iran has changed, or perhaps changed back. As sweeping as it was, the revolution did not obliterate the Westernized society built up by Shah Mohammed Reza Pahlevi, in which women had begun to play a major role. Many secular professional women fled; many others lost their power and jobs, some even their lives. But many stayed behind, making an uneasy peace with the new rulers, continuing to function as doctors, lawyers, academics and businesswomen.

Finally, and most important, the masses of Iran's women have changed. Under the Shah, Iran was the most secularized state in the Persian Gulf. But the freedom enjoyed by the professional, Western-educated female elite of Teheran did not mean much to the majority of lower-class religious women who had never stopped wearing the veil.

The revolution politicized these women, promising them liberation, or at least a place in society. But the promises were broken, and many women felt betrayed. They began to rebel, quietly, against the constraints of their lives. As the economy contracted, as they lost their husbands and sons in eight years of war with Iraq, they often had no choice but to work to support their families. And in a country where 50 percent of the population has been born since the revolution, the mullahs have discovered that they simply cannot exclude women, particularly young women, from government, employment and education.

All these changes created a political opening that the regime women have been eager to exploit. It is a tiny group—perhaps three dozen women at most. Among them are an adviser to the President on women's affairs, a deputy minister, a mayor of a district of Teheran and 13 members of the 270-member Parliament. Loyal to the revolution, with powerful fathers and husbands and brothers to protect them, they have mastered the Iranian art of operating in narrowly defined political spaces, of testing the limits and running for cover.

Their strategy has produced some small, but noteworthy, gains, particularly in the Parliament: the granting of back wages for housework for women whose husbands divorce them; four-month compulsory maternity leave; an equal opportunity labor law. Last summer, for the first time since the revolution, abortion to save the life of the mother was legalized. The punishment for a woman who fails to cover her head and body properly is no longer up to 74 lashes. It's a jail term—from 10 days to 2 months.

Still, these women must navigate treacherous political waters, in which Fatimeh's inviting me to dinner is a bold act. In fact, the written description of women like her in Western dress could spark criticism that they have been seduced by Western ways or lost their religious devotion. "Do not write too many details—what my hair looks like or the shape of our bodies," she says at the end of our evening together.

But Fatimeh's desire to portray herself and her guests as they really look prevails. Two days later in her office, we negotiate what can be written. Her suit, her pearls, her hose, her shoes can be described; the shape of her body and the color and length of her hair cannot. "Don't talk about hair," she says. "That's going too far."

It is not hard for a woman, especially a foreigner, to go too far. The Hejab ("Islamic Dress") Club, a huge state-run sports facility for women in the heart of Teheran, provides athletics for the Islamic masses. Unlike the chic, private gyms in north Teheran, it is a place where ordinary women can pursue sports like basketball, karate, squash, judo and hockey far from the gaze of men. But there are rules.

"You can't go inside dressed like that," a young, sour-faced woman in a black chador barks at me as she blocks my entry into the cavernous building. "Take off your lipstick and cover your head better."

I tell her, loudly and in English, that she has no right to stop me—I'm a foreigner, a non-Muslim and a guest of Faezeh Hashemi, the President's second daughter, who as the head of the Women's Sports Federation is her boss. A female interpreter with whom I am working dutifully translates. The guard, confused, frowns and eventually steps aside.

Why she is so concerned about my appearance is baffling. Inside, I find an enormous overheated swimming pool where about 200 women in colorful bathing suits and caps are taking lessons and practicing their strokes. "You see, the rumors that women wear black chadors to swim is not true," Fatemeh Karamzadeh, the club's deputy director, dressed in a polo shirt and denim shorts. What surprises me even more, given the guard's vigilance, are the women casually walking around the locker rooms totally naked.

I am shown only what the officials of the club want me to see, but as often happens in Iran, more is revealed. In the midst of my tour of the medical clinic and emergency room attached to the club, Dr. Elham Rahimian, an English-speaking radiologist who works here as a volunteer, says matter-of-factly that most of the women who come for full-scale examination are diagnosed with low-level depression. "Most of them are not even aware of it," she adds. "It is the economic pressures, the psychological pressures."

It is that reality that Faezeh is trying to fight. "If women are not active, they will become susceptible to disease and depression," she says. "And sports can fill empty times for young women. It gives them the strength and courage to be taken seriously. And it will keep them away from addiction and corruption and mischief."

This is more controversial than it may sound to the Western ear. Even today, some religious hard-liners consider exercise for women both frivolous and immoral. Last spring, bands of men beat up female bicyclists in a park outside of Teheran and a group of ayatollahs denounced bike riding, boating, running and horseback riding as sexually provocative. Faezeh argued back, insisting there was nothing un-

Islamic about bike riding. The debate that followed led to the creation of a separate and secluded—but not at all equal—bicycle path for women in the park.

Early last year, she ran for Parliament and received more votes than any candidate except Ali Akbar Nateq-Noori, the Speaker of the Parliament and the front-runner to replace her father in this month's presidential election. It has been rumored that she actually came in first but that the shell-shocked authorities gave Nateq-Noori half the votes of a candidate with a similar-sounding name. Suddenly, she became the most outspoken—and controversial—female public figure in Iran.

There is nothing soft or sentimental about the 35-year-old Faezeh, who refuses bodyguards, drives without a chauffeur, barks at her two children and grew up wanting to be a boy. She skips key debates in Parliament and sometimes forgets appointments. She wears blue jeans and sneakers under her chador, even though she is criticized for wearing Western dress. She streaks her hair. She rejects the "feminist" label because, she says, it suggests "special privileges for women." Married at 17 to a man chosen by her parents, she doesn't believe in romantic love before marriage because, she says, "love before marriage usually doesn't last."

What she does believe in, she tells me, is more power for women. "Socially, artistically, athletically our women are doing better, but in politics women haven't made much progress," she says. "Men don't have to prove themselves to be chosen for high positions, but women always do." She argues for "Islamic dress" for all women in Iran, even female athletes, although that precludes their competing in international events.

She is acutely aware of her political vulnerability. "The clerics are very powerful in this country," she says, sounding not at all like the daughter of one of the country's most powerful clerics. "And we have to do things in a way that they all agree with us. Otherwise, we could not do anything. What bothers me is when I'm portrayed as someone trying to stop the Government from doing things. If that kind of idea grows, it's going to stop me instead."

Not surprisingly, westernized secular Iranian woman scoff at Faezeh's brand of Islamic femi-nism. They call her arrogant and superficial, someone who creates public storms but doesn't follow through with concrete actions. But I was surprised to discover that some of the chador-clad women in the Government also dismiss her as a publicity seeker.

One of those women is Marzieh Vahid Dastjerdi, a 37-year-old obstetrician, surgeon, mother of two and member of Parliament. While Faezeh seizes the headlines with her radical-sounding pronouncements, Dastjerdi is waging a quieter battle to change the laws.

Over lunch in the modest apartment she gets free as a member of Parliament, Dastjerdi tells me how Faezeh is fighting the wrong battles. "She gives interviews and says what she wants to say, but if you really want to get things done, you have to do things in the Parliament," says Dastjerdi in English. "If we women say nothing and do nothing in the Parliament, men will accuse us of just occupying a chair."

In the privacy of her home, Dastjerdi is dressed in a velour print pullover and brown pants; her two daughters—ages 9 and 11—are wearing chadors over their backpacks when they arrive home from school. Dastjerdi believes so strongly in proper Islamic dress that when she escorted Benazir Bhutto, who was then the Prime Minister of Pakistan, into Iran's Parliament last year, she told her to cover up better.

Dastjerdi's agenda is ambitious, if somewhat unrealistic: to persuade Iran's clerics to allow women to serve as judges again, to prevent men from divorcing their wives at will, to prevent fathers from forcing their daughters into marriage, to open shelters for battered women, to allow non-Muslim foreign female visitors to Iran to wear hats instead of scarves.

But even the most modest proposals face determined opposition. For several days in December, I watched a rancorous debate in Parliament about whether to adjust for inflation the money a newlywed husband customarily puts in reserve for his wife in the event of a divorce. Those men who opposed it argued that it would require all debts to be adjusted for inflation and create widespread economic instability.

At one point, Abbas Abbassi, a male member of Parliament from Bandar Abbas, said: "A woman who gets married at a young age is of a high value to her husband, and as she becomes older, her value declines. So it is not right to adjust upward for inflation because she is worth less."

The female members were outraged. "He believes that women are created to be used by men, that they are the second sex which should be in man's service," Soheyla Jelowdarzadeh, a member of Parliament and an engineer, shot back. "This is against the Koran." Eventually, the measure passed by a comfortable margin.

As I move around Teheran, chatting with the English-speaking elite, I can't help thinking about a young woman I interviewed on a day trip to the holy city of Qom. "We think a woman in Islam is a tender creature, a rose flower," said the woman, a 32-year-old student at an all-women seminary and a mother of three. "And you should pay more attention to your roses than any other flower. The restrictions for women exist because Islam respects women." But those conservative views are not broadly shared, even in some of the country's most remote towns and villages. When I travel to the rural town of Rafsanjan, the birthplace of Iran's President and the center of Iran's vast pistachio-growing empire in the south, I find young women eager to liberate themselves from the constraints of men altogether. On a day honoring the prophet Mohammed, about 100 women and 30 girls meet for an afternoon party at the house of a cousin of the President's wife: girls in frilly party dresses, elderly women in ill-fitting blouses and skirts, young women in Iranian imitations of Western fashion. In the middle of the floor, two teen-age girls with long hair dance to a rhythmic drum in movements of erotic undulation.

In religious families like these, in which dating before marriage is forbidden and marriages within the family are prized, the dancing is designed as much to attract the attention of prospective mothers-in-law as to entertain. The all-female audience encourages the dancers with whistles and claps. But Nedah Salari, an 18-year-old law student at the local university, does not join in. "I don't want to get married," she says. "I don't want to take orders from a man."

Later, back in Teheran, I have a chance to meet Fatimeh and Faezeh's mother, Iran's First Lady, Effat Marashi. When I first asked Fatimeh if I could call on her mother at home, she said, "Don't even ask such a thing." Now we all are together in the living room of a modern but surprisingly modest house, drinking tea and eating pastries.

Marashi seems a bit uncomfortable sitting unveiled in a dark blue dress with tiny white flowers. She begins to relax as she explains how she never worked outside the home herself, but how she was a political rebel who opposed the Shah alongside her husband. She raised her daughters to be equal to her sons during the many years he spent in prison. And once, when his enemies tried to assassinate him, she threw herself over his body; he was badly wounded but not killed. Today, she sounds more like a militant feminist than the wife of an Iranian cleric.

"Every Iranian woman should become educated and use her knowledge to work outside the home," she says. "Women have been deceived, cheated. It's like this all over the world. It's time for them to go out and be active in society, to gain their own rights. There is no need to stay at home and do the housework."

So the struggle continues, as the tensions and contradictions play out in the political debates and on the streets. Newspapers continue to be shut down and intellectuals silenced. But then the regime allows someone like Shahla Sherkat to publish a provocative monthly women's magazine, Zanan, with headlines like "Why Should Only Women Be Receptionists?" "Is Your Baby Sitter Your Husband's Doll?" and "Sir, Have You Ever Beaten Your Wife?" Yet when Zanan published a photograph of a popular young Iranian film maker, dressed in a colorful print scarf, fashionable sunglasses and a garment that exposed her wrist and bangs, the magazine was swiftly confiscated.

It is also an atmosphere in which women must ride in the back of the bus, but can sit thigh-to-thigh between two male strangers in a public taxi. Women may be segregated from men in governmental offices, but squeeze close to them in the buildings' overused elevators. There are separate entrances for men and women at airports, but they sit next to each other on domestic flights.

Even what a woman wears is often a political statement. For the true believers, the uniform of revolutionary Islam remains the classic black chador. A more comfortable but still acceptable covering is a loose-fitting, drab-colored longish coat worn over a long skirt or pants and a hood that covers the head and neck. The most anti-regime dress is any kind that looks stylish, as well as accessories like jewelry or colorful kerchiefs that reveal a little hair. Sunglasses, see-through hose, jean jackets, bright colors, makeup and nail polish—all available in the clothing stores of Teheran—are clearly considered subversive in public, although they are sometimes permitted.

But even a firebrand like Faezeh isn't calling for open rebellion, because it might invite greater repression. The struggle will continue in guerrilla fashion, with women testing the limits of the rules and the tolerance of the rule makers. Subversion rather than revolution. Minimal compliance rather than outright disobedience. Dissimulation rather than defiance.

And while the older generation of secular women has little use for Faezeh and women like her, there is the beginning of at least grudging respect. "It's important that they are there," says Mehrangiz Kar, a 52-year-old Westernized lawyer who dons Islamic dress to represent female clients in divorce cases. "They have an advantage over us. They speak the language the clerics speak. They answer a verse with a verse, a saying with a saying. If they can become more courageous and solve women's problems in a shorter time than we can, more power to them."

DISCUSSION QUESTIONS

The Chanel Under the Chador

1. Sciolino compares the dilemma of gender in Iran to the dilemma of race in America. How are each of these dilemmas reflected in dress?

2. Speculate as to why plain dress for women in public is part of Islamic culture (also in Mennonite culture and women religious).

76   For Stylish Orthodox Women, Wigs That Aren't Wiggy
Elizabeth Hayt

To express joy on a festive Jewish holiday, it is traditional to wear something new. Last week, for a Passover seder at her parents' home in Borough Park, Brooklyn, Suzy Berkowitz, 50, upheld tradition from head to toe. Exemplifying the Diana Vreeland dictum that elegance is restraint, she wore new Gucci pumps and a new Armani suit, hemmed discreetly just below the knee. She also wore a custom-made wig bought for the occasion.

Like many other Orthodox women who follow Halakha, Jewish law, Mrs. Berkowitz has worn a wig since her wedding day. Women's hair exudes sensual energy, the Talmud teaches, and covering it insures a married woman's modesty.

But the Talmud also obliges a wife to care for her appearance, so though a hat or scarf will do, many Orthodox women favor wigs, the more natural looking the better.

In fact, it was impossible to tell that Mrs. Berkowitz's rich, auburn hair—bobbed chin length with soft bangs brushed off her face—was actually a wig. Stylish Orthodox women like Mrs. Berkowitz eschew synthetic ready-made wigs for custom ones of human hair that closely approximate their own tresses. And much attention is paid, from purchase to the cut and style (new high-end wigs come straight and uncut).

"We talk about wigs the way women who don't wear them talk about their hair," said Liba Noe, 45, of Borough Park, who with her husband owns Eshel Jewelry Manufacturing in Manhattan and who owns a Claire, called by its aficionados the Rolls-Royce of Orthodox wigs. "When women get together at a wedding or a party they ask, 'Where did you get your shoes, dress and wig?' They even ask, 'Who did it?'"

For Passover, Suzy Berkowitz chose a $2,000 Olga, made by Olga Berman, a Hungarian wig maker in Bensonhurst (Mrs. Berkowitz also owns a Claire and an equally high status Ralph). For that critical cut and style, she turned to Mark Garrison, whose Madison Avenue salon serves dozens of Orthodox clients who pay at least $600 to have their wigs transformed.

"Orthodox women want something contemporary and realistic, and don't want a wig to look like what it is," said Mr. Garrison as he began the slow, tedious process— three to four hours—required to shampoo, cut and style a wig. "It's a challenge. You can't rely on next time. There is no next time."

Most swank stylists, including Frederic Fekkai, John Barrett, Oribe, John Sahag and Oscar Blandi, do wigs for Orthodox women. They aim to make them modest but not matronly and definitely not wiggy, the word Orthodox women use to describe the heavy appearance of wigs.

Taking the idea of verisimilitude further, Mr. Fekkai suggested: "An Orthodox woman should have several wigs. A real haircut grows out at different lengths. You need more than one wig at different lengths."

Given the code of modesty that Orthodox women abide by, including clothes that must cover the knees, elbows and collar bone, is it a contradiction to wear a wig, especially a stylish one?

"When the practice of wearing a wig first emerged, there was quite a protest," said Rabbi Rafael Grossman, the president of the Rabbinical Council of America, the world's largest body of Orthodox rabbis. "There are those authorities who strongly object. A wig would seem to contradict the basic principle of avoiding incitement. But my personal view is that it is acceptable because the rudiments of Halakha only require women not to expose their hair, though a woman should avoid wearing a wig that could appear to be sensual."

Rabbi Avi Weiss, of the Hebrew Institute of Riverdale in the Bronx, agreed. "I would distinguish between being stylish and being immodest," he said. "Jewish law is not monolithic. There can be two views, and they can be both opposite and correct."

Wearing a wig is a fairly modern Jewish practice. Before the 19th century, proper Jewish women covered their hair with shawls or veils. In feudal times, some women actually shaved their heads to detract from their appearance and thwart rapacious landlords who had the right to claim a bride's virginity before the groom did. Today, some women who are Hasidic, an Orthodox sect, still shave their heads as an added measure of propriety. But by and large, women either pin their hair up or cut it short and wear a wig.

Many young Orthodox brides insist on wigs that match their hair in style, texture and color; which also helps ease the jitters when a newlywed first dons a wig. "I want my wig to look exactly like my hair," said Elky Stern, 22 and a student at Touro College in Brooklyn, whose long blond hair will be covered when she gets married in June. "At college, everyone who is engaged discusses wigs. Even the guys talk about it because they know the girls are nervous."

Before she was married two years ago, Rifka Locker, 20, a fourth-grade teacher from Lakewood, N.J., had Mr. Garrison style her straight, red hair. He cut it above her shoulders, angled it around her face, and layered the top in a style that became the prototype for her straight, red wig. (Orthodox rabbis frown on male stylists working on a woman's real hair once she is married). Putting on the wig the morning after her wedding, Mrs. Locker remembered: "I was confident wearing it. No one could even tell I got married."

Mrs. Locker bought her two wigs—custom-made for special occasions, ready-made for everyday—at Claire's Accuhair in Midwood, Brooklyn.

Claire Grunewald, who is Zsa Zsa Gabor-like with her false eyelashes, rhinestone-rimmed glasses and strawberry blond bob with honey highlights, is an expert sheitel macher, or wig maker. A Holocaust survivor from Hungary, she spent three years after the war in a displaced people's camp, where she was an apprentice to a German wig maker. Mrs. Grunewald immigrated to the United States in 1949, at age 17, and has devoted most of her 65 years to Orthodox women.

"I had the most beautiful strawberry blond hair and didn't want it covered when I got married, but my religion dictated it," she said. "To make matters worse, no one could style my sheitel the way I liked it. At 19, it made me look 35. So I started making my own wigs. Then I had a dream to manufacture a beautiful wig for the Jewish community. I had a dream that when you walked down a street, you wouldn't be able to say, This young woman is wearing a wig."

The women who make up most of Claire's affluent clientele travel from as far away as California and Israel for the wigs made on the premises of her family-run shop, complete with private fitting rooms. Of the 15 female workers, many sit at banquet tables, ventilating, or tying, strands of hair into wig foundations. The three male workers, who are not permitted in the salon where women try on wigs, sort unrefined hair, primarily imported from Eastern Europe, where a woman's braid sells for enough to feed a family for a month, Mrs. Grunewald said.

Six to eight braids per wig are woven into a lightweight, durable silk or lace-fitted cap. If styled, the process can take 40 to 60 hours. The cost is $1,700 for a Contessa, the ready-made style, and up to $4,000 for a custom design, depending on length and quality of hair. The expense, by tradition, falls on the bridegroom's parents.

"A Claire wig is a designer thing," said Chaya Nachsoni, the executive secretary of the company and one of Mrs. Grunewald's three daughters working at the shop. "People say to me, 'Oh, a Claire,' the wig everyone wants but no one can afford. It's the Rolls-Royce of wigs."

The status attached to a Claire wig is matched only by a Ralph, as in Raffaele Mollica, who works out of an atelier at 75th Street and York Avenue in Manhattan, where the floor is strewn with strands of hair and the walls lined with every variety of wig imaginable. There are long, dark Cher tresses, short, gray Geraldine Ferraro coifs, curly red Chelsea Clinton locks. Mr. Mollica, a native of Sicily, says he has had hundreds of Orthodox customers over the years, paying $2,700 to $3,500 for a wig that may take up to a year to make. Ralph devotees say it is well worth the wait.

Mr. Mollica got his start making wigs for Vidal Sassoon, who led the hair revolution of the 1960's, from set-and-tease to loose, flowing styles. Mr. Mollica has adapted his mentor's vision to wigs.

"He makes a wig cap which is white like my scalp," said Elisa Mermelstein, 29, a customer from Kew Gardens, Queens. "Also, the hair is thin, which prevents the wig from looking bulky. A white scalp and flat hair. Those are Ralph's trademarks. They make for a natural-looking wig."

With all the attention devoted to wigs, is there ever an opportunity for women to let down their real hair?

"Whatever the Torah prohibits the Torah permits," said Rabbi Mayer Fund, founder of the Flatbush Minyona, a synagogue in a largely Orthodox section of Brooklyn.

Since swimming is segregated by sex in Orthodox communities, women swim bare-headed, allowing their hair, which darkens from lack of sunlight, to have a fleeting chance to highlight naturally. And when Orthodox women are at home, where many wig-wearers don only a scarf lest an unexpected visitor appears, they will uncover their hair when ready for bed.

"You're keeping your hair for your husband, "Mrs. Mermelstein explained. "He's the one who gets to see it."

For Stylish Orthodox Women, Wigs That Aren't Wiggy

1. Orthodox Jewish women must wear a wig after marriage to ensure modesty. Mennonite women and Islamic women are also required to cover their hair, especially when in public places. Why do you think covering a woman's hair is so important to these religious cultures?

2. Do you often think that religious dress and being fashionable are not compatible? How has this article affected your thinking on this issue?

77 Clothing, Control, and Women's Agency: The Mitigation of Patriarchal Power

Linda Boynton-Arthur

It is "part and parcel of daily experience to feel both free and enchained, capable of shaping our own future and yet confronted by towering, seemingly impersonal, constraints."
—M. Archer, *Culture and Agency*

In this chapter, by examining how clothing can simultaneously symbolize agency and constraint, I examine the ways women move between both. I do so in a particularly rigid social context which seems to offer little opportunity for resistance—a conservative Holdeman Mennonite community.[1] Holdeman Mennonite women live within but also negotiate the boundaries of their lives, and they do so in a tightly controlled and highly patriarchal world.[2] Metaphorically referred to as "a mirror to the soul," women's clothing is considered by the Holdeman Mennonite community to be the external manifestation of inner attitudes. For Holdeman Mennonites, then, dress provides a visual display of religiosity.[3]

Sociologically speaking, it does more than this. Dress and, by extension, the body are the sites where different symbolic meanings are constructed and contested. This case substantiates Mary Douglas's thesis that the human body is a symbol for the social body, that is, that persons' bodies represent the values of the culture to which they belong. She explains that such symbols arise from pressures within a culture to create consonance between physiological and social experiences. The more value people give to social constraints, the more value they set on symbols of bodily control (Douglas 1970:67). Further, she argues that when social groups are threatened, they use the body in a symbolic manner to define and defend their boundaries (Douglas 1982a:9).

Thus the control of women's clothing by Mennonite ministers as well as the ways women resist this contest represent a negotiation of symbolic meaning for their society at large. From this perspective, neither social control nor collective resistance is a clear-cut phenomenon. These issues are negotiated in everyday interaction in even the most tightly controlled communities.

While compliance with group norms or personal control is required for all Holdeman Mennonites, for women of the community, constraints involve both formal and informal con-

---

Reprinted with permission from Linda Boynton-Arthur.

FIGURE 12.2 *Dresses worn by Holdeman Mennonite women express both a religious affiliation and status (i.e., unmarried, married, and Orthodox) within the group.*

trols that regulate almost every facet of life. The church community regulates social roles and social activities. If there is no specific rule, then usually a custom dictates the correct procedure for any activity. Diversity in any manner is frowned on. Following tradition is the rule which leads to homogeneity. Nevertheless, the women experience a measure of ambivalence. They find comfort in sameness but yearn for variety, especially in clothing.

Although Mennonites as a group feel threatened by the outside world, Holdeman Mennonite women in addition feel threatened by the men of the community. Because the women's need for variety and self-expression is expressed through subtle variations in their dress, clothing is a source of conflict between men and women. In this conflict men exercise control, with ministers having the most power. Women, however, walk a fine line between obedience to the norms and self-assertion when they react to the control exercised by men.

Plagued by anxiety, women nevertheless maneuver in a subtle manner. Through individual and group deviance from the norms, they attempt to change the details of their traditional dress. In doing so they confront the established image and

carefully fashion an alternative to the image defined by men, resisting what appear to be overwhelming constraints. Subtle changes in dress, then, function symbolically to establish solidarity among women and to circumvent patriarchal control.

Since resistance to change is characteristic of Holdeman Mennonite culture, the changes that do occur are, as we would expect, minute. Nevertheless the tension between agency and constraint, or power and resistance, becomes apparent in these subtle struggles over the symbolic meaning of woman's dress.

POWER AND RESISTANCE

Power and resistance are often examined in terms of their public impact. Control of women, however, is also an intensely personal matter tied to conceptions of self. Merten and Schwartz (1982) note that by transgressing the conventional boundaries between public and private, symbolic process in nonritual contexts acquires power to represent the self. They argue that by implicating the self in the constitution of new metaphors, symbolic process in everyday life gives meaning to normative conflict. Symbolic processes involved in normative conflict are frequently not investigated in depth in the social control literature.

Most research on social control tends to be macroscopic in nature and focuses on the use of formal/legal means of control. Goffman (1963, 1971) was among the first to remind us that there is an alternative: we could focus more microscopically in order to investigate symbolic processes. From this perspective, social control would be conceptualized as a social process which, while normatively governed, occurs in everyday interactions. The norms governing social behavior in any situation are implicit. They go unnoticed until they are violated. Then sanctions can be applied to bring behavior back into normative compliance. Here infractions are discouraged by others.

Goffman goes on to specify three forms that normative controls can take. First, there is *personal social control*. The individual refrains from improper behavior by self-regulation. If she or he has acted improperly, the offense is admitted and reparations are undertaken in order to reestablish the social norms. Second, there is *informal social control*. When the individual begins to offend, peers may warn that disapproval is imminent and that sanctions may be applied. Increasing pressure may be exerted until the offender is brought into line, which reaffirms social norms (Goffman 1971:346–347). This feedback is one of the main mechanisms of socialization. Third, the threat that an offender introduces to the social order is managed through *formal social control*. These social sanctions are administered by specialized agents such as the police. Criminals break social rules and ideally are punished. In sum, personal, informal, and formal controls are the means by which conformity to social norms is effected. Deviation is inhibited or corrected, and compliance is assured (Goffman 1971:347–348). Similarly, Douglas (1982a:5) has argued that "people who've banded together...will tend to coerce one another to develop the full implications of their style of life."

Further, Douglas (1982b) claims that all conflict within families, churches, and social groups is really about the boundaries of each institution. The dissent centers on how to deal with normative behavior that becomes encoded as rules. The rules may be as simple as dress codes or as complex as laws. Nonetheless, social control measures are used effectively by society to protect the institution's boundaries. The social body then, constrains the physical body. As a result, the body (including its care and grooming) is a highly restricted medium of expression.

One of the most significant boundaries in society is the line drawn between male and female. The gender system is defined by Schur (1984) as a pervasive network of interrelated norms and sanctions through which female (and male) behavior is evaluated and controlled. Gender-related norms maintain their dominance in society and influence the "micropolitics" of routine interactions (Emerson and Messinger 1977).

In this chapter I take Goffman's recommendation to examine social control microscopically as my analytic starting place. From this position, and using an analysis of dress, I explore both the cultural constraints on Holdeman Mennonite women and their resistance to those constraints. l argue that even in the rigid structure of Holdeman Mennonite life, where men in general and ministers in particular have the power to exercise formal social controls, women resist. Since self-control is a basic requisite of life in Mennonite societies, individual women exercise personal control. In addition, women working together in groups exercise informal collective control. These controls both reinforce dress code norms and contest them.

Holdeman Mennonite women resist not through massive insurrection, but through the most minute everyday practices. By examining how social control is both exercised and resisted within their community, we not only get a picture of the women's never-ending creativity, but we add to the theoretical discourses on social control. Drawing on the insights of Douglas (1970) and Mauss (1936), we can understand women's bodies as an image of society, as giving visual expression to sociocultural values. In other words, women's bodies must be analyzed in conjunction with this social dimension.

Thus control of the Holdeman Mennonite women's clothing by their ministers and the women's resistance to it represent a negotiation of symbolic meanings about both women's bodies and the social body. Negotiations about women's dress are also negotiations about gender and power. As ministers and women struggle over dress codes, ministers symbolically reinscribe themselves as powerful and women as other. Women's bodies, clothed as they are, are symbolically marked and located on the margins. The social body is male. As women resist the dress code, they also restrict their otherness, their location on the margins of power. These struggles take place in the context of an ever-present historical past, which continues to have a great deal of influence on the Holdeman Mennonites' everyday life. History and tradition are used to maintain the status quo and prevent change.

SOME HISTORY

Branded in Europe as heretics, Mennonites migrated throughout the Continent from the sixteenth century on, hoping to escape religious persecution. Eventually some came to North America, where they established isolated communities required to "live and dress simply in avoidance of the world" (Boynton 1986; Hiebert 1973:25). This separation was facilitated by strict social control measures.

The theme that links social control and clothing norms is the historical pattern of "avoidance" or separation from the world. Mennonites believe that there are two kingdoms—the kingdom of God and the kingdom of the world. Separation from "the world" was a simple matter while the Mennonites were physically isolated in remote communities. However, as non-Mennonites moved in among these sectarians, Mennonites began to feel their influence, and many became acculturated. For conservative Mennonites who saw acculturation as a threat, separation from the world became a divisive issue that led to several schisms, including the Holdeman schism of 1859.

Alluding to acculturation and citing the loss of Mennonite distinctiveness, John Holdeman and his followers left the Old Mennonite church. For them, separation from the world was accomplished symbolically by retention of many of the old traditions, including plain dress,[4] formalized in both proscribed and prescribed dress codes. According to Hiebert (pers. comm. 1980), in the early days of the sect Holdeman had prescribed a dress code for women which was characterized by a cape dress with a high neck, loose bodice, and fitted waist.

The historical pattern of modest and plain clothing has continued. Like other "plain people," the Holdemans believe that a lack of emphasis on external beauty leads to the expression of spirituality (Scott 1986:15). Clothing, as all of life, has to be brought under the scrutiny of New Testament standards. The most salient symbol of a woman's Christianity is her black head-covering, worn to symbolize her submission to God, to men in general, and to her husband in particular.

Within Mennonite culture, women have always been subservient to the men. According to the Holdeman Mennonites, male power and female submission are divinely ordered and are rooted in the Bible, the authoritative word of God. This belief results in gender-based segregation within the sect. Men hold all positions of formal power. A group of ten to twelve ministers and deacons are expected to define and eliminate deviance in behavior and appearance. For these patriarchs, control of deviance seems a straightforward matter. Guidelines are based on tradition and the communal goal of living a good Christian life. Through consensus among themselves they determine where the boundaries of deviance are drawn—boundaries that make most change deviant.

If men have the formal power in the family and community, women have informal power rooted in their age-sets. Deliberately emphasizing the corporate nature of social groups, age-sets are a particular type of social organization, a permanent grouping of individuals by age and sex. The Holdemans are patrilocal, so as women marry into a congregation, they are accepted into an age-set.[5] Usually persons enter the set as children and pass through the age-grades as a group; as a consequence, "I" becomes "we" and suppresses individuality (Gulliver 1968:157–161).

In church and other social situations, such as picnics and dinners at the social hall, the sexes remain separate.[6] A Holdeman Mennonite woman, then, interacts primarily in a world of women organized by age-sets. These groups comprise not just a social network, but a working social organization whose complex function is devoted to affirming social norms. It monitors its own behavior in order to insure compliance to religious norms, while at the same time supporting some infractions of the norms. As a consequence, the age-set provides an informal female channel that subverts the formal channels of male control.

THE STUDY COMMUNITY

I studied a specific Holdeman Mennonite community called Bend in northern California, a farming community of 310 persons on the Sacramento River.[7] The community is comprised of sixty-five families. Because land is inherited patrilineally, it is common for several generations of a family to live on farms near each other. Most of the men in the community are farmers, and all of the married women are housewives. Large families are the norm (five children average), and raising children as good Christians is the central focus for all.

The community interacts extensively with the other West Coast Holdeman Mennonite congregations beyond Bend. These communities are linked through a national church conference, missionary work, and marriage. Since the Holdeman Mennonites are religiously endogamous, approximately half the young women leave to marry men from other congregations. The combination of endogamy, patrilocal residence, and few converts creates a community in which most people are related (at least distantly) to each other.

I collected data in two phases. During the first phase of fieldwork, which was intermittent and occurred over a forty-month period, I observed and conducted casual interviews with church members (1979–1984).[8] During the second phase, which occurred between 1985 and 1987, with follow-up interviews in 1991, I interviewed, in groups and individually, most of the local people who had left the church. Almost all of them had been formally expelled. These interviews were tape-recorded and transcribed. Because these people had not returned to the church even under the intense pressure of shunning, they were acutely aware of the power of tradition, history, and social control in Mennonite society.

Tradition and control within the community overlap in the women's clothing. Dresses have changed little since the early days of the sect. Following the styles of their forebearers, women and girls wear shirtwaist dresses characterized by a wide, long skirt and a fitted bodice with buttons down the center to the waist. There is generally a small collar and belt. The uniform attire of Holdeman Mennonite women attests to separation from external society as well as separation of the sexes. Dress reflects the assumed natural gender differences that underlie patriarchal family and social systems.

A MIRROR TO THE SOUL: CONTROLLING THE IMAGE

Since nearly all members of the Holdeman Mennonite community attend every church activity, objective evaluation of a person's commitment to the faith is impossible, so symbolic measures such as dress codes are employed instead. The sexes have different standards as to proper Mennonite dress. While the women dress in a uniquely Mennonite style, the men dress in Levis and plaid shirts, much like outsiders. John and his wife were expelled for differing with the ministers over interpretation of doctrine. He explained: "It's always been that way. Women have always had to dress more carefully. It's a way of the men controlling the women. Holdeman men *need* to control women [because] they feel so controlled themselves." According to his wife, "The men feel like they're accomplishing something if they can get someone to do what they require of them. That is control—women's clothing shows they are being controlled—they have to dress plainer than the men."

A person's religious commitment is exhibited through personal control, so formal measures of social control are not often needed.

However, cases such as those described below serve a preventative function in that they demonstrate to women the price they must pay for deviating from norms enforced by both informal and formal social control.

Formal Control

Ministers and deacons (all men) mete out in public formal measures of social control, including general displays of power, formal reprovals, denial of communion, a practice known as "church repentance," and expulsion. Most of their formal social control of women is related to Mennonite men's particular image of a "proper" Mennonite woman. She should be sober in demeanor and appearance. She is expected to be thin and modestly dressed, visually testifying to her self-control over what are termed "lusts of the flesh." Sensory enjoyment is considered sinful; consequently, such pleasures as eating and sexual and emotional expressions are repressed. Any activity done solely for fun, or to excess, is prohibited. Self-denial is the rule in Mennonite life and is expected to be visible in appearance.

A woman's head covering is a potent symbol of her self-denial, submission, and acceptance of group norms. The following incident over such a head covering, related by an expelled woman, reflects conflict between women and ministers:

> We went through a period of time where we were having some trouble about the head covering. It is a three-cornered black flat scarf, which only becomes round when you shape and fold it around the bun. If you have a lot of hair, this is hard to do—you pin it on at the top, bring it down, fold in each side, tie it under, tuck the bottom tail around, and then it looks like a cap. What we began to do was to sew caps so we could just slap them on and pin them down. That wasn't allowed because the ministers said it wasn't traditional—but they only look at history if they can use it to their advantage.

Women often get into "church trouble," which usually starts with public reprovals. These typically began at a staff meeting (a weekly meeting of all the ministers and deacons), where the men discuss behavior considered deviant. And because rigid conformity is the norm for this sect, it does not take much to be labeled deviant. Women who are so labeled are continually watched by the staff for symbols that are perceived as deviations from established rules. An individual's behavior is interpreted in light of the deviance label, and this results in unequal enforcement of the rules. For example, Leah was in "church trouble" from the time she reached puberty until her midthirties, when she was expelled from the church. She recounted a reproval by the ministers:

> I was eight-and-a-half months pregnant and overweight, and I had borrowed a maternity dress from my older sister Jane [an orthodox member], and I was sitting there and they were giving me the third degree—asking why I do this, or that—and I was crying and they asked why couldn't I please my husband. And one of the ministers said, "Just take for instance that dress you're wearing." It was a decent dress, but he said, "That dress is loud—a woman like you wearing such a dress is offensive." Jane wore it many times after I did, and never was reproved for it. I was the only one who was; it was because they saw me as a threat, because I have always been attractive and not ashamed of it. Ministers always kept their eyes on me.

This incident occurred at the church and involved only the ministers, Leah, and her husband. Formal reproval most often occurs in this manner. It is also common, however, for the errant member to be brought before the entire congregation for a public reproval. "Men do not get reproved very often: women are reproved by men in order to control them," Sharon reports during a group interview. As a member becomes more recalcitrant, the increasingly public and formal nature of the social control becomes evident.

Denial of communion and "church repentance" are formal declarations of deviant status. Leah stated: "The last few years they weren't allowing me to go to communion. They didn't really have anything on me except for my clothes, which was what they harped on. And my clothes were pretty much like everyone else's." "Church repentance" is a period of formal censure. According to an expelled woman, "repentance is like purgatory, like hell, like being shunned, but not quite. You're untouchable. People look at you and weep, because they know you're going to hell." In general these measures are effective in controlling deviance. Some women, however, are unable to accept the power of the ministers and are expelled.

The most drastic form of formal social control, expulsion, is followed by shunning (social ostracism). After appropriate deliberations, ministers expel people at a members' meeting. In Bend, 22 percent of members are expelled, which supports the national figure of 20 percent cited by Hiebert (1973:402). When expelled, a person is not allowed to eat at the same table with the family or have social or economic interactions with church members. The intense pressure generally is successful in returning the member to the fold.

Becky, who has been expelled five times, is one such member. She stated she could foretell her own impending church trouble when she began to experience an increasingly negative attitude toward Mennonite clothing:

> It felt suffocating, as though when I put on the clothes, I put on the church's rules. I was a different person in worldly [fashionable] clothing—I was uncontrolled. The church's rules didn't apply to me. As I got back into the frame of mind that is expected, I grew to appreciate that God wants me in the church; as that happened, I no longer wanted worldly clothes. Eventually, putting on the Mennonite clothes and head covering felt right.

Thus Becky's crisis was apparent visually in her appearance. This illustration points to the ability of clothing to symbolize not just group affiliation, but the construction and affirmation of both personal and cultural identity.

Informal Control

Maintaining group norms is the expressed purpose of informal social control measures. Using methods ranging from gossip to reproval (formal criticism), women insure conformity to norms and function as social control agents within their age-sets. They spend a great deal of time in the company of their friends, and the other members of the community are the main topic of conversation. Since intense scrutiny is considered a sign of Christian love, nothing goes unnoticed. When she breaks a norm, a woman knows the transgression will be noticed and become a current topic of conversation. If that threat is ineffective in redirecting her behavior, a woman's best friends will talk to her directly and express their concern for her spirituality. Members are continually aware of clothing and use it to gauge a person's submission of self to the group. Anna stated that "when Leah was expelled, it was so sudden. There were no signs that she was in trouble....Even her clothing was the same—I'd have expected to see some changes, like her dresses getting fancy or something, 'cause clothing was so important to her."

In the last months prior to her expulsion, Leah's conformity to clothing norms continued in spite of her ongoing difficulty with the ministers and deacons. This example illuminates a larger issue; women derive satisfaction from their social ties, and to retain them, the self is always subjugated to the will of the group. Deviation from the group standard is equated (negatively) with pride. Signs of individuality are seen as a rejection of group norms and values. Naturally, the expression of individuality in clothing is too obvious to be ignored. Charity, a minister's daughter who left the church in 1970 but still lives in Bend, concluded:

> If your clothes are straight down the lines as to the rules of the group, then everyone can see that you are submitting your will to the church. The Mennonite dress is like a uniform—it indicates that you're keeping everything under control. When you're having trouble with the rules, your clothing can show it. This is why everyone watches what everyone else is wearing and how they are wearing it, because clothing shows acceptance of all the rules of the church.

Some women resent the amount of control men exert over women, especially in regard to dress. Leah stated: "We have to conform to whatever the men want, whether it's the way we dress or our behavior. They think it's scriptural. I think it's just another way to *tame women down* [her emphasis]. The men say 'women, submit your-selves to your husbands.'" And submit they do to both formal public reprovals and informal pri-vate reprovals which generally occur between two women. One woman recalled: "On the first Sunday that my daughter wore little anklets with lace around them, Rachael reproved me. She was really on her toes to catch that the first time they were worn!" Rachael's daughter explained: "In her heart, my mother despises confronta-tions. She comes from a long line of ministers, and will do anything to avoid getting into con-flict with them." In order to prevent such con-flict with the ministers, Rachael reproved other women out of sisterly concern.

It is in the best interest of all the women to keep each other committed to the social norms, in order to insulate themselves from formal control by the ministers. An expelled woman described reprovals she experienced while still a member:

> I was reproved for wearing a low-neck dress—it was a dress which was unbuttoned to just below the collarbone. The woman who reproved me was wearing a neckline lower than mine—but reproved me anyway....I was occasionally reproved for my daughter's dresses—I made her beautiful dresses which were a little bit on the fancy side. She loved them! Now that I've been expelled, the Mennonite women make ugly, plain dresses for her that she prefers to wear. She won't wear anything that I made anymore.[10]

Women are reproved for any number of infractions, but clothing is one of the more fre-quent topics. Katie said that "for instance, if my sister or a friend started wearing shorter skirts, I would worry that she was losing her spirituality. I would express my concern about this, and she would probably lower her hems." Holdeman women do not see this gesture as interference; instead they accept the informal reprovals as indicative of sisterly concern. The consensus is that women maintain vigilance over each other to keep themselves from straying too far from the norms and risking formal reprovals.

Through vigilance within their age-sets, women informally control their own dress, whereas men exert formal control over women

and their appearance. These forms of control function quite differently. By enforcing a particu-lar image of "proper" Mennonite dress for women and not allowing deviations from the clothing norms, the ministers exert a great deal of power and try to inhibit resistance. As they con-trol women's dress, men both reflect and rein-force a particular image of women's bodies and the social body—an image that sustains their patriarchal power. By contrast, when women control women's dress, they provide some resis-tance to that power. They offer an alternative, no matter how minute—an alternative that mitigates against patriarchal power. They assert collective independence by using hypertraditional dress in order to bring about changes in the less salient aspects of Holdeman Mennonite dress. Dressing more traditionally than men keeps women above male reproach. By informally enforcing dress codes among themselves, they actively deny men the opportunity to exert formal control. They actively deny men the opportunity to reinforce their patriarchal authority. Not only do women resist by depriving men of the opportunity to rein-force their definition, but they participate in shaping an alternative image of both women's bodies and the social body.

A MIRROR TO THE SOUL: SHAPING AN ALTERNATIVE IMAGE

By working together, Mennonite women are able to balance the restrictions imposed by min-isters with some measure of individual expres-sion. This process is empowering and results in some deviations from the usually explicit dress code. While not all the women approve of these variations, they stand together and do not inter-fere with the changes. The most obvious devia-tions occur among young women.

The community generally understands that adolescence is a period fraught with tension. Men defer to their wives in raising daughters, and the girls are given some leeway with the dress code. Girls exhibit rebellion by secretly wearing "worldly" clothing. Mary recalled that when she went to public high school (late

1960s), many of the Mennonite girls kept worldly clothing in their school lockers. Charity agreed: "I'd sneak them out of the house; I kept some worldly things at school. I also wore two-inch-wide belts, so that when I rolled up the waistband to shorten the skirt, the roll wouldn't show. This way, dresses could be long around adults and short at school like the other [non-Mennonite] girls." Leak was in public school at about the same time as Charity and Mary and recalled that "It was in high school that I really wanted to dress different than the Mennonites.... My friends and I all dressed in worldly clothes when we got the chance. But they didn't have to sneak the clothes out as much as I did, 'cause my parents were so conservative. They could get by with fancier clothes…than I could."

Girls are not allowed to wear makeup, other than a medicinal foundation if they have acne. However, it is typical for Mennonite girls to use foundation and minimal makeup. According to Charity, "makeup has always been forbidden, but we used to sneak out mascara….I would dye my eyelashes with this stuff called Dark Eyes. Mom wondered why my lashes got so dark! The girls in the church now are wearing makeup, but they're sneaking it. They only wear enough that it barely shows." The ministers are apparently unable to discern subtle makeup from the absence of makeup. Leah stated that "the ministers would ask, 'do you wear eyebrow paint'? I'd say no. I wore mascara but I figured that if they didn't know the name for it, I wasn't gonna help them out. They didn't even know the difference."

In addition to using makeup, young women have more latitude with their wardrobes. The most overt instance of rule bending concerned Charity's sister-in-law who converted just before she married. Although "she's a total Mennonite today, she did rebel a little, for a while [just after she married] she left her hair down and wore jeans." Although this is generally unacceptable, the women in the congregation knew about it and looked the other way.

Similarly, the more conservative women overlook the tendency for young women to invest a great deal of time, energy, and money in their wardrobes. While Mennonite women agree that it is required that clothing be modest, single women wear dresses that fit snugly. Charity remarked: "If you're single, clothes are for sexual attraction, but you can't be too obvious. Once you've caught a man, there's no need to put so much time in extensive wardrobes.…When you have to wear one basic style, the only way to get variety is to have a lot of dresses. Many girls have extensive wardrobes." Becky concurred: "girls spend a lot of time designing dresses to be different from everyone else's. We find details to add that won't be objectionable. That's one reason why our dresses look different from the married ladies'—they don't have the time, or need to attract male attention!" The differences alluded to include such structural details as tucks, pleats, and yokes. Applied details are never acceptable, although details that could be considered functional are overlooked. There is an understanding that the rules of modesty can be bent during this short time in a woman's life, since marrying is of utmost importance.

A woman is not considered an adult until she has borne a child, so until then she is able to bend the rules somewhat. With motherhood, however, comes full adulthood and the expectation that a woman will become more settled and submissive. This expectation is apparent in the clothing of married women; they exhibit greater acceptance of the dress code, which reflects the corporate nature of the age-set. When deviations do occur, they are typically collective in nature.

Shoes (other than tennis shoes) must be black or brown, following tradition. They may not have heels smaller than a dime, and no open heels or toes are permitted. This effectively limits shoe selection to flat, unfashionable styles. Most Mennonite women, however, are short and want to appear taller, so when three-inch-high wedge-heeled shoes came into style in the 1970s, they were quickly bought by Mennonite women. Anna remembered that "the ministers complained that these were too worldly, but what could they do? We'd found the perfect solution to get around the rules!" Additionally, when black and brown shoes were no longer fashionable and became unavailable, Mennonite women dyed white shoes in an apparent attempt to get the acceptable colors. However, the accuracy of shoe dyes left much to be desired and some color variation came into the wardrobes of grateful Mennonite women. Katie remarked that "I used brown dye but got mauve—and I like it! [The minister] couldn't say anything, 'cause it'd be a waste to throw them out!"

Adherence to tradition, a major goal of the ministers, runs into conflict when it comes up against technological change. For example, women may not replace buttons with zippers. Nevertheless, the women found a way to circumvent the ministers' decision: "Changes happen that the ministers say don't follow tradition—we wanted to use zippers in the 1960s to save work. It takes a lot of time to make a dress that buttons," recalled Charity. (Several hours could be saved by constructing a garment that closes with a zipper rather than buttons.) However, the ministers sensed a redesign of the costume and could not be persuaded to accept the change, so the women agreed to keep the buttons and buttonholes down the front of the dress but to insert a zipper in the side seam to make getting dressed easier.

Traditionally, Mennonite women made their dresses out of printed cotton fabrics, but in the 1970s polyester knit fabrics were rapidly adopted when they became available. Not only is it quicker and easier to make dresses of polyester knit, but the fabric needs no ironing. Mennonite women consciously choose fabrics that resemble the old cotton calico prints they traditionally used in order to make a significant change without drawing the attention of the ministers.

Resistance to the image of the "proper" Mennonite woman as proscribed by the ministers is subtle. The most obvious examples of resistance are found in deviations from the clothing norms. In recent years, weight has also been a subject of quiet revolution. According to the local physician, in the early 1980s the obesity rate for adult Mennonite women was 15 percent, compared to thirty-five percent for women in the surrounding community (J. Bradshaw, pers. comm., 1988). Mennonite women kept their weight down through weight-loss programs and exercise. Recently, however, the obesity rate of

Mennonite women is increasingly noticed by their non-Mennonite neighbors, one of whom said, "It used to be that Mennonite women were always thin, and we were fat. Now, they're as chubby as we are!" (J. Perez, pers. comm., 1991). One Mennonite woman explained, "We spend most of the day cooking, and it's hard not to eat. But our husbands want us thin—that's so hard to do when we're always in the kitchen. It's getting hard to keep them [husbands] happy." The increased obesity rate of Mennonite women could be interpreted as a covert attempt to defy their husbands' control over their bodies.

The preceding examples demonstrate Holdeman Mennonite women's subtle resistance to both private (family) and public (societal) patriarchy. There is no mindless subjugation of self. While the women may appear submissive, their motivations are complex. They reinforce the dress norms while also resisting the image proscribed for them by the ministers. While there is overt submission, on a more covert level there is collective resistance which supports women's dissension. Women work together, within the age-set, to protect themselves from men's control by monitoring their own behavior. Through their own informal control, women protect themselves from male censure and fashion an alternative image to counteract the image proscribed by men.

While individual men spend much of their time alone, women are constantly involved with other women. Friendship between the sexes is exceedingly rare, and interaction between husband and wife is kept to a minimum. As a consequence, men are excluded from women's lives and are intentionally kept in the dark about things of interest to women. Women take advantage of male ignorance and through their age-sets are able subtly to circumvent the rules. Both resistance and reinforcement of the norms are possible because women's age-sets build solidarity. An individual alone is unable to bend the rules, but women as a group are able to make small changes in the dress codes. The result of this corporate resistance is creation of alternatives to male characterizations of both women's bodies and the social body. These alternatives resist rather than reinforce patriarchal authority.

Conclusions

The constraints on Mennonite women seem overwhelming. However, these women were raised to suppress individual needs and to yield to group control. The formal structure of the Holdeman Mennonite community as a whole is expressed by men, while the informal structure of the women's age-set supports both community norms and some deviances. The age-set is a first line of defense against the structure imposed by men. Clothing is a major source of conflict between men and women. It is the site of struggle—a struggle between the patriarchal social system and the collective agency of the women's age-set groups. It is also a source for building solidarity among women.

In these struggles, it is not only clothing per se that is negotiated. Dress is the site of conflict in which symbolic meanings are negotiated and contested. Dress is a metaphor; it is interpreted as a visual symbol of the suppression of the self to the demands of the community. In this conflict, the physical body becomes a symbol for the social body. In the case of the Holdeman Mennonites, women's bodies become the focus of a symbolic struggle over both personal and group identities—a struggle that draws attention to the ways freedom and constraint go hand in hand.

Freedom and constraint are apparent in conflict over the Mennonite dress code. While men exercise both private and public power over the female body, women help keep each other in line and overlook some deviations from normative behavior. Thus they both reinforce and resist normative constraints. There is a double nature to the agency of Mennonite women. Both actions resist the characterization of a social body ruled entirely by men. Both empower women and build solidarity within the age-sets and for women as a whole.

Religious dogma is used to rationalize admonishing women for infractions of a rigid dress code, since clothing is seen as evidence of either religious conformity or deviance. The greater the deviance from the dress code, the more likely the woman will be reproved by the ministers. The women's age-sets are able to enforce and mitigate that discipline, however.

Resistance of this kind points to the need to go beyond narrowly defined descriptions of agency. A singular focus on either structural constraints or personal agency seems inadequate to analyze the Holdeman Mennonite case. It is through a constant process of negotiation that boundaries are delineated, negotiated, and redefined.

Notes

1. There are about 300,000 Mennonites in the United States today. The Mennonites are prone to schisms, and at least twenty major divisions represent liberal, mainstream, and conservative philosophies. One of the most conservative sects is the Holdeman Mennonites, who number over 10,000 in the United States (Scott 1986:35). Formally known as the Church of God in Christ, Mennonite, members of this branch are called Holdemans, Holdeman Mennonites, or (by the local outsiders) Mennonites. In this chapter, I generally refer to the group as Holdeman Mennonites. When the term *Mennonite* is used, it refers to the larger body of Mennonites.

2. *Patriarchy is* used here to indicate both a family system in which men control women and children in the private sphere, and a social system, characterized by the formal and public control of society by men. This usage follows Carol Brown's (1981) discussion of private and public patriarchy.

   Brown distinguishes between public patriarchy (i.e., a patriarchal social system) and private patriarchy. She states that private patriarchy includes the individual relations found in the traditional family, in which men have control over women, their labor (productive and reproductive), and their children. However, Brown notes that patriarchy is not just a family system. In the social system, we find public aspects of patriarchy that function to uphold rights and privileges of the collective male sex. A husband's control of his wife's daily life is reinforced by the larger-scale monopolization of the social and economic world by men. In current U.S. family law, private patriarchy intersects with public patriarchy (Brown 1981:240). In most of the United States today, it is public not private patriarchy that is problematic for women. For the Mennonites, however, public and private patriarchy constantly intersect, which functions to keep power firmly in male hands.

3. For a discussion of clothing as a metaphor of religiosity, see Boynton 1989 and Poll 1962.

4. "Plain dress" is required by most conservative Amish, Mennonite, and Hutterite churches. It illustrates the values of modesty, piety, economy, and simplicity and provides visual testimony to the commitment and fellowship of the group. For further reading on this topic, see Scott 1986.

5. In Holdeman Mennonite society, the major age-sets for women are girls (sixteen and older, unmarried), mothers (married to age thirty-five), and older women (over thirty-five). Mennonite women refer to unmarried young women as girls. Spinsterhood is rare. It is acknowledged that, without a husband, a woman has few options and a nebulous status. The good things in life, family and children, only come to married women.

6. One woman in the community explained this separation in the following way: "well, you want to be with your friends, the ones you grew up with. After all, you can talk to your husband at home." It is only in the homes that the sexes mingle.

7. I've changed the names of persons and places to insure anonymity.

8. Sixty-three of the seventy-eight adult women, both married and unmarried, were interviewed.

9. A person who will not be controlled by the church is expelled and shunned, which means the expelled person is cut off socially and economically from everyone in the group. As a result of this pressure, the person usually begs for forgiveness and returns (85 percent return to the church). During the second phase of my fieldwork I interviewed

95 percent of the ex-Mennonites who lived within a hundred-mile radius of Bend.

10. This situation was highly unusual. The woman was expelled while she and her husband were having marital problems that ultimately ended in divorce. Initially she was unjustly accused of adultery, after which she became bitter and did have an affair. Eventually she left her husband and was denied access to her children, so the women in the community took over their care. In this instance, public and private patriarchy clearly intersected. Only one other divorce occurred in the history of this community.

References

Archer, M. 1988. *Culture and Agency: the Place of Culture in Social Theory.* Cambridge: Cambridge University Press.

Boynton, L. 1986. *The Plain People: An Ethnography of the Holdeman Mennonites.* Salem, Wisc.: Sheffield Press.

— —.1989. "Religious Orthodoxy, Social Control and Clothing: Dress and Adornment as Symbolic Indicators of Social Control among Holdeman Mennonite Women." Paper presented at the American Sociological Association annual meetings, San Francisco.

Brown, C. 1981. "Mothers, Fathers and Children: From Private to Public Patriarchy." In *Women and Revolution: A Discussion of the Unhappy Marriage of Marxism and Feminism,* ed. L. Sargent. Boston: South End Press.

Douglas, M. 1970. *Body Symbols.* Oxford: Blackstone.

— —. 1982a. *Essays in the Sociology of Perception.* London: Routledge and Kegan Paul.

— —.1982b. *Natural Symbols.* New York: Pantheon Books.

Emerson, R.M., and S. Messinger. 1977. "The Micro-Politics of Trouble." *Social Problems* 25 (December): 121–134.

Goffman, E. 1963. *Stigma: Notes on the Management of Spoiled Identity.* Englewood Cliffs, N.J.: Prentice-Hall.

——. 1971. *Relations in Public.* New York: Harper and Row.

Gulliver, P. H. 1968. "Age Differentiation." In *International Encyclopedia of the Social Sciences.* New York: Macmillan.

Hiebert, C. 1973. *The Holdeman People.* Pasadena, Calif.: William Carey Library.

Mauss, M. 1936. "Les techniques du corps." *Journal de la Psychologie* 32 (March/April): 372–383.

Merten, D., and G. Schwartz. 1982. "Metaphor and Self: Symbolic Processes in Everyday Life." *American Anthropologist* 84:796-810.

Poll, S. 1962. *The Hasidic Community in Williamsburg.* New York: Free Press.

Schur, E. 1984. *Labeling Women Deviant: Gender, Stigma and Social Control.* New York: Random House.

Scott, S. 1986. *Why Do They Dress That Way?* Intercourse, Pa.: Good Books.

DISCUSSION QUESTIONS

Clothing, Control and Women's Agency: The Mitigation of Patriarchal Power

1. What are the subtle changes Mennonite girls and women make to their dress in order to combat the strict dress code set by male ministers?

2. Are changes made by individuals typically successful? Why or why not?

78 From Habit to Fashion: Dress of Catholic Women Religious

Susan O. Michelman
University Of Massachusetts/Amherst

This article focuses on data with 26 Roman Catholic nuns, or as those in noncloistered orders prefer to be called, "women religious" who relinquished religious habits for secular dress. It examines dynamics of personal identity announcements and social identity placements that are not congruous. Prior to the 1960s, women's religious orders were quite homogeneous both in exterior manifestations such as their dress in the habit, and in the purpose and spirit that permeated them (Ebaugh, 1977). Their personal and social persona were one and the same. The life of a woman religious was highly prescribed and routinized. During the

1960s and 1970s, the majority of women in non-cloistered orders of the Roman Catholic Church, as part of larger reforms dictated by Vatican II in 1962, relinquished religious habits for secular fashions. Many had worn habits for a large portion of their lives, often between 20 and 35 years, dressing in them from the moment they arose in the morning until they retired in the evening. Their social identities were more outwardly visible than their personal identities, as they had relinquished individuality for social

Original for this text.

control of their bodies by the Church. From the time that women religious first wore religious attire as novices, they were instructed to view themselves not as individuals, but as representatives of a group. Their habits symbolized their commitment and vows to the Church, which superseded their individual identities (Griffin, 1975). (See Figures 12.3a and b.)

Prior to Vatican II, which occurred in 1962, for many women in noncloistered religious orders, the habit came to be viewed in a more negative than positive light. Their perception was that this dress communicated a social identity that inhibited their ability to express personal identities that would allow them to function more fully in secular environments. The habit clearly symbolized their total commitment to their order, but it was described by them as a social control in their ability to interact and communicate freely as individuals. As described by women in this study, the habit made them feel less than fully human.

Ebaugh (1977), in her research on religious orders, confirmed that personal identity issues were not addressed by the Church prior to Vatican II. She describes the indoctrination of women religious as demanding ideological totalism (Lifton, 1961). In her research, she discussed the mechanisms of social control that made totalism work. The symbolic gesture of exchanging secular dress for black religious garb was "the first symbolic gesture of 'putting off the world' and entering into a new life" (Ebaugh, 1977):

The uniform was characterized by complete simplicity and modesty, being high-necked, long-sleeved, and ankle length. In addition to the uniform, feminine lingerie was exchanged for simple white cotton underwear, indicating that the postulant was exchanging her womanly enjoyments for austere dress that would now symbolize her as the spouse of Jesus Christ. In addition, henceforth the woman

a

b

FIGURE 12.3 *Sisters of Providence dressed in (a) modified habit and (b) full habit.*

was no longer to be distinguished by dress from the other women in the institute with whom she would live.

Historically, the habit did not start as a symbol of religious life, rather, it was the widow's dress of the day. In the case of the Sister's of St. Joseph, it started with six women in France in the 17th century, who went out two by two to minister to the needs of the people (Aherne, 1983). They wore modest black dresses and veils, because women who were widows were allowed more personal freedom than those who were single or married. They could travel without male chaperones. These women were able to circumvent both church and state regulations. This early "habit" was a protection in a sense, and it allowed them to be free to do the work they wanted. Some of the women in this study felt that prior to Vatican II, the Church saw the habit as a protection against the "evils of the world." The voluminous layers of black serge and veiling covering their bodies, heads, and necks cloaked both femininity and sexuality. In the eyes of the women in this study, it also suppressed their personal identity. Ironically, whereas the "habit" had historically begun as a way of achieving autonomy, this type of dress had evolved into a way of suppressing personal identity, through the social control of their bodies. It is important to bear in mind that the women in this study did not leave religious orders after Vatican II; rather, they had remained as members and had negotiated their identity within the boundaries of the Church. They negotiated some social control issues with the Church symbolically by discarding the habit for secular dress.

The women in my study dressed in contemporary fashions that made them indiscernible from any other modestly dressed professional woman in American society. Some orders like their members to wear some visible indication of their affiliation as women religious, such as a ring or cross (Ebaugh, 1993), but many of the women in my study did not. The habit, for many women in noncloistered religious orders, came to be viewed by them prior to Vatican II, in a more negative than positive light. Their perception was that dress inhibited their ability to

have positive social interactions as people; rather, they were frequently stereotyped by the symbolic nature of the habit. The habit visually symbolized and promoted interactions with others that reinforced this belief.

> Interviewer: If you were sitting there in a habit, I would feel differently. I would feel a little more inhibited, more cautious, more formal.
>
> Respondent: Your experience is the other end of what I'm trying to describe to you about coming out of habit.
>
> Interviewer: You are talking about it being an inhibition for you—an inhibition in social interaction?
>
> Respondent: Yes it was—because immediately when people saw us, they didn't see us as the individual that you were. They saw you as the woman religious and they immediately raise you above the human level. We had privilege and prestige and we were considered to be in a holier state of life. That's not true. I've chosen another way to live but it is not a holier way—it's a different way.

At the present time, the work and lifestyles of women religious in active orders is highly liberated in contrast to the period prior to Vatican II. When the habit was relinquished, social control of the body by the Church decreased. For example, today, women exhibit a high degree of personal autonomy, many living alone or in small groups instead of orders, fully integrated into the noncelibate lay community (Ebaugh, 1993). Dress, in light of many social changes for women religious, has been critical in not only reflecting, but also helping them to construct social change, specifically by its role in symbolic interaction processes related to the formation and perpetuation of personal identity.

EMERGING FROM THE HABIT: FASHION AND SECULAR CLOTHING

After Vatican II, which was a period of emerging personal identity, the women experienced profound conflicts surrounding dress and its complex relationship with their vow of poverty. The essence of the vow of poverty of spirit is humility, which is facilitated by material poverty (Metz, 1968). The habit had come to be accepted as a visible symbol of humility, while fashion and cultural issues of women's appearance, such as makeup and hairstyle, were historically associated with worldliness and materialism (i.e. fashion). Yet, women religious found themselves visibly reentering the secular world from the perspective of appearance. Because of their vow of poverty, there was little money for clothing. Most of their post-habit attire came as hand-me-downs, or from thrift shops or sales.

The following quote is from a woman religious who worked in a career in women's clothing sales for 13 years prior to entering religious training. She expresses ambivalence about her love of clothes:

> I maintained my ability over the years [while in habit] to be a very good shopper. I would go to Steigers [Department Store]—the girls [clerks] would really get to know me. Many of them I had known throughout the years and they would know when the bargains were coming in. I became a shopper for several other people, especially in the early days [of transition from habits]. Now I struggle tremendously. I have far too many clothes. I'm good for a while but I have to keep looking. Someone else might not see me as a person that has a lot of clothes.

The habit had obscured visible markers of womanhood such as the hair and figure. In my interviews, much discussion focused on the personal discomfort and even trauma of reemerging into secular society. Skills related to personal appearance had to be relearned. Hair was discussed frequently as the focus of anxiety. After years of deprivation from air and light under the habit, hair loss was common. In this interview segment, a woman religious discusses her personal viewpoint on hair.

> Respondent: I saw older women buying wigs who had lost their hair because of the habit.
> Interviewer: Was that because of rubbing?

Respondent: Yes, and also because they didn't get air. Even at night they wore caps.
Interviewer: Was this a permanent hair loss?
Respondent: Yes, for some. But for some it was O.K. [it grew back]. I color my hair. It's something I do for myself. In the 1960s we began to do a lot of more personalized and psychological study of ourselves. The spiritual was always part of it. How can you separate the spiritual and emotional? It's holistic.

The habit had given women religious surprising freedom from the tyranny of appearance experienced by women in North American culture. Women religious were confronted with issues of body weight that had previously been obscured under the folds of black serge. Some women interviewed went on diets. Their awareness of style and fashion became evident. Women made personal choices about makeup, jewelry, modesty issues (length of skirt, neckline) and even hair coloring. The move to secular dress had a dramatic impact on both women religious and society in general. "It revealed to the world in general the human being underneath the habit. But more important, it revealed the nun to herself: It was an experience in recognition" (Griffin, 1975).

Women emerged from habit during the turbulent period of the Civil Rights Movement, the Vietnam War, and the Women's Movement. Whether in habit or not, women religious are known for their involvement in social causes. Several women in the study referred to themselves as feminists, noting that historically they were role models for women who chose lives of dedication rather than marriage and family. Women religious also acknowledged their identities as single, professional women, and their continuing conflicts with the patriarchal structure of the Vatican. They have been active participants in social activism and the dual labor market of the parish, where they have frequently, despite achieving higher education than priests, been denied positions of authority and participation in aspects of the liturgy.

Their emergence from habit to secular fashion not only reflected gender controversy within the Church but also helped women construct new identities as educated and professional women religious, rather than cloistered icons of the Church. Two women in my study referred to identities of women prior to Vatican II as "women of service" or more derogatorily, "handmaids of the Church." In a symbolic feminist action after Vatican II that coincided with elimination of the habit, many women religious dropped the male component of their chosen names and reassumed the female. The names of male saints who possessed desirable virtues were assigned to the women by their Mother Superior before the women took their final vows.

> There was something else going on…we were changing our clothes and we were also changing our names. It didn't happen like Friday and Saturday, but it happened that we just kind of rebelled against having men's names—Sister Mary Peter, Sister Mary John, Sister Mary Bartholomew. Many women religious were moving out of their dress identity and they were changing their names back. All that was happening at the same time.

Discarding the habit was perceived by the women in this study as a positive step toward allowing them to work and interact as human beings while interpersonal distance lessened. In a positive sense, the Church, prior to Vatican II, had viewed the habit as a protection against the evils of the world, yet that caused many women religious to perceive themselves as isolated and inhibited from mingling with the people. The women's bodies were restrained and controlled by the Church within the confines of the habit. Women religious in this study perceived secular dress as essential in allowing them normal, daily, human interactions, which greatly enhanced their ability to provide social service within the community. They symbolically reclaimed their bodies as they discarded the habit.

> From 1983 to 1987, I was in Kentucky in Appalachia. I could never have done down there in the habit what I did in my [secular] clothes. It would have been an absolute impossibility. My freedom would have been restricted. I was living in a county where there were only 30 Catholic families. I didn't go in as a Sister, I went in as a person named Mary.

THEORETICAL ISSUES

Symbolic interaction theory asserts "that the self is established, maintained, and altered in and through communication" (Stone, 1962). Stone widened the perspective of symbolic interaction studies to include appearance as a dimension of communication, usually the precursor to verbal transactions. Furthermore, Stone asserted that appearance is a critical factor in the "formulation of the conception of self" (Stone, 1962). Appearance establishes identity by indicating to others what the individual projects as his or her "program" (i.e., one's social roles of gender, age, occupation). In turn, these are "reviewed" by others, thereby validating or challenging the self (Stone, 1962):

> It [identity] is not a substitute word for "self." Instead, when one has identity, he is situated—that is, cast in the shape of a social object by the acknowledgment of his participation or membership in social relations. One's identity is established when others place him as a social object by assigning him the same words of identity that he appropriates for himself or announces. It is in the coincidence of placements and announcements that identity becomes a meaning of the self and often such placements and announcements are aroused by apparent symbols such as uniforms. The policeman's uniform, for example, is an announcement of his identity as policeman and validated by others' placements of him as policeman.

Stone (1962) describes identity as being established by two processes, apposition and opposition, a bringing together and setting apart. "To situate the person as a social object is to bring him together with other objects so situated, and, at the same time to set him apart from still other objects. Identity, to Stone, is intrinsically associated with all the joinings and departures of social life. To have an identity is to join with some and depart from others, to enter and leave social relations at once."

In contrast to Stone, Goffman (1963) defines personal identity as "the assumption that the individual can be differentiated from all others." From an interactionist perspective, this was a real dilemma for some women religious in habit. Their dress clearly symbolized their total affiliation to their work in the order, but was described by them as "restricting" in their ability to interact and communicate freely. The consequences of these symbolic limitations led to a paradox described by the women as causing them to "feel less than fully human."

Fred Davis (1992) addressed the concept of ambivalence and appearance more directly than other symbolic interactionists who preceded him. He argued that personal identity announcements and social identity placements might not be congruous. For example, a person might dress as a police officer for a costume party and be incorrectly identified as someone who is actually responsible for law enforcement. Davis (1992), maintaining that dress serves as "a kind of visual metaphor for identity...registering the culturally anchored ambivalence that resonates with and among identities," suggests that personal and social identity incongruity occurs regularly because dress is often an ambivalent form of communication. Davis (1992) is broadly interested in dress and its symbolic relationship to identity, but more specifically, he discusses his theories within the framework of fashion. Davis defines fashion by distinguishing it from style, custom, conventional or acceptable dress, or prevalent modes by stressing the importance of the element of change. While the term "dress" communicates elements of stability, use of the term "fashion" implies the added element of social change (Roach-Higgins & Eicher, 1993).

A symbolic interaction perspective emphasizes social process and meaning(s) and is relevant for explaining how and why these women negotiated their visual and verbal awareness of their appearance (Kaiser, Nagasawa & Hutton, 1995). When the women emerged as visible females from the self-described "androgyny"[1] of how they felt in the habit, identity conflicts surfaced. Davis (1992) described how dress serves as "a kind of visual metaphor for identity...registering the culturally anchored ambivalences that resonate with and among identities." Ambivalence is acknowledged by Davis (1992) to be natural and integral to human experience and can be exhibited in symbolic issues of appearance.

The dialectic of the women's physical bodies, symbolized by their dress, to the social body of the Roman Catholic Church, is a critical one in understanding the power of dress in both reflecting and constructing social change for women religious. For example, both Marx (1967) and Durkheim and Mauss (1963) argued for the dialectic between the "natural" and "social" body. Other social scientists have viewed the body as the *tabula rasa* for socialization. Van Gennep (1960), Mauss (1973), Bordieu (1977), and Douglas (1966, 1970) have argued this dialectic to demonstrate the social construction of the body.

Conclusion

This study of women religious provides a model for examining how changes in enduring modes of dress such as habits can be examined not only in relation to the more predominantly held view of changing social roles but also from the perspective of personal identity. The relationship between dress and social change must be carefully examined, as with women religious, by examining their relationship to social roles, issues of social and personal identities, and their mediation through the symbol of dress.

Davis (1992) uses the term "fault lines" to describe "culturally induced strains concerning who and what we are" that find expression in dress. Vatican II certainly created an enormous quake for women religious, but the forces of change within orders ultimately came from the women themselves in the form of human agency. Women religious were poised and ready to address issues of roles, identities, and social change.

[1]Some women in the study used this word to elaborate on how they felt when wearing a habit. This is not my choice of words. The term "androgyny" is derived from the Greek word "andro" (male) and "gyn" (female). Heilbrun (1964) uses this term to define a condition in which the characteristics of the sexes and the human impulses expressed by men and women are not rigidly assigned. Therefore, the term may be more closely associated with perceptions of identity than solely with characteristics associated with physical appearance.

References

Aherne, M. C. (1983). *Joyous service: The history of the sisters of Saint Joseph of Springfield.* Holyoke, MA: Sisters of Saint Joseph.

Bordieu, P. (1977). *Outline of a theory of practice.* (R. Nice, trans.) Cambridge, England: Cambridge University Press.

Davis, F. (1992). *Fashion, culture and identity.* Chicago, IL: University of Chicago Press.

Douglas, M. (1970). *Nature symbols.* New York: Vintage Books.

Ebaugh, H. (1977). *Out of the cloister: A study of organizational dilemmas.* Austin: University of Texas Press.

Ebaugh, H. (1993). *Women in the vanishing cloister.* New Brunswick, NJ: Rutgers University Press.

Goffman, E. (1963). *Stigma: Notes on the management of a spoiled identity.* Englewood Cliffs, NJ: Prentice Hall.

Griffin, M. (1975). *Unbelling the cat: The courage to choose.* Boston: Little, Brown.

Heilbrun, C. (1964). *Toward a recognition of androgyny.* New York: Alfred A. Knopf, Inc.

Kaiser, S. Nagasawa, R. & Hutton, S. (1995). Construction of an SI theory of fashion: Part 1, ambivalence and change. *Clothing and Textiles Research Journal 13 (3),* 172–183.

Mauss, M. (1973). Techniques of the Body. (B. Brewster, trans.) *Economy and society 2 (1),* pp. 70–88.

Metz, J. (1968). *Poverty of spirit.* New York: Paulist Press.

Roach-Higgins, M., & Eicher, J. Dress and identity. *ITAA special publication #5.*

Stone, G. (1962). Appearance the self. In A. Rose (Ed.), *Human behavior and social processes: An interactionist approach,* pp. 86–118. New York: Houghton, Mifflin, Co.

DISCUSSION QUESTIONS

From Habit to Fashion: Dress of Catholic Women Religious

1. Uniforms (such as a nun's habit) make the wearer easy to identify but can also create barriers that make accessibility to the person wearing the uniform difficult. Can you think of other examples of a uniform dress that creates the same effect?

2. Describe the origin of the nun's habit and what freedoms and/or restrictions were placed on the wearer at the time of its origination.

79 Worldly Lessons
Lynda Edwards

Bob Jones University, nestled here in the South Carolina hill country, is all butter-yellow buildings bordered by purple magnolia blossoms and a fountain sparkling with pink and blue-lighted spumes; the paint-box colors belie a serious house on serious earth. In a classroom where 20 female students sat recently, Bibles and notebooks stacked neatly before them, facing half a dozen headless dress forms draped in deft knockoffs of Todd Oldham and Donna Karan, Prof. Diane Hay of the home economics department was teaching one of her popular "safe beauty classes."

Like all B.J.U. classes, this one begins with prayer. Mrs. Hay—61, tall, slender and elegant—invoked God to help the girls absorb the lecture and guide them to ideal careers. Then she held up the image consultants' bible: "Dress for Success" by John T. Malloy. "I know you're familiar with this book," she said, "but what I want to talk about today is God's dress-for-success program."

She opened her Bible to I Corinthians 6:19: "...Ye are not your own. For ye are bought with a price; therefore glorify God in your body, and in your spirit, which are God's." The girls bowed their heads to take notes, then looked up.

"Ye are bought with a price." Mrs. Hays repeated softly. "Your beauty, the talent and luck that will pave your way, have been paid for by your Lord. He must be your guide to the outside world." It was so quiet you could hear bees buzzing outside. "In the workplace," she went on, "it is wrong for any girl to wear a garment that rouses in any man desires that cannot be righteously fulfilled outside of marriage. The Bible also warns us not to be so masculine that we threaten men. If your talk is spiritual, but your look is cold, hard, carnal and calculating, the outside is what's believed."

Mrs. Hay rested a hand on a dress form clad in a chic cream wraparound blouse, slim brown skirt and leopard print belt. "I want you to look like you belong in the 1990's—your time—not the 1950's," she said smiling. "Style is your armor. Fashion says take off, forget your feelings, get used to this. Style comforts you, gives you confidence. Then, beauty serves you."

Like the feminist author Camille Paglia, fundamentalists (those who interpret the Bible literally, as opposed to evangelicals, who interpret it individually) have always believed that feminine beauty wields a nearly occult power, wreaking havoc if unharnessed, having a redemptive effect if properly cast. In 1986, Beverly LaHaye, president of Concerned Women of America, a group of female religious advocates drawn from both the fundamentalist and evangelical movements, wrote of the "supernaturalism" inherent in a woman's beauty, and its potential for good or evil in the workplace.

Such a belief made women's presence at work problematic. So for decades, fundamentalist women were directed to find safe harbors working in the home or in low-wage jobs at Christian hospitals or schools, said Paul Hetrick, the public affairs director of the Family Research Council, a Washington research organization that calls itself a "conservative pro-family advocate." The council is lobbying to alter the tax code to favor married couples with children, and mothers without paying jobs.

But since the late 1980's, fundamentalist women, like many other conservative American women, have had to adapt to the new economic realities and enter the workplace. In "Children at Risk," his 1990 book on family values, Gary Bauer, the president of the Family Research Council, extols working mothers who "believe in responsible living, the traditional standards of right and wrong, and in the God of our fathers." And last November, the child psychologist Dr.

James Dobson, on his popular radio program, "Focus on Family," implored churches to show "respect, compassion and justice" to fundamentalist career women. Such women, Mr. Bauer and Dr. Dobson assert, are engaged in the "ministry of business."

At Bob Jones, besides professional skills, women learn to navigate a money-fueled culture that, when deconstructed, seems as ritualistically complex and socially treacherous as Edith Wharton's belle epoque. Through Bible-based lessons, female students learn how faith should inform their dress, deportment, conversational skills, etiquette and business ethics. If the lessons hold, they forge a lifelong spiritual cordon sanitaire around the fundamentalist as she encounters the snares of the secular office.

B.J.U., which has about 5,000 students, was founded in 1927 to combat liberalism, according to its recruiting brochure, and is influential enough to have snagged Presidents Ronald Reagan and George Bush as speakers. Although it is not accredited, it attracted recruiters from 40 corporations last year, including Dun & Bradstreet, Arthur Andersen and KPMG Peat Marwick. A CNN recruiter asked the career services director, Dave Williams, whether fundamentalists proselytize fellow workers. "I told him the stereotype of church ladies pushing leaflets in a parking lot is out of date," Mr. Williams said. "The best on-the-job witness we can give is being the company's best employee."

Other fundamentalist Bible colleges do not trivialize the Bob Jones charm and beauty courses; in fact, schools like Liberty College, founded by the Rev. Jerry Falwell, have less elaborate versions. They are viewed as a smart way to tackle a public relations problem. When consumers hear I.B.M. they think of computers; say fundamentalism, and even some fundamentalists concede that people think of Jimmys—Swaggart and Bakker—and bad women with big hair.

In her book, "Beauty and the Best," Beneth Jones, the wife of the university's president, Bob Jones 3d, rebuts the myth that equates the fashions of the wholesome 50's with holiness: "The hold-on-to-the-death attitude of Christian women with bouffant hair is a case in point. All that backcombing and high-piling was so hopelessly outmoded by the blow-dry era that those who clung to it made spectacles of themselves."

Mrs. Hay was discussing legs. The students wore floral prints and pastel silks that swept their ankles; B.J.U. requires that skirts cover the knee whether a woman is standing or sitting.

"A man's eye travels from the floor up," Mrs. Hay said. "A Christian woman wants to do everything she can to draw his eye to her face because that is where her character is revealed. Accessories can guide his eye." She held silvery earrings up for the class to see. "An honest, brave, lovely face does more for your career than any dress can."

For most of the students, these classes, which are introduced to freshmen as an interdisciplinary orientation program, provide the first glimpse of the secular business world. "Most of our girls have college-educated parents earning low incomes—or nothing, if they're missionaries," said Bobbie Yearick, a drama professor. And, she theorized, upper-income managers, male and female, suspect working-class prettiness as being somehow insubordinate. She tells her students: "You're being scrutinized all the time. Be aware of what your face and voice are expressing at all times."

Since Proverbs 15:13 advises believers that "a merry heart maketh a cheerful countenance," and because even the grimmest of corporate cultures demand some measure of jollity and faux camaraderie, a happy face is a high priority. Mrs. Hay and Mrs. Yearick cited the perky countenance of Mary Hart on "Entertainment Tonight" as scripturally ideal.

"A woman must be sure her eyes inspire friendliness, not familiarity, in male co-workers," Mrs. Yearick said. No half-lowered lids or fluid gazes. "The voice should be bright, firm and free of all inflection. Men will claim to read anything in a tone."

But most female students at B.J.U. say they don't worry about inciting uncontrollable lust. What they do worry about is being mistaken for what fundamentalist preachers call "she-men": power-mad, humorless, Joan Crawford-y boss women who emasculate male, and backstab female subordinates. Erin Rodman, a red-haired education major who looks like a runway model, began working at 14 on a bean farm, then was a waitress at a pizza parlor to help pay family bills. "I was always very aloof, very professional to avoid harassment," she said. "But a man who wants to harass you will."

Mrs. Hay recounted this tale of one fraught encounter: A student was at her part-time job when a male co-worker made a pass at her. She told him to leave her alone and walked toward the door. He yanked her blouse collar and shouted, "Why do you advertise if you don't deliver?" She came to Mrs. Hay in tears. "We thought her dress might have caused him to misjudge a good book by a flashy cover," Mrs. Hay said, adding the skirt was "a little too short" and the blouse "a little too unbuttoned."

"We spent six months reforming her style," she said.

Later, Dave McQuaid, director of media relations at Bob Jones, having heard that Mrs. Hay had recounted the story, said: "Journalists rap us as saying women bring harassment on themselves when we don't think that. Understand that Mrs. Hay's expertise is esthetics."

Miss Rodman wants a career in public school administration. "Most of us going on to work in the real world worry about having to wear a tough shell," she said. "It's the emphasis on feminity, especially Mrs. Jones's lessons, that's most useful to us."

Mrs. Jones teaches on a stage before 500 freshmen in a sea-foam-green room ordinarily used for chamber music recitals. The stage, backed by an emerald scrim, is scattered with a few strangely numinous props—a podium, a chair, a coat rack, wooden steps. Mrs. Jones was once a B.J.U. drama major. On stage, she acts out what her book calls "Special Challenges to Grace: Putting On or Removing a Coat; Exiting a Car; Sitting on Table-Attached Picnic Benches." The basics, too: walking and sitting in a chair.

For table-etiquette lessons, the students study diagrams, mapping the way from salad knife to shellfish fork. "I remind that in the real world, even if their business lunch is at McDonalds, they're representing not just their company but their faith," she said.

Students practice being an envoy for both at the university's "management house," a three-

bedroom ranch house on campus built of lavender brick. It was originally intended to be a place for future homemakers to hone cooking and housekeeping skills. Now, it's also a laboratory for making parties and conversations. Students attend on-campus operatic and philharmonic productions to learn how to recognize arias, movements and au courant wear. Their aim is to be able to move among the cultural elite.

Four girls live at the house in four-week stints, during which a faculty member rates their progress as they plan and cook 56 meals, including a formal seven-course dinner. Faculty members are guests, simulating the roles of boss and boss's spouse. Students are graded on being hosts (giving the house tour, correctly matching dinner partners), culinary skills, presentation and conversation.

"I was shy and got an unfavorable critique for allowing long conversation pauses at the parties when I was hostess," said a business major and international banking aspirant who would not give her name because she had several job interviews lined up. "I also performed badly on icebreakers."

The faculty adviser gave her some pointers: Observe body language. Practice discussing stories in U.S. News & World Report, Fortune, the local paper and The New York Times. Quote The Times for the definitive secular view of the world. Ask the shyest person an open-ended question every 20 minutes. Keep any purpose to your social chat unstated, thus preserving the lightness of chance.

"I was so depressed I thought I'd never get it," the student said. "I thought maybe the Lord was pointing me to a job where I'd just deal with numbers."

The adviser made her the host of the formal dinner. She prayed for an hour before dawn. That evening, lulls occurred only when everyone was eating, wallflowers bloomed, and each guest exhibited his or her store of interesting shop talk. Two guests gave her business cards. "It was a sign," she said. "I'm not to be shy anymore."

In the business school, the hallways are dotted with Bible verses in calligraphy: "Servants, be obedient to them that are your masters...not with the eye-service as men-pleasers but doing the will of God from the heart," reads one; there are verses about quenching eternal thirst above the water fountains. All the classroom doors were open; a teacher could be heard drilling students on oil and soybean futures.

Alan Carper, 37, spent over a decade in the corporate world before coming here to teach B.J.U.'s senior management classes. One lesson focuses on the fundamentalist manager's dual responsibility to an H.I.V.-positive employee—defend his privacy and protect him from ostracism by colleagues—based on Christ's ministry to the sick. Another focuses on the Bible's exegesis of sexual harassment.

"And the bottom line is, no one asks for it," he said. "It's not a sexual crime. A harasser's aggression and rages would come out in other ways if the woman didn't exist. It's a crime of power. A female supervisor could harass a male subordinate, as in the story of Joseph and Potiphar's wife."

He follows the politically correct route of all American business schools till he hits a dead-man's curve: whistleblowing. "If a Christian employee witnesses harassment of a co-worker, he or she must come to the co-worker's aid and corroborate her testimony," he said. "The Bible says not to give false witness, even if lying wins you favor with the powers that be." If a corporation sides with the harasser, the fundamentalist may have to resign. "We believe God will open up a path to an ethical corporation to replace the one that is lost," he explained.

It seems a hard fate for a young professional woman, especially after B.J.U. has invested so much time and energy in grooming her for the workplace. "But we don't want our career women to have their egos depend on some corporation," Mrs. Yearnick said. "Fundamentalism is our path. The only real power is the power to walk away.

"It's like soldiers: all you have for protection are the things you can carry. For a young woman, that is her faith, her grace and a lovely face."

DISCUSSION QUESTIONS

Worldly Lessons

1. Several of the readings on religion make reference to social class. Identify the social class issues in each of the readings and note how these issues are related to dress.

2. What is your opinion of "safe beauty classes" that prepare women at Bob Jones University for professional positions among the cultural elite of U. S. society?

CHAPTER 13

Dress and Social Change

Susan O. Michelman

AFTER YOU HAVE READ THIS CHAPTER, YOU WILL COMPREHEND:

- Social change is any significant alteration, modification, or transformation in the organization and operation of social life that includes, among other factors, dress and appearance.

- How cultural assimilation, exemplified by dress, is a process by which ethnic and racial distinctions between groups disappear and the social boundaries of the assimilated individual are largely determined by the majority society.

- How social change, as it relates to appearance, can be influenced by innovations, social conflict, individuals in power, or the economic system.

The old saying goes, "The one thing you can count on is change." Throughout this book, you have been introduced to articles on dress and appearance that have challenged your preconceptions about how the human behavior of dressing the body is related to such issues as race, ethnicity, gender, class, religious beliefs, and politics. The common theme running through all of the articles is how dress and appearance communicate social, cultural, political, religious, and economic stability or social change. This chapter will focus on concepts of social change and how they relate to human appearance.

Social change is defined as any significant alteration, modification, or transformation in the organization and operation of social life (Ferrante, 1995). For example, in an article in this chapter, "Hmong American New Year's Dress: The Display of Ethnicity," Annette Lynch examines how Hmong refugees from Laos have experienced radical changes in all aspects of their social life as they have moved from their life in isolated and traditional hill tribes in Laos to crowded, technologically sophisticated existences in the United States. The study examines how wearing Hmong traditional clothing helps perpetuate cultural beliefs and the social mores of their native land, which many young Hmong have never seen and to which some older Hmong will never return. Lynch also discusses how the effects of American culture have similarly had an impact on the modification or abandonment of traditional dress, particularly among the younger Hmong not born in Laos. The article provides an example of **cultural assimilation**, a process that occurs when one group moves to or integrates with another group.

During assimilation, ethnic distinctions between groups disappear and the social boundaries of the assimilated individual become largely determined by the majority society (Gans, 1982). Sociologists have delineated progressive stages a group must complete to be completely "absorbed" into the dominant group. In the first stage, called **acculturation**, members of a group internalize some values and behavioral patterns (e.g., language, food, religion, dress, and so forth) of a majority society but are not fully admitted to intimate groupings of the majority (Kaiser, 1997). For complete assimilation, the minority group becomes fully accepted into the majority society. The minority group abandons its original cultural identity, or parts of its uniqueness are incorporated into the dominant group.

It is frequently difficult to identify just one factor that causes social change. Change usually results from a complex sequence of events that unfold over time. Many fashion theorists argue that fashion itself is a reflection of social, economic, political, and cultural changes (Lauer & Lauer, 1981; Bush & London, 1960; Wilson, 1985). For example, in the article "From Hoop Skirt to Slam Dunk Chic," Ira Berkow traces the historical progression of women's basketball attire from turn-of-the-century wool and corseted gowns to the current tank tops and shorts that were not just borrowed from men's teams but rather designed to fit women's bodies. The history of both women's sports and its associated dress reflects social and political changes for women that occurred over the course of the 20th century.

The following sections discuss and explain some key events that may trigger changes in social life (Ferrante, 1995).

Innovation

Innovation is the development of something new, whether a thought or idea, a practice, or a tool or implement. For example, hats, helmets, scarves, and goggles were worn by motorcar drivers and passengers in the early 1900s. Later, as automobiles were constructed to be enclosed, this type of clothing quickly went out of style. In this case, innovations in auto design influenced fashion innovations. Similarly, the invention of pantyhose in the early 1960s made girdles and corsets (necessary for holding up hosiery) become somewhat obsolete (Sproles & Burns, 1994). Present-day ecological concerns are discussed in the article "Eco-Friendly Fashions Are 'Cool' " by Wendi Winters. Successful industries have grown out of innovation of earth-friendly products and materials such as certified organic cotton fabric and Tencel (a rayonlike fiber without rayon's eco-messy production process).

Powerful Influences

People in **power** may influence others to change their way of life, either by force or because of their compelling personal style. After the communists took power in China in 1949, the androgynous "Mao suit" was mandated by Chairman Mao Zedong to symbolize the philosophy of the new social order—classless, nonsexist, nonmaterialistic, and organized around the common good. This attire visually assisted the Chinese in making the massive changes required to attain a new social order (Storm, 1987). In another example, during the Third Reich in Germany (1932–1945) various political groups tried to convince German women that a Nazi-style fashion should be adopted (Guenther, 1997). Similarly, the personal style of leaders can influence populations. President Clinton, as well as other U. S. presidents since Jimmy Carter, have undoubtedly influenced American culture with their casual way of dressing for some public appearances (see Figure 13.1). The article by Adler, "Have We Become a Nation of Slobs?" points out that formal dress, even for social occasions such as church, may be a thing of the past.

A striking example of social change in the workplace is the trend toward replacing the traditional business suit with more casual dress (see Chapter 7). Business owners and CEOs are implementing this change in dress of their employees. According to a recent survey of human resource managers, 90 percent of companies allow office workers to wear casual businesswear at least one day of the month. And of these, 33 percent allow casual dress any day of the week, unless an employee is meeting with a client. That's up from 19 percent in 1992 (Evans Research Associates, 1995). According to this study, human resource managers agreed with the following:

FIGURE 13.1 *President Clinton flips through comics without jacket, tie pulled away from his shirt, and holds sunglasses in his mouth.*

- Casual dress improved morale—85 percent.
- Casual dress policies would be perceived by employees as a benefit—82 percent.
- Employees are able to save money because of casual dress—72 percent.
- Casual dress policies could be used to attract new employees—66 percent.
- Wearing casual clothing improves productivity—45 percent.

Conflict

Conflict is perhaps one of the greatest agents of change. In its most basic form, conflict involves controversy between groups over issues of wealth, power, prestige, and other valued resources (Ferrante, 1995). Sometimes conflicts are resolved through social resistance to the norms and mores of the broader society. Frequently, resistance is demonstrated by the use of dress that sets a group apart from mainstream society. Two very different contemporary examples of this phenomenon are the Amish and Rastafarian communities.

The Amish who settled in Pennsylvania in the early 1700s had fled religious persecution in Europe and wanted to live without interference from the outside world, which they consider corrupt. Clothing is a major method the Amish use to maintain their distinct social identity and to ensure conformity to group norms (Rubinstein, 1995). Amish dress, for both men and women, conforms to a uniform ideal, in which individuality in appearance is rejected. Clothing is quite plain and devoid of zippers and other "modern" accessories. The Amish maintain their use of styles from 17th- and 18th-century dress. In this case, rejection of the fashion system through relatively unchanging styles is the form of social resistance.

Similarly, the Rastafarian way of life and its associated appearance promotes spiritual resilience in the face of contemporary poverty and oppression. Rastafarians have rejected the neocolonial reality of Jamaica and have drawn upon African and Hebrew traditions and, to a lesser extent, Anglo-Hispanic. Most notable about Rastafarian appearance are their dreadlocks and unkempt beards (Rubinstein, 1995). The dreadlocks resemble the mane of a fierce lion and are meant to distance the individual from society. Rastafarian clothing is quite simple, indicating **asceticism**, or desire for nothing beyond the basic necessities of life. Interestingly, Rastafarian dreadlocks, a symbol of distance from mainstream materialism, have influenced some avant-garde hairstyles during the 1980s and 1990s (see Figure 13.2).

Capitalism

Capitalism is an economic system in which natural resources and the means of production and distribution are privately owned (Ferrante, 1995). This system is motivated by competition, profits, and a free market and is responsible for the enormous rate of increase in the amount of goods and services produced since the Industrial Revolution. Fashion flourishes in a capitalistic system in which multiple models are proposed each season by clothing designers and manufacturers. This creates a competitive environment in which items are selected by consumers (Blumer, 1969). Consider the article, "Sheer Madness" by Janet Wells, which analyzes the decline in sales of nylon hosiery. Nylon stockings have been an intrinsic part of most women's wardrobes since the late 1930s. Does this indicate that women are tiring of nylon stockings or does it attest to the fact that there are more options in legwear from which to choose? Is it only economic

FIGURE 13.2 *Bob Marley in concert jams on his guitar while he performs on stage at the Santa Monica Civic Auditorium.*

competition that has driven the decline of nylon stockings? Wells examines lifestyle changes in U. S. culture that work in congruence with the economic system to bring about this change in fashion.

As consumers, we are constantly challenged by provocative images in advertising, the media, and technology that are driven by social change. We are constantly required to reexamine our personal and professional ethics, values, and beliefs about issues of appearance. In "Turning Boys Into Girls," author Michelle Cottle makes a strong point that many popular magazines aimed at males are promoting a standard of male beauty "as unforgiving and unrealistic as the female version sold by those dewy-eyed preteen waifs draped across the covers of *Glamour* and *Elle.*"

Perhaps nothing sartorial symbolizes social change better than examining the history of denim clothing in the past 35 years, as discussed in the article "Rebel, Rebel" by Elizabeth Wilson. As noted by Wilson, denim made a radical switch from utility to fashion between the 1930s and 1950s. Denim jeans are readily associated with the youth and music rebellion of the 1950s, 1960s, and early 1970s when they symbolized a distancing from the "uptight" culture of the youths' parents. Even the punk movement of the 1980s utilized denim as a backdrop for its style, but in a totally different context than the 1960s and 1970s. More recently, denim has been used by such couturier designers as Karl Lagerfeld and Jean Paul Gaultier who more typically design with the world's most extravagant fabrics. Concurrently, Ralph Lauren and Calvin Klein have been highly successful selling their "designer" jeans on a global market for prices seemingly too high for lowly denim. Examining the history and symbolic social meaning of denim provides an excellent case study of how appearance can be influenced by innovations, social conflict, individuals in power, or the economic system.

Summary

This chapter addresses social change as it relates to issues of appearance influenced by innovations, social conflict, and individuals in power. Articles examine how cultural assimilation and acculturation can impact dress. Capitalism, the predominant world economic system, is motivated by profit and a free market that supports competition in the media and advertising that entices viewers and readers to buy. Denim apparel that has transitioned from function to fashion is examined as a successful example of clothing that has adapted well to the needs of social change.

Suggested Readings

Ash, J., & Wilson, E. (1992). *Chic thrills*. Berkeley: University of California Press.

Banner, L. (1983). *American beauty*. Chicago, IL: University of Chicago Press.

Blumer, H. (1979). Fashion: From class differentiation to collective selection. In L. Gurel & M. Besson (Eds.). *Dimensions of dress and adornment*. Dubuque, IA: Kendall/Hunt Publishers.

Gaines, J., & Herzog, C. (Eds.). (1990). *Fabrications, costume and the body*. New York: Routledge.

Michelman, S., & Erekosima, T. (1992). Kalabari dress in Nigeria: Visual analysis and gender implications. In R. Barnett & J. Eicher (Eds.), *Dress and gender: Making and meaning*. Oxford, England: Berg Press.

Nakagawa, K., & Rosovsky, H. (1965). The case of the dying kimono. In M. L. Roach & J. Eicher (Eds.), *Dress, adornment, and the social order*. New York: John Wiley & Sons.

Steele, V. Appearance and identity. In C. Kidwell & V. Steele (Eds.). *Men and women dressing the part*. Washington, D. C.: Smithsonian Institution Press.

Wilson, E. (1993). Deviancy, dress, and desire. In S. Fisher & K. Davis (Eds.), *Negotiating at the Margins: The Gendered Discourses of Power and Resistance*. New Brunswick, NJ: Rutgers University Press.

Wilson, E. *Adorned in dreams: Fashion and modernity*. London: Virago Press.

LEARNING ACTIVITY

Style Shifts and Social Change—Examining Meaning Through Photographs

Objectives: To understand how dress is a symbolic expression of social change.

This assignment will utilize old photographs to examine social, political, historical, and economic issues of social change symbolized by dress. Social change is defined as any significant alteration, modification, or transformation in the organization and operation of social life. Knowledge of both the student's past and present social and historical events will be called upon to examine how dress is influenced by innovations, social conflict, individuals in power, or the economic system.

Procedure

Obtain a photograph of a parent, relative, or friend who at the time of being photographed was approximately the student's age. This person should have been born prior to 1960 and should be the same gender as the student. The photograph should be one that is full length and shows an entire clothing ensemble.

Compare this photograph to current styles of dress, including such aspects as body type (e.g., weight, height, muscle tone), hairstyle, makeup, body adornment (e.g., tattoos, body piercing), jewelry, and so forth.

Discuss with the person in the photograph those factors that influenced them in the chosen aspects of their dress and appearance. Record answers to the following factors:

- Religion.
- Political events.
- Economic factors.
- Family.
- Other friends or their peer group(s).
- Ethnic influences.
- The media, including music, television, or movies.
- Influential people such as political leaders, movie stars, celebrities, and so forth.

Writing Activity

Record how these factors have influenced your own dress and appearance.

List comparisons and contrasts between you and your partner on issues of dress. What issues have been affected by social change?

Discussion

As a class, students will share their comparisons and contrasts with the class, and discuss how issues of social change have affected dress and appearance. Discuss from what you have learned in this assignment what social, political, and economic influences have caused the greatest changes in the way people construct their appearance.

References

Blumer, H. (1969). Fashion: From class differentiation to collective selection. *Sociological Quarterly 10*, pp. 275–291.

Bush, G., & London, P. (1960). On the disappearance of knickers: Hypotheses for the functional analysis of the psychology of clothes. *Journal of Social Psychology 51*, 359–66.

Evans Research. (1992 & 1995). *Human resource manager surveys*. San Francisco, CA: Author.

Ferrante, J. (1995). *Sociology: A global perspective*. Belmont, CA: Wadsworth Publishing Co.

Gans, H. J. (1982). *The urban villagers*. New York: The Free Press.

Guenther, I. (1997, March). Nazi "chic"? German politics and women's fashions, 1915–1945. *Fashion Theory,1*, 29–58.

Kaiser, S. (1997). *The social psychology of clothing* (2nd edition, revised). New York: Fairchild.

Lauer, J., & Lauer, R. (1981) *Fashion power: The meaning of fashion in American society*. Englewood Cliffs, NJ: Prentice-Hall.

Rubinstein, R. (1995). *Dress codes: Meanings and messages in American culture*. Boulder, CO: Westview Press.

Sproles, G., & Burns, L. *Changing appearances: Understanding dress in contemporary society*. New York: Fairchild.

Storm, P. (1987). *Functions of dress: Tool of culture and the individual*. Englewood Cliffs, NJ: Prentice-Hall.

Wilson, E. (1985). *Adorned in dreams: Fashion and modernity*. London, England: Virago Press.

80 Hmong American New Year's Dress: The Display of Ethnicity

Annette Lynch

Hmong Americans are refugees from Laos who settled in the United States as a result of the Vietnam conflict. The Lao Hmong living in the United States originally migrated out of China in the early nineteenth century into northern Lao hill country. During the Vietnam War, Hmong were recruited by the American forces to fight against the Laotian communists. Immigration to the United States began in 1975 after the withdrawal of the American army and the assumption of political power by the Laotian communists. Fieldwork (Lynch 1992) supporting this article was conducted in St. Paul and Minneapolis, Minnesota, in a community of approximately 18,000 Hmong Americans.

Within the Hmong American community, textile arts and dress have continued to play a traditional role in structuring social life and marking significance. *Paj ntaub* (flower cloth) is the general term used to refer to all the varied textile arts created by Hmong women. Techniques used include embroidery, appliqué, reverse appliqué and batik as well as the additive arts of assemblage. These arts, like other *kev cai* (customs) discussed by Tapp (1988), have been self-consciously practiced by Hmong Americans as they have used the customs of the past to fashion meaningful lives in the diaspora.

Drawing generally from the academic literature on the expression of cultural difference within modern nation states (Moerman 1964; Barth 1969; Cohen 1973; Glazer and Moynihan 1975; Epstein 1978; Roosens 1989 and Glick-Schiller and Fouron 1990) and specifically upon the work of Sarna (1978) and Comaroff (1987), I will focus upon Hmong American use of New Year's dress as a marker of ethnic identity and pride. I present this Hmong American case study as an argument for a definition of ethnic dress based on its descriptive role in identifying conceptually distinct types of social boundaries marked by the dressed body.

THE CONCEPT OF ETHNICITY

Sarna (1978), writing on the American immigrant experience, argued that American immigrant groups identify themselves by region, village, or family when they enter the United States but are labeled and treated as a homogenous ethnic group by American institutions and power structures. He goes on to argue that ethnic groups use cultural content to construct symbols of cohesiveness and pride as a defensive response to discrimination based on ethnic identity. In this way fragmented clusters of immigrants become cohesive ethnic groups by accepting and eventually symbolizing externally drawn ethnic boundary lines. Cultural content, which is often an eclectic mix of cultural elements drawn from throughout the ethnic group membership, is used both to accommodate and resist dominant American power structures.

Comaroff (1987) posited that the "marking of contrasting identities—of the opposition of self and other, we and they—'is primordial'" (p. 306). He argues that, despite social and cultural differences, all human groups classify themselves in relationship to others. His argument offers a conceptually distinct definition of ethnicity premised on the fact that the substance underlying boundary lines between groups differs depending upon social and cultural circumstances. Using Comaroff's distinctions, totemic (as opposed to ethnic) boundary lines are established between equally powerful and structurally similar groups. In contrast ethnic boundaries are asymmetrical power-based relationships between structurally dissimilar groups.

In the following analysis I will show that as the Hmong people experienced social and cultural upheaval, they moved from using dress to mark totemic boundaries to using dress to display ethnic identity.

LAO HMONG DRESS

Different Hmong dress styles were historically associated with different regions of Laos and Thailand and with different linguistic subgroups of Hmong. The clearest distinctions existed between the two broad categories of Green and White Hmong dress, which in turn corresponded to two major linguistic subgroups. Green Hmong handwork can be most simply identified by the use of blue batik to produce pattern. White Hmong handwork used the reverse appliqué technique to produce intricate white patterns.

The dress of White Hmong women included a white pleated skirt with black leggings worn with a black shirt with blue cuffs and front edging. A rectangular collar at the back of the shirt was heavily decorated with handwork. The ensemble included a black apron and was worn with belts adorned with silver coins. In contrast, the dress of a Green Hmong woman customarily included a pleated skirt dominated visually by a wide central panel of blue batik work and decorated with appliqué and embroidery. They wore dark shirts similar to the White Hmong women, but their collars were worn face down. Both groups of women wore a version of a dark wrapped turban form, which generally featured a black and white striped turban tie.

White Hmong men wore black shirts with blue cuffs and black flared pants. Accessories included a dramatic pink or red waist sash, narrow coined belts and black skullcaps with red topknots. Green Hmong men's pants were also black but were cut large with a low crotch and fitted ankles. They also wore dark cuffed shirts and black skullcaps (Cubbs 1986).

Scholars trace the roots of the Lao Hmong subgroups which are marked by corresponding differences in dress styles to China where the Han Chinese ascribed separate status to various sub-categories of Miao (Geddes 1976; Dewhurst

and MacDowell 1983; Cubbs 1986). Sub-styles of dress in the Lao context were internally perceived and understood categories. Peterson (1990) pointed out the extensive information that was carried by dress in Lao Hmong communities:

> the individual is recognized as Hmong by other Hmong, who with a glance will know if the stranger they meet shares their dialect, marriage customs, house style, spiritual offerings, standards of beauty in clothing and song, and other cultural facets that distinguish one subgroup from another. They mutually recognize, in a twinkling, what kinds of limits might structure their future relationship. (p 118)

Dress thus immediately sets up a relationship between the Hmong individual wearing the dress and the Hmong individual perceiving the dress. The two individuals knew how to respond socially to one another and what relationships were possible based upon internally understood visual cues.

Lao Hmong dress marked what Comaroff (1987) would call a totemic boundary between the related subgroups. The bounded groups were structurally similar and had roughly the same amount of power. The subgroups of Lao Hmong spoke different versions of the same language and tended to perform rituals in slightly different ways. These cultural differences, while internally perceived, were often not externally appreciated. Dress as a visible sign was more often noticed and commented upon by outsiders, thus perhaps accounting for the use of dress by the outside world to label the differing subgroups.

HMONG AMERICAN NEW YEAR

Hmong-style dress, worn on an everyday basis in Laos, is reserved for special occasions in the United States. Hmong American women are typically married in Hmong-style dress and families dress up for family photographs in the summer. The largest public display of Hmong American dress is the annual public celebration of New Year, generally held in St. Paul over the Thanksgiving weekend. My research focused specifically upon the meaning of dress worn within the context of the public celebration of the New Year.

Hmong New Year as celebrated in the Lao village context was the single annual holiday celebrated at the close of a busy agricultural season. It was an opportunity for families and friends to gather and renew the bonds tying the community and family together. Clan leaders and shamans performed rituals of renewal to usher in the New Year, banish the cares of the old year, and make peace with the spirit world in order to safeguard the community for the coming year. Women sewed throughout the year to prepare new clothing to be worn first for the New Year celebration and subsequently throughout the year for everyday attire. Treasured and costly clothing not worn on a daily basis was taken out of the storage baskets to add additional pomp to the newly sewn ensembles. A ball toss courtship ritual was played throughout the holiday season and provided an opportunity for young Hmong men and women to meet and get to know each other. Many marriages followed the holiday season.

The New Year as celebrated in the United States is a rare opportunity for public display of ethnic pride. While for much of the year community members try hard to fit into American culture, the New Year is an opportunity to be Hmong again in a supportive environment. Lao Hmong who relocated to the United States arrived relatively unprepared for life in the industrialized West. Most (92%) came from rural backgrounds and many (72%) were not able to read or write in their native language (Mallinson, Donnelly, and Hang 1988: 21). Resulting high rates of welfare dependency have made it difficult for youth to be proud of their heritage and families. Teenagers enrolled in public schools are particularly sensitive to the judgments of their peers. For example, one young man attempted to mask his ethnic identity by claiming to be a member of the more culturally assimilated Vietnamese community. For these teenagers and for the community at large, the New Year provides an arena in which ethnic identity is affirmed and displayed.

The public celebrations of Hmong New Year held in St. Paul in the late 1980s, like comparable nineteenth century immigrant celebrations discussed by Bodnar (1985), drew upon long-standing practices yet were adapted to the new American context. Focusing primarily on youth, the public celebrations in St. Paul juxtaposed ancient Hmong ritual and American popular culture. The auditorium floor was dominated by a ball toss courtship ritual by day and a rock and roll dance by night. The stage featured spectacles ranging from shamanistic rituals to heavy metal rock and roll performed by punk Hmong teenagers. The conflicts inherent in the position of Hmong teens as the generation between Hmong and American cultures were acted out in plays written in local schools, in speeches delivered by Hmong teenage leaders, and in the structure of the celebration, which in 1989 moved from an opening day focused on the Hmong past to a closing day focused on the Hmong future in America.

Dress styles derived from Lao Hmong prototypes were worn to the public celebration by many Hmong American teenagers and some Hmong American children and adults (see Figure 13.3). Hmong American teenagers used dress throughout the two-day festival to mark movement from one cultural world into the other. One Hmong teenager explained the use of clothing by saying that "at the New Year if we do something Hmong we wear Hmong clothes, and if we do something American we wear American clothes" (AL-F-03),[1] thereby indicating a conscious association of dress with cultural identity.

While Hmong style dress was most typically worn by youth at the New Year celebration, it was generally designed by older women in the community. Older styles of Lao Hmong dress were transformed through the process of cultural authentication[2] to reflect American as well as Hmong culture. Teenagers and the older women who sewed the garments drew inspiration from the range of cloth and trims available in American fabric stores to create ensembles that, while rooted in Lao Hmong prototypes, were a creative blend of both Hmong and American influences. As will be outlined, the

FIGURE 13.3 *Young women dressed in New Year finery playing ball toss.*

transformation of Lao Hmong dress marking subgroup membership into Hmong American dress marking cohesive group identity is an apt illustration of Sarna's concept of ethnic group formation and Comaroff's distinction between totemic and ethnic boundary lines.

DRESS: THE DISPLAY OF ETHNICITY

At my first Hmong American New Year in November of 1988, I naively assumed that teenagers were wearing distinct substyles of dress associated with their family and region of origin.

I was therefore surprised when a girl told me to be sure to watch for her the next day as she would be wearing a costume associated with a different subgroup. Teenage girls typically owned and wore a variety of substyles of dress. When I interviewed the winner of the 1989 Teen of the Year contest, she proudly showed me photographs of her taken in four different substyles of dress.

Teenagers were perplexed when I asked them why they wore the substyles of other groups and generally attributed little meaning to the practice. Most teenagers simply told me it was the new style, the American way. But importantly, being a Hmong American rather than a Lao Hmong was often associated with the freedom to wear other subgroups' styles. For example, the following is drawn from an interview with a Hmong American female Teen of the Year contestant:

> See, that is the change now. Now we can wear any one—any kind. I could be a Green Hmong, I could wear White Hmong clothes, it doesn't really matter. It doesn't really matter in Laos too, but in Laos you wear what you are. But now it is the style—if you like it you wear it. We are becoming more Americanized in that way. (AL-F-01)

It was typical that the teenagers discussed the impulse to wear the other styles or to mix the styles as a fashion impulse or as an aesthetic choice. "It looks good" and "it is the new style" were often the words used by the teenagers. The following response concerns the practice of mixing the different substyles within a single ensemble: "I usually mix them up. I wear the hat with the White, and the hat doesn't go with the White dress. It doesn't really matter but it surely looks good so why not?" (AL-F-05).

The practice of mixing the substyles together and wearing those of groups other than one's own was documented throughout the United States. Sally Peterson (1990) commented that "there are not many Green Hmong families in Philadelphia, but almost every family with daughters owns a Green Hmong skirt— particularly if it is made in the new style."[3] (p. 94). In Missoula, Montana, Susan Lindbergh's (1990) research compared how Hmong American teenage girls dressed for the New Year with the way their mothers dressed in Laos:

> Transition is evident in the costumes that the girls wear. Whereas their mothers dressed for the New Year's in Sam Neua (White Hmong substyle) or Xieng Khouang costumes, depending on the subgroup into which they were born, the young women in this study each own costumes representative of at least two, if not three, different subgroups from which they select one to wear, depending upon personal preference. Wealthy girls may wear a different costume for each night of the New Year celebration to display their riches.

> Frequently subgroup garments are mixed, creating a hybrid costume. (p. 45)

In a similar vein, Joanne Cubbs (1986) reported that new style ensembles worn by teenagers at the New Year in Sheboygan, Wisconsin combined elements of White Hmong and Green Hmong dress (p. 71). The pattern of mixing substyles I discovered at the New Year in St. Paul was thus a national trend moving toward the use of dress to express shared group (ethnic) identity rather than distinct subgroup (totemic) identity.

Lindbergh (1990) discussed the possibility of the above interpretation, but in the end dismissed it as an outsider's perception without internal validity. She provided an example of a response she received when she asked a young woman about the meaning of the blurring of the lines between the subgroup styles:

> When asked whether the blurring of lines between costume subgroups meant that the Hmong were beginning to identify with all Hmong rather than with their individual subgroups, a conclusion an outsider might draw, one young woman seemed confused by the question. Ties with her family, her husband's family, their places of origin and shared experiences within their lineages are still more important to her than any general sense of being Hmong. She feels tremendous loyalty to being from Sam Neua (a White Hmong subgroup), even though in the United States as a teenager she chose to wear a variety of different costumes, and though as an adult she continues to collect them for herself and for her daughters. (p. 50)

In contradiction to Lindbergh, I hold that the outsider sometimes sees the bigger picture missed by insiders who tend to offer more personalized interpretations centered upon their own individual experiences rather than the ethnic group as a whole. The fact that the woman quoted above both values her own substyle of dress and collects a variety of other substyles likely indicates that Hmong-style dress has a myriad of meanings to her, some of which are perhaps more easily articulated than others. The nationwide trend to mix the substyles together into hybrid ensembles and to wear the substyles of other groups indicates that Hmong-style dress had group as well as individual significance, an insight that is perhaps more easily perceived by a more objective outsider's eye.

While most forms of new style dress worn to the New Year were tied by their wearers to Lao Hmong prototypes, the popular rooster style women's New Year hat, a highly decorated cloth hat topped with dramatic coxcomb, was consistently classified as Hmong American despite evidence that similar hat styles did exist in historical Green Hmong dress (Cubbs 1986; Peterson 1990; AL-F-03; Lynch, Detzner, and Eicher, 1995). Early versions of the American-style New Year hat combined White Hmong handwork with a Green Hmong children's hat style. The dramatic mixing of the two major substyles of dress within a single form makes the hat a prime example of dress expressive of a cohesive ethnic identity. The more contemporary versions of the hat integrated elements of American material culture into the design. Sequins, lace, and American trims were borrowed and creatively integrated through the process of cultural authentication into striking symbols of Hmong American identity.

SUMMARY AND CONCLUSIONS

Hmong Americans entered the Thai refugee camps and later the United States in fragmented groups and continued to categorize themselves by what I would label a totemic classification. However as the integrity of their world was threatened by outside forces they became defensive and thus more conscious of their ethnic as opposed to totemic identity. While allegiance to the White or Green Hmong subgroup or to a specific clan was of fundamental importance in the Lao village context, it became progressively less important as the Hmong were threatened and discriminated against on the basis of their more inclusive ethnic identity.

Sarna posits that as ethnic groups endure discrimination based upon an externally ascribed ethnic boundary line, that line becomes impor-

tant internally as well. When the Lao Hmong were targeted for extermination by the communists based upon their ethnic identity, the Hmong themselves began to assign more salience to their ethnic as opposed to totemic identity. Allegiances to totemic classifications became less important as the once separate Hmong subgroups became vulnerable to outsiders based upon their more inclusive ethnic identity. As Hmong refugees were moved into camps in Thailand and later relocated to the United States, they continued to be treated as a cohesive ethnic group and received both positive and negative treatment based upon that identity.

The transformation of regional substyles of Lao Hmong dress into a cohesive Hmong American style can be interpreted as symbolic of Hmong American ethnicity. As the generation most acutely experiencing discrimination based on their ascribed ethnic identity, teenagers wear dress which expresses Hmong cohesiveness and pride. By wearing a mix of Hmong substyles teenagers visibly accept and celebrate their ascribed ethnic identity both as individuals and as corporate representatives of their families and community.

In conclusion, I propose a classification system for dress that marks opposing cultural identities. My classification system differentiates between dress expressing symmetrical totemic relationships between structurally similar groups, and dress expressing asymmetrical ethnic relationships between structurally dissimilar groups. I propose that regionally distinct Hmong dress styles worn in Lao villages marked totemic differences between similar and equally powerful Hmong subgroups. In contrast, Hmong American style dress worn at New Year marks an ethnic boundary between the Hmong and what they perceive to be more politically and economically powerful groups.

The term ethnic is often used as a convenient substitute for academically dated terms such as tribal and primitive (see Chapman, McDonald and Tonkin 1989: 14). Because of this convenient quality, ethnicity (and the related term, ethnic dress) is a slippery concept that has been used in many different ways in many different places. The use of the term "ethnic dress" to refer to defined characteristics of a specific type of social boundary, as suggested in this chapter, transforms it from a convenient label into a useful concept. Further, it begins to build necessary linkages between academic literature focused upon defining ethnic identity and research on dress.

Notes

1. Interview data is coded according to the author's initials and subject number through the manuscript.

2. Cultural authentication is a process by which a borrowed cultural element works its way into the culture through language (being assigned a specific name), patterns of significant use, and aesthetic transformation (Ereksomia and Eicher 1981).

3. New style Green Hmong skirts are more heavily embroidered and appliquéd than the older style skirts—the more heavily embellished the better is an underlying aesthetic criteria of the new style.

References

Barth, F. (1969), *Ethnic Groups and Boundaries: The Social Organization of Cultural Difference*, Boston: Little Brown.

Bodnar, J. (1985), *The Transplanted*, Bloomington: Indiana University Press.

Chapman, M., McDonald, M., and Tonkin, E. (1989), "Introduction" in *History and Ethnicity*, London and New York: Routledge.

Cohen, A. (1973), *Urban Ethnicity*, London: Tavistock Publications.

Comaroff, J.L. (1987), "Of Totemism and Ethnicity: Consciousness, Practice and the Signs of Inequality, *Ethnos*, vol. 52, nos. 3–4, pp. 301–23.

Cubbs, J. (1986), "Hmong Art: Tradition and Change," In *Hmong Art: Tradition and Change*, Sheboygan, WI: John Michael Kohler Arts Center.

Dewhurst, C.K., and MacDowell, M. (1983), "Michigan Hmong Arts," *Publications of the Museum, Michigan State University Folk Culture Series*, vol. 3, no. 2.

Epstein, A.L. (1978), *Ethos and Identity*, London: Tavistock.

Erekosima, T., and Eicher, J. (1981), "Kalabari Cut-thread and Pulled-thread Cloth," *African Arts*, vol. 14, no. 2, pp 48–51, 87.

Geddes, W.P. (1976), *Migrants of the Mountains: The Cultural Ecology of the Blue Miao of Thailand*, Oxford: Clarendon Press.

Glazer, N., and Moynihan, D.P. (1975), *Ethnicity, Theory and Experience*, Cambridge, MA: Harvard University Press.

Glick-Schiller, N., and Fouron, G. (1990), "Everywhere We Go, We Are in Danger: Ti Manno and the Emergence of a Haitian Transnational Identity," *American Ethnologist*, vol. 17, no. 2, pp. 329–6.

Lindbergh. S M. (1988), "Traditional Costumes of Lao Hmong Refugees in Montana: A Study of Cultural Continuity and Change, unpublished Master's thesis, Minneapolis: University of Montana.

Lynch, A. (1992), "Hmong American New Year's Dress: A Material Culture Approach," unpublished Ph.D. dissertation, Minneapolis: University of Minnesota (*Dissertation Abstracts International*, 53, 228B).

Lynch, A., Detzer, D., and Eicher J. (1995), "Hmong American New Year Rituals: Generational Bonds through Dress," in *Clothing and Textiles Research Journal*, vol. 13, no. 2, pp. 111–20.

Mallinson, J., Donnelly, N., and Hang L. (1988), *Hmong Batik:. A Textile Technique from Laos*, Seattle, WA: Mallison/Information Services.

Moerman, M. (1964), "Ethnic Identification in a Complex Society: Who Are the Lue?" *American Anthropologist*, vol. 67, pp. 1215–30.

Peterson, S.N. (1990), "From the Heart and the Mind: Creating *paj ntaub* in the Context of Community," unpublished Ph.D. dissertation, University of Pennsylvania (*Dissertation Abstracts International*, 51, 1724A).

Roosens, E.E. (1989), *Creating Ethnicity: The Process of Ethnogenesis*, Newbury Park: Sage.

Sarna, J. (1978), "From Immigrants to Ethnics: Towards a New Theory of 'Ethnicization'," *Ethnicity*, vol. 5, pp. 370–8.

Tapp, N. (1988), "The Reformation of Culture: Hmong Refugees from Laos," *Journal of Refugee Studies*, vol. I, no. I, pp. 20–37.

DISCUSSION QUESTIONS

Hmong American New Year's Dress: The Display of Ethnicity

1. How is the roaster hat worn by Hmong teenagers on New Years symbolic of both their ethnic identity and assimilation into American culture?

81   From Hoop Skirt to Slam Dunk Chic

Ira Berkow

The first organized women's basketball game was held at Smith College in 1892. Signs were posted outside the gymnasium: MEN ARE NOT PERMITTED TO WATCH. And the hoopsters wore long dresses.

It's a long, long way from the fin de siècle.

Many bloomers and baggy men's shorts later, the country's newest league, the Women's National Basketball Association, begins play on June 21. And the players will be dazzling (that's as in the fabric, if not the fast break as well) in new ergonomic tops and shorts.

Eager to make a name for itself in the sweaty, rough-and-tumble world of sport and commerce, the W.N.B.A., the Adam's rib of the N.B.A., has set out to get the best players available. The organizers know that if the women can't fill up the hoop, the league, whose season runs to Aug. 30, will be a disaster. But the belief is also that apparel oft proclaims the woman, and the sweeter the style of the uniform on such as Lisa Leslie, Rebecca Lobo and Sheryl Swoopes, the swifter the click of the turnstile.

So last October, the league began to plot the future of women's basketball couture, snaring people for consultation and focus groups from the N.B.A.'s television broadcasting division, from its marketing group, from its basketball operations unit, from the teams, and perhaps some startled others who might have just been staring out the window. They hired the fashion mavens at Champion and set up a committee of active-wear designers to dress their eight teams in a uniform that, they say, has been especially configured not for sex appeal but to improve the performance of the players.

The W.N.B.A. plans to introduce its new uniform at Madison Square Garden on Wednesday.

"These women have a job to perform, and we wanted to make sure that this uniform has all

FIGURE 13.4 *Kathy Coiner plays women's basketball at University of Massachusetts—Amherst and dresses in contemporary active wear.*

the strengths and attributes that the men's uniform has," said Linda Jameison, director of the N.B.A.'s apparel group. "What's been happening in professional and college uniforms is that it's been a male focus. So what they've done is take a traditional male tank and short and put that on female players. It doesn't fit the same. It's a female form versus a male form. And it holds a garment differently."

So, beyond the requisite jumpers, as in jump shots, and players threading the needle on passes and hitting the open woman, the spectator at W.N.B.A. games can also expect to see tops that have a tapered waist and flair out a bit at the hips, wider shoulder straps that cling better on women's narrower shoulders, lighter fabrics—dazzle (a nylon or polyester with a sheen that appears to glow under arena lights), striped dazzle and two

kinds of mesh—and shorts that are slightly shorter than men's and cut fuller in the leg.

"It won't look like a skirt," Ms. Jameison insisted. "Movement is still of the essence."

The rival American Basketball League, not to be outdone by the frock-conscious W.N.B.A., is busy adapting its more conventional men's-style shorts and jerseys for women, adding dazzle and V-necks and assigning the fashion mavens at Reebok to tailor each of the players on its nine teams personally. (The bigger women generally prefer baggier pants, while the shorter ones like their shorts short, so as not to look too short.)

It used to be that women chased around a basketball court wearing hoops while trying to throw a ball through one. Basketball was invented by Dr. James Naismith, who was instructed in late 1891 by his superiors at the Springfield (Mass.) Y.M.C.A. to devise an indoor game from which its members could get good wintertime exercise.

At that time, women were still encased in the petticoats and tightly laced corsets that "threatened their vigor and stamina," according to "A Century of Women's Basketball," edited by Joan S. Hult and Marianna Trekell (1991). "Early in sporting experiences, women wore their tight clothing including corsets for tennis, croquet and archery."

But as the last decade of the 19th century wound down, Ms. Hult noted, "they moved to the bloomer attire and wore modified versions of male attire—shirt and skirt. If bloomers could appear outside on cycling paths, they could also be acceptable on basketball courts."

Perhaps the most stylish women's team was the All-American Red Heads of the first half-century, a barnstorming group that competed against men, shooting trick shots, whipping passes behind the back and wowing the crowds with their appearance as well. All the players were redheads, in one fashion or another—natural, dyed or wigged.

Their uniforms, when they were organized in 1936, were black and white, but they soon switched to green, the better to highlight their red crests. Wool uniforms were a problem, since the whirlwind travel of some 135 games a season meant that they took a long time to dry after washing—and this was before laundromats. "So the players didn't like to wash them," said Tom O'Grady, director of the N.B.A.'s creative services division, "and they smelled foul."

It was a pleasure for player and spectator alike, then, when wool uniforms gave way to rayon and nylon and washing machines and dryers.

But there are still olfactory memories associated with uniforms. "We wore polyester uniforms that were heavy and not cool," said Carol Blazejowski, general manager of the New York Liberty team in the W.N.B.A. and an all-America at Montclair State College, who played one year, 1981, for the New Jersey Gems of the Women's Basketball League, which no longer exists. "The smell hung around. We had polo shirts with sleeves. Our shorts were boxy and real short. Nothing to flatter the leg. And primary colors. Just the average dumb red. The uniform was a function. Today the uniform is fashion *and* function."

The W.N.B.A. and A.B.L. uniforms are still a new world from even 20 or 30 years ago.

"I played in high school in what I used to wear to gym class," recalled Tara VanDerveer, head coach of the Stanford University women's basketball team. "It was a long, flowing navy-blue pleated skirt—not quite a kilt—and we put it over a white blouse that came down to above the knees, and a sash and shorts underneath."

Taking note of the general change in women's uniforms, she added: "Uniforms had become big. Women were falling out of them. Jog bras showed. Now, they are fitting better. Classic lines and a clean look. Very nice."

Ann Meyers, a former all-America at the University of California at Los Angeles and a Gems teammate of Ms. Blazejowski's, prefers the looser fit in shorts. At U.C.L.A., the pants were rather tight, though not, she said, "a bun hugger like we call the uniforms of the European teams."

Baggy shorts can be a problem, however.

"When I was a freshman in college," said Rebecca Lobo, the former University of Connecticut star, "I jumped to block a shot against another player. and our bodies got caught. I had forgotten to tie the drawstring, and my shorts fell down! I couldn't believe it! I learned to tie a drawstring after that."

Ms. Lobo, a member of the new Liberty team, can now choose shorts with elastic waistbands so she won't have to be concerned with drawstrings. Then again, she anticipates that the league will sell itself on the skills of the players, and not of the fashion designers.

"I hope people are more interested in how we play," she said, "and not how we look."

As for habiliments in the A.B.L., some players have been perfectly happy.

"I don't really see a need for changes," Karen Deden of the New England Blizzard said. "Men's gear fit fine. Most of us are used to wearing them. In fact, I like men's shorts because they sit lower on the hips and don't ride up."

And some A.B.L. players wonder about the effects. "I think it's great they're spending time on making new uniforms for women," said Lin Dunn, head coach of the Portland Power. "But whether it'll make the W.N.B.A. play better remains to be seen."

Valerie Still, star forward of the A.B.L. champion, the Columbus Quest, maintains doubts about the summertime league. "I don't think it'll work," she said, "unless the girls play on a beach in string bikinis."

DISCUSSION QUESTIONS

From Hoop Skirt to Slam Dunk Chic

1. How have technological advances in fabrics had a direct impact on women's basketball uniforms?

2. Why have some women basketball players downplayed the interest in what women wear on the court?

Wendi Winters

A few years back there was a ripple of interest in eco-friendly clothing.

The idea was to dress responsibly without scalping the planet. But after a flood of scratchy clothes with a homemade look, the buzz died, and the fashion world cantered off in hot pursuit of the next new trend.

Though it has had some notable flops, the eco-fashion movement isn't dead. Instead, it's heading for mainstream acceptance in several categories— jeans wear, sportswear, sweaters, shirts, lounge wear, outerwear and children's clothing.

The Los Angeles-based O Wear, dubbed "America's first 100 percent certified organic cotton clothing company," was founded in 1989 by fashion industry veteran George Akers. Organic cotton was scarce, but he encouraged area farmers to grow more for his company, which projects sales of more than $20 million by decade's end.

Blue Fish, of Frenchtown, N.J., is a designer, manufacturer, wholesaler and retailer of New Age clothing made of organic or recycled materials finished with hand-blocked linoleum prints created by local artisans. Though its public relations director, Ta Kimble, is the company's "Spirit Keeper," Blue Fish is not a hippie pipe dream. It has sales in the millions, and its stock is publicly traded.

AVEDA FASHIONS FAILED

But Aveda, well-known for its extensive collection of ecologically correct cosmetics, hair products and fragrances, failed in a bid to add socially responsible fashion to its line. Nicole Rechelbacher of Minneapolis, daughter of Aveda's founder, started Anatomy "to show other designers it can be done." Alas, it didn't fly.

Other failures include Wrangler's Earth Wash jeans, stone washed in a way that reduced waste, and Code Bleu's much ballyhooed Soda Pop denim jeans, made from a blend of recycled soda bottles and cotton.

"There was no demand or interest from the consumer and very little support from retailers," according to Code Bleu's Lainey Goldberg, Executive Vice President of Sales.

One area where it was successful, Goldberg said, was in the children's market. "Schools are doing a good job teaching ecology, and kids are much more committed to taking care of the environment."

Yet other manufacturers, such as Columbia Sportswear Co. in Portland, Ore., produce BioWashed Jeans, a biodegradable alternative to chemically stone-washed denims.

And there's Trio Eco-Blend Denim, "a high-tech blend with an ecological conscience." Trio, a jeans wear fabric, is made of Tencel, a rayon-like fiber without rayon's eco-messy production process; and EcoSpun fiber produced from recycled soda pop bottles, and cotton.

HANDBOOK OF SOURCES

Since 1994, Men's Health magazine has periodically published *Eco-Style Guide*, a handbook listing sources for clothing, accessories and footwear "made with the Earth in mind, with new fabrics and new production processes."

Warren Christopher, the magazine's fashion and grooming editor, notes, "The companies listed in our guide have more than doubled from the first issue. While the eco market is still in its early stages, its growth reflects a shift from a cottage industry to a dedicated niche market. A lot of our younger readers are living ecologically correct lives. In college or newly graduated, they are in tune with the environment. They're buying the

Winters, Wendi, "Eco-friendly Fashions are 'Cool." *The Indianapolis Star* (May 29, 1997).

unbleached and recycled cottons, the hemp fabric clothes and the soda bottle skiwear."

Almost as lengthy is the listing of apparel companies using Wellman Inc.'s EcoSpun fiber, introduced in 1993. Judith Langan, communications director, says sales have since risen 450 percent.

"Although we launched it for outerwear, it's used in dozens of categories now," she says. "Products and garments made of EcoSpun are sold around the world. The Japanese, especially, love the concept."

Eventually, according to Jim Casey, president of the fibers division, EcoSpun production could recycle approximately 3 billion bottles per year.

Manufacturers currently using EcoSpun include Patagonia, Colombia Sportswear, Eileen Fisher and Levi's.

Deep in the heart of Texas, another "green" fiber revolution is brewing. The Texas Organic Cotton Marketing Cooperative, growers of organic cotton certified and regulated by the state agriculture department, have organized a marketing arm, Cotton Plus Ltd., to promote their growing catalog of products, yarns and fabrics.

ORGANIC COTTON, HEMP

Certified organic cotton is cotton that is grown on land that remained free of synthetic chemicals, pesticides and fertilizers for at least three years. Though this chemical-free cotton is more expensive to buy, as it is more difficult to grow

and process, growers say supply is out-paced by demand.

Hemp, a product of the marijuana plant, is trying to rehabilitate its image. Once used nearly worldwide in rope-making, paper and apparel, hemp in the United States and many other countries was outlawed earlier in the century.

While growing hemp is still illegal in the United States, it is not illegal to import hemp fabric from the handful of countries that grow it. Hal Nelson, founder of the American Hemp Mercantile in Seattle, imports hemp apparel and other hemp products for more than 1,000 stores, many in California.

Nelson says the type of cannabis plant cultivated for hemp fiber has a much lower THC content than that grown for drug use. American Hemp had sales of $1.5 million in 1995 and $1.8 million last year.

"The popularity of hemp apparel is growing," Nelson says. "The quality is improving. In three years we have gone from selling beige sack dresses to clothes that are colorful and stylish.

"Manufacturers are investing money for better dyeing, finishing and detailing. Consumers are finding hemp fabrics are better than cotton. The fibers of hemp are long and strong like a supima cotton, yet fewer harsh chemicals are used in its cultivation and processing."

But, he adds, consumers aren't buying because it is eco-friendly. "Consumers are buying it because it's 'cool.' We have to do more education."

Eco-friendly Fashions Are Cool

1. Give reasons why an eco-friendly fashion might fail as a business venture. Give reasons why it could be successful.

2. Why has hemp become a desirable eco-friendly fabric? How has marketing added to the popularity?

83 Have We Become a Nation of Slobs?

Jerry Adler

When Sam Albert went to work for IBM in 1959, he assumed he'd be wearing a suit for the rest of his life. In fact, the *same* suit (single-breasted dark blue or gray worsted), over dark socks suspended rigidly from garters and a white shirt with a detachable collar starched to the stiffness of an annual-report cover. Feet planted in black wingtips, heads encased in steel-gray fedoras, the men of IBM achieved an uncanny uniformity, signifying not just business, but business *machines*. When Albert retired in 1989 as a top marketing executive, he counted 35 dress shirts in his closet, all of them white. So when he returned as a consultant to IBM's Armonk, N.Y., headquarters last week, wearing a dress shirt, suit and tie, he was prepared for anything but the sight of employees lined up for lunch in sweaters and slacks. "They looked at me," he says, "like they were asking, 'Who is this guy with the suit on?'"

By rights, this age should mark the apotheosis of the suit. From Eastern Europe to Latin America, the broadcloth-backed armies of capitalism are on the march. Bustling Pacific Rim societies such as Singapore illustrate the perverse rule that the more inhospitable the climate of a given country, the more closely cinched the ties around the necks of the ruling class. America, for its part, has elected new leaders drawn from the ranks of small-town Southern professionals and college teachers for whom drab gray suits are expressive of their very nature, like fatigues for Castro. The last election was a landslide for the values the suit stands for: tradition, hierarchy, conformity and, well, money.

Yet even as the idea of the suit has triumphed, the garment itself is losing ground. The most recent sign came on Friday, Feb. 3, when IBM chairman Louis V. Gerstner Jr. relaxed the inviolable, though unwritten, dress code for the 800 workers at the innermost sanctum of American capitalism. "Dress down" days, a phrase that first appeared in print barely five years ago, now affect, by some estimates, more than half of all U.S. office workers. Major banks and law firms

are among the companies that lift the burden of neckties and nylons on employees in honor of the impending weekend; so is the Central Intelligence Agency. At least one governor, Oregon's John Kitzhaber, has proclaimed casual Fridays for himself, keeping his normal schedule in crisply pressed Levi's button-fly jeans. American men bought only around 13 million suits last year, down by 1.6 million since 1989, according to NPD Research, Inc. This implies that every adult male in the country buys a suit every seven years. Since the average American doubles his weight in that time, he presumably has long since stopped buttoning the last one.

HATS AND GLOVES

Nor is this phenomenon confined to office wear. You don't have to be very old to recall when middle-class men routinely wore a jacket and tie in public, even to a baseball game, or when women would put on a dress, hat, gloves, heels, nylons and jewelry to go to a department store. At a ball game today most people are grateful if the person in the next seat has on a *shirt*. Travel once called for dressing up—one is, after all, representing oneself to strangers—but now it seems to bring out people's worst fashion instincts. Bert Hand, chairman of the menswear company Hartmarx, identifies these as sweat pants and jogging suits. "Maybe," he says, "there should be a jogging-suit airline."

As tourists, Americans have given up pastel Bermuda shorts, only to replace them with Gap jeans, golf shirts, Nike jackets and $100 sneakers. These invite less ridicule but, if anything, even more contempt. Parisians assume not merely that Americans dress badly but that they don't even know the difference. The bright swirls and stripes of American sports logos seem especially glaring in the gloom of an 800-year-old church. "People are pretending that dress has no symbolic significance," says Judith Martin, the "Miss Manners" columnist, "but it does."

As for worship, Americans who long ago gave up wearing ties to services are starting to treat socks as optional. "We have lost the ideal of adult self-respect, and we're dressing like rebellious children," remarks the fashion historian Anne Hollander ("Sex and Suits"). "When you go to church, or to the opera, you now have the idea that you do not need to express respect in your costume—that if you do, you somehow feel like one of the oppressed." Morticians are seeing more street clothes at funerals. That includes on corpses. Boston funeral director Arthur Hasiotis says families sometimes request casual burial wear for decedents who never put a tie around their necks while they were alive.

SHORTS AND CAPS

Slovenliness jeopardizes our precious national iconography. Presidents used to dress like presidents, not like a guy from the block, lumbering by every morning in shorts and a baseball cap. Movie stars used to dress like stars; Brad Pitt, arriving for the premiere of "Legends of the Fall" last year in a baggy gray sweater, could have been mistaken for the projectionist. Many people's memories of Jackie Onassis will forever bear the nagging footnote that the day after her death, Daryl Hannah showed up at her apartment in jeans and a T shirt, looking like she was planning to clean out the closets. Hannah's controversial Rollerblading visit to Onassis just before she died was a watershed in casual history. Many people were offended, but Richard Martin, curator of the Costume Institute of the Metropolitan Museum of Art, came to her defense. "It seems to me that at the point of death one wants to affirm life," he says. "Rollerblading was an affirmation of life. Dressing mournfully is a pretty hollow ceremony."

Even gangsters don't dress up for work any longer. John Gotti showed that you can be an animal without dressing like one, but now mob power in New York has allegedly passed to Vincent (the Chin) Gigante, who wanders the streets of Little Italy in a bathrobe and bedroom slippers. Hollywood big shots used to dress like…well, never mind. But even on their worst days any three of them could have come up with more than the one necktie Jeffrey Katzenberg, Steven Spielberg and David Geffen mustered last October to announce the formation of their colossal new studio.

The photograph of the moguls at their press conference is worth deconstructing, because it shows the many nuances of slovenliness. Katzenberg is relatively neat in a tie and a dress shirt with sleeves rolled up—a look that says, "OK, hey, I left my jacket in the office, you think starting a new studio is all I have to do today?" Geffen, known as "Mr. Gap," wears a shirt open at the collar and a casual vest, an outfit whose message is, "I can wear anything I want—you got a problem with that?" But Spielberg is dressed in rumpled pants and a plaid shirt that might have come from JCPenney, a white blotch of undershirt showing at the collar—a look that says only, "This was on the front hanger in my closet."

Of course, Spielberg, being Spielberg, can dress however he pleases. But that's the point: Americans used to *want* to dress up. Wearing a suit was a privilege of adulthood; Spielberg's outfit looks like something his mother might have dressed him in in fourth grade. One of the fastest-growing apparel categories is sweat suits, known in the trade as "fleece wear." Especially on airplanes, Americans love to curl up among their cuddly folds, like oversize babies, surrounded by the comforting sensations of infancy.

COLLARS AND GARTERS

Comfort, of course, is the one unanswerable argument in favor of casual dressing. No one bothers putting on a suit or high heels to work at home, certainly. IBM's long-suffering employees of the 1950s didn't just sit at their desks in starched collars and garters; they rode to work in them on stifling buses or subways. You couldn't pay people enough to do that today—not, anyway, once they heard about how Lester Brown, president of WorldWatch Institute, works all summer in neat walking shorts. The other advantage of casual dress is that it is cheaper than suits—except, of course, for workers who may already have a closet full of suits, and find they now have to buy a bunch of sweaters as well. "Not having to wear nylons," an IBM worker in Atlanta told her boss "is like getting a raise."

But comfort and economy are nothing new. What has changed is the maturing of the first generation that was allowed to wear blue jeans to high school. The formative moment for today's leaders, according to fashion editor Alan Millstein, was their first glimpse of a classmate's rear end in tight Levi's. "That was the ultimate sex symbol, the 501s," Millstein says, explaining that the experience permanently turned them away from baggy suits and dresses.

This is also a generation that defined itself by rebellion. Some of the earliest acts of student activism were directed at dress codes. For many people in their 30s and 40s, going without a suit is still a step on the road to self-actualization. Bart Kosko, a 34-year-old computer scientist, began his career in the aerospace industry, where a suit and tie was a badge of loyalty in the cold war. When he came to the University of Southern California in 1988 as an associate professor in "neural fuzzy logic," he began to question his old values, including what was in his closet. "I asked myself: 'Do you have the courage to dress as you please?' Was I afraid of what people think?" Over time Kosko pared his outfit to the irreducible minimum of tank top and shorts, something that would have been literally inconceivable a generation ago. In the 1950s a suit was not a lifestyle choice; it was just what men wore, unless they were manual laborers. "There was a much narrower view of the world," says Boston University sociologist Bernard Phillips. "You didn't step outside of your role. The role dominated you."

UNBUTTONED STRAP

It is also no coincidence that suits and ties became dispensable in the 1980s, just as people started seeing billionaires in khaki pants. High-tech start-up companies were notorious for being populated by overgrown college boys wandering the halls in socks, shorts and T shirts. "The first time I interviewed here there was a woman in bare feet and overalls with one strap unbut-

toned," says Cindy Wilson of Velocity, a San Francisco multimedia company. The absence of ties is still linked in people's minds with creativity, imagination and $50 million Initial Public Offerings. "Your look is *entrepreneurial* when you dress down," says Timberland "wardrobe consultant" Barbara Seymour, using the hottest new catchphrase in fashion. "You can really *own your own look*."

Of course, not everyone wants to look "entrepreneurial." In Dallas, where the chic thing is to look as if you already have all the money in the world, "'casual' means you don't bring a gift," says *Dallas Morning News* columnist Maryln Schwartz. "A friend of mine called and said, 'I'm having people over for takeout,' and I'm thinking, you know, jeans. I go there and she was wearing pants, but they were Chanel pants."

But wearing a $1,200 outfit to eat chop suey at home is mere decadence. For sheer panache in dressing up, you can't beat a middle-class black church in the South. For generations church was the only institution where Southern blacks were allowed to dress up. On a recent Sunday the congregation arrived at Sardis Baptist in Birmingham, Ala., as if hoping to knock God's eyes out. The men wore immaculate black vested suits, French-cuffed shirts and top hats, the women…let's see: a formal black dress with matching blazer, saucer-shaped onyx earrings and a gold choker, a blue-black rhinestone-trimmed hat whose bobbing feathers stretched almost to the wearer's nose and, oh yes, a full-length black mink coat, on 53-year-old Laquita Bell, executive director of the Urban League of Birmingham. "You have to go to a little more trouble when you go to the house of the Lord," says Bell modestly. At around the same time, at First Baptist in a suburb north of Atlanta, a predominantly white congregation sauntered into the pews in jogging suits, jeans and sweaters. "It really doesn't matter what you wear," says Margaret

Sulpy, strolling toward the "worship center" (a converted warehouse) in a pink and white warm-up suit. "The Lord don't care, as long as you come."

There it is, in a nutshell, the philosophic question that everyone from the chairman of

IBM to Daryl Hannah has to wrestle with: is "dressing down" a more democratic and authentic way of life, or a sign that we just can't get it together in the morning? Robert Goldberg, a senior research fellow at Brandeis University, has noticed the curious phenomenon that two people meeting for a business deal on a Friday will each put on a suit as a token of respect, even if it's dress-down day in their respective offices. To him, this signifies that the whole concept is flawed, because why should one's own co-workers be any less deserving of the minimal effort it takes to put on a necktie? More fundamentally, are clothes mere vanities, or do they express something essential about how we view ourselves and society? "In this country we say, 'To heck with facades, we have to have the truth',' Hollander says. "We have our Puritan Protestant ideals telling us that being vain is wicked. All this we have internalized hopelessly so that good people cannot wear earrings, they have to wear running shoes."

A lot is riding on the answers to these questions, because the fashion industry has ingeniously turned the "dress down" phenomenon into a way to sell people even more clothes—a new wardrobe *just for Fridays*. To the cotton industry, casual wear is the greatest boon since the Civil War. Eddie Bauer, the manufacturer of rugged outdoorsy sportswear, is starting two new lines to meet the demand for garments in such esoteric categories as "formal casual," "business alternative" and "dress sportswear." Hush Puppies, a company that has an obvious stake in casual wear, has produced a video guide to "the growing trend toward the unstructured." "The shift creates new challenges for human resources professionals," the video notes cheerfully. "The human-resources department has got to do a better job of communicating what they mean by a Henley sweater or stretch leggings." Last year this kind of communication helped Hush Puppies sell the rest of the country 37 percent more shoes.

FROCK COATS

And something else is at stake, the very face, if not the soul, of America. Fashion usually proceeds in cycles and so may the fashion for dressing down. But there is also a long-range trend toward informality that may prove unstoppable. What we know as the three-piece business suit was known at the turn of the century as the "lounge suit," a casual garment for wearing at home or in the country. A banker or senator would ordinarily wear a frock coat to his office. In "Sex and Suits," Hollander notes that in the middle of the last century, when formal dress consisted of white tie and tails, the bewigged footmen at a ball were dressed in the gentleman's costume of a century earlier. Today, the headwaiter in a fancy restaurant may wear a dinner jacket as he greets patrons dressed in business clothes. If the pattern continues, the ordinary suit may be fated to become a ceremonial garment, worn mostly by waiters in restaurants whose patrons wear…better not to think about it.

Have We Become a Nation of Slobs?

1. Because casualness in appearance is currently a well-accepted trend, what are some of the negative aspects of this social change? What are the positive aspects?

2. Give three reasons why you feel our society is moving toward the trend of casualness in appearance.

84   Sheer Madness

Janet Wells

Consider the heraldic beginnings of nylon stockings. In 1939, the first 40,000 pairs—limit two per woman—sold out in three hours.

A few years later, when a survey asked 60 women what they missed most during World War II, one-third, responded, "Men." The pragmatic other two-thirds, remembering all the nylon fabric commandeered for parachutes and tents, lamented, "Nylons."

Indeed, 10,000 women rioted in San Francisco in 1945 to get at the first postwar hosiery shipment, breaking storefront windows. A headline read, "Women Risk Life and Limb in Bitter Battle for Nylons."

Women have been crazy for nylons ever since the 1930s, when a Du Pont scientist stumbled upon the stretchy stuff and advertised it to be "as strong as steel yet as fine as a spider's web."

Now the unimaginable has finally happened. Women's obsessive love affair with sheer hosiery is over. It took more than 50 years of runs, fickle fashions and changes in lifestyle, but for the first time, sales of sheer hosiery are tumbling.

"There was a day five years ago, when working women wore sheer pantyhose as a social custom. It was an obligation, a part of a uniform," said Frank Oswald, marketing consultant for Du Pont, the world's biggest supplier of yarns to the hosiery industry. "That's changed. Leg wear is going through a lot of soul-searching." Women are looking for casual and comfortable.

"No woman in the Bush administration would ever go into the White House without pantyhose," former Bush press assistant Kirstin Hyde told Newsweek recently as she bemoaned the fashion standards of the Clinton crowd. "Even in the wee hours of the night. Even on the weekends."

Through the mid-1980s, sales of sheer hosiery grew at double-digit rates to a high of $3.4 billion in 1985. By last year, sales had slipped to $2.3 billion.

Hosiery makers, hoping the decline was a phase rather than a trend, continued to increase production. But after manufacturing an overrun of 34 million dozen pairs of sheer hose over the last three years, makers have been forced to consolidate and close plants nationwide.

While sales of sheer pantyhose and stockings have fallen through the floor, however, sales of tights and opaque hose have soared through the roof. Tights, which didn't even have a separate marketing category until 1990, jumped 281 percent in sales last year, up to $409 million.

"When I was in college, wearing black tights was the hippie thing to do. Now it's mainstream," said Heidi Benson, fashion editor at San Francisco Focus magazine. You saw Hillary Clinton wearing opaque black hose during the campaign. It seemed very strange, but it's the trend."

Some say the change in loyalty stems from cost and comfort-consciousness. Tights last up to a year without a run and usually are a dramatic improvement over the sausage-casing-like squeeze of pantyhose.

Others say fashion still is the dictator and that women are just following designer dictums by sporting tights, funky socks and bare legs.

"When Christian Lacroix put the famous power suit on the runway in the late 1980s and teamed it with black tights, millions and millions of women voted with him," Du Pont's Oswald said. "If he put a dress on the runway that was just above the knee with sheers, women would buy sheers.

"The casual lifestyle is the major threat to sheers, and I don't think that's going to go away," he said. "It has hurt the industry. The business is in the throes of a real transition."

Du Pont, like many companies, has casual day on Fridays, when men leave their neckties in the closet and women don leggings and jeans.

"That has removed (one-seventh) of the opportunity to wear pantyhose," Oswald mourned. "Dressing down doesn't seem like a benefit to me, but obviously I'm in the minority."

Janet Wells, *San Francisco Chronicle*, Sept. 8, 1993, p. 1. Reprinted by permission.

Manufacturers are hardly conceding defeat over sheer pantyhose. Companies intend to turn the trend into an opportunity by persuading women to buy a drawer full of leg wear, rather than a few pairs of staple pantyhose.

"Price used to be based on hostility—women would pay only a finite amount when hosiery was viewed simply as a leg covering," Oswald said, "but when I promise you I can dress up your legs to make your outfit, you'll pay anything."

Women are snapping up tights, opaque hose and leggings at $10 to $30 a pop, while pantyhose, even at sale prices, languish on the shelves.

Even so, Francisco's Financial District is proof that while the market for sheer hosiery may be lagging, it will never die.

"For some women, it's always appropriate for work, and for the holidays, the No. 1 seller is still jetblack sheer," said Jane Harmon, a Macy's fashion coordinator.

"Women will never stop buying (pantyhose)," agreed Kathryn Cordes, publicity director for Hanes Hosiery in New York, "but you're not going to find women with a drawer full of skin-colored hosiery anymore. There's so much more choice now."

Sheer Madness

1. What reasons does the author give for the decline in popularity of the nylon stocking?

2. What is the relationship between the decline in interest in nylon stockings and the increased casualness of American dress?

85   Turning Boys Into Girls

Michelle Cottle

I love *Men's Health* magazine. There. I'm out of the closet, and I'm not ashamed. Sure, I know what some of you are thinking: What self-respecting '90s woman could embrace a publication that runs such enlightened articles as "Turn Your Good Girl Bad" and "How to Wake Up Next to a One-Night Stand"? Or maybe you'll smile and wink knowingly: What red-blooded hetero chick *wouldn't* love all those glossy photo spreads of buff young beefcake in various states of undress, ripped abs and glutes flexed so tightly you could bounce a check on them? Either way you've got the wrong idea. My affection for *Men's Health is* driven by pure gender politics—by the realization that this maga-

zine, and a handful of others like it, are leveling the playing field in a way that *Ms.* can only dream of. With page after page of bulging biceps and Gillette jaws, robust hairlines and silken skin, *Men's Health* is peddling a standard of male beauty as unforgiving and unrealistic as the female version sold by those dewy-eyed pre-teen waifs draped across the covers of *Glamour* and *Elle*. And with a variety of helpful features on

Reprinted with permission from *The Washington Monthly.* Copyright by The Washington Monthly Company, 1611 Connecticut Ave., N.W., Washington, D.C. 20009 (202)462-0128.

"Foods That Fight Fat," "Banish Your Potbelly," and "Save Your Hair (Before It's Too Late)," *Men's Health* is well on its way to making the male species as insane, insecure, and irrational about physical appearance as any *Cosmo* girl.

Don't you see, ladies? We've been going about this equality business all wrong. Instead of battling to get society fixated on something besides our breast size, we should have been fighting spandex with spandex. Bra burning was a nice gesture, but the greater justice is in convincing our male counterparts that the key to their happiness lies in a pair of made-for-him Super Shaper Briefs with the optional "fly front endowment pad" (as advertised in *Men's Journal*, $29.95 plus shipping and handling). Make the men as neurotic about the circumference of their waists and the whiteness of their smiles as the women, and at least the burden of vanity and self-loathing will be shared by all.

This is precisely what lads' mags like *Men's Health* are accomplishing. The rugged John-Wayne days when men scrubbed their faces with deodorant soap and viewed gray hair and wrinkles as a badge of honor are fading. Last year, international market analyst Euromonitor placed the U. S. men's toiletries market—hair color, skin moisturizer, tooth whiteners, etc.—at $3.5 billion. According to a survey conducted by DYG researchers for *Men's Health* in November 1996, approximately 20 percent of American men get manicures or pedicures, 18 percent use skin treatments such as masks or mud packs, and 10 percent enjoy professional facials. That same month, *Psychology Today* reported that a poll by Roper Starch Worldwide showed that "6 percent of men nationwide actually use such traditionally female products as bronzers and foundation to create the illusion of a youthful appearance."

What men are putting on their bodies, however, is nothing compared to what they're doing *to* their bodies: While in the 1980s only an estimated one in 10 plastic surgery patients were men, as of 1996, that ratio had shrunk to one in five. The American Academy of Cosmetic Surgery estimates that nationwide more than 690,000 men had cosmetic procedures performed in '96, the most recent year for which figures are available. And we're not just talking

"hair restoration" here, though such procedures do command the lion's share of the male market. We're also seeing an increasing number of men shelling out mucho dinero for face peels, liposuction, collagen injections, eyelid lifts, chin tucks, and, of course, the real man's answer to breast implants: penile enlargements (now available to increase both length and diameter).

Granted, *Men's Health* and its journalistic cousins (*Men's Journal, Details, GQ,* etc.) cannot take all the credit for this breakthrough in gender parity. The fashion and glamour industries have perfected the art of creating consumer "needs," and with the women's market pretty much saturated, men have become the obvious target for the purveyors of everything from lip balm to lycra. Meanwhile, advances in medical science have made cosmetic surgery a quicker, cleaner option for busy executives (just as the tight fiscal leash of managed care is driving more and more doctors toward this cash-based specialty). Don't have several weeks to recover from a full-blown facelift? No problem. For a few hundred bucks you can get a microdermabrasion face peel on your lunch hour.

Then there are the underlying social factors. With women growing ever more financially independent, aspiring suitors are discovering that they must bring more to the table than a well-endowed wallet if they expect to win (and keep) the fair maiden. Nor should we overlook the increased market power of the gay population—in general a more image-conscious lot than straight guys. But perhaps most significant is the ongoing, ungraceful descent into middle age by legions of narcissistic baby boomers. Gone are the days when the elder statesmen of this demographic bulge could see themselves in the relatively youthful faces of those insipid yuppies on "Thirtysomething." Increasingly, boomers are finding they have more in common with the *parents* of today's TV, movie, and sports stars. Everywhere they turn some upstart Gen Xer is flaunting his youthful vitality, threatening boomer dominance on both the social and professional fronts. (Don't think even Hollywood didn't shudder when the Oscar for best original screenplay this year went to a couple of guys barely old enough to shave.) With whippersnappers looking to steal everything from their jobs to their women, post-pubescent men have at long last discovered the terror of losing their springtime radiance.

Whatever combo of factors is feeding the frenzy of male vanity, magazines such as *Men's Health* provide the ideal meeting place for men's insecurities and marketers' greed. Like its more established female counterparts, *Men's Health* is an affordable, efficient delivery vehicle for the message that physical imperfection, age, and an underdeveloped fashion sense are potentially crippling disabilities. And as with women's mags, this cycle of insanity is self-perpetuating: The more men obsess about growing old or unattractive, the more marketers will exploit and expand that fear; the more marketers bombard men with messages about the need to be beautiful, the more they will obsess. Younger and younger men will be sucked into the vortex of self-doubt. Since 1990, *Men's Health* has seen its paid circulation rise from 250,000 to more than 1.5 million; the magazine estimates that half of its 5.3 million readers are under age 35 and 46 percent are married. And while most major magazines have suffered sluggish growth or even a decline in circulation in recent years, during the first half of 1997 *Men's Health* saw its paid circulation increase 14 percent over its '96 figures. (Likewise, its smaller, more outdoorsy relative, Wenner Media's *Men's Journal*, enjoyed an even bigger jump of 26.5 percent.) At this rate, one day soon, that farcical TV commercial featuring men hanging out in bars, whining about having inherited their mothers' thighs will be a reality. Now *that's* progress.

VANITY, THY NAME IS MAN

Everyone wants to be considered attractive and desirable. And most of us are aware that, no matter how guilty and shallow we feel about it, there are certain broad cultural norms that define attractive. Not surprisingly, both men's and women's magazines have argued that, far from playing on human insecurities, they are merely helping readers be all that they can be — a kind of training camp for the image impaired. In recent years, such publications have embraced the tenets of "evolutionary biology," which argue that, no matter how often we're told that beauty is only skin deep, men and women are hardwired to prefer the Jack Kennedys and Sharon Stones to the Rodney Dangerfields and Janet Renos. Continuation of the species demands that specimens with shiny coats, bright eyes, even features, and other visible signs of ruddy good health and fertility automatically kick-start our most basic instinct. Of course, the glamour mags' editors have yet to explain why, in evolutionary terms, we would ever desire adult women to stand 5'10" and weigh 100 pounds. Stories abound of women starving themselves to the point that their bodies shut down and they stop menstruating — hardly conducive to reproduction — yet Kate Moss remains the dish du jour and millions of Moss wannabes still struggle to subsist on a diet of Dexatrim and Perrier.

Similarly, despite its title, *Men's Health* is hawking far more than general fitness or a healthful lifestyle. For every half page of advice on how to cut your stress level, there are a dozen pages on how to build your biceps. For every update on the dangers of cholesterol, there are multiple warnings on the horrors of flabby abs. Now, without question, gorging on Cheetos and Budweiser while your rump takes root on the sofa is no way to treat your body if you plan on living past 50. But chugging protein drinks, agonizing over fat grams, and counting the minutes until your next Stairmaster session is equally unbalanced. The line between taking pride in one's physical appearance and being obsessed by it is a fine one — and one that disappeared for many women long ago.

Now with the lads' mags taking men in that direction as well, in many cases it's almost impossible to tell whether you're reading a copy of *Men's Health* or of *Mademoiselle*: "April 8. To commemorate Buddha's birthday, hit a Japanese restaurant. Stick to low-fat selections. Choose foods described as *yakimono* which means grilled," advised the monthly "to do list" in the April *Men's Health*. (Why readers should go Japanese in honor of the most famous religious leader in *India's* history remains unclear.) The

January/February list was equally thought provoking: "January 28. It's Chinese New Year, so make a resolution to custom-order your next takeout. Ask that they substitute wonton soup broth for oil. Try the soba noodles instead of plain noodles. They're richer in nutrients and contain much less fat." The issue also featured a "Total Body Workout Poster" and one of those handy little "substitution" charts (loathed by women everywhere), showing men how to slash their calorie intake by making a few minor dietary substitutions: mustard for mayo, popcorn for peanuts, seltzer water for soda, pretzels for potato chips....

As in women's magazines, fast results with minimum inconvenience is a central theme. Among *Men's Health's* March highlights were a guide to "Bigger Biceps in 2 Weeks," and "20 Fast Fixes" for a bad diet; April offered "A Better Body in Half the Time," along with a colorful four-page spread on "50 Snacks That Won't Make You Fat." And you can forget carrot sticks—this think-thin eating guide celebrated the wonders of Reduced Fat Cheez-its, Munch 'Ems, Fiddle Faddle, Oreos, Teddy Grahams, Milky Ways, Bugles, Starburst Fruit Twists, and Klondike's Fat Free Big Bear Ice Cream Sandwiches. Better nutrition is not the primary issue. A better butt is. To this end, also found in the pages of *Men's Health* is the occasional, tasteful ad for liposuction—just in case nature doesn't cooperate.

But a blueprint to rock-hard buns is only part of what makes *Men's Health* the preeminent "men's lifestyle" magazine. Nice teeth, nice skin, nice hair, and a red-hot wardrobe are now required to round out the ultimate alpha male package, and *Men's Health* is there to help on all fronts. In recent months it has run articles on how to select, among other items, the perfect necktie and belt, the hippest wallet, the chicest running gear, the best "hair-thickening" shampoo, and the cutest golfing apparel. It has also offered advice on how to retard baldness, how to keep your footwear looking sharp, how to achieve different "looks" with a patterned blazer, even how to keep your lips from chapping at the dentist's office: "[B]efore you start all that 'rinse and spit' business, apply some moisturizer to your face and some lip balm to your lips. Your face and lips won't have that stretched-out dry feeling...Plus, you'll look positively radiant!"

While a desire to look good for their hygienists may be enough to spur some men to heed the magazine's advice (and keep 'em coming back for more), fear and insecurity about the alternatives are generally more effective motivators. For those who don't get with the *Men's Health* program, there must be the threat of ridicule. By far the least subtle example of this is the free subscriptions for "guys who need our help" periodically announced in the front section of the magazine. April's dubious honoree was actor Christopher Walken:

> Chris, we love the way you've perfected that psycho persona. But now you're taking your role in "Things to do in Denver When You're Dead" way too seriously with that ghostly pale face, the "where's the funeral?" black clothes, and a haircut that looks like the work of a hasty undertaker....Dab on a little Murad Murasun Self-Tanner ($21)...For those creases in your face, try Ortho Dermatologicals' Renova, a prescription antiwrinkle cream that contains tretinoin, a form of vitamin A. Then, find a barber.

Or how about the March "winner," basketball coach Bobby Knight: "Bob, your trademark red sweater is just a billboard for your potbelly. A darker solid color would make you look slimmer. Also, see 'The Tale of Two Bellies' in our February 1998 issue, and try to drop a few pounds. Then the next time you throw a sideline tantrum, at least people won't say, 'look at the crazy *fat* man.'"

Just as intense as the obsession with appearance that men's (and women's) magazines breed are the sexual neuroses they feed. And if one of the ostensible goals of women's mags is to help women drive men wild, what is the obvious corollary objective for men's magazines? To get guys laid—well and often. As if men needed any encouragement to fixate on the subject, *Men's Health* is chock full of helpful "how-tos" such as, "Have Great Sex Every Day Until You Die" and "What I Learned From My Sex Coach," as well as more cursory explorations of why men with larger testicles have more sex ("Why Big Boys Don't Cry), how to maintain orgasm intensity as you age ("Be one of the geysers"), and how to achieve stronger erections by eating certain foods ("Bean counters make better lovers"). And for those having trouble even getting to the starting line, last month's issue offered readers a chance to "Win free love lessons."

THE HIGH PRICE OF PERFECTION

Having elevated men's physical and sexual insecurities to the level of grand paranoia, lads' mags can then get down to what really matters: moving merchandise. On the cover of *Men's Health* each month, in small type just above the magazine's title, appears the phrase "Tons of useful stuff." Thumbing through an issue or two, however, one quickly realizes that a more accurate description would read: "Tons of expensive stuff." They're all there: Ralph Lauren, Tommy Hilfiger, Paul Mitchell, Calvin Klein, Clinique, Armani, Versace, Burberrys, Nautica, Nike, Omega, Rogaine, The Better Sex Video Series....The magazine even has those annoying little perfume strips guaranteed to make your nose run and to alienate everyone within a five-mile radius of you.

Masters of psychology, marketers wheel out their sexiest pitches and hottest male models to tempt/intimidate the readership of *Men's Health*. Not since the last casting call for "Baywatch" has a more impressive display of firm, tanned, young flesh appeared in one spot. And just like in women's magazines, the articles themselves are designed to sell stuff. All those helpful tips on choosing blazers, ties, and belts come complete with info on the who, where, and how much. The strategy is brilliant: Make men understand exactly how far short of the ideal they fall, and they too become vulnerable to the lure of high-priced underwear, cologne, running shoes, workout gear, hair dye, hair strengthener, skin softener, body-fat monitors, suits, boots, energy bars, and sex aids. As Mark Jannot, the grooming and health editor for *Men's Journal*, told "Today" show host Matt Lauer in January, "This is a huge, booming market. I mean, the marketers have found a group of people that are ripe for the picking. Men are finally learning that aging is a disease." Considering how effectively *Men's Health* fosters this belief, it's hardly surprising that the magazine has seen its ad pages grow 510 percent since 1991 and has made it onto *Ad-week*'s 10 Hottest Magazines list three of the last five years.

To make all this "girly" image obsession palatable to their audience, lads' mags employ all their creative energies to transform appearance issues into "a guy thing." *Men's Health* tries to cultivate a joking, macho tone throughout ("Eat Like Brando and Look Like Rambo" or "Is my tallywhacker shrinking?") and tosses in a handful of Y-chromosome teasers such as "How to Stay Out of Jail," "How to Clean Your Whole Apartment in One Hour or Less," and my personal favorite, "Let's Play Squash," an illustrated guide to identifying the bug-splat patterns on your windshield. Instead of a regular advice columnist, which would smack too much of chicks' magazines, *Men's Health* recently introduced "Jimmy the Bartender," a monthly column on "women, sex, and other stuff that screws up men's lives."

It appears that, no matter how much clarifying lotion and hair gel you're trying to sell them, men must never suspect that you think they share women's insecurities. If you want a man to buy wrinkle cream, marketers have learned, you better pitch it as part of a comfortingly macho shaving regimen. Aramis, for example, assures men that its popular Lift Off! Moisture Formula with alpha hydroxy will help cut their shave time by one-third. "The biggest challenge for products started for women is how to transfer them to men," explained George Schaeffer, the president of OPI cosmetics, in the November issue of *Soap-Cosmetics-Chemical Specialties*. Schaeffer's Los Angeles-based company is the maker of Matte Nail Envy, an unobtrusive nail polish that's proved a hit with men. And for the more adventuresome shopper, last year Hard Candy cosmetics introduced a line of men's nail enamel, called Candy Man, that targets guys with such studly colors as Gigolo (metallic black) and Testosterone (gunmetal silver).

On a larger scale, positioning a makeover or trip to the liposuction clinic as a smart career move seems to help men rationalize their image obsession. "Whatever a man's cosmetic short-coming, it's apt to be a career liability," noted Alan Farnham in a September 1996 issue of *Fortune*. "The business world is prejudiced against the ugly." Or how about *Forbes'* sad attempt to differentiate between male and female vanity in its Dec. 1 piece on cosmetic surgery: "Plastic surgery is more of a cosmetic thing for women. They have a thing about aging. For men it's an investment that pays a pretty good dividend." Whatever you say, guys.

The irony is rich and bittersweet. Gender equity is at last headed our way—not in the form of women being less obsessed with looking like Calvin Klein models, but of men becoming hysterical over the first signs of crows feet. Gradually, guys are no longer pumping up and primping simply to get babes, but because they feel it's something everyone expects them to do. Women, after all, do not spend $400 on Dolce & Gabbana sandals to impress their boyfriends, most of whom don't know Dolce & Gabbana from Beavis & Butthead (yet). They buy them to impress other women—and because that's what society says they should want to do. Most guys

haven't yet achieved this level of insanity, but with grown men catcalling the skin tone and wardrobe of other grown men (Christopher Alien, Bobby Knight) for a readership of still more grown men, can the gender's complete surrender to the vanity industry be far behind?

The ad for *Men's Health's* web site says it all: "Don't click here unless you want to look a decade younger…lose that beer belly…be a better lover…and more! Men's Health Online: The Internet Site For Regular Guys." Of course, between the magazine's covers there's not a "regular guy" to be found, save for writers or editors—usually taken from a respectable distance. The moist young bucks in the Gap jeans ads and the electric-eyed Armani models have exactly as much in common with the average American man as Tyra Banks does with the average American woman. Which would be fine, if everyone seemed to understand this distinction. Until they do, however, I guess my consolation will have to be the image of thousands of once-proud men, having long scorned women's insecurities, lining up for their laser peels and trying to squeeze their middle-aged asses into a snug set of Super Shaper Briefs—with the optional fly front endowment pad, naturally.

DISCUSSION QUESTIONS

Turning Boys Into Girls

1. As women grow more financially independent, what effect do you feel this has on how men perceive their own appearance?

2. What are some present-day social factors that might make men more insecure about their appearance than in the past?

86   Rebel, Rebel

Elizabeth Wilson

There can surely be nothing more to say about denim. Blue jeans must be the biggest sartorial cliché of all time. But no—rather bravely in the circumstances—the Brighton Museum and Art Gallery, known for its innovative displays, has mounted an exhibition about the ubiquitous blue cloth, which explores the history of the fabric and its metamorphosis from workwear to high fashion.

In itself there is nothing especially unusual about this trajectory. There is a widespread belief that fashion "trickles down" from the rich, who are always fashion innovators, to the middle classes and ultimately everyone. This belief is based on the oversimplified ideas of Thorstein Veblen, who saw fashion—and culture itself—primarily in terms of emulation and the display of wealth.

In reality things are more complicated. There are plenty of examples of the reverse process; it has historically been quite common for both sports and workwear to be taken up and turned into fashion. In the revolutionary atmosphere of the 1790s, for example, working men's coats were transformed into dandified chic. In cases such as these an article or articles of clothing are chosen to represent a new idea. Indeed, Veblen's belief that dress was about *display* harked back to an outdated, pre-industrial world in which that was much more the case; in the industrial societies of the past 200 years the much wider availability of fashionable clothes has enabled dress to be used to create a whole range of meanings, including a critique of display and "conspicuous consumption".

The fact that the transformation of working people's clothes into high fashion has occurred in the past does not, however, explain why denim in particular should have crossed the line between utility and glamour at some time between the 1930s and 1950s. Clearly the heavy cotton has a number of built-in practical advantages. It is above all versatile: as well as being hard-wearing, it is cool enough to wear in hot weather, yet warm in winter; it can be preshrunk, and does not crease. It is a material worn by men, women—and children.

Yet it does not seem as if even this is quite enough to explain its unique place in the fashions of the past 35 years. However, the current exhibition[1] usefully traces the process whereby denim moved out of the American West and into first youth and then mainstream fashion. Interestingly enough, American *Vogue* appears to have done something to promote the fashion potential of denim jeans and "overalls" (dungarees to us) in the thirties; in 1935 *Vogue* was advising readers that:

"True western chic was invented by the cowboys...your uniform for a dude ranch is simple-but-severe blue jeans or Levis, turned up at the bottom once, laundered before wearing (to eliminate stiffness), cut straight and tight fitting, worn low on the hips, in the manner of your favourite dude wrangler. With these jeans go a simply tailored flannel or plaid cotton shirt, or possibly a Brooks sweater; a plain silk kerchief knotted loosely; a studded leather belt; high-heeled western hoots; a Stetson hat; and a great free air of bravado."

Here the jeans appear to have been envisaged as part of a more or less "western" dress, treating western style as almost a form of folk costume. As such, its qualities of regionalism and timelessness are to the fore; the outfit signifies sportiness in a general way, and also "Americanness", but in addition there is a suggestion of the glamorisation of casual wear; clothes originally intended for riding the range (and worn principally by men) are now being adapted for passive spectatorship, and function has ceded to a semiotic code which creates a myth of "far western-

Wilson, Elizabeth, "Rebel, Rebel," *New Statesmen & Society*, June 15, 1990. Reprinted with permission.

ness". The "great free air of bravado" is nothing but hot air. The women for whom this appropriation of western chic was intended were living in the American suburbs and were not about to go riding the range.

Denim jeans did not become a common component of fashion until taken up by the youth music cults of the 1950s. After the second world war jeans in fact became—to outraged Europeans at least—a symbol and indicator of the cultural imperialism of the United States: blue jeans and Coca Cola were subverting the youth of France, Italy, Britain. Worn by Elvis Presley, by James Dean in *Rebel Without A Cause* (precisely) and by Marlon Brando in *The Wild One*, jeans signified youth in revolt, signalled nihilism, outrage and aggression. In *The Feminine Mystique*, Betty Friedan identified the formless disquiet of women in the wealthy suburbs of America as "the problem that has no name"—the rebellion against anomie, materialism, the regulation of mass society—and these women used jeans to symbolise this.

Jeans were still essentially casual wear, but their message was about counter cultures, not about sport. Or perhaps it would be more accurate to say that jeans were now commercially marketed as casual wear for the young, when to the young themselves they signified not so much the casual or sporty as the angry, and as a form of distancing from the parent culture.

The mass production fashion industry has consistently tried to cash in on the popularity of jeans, yet has in terms of strict chic never got it quite right. Jeans designed for women were introduced as early as the 1940s—yet to look really smart a woman has to wear men's jeans. There were commercial attempts to copy early 1970s hippy bricolage: patches, embroidery and so on, but it always had an ersatz look. "Designer jeans" were introduced in the late 1970s—but they could never achieve the genuine look of "real" Levis. Techniques have been developed whereby denim can be "distressed", "stone washed" or just bleached in order to give the right appearance of ageing; but none of these can compete with use and wear, so in recent years the most "correct" jeans were imported second-hand ones, costing far more than Taiwanese copies, while the mid-eighties vogue for original Levi 501s with buttons instead of a zip became almost a postmodern pastiche cult.

Denim achieved its greatest hour in the late 1960s and early 1970s. Garments from this period on display at Brighton are quite extraordinarily evocative to those who remember that defunct period. It was not just that jeans became, even more than in the 1950s, a symbol of revolt for the 1968 student generation. Combined with various hippy, ethnic modes denim became less a material than a way of life, less garments than the essential precondition of all other forms of dress. Suddenly a universal cottage industry sprang up; every hip woman under 30 was embroidering her jeans, cutting them up to turn them into a skirt, adding beads and a hand-crocheted tank top.

I remember how disgusted and amused we were when one member of my women's group told us of her visit to the Tavistock Institute. The psychoanalyst who interviewed her took exception to her jeans, the flies of which were embroidered with flowers, and accused her or [sic] thus instigating a deliberate attempt at his seduction. We thought this was hilarious—didn't the silly old gaffer know that embroidery was simply a beautiful form of women's art, and who would want to seduce him anyway.

There are some amazing examples of this art form in the exhibition; notably a midi-skirt hand-embroidered with the names of pop groups of the period (including Cat Stevens—oh dear). This was the moment at which a universal uniform could *simultaneously* express the highest level of individualism. Thus at a transcendent moment, denim could distil the paradox of all fashion: that it must express both conformity and difference at one and the same moment.

Although punk began as a reaction against the droopiness and flares of the hippie counterculture, it too created an alternative form of dress that depended in part on individual creativity, superimposed upon mass manufactured items of clothing—often, indeed the same ones, as jeans could still be worn, although in a very different way. We can in retrospect see the similarities between these two countercultures, and how one grew out of the other, although they appeared so totally different at the time.

More recent attempts by avant garde designers such as Jean Paul Gaultier and Katharine Hamnett to elevate denim to classic status are also featured in the exhibition. There is even one garment that combines denim with classic worsted suiting. In 1988 Charlotte Du Cann claimed that the leather and jeans uniform of rebellion had completely lost all its radical potential, becoming yet another empty allusion (or illusion). For Gaultier it has become part of a minimalist uniform consisting of jeans, a white shirt and a jacket. This is to overstate the acceptability of jeans in the office; nevertheless it contains a grain of truth. Yet jeans can also incorporate the desire for change which fuels fashion; one year it can be 501s, another year black jeans, today white "new age" jeans (whitened, one hopes, without the use of ecologically harmful bleach). Perhaps in the end, jeans are the ultimate "empty signifier", the symbolic vessel into which any and every aspiration about one's identity can be poured, the ultimate conveyor of that greatest fashion paradox: how to be just the same as, yet entirely different from everyone else.

Note

1. "Denim: From Workwear to High Fashion," exhibit at the Museum and Art Gallery, Church St., Brighton, 1990.

DISCUSSION QUESTIONS

Rebel, Rebel

1. How is today's image of designer jeans different from the past image associated with people like Elvis Presley and James Dean? Why are jeans more popular than ever?

2. Why do people from other countries (for example Japan, China, Eastern Europe) love American jeans? Give five reasons.

CHAPTER 14

Future Trends

Mary Lynn Damhorst

AFTER YOU HAVE READ THIS CHAPTER, YOU WILL COMPREHEND:

- How forecasting the future of dress in society is a useful endeavor.

- Why it is necessary to make alternative rather than single forecasts for dress in the future.

- Multiple factors influencing future trends.

What will you be wearing in the year 2020? Will your attire resemble a space suit, with high-tech, shiny fabrics inspired by clothing adapted and invented for colonists on the moon or Mars? Will we need to wear actual space suits to protect ourselves from elevated levels of pollution here on Earth? Will our garments and accessories have communication systems and voice command computers engineered into the materials? Or will the hottest fashions be similar to what we wear today as a result of a nostalgic revival of 1990s styles? Chances are, clothing in 2020 will not be radically different from what we wear today, except for new silhouettes and fashion details reflecting the times and fiber innovations reflecting technological trends. But who knows?

We cannot know exactly what people will be wearing next season or three years from today. But we can look at today's trends and other data that give probable indication of what societal conditions will be 20 years from now. Those projections are a type of **futuring** that can help us imagine what life and dress will be like in the future. To do a respectable job of futuring we must always keep in mind, however, that we are dealing with probabilities. Forecasts about the future must be tentative, and multiple probabilities or possibilities must be examined. For example, in the 1982 book *Fashion 2001* by Lucille Khornak, forward-thinking designers proposed what they thought would be in fashion about 20 to 25 years into the future. None of the designers was completely correct, knowing what we know today. But across their imaginative forecasts, a number of designers' ideas were quite right. Their forecasts in sum, rather than one individual prediction, helped us look into the future.

Futuring is not about making specific and detailed predictions. Instead, we will look at a few present-day trends and consider several directions in which those trends might go in the future. We are making **forecasts** rather than **predictions**; forecasts are estimations of probable occurrences based on present and past information. We will have to be diligent about not thinking too linearly, however. Only a very few trends are linear, with continuing increases or decreases over time. Most trends happen in cycles, spurts, and curvilinear waves. Sometimes exponential increases occur, blowing the trend way out of existing proportions.

Thinking about the future helps individuals and organizations, such as retailers and apparel producers, plan for what might happen. Such planning can help in choosing career directions, selecting educational experiences, making investments, planning business strategies, and shaping government policy. Thinking about the future is also a lot of fun and a great mental workout, requiring the juggling of multiple ideas and data at one time while allowing for creative leaps of imagination. And thinking about future possibilities can make things happen. If we examine possibilities and consider any of them desirable, we might be more apt to make them happen.

Future forecasting could go on endlessly; therefore, for this chapter, we will establish some parameters for choosing what to consider. We base our forecasts on the assumption, which is possibly flawed, that during the next 20 years the world as a whole will not experience any catastrophic changes that destroy much of life on earth or radically alter human existence as we know it today. For example, we will *not* consider what might happen if worldwide nuclear devastation occurs, if global warming becomes so severe that only the arctic regions are inhabitable, if a worldwide economic collapse occurs rendering all monetary systems useless, if a giant comet strikes the earth, or if beings from outer space take over the Earth and make us all slaves. Some of these situations might be interesting to ponder, but we will not entertain these possibilities here just for the sake of limiting our projections.

Instead, we will look at technological, population, and social trends that are already starting to happen and that most probably will affect our lives during the next 20 years. Four trends we examine include:

1. the increasing proportion of ethnic minorities in the U. S. population;

2. increasing proportions of older people in many nations throughout the world;

3. technological innovations that might influence how we dress and how we manage our presentation of self, including the increasing potential of computerization and robotization to customize sizing and styling of garments for each individual, and expanded modes of shopping via mail, TV, and Internet to vastly expand accessibility of diverse and customized designs; and

4. growing concerns about the environment that may lead to increased caution about our use of technology and the toll that our consumption of products—including apparel—has on the environment.

We will discover that all of these trends are, to some extent, interconnected. No cultural trend occurs in isolation. In addition, we will try to consider a few alternative projections for the future. Although data may indicate strong possibility for a future trend, we can never know what might occur to radically alter what seems most plausible now. Probable trends may pan out in ways we never could have suspected. So thinking about the future requires consideration of alternative possibilities to help us remember that we can only make projections; we cannot look into a crystal ball and predict exactly what will happen. Nevertheless, thinking about the future helps individuals, businesses, government, and organizations ready themselves to plan flexibly for changes to come.

TRENDS IN ETHNICITY AND CULTURAL IMAGES OF ATTRACTIVENESS

By the year 2020, substantial increases in proportions of ethnic minority groups in the United States are very likely. There may be some geographical regions of the United States in which little ethnic diversity occurs, perhaps because of historical patterns of migration to an area or resulting from racism or exclusionary social and political practices in the local area. However, to remain a viable and livable part of society, any community in the United States must at least do business with the rest of the country and the world. Individuals or communities who cannot operate within conditions of pluralism will not be effective or successful in the increasingly multicultural society that is and very likely will continue to be the United States of America. Career options will be limited for individuals who cannot interact successfully with diversity. That is one forecast we can make with a great amount of certainty.

The year 2000 census will update the population projections listed in Table 14.1. For the first time in that upcoming census, individuals will be able to claim multiple categories to reflect mixed race and ethnicity. Minority representation in the United States is probably undercounted in the figures listed in Table 14.1, in part as a result of prior census data-collection methods that did not allow indication of mixed heritage. But even the 1990 figures paint a picture of increasing ethnic and racial diversity in the United States. According to estimations based on 1990 census data, the proportion of European Americans in the United States will be approximately 50 percent by the year 2050. As a result, the United States is rapidly moving to a situation in which there is no

TABLE 14.1

Census Projections: Ethnic Representation in U.S. Population

	1990	2010	2050
European American	75.7	67.7	50.3–56.5
African American	11.8	12.6	13.6–13.7
Hispanic American	9.0	13.5	20.2–24.6
Asian American	2.8	5.4	8.7–10.6
Native American	0.7	0.8	0.8–1.0

SOURCE: U. S. BUREAU OF THE CENSUS, 1993

ethnic majority group. What consequences will increases in diversity have on how people dress and how people think about their bodies?

In a society with pervasive diversity of skin colors, body shapes, and facial features, ideals of attractiveness are apt to change. Let's imagine three scenarios or possibilities of what could happen: 1) true equality, 2) white supremacist takeover, and 3) white backlash.

True Equality

This first scenario is probably too optimistic. If ethnic minority groups increase proportionately in the U. S. population and also increase levels of educational and occupational achievement, by 2020 the United States might see greater levels of pluralism and decreasing focus on white or European American hegemony. With diversity characterizing men and women in powerful and successful positions in society, standards of attractiveness should also tend to diversify. A wider variety of facial features and skin colors would be seen in models and glamorous celebrities. People from diverse ethnicities will have greater impact on fashion trends. Will greater variety in heights and weights also be seen as attractive in men and women? Twenty years is a short time to escape the shackles of thinness standards. But appreciation of greater variety in body shapes may begin to become evident as diversity in racial characteristics is appreciated.

White Supremacist Takeover

An opposite scenario foresees a rising tide of ethnic protectionism among the shrinking white, European American majority over the next 20 years. Threatened by Affirmative Action policies, increasing numbers of minorities into positions of power and achievement, and government policies favoring diversity in schools and other public institutions, wealthy groups of white European Americans seeking to hold on to privilege and opportunities afforded in the prior hegemonic situation may band together to influence business leaders, politicians, religious leaders, and media moguls to support new policies and practices that tend to exclude minority groups from the upper echelons of society. Claiming that acceptance of diversity has weakened the nation and reduced its productivity and leadership on the world scene, these white supremacists would increase their support base among whites who feel lost and fearful in a nation of increasing diversity. Supremacist media "plots" would unfold to emphasize and idolize whiteness, diminish inclusion of nonwhite appearances in the media, and seek passage of laws and public policy that do not favor or accommodate ethnic minority groups in any way. A portion of the mainstream fashion industry, owned by white supremacist leaders or threatened by boycotts from supremacist consumers, might move to ignore needs of ethnic minority consumers and inclusion of diversity in advertising. This scenario seems counter to today's trends emphasizing ethnic marketing (see "Black, Hip, and Primed to Shop" in Chapter 10 and "Styles with a Sizable Difference" in Chapter 11) and minority group influences on fashion (see "Marketing Street Culture" in Chapter 11). Under future conditions of a weak economy and high crime rates, however, fringe elements in society can grow in influence if their message helps to allay fears of a segment of the population that feels its quality of life is diminishing. Minority protest and violence would erupt throughout the nation as a response to escalating exclusion, further convincing the supremacists that minority groups must be controlled and segregated from whites and positions of power.

White Backlash

A third possibility could be that increasing diversity in the population could move toward emphasis on ethnic minorities as attractive and anything white or European American as unattractive, unfashionable, and unappealing. Diversity could become popular and acceptable only if it is NOT WHITE. Such a backlash against European heritage could send youthful whites into a frenzy to acquire darker skin tones via excessive sun tanning or staining lotions. Those who can afford it would seek physicians who dispense drugs that darken skin color all over the body. Entertainers and sports stars with ethnic minority heritage would lead fashion trends. Fashion magazines would include few white, European-looking models. Those who looked European would be considered "uncool," poor, or elderly.

We can see that each of these scenarios leads to a different projection of trends in dress and attractiveness standards. What will emerge remains to be seen.

INFLUENCE OF AGING POPULATION ON CONCEPTS OF BEAUTY

In Chapter 9, we projected that about 16 percent of the population would be 65 years and older in 2020. A historically unprecedented number of individuals will move into that age group after 2020 in the United States, Canada, Japan, and many countries in Europe. How will these countries deal with so many older individuals? Three following possibilities are proposed.

The Fashionable, Aged Baby Boomer

With relatively so many individuals in their elder years, the fashion and cosmetics industries may pay substantial attention to aging consumers. Perhaps attractive images of older men and women will appear in apparel and cosmetics ads. Designer and brand name clothing, specially designed for the changing aging body, may become common. "Gray Power" could become increasingly important to politicians, businesses, and cultural institutions. It might even become chic to be 60-something or 70-something. Aging might be seen as "graceful" and beautiful in its own way, a time to retire and explore activities one has always wanted to pursue. Perhaps some fashion trends would start with innovative baby boomer consumers and be picked up by young adult fashion opinion leaders inspired by the plucky, independent oldsters.

Old Is Out

In contrast, deep and long-lasting economic recession could wipe out retirement savings and push a substantial proportion of elderly below the poverty level. The great numbers of impoverished elderly would be seen as a burden on society rather than attractive as a market segment. The fashion industry would probably ignore this lifespan group to a great extent, leaving them out of advertising, product development focus, and marketing efforts in general.

Instead, the fashion industry would continue to focus on youthful markets. By 2020 technological developments might make cosmetic surgery less expensive and less painful, giving more individuals incentive to sculpt their bodies to desired youthful shapes and condition. Exercise equipment and trainers, in combination with drug therapies, would make muscle toning and development easier. Fashionable sleek bodies would be clothed in spray-on materials or synthetic skins to show off every muscle and curve (Richards, 1997).

The elderly who could afford it would procure all techniques available to look as youthful as possible. But the elevated levels of poverty and low incomes among the old will leave many out of the quest for a youthful-looking body. Body dissatisfaction among the elderly in general would soar. Problems such as anorexia, bulimia, and drug misuse related to appearance management would increase among older consumers.

Diversity Among Older Segments

What is quite probable by 2020 is a blend of the prior two scenarios. Some middle aged and older consumers might embrace the new technologies of beauty and chase relentlessly after a medically chiseled, youthful, trim body. Other baby boomers, a generation questioning the status quo to the end, might reject artificial means of looking young and insist on aging naturally. They would wear their wrinkles and gray hair as badges of honor. These radical elders might begin to forge new meanings of aging for generations to follow.

TECHNOLOGY AND THE CONSUMER

Advances in cosmetic surgery technology and innovations in age-retarding and youth-enhancing drugs will develop over the next several decades. People around the world will continue to negotiate the meanings and acceptability of these procedures and products for modifying the body. Each cultural group may derive different or particular meanings for these technological advancements. Technology will also change the way we shop and introduce product changes that may have profound impact on how and what we acquire as dress and how we feel about our bodies.

Customization and Multiple Modes of Access

Computerized systems are currently under development to make virtual images that capture actual measurements, proportions, movements, and appearance of the real human body. These three-dimensional images can already be combined with images of apparel to help designers adjust style design for size variations, help consumers electronically "try on" clothing to see how it looks on them before ordering an actual garment, and eventually will allow consumers to order a custom-made garment that perfectly fits their actual bodies and their personal tastes (Gray, 1998). Computers could someday translate computerized body measurements into pattern adjustment commands that will guide robotized production systems to cut and sew a garment to fit an individual person precisely. In addition, the robotized system could allow the customer to select fabric, color, and style details such as sleeve length, pant leg fullness, and pocket style from an array of options offered through the system. Not only would fit be customized, but the consumer would take part in designing the style of garments she or he wants. Apparel industry experts often refer to custom-fit garments ordered through a mass retailer or producer as **made-to-measure** (Gellers, 1998). Garments ordered through a mass retailer or producer for which the consumer has made personal style design choices are termed **mass customized** (Pine, 1993).

Much of this ordering of mass customized and made-to-measure apparel could be done at home through the Internet via on-line catalogs, mall kiosks, or through retail stores. The customer might have a file containing a computerized image of his or her body, an image that could easily be updated for a small fee at a local mall shop with imaging equipment. Or we might eventually be able to stand in front of our personal computers with built-in camera connections that would record our current body dimensions. Bandwidth of phone or cable line connections between home and Internet would have to be ample to provide enough speed and capacity to effectively use three-dimensional images on home computers, but equipment advances and access to pipelines with increased image speed and clarity are already on their way in many communities throughout the United States (Lehr, 1998; Rose, 1998). Made-to-measure and mass customized apparel is available today, but advances in computerized imaging and production systems probably will make customized apparel more readily accessible and less expensive sometime during the next 20 years.

Certainly, there are many consumers who will never attempt to buy anything through the Internet, much less order a garment customized to their body size and their style preferences via computer. Today, only a minority of consumers purchase garments frequently via mail while approximately 45 percent of a recent national sample have at some time purchased apparel by mail (Yoh, 1999). Only a tiny minority (about nine percent) purchase apparel through the Internet (Yoh, 1999). Few consumers have garments custom-made on a regular basis, and computerized robotic systems for customizing fit and style are not yet fully operable. So why should we consider that these modes of shopping will play any substantial role in how consumers shop within the next 20 years?

First of all, population segments who are more inclined to purchase by mail are increasing in numbers. Aging individuals are more apt to experience health conditions that make shopping in stores very time-consuming and physically inconvenient. The majority of individuals in their 60s and 70s in the year 2020 will have had experience using computers, because of present and upcoming job demands. For most of these consumers and consumers of all younger ages, using the Internet will be a common experience. Also, more women will probably be working in jobs other than homemaking, leaving little time for women and their families to get out and shop. With the aging population and increasing diversity in ethnicities in the United States, garment-size needs are also becoming more diverse, but it will be extremely difficult for most store retailers to have in stock the wide array of clothing sizes necessary to fit their customers.

Apparel and footwear purchases via Internet catalogs is fairly limited so far, but growing. About $92 million was spent on apparel and footwear ordered via Internet in 1997. That amount is predicted to increase fourfold by the year 2000 (Green, DeGeorge, & Barrett, 1998). At present, most Internet catalogs tend to be simple electronic versions of printed mail-order catalogs. Interesting and creative innovations will be needed to lure more consumers onto the Internet. Some Internet stores allow the customer to dress a model with different items from the catalog to see how a combination of pieces will look together. ModaCAD is developing a virtual shopping mall that allows the customer to order from many New York City stores and compare garments across stores (Rose, 1998). Yoh (1999) has found that many consumers would be attracted to the Internet if there were indexing services that would find similar items (navy blazers, perhaps) across all shopping sites. They are also interested in being able to click in images of themselves as models to see how garments would look on their body size and shape. Easy search, comparison, and try-on features for some consumers might compensate for the wait to receive a garment by mail rather than through immediate, in-store experiences. The access to nationwide and even worldwide offerings in styles might increase diversity of style and size offerings on the market.

Would availability of made-to-measure infinite sizes help some consumers feel less discriminated against or left out because of non-normative body size or shape? And will an "underclass" of people who cannot afford made-to-measure apparel develop, marked as lower status by their imperfectly fitting clothing and off-the-rack wardrobes? Both positive ramifications for some individuals' body satisfaction and negative effects on others' self-esteem could be the result of made-to-measure advances.

Chances are that a variety of modes of shopping will continue on through the next 20 years. Made-to-measure apparel will require extensive development of computer systems and also new ways of shopping. For example, what happens if you purchase a custom-fit garment that was made specifically for you but you want to return it? What will the retailer do with your rejected, perhaps oddly sized garment? And how will the average consumer deal with the expanded array of choices if mass customized style choices become common? Will retailers need to provide style consultants who can help the choice-overloaded consumer make decisions about what style details to order in a customized garment?

Internet catalogs can take the consumer directly to the manufacturer or designer. Will some designers develop such close connections with consumers that they ask regular on-line customers to "vote" on new seasonal offerings? With such bypassing of traditional retail buyers as gatekeepers to style selection, will consumers gain more direct impact on style options available to them? Individual choice and innovativeness may be facilitated by direct and personal connections with designers. Style design could become highly individualized if customized ordering for made-to-measure apparel becomes more affordable. How will that influence fashion diffusion? Will fashion changes become even more rapid when designers are linked directly to consumers and can propose new style ideas any time of the year?

The eventual changes in the fashion system that could result from widespread use of electronic catalogs and made-to-measure and mass customized ordering are almost too immense to comprehend, but certainly intriguing. Increased variety and diversity in appearances and more uniqueness in what can be purchased could certainly emerge. Would more people develop independence and confidence in ordering styles they want rather than slaving to the latest fashion trends? Or would major segments of the population be confused and crave dictation of simple styles by mainstream fashion designers? Perhaps all these trends could occur simultaneously. The fashion system will probably become increasingly complex during the 21st century.

ENVIRONMENTAL CONCERNS

Advances in technological innovations could be accompanied by increased concern about what all this technology is doing to our lives and the environment. Consumers in the United States so far have limited knowledge of the environmental impacts of apparel textiles and show fairly low levels of interest in purchasing environmentally friendly garments (Kim & Damhorst, 1998). Wendi Winters in "Eco-Friendly Fashions Are 'Cool'" (Chapter 13) contends that the eco-fashion market is just beginning to take off. But is it?

Let's imagine what might happen if environmental concern became widespread and deeply ingrained in consumer thinking and behavior. Would consumers buy less and wear each garment longer to get more use from each item before discarding? Esprit Inc. once suggested this idea in an ad campaign (see Figure 14.1). A massive consumer movement in this direction would probably slow the pace of fashion change.

A Plea for Responsible Consumption

So often our needs are defined by things that don't get us much: the comfort of having lots of stuff, the image we want to portray, the social pressure to appear to be affluent, the bizarre idea of having something new for its own sake, like a new car or new TV or the latest fashion. For years, we have spoken to our customers about the difference between fashion and style. We've tried our best to encourage style and reinforce the concept that style isn't a fad. It comes from your imagination and is developed slowly. It's a reflection of your values.

Today, more than ever, the direction of an environmentally conscious style is not to have luxury or conspicuous consumption written all over your attire. This is still our message. We believe this could be best achieved by simply asking yourself before you buy something (from us or any other company) whether this is something you really need. It could be you'll buy more or less from us, *but only what you need*. We'll be happy to adjust our business up or down accordingly, because we'll feel we are then contributing to a healthier attitude about consumption. We know this is heresy in a growth economy, but frankly, if this kind of thinking doesn't catch on quickly, we, like a plague of locusts, will devour all that's left of the planet. We could make the decision to reduce our consumption, or the decision will soon be made *for* us.

We are optimistic that we can change course and avoid the disastrous destination toward which we're heading. We also believe that there are many events occurring throughout the world right now which support this outlook. We've experienced big changes in people's attitudes about some extremely important philosophical issues and values: racial, feminist, and economic systems such as what we're witnessing in Eastern Europe.

Our purchasing habits have enormous influence. By changing the things that make us happy and buying less stuff, we can reduce the horrendous impact we have been placing on the environment. We can buy for vital needs, not frivolous ego-gratifying needs. We do need clothes? yes, but *so many?*

While we're lobbying for responsible consumption, we want to suggest one more idea. What you save, if you do, through changing your purchasing habits, consider contributing to one of the thousands of social and environmental organizations that are working to correct, repair, preserve or halt the damage to which our consumptive ways and economic system have led us.

We all have to work together to preserve the continuity of natural cycles and processes. If we don't, we'll have no inheritance to bestow to our grandchildren. All will be gone. Our place in history will be that of the greatest mismanagers of the Earth, not such a loving way to be remembered!

FIGURE 14.1. *1990 Esprit ad.*

Addition of color to yarns and fabrics and bleaching before dyeing or to whiten introduces chemical waste into the environment (Kadolph & Langford, 1998). Emphasis on undyed organic cotton and naturally colored organic fibers could make much of fashion neutral and subdued in color. It also might become "unhip" to wear anything dyed—even hair. Or we might end up wearing mostly synthetic fibers—techno-fibers that perform better than natural fibers and that are made in tightly controlled factories that do not pollute with the overuse of chemicals or require spraying insecticides and pesticides on crops. Fibers such as hemp, that require no pesticides during growth, may also become more common in apparel (Kadolph & Langford, 1998). Companies such as Patagonia and Harmony have been featuring hemp in limited apparel offerings in their 1998 catalogs. Recycled fibers may become so politically correct that most consumers will take garments that are worn out or don't fit to recycling centers that send textiles off to be reengineered into fabrics for further use. Consignment and second-hand shops could become so common that nostalgic revivals of old styles would continue to be popular. Ordering apparel through the Internet also could decrease the paper waste incurred by use of mail-order catalogs.

Of course, the alternative also could very well occur—that few consumers ever connect apparel purchases with the environment or care much about the impact of fashion obsolescence on waste dumps. Rapid fashion change would continue, and perhaps at a pace even faster than today. The textile industry is concerned about government regulation of the industry, and the industry itself may make improvements in environmental consequences of production techniques, taking care of the problem for the vast majority of uninvolved and unconcerned consumers. Even without consumer and government action, however, much of the textile industry worldwide is apt to adopt environmentally friendly production practices.

ON TO THE FUTURE

We cannot be sure if any of the above trends will actually happen. As with any forecasting exercise, only time will tell. Nevertheless, pondering the future is a good exercise in using some of the theories and ideas we have encountered throughout this book. Two things are pretty much a certainty in the future, however: 1) Changes in society and people's lives are bound to occur, and 2) dress will reflect those changes in some way.

Summary

In this chapter we have examined brief scenarios built around four future trends: minority ethnicity in the United States, the aging population, customized and computer-purchased apparel, and environmental issues. Three alternative scenarios relate to projected increases in diversity in U. S. minority ethnic populations. We considered how attractiveness standards and appearances might be affected if alternative situations of true equality among ethnic groups, white supremacist dominance, and reverse discrimination against European Americans occur. Three scenarios examine what might happen to attractiveness standards and fashion trends as a result of increasing proportions of elderly individuals in many industrialized countries around the world. Possibilities include the older consumers having some influence on fashion trends, elderly becoming undesirable, and diversity of older consumer responses to aging. Internet shopping systems combined with made-to-measure and mass customization were considered for possible impacts on the fashion process and individuality and conformity in self-expression through dress. The last trend we considered is the environmental impact of apparel production and consumption. Consumer versus industry actions were pondered. The following learning activity encourages evaluation of the trends.

LEARNING ACTIVITY
Evaluating Trends

Objective: To help you think about and prepare for the future. Discuss the future scenarios presented and develop additional scenarios to evaluate how you and your classmates feel about future possibilities. Consider actions that might be taken to encourage or prevent the scenarios from happening.

Procedure

Divide into groups of three to seven people. Each group will be assigned one of the trend topics in this chapter. Discuss the scenarios and different possibilities presented for your group's trend. Are there positive and negative ramifications of each scenario or projection? Which scenarios and projections do you like the most? What seems most undesirable or dangerous to you? What needs to be done during the next 20 years to make positive things happen and to diminish negative possibilities? Who needs to take action?

Each group should also select another topic discussed somewhere else in this book and develop two or three alternative scenarios around that topic. Look back through the chapters and think about potential changes in age roles, work roles, religions, gender roles, sexuality, sports, social status divisions, globalization, and so forth. What might happen to dress and appearance in each of your scenarios? After developing the scenarios, consider the positive and negative outcomes of each, what needs to be done, and who needs to take action, as discussed for this chapter's scenarios.

References

Gellers, S. (1998, July 8). Made-to-measure: Raising the stakes for better clothing. *DNR*, pp. 9, 16.

Gray, S. (1998, February). In virtual fashion. *IEEE Spectrum*, pp. 18–25.

Green, H., DeGeorge, G., & Barrett, A. (1998, January 26). The virtual mall gets real. *Business Week*, pp. 90–91.

Kadolph, S. J., & Langford, A. L. (1998). *Textiles* (8th edition). Upper Saddle River, NJ: Merrill.

Kim, H-S., & Damhorst, M. L. (1998). Environmental attitude and commitment in relation to ad message credibility. *Clothing and Textiles Research Journal, 16*(3), pp. 126–133.

Khornak, L. (1982). *Fashion 2001*. New York: The Viking Press.

Lehr, C. J. (1998, March 12). *High bandwidth at home: Now or never?* http://lehr.ne.mediaone.net/hiband/ [Online].

Pine, B. J., II. (1993). *Mass customization: The new frontier in business competition.* Boston, MA: Harvard Business School Press.

Richards, R. W. (1997, October 14). Fashion 2027. *The Advocate*, p. 103.

Rose, F. (1998, May 14). ModaCAD aims to bridge real gaps in virtual mall. *The Wall Street Journal*, p. B6.

Yoh, E. (1999). *Consumer adoption of the Internet for apparel shopping.* Doctoral dissertation, Iowa State University, Ames, IA.

LIST OF READINGS

Adler, J. (1995, February 20). Have we become a nation of slobs? *Newsweek, pp. 56-62.* Chapter 13

al-Shaykh, H. (1994). Inside a Moroccan bath. In P. Foster (Ed.), *Minding the Body* (pp. 193-208). New York: Anchor Books. *Chapter 9*

Armstrong, M. L., & Murphy, K. P. (1997, November). Tattooing: Another adolescent risk behavior warranting health education. *Applied Nursing Research, 10* (4), 181-189. *Chapter 2*

Arthur, L. B. (1993). Clothing, control, and women's agency: The mitigation of patriarchal power. In S. Fisher & K. Davis (Eds.), *Negotiating at the Margins* (pp. 66-84). New Brunswick, NJ: Rutgers University Press. *Chapter 12*

Associated Press (1997, January 16). Tots grow up fast in pageant world. Published in *Des Moines Register,* pp. 1, 5A. *Chapter 8*

Associated Press (1994, September 6). Vintage jeans hot in Japan. Published in *Des Moines Register,* p. 6S. Chapter 3

Berkow, I. (1997, May 18). From hoop skirt to slam dunk chic. *New York Times,* pp. 35-36. Chapter 13

Berner, R. (1997, May 27). Now even toddlers are dressing to the nines. *Wall Street Journal,* p. B1, B2. *Chapter 8*

Bernstein, N. (1995, March/April). Goin' gangsta. *West Magazine,* Sunday supplement to the San Jose Mercury News, pp. 85-90. *Chapter 10*

Bird feathers. (1997, July/August/September). *The Wind River Rendezvous, 27*(3), pp. 13-14. *Chapter 4*

Bordo, S. (1993). Slenderness and the inner state of the self. Excerpt from *Unbearable weight: Feminism, western culture, and the body* (pp. 191-198). Berkeley, CA: University of California Press. *Chapter 10*

Brodman, B. (1994). Paris or perish: The plight of the Latin American Indian in a westernized world. In S. Benstock & S. Ferriss (Eds.), *On fashion* (pp. 267-283). Piscataway, NJ: Rutgers University Press. Chapter 11

Brubach, H. (1996, June 23). The athletic esthetic. *New York Times Magazine,* pp. 48-51. *Chapter 5*

Caminiti, S. (1996, November 11). Ralph Lauren: The emperor has clothes. *Fortune, 134* (9), pp. 80-84, 88, 92. *Chapter 11*

Carlin, K. (1996, June 1). You become what you wear. *Commonweal, 123,* 31. *Chapter 10*

Coffman, C., & Jurta, A. (1996, December). Do school uniforms make the grade? *Textiles and Apparel News, 11* (3), pp. 3-4. Cornell Cooperative Extension, New York State College of Human Ecology, Cornell University, Ithaca, NY 14853-4401. *Chapter 6*

Cottle, M. (1998, May). Turning boys into girls. *The Washington Monthly,* pp. 32-36. *Chapter 13*

Dalby, L. (1983). Kimono schools. Excerpt from *Geisha* by L. Dalby (pp. 290-293). New York: Vintage Books. *Chapter 3*

Damhorst, M. L., & Fiore, A. M. (1999, original for this text). Women's job interview dress: How the personnel interviewers see it. *Chapter 3*

Darling, L. (1994, January 23). Age, beauty and truth. *New York Times,* pp. 1, 5. *Chapter 9*

Edwards, D. (1996, November 23). Seinfeld and the *real* John Peterman. *Lexington Herald-Leader,* p. C3. *Chapter 11*

Edwards, L. (1993, May 30) Worldly lessons. *New York Times,* pp. C1, C9. *Chapter 12*

Egan, J. (1996, February 4). James is a girl. *New York Times Magazine,* pp. 26-35, 38-39, 51-52, 63. *Chapter 8*

Eggen, D. (1995, November 7) Saving face: Here's how it's done. *Des Moines Register,* pp. 1T-2T. *Chapter 6*

Farnham, A. (1996, September 9). You're so vain: I bet you think this story's about you. *Fortune, 134,* 66-71, 74, 76, 78, 80, 82. *Chapter 9*

Farr, B. R. (1999, original for this text). Plus-size modeling: The industry, the market, and reflections as a professional in the image industry. *Chapter 11*

Farrell-Beck, J. (1999, original for this text). Not so new: Casual dress in the office. *Chapter 7*

Fisher, C. (1996, September). Black, hip, and primed (to shop). American Demographics, 18(9), pp. 52-58. *Chapter 10*

Garner, D. M. (1997, January/February). The 1997 body image survey results. *Psychology Today, 30* (1), 30-44, 75-76, 78, 80, 84. *Chapter 2*

Grealy, L. (1994). Pony party. Excerpt from *Autobiography of a Face* by Lucy Grealy (pp. 5-13). Boston: Houghton Mifflin. *Chapter 8*

Greco, A. J. (1986). The fashion-conscious elderly: A viable, but neglected market segment. *The Journal of Consumer Marketing, 3* (4), 71-74. *Chapter 9*

Hamilton, W. L. (1998, February 19). The school uniform as fashion statement: How students crack the dress code. *New York Times,* p. A19. *Chapter 6*

Hart, J. (1998, June 8). Northampton confronts a crime, cruelty. *Boston Globe,* pp. A1, A12. *Chapter 5*

Hayt, E. (1997, April 27). For stylish Orthodox women, wigs that aren't wiggy. *New York Times,* pp. 43, 48. *Chapter 12*

Hegland, J. E. (1999, original for this text). Drag queens, transvestites, transsexuals: Stepping across the accepted boundaries of gender. *Chapter 5*

Heightism: Short guys finish last. (1996, December 23). *The Economist,* pp. 19-22. *Chapter 2*

James, G. (1994, November 27). Sharper image: The N.Y.P.D. dresses for success. *New York Times,* Section 4, p. 6. *Chapter 7*

Janeczko, J. (1992, May 5). Bennett: A non-conformist immune to criticism. *Iowa State Daily,* pp. 1, 3. *Chapter 6*

Janus, T., Kaiser, S. B., & Gray, G. (1999, original for this text). Negotiations @ work: The casual businesswear trend. *Chapter 7*

Jefferson, M. (1997, January 30). Dennis Rodman, bad boy as man of the moment. *New York Times*, pp. C13, C20. *Chapter 6*

Kaiser, S. B. (1999, original for this text). Identity, postmodernity, and the global apparel marketplace. *Chapter 3*

Kakutani, M. (1997, February 16). Common threads. *New York Times Magazine*, p. 18. *Chapter 10*

Kimle, P. A., & Damhorst, M. L. (1999, original for this text). Women's images in corporate culture: The case of casual day. *Chapter 7*

Kissel, W. (1993, June 18). Styles with a sizable difference. *Los Angeles Times*, pp. E1, E3. *Chapter 11*

Kristoff, N. D. (1996, April 29). Young Japan is dyeing (It's anything but natural). *New York Times*, p. A4. *Chapter 3*

Kunkel, C. A. (1999, original for this text). A visual analysis of feminist dress. *Chapter 5*

Levin, J. (1993). Fat chance in a slim world: We believe it's the size of a book's cover that counts. In *Sociological Snapshots* (pp. 11-14). Thousand Oaks, CA: Pine Forge Press. *Chapter 2*

Lillethun, A. (1999, original for this text). An interpretation of negative press coverage of casual dress. *Chapter 7*

Littrell, J. M. (1999) Employing clothing for therapeutic change in brief counseling. *Chapter 4*

Lynch, A. (1995). Hmong American New Year's dress: The display of ethnicity. In J. B. Eicher (Ed.), *Dress and ethnicity: Change across space and time* (pp. 255–267). Oxford, England: Berg Publishers. *Chapter 13*

Majors, R., & Billson, J. M. (1992). Excerpt from *Cool pose: Dilemmas of black manhood in America* by R. Majors and J. M. Billson (pp. 79-85). New York: Lexington Books. *Chapter 10*

May, L. (1996, November 22). Students' rights not as broad as those of public. *Lexington Herald-Leader*, pp. B1, B2. *Chapter 6*

McLeod, H. (1999, original for this text). Business casual dress: An African American male perspective. *Chapter 7*

Michelman, S. O. (1999, original for this text). From habit to fashion: Dress of Catholic women religious. *Chapter 12*

Michelman, S. O. (1999, original for this text). Is thin in? Kalabari culture and the meaning of fatness. *Chapter 2*

Miller, K. A., & Hunt, S. A. (1999, original for this text). It's all Greek to me: Sorority members and identity talk. *Chapter 6*

Mithers, C. L. (1994, December). A new look at beauty, aging and power. *Glamour*, 92 (12), 184-5, 246-249. *Chapter 9*

Olson, J. (1997, October 23). Bulldog with character makeup. *Des Moines Register*, p. 3S. *Chapter 4*

O'Neal, G. S. (1998, Spring). African American women's professional dress as expression of ethnicity. *Family and Consumer Science Research Journal*, 90 (1), 28-33. *Chapter 10*

Parker, S., Nichter, M., Nichter, M., Vuckovic, N., Sims, C., & Ritenbaugh, C. (1995). Body image and weight concerns among African American and white adolescent females: Differences that make a difference. *Human Organization*, 54 (2), 103-114. *Chapter 8*

Polhemus, T. (1994). Tribal Styles. Excerpt from *Street style* by T. Polhemus (pp. 13-16). New York: Thames and Hudson. *Chapter 11*

Reed, J. D. (1992, April). Hail to the T, the shirt that speaks volumes. *Smithsonian*, 23 (1-3), 96-102. *Chapter 4*

Respers, L. (1996, February 23). Day-care dress up not amusing to boy's dad. *Lexington-Herald-Leader*. *Chapter 5*

Rich, C. (1983/90). Ageism and the politics of beauty. In B. Macdonald (with C. Rich), *Look me in the Eye* (2nd ed.) (pp. 139-146). Duluth, MN: Spinsters Ink. *Chapter 9*

Rodriguez, R. (1982). Complexion. Excerpt from *Hunger of Memory* by R. Rodriguez (pp. 113+). Boston, MA: David R. Godine, Publisher. (pp. 265-278). Cambridge, MA: MIT Press. *Chapter 10*

Roome, L. (1998). What is mehndi? Excerpt from *Designs for the hands: The timeless art of henna painting by* L. Roome (pp. 1-2, 6-12, 41-51). New York: St. Martin's Press. *Chapter 3*

Rucker, M. (1999, original for this text). Economic impacts of casual business attire on the market for textiles and apparel. *Chapter 7*

Russell, A. (1992, May) Fine-tuning your corporate image. *Black Enterprise*, 22, pp. 72-74+. *Chapter 7*

Sanders, C. R. (1991, Winter). Memorial decoration: Women, tattooing, and the meanings of body alteration. *Michigan Quarterly Review*, 30 (1), 146-157. *Chapter 4*

Saturn Corporation: A casual businesswear case study. (no date available). Levi Strauss & Co. *Chapter 7*

Schneider, A. (1998, January 23). Frumpy or chic? Tweed or Kente? Sometimes clothes make the professor. *The Chronicle of Higher Education*, 44 (20), A12-A14. *Chapter 7*

Schneider, K. S. (1996, June 3). Mission impossible. *People*, 45(22), 64-68, 70-71, 73-74. *Chapter 2*

Schulze, L. (1990). On the muscle. In J. Gaines & C. Herzog (Eds.) *Fabrications, costume and the female body* (pp. 59-65, excerpt). New York: Routledge. *Chapter 2*

Sciolino, E. (1997, May 4). The Chanel under the chador. *New York Times Magazine*, pp. 46-51. *Chapter 12*

Siebert, C. (1996, July 7). The cuts that go deeper. *New York Times Magazine*, pp. 20-25, 34, 40, 43-45. *Chapter 3*

Smith, L. (1996, March 11). The changing image of childhood. *Los Angeles Times*. Published in *Des Moines Register*, pp. 1T-2T. *Chapter 8*

Spiegler, M. (1996, November). Marketing street culture: Bringing hip-hop style to the mainstream. *American Demographics*, 18 (11), 29-34. *Chapter 11*

Spindler, A. (1994, September 25). Men in uniformity. *New York Times Magazine*. Men's fashions of the times, pp. 16, 18. *Chapter 5*

Teilhet-Fisk, J. (1996). The Miss Heilala beauty pageant: Where beauty is more than skin deep. In C. Cohen, R. Wilk, & B. Stoeltje (Eds.), *Beauty queens on the global stage* (pp. 185-202). New York: Routledge. *Chapter 2*

Wells, J. (1993, September 13). Sheer madness. *San Francisco Chronicle*, p. 1. *Chapter 13*

White, J. (1997, June 15). Saving grace: Clothes savers have memories and feelings hanging in their closets. *The Kansas City Star*, pp. H5, H6. *Chapter 9*

Wickliffe, V. P. (1999, original for this text). Culture and consumer behavior. *Chapter 6*

Wilkie, M. (1995, August). Scent of a market. *American Demographics*, 17 (8), 40-43, 46-47, 49. *Chapter 4*

Wilson, E. (1990, June 15). Rebel, rebel. *New Statesman & Society*, 3(2), 40-41. *Chapter 13*

Winters, W. (1997, May 29). Eco-friendly fashions are 'cool.' *The Indianapolis Star*, p. 3. *Chapter 13*

Wood, T. (1993, November). The magic of dress-up. *Parents*, 68 (11), pp. 172-174. *Chapter 8*

LIST OF PHOTO CREDITS

Chapter 1

Figure 1.2 *(a) Universal (Courtesy Kobal). (b) Fairchild Publications, Inc.*

Figure 1.3 *Photo from Goudge, B.S. (1985). Attributions for job acquisition: Job skills, dress, and luck of female job applicants. Master's thesis, Iowa State University, Ames.*

Figure 1.4 *Photo by T. Campion, Sygma Photo News.*

Figure 1.5 *Marla Berns, Director of the University Museum at University of California, Santa Barbara.*

Chapter 2

Figure 2.1 *National Gallery of London.*

Figure 2.2 *Photo by Larry White.*

Figure 2.3 *Photo by Tim Graham, Sygma Photo News.*

Figure 2.6

Figure 2.7 *Courtesy of Susan O. Michelman. (b, c).*

Chapter 3

Figures 3.1 *Cotbis / Mitchell Gerber.*

Figure 3.2. *© 1988 from The New Yorker Collection. All Rights Reserved.*

Figure 3.3 *Corbis / Peter Turnley.*

Figures 3.7, 3.8, 3.9 *Courtesy of Mary Lynn Damhorst.*

Figure 3.10 *Photo by Tracey Eller © 1998.*

Figure 3.11 *Corbis / Michael S. Yamashita.*

Chapter 4

Figure 4.1 *Saba Press Photos Inc.*

Figure 4.2 *Sipa Press (photo of Pope John Paul II.); graphics courtesy of Time Life Syndication.*

Figure 4.3 *Berger, E.A. (1984). Clothing cues and occupation: Influence on person perception. Master's thesis, Iowa State University, Ames.*

Figure 4.5 *Corbis / Charles and Josette Lenars.*

Figure 4.6 *Corbis / Philip James Corwin.*

Figure 4.7 *Photo by Doug Wells © 1997. The Des Moines Register and Tribune Company. Reprinted with permission.*

Chapter 5

Figure 5.1 *Courtesy of Susan O. Michelman.*

Figure 5.2b *La Oranba Maria (Hail Mary), Paul Gauguin, French, 1848–1903. Oil on canvas, 44 ?? × 34 ??, 1891. The Metropolitan Museum of Art, Bequest of Sam A. Lewisohn, 1951, 51.112.2.*

Figure 5.3 *Courtesy of Charlotte A. Kunkel, Ph.D., Luther College.*

Figure 5.4 *Courtesy of Jane E. Hegland, New Mexico State University.*

Chapter 6

Figure 6.1 *Crox San Jose Mercury News, Sipa Press.*

Figure 6.2 *Corbis / Mitchell Gerber.*

Figure 6.3 *The Des Moines Register: (a) Modersohn and (b) Nandell.*

Figure 6.4 *Suzanne DelChillo / NYT Pictures.*

Chapter 7

Figure 7.1 *Carhartt.*

Figure 7.2 *Chris Hildreth Director, University Photography, Duke University.*

Figure 7.3 *AP / Wide World Photos.*

Figure 7.4 *The British Library, London.*

Figure 7.5 *Photo by Gary Tartakov.*

Chapter 8

Figure 8.1 *Photo by J.R. Campbell. Dolls courtesy of Carol Hall.*

Figure 8.2 *Photo by Donna Pang.*

Figure 8.3 *AP / Wide World Photos.*

Figure 8.4 *Top by Diesel, dress by Fragile, tights by Mentor Sox, shoes by Bopy.*

Figure 8.5 *Photo by NanGoldin © 1999.*

Chapter 9

Figure 9.2 *Rob Hernandez, Copyright, 1993, Los Angeles Times. Reprinted by permission.*

Chapter 10

Figure 10.1 *Courtesy Huntington Historical Society, Huntington, NY.*

Figure 10.2 *Fairchild Publications, Inc.*

Chapter 11

Figure 11.1 *Fairchild Publications, Inc.*

Figure 11.2 *Corbis / Bradley Smith.*

Figure 11.3 *Courtesy of Mary Lynn Damhorst.*

Figure 11.5 *Photo by E.J. Carr.*

Figure 11.6 *Corbis / Richard Oliver.*

Chapter 12

Figure 12.1 *Photo by Lise Sarfati, Magnum Photos, Inc.*

Figure 12.2 *Illustration by Mary Lou Carter.*

Figure 12.3 *Courtesy of Susan O. Michelman*

Chapter 13

Figure 13.1 *Corbis / Joseph Sohm; ChromoSohm Inc.*

Figure 13.2 *Corbis / Neal Preston*

Figure 13.3 *Photo by Annette Lynch, Ph.D., The University of Northern Iowa.*

Figure 13.4 *University of Massachusetts, Photo Services*

Chapter 14

Figure 14.1 *Courtesy of Esprit.*

AUTHOR INDEX

SUBJECT INDEX

by men, 193–205
by noncomformists, 209, 218–220
reasons for, 194–195
transsexuals, 195–196
transvestites, 196–198
understanding, 199–200
visual typology of, 195
by women, 194
See also Homosexuals
Cultural assimilation, 495
Cultural authentication, 508
Cultural ideals, 13–14
of beauty, 19–20, 364–370
feminist critiques of, 19
and gender, 15–16
globalization of, 66
and the individual, 16–18
and power, 15
in the United States, 14–18
See also Body image; Body weight
Cultural imperialism of the United States, 526
Cultural norms, 2, 168–169, 473
Cultural stereotypes, 18
Cultural system in the fashion continuum, 410–412
Cultural universals, 206
Culture, 3–5
African American heritage, 391–392
and context of dress, 84
and diversity, 8–9
Hmong Americans, 373, 495, 502–509
Latin American Indians, 412, 429–438
obsessed with youthfulness, 331, 352
popular, 218
See also Acculturation; Bicultural
Cuna people, 411
Customization, 533–535

D

Dazzle fabric, 510
Death, fear of, 355
Definition of situation in dress messages, 128

Demographics, 237
Denim clothing, 498
embroidering, 526
history of, 525–527
synthetic, 512–513
See also Blue jeans
Denotation in meanings of dress, 132
Department stores, 384
Depilatories, 343
Dermabrasion, 117
Dermatologists, 13
Designer clothing for children, 171, 289–290
Designer jeans. *See* Jeans
Designer labels, 108, 414
Designers, fashion, 63, 438–444, 523, 535
Diet industry, 36
organizations for weight loss, 52
revenues in, 43
Diet pills, 27, 45
Dieting, 2
advertising for, 25
and African American adolescent females, 308
in children, 36, 42, 43, 283, 296
excessive, 17
in the media, 52
percentage of dieters, 43
rebellion against, 52
and self-esteem, 17, 36
by White adolescent females, 303
See also Body weight; Fat people
Diffusion of fashions, 6
Diffusion of styles, 414
Disabilities. *See* People with disabilities
Disc jockeys, 448
Discount department stores, 384
Discourse in meanings of dress, 132
Discretionary income, 236, 383, 410
Discrimination
body size, 18, 51–53
height of men, 12, 18, 54–58

lawsuits, 385
pervasive, systematic, and irrational, 56
in the United States, 381
See also Diversity; Ethnicity; Minority groups; Prejudice; Stereotypes
Disfigurements, 119
facial, 285, 313–316
Dissatisfaction with the body. *See* Body dissatisfaction
Diuretic abuse, 27, 61
Diversity, 8–9, 411, 530, 532
See also Discrimination; Ethnicity; Minority groups; Prejudice; Stereotypes
Divorce, 331, 482
Double consciousness in African Americans, 308, 390–391
Double standard in aging, 329, 340, 342, 352, 355
Downward mobility, 374
Drag queens, 108, 108–199, 202, 203
See also Cross-dressing; Homosexuals
Dreadlocks, 497
Dress
in adulthood, 328–370
as behavior, 2
conformity and individuality, 206–237
from infancy to adolescence, 279–327
future trends in, 528–538
and gender, 168–205
and group identity, 210
in human interaction, 127–167
as nonverbal communication, 78–126
and sexuality, 458–459
and social change, 459–460, 494–527
for specific needs, 241
in the workplace, 238–278
and world religions, 455–493

Dress codes, 214–217, 231, 232

Dress codes, *See also* Dressing down; School uniforms

Dress communication systems, 80–86
    channels of communication, 80–81
    context of use, 83–86
    elements of dress signs, 82–83
    grammar of dress, 81–82
    See also Nonverbal communication

Dress messages, 128

Dress up play, 171, 182, 282–283, 291–293
    See also Costumes

Dressing down, 514–517, 518
    church dress, 515, 516
    collars and garters, 515–516
    comfort and economy, 515–516
    frock coats, 517
    gangsters, 515
    hats and gloves, 514–515
    shorts and caps, 515
    See also Business dress; Casualization of dress; Dress codes

Drug abuse, 418

Dwarfs, 57

Dynamic lifespan process, 334, 335–336, 362–364

E

Early adolescence, 283
    See also Adolescence
Early adopters of styles, 414
Early adulthood, 329
    See also Adulthood
Early childhood, 280
    See also Childhood
Eating disorders, 25, 42–43
    in African Americans, 299
    and beauty pageants, 294
    extreme weight control, 27, 28, 33–36
    in female athletes, 180
    increases in, 108
    influence of media, 37

    in men, 16, 41, 43
    percentages of incidence, 43
    professional help for, 39
    and self-control, 407
    See also Anorexia; Bulimia

Eclecticism in postmodern times, 86, 109, 111, 114

Eco-friendly fashions, 495, 512–513
    See also Environmental concerns

Economic collapse, 529

Economic impacts of casualization of dress, 275–278

Egypt, ancient tattooing in, 141, 143

El Salvador, 429

Elaborated code of dress for women, 173

Elderly, 332
    fashion-conscious, 358–362
    poverty of, 532–533
    shopping by, 534
    See also Ageism; Aging

Elements of dress signs, 82–83

Embroidering denim clothing, 526

Empty nest syndrome, 330–331

Endogamy, 475

Environmental concerns
    future trends in dress, 535–537
    See also Eco-friendly fashions

Epinephrine, 119

Equal Employment Opportunity Commission, 57

Escape and dress, 135–136

Ethical responsibilities of the fashion industry, 417–419

Ethnic boundary lines, 502–509

Ethnicity, 5, 20, 57
    and appearance, 373–374
    census projections, 530–531
    claiming, 395, 396
    expression by African American women, 388–394
    future trends in dress, 530–532

    gangsta dress, 235–236, 274, 394–397
    hip-hop style, 6, 398–399, 408, 414, 445–450
    Hmong Americans, 373, 495, 502–509
    mixed race and ethnicity, 530
    stereotypes, 376–377
    true equality, 531

Ethnocentrism, 9, 19

Euphemisms, fat and black, 53

Euro-American hegemony, 531

Euro-American ideals, of body weight, 12

European aristocracy, and tattoos, 142

European Convention on Human Rights, 57

Exercise, 2
    excessive, 17
    and positive feelings, 31, 32–33, 37, 38
    reasons for, 16, 36

Exfoliating, 349

Exhibitionism, 196–197

Expulsion, 476, 477, 482

Extreme weight control, 27, 33–36

Eyebrow rings, 13

Eyelid surgery, 121, 520

F

Fabrics, condition of, 84

Face lifts, 13, 19, 117, 121, 343, 520

Face paint for football games, 159–161

Face peels, 117, 347, 348, 520

Facial disfigurement, 285, 313–316

Facial expressions, 79

Facial hair, 13, 195

Facial implants, 117

Facial peels, 13

Fashion, 2, 5
    as a conforming behavior, 207
    definition of, 332, 409–410
    diffusion of, 6

G.I. Joe, 171
Girdles, 344, 495
Girls Incorporated, 41
Glass ceiling, 96, 109, 240
Global marketplace
    and postmodernity, 106–115
    and stereotyping, 18, 20
Global warming, 529
Globalization
    of cultural ideals, 66, 67–77
    of ideals of beauty, 20
Government regulation of the textile industry, 537
Governmental dress, 130
Graffiti, 448
Grammar of dress, 81–82
Gray power, 532
    See also Aging
Green Hmong dress, 503, 506, 507, 508
Grooming products, men using, 343, 347, 349, 350
Group identity, 506
    See also Ethnic boundary lines
Group identity and dress, 210
Grunge look, 6
Guatemala, 429–438, 437
Gynecomastia (male breast reduction), 118

H
Hair
    body, 195
    and cultural traditions, 73
    dyeing, 13
    dyeing hair in Japan, 83, 90–91
    facial and body, 195
    loss of, 13
    and nuns, 486
    and sexuality, 458, 459, 465
    wigs and toupees, 13, 344, 468–471
Hair replacement, 520
    nonsurgical, 343–344
    surgery for, 13, 117, 346–347, 348
Hair salons, 13
Half-stepping, 402
Halo effect, 212, 229

Hand book of sources for eco-friendly fashions, 512–513
Hand gestures, 79
Hand painting. See Mehndi
Haptics, 79
Hasidic sect of Judaism. See Judaism
Hate crimes, 190, 221
    See also Homophobia
Hats and gloves in dressing down, 514–515
Haute couture designs, 412, 423
Head coverings, 476
Health in adulthood, 332–334
Health insurance and plastic surgery, 118
Hedonic power, 15
Hegemony, 4–5
    European American, 531
    and female bodybuilders, 60, 62
    in patriarchical societies, 19
Height of men, 12, 18, 54–58
Hemp fabrics, 513, 537
Henna hand painting. See Mehndi
High–heeled shoes, 9, 19
Hindus
    bridal adornment, 98
    See also Mehndi
Hip–hop style, 6, 392–399, 408, 414
    marketing, 445–450
Hippies, 2, 526
Hispanics, 58, 378–382
History
    of casualization of dress, 259–261
    of denim clothing, 498, 525–527
    dynamic lifespan process, 334, 335–336, 362–364
    of plastic surgery, 121
    of the plus-size market, 424–426
    self–history, 334, 335–336, 362–364
    of tattoos, 142–143
History of dress, 2
    costume histories, 130–131
    cross-dressing, 201–203

and gender, 15, 173–174
    nineteenth century S-shape, 170
    trends in, 112
    in twentieth century, 180
HIV and tattoos, 17
Hmong Americans, 373, 495, 502–509
Holdeman Mennonites, 471–483
    See also Christianity
Holistic approach, 3
Homeless people, 374, 405–406
    See also Poverty
Homo–punk, 220–221
Homogenizing effect, 110
Homophobia, 172
    and female bodybuilders, 19, 60
    and men's cross-dressing, 194
    and school violence, 189–191
Homosexuals
    and cross-dressing, 203
    definition of, 172
    homo-punk, 220–221
    market power of, 520
    and patriarchy, 19
    See also Bisexuals; Cross-dressing; Drag queens; Lesbians; Sexual orientation
Human interaction and dress, 127–167
Human rights, 429–438
Hutterites, 211, 482
Hybrid tribal styles, 415
Hypodescent rule, 372

I
Identity, 7–8
    and fashion, 104
    multiple, 128–129
    and postmodernity, 106–115
    and self, 487–488
Identity politics, 422
Ideological statements of dress, 412, 456
Image consultants, 242, 247–250
Image enhancement, 123
Image industry, 422–429

Plastic surgery, 16, 17, 86–87, 117–126
   advances in, 533
   breast augmentation, 108
   computer-imaging, 117
   French performance artist, 122
   history of, 121
   increase in, 108
   increase in men, 118, 174, 343–351, 520, 524
   and Judeo-Christian precepts, 121
   psychological impact of, 125
   See also specific types of
Play with dress. *See* Dress up play
Pluralism, 9, 411, 530, 531
Plus size fashion, 53, 411, 422–429
Police uniforms, 80, 209, 242, 255–257
Political statements of dress, 412
Pollution, 528
Polynesian culture, 20
   See also Tongan people
Polysemic behavior, 80
Polytheism, 456
Pomanders, 155
   See also Scents
Popular culture, 218, 411, 414, 446
Portable billboards, 135
Postmodern times, 86–87, 106–115
   choice, 109–111
   confusion, 111–112
   creativity, 112–114
   eclecticism, 86
   nostalgia, 86
   questioning of traditions and rules, 86
   reflected in dress, 411
   simulation, 86–87
Poverty, 281, 374
   and skin color, 380
   and violence, 392
   See also Homeless people
Power
   in aging of women, 338–342
   and cultural ideals, 15
   issues for women, 26
   traditional notions of, 109

Power Rangers, 171
Powerful influences on social change, 496–497
Precontemplation in the change model, 162
Predictions versus forecasts, 529
Pregnancy
   cultural standards over time, 21–23
   decisions to have children, 30, 37
   dress for, 241
   teen, 283
Prejudice, 3
   and stigmatization, 18
   See also Discrimination; Diversity; Ethnicity; Minority groups; Stereotypes
Preparation in the change model, 162, 164, 166
Presidential candidates, 240
Prestige, 239
Primary sex characteristics, 169
Prison uniforms, 7
Production and exchange of meanings, 80
Profane, 456
Professional counseling, 39
Professional dress. *See* Business dress
Programs of dress, 7
Prominent adam's apple, 195, 196, 203
Protestants, 457
   See also Religion
Proxemics, 79
Psychotherapy. *See* Therapy
Punk subculture, 415, 447, 453, 498, 526
   See also Styletribes

Q
Quality of life, 122
Questioning of traditions and rules in postmodern times, 86

R
Race
   and appearance, 371–373

   definition of, 371–372
   and ethnicity, 389
   mixed race and ethnicity, 530
   true equality, 531
Race, ethnicity, and class, 371–407
   ethnic stereotypes, 376–377
   ethnicity and appearance, 373–374
   race and appearance, 371–373
   social class and appearance, 374–375
Racism, 372–373, 380
   and cool pose, 403
   See also Discrimination
Rap music, 398–399, 414, 415, 445–450
Rastafarians, 497
Recessions, 277
Recreational shopping, 384, 385
Recycled fibers, 537
Recycled soda pop bottles, 512–513
Red
   meanings in different cultures, 84
   See also Color
Relationships, abusive, 38
Relationships in dress messages, 128
Relativism, 5–7
Religion, 5
   and cross-dressing, 202
   definition of, 456
   and dress, 130, 455–493
   See also Christianity; Islam; Judaism
Reproval, 477–478
Responsible consumption, 536
Restricted codes of dress for men, 173
Retail buyers, 412, 414, 535
Retailing displays, 413
Retailing industry, 265, 277
   and African Americans, 373, 383–387
Reverse discrimination, 532, 537
Reviews of dress, 7, 8
Rhinoplasty, 117, 121

Rhytidectomy. *See* Face lifts
Rights of students, 213, 230,
    231–232
Rites of passage, 98, 451
Rituals, 129–130
    and tattooing, 141
Robotized production, 533
Rock music, 453
Role-related dress, 242
Roles, 7
    achieved and ascribed, 239
    conflicts in women, 36
Roman Catholic Church, 132,
    455, 457, 459, 483–489
    See also Religion
Rules of dress, 81–82

S
"Sack suit," 114, 260
Sacred meanings, 130, 456
"Safe beauty classes," 490–493
Sales associates, 207
Samskara (rite of passage), 98
Sarongs, 169
Saudi Arabia, 462
Scarification (cicatrization), 9, 19,
    141
Scents, 131, 154–159, 413
    allergic reactions to,
        158–159
    as aphrodisiacs, 158
    aramotherapy, 154, 158
    functional use of, 156
    in motivation to work harder
        or buy more, 157–158
    perfume images, 156–157
    sense of smell, 155
School uniforms, 108, 212–213,
    228–235
    benefits of, 228–229
    children liking, 282
    as fashion statement,
        232–235
    pros and cons, 214–217
    and school violence, 212,
        229
    See also Dress codes
School violence
    and homophobia, 189–191
    and school uniforms, 212,
        229

Screenwriters, 44
Second-hand shops, 537
Secondary sex characteristics, 169
Self, 7–8
    definition by African
        Americans, 390–391
    and identity, 487–488
    See also Individual
Self–employment, 423
Self-esteem, 17
    in African American adoles-
        cent females, 308
    criteria for, 38
    ethnic differences, 297–300
    high levels of, 208
    and violence, 392
Self-fulfilling prophecy, 212
Self-hatred, 17, 28
Self-history, 334, 335–336,
    362–364
Self-indication, 7
Self-perception, 42, 212
Semiotics, 10
Senior citizens. *See* Ageism;
    Aging; Elderly
Sense of smell. *See* Scents
Senses, physiological, 80–81
Sensory enjoyment, 476
Sephardic traditions
    bridal adornment, 98
    See also Mehndi
Sex
    and body image, 31, 37
    in childhood, 283
    defintion of, 169
    and dress, 458–459
    primary and secondary char-
        acteristics, 169
Sexism, 52, 171–172
Sexual abuse, 33, 37
    of children, 283
Sexual excitement and dress, 135
Sexual harassment, 95
    definition of, 172
    and dress in the workplace,
        134, 492, 493
    of homosexuals, 172
    and physical contact, 250
Sexual identity kit, 171–174
Sexual orientation, 168–205

See also Bisexuals;
    Homosexuals; Lesbians
Shape Up America, 28
"She-men," 491
Shoes, 479–480
Shopping
    in adolescence, 285
    by African Americans, 373,
        383–387
    on the Internet, 285, 329,
        534–535, 537
    in late adulthood, 358–362
    mail-order, 329, 332, 534,
        537
    recreational, 384, 385
Short men. *See* Height of men
Shorts and caps in dressing down,
    515
SHRIMPS. *See* Height of men
Shunning, 475, 477, 482
Sign versus symbol, 10
Simulation in postmodern times,
    86–87
Single-parents, 329
Skateboarders, 448, 449
Skin care products, 334
Skin cells, 122
Skin color, 369, 372, 378–382, 532
Skin tags, 13
Skin tone, 13
Slavery, 372, 389
Slenderness and self-mastery,
    405–407
    See also Body weight;
        Dieting
Slovenliness in dress. *See* Dressing
    down
Snowboarders, 448
Social activism, 486
Social activity in late adulthood,
    332
Social boundaries, 502–509
Social change and dress, 459–460,
    494–527
    acculturation, 495
    capitalism, 497–498
    conflict, 497
    cultural assimilation, 495
    innovation, 495
    powerful influences,
        496–497

Termination in the change model, 162
Testosterone, 61
Textile arts, 502
Textile industry, 114, 244, 275–276
    in China, 412
    government regulations, 537
    and Latin American Indians, 430–437
Thailand, 503, 507
Therapy
    and dress, 135–136, 161–167
    See also Brief counseling
Third Reich in Germany, 496
Tights and leggings, 518–519
Timbira people and height discrimination, 55
Toddler stage, 280
    See also Childhood
Toiletries market, 520
Tongan people
    California-Tongan contestants, 70–71
    expatriates, 76
    factionalsim and cultural unity, 71
    ideal for body weight, 20
    Miss Heilala Beauty Pageant, 20, 67–77
    Miss *Tau'olunga*, 71–72, 76
    social hierarchy of, 69–70
    swimwear of, 74
Totemic boundary lines, 502–509
Touch, 79, 80
Touching, physical, 249–250
Toupees, 13
Toys, gender-specific, 171
Traditional acculturation, 390
Traditional dress, 411
Transsexuals, 195–196, 202
    See also Cross-dressing
Transvestites, 196–198, 202
    See also Cross-dressing
Trial consultants, 210, 222–223
Tribal designs, 429–438
Tribal styles, 451–454
Trickle-across diffusion, 415
Trickle-down theory, 415, 525

Trickle-up theory, 374, 415
Trobriand Islanders and height discrimination, 55
True equality, 531
True hermaphrodite, 169
Tummy tuck (abdominoplasty), 118, 121

U
Undercoding, 80
Uniforms, 4
    Boy Scout, 132, 282
    military, 80, 255
    police, 80, 209, 242, 255–257
    prison, 7
    school, 108, 212–213, 228–235, 282
    women's basketball, 509–511
Uniqueness theory, 207–208
Unisex, 173
United Nations, 57
United States
    consumers in, 213–214, 235–237
    cultural ideals, 14–18
    cultural imperialism of, 526
    discrimination in, 381
    immigration to, 502
    individualism in, 213, 235
    tattooing history in, 142–143
Upward mobility, 374
Urban dress, 201
Urbanization, 236

V
Vanity of men, 519–524
Variety in adulthood, 329
Vatican II, 483–489
    See also Roman Catholic Church
Veiling. *See* Islam
Verbal expression, 79
Vertical mobility, 374
Victorian era, 22
Vietnam War, 486, 502
Vintage clothes, 362–364, 537
Vintage jeans, 116–117
Violence

and poverty, 392
and self-esteem, 392
Visual typology of cross-dressing, 195
Voice characersitics, 79
Voice command computers, 528
Vomiting
    self-induced, 17, 19, 27
    See also Bulimia; Eating disorders
Vow tattoos, 145

W
Warts, 13
Weaving, 431–437
Wedding rituals. *See Mehndi*
Weight. *See* Body weight
West Africa, 169
Western colonialism, 429–438
Western dress, 201, 236
Whistleblowing, 493
White adolescent females
    competition among, 303–304
    ideals of beauty, 301–302
White backlash, 532, 537
White collar dress, 240
White Hmong dress, 503, 506, 507
White Negro, 219
White supremacist takeover, 531
Wiggers, 394–397, 399, 449
Wigs and toupees, 13, 344
    Orthodox Jewish women, 456, 459, 460, 468–471
Women
    African American professional dress, 388–394
    African Americans satisfied with bodies, 41
    and aging, 329, 338–342, 351–354
    as athletes, 177–181, 210
    and basketball, 495, 509–511
    as bodybuilders, 19, 58–63, 179
    and casualization of dress, 267, 269–271
    cross-dressing, 84, 194, 201